ANECDOTES: Religious, Moral and Entertaining

ANECDOTES,

RELIGIOUS, MORAL, AND ENTERTAINING,

BY THE

LATE REV. CHARLES BUCK,

Author of Theological Dictionary.

ALPHABETICALLY ARRANGED, AND INTERSPERSED WITH A VARIETY
OF USEFUL OBSERVATIONS.

WITH

A PREFACE,

BY ASHBEL GREEN, D. D.

SOME TIME PRESIDENT OF PRINCETON COLLEGE.

TWO VOLS. IN ONE

VOL. I.

Solid Ground Christian Books
Birmingham, Alabama USA

Solid Ground Christian Books
2090 Columbiana Rd, Suite 2000
Birmingham, AL 35216
205-443-0311
sgcb@charter.net
http://solid-ground-books.com

ANECDOTES: Religious, Moral and Entertaining

Charles Buck (1771-1815)

Taken from the 1832 edition by J.H. Turney, New York

Solid Ground Classic Reprints

First printing of new edition June 2005

Cover work by Borgo Design, Tuscaloosa, AL
Contact them at nelbrown@comcast.net

Cover photo used by permission of Ric Ergenbright.
Visit and view his work at http://ricergenbright.org

ISBN: 1-932474-84-6

RECOMMENDATIONS.

I HAVE read so much of those volumes of the works of the Rev. Charles Buck, which contain his collection of moral and religious anecdotes, as to satisfy me that it is a very entertaining and useful compilation. So far as my examination has extended, Mr. Buck appears to have been judicious in his selections, and to have given the anecdotes a dress calculated to invite the attention and benefit the hearts of his readers.

July 1831.   JAMES MILNOR,
                        D. D. Rector of St. George's Church, N. Y.

I am pleased that Buck's Anecdotes are to be republished in this country —they are a fund both of amusement and instruction, and may be read with profit by persons of almost every order of understanding.

Phila. July 1, 1831.   THOS. H. SKINNER,
                    D. D. and Pastor of 5th Presbyterian Church, Phil.

There are few publications in the present day, which in my opinion merit a more extensive circulation than Buck's Anecdotes. The work has been compiled with great industry, is in good taste, systematically arranged, and subservient to the purposes of morality and religion.

I can therefore confidently recommend it to the reading public, particularly the youth of our country, as a fund of useful entertainment.

Phila. July 5th, 1831.   GEORGE G. COOKMAN,
                          *Minister of the Methodist Episcopal Church,
                                N. Fifth-street, Philadelphia.*

I have repeatedly read Buck's Religious Anecdotes with pleasure and profit. They have been published and republished in detached parts, in a great variety of forms. I am glad to learn that Mr. John C. Riker, of New York, is about to stereotype them, so that he will be able to furnish at a cheap rate, an abundant supply for the religious community. They are hereby recommended, especially to all those persons who must have *entertainment* as well as *profit* from their reading.

Phila. June 1, 1831.   EZRA STILES ELY, D. D.

BUCK'S ANECDOTES is a very amusing, instructive, and valuable work— of which the matter is mainly authenticated facts, the style sprightly and interesting, and the scope beneficial. While I devoutly wish the word of God were read and understood more extensively, and that *no other volume* might in any degree take precedence of that which is alone inspired, I would not disparage the utility of such a little religious Museum as that which is now becoming scarce, and of which it is proposed to issue a new edition.

N. York, April 30, 1831.   SAMUEL H. COX, D. D.

RECOMMENDATIONS.

Buck's works are highly useful and important to the Christian reader and student. I have been conversant with them for the last twenty years, and can cordially recommend them to the attention and study of all persons desirous of improvement in knowledge and purity.

Phila. June 27, 1831.   W. T. BRANTLY,
Pastor of the 1st. Baptist Church and Editor of
the Columbian Star and Christian Index.

I heartily concur with the above recommendation of Buck's Anecdotes. Parents will find them very useful in the religious instruction of their children.

N. Y. April 30th, 1831.   H. G. LUDLOW.

Having made a cursory examination of the above named work of Buck, I coincide with Doctor Green, in his favourable opinion. See the preface.

Phila. June 27th, 1831.   G. T. BEDELL, D. D.

PREFACE.

The Reverend Charles Buck was a Dissenting minister of South Britain, who died a few years since; a man of considerable erudition, of an inquisitive and discriminating mind, and of fervent piety. His most elaborate work was his Theological Dictionary, which has passed through several editions, and is still held in high and just esteem. Besides this he published several volumes of Miscellanies, all of which have a considerable degree of merit, and have had a pretty extensive circulation. But of all his works, that which is here offered to the public, and which forms a part of his Miscellanies, blends the useful with the pleasant, in the greatest degree. Of his "Anecdotes, Religious, Moral and Entertaining, alphabetically arranged and interspersed with a variety of useful observations," I hesitate not to say, that I know of no work, which more happily unites instruction with entertainment. It requires no effort of the mind to be understood, and can weary no one by a long demand of attention to a particular subject. It cannot be read without interest, and it is, in every part, calculated to leave an impression on the mind favourable to virtue, piety or benevolence. It instructs by example. It can be taken up at a leisure moment, and laid down at pleasure, without leaving a subject unfinished. All who read serious books at all, I am ready to suppose, would like to have in their possession, such a book as this. It is a book of amusement for the scholar, and of profitable instruction to those who read but little. The character given of it when first published, in the Evangelical Review, was as follows. " This work is " well calculated for young persons, and may prove in many " cases, a very acceptable present to them, as it conveys much " instruction, mingled with entertainment. It will also serve " for a pleasing companion to the traveller in the chaise or the " stage coach. In short, it affords a copious fund of rational " amusement for a leisure hour. We have no doubt but it " will obtain, as it certainly merits, an extensive circula- " tion."

ASHBEL GREEN.

Philadelphia, Aug. 3d, 1831.

AUTHOR'S PREFACE.

To inform the mind, affect the heart, and promote the best interests of mankind, must ever be considered as a pleasing and honourable employ. Various means, indeed, may be made use of in order to accomplish these ends. Some do good by wise and judicious conversation: others by constant and laborious teaching; and many by an excellent and uniform character. The Compiler of these volumes has here attempted to contribute something towards so good and desirable a work.

It need not be observed, that men are naturally indifferent about their duty to God, and unconcerned as to the welfare of their immortal souls. Any attempt, therefore, to set before them the grand object of veneration and worship, to rouse them to duty, to facilitate their happiness, to show them the deformity of vice, and to inspire them with true and exalted views of the sacred Religion of Jesus, cannot, I think, be considered as unworthy of attention. How far this Work will conduce to these ends, must be left to the judgment of the Reader.

Volumes of Anecdotes have already been presented to the public under various titles; but none that I know of which have been more particularly selected as *religious*, and more immediately calculated to lead men to genuine devotion and solid piety. It is to be lamented, that while many write merely to amuse the imagination, the *real profit* of the mind is not thought of. The passions, perhaps, are affected, and the fancy pleased, while the temper remains unsubdued, the heart unimpressed, and the conduct unstable and irregular. Now, without incurring the charge of egotism, I hope the present Work, while it affords a degree of entertainment to the Reader, will also tend to excite reverence for the best of Beings ; a regard for the noble and delightful system of Christianity ; together with benevolence to our fellow mortals, and an earnest desire to devote ourselves to the glory and service of our God and Saviour.

The Reader will evidently see that *novelty* has not been so much my design as *utility*. If any object, however, to the Work on this account, I can only say in reply, that Anecdotes *cannot be made*. In writing on any system, invention may be displayed, and the ideas of the author may bear the air of novelty : but in a Work of this kind, we must confine ourselves to our materials. I own it is not difficult to find, now and then, an original Anecdote ; but, in this age of writing and publishing, it would be very difficult indeed to find a *volume* of them, since almost every thing of importance is speedily conveyed to the press for the public benefit. We must, therefore, take them as we find them, and make the best improvement of them we can.

I am conscious that every Anecdote will not strike the mind of the Reader with equal importance : nor can it be expected, that, in a selection of some hundreds, it should be so. Besides, men are of different tastes ; they form different views, and are situated in different circumstances : each one, therefore, will judge favourably of *that* which is most congenial to his own ideas. The compiler, however, deprecates the severity of the critic, and hopes that candour will perform the office of a kind friend, who is more disposed to pardon than to indulge a spirit of invective. In respect to authenticity, which is of considerable importance in a work of this kind, I have carefully avoided what appeared to be apocryphal, and bore but scrupulous evidence; yet, after all, if any thing should be found of this kind, (which I am ignorant of, if there be,) still its moral or use will be found beneficial, pointing the Reader to view religion and morality as worthy of his sincere regard and constant pursuit.

To conclude: if any good be done, any mind instructed, any comfort derived; if love to men, gratitude to our adorable Redeemer, and a firm adherence to the truth, be excited or promoted by this selection, it will abundantly compensate the little labour and feeble efforts of the Compiler.

C. B.

INDEX TO VOL. I.

6

INDEX

ANECDOTES

AFFLICTIONS.

WHOEVER considers the manifold calamities to which mankind are exposed in the present state, must feel some emotion of sorrow. Sin has introduced great misery and universal disorder into the world. No person, however mean and obscure, or eminent and exalted, can stand invulnerable against the arrows of adversity. It is, however, the peculiar privilege of a good man, that though, alike with others, he partakes of the sufferings of humanity, yet he sees a wise hand directing every event, and rendering all subservient to a grand and glorious end. He desires to learn the noble lessons of patience and submission, while his heart glows with gratitude to Him, to whom he is indebted for every comfort he enjoys, and without whose permission he knows no evil can transpire.

Ebenezer Adams, a celebrated Quaker of Philadelphia, on visiting a lady of rank, whom he found six months after the death of her husband sitting on a sofa covered with black cloth, and in all the dignity of wo, approached her with great solemnity, and gently taking her by the hand, thus accosted her :—" So, *friend, I see that thou hast not yet forgiven God Almighty.*" This seasonable reproof had such an effect upon the person to whom it was addressed, that she immediately had all her trappings of grief destroyed, and went about her necessary business and avocations. " A word spoken in due season, how good is it !"

Afflictions, though not blessings in themselves, yet when sanctified are productive of great good to them who are exercised thereby. Even Demetrius, a heathen, could say, " That nothing could be more unhappy than a man who had never known affliction." And one who was not a heathen has left it on record, That it was good for him to be afflicted. Let us not therefore sink into despondency under a view of approaching difficulties, nor suffer our imaginations to dwell with horror on supposed future events. "The evils and afflictions of this life, indeed, appear like rocks and precipices, rugged and barren, at a distance ; but at our nearer approach we shall find little fruitful spots, and refreshing springs, mixed with the harshness and deformities of nature."

A Minister was recovering of a dangerous illness, when one of his friends addressed him thus : " Sir, though God seems to be bringing you up from the gates of death, yet it will be a long time before you will sufficiently retrieve your strength, and regain vigour enough of mind to preach as usual." The good man answered, "You are mistaken, my friend; for this six weeks' illness has taught me more divinity than all my past studies and all my ten years' ministry put together."

It is related of one, who, under great severity, had fled from the worst of masters to the best, (I mean he had sought rest in the bosom of Jesus Christ, the common friend of the weary and the heavy laden,) that he was so impressed with a sense of the benefit he had derived from his afflictions, that lying on his death-bed, and seeing his master stand by, he eagerly caught the hands of his op-

1*

pressor, and kissing them, said, " These hands have brought me to heaven." Thus many have had reason to bless God for afflictions, as being the instruments in his hand of promoting the welfare of their immortal souls !

It is said of Dr. W., that from his most early infancy to his dying day, he scarcely ever knew what health was ; yet we are told that he looked upon this affliction as the greatest blessing of his life. And the reason he assigned for it was, that, being naturally of a warm temper and an ambitious disposition, these visitations of Divine Providence weaned his affections from the world, and brought every passion into subjection to the Divine will.

AVARICE.

OF all characters, perhaps, none are so truly wretched as the miser. The prodigal, it is true, spends his substance, but then he attempts to enjoy himself, and to make others happy around him ; whereas the covetous man does neither.—Avarice is a principle not only detestable in its nature, but prejudicial to the possessor of it ; inasmuch as it alienates the mind from God, frequently leads to dishonesty among men, and, what is worse, is a disorder hardly ever cured. "Other passions have their holidays, but avarice never suffers its votaries to rest."

"Oh cursed lust of gold ! when for thy sake
The fool throws up his interest in *both*
        worlds,
First starv'd in this, then damn'd in that
    to come."   BLAIR.

"Joshua," says Ambrose, " could stop the course of the sun, but all his power could not stop the course of avarice. The sun stood still, but avarice went on. Joshua obtained a victory when the sun stood still ; but when avarice was at work, Joshua was defeated."

In December, 1790, died at Paris, literally of want, Mr. Ostervald, a well known banker. This man felt the violence of the disease of avarice

(for surely it is rather a disease than a passion of the mind) so strongly that, within a few days of his death, no importunities could induce him to buy a few pounds of meat, for the purpose of making a little soup for him. " 'Tis true, (said he,) I should not dislike the soup, but I have no appetite for the meat ; what, then, is to become of that ?" At the time that he refused this nourishment, for fear of being obliged to give away two or three pounds of meat, there was tied round his neck a silken bag which contained 800 assignats, of 1,000 livres each. At his outset in life, he drank a pint of beer, which served him for supper, every night at a house much frequented, from which he carried home all the bottle corks he could come at : of these, in the course of eight years, he had collected as many as sold for 12 louis d'ors ; a sum that laid the foundation of his future fortune, the superstructure of which was rapidly raised by his uncommon success in stock-jobbing. He died possessed of 125,000*l.*sterling.

There have been few persons in whom avarice has predominated more than in the late Mr. Elwes. His mother, indeed, was excessively avaricious, and though she was left nearly 100,000*l.* by her husband, yet she absolutely starved herself to death. Mr. Elwes seemed not less wretched than his mother. At his house at Stoke, in Suffolk, if a window were broken, it was mended by a piece of brown paper, or by patching it with a small bit of glass ; and this had been done so frequently, and in so many shapes, that it would have puzzled a mathematician to say what figure they represented. To save fire, he would walk about the remains of an old green-house, or sit with a servant in the kitchen ! In the advance of the season his morning employment was to pick up chips, bones, or any thing he could find, and carry them home in his pocket for fire ! One day he was surprised by a neighbouring gentleman in the act of pulling down, with great difficulty, a crow's nest for this purpose ; and when the gentleman wondered why he should give himself so much trouble, "O, Sir," replied Elwes, "it is really a shame that these creatures should do so; do but see what waste they make. They don't care how extravagant they are." He would almost eat any thing to save expense. At a time when he was worth eight hundred thousand pounds, he would eat game at the last state of putrefaction, and meat that no other person could touch! As to his dress, any thing would do. He wore a wig for a fortnight which he picked up in a rut in the lane, when riding with another gentleman. His shoes he never suffered to be cleaned, lest they should be worn out the sooner. As the infirmities of old age, however, came upon him, he began to be more wretched. It is said, that he was heard frequently at midnight as if struggling with some one in his chamber, and crying out, " I will keep my money; nobody shall rob me of my property." There are many other remarkable circumstances related of him, but what we have already quoted afford a striking proof of the vanity of sublunary things, and of the insufficiency of riches to render mankind happy.—See his Life.

Daniel Dancer, Esq. was remarkable for a miserly disposition. Lady Tempest was the only person who had the least influence on this unfortunate man. She had one day the pleasure of prevailing on him to purchase a hat (having worn his own for thirteen years) from a Jew for a shilling; but to her great surprise, when she called the next day, she saw the old *chapeau* still covered his head! On inquiry it was found that, after much solicitation, he had prevailed on old Griffiths, his servant, to purchase the hat for *eighteen pence*, which Mr. Dancer bought the day before for a shilling! He generally, in severe weather, laid in bed to keep himself warm: to light a fire he thought expensive, though he had 3,000*l*. per annum, besides immense riches! He never took snuff, for that was extravagant, but he always carried a snuff-box. This probably he would fill in the course of a month, by pinches obtained from others! When the box was full, he would barter the contents for a farthing candle at a neighbouring green grocer's : this candle was made to last till the box was again full, as he never suffered any light in his house, except while he was going to bed. He seldom washed his face and hands but when the sun shone forth ; then he would betake himself to a neighbouring pool, and used sand instead of soap : when he was washed, he, would lie on his back, and dry himself in the sun, as he never used a towel, for that would wear, and, when dirty, the washing was expensive. Since his death there have been jugs of dollars and shillings found in the stable. At the dead of night he has been known to go to this place, but for what purpose even *Old Griffiths* could not tell ; but it now appears he used to rob one jug to add to the other.

M. Vandille was the most remarkable man in Paris, both on account of his immense riches and his extreme avarice. He lodged as high up as the roof would admit him, to avoid noise or visits ; maintained one poor old woman to attend him in his garret, and allowed her only seven sous per week,or a half penny per day. His usual diet was bread and milk, and, by way of indulgence, some poor sour wine on a Sunday. This prudent economist had been a magistrate or officer at Boulogne, from which obscurity he was promoted to Paris, for the reputation of his wealth, which he lent upon undeniable security to the public funds, not caring to trust individuals with what constituted all his happiness. While a magistrate at Boulogne, he maintained himself by taking upon him to be milk taster-general at the market, and from one to another filled his belly and washed down his bread without expense to himself.

8   RELIGIOUS, MORAL, AND

When he was become exceedingly rich, he one day heard a woodman go by in summer, at which season they stock themselves with fuel for the winter. He agreed with him at the lowest rate possible, and stole from the poor man several logs, with which he loaded himself to his secret hiding hole, and thus contracted, in that hot season, a fever. He then sent, for the first time, for a surgeon to bleed him, who, asking half a livre for the operation, was dismissed; he then sent for an apothecary, but he was as high in his demand. He next sent for a poor barber, who undertook to open a vein for three pence a time; but understanding from the barber that he should be blooded three times, he asked what quantity of blood it was meant to take at once. 'About eight ounces each time,' answered the barber.—'That will be nine-pence :—too much, too much!' says the old miser: 'I have determined to go a cheaper way to work; take at once the whole quantity you designed to take at three times, and that will save me sixpence;' which being insisted on, he lost twenty-four ounces of blood, and died in a few days, leaving all his vast treasure to the King, whom he made his sole heir. Thus he contracted his disorder by pilfering, and his death by an unprecedented piece of parsimony.

INSTANCES OF BENEFICENCE,
AND CHARITY.

"It is more blessed to give than to receive," says our Lord. Happy is he who can subscribe sincerely to this truth, and whose felicity arises in proportion as he alleviates the distresses of others. To do good is to resemble the best of Beings. It is, indeed our honour, and renders us valuable and useful in society. A compassionate heart and a liberal hand form a degree of amiableness ever worthy to be venerated. There is a threefold pleasure in doing good. It is pleasant to God for his creatures to be like him; it is pleasant to ourselves to discharge our duty; and it is pleasant to the object who is relieved by our munificence.

It was a common saying of Julius Cæsar, "that no music was so charming in his ears as the request of his friends, and the supplication of those in want of his assistance." Let Christians learn to imitate this Pagan.

The King of Prussia once rang the bell of his cabinet, but as nobody answered, he opened the door of the antichamber, and found his page fast asleep upon a chair. He went up to awake him, but coming nearer he observed a paper in his pocket, upon which something was written. This excited his curiosty. He pulled it out, and found that it was a letter from the page's mother; the contents of which were nearly as follow : " She returned her son many thanks for the money he had saved out of his salary, and had sent to her, which had proved a very timely assistance. God would certainly reward him for it, and if he continued to serve God, and his King faithfully and conscientiously, he could not fail of success and prosperity in this world." Upon reading this, the King stept softly into his closet, fetched a rouleau of ducats, and put it with the letter into the page's pocket. He then rang so long till the page awoke, and came into his closet. " You have been asleep, I suppose," said the King. The page could not deny it, stammered out an excuse, put (in his embarrassment) his hand into his pocket, and felt the rouleau of ducats. He immediately pulled it out, turned pale, and looked at the King with tears in his eyes. " What is the matter with you?" said the King. " O," replied the page, "somebody has contrived my ruin : I know nothing of this money." " What God bestows," resumed the King, "he bestows in sleep.* Send the money to your mother: give my respects to her, and inform her that I will take care of both her and you."

It is said of the excellent Lord Chief Justice Hale, that he frequently invi-

* A German Proverb.

ted his *poor* neighbours to dinner, and made them sit at table with himself. If any of them were sick, so that they could not come, he would send provisions to them, warm from his own table : and he did not confine his bounties to the poor of his own parish, but diffused supplies to the neighbouring parishes as occasion required. He always treated the *old*, the *needy*, and the *sick*, with the tenderness and familiarity that became one who considered they were of the same nature with himself, and were reduced to no other necessities but such as he himself *might* be brought to. Common beggars he considered in another view : if any of these met him on his walks, or came to his door, he would ask such as were capable of working, *why they went about so idle?* If they answered, *it was because they could not get employ*, he would send them to some field, to gather all the stones in it, and lay them in a heap ; and then paid them liberally for their pains. This being done, he used to send his carts, and cause them to be carried to such places of the highway as needed mending.

Mr. Gilpin, who was called the Apostle of the North, was such an hospitable man, that every Thursday throughout the year he had a very large quantity of meat dressed wholly for the poor ; and every day they had what quantity of broth they wanted. Twenty-four of the poorest were his constant pensioners. Four times in the year a dinner was provided for them, when they received from the steward a certain quantity of corn, and a sum of money ; and at Christmas they had always an ox divided among them. During some part of the year, from Michaelmas to Easter, he expected to see all his parishioners and their families. For their reception he had three tables well covered ; the first was for gentlemen, the second for husbandmen and farmers, and the third for day labourers. This piece of hospitality he never omitted, even when losses or a scarcity of provision made its contrivance rather difficult to him. Even when he was absent, no alteration was made in his family expenses ; the poor were fed, and his neighbours entertained as usual. Strangers and travellers found a cheerful reception ; all were welcome that came ; and even their beasts had so much care taken of them that it was humorously said, " if a horse was turned loose in any part of the country, it would immediately make its way to the rector of Houghton."

Whatever plans of liberality we may have before us, it is well not to procrastinate, but to embrace the first opportunity of executing them.

When Mr. Baxter lost a thousand pounds, which he had laid up for the erection of a school, he used frequently to mention the misfortune as an excitement to be charitable while God gives the power of bestowing, and considered himself as culpable in some degree for having so long delayed the performance of a good action, and suffered his benevolence to be defeated for want of quickness and diligence.

Dr. Tillotson (afterwards Archbishop) gave the most exemplary proof of his charity. The revocation of the Edict of Nantz having driven thousands of the Huguenots to this country, many of them settled at Canterbury, where their posterity still continue. The King having granted briefs to collect alms for their relief, Dr. T. was peculiarly active in promoting their success; and when Dr. Beveridge, one of the Prebendaries of Canterbury, refused to read the briefs, as being contrary to the rubric, he was silenced by Dr. T. with this energetic reply, " *Doctor, Doctor, charity is above rubrics.*"

A wealthy merchant having lost by one shipwreck to the value of 1,500*l.* ordered his clerk to distribute 100*l.*, among poor ministers and people ; adding, that if his fortune was going by 1,500*l.* at a lump, it was high time to make sure of some part before it was gone.

Of Dr. Samuel Wright it is said, that his charity was conducted upon rule; for which purpose he kept a purse, in which was found this memorandum: "Something from all the money I receive to be put into this purse for charitable uses. From my salary as minister, which is uncertain, a tenth part—from occasional and extraordinary gifts, which are more uncertain, a twentieth part—from copy money of things I print, and interest of my estate, a seventh part."

When a gentleman who had been accustomed to give away some thousands was supposed to be at the point of death, his presumptive heir inquired where his fortune was to be found? To whom he answered, "that it was in the pockets of the indigent."

When some bedding was to be given away to the poor at O———, a poor woman carried home two pair of blankets, a pair for herself and husband, and a pair for six children. As soon as the children saw them, they jumped out of their straw, caught them in their arms, kissed and blessed them, and danced for joy. A very old woman, the first night she found herself so comfortably covered, could not sleep a wink; being kept awake by the contrary emotions of transport on the one hand, and fear of not being thankful enough on the other.

A poor cottager within a few miles of London, who had a wife and six children, was seized on for his rent; and whilst the poor woman was imploring the mercy of the officers, a person came by, and inquiring into the cause of her distress, immediately discharged the debt, amounting to eleven pounds, and walked away. For this timely and truly generous action, the distressed family were indebted to a tradesman on Ludgate Hill. The name is concealed, but the action shall not be forgotten.

When a collection was made in Wales for the Bible Society, we are told that a poor servant maid put down one guinea on the plate, being one third of her wages. That it might not be perceived what she put down, she covered the guinea with a halfpenny.—One little boy had with much trouble reared a brood of chickens : when the collection came to be made, he sold them all, and gave every farthing he got for them towards it, and this was his whole stock, and all the living that he had.

The following anecdote of Bishop Barrington does high honour to his liberality and piety. A relation of Mrs. Barrington having experienced some embarrassments and disappointments in life, wished to amend his situation, (being a military officer) by entering into the church, thinking that the Bishop would provide handsomely for him. On making the necessary application to his kinsman, he was asked what preferment would satisfy him? To this home question he readily answered, that about 500*l.* a year would make him a happy man. "You shall have it," said his lordship, "but not out of the patrimony of the church. I will not deprive a worthy and regular divine to provide for a necessitous relation. You shall have the sum you mention out of my own pocket."

While Lord Thurlow was at College, he was often too licentious with his tongue, and, entering once into a dispute with an elective and temporary officer, he was asked "whether he knew that he was talking to the *Dean?*" "Yes, Mr. *Dean,*" replied Mr. Thurlow, and never afterwards saw him without reiterating, "Mr. Dean, Mr. Dean," which set them at variance. When he became Attorney General, they met by accident; and he addressed his old friend *unwittingly,* "How do you do, Mr. *Dean?*" which so hurt the old *cantab,* that he left the room without making him any reply. On his obtaining the office of Lord Chancellor, he took an opportunity of meeting once more with his quondam acquaintance, and again addressed him with, "How do you do, Mr. *Dean?*"—"My Lord," replied the other sullenly, "I am not now a dean, and therefore do not deserve the title." "But you *are* a Dean," said his Lordship :—" and, to satisfy you that it is so, read this paper, by which you will find that you are Dean of —— : and I am so convinced that you will do honour to the appointment, that I am sorry any part of my conduct should have given offence to so good a man."

It would be injustice here to omit the name of that great philanthropist, Mr. John Howard, who, after inspecting the receptacles of crime, of poverty, and misery, throughout Great Britain and Ireland, left his native country, relinquished his own ease, to visit the wretched abodes of those who were in want, and bound in fetters of iron, in other parts of the world. He travelled three times through France, four through Germany, five through Holland, twice through Italy, once through Spain and Portugal, and also through Denmark, Sweden, Russia, Poland, and part of Turkey. These excursions occupied (with some short intervals of rest at home) the period of twelve years.

Never before was such a considerable portion of the life of man applied to a more benevolent and laudable purpose. He gave up his own comfort that he might bestow it upon others. He was often immured in prison, that others might be set at liberty. He exposed himself to danger, that he might free others from it. He visited the gloomy cell, that he might inspire a ray of hope and joy in the breasts of the wretched. Yea, he not only lived but died in the noble cause of benevolence ; for, in visiting a young lady who lay dangerously ill of an epidemic fever, in order to administer relief, he caught the distemper, and fell a victim to his humanity, on January 20, 1790.

Mr. Howard's worth seems to be appreciated by two or three singular circumstances. The first was, that a liberal subscription was opened to defray the expenses of erecting a statue to his honour, *while yet alive*, and the sum of 1,533*l.* 13*s.* 6*d.* was actually subscribed. But the principles of Howard were abhorrent from ostentation, and when he heard of it, " Have not I," said he, "one friend in England who would put a stop to such a proceeding ?" The business was accordingly dropped.—Another circumstance was, that his death was announced in the London Gazette, a compliment which no private subject ever received before.—And a third circumstance deserves to be noticed, that, though a Dissenter, a monument was erected to his memory in St. Paul's Cathedral. The inscription tells us with truth, " That he trod an open but unfrequented path to immortality, in the ardent and unremitted exercise of Christian charity." And concludes, " May this tribute to his fame excite an emulation of his truly honourable actions."

Mr. Burke justly observed of this great man, "that he visited all Europe (and the East) not to survey the sumptuousness of palaces or the stateliness of temples ; not to make accurate measurements of the remains of ancient grandeur, nor to form a scale of the curiosity of modern art ; not to collect medals, or to collate manuscripts : but to dive into the depth of dungeons ; to plunge into the infection of hospitals ; to survey the mansions of sorrow and of pain ; to take the gauge and dimensions of misery, depression and contempt ; to remember the forgotten ; to attend to the neglected ; to visit the forsaken ; and to compare and to collate the distresses of all men and in all countries. His plan is original, and it is as full of genius as it is of humanity. It is a voyage of discovery, a circumnavigation of charity ; and already the benefit of his labour is felt more or less in every country."

The late John Thornton, Esq. of Clapham, was distinguished by great liberality ; he disposed of large sums in various charitable designs, with unremitting constancy, during a long course of years. His charities were much larger than is common with wealthy persons of good reputation for beneficence, insomuch that he was almost regarded as a prodigy. He was the patron of all pious, exemplary, and laborious Ministers of the Gospel; frequently educating young men whom he found to be religiously disposed, and purchasing many livings, which he gave to Ministers, in order that the Gospel might be preached in those places where he supposed the people were perishing for lack of knowledge. He also dispersed a very great number of Bibles in different languages, in distant countries, perhaps in all the four quarters of the globe, and with them vast quantities of religious books, calculated to alarm the conscience and affect the heart with the importance of eternal things. He also patronised every undertaking which was suited to supply the wants, to relieve the distresses, or to increase the comforts of the human species, in whatever climate, or of whatever description, provided they properly fell within his sphere of action. Perhaps it would even be difficult to name one public or private charity of evident utility to which he was not a benefactor.—May such noble and benevolent characters be found in every age!

BISHOPS.

THE office of a Bishop is certainly honourable: but it should be recollected, at the same time, that it is very important. He, therefore, who undertakes it for the sake of emolument, and not from a love to souls, may suspect himself of having run before he was sent.

Bishops have it greatly in their power to do good, and it is well when they are convinced of the duties of the situation they sustain, and act with proportionate zeal and activity Out of the vast number who have arrived to this honour, we have had some instances of men who have made use of their authority to promote the best ends, and "who did not count their lives dear unto themselves."

" Old Bishop Latimer, it is said, in a coarse frieze gown, trudged afoot,

his testament hanging at one end of his leathern girdle, and his spectacles at the other, and, without ceremony, instructed the people in rustic style from a hollow tree; while the courtly Ridley, in satin and fur, taught the same principles in the cathedral of the metropolis."

Archbishop Williams once said to a friend of his, " I have passed through many places of honour and trust, both in church and state, more than any of my order in England these seventy years before; yet were I but assured that by my preaching I had converted but one soul to God, I should take therein more spiritual joy and comfort than in all the honours and offices which have been bestowed upon me."

Of Archbishop Matthews it is said that he had an admirable talent for preaching, which he never suffered to be idle; but used to go from one town to another, to preach to crowded audiences. He kept an exact account of the sermons which he preached after he was preferred; by which it appears, that he preached, when Dean of Durham, 721; when Bishop of that diocese, 550; and when Archbishop of York, 721; in all 1992. Preferment, it seems, did not injure him.

Archbishop Sheldon expended in public and private benefactions, and acts of charity, no less than 66,000l. as appeared from his accounts; much of this money was appropriated to the relief of the necessitous in the time of the plague, and to the redemption of Christian slaves.

Archbishop Leighton was a most exemplary character : Bishop Burnet says, " he had the greatest elevation of soul, the largest compass of knowledge, the most mortified and heavenly disposition, that I ever yet saw in mortal. He had the greatest parts as well as virtue, with the most perfect humility, that I ever saw in man; and had a sublime strain in preaching, with so grave a gesture, and such a majesty both of thought, of language, and pronunciation, that I never once saw a wandering eye where he preached, and I have seen whole assemblies often melt in tears before him; and of whom I can say, with great truth, that in a free and frequent conversation with him for above two and twenty years, I never knew him say an idle word, or a word that had not a direct tendency to edification; and I never once, saw him in any other temper but that I wished to be in, the last moment of my life."

It is said of Bishop Burnet that he was extremely laborious in his episcopal office. Every summer he made a tour, for six weeks or two months, through some district of his diocese, daily preaching, and confirming from church to church; so as in the compass of three years, besides his triennial visitation, to go through all the principal livings in his diocese.

It is a favourable circumstance when bishops are disposed to countenance those clergymen who are determined to be active and diligent in promoting the welfare of their parishioners. Not long since, at a visitation in Ireland, the name of Mr. Shaw, a pious and useful clergyman was mentioned. "What!" said a clergyman, "what *mad Shaw!*" The bishop answered, "Sir, if Mr. Shaw is mad, I wish he may bite all the clergy in my diocese."

Of Archbishop Secker we are informed that he kept two paper books, one called the *black*, the other the *white* book; in which he entered down such notices as he received concerning the different character of each of his clergymen, as they happened to suit the design of either book: those whose character he found to be bad, he resolved never to promote, nor did, paying no regard to any solicitation made in their behalf; and those of good character he always encouraged. Whenever any publications came to his knowledge that were manifestly calculated to corrupt good morals, or subvert the foundation of Christianity, he did his utmost to stop the circulation of them;

yet the wretched authors themselves he was so far from wishing to treat with any undue rigour, that he more than once extended his bounty to them in distress. And when their writings could not properly be suppressed by lawful authority, he engaged men of ability to answer them, and rewarded them for their trouble. Even the falsehoods and misrepresentations of writers in the newspapers on religious or ecclesiastical subjects he generally took care to have contradicted. What was also greatly to his praise, he was no bigot. With the Dissenters, it is said, he was sincerely desirous of cultivating a good understanding; he considered them, in general, as a conscientious and valuable class of men: with some of the most eminent of them, Watts, Doddridge, Leland, Chandler, Lardner, he maintained an intercourse of friendship or civility. Such liberality is worthy to be imitated.

Dr. Thomas Wilson, Bishop of Soder and Man, is reported to have expended more than ten thousand pounds in acts of charity and beneficence. He preached every Lord's-day at eighty-three years of age.

As Queen Caroline was once in conversation with several of our English bishops, his Lordship of Man came in to pay his respects. She no sooner glimpsed him at a distance, than she said to the prelates who were present, "My Lords, here comes a Bishop, whose errand is not to apply for a translation; he would not part with his spouse (his diocese) because she is poor." With regard to the rights of conscience in others, he exercised the most candid and benevolent moderation. He admitted Dissenters to the holy communion, and administered it to them, either sitting or standing, as they themselves approved. Such amiable and uniform moderation had so favourable an effect that, a few years after his settlement in the island, not a single dissenting congregation of any kind was to be found in it.

B

BLIND—BLINDNESS

It is somewhat remarkable, that, where there is a deficiency in the organs of the human frame, we often find it amply compensated by a superiority of mental excellence, and particularly in the case of blindness. Though one would imagine that of all others, the blind would be most peevish and fretful, yet their behaviour is often highly expressive, not only of resignation, but of cheerfulness. Indeed, "the common Parent of nature, whose benignity is permanent as his existence, and boundless as his empire, has neither left his afflicted creatures without consolation or resource. Even from their loss, however oppressive and irretrievable, they derive advantages; not indeed adequate to recompense, but in some degree sufficient to alleviate their misery. The attention of the soul is not dissipated by the immense multiplicity of surrounding objects. Her contemplations are more uniformly fixed upon herself, and the revolutions of her own internal frame. Hence her perceptions of such external things as are contiguous and obvious to her observation become more lively and exquisite. Hence, even her instruments of corporal sensation are more assiduously cultivated and improved, so that from them she derives such notices and presages of approaching pleasure or impending danger, as entirely escape the attention of those who depend for security on the reports of their eyes."

Mr. Henry Moyes, though blind from his infancy, by the ardour and assiduity of his application, and by the force of a genius to which nothing is impenetrable has not only made incredible advances in Mechanical Operations, in Music, and in the Languages, but is likewise profoundly skilled in Geometry, in Optics, in Algebra, in Astronomy, in Chemistry, and in all the other branches of Natural Philosophy, as taught by Newton, and received by an admiring world.

Blacklock is said to have seen the light only for five months. Besides having made himself master of Greek, Latin, Itatian, and French, he was also a great poet.

A French lady, who lost her sight at two years old, was possessed of many talents which alleviated her misfortune. " In writing to her," it is said, " no ink is used, but the letters are pricked down on the paper; and, by the delicacy of her touch, feeling each letter, she follows them successively, and reads every word with her fingers' ends. She herself in writing makes use of a pencil, as she could not know when her pen was dry: her guide on the paper is a small thin ruler, and of the breadth of her writing. On finishing a letter, she wets it, so as to fix the traces of her pencil, that they are not obscured or effaced; then proceeds to fold and seal it, and write the direction, all by her own address, and without the assistance of any other person. Her writing is very straight, well cut, and the spelling no less correct. To reach this singular mechanism, the indefatigable cares of her affectionate mother were long employed, who, accustoming her daughter to feel letters cut in cards of pasteboard, brought her to distinguish an A from a B, and thus the whole alphabet, and afterwards to spell words; then, by the remembrance of the shape of the letters, to delineate them on paper; and, lastly, to arrange them so as to form words and sentences. She sews and hems perfectly well, and in all her works she threads the needle for herself, however small."

Dr. Nicholas Saunderson, born in 1682, may be considered as a prodigy for his application and success in mathematical literature, though he lost his sight by the small-pox before he was a year old. When young, he could make long and difficult calculations. without having any sensible marks to assist his memory. At eighteen he was taught the principles of Algebra and Geometry. He went to Christ College Cambridge, at twenty-five. His reputation was soon spread through the University, and numbers attended to hear his Mathematical Lectures. He made such proficiency, that he was afterwards elected Lucasion Professor of Mathematics in 1771, and in 1736 he was admitted member of the Royal Society. He invented, for his own use, a palpable Arithmetic; that is, a method of performing operations in Arithmetic solely by the sense of touch. His sense of touch was so perfect, that he could discover, with the greatest exactness, the slightest inequalities of surface, and could distinguish, in the most finished works, the smallest oversight in the polish.

We have a remarkable instance of a blind guide in John Metcalf, of Manchester, who very lately followed the occupation of conducting strangers through intricate roads during the night, or when the tracks were covered with snow. And, strange as this may appear to those who can see, the employment of this man was afterwards that of a projector and surveyor of highways in difficult and mountainous parts! With the assistance only of a long staff, he has been several times seen traversing the roads, ascending precipices, exploring valleys, and investigating their several extents, forms, and situation, so as to answer his designs in the best manner. Most of the roads over the Peak in Derbyshire have been altered by his directions, particularly those in the vicinity of Buxton; and he has since constructed a new one betwixt Winslow and Congleton, with a view to open a communication to the great London road, without being obliged to pass over the mountains.—See the account by Dr. Bew, published in the Transactions of the Manchester Society.

BURYING-PLACE OF CAPUCHINS.

[Related by Mr. Brydone.]

"At Bologna they shewed us the skeleton of a celebrated beauty, who died at a period of life when she was still the object of universal admiration. By way of making atonement for her own vanity, she bequeathed herself as a monument to curb the vanity of others. Recollecting on her death-bed the great adulation that had been paid to her charms, and the fatal change they were soon to undergo, she ordered that her body should be dissected, and her bones hung up for the inspection of all young maidens who are inclined to be vain of their beauty."

"Our late visit to the famous Convent of Capuchins about a mile without the city of Palermo, brought the above anecdote to my remembrance. This Convent contains nothing very remarkable but the burying-place, which, indeed, is a great curiosity. This is a vast subterraneous apartment, divided into large commodious galleries, the walls on each side of which are hollowed into a variety of niches, as if intended for a great collection of statues. These niches, instead of statues, are all filled with dead bodies, set upright on their legs, and fixed by the back to the inside of the nich. Their number is about three hundred. They are all dressed in the clothes they usually wore, and form a most respectable and venerable assembly. The skin and muscles, by a certain preparation, become as dry and hard as a piece of stockfish; and although many of them have been here upwards of 250 years, yet none are reduced to Skeletons. The muscles, indeed, in some, appear to be a good deal more shrunk than in others; probably because these persons had been more attennuated at the time of their death. Here the people of Palermo pay daily visits to their deceased friends, and recal with pleasure and regret the various scenes of their past life. Here they familiarize themselves with their future state, and choose the company they would wish to keep in another world. It is a common thing to make choice of their nich, and to try if their body fits it, that no alternations may be necessary after they are dead; and sometimes, by way of a voluntary penance, they accustom themselves to stand for hours in these niches. The bodies of the princes and first nobility are lodged in handsome chests or trunks, some of them richly adorned These are not in the shape of coffins, but all of one width, and about a foot and a half or two feet deep. The keys are kept by the nearest relations of the family, who sometimes come and drop a tear over their departed friends. I am not sure if this be not a better method of disposing of the dead than our's. These visits must prove admirable lessons of humility; and I assure you they are not such objects of terror as you would imagine. They are said, even for ages after death, to retain a strong likeness to what they were when alive; so that, as soon as you have conquered the first feelings excited by these venerable figures, you only consider this as a vast gallery of original portraits, drawn after the life by the justest and most unprejudiced hand. It must be owned that the colours are rather faded; and the pencil does not appear to have been the most flattering in the world. But no matter: it is the pencil of truth, and not of a mercenary who only wants to please. We were alleging, too, that it might be made of very considerable utility to society, and that these dumb orators could give the most pathetic lectures upon pride and vanity. Whenever a fellow began to strut, or affect the haughty or supercilious air, he should be sent to converse with his friends in the gallery; and if their arguments did not bring him to a proper way of thinking, I would give him up as incorrigible. If the lady above mentioned had been preserved in this moral gallery, the lesson would have been stronger: for those very features that had raised her vanity would still have remained, only divested of all their powers, and disarmed of every charm. Some of the Capuchins sleep in these galleries

every night, and pretend to have many wonderful visions and revelations; but the truth is, that very few people believe them.

CARDS.

CARDS were first invented under the reign of Charles VI. King of France, to amuse him during the intervals of the disorder which carried him to the grave. The world would have sustained no loss had his Majesty been suffered to die in peace without this invention. They seem, however, to be the delight of vast numbers of mankind; and even men who profess to have a superiority of taste and a greater extent of knowledge than the generality, pass away too much of their time in this useless and often injurious pursuit. The following is a very pointed and suitable reproof to such:

Mr. Locke having been introduced by Lord Shaftesbury to the Duke of Buckingham and Lord Halifax, these three noblemen, instead of conversing with the philosopher, as might naturally have been expected, on literary subjects, in a very short time sat down to cards. Mr. Locke, after looking on for some time, pulled out his pocket-book, and began to write with great attention. One of the company observing this, took the liberty of asking him what he was writing. "My Lord," said Locke, "I am endeavouring, as far as possible, to profit by my present situation; for, having waited with impatience for the honour of being in company with the greatest geniuses of the age, I thought I could do nothing better than to write down your conversation: and, indeed, I have set down the substance of what you have said for this hour or two." This well-timed ridicule had its desired effect, and these noblemen, fully sensible of its force, immediately quitted their play, and entered into a conversation more rational, and better suited to the dignity of their characters.

"I think it very wonderful," says Addison, "to see persons of the best sense passing away a dozen hours together in shuffling and dividing a pack of cards, with no other conversation but what is made up of a few game phrases, and no other ideas but those of black or red spots ranged together in different figures. Would not a man laugh to hear any one of this species complaining that life is short?"

Mr. Dodd, an eminent minister, being solicited to play at cards, arose from his seat, and uncovered his head. The company asked him what he was going to do. He replied, "To crave God's blessing." They immediately exclaimed, "We never ask a blessing on such an occasion." "Then," said he, " I never engage in any thing, but what I beg of God to give his blessing."

A lady who once heard Mr. Romaine, expressed herself mightily pleased with his discourse, and told him afterwards, that she thought she could comply with his doctrine, and give up every thing but one. " And what is that, madam?" "Cards, Sir."—" You think you could not be happy without them?" " No, Sir ; I know I could not."—" Then, Madam, they are your god, and they must save you." This pointed and just reply is said to have issued in her conversion.

CATECHISING.

CATECHISING is an excellent mean of informing the mind and impressing the heart, and should be attended to by all who wish well to their children. No Minister of the Gospel, who has opportunity, should neglect this part of his work. The late Mr. Hervey's method of instructing young people was such, that while it afforded profit to them, it was a mean of reproof to others.

Some of his parishioners having laid in bed on a Sunday morning longer than he approved, and others having been busy in foddering their cattle when he was coming to church, and several having frequented the ale-house, he thus catechised one of

the children before the congregation. " Repeat me the fourth commandment."—" Now, little man, do you understand the meaning of this commandment?" "Yes, Sir."—" Then if you do, you will be able to answer me these questions : Do those keep holy the Sabbath-day who lay in bed till eight or nine o'clock in the morning, instead of rising to say their prayers and read the Bible?" " No Sir."—" Do those keep the sabbath who fodder their cattle when other people are going to church?" " No, Sir."—" Does God Almighty bless such people as go to ale-houses, and don't mind the instruction of their minister?" " No, Sir."—" Don't those who love God read the Bible to their families, particularly on Sunday evenings, and have prayers every morning and night in their houses." " Yes, Sir." A great variety of such pertinent and familiar questions he would frequently ask, in the most engaging manner, on every part of the Catechism, as he thought most conducive to the improvement and edification of his parish.

CHRISTIANITY.

NOTWITHSTANDING all the objections which infidels and sceptics have brought against Christianity, yet it has nothing to fear from impartial examination. It will bear the closest inspection of the most wise, and outstand all the virulent attempts of the most wicked. It will afford instruction to the philosopher, however exalted, and render consolation to the ignorant, however wretched. Its doctrines are sublime, just, and pure. Its precepts are founded on the most consummate wisdom, truth, and love, every way calculated to promote the holiness, peace, and interest of mankind. Its privileges are great and extensive, allowing its votaries the most noble and refined pleasures in the present state, and opening before them a boundless prospect of immortality and glory in the future.

As to the effects of Christianity, they have been and still are considerable, and afford at least a collateral proof of the superiority and excellency of the system. " Destitute of all human advantages," says one, " protected by no authority, assisted by no art; not recommended by the reputation of its authors, not enforced by eloquence in its advocates, the word of God grew mightily, and prevailed. Twelve men, poor, artless, and illiterate, we behold triumphing over the fiercest and most determined opposition ; over the tyranny of the magistrate and the subtleties of the philosopher; over the prejudice of the Gentile and the bigotry of the Jew."

" The religion of Jesus," says Bishop Taylor, " trampled over the philosophy of the world, the arguments of the subtle, the discourses of the eloquent, the power of princes, the interest of states, the inclination of nature, the blindness of zeal, the force of custom, the solicitation of passions, the pleasure of sin, and the busy arts of the devil."

Sir Isaac Newton set out in life a clamorous infidel, but, on a nice examination of the evidences for Christianity, he found reason to change his opinion. When the celebrated Dr. Edmund Halley was talking infidelity before him, Sir Isaac addressed him in these or the like words :— " Dr. Halley, I am always glad to hear you when you speak about astronomy, or other parts of the mathematics, because that is a subject you have studied, and well understand; but you should not talk of Christianity, for you have not studied it. I have, and am certain that you know nothing of the matter." This was a just reproof, and one that would be very suitable to be given to half the infidels of the present day, for they often speak of what they have never studied, and what, in fact, they are entirely ignorant of. Dr. Johnson, therefore, well observed, that no honest man could be a Deist, for no man could be so after a fair examination of the proofs of Christianity. On the name of Hume being mentioned to him, " No, Sir," said he : " Hume owned to a

clergyman in the bishopric of Durham, that he had never read the New Testament with attention."

The late Lord B——e, the celebrated infidel, was one day reading in Calvin's Institutions.—A clergyman of his Lordship's acquaintance coming on a visit, Lord B. said to him, " You have caught me reading John Calvin. He was indeed a man of great parts, profound sense, and vast learning. He handles the doctrines of grace in a very masterly manner." " *Doctrines of grace!*" replied the clergyman. "The doctrines of grace have set all mankind together by the ears." " I am surprised to hear you say so," answered Lord B. " you profess to believe and to preach Christianity. Those doctrines are certainly the doctrines of the Bible, and if I believe the Bible, I must believe them ; and let me seriously tell you, that the greatest miracle in the world is, the subsistence of Christianity, and its continued preservation as a religion, when the preaching of it is committed to the care of such unchristian wretches as you."

Lord Bacon, towards the latter end of his life, said, that a smattering of philosophy would lead a man to Atheism, but a thorough insight of it will lead a man back again to a first cause, and that the first principle of right reason is religion : and seriously professes, that, after all his studies and inquisitions, he durst not die with any other thoughts than those of religion, taught, as it is professed, among the Christians. To the above we may add the names of Mr. Charles Gildon, Lord Lyttleton, Gilbert West, Esq. Soame Jenyns, Esq. and the late Sir John Pringle, who, though they had imbibed Deistical principles, were afterwards converted to the Christian faith, and four out of the five wrote in defence of it.

Infidels should never talk of our giving up Christianity, till they can propose something superior to it. Lord Chesterfield's answer, therefore, to an infidel lady was very just. When at Brussels, he was invited by

Voltaire to sup with him, and with Madame C. The conversation happening to turn upon the affairs of England, " I think, my Lord," said Madam C. " that the parliament of England consists of five or six hundred of the best informed and most sensible men in the kingdom." "True, madam, they are generally supposed to be so."—" What, then, my Lord, can be the reason that they tolerate so great an absurdity as the Christian religion ?" " I suppose, madam," replied his Lordship, " it is because they have not been able to substitute any thing better in its stead : when they can, I don't doubt but in their wisdom they will readily adopt it."

Christianity is the best system for raising the standard of morals, and promoting the happiness of a government. The French, after making the boldest experiment in profaneness ever made by a nation in casting off its God, and who for a time seriously deliberated whether there should be any god at all; who, after madly stamping on the yoke of Christ, attempted to establish order on the basis of a wild and profligate philosophy; was obliged at length to bid an orator tell the abused multitude, that, under a philosophical religion, every social bond was broken in pieces; and that Christianity, or something like it, must be re-established to preserve any degree of order or decency.

With respect to the propagation of Christianity, it is with pleasure I observe, that though some of its professors are nominal, yet there is every reason to believe that it is making progress in the world. The judgments of God, indeed, are in the earth, but his love and mercy are there also. The various commotions among the different states render the book of Providence difficult to be read in many respects; but it certainly must be pleasing to consider, that there never, perhaps, was a more general zeal, or greater efforts made for the instruction of the igno-rant, than in the present day. I think myself happy to live in a time when there are so many wise, excellent, and faithful ministers, such a multitude of serious people, so many Bibles and other good books distributed, and so great a number of public societies for the purpose of concerting schemes and adopting plans for the general good.

CIVILITY.

RUDENESS ill becomes men possessed of ability, power, riches, or religion. It is a law, not to be dispensed with—"To honour all men." Christians especially are called upon to show respect and kindness to mankind. " Sanctified civility is a great ornament to Christianity." Piety of disposition, connected with urbanity of manners, characterize both the Christian and the gentleman. We should always be careful not to hurt or injure others by a careless, wanton, or unkind conduct. "As every action may produce effects over which human power has no influence, and which human sagacity cannot foresee, we should not lightly venture to the verge of evil, nor strike at others, though with a reed, lest, like the rod of Moses it become a serpent in our hand."

" If a civil word or two will render a man happy," said a French king, " he must be a wretch indeed who will not give them to him." Were superiors to keep this in view, yea, were all mankind to observe it, how much happier would the world be than what it is ? We may say of this disposition, " that it is like lighting another man's candle by one's own, which loses none of its light by what the other gains."

Frederic II. King of Prussia, made it a point to return every mark of respect or civility shewn him in the street by those who met him. He one day observed at table, that, whenever he rode through the streets of Berlin, his hat was always in his hand. Baron Pollnitz, who was present, said, "That his Majesty had no occasion to notice the civility of every one who pulled his hat off to him in the street." " And why not ?" said the King, in a lively tone : " are they not all human beings as well as myself ?"

It was a maxim of a celebrated minister, "that if a child but lisped to give you pleasure, you ought to be pleased." When occasionally preaching in the villages, he used to be delighted in visiting the poor, and, when solicited, would regale himself with their brown bread and black tea ; but took care, at the same time, that they should lose nothing by their attention. " When a poor person shows anxiety to administer to your comfort," he would say, " do not interrupt him. Why deprive him of the pleasure of expressing his friendship ?"

CONSCIENCE.

Of all the horrors human beings can feel, none perhaps are equal to those of a guilty conscience. It embitters every comfort, it dashes every pleasure with sorrow, it fills the mind with despair, and produces wretchedness in the greatest degree. " To live under such disquietude," says Blair, " is already to undergo one of the most severe punishments which human nature can suffer. When the world threatens us with any of its evils, we know the extent and discern the limits of the danger. We see the quarter on which we are exposed to its attack. We measure our own strength with that of our adversary, and can take precautions either for making resistance, or for contriving escape. But when an awakened conscience places before the sinner the just vengeance of the Almighty, the prospect is confounding, because the danger is boundless. It is a dark unknown which threatens him. The arm that is stretched over him he can neither see nor resist. No wonder that the lonesome solitude, or the midnight hour, should strike him with horror."

The following, we are informed, is a true relation of an event which happened in a neighbouring state, not many years ago :—A jeweller, a man of good character and considerable wealth, having occasion, in the way of business, to travel some distance from the place of his abode, took along with him a servant : he had with him some of his best jewels, and a large sum of money, to which his servant was likewise privy. The master having occasion to dismount on the road, the servant watched his opportunity, took a pistol from the master's saddle, and shot him dead on the spot ; then, rifling him of his jewels and money, and hanging a large stone to his neck, he threw him into the nearest canal. With this booty he made off to a distant part of the country, where he had reason to believe that neither he nor his master were known. There he began to trade, in a very low way at first, that his obscurity might screen him from observation ; and in the course of many years seemed to rise up, by the natural progress of business, into wealth and consideration; so that his good fortune appeared at once the effect of industry and the reward of virtue. Of these he counterfeited the appearance so well, that he grew into great credit, married into a good family, and, by laying out his hidden stores discreetly, as he saw occasion, and joining to all an universal affability, he was at length admitted to a share of the government of the town, and rose from one post to another, till at last he was chosen chief magistrate. In this office he maintained a fair character, and continued to fill it with no small applause, both as governor and judge ; till one day, as he sat on the bench with some of his brethren, a criminal was brought before him, who was accused of murdering his master. The evidence came out full ; the jury brought in their verdict that the prisoner was guilty, and the whole assembly waited the sentence of the president of the Court (which happened to be himself) in great suspense. Meanwhile he appeared to be in unusual disorder and agitation of mind; his colour changed often; at length he arose from his seat, and, coming down from the bench, placed himself just by the unfortunate man at the bar, to the no small astonishment of all present. "You see before you, (said he, addressing himself to those who had sat on the bench with him,) a striking instance of the just awards of Heaven, which this day, after thirty years' concealment, presents to you a greater criminal than the man just now found guilty." Then he made an ample confession of his heinous offence, with all its peculiar aggravations: "Nor can I," continued he, "feel any relief from the agonies of an awakened conscience, but by requiring that justice be forthwith done against me, in the most public and solemn manner." We may easily imagine the amazement of all, especially his fellow judges. They accordingly proceeded, upon his confession, to pass sentence upon him, and he died with all the symptoms of a penitent mind. See Fordyce's Dialogue on Education, and Encyclopædia Britannica.

A Mr. Thoroughgood, of the 17th century, having reproved the sin of swearing, one of his hearers, sensible of his guilt, and thinking he was the person particularly intended, resolved to kill him; and in order to do it, he hid himself behind a hedge, which he knew Mr. Thoroughgood would ride by when he went to preach his weekly lecture. When Mr. T. came to the place, he offered to shoot him, but his piece failed, and only flashed in the pan. The next week he lay in the same place, with the same intent. When Mr. T. came up, the wretch offered to fire again; but the piece would not go off. Upon this, his conscience accusing him for such a wickedness, he went after him, and, falling down on his knees, with tears in his eyes, related the whole to him, and begged his pardon. This Providence was the mean of his conver-

sion, and he became, from that time, a serious good man.

The famous Mr. Gilpin, who was called the Father of the Poor, and the Apostle of the North, once had his horses stolen. The news was quickly propagated, and every one expressed the highest indignation at it. The thief, however, was rejoicing over his prize, when, by the report of the country, he found whose horses he had taken. Terrified at what he had done, he instantly came trembling back, confessed the fact, returned the horses, and declared he believed the devil would have seized him directly, had he carried them off when he knew they belonged to Mr. Gilpin.

Experienced ministers sometimes describe the feelings and situations of their hearers so exact, that, while the serious part are profited, the ignorant are astonished. It is related of Mr. Richard Garrat, that he used to walk to Petworth, every Monday. In one of these walks, a country fellow, that had been his hearer the day before, and had been cut to the heart by somewhat he had delivered, came up to him with his scythe upon his shoulders, and in mighty rage, told him, "he would be the death of him, for he was sure he was a witch, he having told him the day before what no one in the world knew of him but God and the devil, and, therefore, he most certainly dealt with the devil."

One of the most sensible men I ever knew, says one, but whose life as well as creed had been rather eccentric, returned me the following answer, not many months before his death, when I asked him, "Whether his former irregularities were not both accompanied at the time, and succeeded afterwards, by some sense of mental pain?" "Yes," said he; "but I have scarce ever owned it until now. We (meaning we infidels and men of fashionable morals) do not tell you all that passes in our hearts!"

James Le Fevre, of Etaples, did not outwardly depart from the Church of Rome, but at the bottom of his heart was a Protestant. He was protected by the Queen of Navarre, sister to Francis I.; and, dining with her in company with some other learned men, whose conversation pleased the Queen, he began to weep; and, when the Queen asked him the reason of it, he answered, "the enormity of his sins threw him into that grief! It was not the remembrance of any lewdness he had been guilty of, and with regard to other vices he felt his conscience easy enough : but he was pricked in his conscience, that, having known the truth and taught it to several persons who had sealed it with their blood, he had the weakness to keep himself in an asylum far from the places where crowns of martyrdom were distributed." He went to bed, where he was found dead a few hours after.

An instance of the power of conscience we have in Lord Rochester. "One day," says he, "I was at an atheistical meeting at a person's of quality : I undertook to manage the cause, and was the principal disputant against God and piety, and for my performance received the applause of the whole company ; upon which my mind was terribly struck, and I immediately replied thus to myself— 'Good God! that a man that walks upright, that sees the wonderful works of God, and has the use of his senses and reason, should use them to the defying of his Creator!' "

THE CONSCIENTIOUS JUDGE.

Sir Matthew Hale, when Chief Baron of the Exchequer, was very exact and impartial in his administration of justice. He would never receive any private addresses or recommendations from the greatest persons, in any matter in which justice was concerned. One of the first Peers of England went once to his chamber, and told him, "That, having a suit in law to be tried before him, he was then to acquaint him with it, that he might the better understand it when it should come to be heard in Court."

Upon which Sir Matthew interrupted him, and said, "He did not deal fairly, to come to his chamber about such affairs, for he never received any information of causes but in open court, where both parties were to be heard alike," so he would not suffer him to go on. Whereupon his Grace (for he was a Duke) went away not a little dissatisfied, and complained of it to the King, as a rudeness that was not to be endured. But his Majesty bade him content himself that he was no worse used, and said, "He verily believed he would have used himself no better, if he had gone to solicit him in any of his own causes."

Another passage fell out in one of his circuits, which was somewhat censured as an affectation of unreasonable strictness; but it flowed from his exactness to the rules he had set himself. A gentleman had sent him a buck for his table that had a trial at the Assizes ; so, when he heard his name, he asked, "If he was not the same person that had sent him venison?" And finding he was the same, he told him, "He could not suffer the trial to go on, till he had paid him for his buck." To which the gentleman answered, "That he never sold his venison, and that he had done nothing to him which he did not do to every Judge that had gone that circuit," which was confirmed by several gentlemen then present ; but all would not do, for the Lord Chief Baron had learned from Solomon, that "a gift perverteth the ways of judgment;" and therefore he would not suffer the trial to go on till he had paid for the present ; upon which the gentleman withdrew the record. And at Salisbury, the Dean and Chapter having, according to custom, presented him with six sugar loaves in his circuit, he made his servants pay for the sugar before he would try their cause.

CONTENTMENT.

Dr. Hammond, it is said, was troubled with a complication of disorders, and, when he had got the gout upon him, he used to thank God that it was not the stone ; and when he had the stone, that he had not both these distempers on him at the same time. Thus we see how Christianity influences the mind, and learns us to be submissive and resigned under adverse providences; and, indeed, however men may boast of their courage or fortitude, they must be strangers to genuine and lasting peace, if they are unacquainted with religion. " Poets, indeed, and novelists, have beautifully described contentment, and have often charmed their admirers into a momentary oblivion of their sorrows : but this has made way for subsequent dissatisfaction with every situation and employment in real life. The citizen fancies that contentment dwells in rural obscurity ; the rustic concludes that it may be found in the splendour and pleasures of the metropolis. Courtiers *pretend to think* that this pleasing companion is inseparable from retirement ; the poor erroneously imagine that it may be found in palaces. Britons amuse themselves with descriptions of Arcadian groves; the Arcadians probably conclude that none are so happy as the inhabitants of this favoured isle. They who have it in their power are continually shifting from one place and pursuit to another : and such as are excluded from this privilege, envy, grudge, and murmur. The world resembles a number of people in a fever, who relish nothing, are always restless, and try by incessant change of place or posture to escape from their uneasy sensations; but all their efforts are in vain. Does not this single consideration prove that godliness is the health of the soul, and that without it there can be no abiding contentment?"

A Mr. Lawrence, who was a sufferer for conscience sake, if he would have consulted with flesh and blood, as was said of one of the martyrs, had eleven good arguments against suffering ; viz. a wife and ten children. Being once asked how he meant to maintain them all, he cheerfully replied, " They must all live on Matthew, vi. 34: 'Take therefore no thought for the morrow,'" &c. Contentment and resignation, in such trying circumstances, are not only blessings to the possessors, but they fill by-standers with astonishment. Hence, said Dr. W. to a poor minister, " I wonder, Mr. W., how you do to live so comfortably ; methinks you, with your numerous family, live more plentifully on the providence of God than I can with the benefits of the parish."

When Archbishop Fenelon's library was on fire—"God be praised," said he, " that it is not the habitation of some poor man."

It is our interest as well as our duty cheerfully to acquiesce in the will of God, whatever befalls us.— " That we may not complain of what *is*, let us see God's hand in all events ; and that we may not be afraid of what *shall be*, let us see all events in God's hands."—"When I was rich," says one, " I possessed God in all; and now I am poor, I possess all in God." Thus a right temper of mind involves blessedness in itself. " I carry all my goods with me wherever I go," said a philosopher. So a Christian may truly say.

While Dr. Doddridge was at Bath on his way to Falmouth, (from which latter place he embarked for Lisbon, for the recovery of his health,) Lady H—'s house at Bath was his home. In the morning of the day on which he set out from thence for Falmouth, Lady H. came into the room, and found him weeping over that passage in Daniel, chap. ix. 11 and 12 verses—"O Daniel, a man greatly beloved," &c. " You are in tears, Sir," said Lady H. "I am weeping, Madam," answered the good Doctor ; " but they are tears of comfort and joy. I can give up my country, my relations, and friends, into the hands of God ; and as to myself, I can as well go to heaven from Lisbon as from my own study at Northampton."

How peculiarly placid must the mind of Dr. Watts have been, when in the prospect of death he said, "I bless God I can lie down with comfort at night, unsolicitous whether I awake in this world or another."

"No doubt," said the late Mr. Brown, of Haddington, "I have met with trials as well as others; yet so kind hath God been to me, that I think, if God were to give me as many years as I have already lived in the world, I would not desire one single circumstance in my lot changed, except that I wish I had less sin. It might be written on my coffin, 'Here lies one of the cares of providence, who early wanted both father and mother, and yet never missed them.'"

CONVERSATION.

It is much to be lamented that professing Christians are engaged so little in religious conversation. Subjects trite and useless often occupy their attention, while topics of a profitable nature are neglected. The following instance shows the necessity and utility of serious converse.

A number of intimate friends being at dinner together on the Lord's day, one of the company, in order to prevent impertinent discourse, said, "*It is a question, whether we shall all go to heaven or not?*" This plain hint occasioned a general seriousness and self-examination. One thought —If any of this company go to hell, it must be myself; and so thought another; even the servants who waited at table were affected in the same manner. In short, it was afterwards found that this one sentence proved, by the special blessing of God upon it, instrumental to their conversion.

For some years before Mr. Hervey's death, he visited very few of the principal persons in his neighbourhood. Being once asked, "Why he so seldom went to see the neighbouring gentlemen, who yet shewed him all possible esteem and respect?" he answered, "I can hardly name a polite family where the conversation ever turns upon the things of God. I hear much frothy and worldly chit chat, but not a word of Christ; and I am determined not to visit those companies where there is not room for my Master as well as myself."

Were clergymen in general to act as Mr. Hervey did, it would reflect more honour on their character than their visiting for the sake of worldly pleasure and sensual enjoyment. But it is to be feared that the case is very different with many. "It is, I think, remarked by some one who went into the company of the clergy at one of their feasts, in hopes of finding among them that elegance and philosophical spirit of converse which he had in vain sought among others, that nothing was talked of with any apparent animation but the flavour of the venison, the fine relish of the hams, the richness of the pie-crust, and the excellence of the claret.— These, indeed, caused the most cordial congratulations; and these, interrupted only by the conjectures of the next vacancies in living, stalls, and mitres, constituted the whole of the discourse, in a symposium consisting of the instructors of mankind. If such be the case, we are not to wonder that the sublimer sort of conversation is rarely to be found in the common ranks, who are often too deficient in education to be able to interchange their sentiments with any considerable advantage to the mind or the morals."

"The gift of speech," says Hervey, "is the great prerogative of our rational nature. And it is a pity that such a superior faculty should be debased to the meanest purposes. Suppose all our stately vessels, that pass and repass the ocean, were to carry out nothing but tinsel, and theatrical decorations; were to import nothing but glittering baubles and nicely fancied toys; would such a method of trading be well judged in itself, or beneficial in its consequences? Articulate speech is the instrument of much nobler commerce, intended to transmit and diffuse the treasures of the mind. And will not the practice be altogether as injudicious ; must not the issue be infinitely more detrimental, if this vehicle of intellectual wealth be freighted only with pleasing fopperies ?"

" In the multitude of words there wanteth not sin." He who talks much, not only often renders himself unpleasant to the company, but is in danger of offending God. There is a happy medium, which sh**o**uld be attended to ; neither to seal up the lips in monkish stupidity, nor, on the other hand, to be guilty of impertinent and trifling loquacity.

Zeno, being present where a person of a loquacious disposition played himself off, said, with an air of concern in his countenance, " I perceive that poor gentleman is ill. He has a violent flux upon him." The company was alarmed, and the speaker stopped in his career. " Yes," added the philosopher, " the flux is so violent, that it has carried his ears into his tongue."

The Rev. Mr. Berridge being once visited by a very loquacious young lady, who, forgetting the modesty of her sex, and the superior gravity of an aged divine, engrossed all the conversation of the interview with small talk concerning herself, when she rose to retire, he said, " Madam, before you withdraw, I have one piece of advice to give you ; and that is, when you go into company again, after you have talked *half an hour* without intermission, I recommend it to you to stop awhile, and see if any other of the company has any thing to say."

Though the above mentioned reproof were suitable, yet it is not to be understood that the gift of conversation is to be lightly appreciated, but only to be used with judgment. They who cannot talk at all are, perhaps, as miserable to themselves, as they who talk much are disagreeable to others.

A gentleman who acquir**e**d a very considerable fortune in trade, was absolutely wretched because he could not talk in company. " I am a most unhappy man," said he. " I am invited to conversations—I go to conversations—but, alas ! I have no conversation." From this instance we may learn how much more conducive to our happiness it is to store our minds with intellectual wealth, than to be heaping up riches in expectation that money will supply the place of every thing else.

Much is to be gained by judicious conversation. Menage once heard Varilles say, that of ten things which he knew, he had learned nine from conversation. " The tongue of the wise," says Solomon, " useth knowledge aright." And again, " The tongue of the just is as choice silver."

In conversation, great care should be taken to introduce subjects with discretion and propriety. A person once harangued on the strength of Samson. " I affirm,' said he, " that this same Samson was the strongest man that ever did or ever will live in the world." " I deny it," replied one of the company : " you yourself are stronger than he."—" How do you make out that ?" " Because you just now lugged him in by head and shoulders."

CONVERSIONS.

To be convinced of the depravity of human nature, to have our understanding enlightened, the will renovated, and our conduct changed from a course of sin to holiness, must ever be considered as the greatest evidences of divine favour, and the most valuable blessings we can be the partakers of.

The accounts given us, indeed of singular, sudden, and extraordinary conversions, certainly deserve close attention, as many have, after all that they have professed, proved themselves still slaves to sin. However, to reject all such instances because some have been counterfeit, is acting injudicious and uncharitable. The following, I beli**e**ve, may be depended on.

3

Mr. Thomas Tregross, of Exeter, dated his conversion, after he had been some time in the ministry, and a sufferer for non-conformity too! And it is a circumstance which deserves remark, that he considered a sermon composed and preached by himself, on Luke xii. 47, as the mean of his conversion!

A godly minister of the Gospel occasionally visiting a gay person, was introduced to a room near to that wherein she dressed. After waiting some hours, the lady came in, and found him in tears. She inquired the reason of his weeping. He replied, "Madam, I weep on reflecting that you spend so many hours before your glass, and in adorning your person, while I spend so few hours before my God, and in adorning my soul." The rebuke struck her conscience. She lived and died a monument of grace.

Doctor Staunton was called the searching preacher. Preaching once at Warborough, near Oxford, a man was so much affected with his first prayer, that he ran home, and desired his wife to get ready and come to church, for there was one in the pulpit who prayed like an angel. The woman hastened away, and heard the sermon, which, under the Divine blessing, was the mean of her conversion, and she afterwards proved an eminent Christian!

A Mr. Woodward, who was Minister at Dursley in Gloucestershire, was brought to think seriously by the following incident. Being out one evening late, as he was coming home, some dogs fell a fighting about him, when he thought himself in great danger, which caused a serious reflection in him, what would have become of his soul if he should have been torn to pieces by them; and so, leaving his former company, he changed it for that of the godly professors at Wotton, who used to pray and repeat sermons, and sing together; which edifying society he found so beneficial, that he used to say, 'though Oxford made him a scholar, the professors of Wotton fitted him for the Ministry."

Lady H—— once spoke to a workman who was repairing a garden wall, and pressed him to take some thought concerning eternity and the state of his soul. Some years afterwards she was speaking to another on the same subject, and said to him "Thomas, I fear you never pray, nor look to Christ for salvation." "Your Ladyship is mistaken," answered the man : "I heard what passed between you and James at such a time, and the word you designed for him took effect on me." "How did you hear it?" "I heard it on the other side of the garden, through a hole in the wall, and shall never forget the impression I received."

When Oliver Cromwell entered upon the command of the Parliament's army against Charles I. he ordered all his soldiers to carry a Bible in their pockets, (the same which is now called Field's.) Among the rest there was a wild, wicked young fellow, who ran away from his apprenticeship in London for the sake of plunder and dissipation. This fellow was obliged to be in the fashion. Being one day ordered out upon a skirmishing party, or to attack some fortress, he returned to his quarters in the evening without hurt. When he was going to bed, pulling the Bible out of his pocket, he observed a hole in it. His curiosity led him to trace the depth of this hole into his Bible ; he found a bullet was gone as far as the 11th chap. of Ecclesiastes, 9th verse. "Rejoice, O young man, in thy youth, and let thy heart cheer thee in the days of thy youth, and walk in the ways of thy heart, and in the sight of thine eyes ; but know thou, that for all these things God will bring thee into judgment." The words were set home upon his heart by the Divine Spirit, so that he became a very serious and sound believer in the Lord Jesus Christ, and lived in London many years after the civil wars were over. He used pleasantly to observe to Dr. Evans, Author of the Christian Temper, that the Bible was the mean of saving his soul and body too.

It is said of a merchant, that talking to his friend who fell down dead before him, he immediately upon it retired, and considered it to so good a purpose, that it became the mean of his conversion.

A certain libertine, of a most abandoned character, happened one day to stroll into a church, where he heard the 5th chapter of Genesis read; importing, that so long lived such and such persons, and yet the conclusion was, "they died." Enos lived 905 years, and he died—Seth 912, and he died—Methusaleh 969, *and he died.* The frequent repetition of the words, *he died,* notwithstanding the great length of years they had lived, struck him so deeply with the thought of death and eternity, that through divine grace he became a most exemplary Christian.

Mr. Flavel being in London in 1673, his old bookseller, Mr. Boulter, gave him the following relation, viz. " That some time before, there came into his shop a sparkish gentleman, to inquire for some play books. Mr. Boulter told him he had none; but shewed him Mr. Flavel's little treatise of ' Keeping the Heart,' intreating him to read it, and assured him it would do him more good than play books. The gentleman read the title ; and glancing upon several pages here and there, broke out into these and such other expressions—' What a fanatic was he who made this book !' Mr. Boulter begged of him to buy and read it, and told him, ' he had no cause to censure it so bitterly.' At last he bought it, but told him he would not read it. ' What will you do with it, then ?' said Mr. Boulter. ' I will tear and burn it,' said he, ' and send it to the devil.' Mr. Boulter told him, ' then he should not have it.' Upon this the gentleman promised to read it; and Mr. Boulter told him, ' If he disliked it upon reading, he would return him his money.' About a month after, the gentleman came to the shop again in a very modest habit, and with a serious countenance addressed him thus : ' Sir, I most heartily thank you for putting this book into my hands—I bless God that moved you to do it :— it hath saved my soul—blessed be God, that ever I came into your shop.' And then he bought an hundred more of those books of him, and told him, ' he would give them to the poor, who could not buy them.' "

A godly faithful minister, of the 17th century, having finished prayer and looking round upon the congregation, observed a young gentleman just shut into one of the pews, who discovered much uneasiness in that situation, and seemed to wish to get out again. The minister feeling a peculiar desire to detain him, hit upon the following singular expedient. Turning towards one of the members of his church, who sat in the gallery, he asked him this question aloud— " Brother, do you repent of your coming to Christ ?" " No, Sir," he replied ; " I never was happy till then. I only repent that I did not come to him sooner." The minister then turned towards the opposite gallery, and addressed himself to an aged member in the same manner—" Brother, do you repent that you came to Christ ?" " No, Sir," said he : " I have known the Lord from my youth up." He then looked down upon the young man, whose attention was fully engaged, and fixing his eyes upon him, said—" Young man, *are you* willing to come to Christ ?" this unexpected address from the pulpit, exciting the observation of all the people, so affected him, that he sat down and hid his face. The person who sat next to him encouraged him to rise, and answer the question. The minister repeated it—" Young man, *are you* willing to come to Christ ?" With a tremulous voice he replied, " Yes, Sir." " But *when,* Sir ?" added the minister, in a solemn and loud one.—He mildly answered, " Now,

Sir," " Then stay," said he," and hear the word of God, which you will find in 2 Cor. vi. 2: Behold *now* is the accepted time, behold *now* is the day of salvation." By this sermon he was greatly affected. He came into the vestry, after service, dissolved in tears. That unwillingness to stay, which he had discovered, was occasioned by the strict injunction of his father, who threatened, that, if ever he went to hear the fanatics, he would turn him out of doors. Having now heard, and unable to conceal the feelings of his mind, he was afraid to meet his father. The minister sat down, and wrote an affectionate letter to him, which had so good an effect, that both father and mother came to hear for themselves. They were both brought to the knowledge of the truth, and father, mother, and son, were together received with universal joy into that church.

The story of poor Joseph is so well known, that it needs not a place here. However, it is pleasing to find that a person was savingly converted by the means of reading that account in a periodical publication.

DEATH

" THE best course of moral instruction against the passions," says Saurin, " is death." The grave is a discoverer of the absurdity of sin of every kind. There the ambitious may learn the folly of ambition ; there the vain may learn the vanity of all human things ; there the voluptuous may read a mortifying lesson on the absurdity of sensual pleasure.

The aggregate population on the surface of the known habitable globe is estimated at 895,300,000 souls. If we reckon, with the ancients, that a generation lasts 30 years, then in that space, 895,300,000 human beings will be born and die ; consequently 81,760 must be dropping into eternity every day, 3407 every hour, or about 56 every minute. Reader, how awful is this reflection! Consider, Prepare—Watch!

The calculation, as it respects death in Great Britain, is as follows : every year, about 332,708 ; every month, about 25,592 ; every week, about 6,398 ; every day, 914 : every hour, 40 ; and every three minutes 2.

Constantine the Great, in order to reclaim a miser, took a lance, and marked out a space of ground of the size of the human body, and told him, " Add heap to heap, accumulate riches upon riches, extend the bounds of your possessions, conquer the whole world, in a few days such a spot as this will be all you will have." " I take this spear," says Saurin ; " I mark out this space among you ; in a few days you will be worth no more than this. Go to the tomb of the avaricious man ; go down and see his coffin, and his shroud ; in four days these may be all you will have."

" Death," says the same author, " puts an end to the most specious titles, to the most dazzling grandeur, and to the most delicious life. The thought of this period of human glory reminds me of the memorable action of a prince, who, although he was a heathen, was wiser than many Christians ; I mean the great Saladin. After he had subdued Egypt, passed the Euphrates, and conquered cities without number ; after he had retaken Jerusalem, and performed exploits more than human in those wars which superstition had stirred up for the recovery of the Holy Land, he finished his life in the performance of an action that ought to be transmitted to the most distant posterity.

" A moment before he uttered his last sigh, he called the herald who had carried his banner before him in all his battles ; he commanded him to fasten to the top of a lance the shroud in which the dying prince was soon to be buried. 'Go,' said he, 'carry the lance, unfurl this banner ; and, while you lift up this standard, proclaim—This, this is all that remains to Saladin the Great (the Conqueror and the King of the Empire) of all his glory.' Christians (says Saurin) I perform to-day the office of this herald. I fasten to the staff of a spear sensual and intellectual pleasures, worldly riches, and human honours. All these I reduce to the piece of crape in which you will shortly be buried. This standard of death I lift up in your sight, and I cry—This, this is all that will remain to you of the possessions for which you exchanged your souls."

Philip, King of Macedon, as he was wrestling at the Olympic games, fell down in the sand ; and, when he rose again, seeing the print of his body in the sand, cried out, " *O how little a parcel of earth will hold* us, *when we are dead,* who *are ambitiously seeking after the whole world whilst we are living !*"

A Sultan amusing himself with walking, observed a Dervise sitting with a human skull in his lap, and appearing to be in a very profound reverie; his attitude and manner surprised the Sultan, who demanded the cause of his being so deeply engaged in reflection. "Sire," said the Dervise, "this skull was presented to me this morning; and I have from that moment been endeavouring, in vain, to discover whether it is the skull of a powerful Monarch like your Majesty, or a poor Dervise like myself." A humbling consideration truly !

Mr. B—— mentioning to Dr. Johnson, that he had seen the execution of several convicts at Tyburn two days before, and that none of them seemed to be under any concern; "Most of them, Sir," said Johnson, "have never thought at all." "But is not the fear of death natural to man ?" said B. "So much so, Sir." said Johnson, "that the whole of life is but keeping away the thoughts of it." There are some exceptions, however, to this remark. Dr. Donne, it is said, some time before his death, when he was emaciated with study and sickness, caused himself to be wrapped up in a sheet, which was gathered over his head in the manner of a shroud, and, having closed his eyes, he had his portrait taken, which was kept by his bed-side as long as he lived, to remind him of mortality.

When Garrick showed Dr. Johnson his fine house, gardens, statues, pictures, &c. at Hampton Court, what ideas did they awaken in the mind of that great man ? Instead of a flattering compliment, which was expected, "Ah ! David, David, David," said the Doctor, clapping his hand upon the little man's shoulder, "these are the things which make a death-bed terrible."

Lewis the XIth of France was so fearful of death, that, as often as it came into his physician's head to threaten him with death he put money into his hands to pacify him. His physician is said to have got 55,000 crowns from him in five months.

"I have heard of a man," says Gurnall, "that would never be present at any funeral; he could not even bear the sight of any of his own grey hairs, and, therefore, used a black lead comb to discolour them, lest, by these, the thoughts of death, which he abhorred, should crowd in upon him."

Mere dignity of station, or worldly affluence, cannot produce real felicity : there is still an uncomfortable reflection, that all will terminate in death. "Hence," said the late popular Mr. W. "I'd rather be a beggar-boy at sixteen, without a shilling, than the Chamberlain of London at seventy !"

That was a pertinent and emphatical reply, which a Fellow of Emanuel College, in Cambridge, made to a friend of his of the same College. The latter, at the Restoration, had been representing the great difficulties (as they seemed to him) of conformity in point of conscience, concluding, however, with these words : "But we must live." To which the other answered only with the like number of words: "But we must (also) die." Than which a better answer could not possibly be given. Let those whom it may concern weigh the answer well.

"Consider death in itself, it is," as a good writer observes, "a sad scene;

3*

and the solemnity of the scene increases as death advances. Every step the last enemy takes, alarms; every fresh symptom strikes terror into the spectators, and spreads silence and gloominess through the dwelling; the disease baffles the power of medicine. They who stand by, observe its progress; the dying man watches their looks; he suspects his case to be desperate. The physician at length pronounces it so; he believes it. Now the wheel of life goes down apace. The vital flame burns faint and irregular; reason intermits, short intervals of sense divide his thoughts and passions: now himself is the object; then his family. His friends, his relations, his children, crowd around his bed, shed their unavailing tears over him, and receive his last blessing. His pulse beats a surrender to the pale conqueror; his eyes swim; his tongue falters; a cold sweat bedews his face; he groans; he expires!"

HAPPY DEATHS.

"BLESSED are the dead who die in the Lord." Nothing can be more consolatory to a pious mind, than the consideration of the happy deaths of believers. The idea of dissolution is, indeed, somewhat terrific in itself; but when we behold the Christian in that moment superior to every fear, and often happy beyond expression, it tends to brighten our hopes, animate our minds, and helps us to look forward to our own exit with a degree of composure and submission. "There is nothing in history," says Addison, "which is so improving as those accounts which we meet with of the deaths of eminent persons, and of their behaviour in that dreadful season."

A happy death, no less than an holy life, is the gift of God. Hence Dr. Guise never prayed in public without thanking God for all who depart in the faith.

Mr. Robert Bruce, the morning before he died, being at breakfast, and having, as he used, eaten an egg, he said to his daughter, "I think I am yet hungry : you may bring me another egg." But having mused a while, he said, " *Hold, daughter, hold ; my Master calls me.*" With these words his sight failed him; whereupon he called for the Bible, and said, " Turn to the 8th chapter to the Romans, and set my finger on the words—'*I am persuaded that neither death, nor life, &c. shall be able to separate me from the love of God, which is in Christ Jesus my Lord.*'" When this was done, he said, "*Now is my finger upon them?*" Being told it was, without any more, he said, "*Now, God be with you, my children ; I have breakfasted with you, and shall sup with my Lord Jesus Christ this night.*" And then expired.

Addison, after a long and manly but vain struggle with his distemper, dismissed his physicians, and with them all hopes of life. But with his hopes of life he dismissed not his concerns for the living, but sent for a youth who was nearly related, and finely accomplished. He came, but, life now glimmering in the socket, the dying friend was silent. After a decent and proper pause, the youth said, " Dear Sir, you sent for me. I believe and I hope you have some commands ; if you have, I shall hold them most sacred." May distant ages not only hear but feel the reply ! Forcibly grasping the youth's hand, he softly said, "See in what peace a Christian can die !" He spoke with difficulty, and soon expired.

Beza, in his younger years, was one day in the church of Charenton, where he providentially heard the 91st Psalm expounded. It was followed with such power to him, that he not only found it sweet and pleasant, but was enabled to believe that the Lord would fulfil to him all the promises of that psalm. At his death, he declared to his Christian friends that he had found it so indeed. That, as he had been enabled to close with the second verse, in taking the Lord for his God, and got a sure claim that he should be his *refuge and fortress*, so he had found remarkably, in the after changes of his life, that the Lord had *delivered him from the snare of the fowler*, for he had been in frequent hazard by the lying in wait of many to ensnare him; and from the *noisome pestilence* (for he was sometimes in great hazard from the pestilence) in those places where he was called to reside; and, amidst the civil wars, which were then so hot in France, he had most convincing deliverances from many imminent hazards, when he was called to be present sometimes with the Protestant Princes upon the field, where *thousands did fall about him*. And thus, when near his end, he found *that* Psalm so observably verified on which he was caused to hope, that he went through all these promises, declaring the comfortable accomplishment of them, how he found the *Lord giving his Angels charge over him, often answering him when he called upon him; how he had been with him in trouble, had delivered him, and had satisfied him with long life.* And now, says he, I have no more to wait for, but the fulfilling of these last words of the Psalm—"*I will shew him my salvation;* which with confidence I long for."

DEATHS, REMARKABLE, AND PRESENTIMENT OF.

Though we are not bound to believe every idle story propagated by the weak and superstitious, yet it must be confessed there have been singular monitions and very remarkable events which have preceded the death of some men, the testimonies for which we cannot reasonably reject. The following, I believe, are attested by indubitable evidence.

The pious Mr. Ambrose had a very strong impulse on his mind of the approach of death, and took a formal leave of his friends at their houses a little before his departure, and the last night of his life he sent his discourse concerning angels to the press. The next day he shut himself up in his parlour, where, to the great surprise and regret of all who saw him, he was found just expiring.

Dr. Willet, in his epistle dedicatory prefixed to his Hexapla upon Exodus, has this expression: "It is most honourable for a soldier to die fighting, and for a bishop or pastor praying; and, if my merciful God shall vouchsafe to grant me my request, my earnest desire is, that in writing and commenting upon some part of the scripture, I may finish my days." This request was granted him, for he was called hence as he was composing a commentary upon Leviticus.

Archbishop Usher often said, he hoped to die with the language of the publican in his mouth; and his biographer tells us, that his wish was fulfilled: he died, saying, " God be merciful to me a sinner."

There was a remarkable circumstance in Dr. Leighton's death. He often used to say, that, if he were to choose a place to die in, it should be an inn; it looking like a pilgrim's going home, to whom this world was all as an inn, and who was weary with the noise and confusion of it. He added, that the officiousness and care of friends were an entanglement to a dying man, and that the unconcerned attendance of those that could be procured in such a place would give less disturbance. He obtained what he desired, for he died at the Bell-Inn, in Warwick Lane, in the year 1684.

The manner of Mr. Saltmarsh's death was so extraordinary, that it deserves a place in this collection. Dec. 4, 1647, being at his house at Ilford in Essex, he told his wife he had been in a trance, and received a message from God, which he must immediately deliver to the army. He went that night to London, and next day to Windsor: being come to the council of officers, he told them that the Lord had left them; that he would not prosper their consultations, but destroy them by divisions among themselves, because they had sought to destroy the people of God, those who stood by them in their greatest difficulties. He then went to the General, and, without moving his hat, told him, that God was highly displeased with him for committing of saints to prison. The like message he delivered to Cromwell, requiring him to take effectual measures for the enlargement of the members of the army who were committed for not complying with the general council. He then took his leave of the officers, telling them he had now done his errand, and must never see them any more. After which he went to London, and took leave of his friends there, telling them his work was done, and desiring some of them to be careful of his wife. Thursday, Dec. 9, he returned to Ilford in perfect health : next day he told his wife he had now finished his work, and must go to his Father. Sunday morning, Dec. 11, he was taken speechless, and about four in the afternoon died.

Dr. James Spener, some days before he died, gave orders that nothing of black should be in his coffin—" For," said he, " I have been a sorrowful man these many years, lamenting the deplorable state of Christ's Church militant here on earth ; but now, being upon the point of retiring into the chuch triumphant in Heaven, I will not have the least mark of sorrow left upon me ; but my body shall be wrapt up all over in white, for a testimony that I die in expectation of a better and more glorious state of Christ's church to come, even upon earth."

The Georgia Analytical Repository, No. 3, contains the following singular account of the death of Mrs. Daniel. On the morning preceding her death, Mr. and Mrs. Daniel junior, left her in perfect health, expecting their return at dinner time ; shortly after this hour they arrived, and found the victuals on the table scarcely cold. To their unutterable surprise, their mother appeared in her grave clothes, having also prepared and taken possession of a suitable place for her corpse. To the earnest and affectionate inquiries which were immediately addressed to her, she calmly replied, " I am admonished by a strong impression on my mind that my departure is at hand ; I hope grace has prepared me for my change : I have no desire to remain any longer in this world. Pray be composed, and resign me to the will of my God. I am going to the rest that I have long desired."

With the best means in their power to re-animate her feeble body, they used all the remonstrances and entreaties that prudence and affection could suggest, to banish from her mind the idea of instant dissolution : observations were made on her case, the natural appearance of her countenance ; and hopes very confidently expressed that she must be mistaken in her views of so sudden a death : in reply she said, " I should be very sorry to find this to be the case, but am under no apprehension of it. I have received an assurance of being in heaven in a short time : my soul is in perfect peace ; I feel no pain, and am happy : compose yourselves, and leave me to my joys. Love and serve God, and you will soon follow me to his presence ! May God bless you, my dear children, and keep you in the way of his holy commandments."

With great composure, she directed a pair of hose and a handkerchief, which she had laid by themselves for the purpose, to be put on her corpse, as the only articles she had omitted in otherwise fitting herself for the coffin. Nothing like distortion was seen in her features ; no symptoms of alarm, nor the slightest degree of derangement, appeared in her conduct or conversation. Life gradually retreated to the extremities of the system ; her breath began to fail, and in the course of a very few minutes she gently departed.

She had been remarkably healthy for many years, and never appeared more so than she was a little before her dissolution. It is supposed, that, within two hours from the time she conceived herself warned to prepare immediately for death, she was in eternity : several of her neighbours, who are worthy of the highest confidence, speak of her as a pious and excellent character. The extraordinary manner of her dissolution is said to have had a happy effect, in connexion with her dying counsel, on her surviving relatives.

DIFFIDENCE.

WHILE we behold some possessed but of little knowledge, and a mediocrity of talent, put on all the consequence of learning and all the boldness of authority, we are sometimes, on the other hand, spectators of men of uncommon worth, fine genius, and extensive abilities, labouring under the fetters of diffidence and fear. It is, however, an unhappy circumstance for such, as it must be injurious to themselves, while it precludes in some respect their usefulness to others.

It is said of the learned Junius, that he had such an invincible modesty, that throughout his life he appeared to common observers under peculiar disadvantages, and could scarcely speak upon the most common subjects with strangers without a suffusion in his countenance. In this respect he seems to have equalled our famous Mr. Addison, who likewise was at once one of the greatest philosophers, as well as one of the most abashed and modest men of his time.

Such was the diffidence of that good man Dr. Conyers, that if he saw a stranger in his congregation, especially if he suspected him to be a minister, it would so disconcert him, as to render him almost incapable of speaking. On these occasions he would sometimes say to Mr. Thornton—" If you expect any blessing under my ministery, I beg you will not bring so many *black coats* with you."

Perhaps there have been martyrs who approached the rack on the stake with less distressing sensations than he has felt when about to enter upon his otherwise delightful work. It is not remembered, that, while he resided at Deptford, he ever preached publicly in the neighbourhood, excepting once, when he accepted an appointment to preach at the Archdeacon's visitation, at Dartford. In this instance he kept his intention an entire secret, lest a multitude should be drawn to hear him. He afterwards mentioned to a particular friend, that from the hour he stood engaged, which was several weeks before the time, he could scarcely think of any thing else ; and that, when the day arrived, his spirits were so extremely agitated, that, for a few minutes after he was in the pulpit, he was deprived of his eye-sight.

DELIBERATION;
Or, the Town Clerk of Ephesus.

DELIBERATION, which is the act of considering things before an undertaking or making choice, is very essential to our honour and comfort in the present state. " I have heard one say (observes Dr. Mather) that there was a gentleman, in the 19th chapter of Acts, to whom he was more indebted than to any man in the world. This was he whom our translation calls the Town-clerk of Ephesus, whose counsel it was to do nothing rashly. Upon any proposal of consequences, it was a usual speech with him—' we shall first advise with the Town-clerk of Ephesus.' One, in a fond compliance with a friend, forgetting the Town-clerk, may do that in haste which he may repent at leisure—may do what may cost him several hundreds of pounds, besides troubles which he would not have undergone for thousands."

DISPUTATION.

So much have the tempers of men been agitated in controversy, and so numerous the quibbles of disputants, that it has, with great propriety, been called a thorny path.

Sir Henry Wotton so disliked it,

that he ordered the following inscription to be put on his monument:

"Hic jacet hujus sententiæ primus auctor—
"Disputandi pruritus ecclesiæ scabies,
     "Nomen alias quære."
" Here lies the first author of this sentence—
"The itch of disputation is the bane of the
     church.
         "Seek his name elsewhere !"

The same person being asked if he thought a Papist could be saved, "You may be saved," replied he, "without knowing that." An excellent answer to the questions of impertinent curiosity in religious matters.

A certain disputant was once labouring a point (in which himself was more interested than God,) and, finding his antagonist hard to be convinced, he so far forgot himself as to reverse the nature of his argument, and, lifting up a dreadful club stick which he had in his hand, says he, " If you won't believe it, I'll make you believe it."

Philip Melancthon being gone to the conferences at Spire in 1529, he made a little journey to Bretten to see his mother. This good woman asked him what she must believe amidst so many disputes, and repeated him her prayers, which contained nothing superstitious. " Go on, mother," said he, " to *believe and pray* as you have done, and never trouble yourself about religious controversies." It is said of this great man, that he longed for death for two reasons: 1. That he might enjoy the much desired presence and sight of Christ, and of the heavenly Church ; and, 2. That he might be freed from the cruel and implacable discords of divines.

Even Luther, who was no small controversialist, used to pray in the following manner : " From a vainglorious doctor, a contentious pastor, and nice questions, the Lord deliver his church."

There are some persons who are habitually disposed to wrangling, and it is curious enough to hear such justify their conduct by a pretence of zeal for the truth. It is not the love of truth, but of victory, that engages them in disputation. " I have witnessed," says Dr. Beattie, " many contests of this kind ; but have seldom seen them lead, or even tend, to any useful discovery. Where ostentation, self-conceit, or love of paradox, are not concerned, they commonly arise from some verbal ambiguity, or from the misconception of some fact, which both parties, taking it for granted that they perfectly understand, are at no pains to ascertain. I once saw a number of persons neither unlearned nor ill-bred meet together to pass a social evening. A dispute arose about the propriety of a certain action, in which some of the company had been interested the evening before. Two parties of disputants were immediately formed, and the matter was warmly argued from six o'clock till midnight when the company broke up. Not being able to enter into the merits of the cause, I did not take any part in the controversy ; but I observed that each of the speakers persisted to the last in the opinion he took up at the beginning, in which he seemed to be rather confirmed than staggered by the arguments that had been urged in opposition. Thus most disputes, if I mistake not, will be found to be equally unprofitable. If a catalogue were to be made of all the truths that have been discovered by wrangling in company, or by solemn disputation in the schools, I believe it would appear that the contending parties might have been employed as advantageously to mankind, and much more so to themselves, in whipping a top, or brandishing a rattle."

" The following little parable or story," says Bishop Patrick, " I have somewhere met with out of Anselm. They were two men, says he, who, a little before the sun was up, fell into a very earnest debate concerning that part of the heavens wherein that glorious body was to arise that day. In this controversy they suffered themselves to be so far engaged, that at last they fell together by the ears, and ceased not their buffetings till they had beaten out each others eyes ·

and so it came to pass that, when a little after the sun did show his face, neither of these doughty champions could discern one jot. So it is often with controversialists."

It must, however, be observed that there is a difference to be made between disputations and the wrong management of them. Disputation of itself is not an evil. "The ministry of our Lord was a perpetual controversy. St. Paul's Epistles are, most of them, controversial. The Apostles came at truth by *much disputing* among themselves, Acts xv. 7, and they convinced Jews and Gentiles by disputing with both, Acts xvii. 17; xix. 8." But the evil arises from the bad spirit with which controversy is often conducted. It is prettily said by Archbishop Tillotson, that those who are transported by passion, by their ill management of a good cause, and by their ungracious way of maintaining the truth, have found out a cunning way to be in the wrong, even when they are in the right. Alas! what a pity that our passions should be such barriers to the promotion of truth and the improvement of our minds!

DRESS.

To say much upon this subject, perhaps, would be considered as impertinent and intruding, since individuals are here supposed to judge for themselves. Let it, however, be observed, that in this, as well as in other things, an extreme should be guarded against. To be led by every fashion which fancy dictates, is a mark of a little, effeminate, and worldly mind; and to be rigidly plain, carries with it an air of affected singularity. There is a simple elegance, connected with uniform neatness, about some persons, that appears more consistent than all the meretricious ornaments of the gay, or the very peculiar dress of those who run to the other extreme.

Philopemen, the greatest soldier of his age in Greece, was usually clad in a very plain dress, and often went abroad without any servant or attendance: in this manner he came alone to the house of a friend, who had invited him to dinner. The mistress of the family, who expected him, (as the General of the Achæans,) took him for a servant, and begged he would give her assistance in the kitchen, because her husband was absent. Philopemen, without ceremony, threw off his cloak, and fell to the cleaving of wood. The husband coming in at that instant, and surprised at the oddness of the sight: "How now, Lord Philopemen?" says he: "what's the meaning of this?" "O," answered the other, "I am paying the interest of my bad looks."

Augustus Cæsar used to wear no other apparel but such as his wife, his sister, or daughter, made him; and used to say, "That rich and gay clothing was either the ensign of pride or the nurse of luxury."

It is said of the celebrated Mr. Whitfield, that he was always very clean and neat, and often said, pleasantly, "That a minister of the Gospel ought to be without a spot."— Sir Edward Coke was very neat in his dress, and it was one of his sentiments, "That the cleanness of a man's clothes ought to put him in mind of keeping all clean within."— Mr. Nelson, the learned and pious author of many excellent books of devotion, was peculiarly elegant in his dress and appearance. Though such an advocate for strict piety, he was willing to convince the world that it did not consist in a monkish habit, or exterior habiliment Men of a studious turn sometimes, however, have been so absorbed in pursuit of intellectual pleasures, that they have paid little attention to their bodies.

Francis Eudes de Mezery, an eminent French historian, was so negligent of his dress, that he might have passed for a beggar rather than what he was. He was actually seized one morning by the archers des pauvres,

36 RELIGIOUS, MORAL, AND

or parish officers; which mistake was so far from provoking him, that he was highly diverted with it, and told them that "He was not able to walk on foot, but, as soon as a new wheel was put to his chariot, he would attend them wherever they thought proper."

Sir Matthew Hale, while a student at Lincoln's Inn, neglected his apparel so much, that he was once taken, when there was a press for the King's service, as a fit person for it. Some that knew him coming by, and giving notice who he was, the pressmen let him go; from which time he began to be more decent in his dress.

It is said of the late Mr. Romaine, that, when at Oxford, the desire of mental improvement had gained such an ascendancy over him as to render him inattentive to that decency of dress which generally distinguishes the clerical order. Passing by the apartments of the master of one of the colleges in his dishabille, a gentleman who was a visitant asked, "What slovenly fellow is that with his stockings about his heels?" The master returned for answer, "That slovenly fellow, as you call him, is one of the greatest geniuses of the age, and is likely to be one of the greatest men in the kingdom."

DRUNKENNESS.

"A DRUNKEN man is a greater monster than any that is to be found among all the creatures which God has made; as indeed, there is no character which appears more despicable and defamed in the eyes of all reasonable persons than that of a drunkard."

Æschines, commending Philip, King of Macedon, for a jovial man that would drink freely, Demosthenes answered, "That this was a good quality in a sponge, but not in a king."

Bonosus, one of our own countrymen, who was addicted to this vice, having set up for a share in the Roman empire, and being defeated in a great battle, hanged himself. When he was seen by the army in this melancholy situation, notwithstanding he had behaved himself very bravely, the common jest was, that the thing they saw hanging on the tree before them was not a man, but a bottle.

Alexander having invited several of his friends and general officers to supper, proposed a crown as a reward for him who should drink most. He who conquered on this occasion was Promachus, who swallowed fourteen measures of wine, that is eighteen or twenty pints. After receiving the prize, which was a crown worth a talent, i. e. about a thousand crowns, he survived his victory but three days. Of the rest of the guests, forty died of their intemperate drinking.

When this same prince was at Babylon, after having spent a whole night in carousing, a second was proposed to him. He met accordingly, and there were twenty guests at table: he drank to the health of every person in company, and then pledged them severally. After this, calling for Hercules' cup, which held an incredible quantity, it was filled, when he poured it all down, drinking to a Macedonian of the company, Proteas by name; and afterwards pledged him again in the same extravagant bumper. He had no sooner swallowed it, than he fell upon the floor. "Here then," cries Seneca, (describing the fatal effects of drunkenness) "this hero, unconquered by all the toils of prodigious marches, exposed to the dangers of sieges and combats, to the most violent extremes of heat and cold, here he lies subdued by his intemperance, and struck to the earth by the fatal cup of Hercules." In this condition he was seized with a fever, which, in a few days, terminated in death. He was 32 years and 8 months old, of which he had reigned 12. No one, says Plutarch, suspected then that Alexander had been poisoned: the true poison which brought him to this end was wine, which has killed many thousands besides Alexander.

"The caution of an heathen prince (see Esther i. v. 8.) even when he would show his generosity, may shame many who are called Christians, that think they do not sufficiently show their good house-keeping, nor bid their friends welcome, unless they make them drunk, and, under pretence of sending the health round, send the sin round, and death with it."

Anachonis, the philosopher, being asked by what means a man might best guard against the vice of drunkenness? he made answer, "By bearing constantly in his view the loathsome indecent behaviour of such as are intoxicated in this manner." Upon this principle probably was founded the custom of the Lacedemonians, of exposing their drunken slaves to their children, who, by that means, conceived an early aversion to a vice which makes men appear so monstrous and irrational.

The famous Bernard Gilpin discovered the seriousness of his disposition very early in life. A begging friar came to his father's house, where, according to the custom of the times, he was received in a very hospitable manner. The friar made too free, and was not sober enough to save appearances. The next morning, however, he ordered the bell to toll; and from the pulpit expressed himself with great vehemence against the debauchery of the times, and particularly against drunkenness. Young Gilpin, then a child by his mother's knee, seemed, for some time, exceedingly affected with the friar's discourse, and at length, with the utmost indignation, cried out—"Oh, Mamma, do you hear how this fellow dares speak against drunkenness, and was drunk himself yesternight at our house?" How careful and circumspect should professors of religion be in their conduct! Even infantine wisdom cannot help discerning and marking the inconsistencies of such.

The Drunkard confounded.

A notorious drunkard, who used, when told of his ungodly life, to shake off all the threatenings of the word, upon a presumptuous hope of the mercy of God, was, at last, laid on a bed of sickness, and which, for a time, scared all his old companions in iniquity from visiting him; but hearing he was cheery and pleasant in his sickness, some of them ventured to see him; whom they found very confident of the mercy of God, whereby their hands were much strengthened in their old ways: but before he died, his tone was much changed; his vain hopes vanished, and his guilty conscience awakened. Now ready to die, he cries out in despair, "O! Sirs, I had prepared a plaister, and thought all was well; but now it will stick no longer." Thus is the word of God verified: "There is no peace to the wicked."

The Drunkard recovered.

The late R. P. of W. was, for some time, awfully ensnared by the sin of drunkenness, but was, at length, recovered from it in the following singular way: he had a tame goat, which was wont to follow him to the alehouse which he frequented. One day, by way of frolick, he gave the animal so much ale, that it became intoxicated. What particularly struck Mr. P. was, that, from that time, though the creature would follow him to the door, he never could get it to enter the house. Revolving this circumstance in his mind, Mr. P. was led to see how much the sin by which he had been enslaved had sunk him beneath a beast, and from that time became a sober man.

DUELS.

THE number of duels that are now fought proves the sad depravity of the times, and of the little sense men have of another world. "If every one," says Addison, "that fought a duel were to stand in the pillory, it would quickly lessen the number of these men of imaginary honour, and put an end to so absurd a practice. "When honour is a support to virtuous principles, and runs parallel with the laws of God and our country, it cannot be too much cherished and encouraged; but when the dictates of honour are contrary to those of religion and equity, they are the greatest depravations of human nature, by giving wrong ambitions and false ideas of what is good and laudable, and should, therefore, be exploded by all governments, and driven out, as the bane and plague of human society."

Gaston, Marquis de Renty, an illustrious nobleman, having a command in the French army, had the misfortune to receive a challenge from a person of distinction in the same service. The Marquis returned for answer, "That he was ready to convince the gentleman that he was in the wrong; or, if he could not convince him, was as ready to ask his pardon." The other, not satisfied with this reply, insisted upon his meeting him with the sword. To which the Marquis sent this answer; "That he was resolved not to do it, since God and his King had forbidden it; otherwise he would have him know, that all the endeavours he had used to pacify him did not proceed from any fear of him, but of Almighty God and his displeasure—that he should go every day about his usual business, and if he did assault him, he would make him repent it." The angry man, not able to provoke the Marquis to a duel, and meeting him one day by chance, drew his sword, and attacked him. The Marquis soon wounded and disarmed both him and his second, with the assistance of a servant who attended him. But then did this truly Christian nobleman show the difference betwixt a brutish and a Christian courage; for, leading them to his tent, he refreshed them with wine and cordials, caused their wounds to be dressed, and their swords to be restored to them; then dismissed them with Christian and friendly advice, and was never heard to mention the affair afterwards, even to his nearest friends. It was a usual saying with this great man, "That there was more true courage and generosity in bearing and forgiving an injury for the love of God, than in requitting it with another; in suffering rather than revenging, because the thing was really more difficult. Adding, that bulls and bears had courage enough, but it was brutal courage; whereas that of men should be such as became rational beings and Christians."

A quarrel having arisen between a celebrated gentleman in the literary world and one of his acquaintances, the latter heroically, and less laconically, concluding a letter to the former, on the subject of the dispute, with, "I have a life at your service, if you dare take it." To which the other replied: "You say you have a life at my service, if I dare take it. I must confess to you, that I dare not take it; I thank my God I have not the courage to take it. But though I own that I am afraid to deprive you of your life, yet, Sir, permit me to assure you, that I am equally thankful to the Almighty Being, for mercifully bestowing on me sufficient resolution, if attacked, to defend my own." This unexpected kind of reply had the proper effect; it brought the madman back again to his reason. Friends intervened, and the affair was compromised.

It is reported of the famous Viscount de Turenne, that, when he was a young officer, and at the siege of a fortified town, he had no less than twelve challenges sent him, all of which he put in his pocket without farther notice: but, being soon after commanded upon a desperate attack on some part of the fortifications, he sent a billet to each of the challengers, acquainting them, "That he had received their papers, which he deferred answering till a proper occasion offered both them and himself to exert their courage for the King's service; that, being ordered to assault the enemy's works the next day, he desired their company, when they would have an opportunity of signalizing their own bravery, and of being witnesses of his." We may leave the reader to determine, in this case, who acted most like a man of sense, of temper, and of true courage.

Two friends happening to quarrel at a tavern, one of them, a man of a hasty disposition, insisted that the other should fight him next morning. The challenge was accepted on condition that they should breakfast together at the house of the person challenged, previous to their going to the field. When the challenger came in the morning, according to appointment, he found every preparation made for breakfast, and his friend with his wife and children ready to receive him : their repast being ended, and the family withdrawn, without the least intimation of their purpose having transpired, the challenger asked the other if he was ready to attend ?—" No Sir," said he, " not till we are more on a par : that amiable woman, and those six lovely children, who just now breakfasted with us, depend, under Providence, on my life for subsistence ; and, till you can stake something equal, in my estimation, to the welfare of seven persons dearer to me than the apple of my eye, I cannot think we are equally matched." " *We are not indeed!*" replied the other, giving him his hand.—These two persons became firmer friends than ever.

Sir Cholmley Deering, member of parliament for the county of Kent, was killed by his intimate friend, Mr. Thornhill, in a duel, the 9th of May, 1711. These gentlemen, having sat too long over a glass of wine, it seems, began to make personal reflections on each other, which produced a challenge ; and both of them were grieved they had quarrelled, some time before they fought ; but, deluded by a false notion of honour, believing their courage would be called in question if they did not fight, they armed themselves with swords and pistols, went, without any malice, in the same coach to the place where the matter was to be decided ; and, on the first discharge of the pistols, Sir Cholmley was mortally wounded, and died a few days after, lamenting the unhappy occasion, and that none of their friends would be so good as to endeavour to make up the matter before they fought ; for it seems some days had elapsed between the challenge and the engagement : nor was Mr. Thornhill less afflicted than his dying friend, for the unfortunate murder which that false notion of honour had incited him to commit on a gentleman in whose defence he would readily have ventured his own life at another time. " I have related this more largely, (says the writer of this article,) that gentlemen, reflecting on this unhappy adventure, may, when passionate words are let fall, deliberate a little before they run headlong to their own destruction. It has been observed, that the Romans, the bravest men that ever ruled the world, gave no encouragement to this practice of duelling. They thought there was more honour in passing by an affront, than resenting it : especially in so outrageous a manner. The highest point of honour among them was, the saving the life of a fellow-citizen ; but, among us, no man is thought brave till he has murdered a friend ; and shall Christians whose very characteristic is a forgiving, benevolent temper, become more savage than heathens, by encouraging these barbarous encounters ? The parliament, it is true, was so sensible of the inhumanity of the practice, that a bill was brought in, in 1711, to prevent the infamous practice of duelling ; but it was unaccountably dropped, and we have *yet* no law that sufficiently restrains gentlemen from cutting the throats of their friends and relations ; for that absurd notion still prevails, *That he is a scoundrel who refuses to be a murderer.*"

D

EARLY RISING.

It cannot be denied that early rising is conducive both to the health of the body and the improvement of the mind. It was an observation of Swift, "That he never knew any man come to greatness and eminence who lay in bed of a morning." Though this observation of an individual is not received as an universal maxim, it is certain that some of the most eminent characters which ever existed accustomed themselves to early rising. It seems, also, that people in general rose earlier in former times than now. In the fourteenth century, the shops in Paris were opened at four in the morning; at present a shop-keeper is scarcely awake at seven. The King of France dined at eight in the morning, and retired to his bed chamber at the same hour in the evening. During the reign of Henry VIII. fashionable people in England breakfasted at seven in the morning, and dined at ten in the forenoon. In Elizabeth's time the nobility, gentry, and students, dined at eleven in the forenoon, and supped between five and six in the afternoon.

Various have been the means made use of to overcome the habit of sleeping long of a morning. Buffon, it is said, always rose with the sun; he often used to tell by what means he had accustomed himself to rise early. "In my youth," says he, "I was very fond of sleep; it robbed me of a great deal of my time; but my poor Joseph (his domestic servant) was of great service in enabling me to overcome it. I promised to give Joseph a crown every time that he could make me get up at six. Next morning he did not fail to awake me, and to torment me, but he only received abuse. The next day after he did the same, with no better success; and I was obliged at noon to confess that I had lost my time. I told him that he did not know how to manage his business; that he ought to think of my promise, and not to mind my threats. The day following he employed force; I begged for indulgence, I bid him be gone, stormed, but Joseph persisted. I was, therefore, obliged to comply, and he was rewarded every day for the abuse which he suffered at the moment when I awoke, by thanks accompanied with a crown, which he received about an hour after. Yes, I am indebted to poor Joseph for ten or a dozen of the volumes of my works."

Frederick II. King of Prussia, rose very early in the morning, and in general allowed a very short part of his time to sleep. But as age and infirmities increased upon him, his sleep was broken and disturbed; and when he fell asleep towards the morning, he frequently missed his usual early hour of rising. This loss of time, as he deemed it, he bore very impatiently, and gave strict orders to his attendants never to suffer him to sleep longer than four o'clock in the morning, and to pay no attention to his unwillingness to rise. One morning, at the appointed time, the page whose turn it was to attend him, and who had not been long in his service, came to his bed, and awoke him. "Let me sleep but a little longer," said the Monarch: "I am still much fatigued." "Your Majesty has given positive orders I should wake you so early," replied the page.—"But another quarter of an hour more." "Not one minute," said the page: "it has struck four; I am ordered to insist upon your Majesty's rising."— "Well," said the King, "you are a brave lad: had you let me sleep on, you would have fared ill for your neglect."

Czar Peter, the famous philosopher, who honoured London so long with his residence, whom Muscovy enjoyed so many years, and whose memory will ever be the admiration of Europe, used constantly to rise before day; and when he saw the morning break, would express his wonder that men should be so stupid not to rise every morning to behold one of the most glorious sights in the universe. " They take a delight," said he, " in gazing on a picture, the trifling work of a mortal, and at the same time neglect one painted by the hand of the Deity himself. For my part," added he, " I am for making my life as long as I can, and therefore sleep as little as possible."

Dr. W. Gouge was very conscionable in spending his time, from his youth to his very death. He used to rise very early both winter and summer. In the winter, he constantly rose long before day-light; and in the summer time, about four o'clock in the morning; by which means he had done half a day's work before others had begun their studies. If he heard any at work before he got to his study, he would say (as Demosthenes did concerning the smith,) ' That he was much troubled that any should be at their calling before he was at his."

Dr. Doddridge, in his Exposition of Rom. xiii. and 13 verse, has these words : " I will here record the observation which I have found of great use to myself, and to which I may say that the production of this work, and most of my other writings, is owing; viz. that the difference between rising at five and at seven of the clock in the morning, for the space of 40 years, supposing a man to go to bed at the same hour at night, is nearly equivalent to the addition of ten years to a man's life, of which (supposing the two hours in question to be spent) eight hours, every day, should be spent in study and devotion."

" The solemn stillness of the morning, just before break of day, (says a good author,) is fit and friendly to the cool and undisturbed recollection of a man just risen from his bed, fully refreshed, and in perfect health. Let him compare his condition with that of half the world, and let him feel an indisposition to admire and adore his Protector, if he can. How many great events have come to pass since I have slept! I feel my insignificance. The heaven-ly bodies have moved on; the great wheels of nature have none of them stood still; vegetation is advanced; the season is come forward: fleets have continued sailing; councils have been held; and, on the opposite side of the world, in broad noon day business and pleasure, amusements, battles and revolutions, have taken place, without my concurrence, consent, or knowledge. Great God what am I in the world? An insect a nothing !

" How many of my fellow-crea tures have spent the whole night ir praying, in vain, for ten minutes sleep; how many, in racking pain, crying, " Would God it were morn ing !" How many in prison! How many in the commission of gree crimes! How many have been ourr out of house and home ! How man have been shipwrecked at sea, or los in untrodden ways in the land ! How many have been robbed and murder ed ; how many have died unpre pared, and are now lifting up thei eyes in torment ! And here stand I a monument of mercy, ' the living, the living, to praise God.' O Lord, thou patient and merciful Being, unto thee will I look up: I will bemoan the vices and sympathize with the distresses of my fellow-creatures : I will try this day to show my gratitude to my Preserver, by taking care not to offend him."

EMINENT PERSONS RAISED FROM LOW SITUATIONS.

This article perhaps will not be found superfluous, when we consider that its tendency is to encourag merit obscured by indigent circum stances, and to suppress pride and vanity in any who, though arrived at the summit of prosperity, have forgotten the humble valley through which they once traversed.

Archbishop Abbot was educated and maintained by public charity. Tillotson's father was a weaver, and does not appear to have been in circumstances sufficient to provide for his

son. Pope Sixtus V. while he was
a boy keeping a neighbour's hogs, a
Franciscian friar, who had lost his
way, applied to him for direction,
which he gave with so good a grace,
and at the same time offered his
services so earnestly to attend him as
a waiting boy, provided he would
teach him to read, that the friar took
him home to his convent. Such was
his first step to the road of preferment, which he pursued so steadily,
that he was admitted to make his
profession at fourteen years of age ;
was ordained a priest, by the name
of Father Montalto, and at last
arrived at the honour of the Popedom.

On his elevation to the *tiara*, he
used to say, in contempt of the pas-
quinades that were made upon his
birth, that he was *domus natus illus-
tri*, born of an illustrious house ; because the sunbeams, passing through
the broken walls and ragged roof,
illustrated every corner of his father's
hut. The poor people of Italy, till
of late, have been accustomed to excite in their children an application
to study, by relating to them the
story of this pope.

Pope Benedict XII. was the son
of a miller, whence he came to be
called the *White Cardinal.* He
never forgot his former condition ;
and when he was upon marrying his
niece, he refused to give her to the
great lord who sued for her, and
married her to a tradesman.

Libussa, princess of Bohemia, first
ennobled, and then married, Primas-
laus, who before was a plain hus-
bandman. In remembrance of his
former condition, he preserved a pair
of wooden shoes. Being asked the
cause of his doing so, he made the
following answer :—" I have brought
these shoes with me for the purpose
of setting them up as a monument in
the Castle of Visegrade, and of exhibiting them to my successors, that
all may know that the first prince of
Bohemia was called to his high dignity from the cart and the plough ; and
that I myself, who am elevated to a
crown, may bear constantly in mind
that I have nothing whereof to be
proud."

John Prideaux, Bishop of Worcester, was originally very poor. Before he applied himself to learning,
he stood candidate for the office of
parish clerk at Ugborow, in Devon-
shire, and to his great mortification
another was chosen into that place.
Such was his poverty on his first
coming to Oxford, that he was employed in servile offices in the Kitch-
en of Exeter College for his support.
He has been often heard to say, that
if he had been elected clerk of Ugborow, he should never have been a
bishop. He was so far from being
ashamed of his former poverty, that
he kept the leather breeches which he
wore at Oxford as a memorial of it.
He died 29th July, 1650, aged seven-
ty-two.

We are told of this great man, that,
towards the latter end of his life, he
suffered so much from plundering
and sequestration, that he was reduced to his original state of poverty.
A friend coming to see him, and saluting him in the common form of
" How doth your   lordship   do ?"
" Never better in my life (said he,)
only I have too great a stomach;
for I have eaten that little plate which
the sequestration left me, I have eat-
en a great library of excellent books,
I have eaten a great deal of linen,
much of my brass, some of my pewter, and now I am come to eat iron ;
and what will come next I know
not."

Isaac Maddox, a famous English
prelate, who was born of obscure parents, whom he lost while he was
young, was taken care of by an aunt,
who placed him in a charity school,
and afterwards put him on trial to
a pastry cook ; but before he was
bound apprentice, the master told
her that the boy was not fit for trade ;
that he was continually reading books
of learning above his (the master's)
comprehension ; and therefore advised that she should take him away,
and send him back to school, to fol-

low the bent of his inclination. He was therefore sent to one of the universities of Scotland ; from thence he went to Cambridge, and rose from one degree to another, until he was made successively the Bishop of Asaph and Worcester.

The names of Parker, Whitgift, Grindal, Potter, and a vast number of others, might here be subjoined, who rose from humble situations in life ; but the above must suffice. Let me, however, add, that no kind of calumny or disrespect whatever should be attached to such characters, whose piety or talents have rendered them conspicuous in the world ; for, "It is no uncommon thing," says one, "in the dispensations of the only wise God, to keep those persons hidden for a time under the veil of obscurity, whom he intends shall make the most illustrious appearance on earth ; and that those whom Infinite Wisdom hath appointed for the emancipation or redemption of others, as preparatory to that, shall themselves experience the hardships of bondage, toil, and labour, so that, like the rising sun, they may more visibly shed their light upon, and sensibly communicate their usefulness to a benighted world."

ENVY.

"Envy," says Johnson, "is, above all other vices, inconsistent with the character of a social being, because it sacrifices truth and kindness to very weak temptations. He that plunders a wealthy neighbour, gains as much as he takes away, and may improve his own condition in the same proportion as he impairs another's ; but he that blasts a flourishing reputation, must be content with a small dividend of additional fame, so small as can afford very little consolation to balance the guilt by which it is obtained."

"Base envy withers at another's joy,
"And hates that excellence it cannot reach."

Cambyses, King of Persia, slew his brother Smerdis out of envy, because he could draw a stronger bow than himself, or any of his followers ; and the monster Caligula slew his brother, because he was a beautiful young man.

Mutius, a citizen of Rome, was noted to be of such an envious and malevolent disposition, that Publius, one day, observing him to be very sad, said, "Either some great evil is happened to Mutius, or some great good to another."

"Dionysius, the tyrant, (says Plutarch,) out of envy, punished Philoxenius, the musician, because he could sing ; and Plato, the philosopher, because he could dispute better than himself."

When Aristides, so remarkable for his inviolable attachment to justice, was tried by the people at Athens, and condemned to banishment, a peasant, who was unacquainted with the person of Aristides, applied to him to vote against Aristides. "Has he done you any wrong," said Aristides, "that you are for punishing him in this manner ?" "No," replied the countryman, "I don't even know him ; but I am tired and angry with hearing every one call him *the just.*"

Let us watch against the first rising of this base spirit, and learn rather to be thankful for what we are, than envy others because we are inferior to them ; remembering that we also have our place and excellence in the scale of being. "It should help to keep us from envying others," says Henry, "when we consider how many there are above whom we are placed. Instead of fretting that any are preferred before us in honour, power, estate, or interest, in gifts, graces, or usefulness, we have reason to bless God, if we, who are less than the least, are not put hindmost."

ETERNITY.

"When I endeavour to represent eternity to myself," says Saurin, "I avail myself of whatever I can conceive most long and durable. I heap imagination on imagination, conjecture on conjecture. First, I consider those long lives which all men wish, and some attain. I observe those old men who live four or five generations, and who alone make the history of an age. I do more: I turn to ancient chronicles, I go back to the patriarchal age, and consider life extending through a thousand years; and I say to myself, all this is not eternity, all this is only a point in comparison of eternity. Having represented to myself real objects, I form ideas of imaginary ones. I go from our age to the time of publishing the gospel, from thence to the publication of the law, from the law to the flood, from the flood to the creation; I join this epoch to the present time, and I imagine Adam yet living. Had Adam lived till now, and had he lived in misery, had he passed all his time in a fire, or on a rack, what idea must we form of his condition? At what price would we agree to expose ourselves to misery so great? What imperial glory would appear glorious were it followed by so much wo? Yet this is not eternity; all this is nothing in comparison of eternity! I go farther still. I proceed from imagination to imagination, from one supposition to another. I take the greatest number of years that can be imagined. I add ages to ages, millions of ages to millions of ages. I form of all these one fixed number, and I stay my imagination. After this I suppose God to create a world like this which we inhabit. I suppose him creating it, by forming one atom after another, and employing in the production of each atom the time fixed in my calculation just now mentioned! What numberless ages would the creation of such a world in such a manner require! Then I suppose the Creator to arrange these atoms, and to pursue the same plan of arranging them as of creating them. What numberless ages would such an arrangement require! Finally, I suppose him to dissolve and annihilate the whole, and observing the same method in this dissolution as he observed in the creation and disposition of the whole. What an immense duration would be consumed! Yet this is not eternity; all this is only a point in comparison of eternity!"

It was a question asked of the brethren, both in the classical and provincial meetings of ministers, twice in the year, if they preached the duties of the times? And when it was found that Mr. Leighton did not, he was censured for this omission, but said, "If all the brethren have preached to the times, may not one poor brother be suffered to preach on eternity?"

A lady having spent the afternoon and evening at cards, and in gay company, when she came home, found her servant maid reading a pious book. She looked over her shoulders, and said, "Poor melancholy soul! what pleasure canst thou find in poring so long over that book?" That night the lady could not sleep, but lay sighing and weeping very much. Her servant asked her once and again, what was the matter? At length she burst out into a flood of tears, and said, "O! it was one word I saw in your book that troubles me: there I saw that word eternity. O how happy should I be if I were prepared for eternity!" The consequence of this impression was, that she laid aside her cards, forsook her gay company, and set herself seriously to prepare for another world.

A religious man, skilled in all literature, was so ardently bent to impress eternity on his mind, that he read over carefully seven times a treatise on eternity, and had done it oftener, had not speedier death summoned him into it.

Awful as the consideration of eternity is, it is a source of great consolation to the righteous. An eminent minister, after having been silent in company a considerable time, and being asked the reason, signified that the powers of his mind had been solemnly absorbed with the thought of everlasting happiness. "O my friends," said he, with an energy that surprised all present, "consider what it is to be for ever with the Lord—for ever, for ever, for ever !"

EXAMPLE.

One of the most effectual means of doing good, and impressing the minds of others, is by example. He who exhibits those excellencies in his life which he proclaims with his tongue, will appear the most amiable and prove the most useful. A fine genius, a retentive memory, an eloquent tongue, may be desirable ; but an enlightened mind and uniform life are every way superior. Well-doing must be joined with well thinking, in order to form the Christian and constitute real excellency of character.

It is observed of Cæsar, that he never said to his soldiers—"Ite," go on ; but, "Venite," come on, or follow me. So our great Exemplar, while he commands us to duty, hath shown us the way. "Follow me," is the divine injunction.

Two architects were once candidates for the building a certain temple at Athens. The first harangued the crowd very learnedly upon the different orders of architecture, and showed them in what manner the temple should be built. The other, who got up after him, only observed, "That what his brother had spoken he could do ;" and thus he at once gained the cause. So, however excellent the discussion or profession of Christianity may be, the practice of it is far more so.

Such is the force of example, that even our enemies are sometimes penetrated with admiration, and constrained to bear a testimony in our favour. It is observed of Bishop Jewel, that his affability of behaviour and sanctity of life made a fierce and bigoted Papist sometimes say to him, "I should love thee, Jewel, if thou wert not a Zuinglian. In thy faith thou art an heretic ; but surely in thy life thou art an angel. Thou art very good and honest, but a Lutheran."

Lord Peterborough, more famed for wit than religion, when he lodged with Fenelon, at Cambray, was so charmed with the piety and virtue of the Archbishop, that he exclaimed at parting, "If I stay here any longer, I shall become a Christian in spite of myself."

FILIAL AFFECTION.

"HONOUR thy father and mother," is part of that sacred law given to mankind, ever worthy to be remembered. It becomes us to revere, obey, and love them to whom we are so greatly indebted. Disobedience to parents hath been awfully marked with God's displeasure, while affection for them and attention to them have been eminently sanctioned by him as the means of promoting their felicity and our own honour and esteem. So justly is filial affection appreciated by the Chinese, that they erect public monuments and triumphal arches in honour of those children who have given proof of great filial affection.

Among the multitude of persons who were proscribed under the second triumvirate of Rome, were the celebrated orator Cicero and his brother Quintus. The latter found means to conceal himself so effectually at home, that the soldiers could not find him. Enraged at their disappointment, they put his son to the torture, in order to make him discover the place of his father's concealment ; but filial affection was proof against the most exquisite torments. An involuntary sigh, and sometimes a deep groan, were all that could be extorted from the youth. His agonies were increased ; but with amazing fortitude he still persisted in his resolution of not betraying his father. Quintus was not far off ; and it may be imagined, better than can be expressed, how his heart must have been affected with the sighs and groans of a son expiring in torture to save his life. He could bear it no longer ; but, quitting the place of his concealment, he presented himself to the assassins, begging of them to put him to death, and dismiss the innocent youth. But the inhuman monsters, without being the least affected with the tears either of the father or the son, answered that they must both die ; the father because he was proscribed, and the son because he had concealed the father. Then a new contest of tenderness arose who should die first ; but this the assassins soon decided, by beheading them both at the same time.

Cinna undertook to get Pomponius Strabo murdered in his tent, but his son saved his life, which was the first remarkable transaction of Pompey the Great. The treacherous Cinna had gained over one Terentius, a confidant of Pompey's, and prevailed on him to assassinate the General, and seduce his troops. Young Pompey being informed of his design a few hours before it was to be put in execution, placed a faithful guard round the prætorium, so that none of the conspirators could come near it. He then watched all the motions of the camp, and endeavoured to appease the fury of the soldiers by such acts of prudence as were worthy of the oldest commanders. However, some of the mutineers having forced open one of the gates of the camp, in order to desert to Cinna, the General's son threw himself flat on his back in their way, crying out, that they should not break their oath, and desert their commander, without treading his body to death. By this means he put a stop to their desertion, and afterwards wrought so effectually upon them by his affecting speeches and engaging carriage, that he reconciled them to his father.

Miltiades, a famous Athenian commander, died in prison, where he had been cast for debt. His son Simon, to redeem his father's body for burial, voluntarily submitted himself a prisoner in his room, where he was kept in chains till the debt was paid.

Epaminondas, without all doubt, was one of the greatest generals and one of the best men Greece ever produced. Before him the city of Thebes was not distinguished by any memorable action ; and after him it was not famous for its virtues, but its misfortunes, till it sunk into its original obscurity, so that it saw its glory take birth and expire with this great man. The victory he obtained at Leuctra, had drawn the eyes and admiration of all the neighbouring people upon Epaminondas, who looked upon him as the support of Thebes, as the triumphant conqueror of all Sparta, as the deliverer of all Greece ; in a word, as the greatest man and the most excellent captain that ever was in the world. In the midst of this universal applause, so capable of making the general of an army forget the man for the victor, Epaminondas, little sensible to so affecting and so deserved a glory ; "My joy," said he, "arises from my sense of *that* which the news of my victory will give my father and my mother."

"Nothing in history seems so valuable to me," says Rollin, "as such sentiments which do honour to human nature, and proceed from a heart which neither false glory nor false greatness have corrupted. I confess it with grief I see these noble sentiments daily expire amongst us, especially in persons where birth and rank raise them above others, who too frequently are neither good fathers, good sons, good husbands, nor good friends ; and who would think it a disgrace to express for a father and mother the tender regard of which we have here so fine an example from the pagan above mentioned."

A gentleman of Sweden was condemned to suffer death as a punishment for certain offences committed by him in the discharge of an important public office, which he had filled for a number of years with an integrity that had never before undergone either suspicion or impeachment. His son, a youth about eighteen years of age, was no sooner apprised of the predicament to which the wretched author of his being was reduced, than he flew to the Judge who had pronounced the fatal decree, and, throwing himself at his feet, prayed " that he might be allowed to suffer in the room of a father whom he adored, and whose loss he declared it was impossible for him to survive." The magistrate was thunderstruck at this extraordinary procedure in the son, and would hardly be persuaded that he was sincere in it. Being at length satisfied, however, that the young man actually wished for nothing more ardently than to save his father's life at the expense of his own, he wrote an account of the whole affair to the King; and the consequence was, that his Majesty immediately despatched back the courier, with orders to grant a free pardon to the father, and to confer a title of honour on his incomparable son. The last mark of royal favour, however, the youth begged leave, with all humility, to decline ; and the motive for the refusal of it was not less noble than the conduct by which he had deserved it was generous and disinterested. " Of what avail," exclaimed he, "could the most exalted title be to me, humbled as my family already is in the dust ? Alas ! would it not serve but as a monument to perpetuate in the minds of my countrymen the direful remembrance of an unhappy father's shame !" His Majesty (the King of Sweden) actually shed tears when this magnanimous speech was reported to him ; and, sending for the heroic youth to Court, he appointed him directly to the office of his private confidential secretary.

Mr. Robert Tillotson went up to London on a visit to his son, when he was Dean of Canterbury, and, being in the dress of a plain countryman, was insulted by one of the Dean's servants, for inquiring if John Tillotson was at home. His person, however, being described to the Dean, he immediately exclaimed,

" It is my worthy father :" and, running to the door to receive him, he fell down upon his knees in the presence of his servants to ask his father's blessing.

It is mentioned, as an amiable part of the character of the judicious Mr. Hooker, that he used to say, " If I had no other reason and motive for being religious, I would strive earnestly to be so for the sake of my aged mother, that I may requite her care of me, and cause the widow's heart to sing for joy."

FLATTERY.

" As there is no character so deformed," says Johnson, "as to fright away from it the prostitutes of praise, so there is no degree of encomiastic veneration which pride has refused. The Emperors of Rome suffered themselves to be worshipped in their lives with altars and sacrifice ; and in an age more enlightened, the terms peculiar to the praise and worship of the Supreme Being have been applied to wretches whom it was the reproach of humanity to number among men, and whom nothing but riches or power hindered those that read or wrote their deification from hunting into the toils of justice, as disturbers of the peace of nature."

" The only coin that is most current among mankind (says another) is flattery : the only benefit of which is, that by hearing what we are not, we may learn what we ought to be."

As Canute the Great, King of England, was walking on the seashore at Southampton, accompanied by his courtiers, who offered him the grossest flattery, comparing him to the greatest heroes of antiquity, and asserting that his power was more than human, he ordered a chair to be placed on the beach, while the tide was coming in. Sitting down with a majestic air, he thus addressed himself to the sea : " Thou sea, that art a part of my dominions, and the land whereon I sit, is mine : no one ever broke my commands with impunity I, therefore, charge thee to come no farther upon my land, and not to presume to wet either my feet or my robe, who am thy Sovereign." But the sea, rolling on as before, and without any respect, not only wets the skirts of his robe, but likewise splashed his thighs. On which he rose up suddenly, and, addressing himself to his attendants, upbraided them with their ridiculous flattery, and very judiciously expatiated on the narrow and limited power of the greatest monarch on earth.

A flatterer one day complimented Alphonso V. in the following words: "Sire, you are not only a King like others, but you are also the brother, the nephew, and the son of a King." "Well," replied the monarch, "what do all these vain titles prove? That I hold the crown from my ancestors, without ever having done any thing to deserve it."

His Majesty, King James the First, once asked Bishop Andrews and Bishop Neale the following question:—"My Lords, cannot I take my subjects' money when I want it, without all this formality in Parliament?" Bishop Neale readily answered, "God forbid, Sir, but you should; you are the breath of our nostrils." Whereupon the King turned, and said to Bishop Andrews "Well, my Lord, what say you?" "Sir," replied the Bishop, "I have no skill to judge of parliamentary cases." The King answered, "No put offs, my Lord; answer me presently." "Then, Sir," said he, "I think it lawful for you to take my brother Neale's money, for he offers it."

It is lamentable to reflect how even good men have been guilty of extravagant adulation and ridiculous flattery. Thus Archbishop Abbot, who manifested such great zeal for the protestant religion, speaking of his Royal Master King James the I. he says, "Whose life hath been so immaculate and unspotted, &c. that even malice itself, which leaves nothing unsearched, could never find true blemish in it, nor cast probable aspersion on it. Zealous as a David; learned and wise: the Solomon of our age; religious as Josias; careful of spreading Christ's faith as Constantine the Great; just as Moses; undefiled in all his ways as a Jehoshaphat and Hezekiah; full of clemency as a Theodosius." If Mr. Walpole had seen this passage, he certainly would not have said that "Honest Abbot could not flatter."

The following passages from the Bishop of Downe's sermon and a letter from General Digby to the Marquis of Ormond show the impious nonsense as well as flattery that was preached and propagated after the death of Charles I. "The person now murdered," says the Bishop, "was not the Lord of Glory, but a glorious Lord, Christ's own vicar, his lieutenant and vicegerent here on earth." [One would imagine he was speaking of his *Holiness* of Rome.] "Albeit he was inferior to Christ as man is to God, yet was his privilege of inviolability far more clear than was Christ's; for Christ was not a temporal prince, his kingdom was not of this world; and, therefore, when he vouchsafed to come into this world, and to become the son of man, he did subject himself to the law; but our gracious Sovereign was well known to be a temporal prince, a free monarch, to whom they did all owe and had sworn allegiance. The parliament is the great council, and hath acted more against the Lord and Sovereign than the other did against Christ. The proceedings against our Sovereign were *more illegal, and in many things more cruel.*"

"From the creation of the world," says General Digby, "to the accursed day of this damnable murder, nothing parallel to it was ever heard of. Even the crucifying our blessed Saviour, if we consider him only in human nature, did nothing equal this," &c. &c.

FORWARDNESS.

NOTHING, perhaps, is more unbecoming young persons than the assumption of consequence before men of age, wisdom, and experience.— The advice, therefore, of Parmenio, the Grecian general, to his son, was worthy of him to give, and worthy of every man of sense to adopt : " My son," says he, " would you be great, you must be less ;" that is, you must be less in your own eyes if you would be great in the eyes of others.

An acute Frenchman has remarked, "that the modest deportment of really wise men, when contrasted to the assuming air of the young and ignorant, may be compared to the different appearance of wheat, which, while its ear is empty, holds up its head proudly, but as soon as it is filled with grain bends modestly down, and withdraws from observation."

Anthony Blackwall, the author of that excellent work, the "Sacred Classics Defended and Illustrated," had the felicity to bring up many excellent scholars in his seminaries at Derby and Bosworth. A gentleman who had been his scholar, being patron of the church of Clapham, in Surrey, presented him to that living, as a mark of his gratitude and esteem. This happening late in life, and Blackwall having occasion to wait upon the Bishop of the diocese, he was somewhat pertly questioned by a young chaplain as to the extent of his learning. " Boy," replied the indignant veteran, " I have forgot more than ever you knew." An answer this much like that of Sergeant Glanville to the young lawyer.

Once, at a meeting of ministers, a question of moment was started to be debated among them. Upon the first proposal of it, a confident young man shoots his bolt presently. " Truly," said he, " I hold it so." " You hold, Sir !" answered a grave minister ; " it becomes you to hold your tongue."

Nothing is more ridiculous than to boast advantages of education which have not been improved. A young clergyman in America was lately boasting, among his relations, of having been educated at two colleges, Harvard and Cambridge. " You remind me,"

said an aged divine present, "of an instance I knew, of a calf that sucked two cows." " What was the consequence ?" said a third person.— " Why, Sir," replied the old gentleman, very gravely, " the consequence was, that he was a very *great calf.*"

A young minister once preaching for Mr. Brewer, evidently laboured to set *himself* off to the best advantage. Being afterwards very solicitous to know of Mr. Brewer what the people said of him, he received the following answer. " Why, Sir, the people said, and I said with them, that *you said* I am a very clever fellow."

A very young clergyman, who had just left college, presented a petition to the King of Prussia, requesting that his Majesty would appoint him inspector in a certain place where a vacancy had just happened. As it was an office of much consequence, the King was offended at the presumption and importunity of so young a man, and, instead of any answer to the petition, he wrote underneath, " 2 Book of Samuel, chap. x. verse 5." and returned it. The young clergyman was eager to examine the quotation, but to his great disappointment found the words, " Tarry at Jericho until your beards be grown."

FRIENDSHIP.

IT has been observed, that a real friend is somewhat like a ghost or apparition ; much talked of, but hardly ever seen. Though this may not be justly true, it must, however, be confessed, that a friend does not appear every day, and that he who has in reality found one, ought to value his boon, and be thankful.

Where persons are united by the bonds of genuine friendship, there is nothing, perhaps, more conducive to felicity. It supports and strengthens the mind, alleviates the pains of life, and renders the present state, at least, somewhat comfortable. " Sorrows," says Lord Verulam, " by being communicated, grow less, and joys greater." " And indeed," observes another, " sorrow, like a stream, loses itself in many channels; while joy, like a ray of the sun, reflects with a greater ardour and quickness when it rebounds upon a man from the breast of his friend."

" Friendship! mysterious cement of the soul,
Sweetner of life, and solder of society,
I owe thee much. Thou hast deserved from me
Far, far beyond what I can ever pay :
Oft have I proved the labour of thy love,
And the warm efforts of the gentle heart,
Anxious to please."
                              BLAIR.

The very ingenious and amiable Bishop Berkley, of Cloyne, in Ireland, was so entirely contented with his income in that diocese, that when offered by the Earl of Chesterfield (the Lord Lieutenant) a bishoprick much more beneficial than that he possessed, he declined it with these words : " I love my neighbours, and they love me ; why then should I begin in my old days to form new connexions, and tear myself from those friends whose kindness is to me the greatest happiness I enjoy ?" Acting in this instance, like the celebrated Plutarch, who, being asked why he resided in his native city, so obscure and so little, " I stay," said he, " lest it should grow less."

Lord Stanhope was at Eton School with one of the Scots noblemen who were condemned after the rebellion of 1715. While the Privy Council were deliberating upon the signing of the warrant for the execution of this unfortunate nobleman, Lord S. requested the life of his old schoolfellow (whom he had never seen since he was at school.) His request was refused, till he threatened to give up his place, if the Council did not comply with it. This menace procured him the life of his associate in early life, to whom he afterwards sent a handsome sum of money. Connexions and friendships are sometimes formed in schools, which are never forgotten through life!

A lady of quality being on a visit to Dr. Watts, at Stoke Newington, the Doctor thus accosted her : " Madam, your Ladyship is come to see me on a very remarkable day !" " Why is this day so remarkable ?" answered the Countess. " This very day, thirty years," replied the Doctor, " I came hither to the house of my good friend, Sir Thomas Abney, intending to spend but one single week under this friendly roof, and I have extended my visit to the length of exactly thirty years." Lady Abney, who was present, immediately said to the Doctor, " Sir, what you term a long thirty year's visit, I consider as the shortest visit my family ever received."

It is said of the late Mr. Smeaton (whom I have noticed under the article Precocity) that, early in life, he attracted the notice of the late Duke and Duchess of Queensbury, from a strong resemblance to their favourite *Gay*, the poet. The commencement of this acquaintance was singular, but the continuance of their esteem and partiality lasted through life.— Their first meeting was at a public place, where, walking with Mrs. Smeaton, he observed an elderly lady and gentleman fix an evident and marked attention on him. At length they stopped him, and the Duchess (of eccentric memory) said, " Sir, I don't know who you are, or what you are, but so strongly do you resemble my poor dear Gay, we *must* be acquainted : you shall go home and sup with us; and, if the minds of the two men accord, as do the countenances, you will find two cheerful old folks, who can love you *well*, and I think (or you are an hypocrite) you can as *well* deserve it." The invitation was accepted, and, as long as the Duke and Duchess lived, the friendhip was as cordial as uninterrupted.

Sir Philip Sidney was a person universally admired for his talents, knowledge and polite attainments.— He was a subject of England, but was honoured with an offer of the crown of Poland. Queen Elizabeth used to call him " her Philip," and the Prince of Orange, " his Master." Lord Brooks was so proud of his friendship, that he would have it part of his epitaph—"*Here lies Sir Philip Sidney's friend;*" and, as a testimony of respect for his memory, his death was lamented, in verse, by the Kings of France and Scotland, and by the two universities of England.

HAPPINESS.

VARIOUS, sincere, and constant, are the efforts of men to procure that happiness which the nature of the mind requires; but most seem to be ignorant both of the source and means of genuine felicity. The estimate which men make of life is generally false, and the objects they pursue, however specious and fascinating, are found in the end delusory and vain, while the very thing they neglect and despise is the most productive of real good; I mean the knowledge and enjoyment of the favour of God. Religion alone can afford true joy and permanent peace.— It is this that inspires fortitude, supports patience, and, by its prospects and promises, darts a cheering ray into the darkest shade of human life. An Italian Bishop struggled through great difficulties without repining, and met with much opposition in the discharge of his episcopal function without ever betraying the least impatience. An intimate friend of his, who highly admired those virtues which he thought it impossible to imitate, one day asked the prelate, if he could communicate his secret of being always easy? "Yes," replied the old man, "I can teach you my secret, and with great facility: it consists in nothing more than making a right use of my eyes." His friend begged him to explain himself.— "Most willingly, (returned the Bishop:) in whatever state I am, I first of all look up to heaven, and remember that my principal business here is to get there; I then look down upon the earth, and call to mind how small a space I shall occupy in it when I come to be interred. I then look abroad in the world, and observe what multitudes there are who are in all respects more unhappy than myself.— Thus I learn where true happiness is placed, where all our cares must end, and how very little reason I have to repine or to complain."

Great part of the infelicity of men rises not so much from their situations or circumstances as from their pride, vanity, and ambitious expectations. In order to be happy, these dispositions must be subdued; "we must always keep before our eyes such views of the world as shall prevent our expecting more from it than it is designed to afford. We destroy our joys by devouring them before hand with too eager expectation.— We ruin the happiness of life when we attempt to raise it too high."— Menedemus being told one day, that it was a great felicity to have whatever we desire, "Yes," said he, "*but it is a much greater to desire nothing but what we have.*"

None are more mistaken than those who imagine happiness consists in extensive riches, splendid retinue, or having a vast number of servants to wait on them. Bishop Mancini staying once on a visit to Monsieur Poussin till it was dark, Mons. P. took the candle in his hand, lighted him down stairs, and waited upon him to his coach. The prelate was sorry to see him do it himself, and could not help saying, "I very much pity you, Monsieur Poussin, that you have not one servant." "And I pity you more, my Lord, (replied Poussin,) that you have so many." Were the happiness of the humble and retired weighed with that of the great, the former, I believe, would abundantly preponderate.

It was a good speech of an emperor, "You," said he, "gaze on my purple robe and golden crown; but, did you know what cares are under it, you would not take it up from the ground to have it." It was a true saying of Augustine: "Many are miserable by loving hurtful things; but they are more miserable by having them."

One saying to a philosopher, "Couldest thou but please Dionysius, thou needest not eat herbs and roots;" the philosopher answered, "Couldest thou but eat herbs and roots, thou needest not please Dionysius." To the humble-minded, temptations to greatness are no great temptations.

He who would wish to maintain happiness through life, must elevate his mind above those little trifling vexations incident to all. A person having behaved very rudely to Mr. Boswell, he went to Dr. Johnson, and talked of it as a serious distress. Dr. Johnson laughed, and said, "*Consider, Sir, how insignificant this will appear twelve months hence.*"—"Were this consideration (says Mr. B.) applied to most of the little vexations of life, by which our quiet is too often disturbed, it would prevent many painful sensations. I have tried it frequently and with good effect."

Dr. Cotton Mather gives the following plain but suitable advice to his son on this head.—"It may not be amiss for you to have two heaps; a heap of *unintelligibles*, and a heap of *incurables*. Every now and then you will meet with something or other that may pretty much distress your thoughts: but the shortest way with the vexations will be, to throw them into the heap they belong to, and be no more distressed about them.

"You will meet with some unaccountable and incomprehensible thing, particularly in the conduct of many people. Throw them into your heap of *unintelligibles*; leave them there. Trouble your mind no farther; hope the best, or think no more about them.

"You will meet with some unpersuadable people; no counsel, no reason, will do any thing upon the obstinate, especially as to the making of due submissions upon offences.—Throw them into the heap of *incurables*; leave them there. And so do you go on to do as you can what you have to do. Let not the crooked things that cannot be made straight encumber you."

HOGARTH'S TAIL-PIECE.

A FEW months before that ingenious artist Hogarth was seized with the malady which deprived society of one of its most distinguished ornaments, he proposed to his matchless pencil the work he has entitled the Tail-Piece. The first idea of this is said to have been started in company at his own table. "My next undertaking," said Hogarth, "shall be the end of all things." "If that is the case," replied one of his friends, "your business will be finished; for there will be an end of the painter." "There will so," answered Hogarth, sighing heavily, "and, therefore, the sooner my work is done the better." Accordingly he began the next day, and continued his design with a diligence that seemed to indicate an apprehension (as the report goes) he should not live till he had completed it.—This, however, he did, in the most ingenious manner, by grouping every thing which could denote the end of all things;—a broken bottle—an old broom worn to the stump—the butt end of an old firelock—a cracked bell—a bow unstrung—a crown tumbled in pieces—towers in ruins—the signpost of a tavern, called the World's End, tumbling—the moon in her wane—the map of the globe burning—a gibbet falling, the body gone, and the chains which held it dropping down—Phœbus and his horses dead in the clouds—a vessel wrecked—Time, with his hour glass and scythe broken; a tobacco-pipe in his mouth, the last whiff of smoke going out—a play-book opened, with *exeunt omnes* stampt in the corner—an empty purse—and a statute of bankruptcy taken out against Nature. "So far good," cried Hogarth; "nothing remains but this," taking his pencil in a sort of prophetic fury, and dashing off the similitude of a painter's pallet broken—"Finis," exclaimed Hogarth: "*the deed is done, all is over.*" It is a very remarkable and well-known fact that he never again took the pallet in hand. It is a circumstance less known, perhaps, that he died about a year after he had finished this extraordinary Tail-Piece.

HUMAN NATURE.

"Lo! this only have I found," saith Solomon, "that God made man upright, but they have sought out many inventions." If just observation, general experience, and the decisions of Scripture, are to be regarded, every one must know that human nature is corrupt, that all our powers are contaminated by sin, yea, that there is not only imbecility, but awful depravity, in the heart of every man. Indeed, the very heathens themselves had some faint glimmering of the consequences of original sin. Xenophon, in his Cyropædia, speaks of a young nobleman of Media, who, having yielded to a temptation he had no distrust of, so confident was he of his own strength, confessed his weakness to Cyrus, and told him he found he had two souls; that one of them, which inclined him to do well, had always the superiority in his prince's presence ; but that the other, which led him to do ill, generally got the better out of his sight. He who boasts of absolute innocence, and supposes that no infirmity attaches to his character, is a stranger both to his heart and his life.

The learned, judicious, and pious Boerhaave relates, "that he never saw a criminal dragged to execution without asking himself, Who knows whether this man is not less culpable than myself? On the days when the prisons of this city are emptied into the grave, let every spectator of the dreadful procession put the same question to his own heart. Few among those that crowd in thousands to the legal massacre, and look with carelessness, perhaps with triumph, on the utmost exacerbations of human misery, would then be able to return without horror and dejection. For, who can congratulate himself upon a life passed without some act more mischievous to the peace or prosperity of others than the theft of a piece of money?"

When some one was talking before that acute Scotchman, Doctor Cheyne, of the excellency of human nature,—" Hoot, hoot, mon," said he, "Human nature is a rogue and a scoundrel, or why would it perpetually stand in need of laws and religion?" And, surely, if a cause be examined by its effect, if a principle be considered by its operation, that man must indeed be blind who will not acknowledge the depravity of human nature.

Dr. Gill once preaching on human inability, a gentleman present was much offended, and took him to task for degrading human nature. "Pray, Sir," said the Doctor, "what do you think that men can contribute to their own conversion?" He enumerated a variety of particulars.—"And have you done all this?" said the Doctor. "Why, no, I can't say I have yet; but I hope I shall begin soon."—"If you have these things in your power, and have not done them, you deserve to be doubly damned, and are but ill qualified to be an advocate for free-will, which has done you so little good."

HUMANITY.

"It is just we should have a superior tenderness for a father, a wife, a child, or a friend ; but there is a sort of affection which we owe to all mankind, as being members of the same family of which God is the Creator and Father. Let us illustrate this by the circular undulations which the fall of a stone causes on the surface of a clear and tranquil water. The agitation in the centre, by communicating itself afar off, forms a great number of trembling circles, the faintness of whose impression is in proportion to the largeness of their circumference, till the last seems to escape from our sight. Here is an image of the different degrees of our affections. We love, principally, that which touches us the most nearly ; and less and less in proportion to the distance. We consider mankind, with relation to us, as divided into different classes, every one of which increasing gradually consists of greater numbers than the former; we place ourselves in the smallest, which is surrounded by others more extended, and from thence we distribute to the different orders of men which they contain different degrees of affection more or less strong, in proportion to their distance from us, in such a manner as that the last has hardly any share of it. These different classes may be ranked in the following order: a wife, children, friends, relations, men of the same religion; next are those of the same trade or profession as ourselves; the other classes comprehend our neighbours, fellow-citizens, and countrymen; the last, which includes all the rest, is the universal class of mankind."

Sir Philip Sidney, at the battle near Zutphen, displayed the most undaunted courage. He had two horses killed under him; and, whilst mounting a third, was wounded by a musket-shot out of the trenches, which broke the bone of his thigh. He returned about a mile and a half on horseback to the camp; and being faint with the loss of blood, and probably parched with thirst, through the heat of the weather, he called for drink. It was presently brought him; but as he was putting the vessel to his mouth, a poor wounded soldier, who happened to be carried by him at that instant, looked up to it with wishful eyes. The gallant and generous Sidney took the bottle from his mouth, just when he was going to drink, and delivered it to the soldier, saying, "Thy necessity is yet greater than mine!"

Queen Caroline, one day, observing that her daughter, the late Princess of Orange, had made one of the ladies stand a long time, while she was talking to her upon some trivial subject, indeed till she was almost ready to faint, was resolved to give her a practical reprimand for her ill behaviour, that should have more weight than verbal precept. When the Princess, therefore, came to her in the evening, as usual, to read to her, and was drawing herself a chair to sit down on, the Queen said,—"No, my dear, you must not sit at present; for I intend to make you stand this evening as long as you suffered Lady —— to remain to-day in the same position. She is a woman of the first quality; but, had she been a nursery maid, you should have remembered she was a human creature as well as yourself."

As soon as the soldiers of the truly gallant Czar of Moscovy were masters of the town of Narva, they fell to plunder, and gave themselves up to the most enormous barbarities. The Czar ran from place to place to put a stop to the disorder and massacre. He even turned upon his own victorious but ungovernable troops, and threatened to drench his dagger in their hearts if they did not immediately desist from rapine and slaughter, and allow quarter to their vanquished foes.

A Chinese Emperor being told that his enemies had raised an insurrection in one of the distant provinces; "Come, then, my friends," said he, "follow me, and I promise you that we shall quickly destroy them." He marched forward, and the rebels submitted upon his approach. All now thought that he would take the most signal revenge, but were surprised to see the captives treated with mildness and humanity. "How," cried the First Minister, "is this the manner in which you fulfil your promise? Your royal word was given that your enemies should be destroyed, and behold you have pardoned all, and even caressed some!" "I promised (replied the Emperor, with a generous air) to destroy my enemies; I have fulfilled my word; for, see, they are enemies no longer: I have made friends of them." Let every Christian imitate so noble an example, and learn "to overcome evil with good."

Henry IV. of France, though a warrior, deserves to be recorded as one who delighted not in the shedding of blood where it could be avoided. When he was advised to take Paris by assault, before the arrival of the auxiliaries which the King of Spain was sending to the succour of the league, he would not give his consent to expose that capital to the horrors which a city taken by storm must experience. "I am," said he, "the real father of my people; I am like that genuine mother who presented herself before Solomon: I would much rather not have Paris in my possession, than possess it in a state of ruin, by the slaughter of so many persons." If those who delight so much in bloodshed would learn to imitate this illustrious monarch, we should not hear of so much carnage and slaughter among mankind. And, as one observes, "if Christian nations were nations of Christians, all war would be impossible and unknown amongst them."

JEWS.

"THE numbers, dispersion, and adherence of the Jews to their religion," says Addison, "have furnished every age, and every nation of the world, with the strongest arguments for the Christian faith, not only as these very particulars are foretold of them, but as they themselves are the depositories of these and all the other prophecies which tend to their own confusion. Their number furnishes us with a sufficient cloud of witnesses that attest the truth of the Bible. Their dispersion spreads these witnesses through all parts of the world. The adherence to their religion makes their testimony unquestionable."— Notwithstanding, however, their general obstinacy and unbelief, many individuals among them have been struck with the evidence produced in favour of our Messiah.

Dr. South informs us, that a Rabbi who lived about fifty years before Christ, upon the consideration of Jacob's prophecy, Gen. xlix. 10. of Daniel's seventy weeks (Daniel, ix.) said, that it was impossible for the coming of the Messiah to be deferred beyond

E

fifty years; a proportion of time vastly different from that of 1800.

At a solemn disputation which was held at Venice, in the 17th century, between a Jew and a Christian —the Christian strongly argued, from Daniel's prophecy of the seventy weeks, that Jesus was the Messiah whom the Jews had long expected from the predictions of their prophets; —the learned Rabbi who presided at this disputation was so forcibly struck by the argument, that he put an end to the business by saying, "Let us shut up our Bibles, for if we proceed in the examination of this prophecy, it will make us all become Christians."—Bishop Watson.

A learned Rabbi of the Jews, at Aleppo, being dangerously ill, called his friends together, and desired them seriously to consider the various former captivities endured by their nation, as a punishment for the hardness of their hearts, and their present captivity, which has continued sixteen hundred years, "the occasion of which," said he, "is doubtless our unbelief. We have long looked for the Messiah, and the Christians have believed in one Jesus, of our nation, who was of the seed of Abraham and David, and born in Bethlehem, (for aught we know,) may be the true Messiah; and we may have suffered this long captivity because we have rejected him. Therefore, my advice is, as my last words, that if the Messiah which we expect do not come at or about the year 1650, reckoning from the birth of their Christ, then you may know and believe that this Jesus is the Christ, and you shall have no other."—Hill's Six Sermons, 1648.

A person travelling some time ago in a stage coach with a Jew, who appeared more intelligent and communicative than most he had ever met with before, conversed with him very freely about the opinions of the modern Jews. Among other things, he asked him, "In what light he viewed his expected Messiah?" To which the Jew replied, with great seriousness, "I think so highly of *him, that I commit my eternal all into his hands, and depend upon him for everlasting life.*"

A Jew went from Paris to Rome, in order to acquire a just idea of the Christian religion, as at the fountain head. There he beheld simony, intrigue, and abominations, of all sorts; and after gratifying his curiosity in every particular, returned to France, where he gave a detail of his observations to a friend, by whom he had been long solicited to abjure Judaism. From such a recital, the Christian expected nothing but an obstinate perseverance in the old worship, and was struck with amazement when the Jew acquainted him with his resolution of requesting baptism upon the following grounds of conviction; That he had seen at Rome every body, from the Pope down to the beggar, using all their endeavours to subvert the Christian faith, which, nevertheless, daily took deeper and firmer root, and must, therefore, be of divine institution.

However dispersed and unbelieving the Jews are at present, we have reason to believe, from the aspect of scripture prophecy, that they shall, in due time, be converted to Christianity. "And might we presume to anticipate the glorious scene, when this conversion shall take place, we might picture to ourselves the heretofore incredulous, but still zealous Jew, with the Books of Moses in his hand, anxiously tracing out the particular outlines of that sacred character to which his attention is now, for the first time, directed. Mark his countenance, speaking the language of increasing astonishment, as the rays of evangelic light, reflected from the different parts of his favourite law, break through the thick cloud that has hitherto obscured his understanding. Behold him placed at the foot of the cross; one while bowed down with shame and compunction for the crying sins of his nation; one while lifting up his eyes, and fixing them in pious adoration on him whom his fathers pier-

ced. In the language of heartfelt rapture hear him crying out, 'Blessed be God, I have at length found him, of whom Moses and the prophets did write; the Lamb of God, slain for the recovery of a lost world. For this is he, of whom it is written, Surely he hath borne our griefs, and carried our sorrows; yet we did esteem him stricken of God and afflicted, &c. Lord, now lettest thou thy servant depart in peace; for mine eyes have seen thy salvation.' "

INSTANCES OF IGNORANCE, AND PROFANITY.

WHATEVER intelligence and purity man possessed in his original state, it is evident that "the gold is become dim, and the most fine gold changed." The scripture does not, in the least, exaggerate, when it declares the understanding to be enveloped in the grossest ignorance, and the heart deceitful above all things, and desperately wicked. Perhaps in no one thing is the mind of man more dark and benighted, than in respect to the fear and knowledge of that God, who is the author of our existence and the source of all our blessings. Converse with men on sublunary things, and the temporal concerns in which they are engaged, and they are all attention, life, and activity; but propose to them their duty to God, and the necessity of being concerned for their souls, and they discover the greatest stupidity, the most awful ignorance connected with the most shocking perverseness of will.—The following instances of ignorance may not be pleasant to the feelings of an enlightened mind; but they are not without their use, as they teach us to value the smallest degree of spiritual knowledge, and to excite us to the most vigorous exertions to diffuse it.

Synesius, though raised to be a bishop in the Christian church, still continued to be a determined Platonist, and had so far imbibed the spirit and doctrine of that school, as to declare his sentiments thus :—" As darkness is most proper and commodious for those who have weak eyes, so I hold that *lies* and *fictions* are useful to the people, and that *truth* would be hurtful to those who are not able to bear its light and splendour." Unhappy Synesius! it is much to be feared truth did not dart its celestial ray on thee, or such gross ignorance would not have beclouded thy mind.

The Rev. Mr. Cochlan asking a lady in the neighbourhood of Norwich, "Whether she knew any thing of Christ?" she answered, "Yes, Sir; I remember that I once saw his picture."

Lady H. being once at Tunbridge, asked a poor man's daughter, "Whether she took any thought for her soul?" The young woman answered, "I never knew that I had a soul."— "Bid your mother call on me to-day," replied the Countess. When the old woman came, my lady said to her, "How is it that your daughter is sixteen years of age, and does not know that she has a soul?" The woman answered, "In troth, my lady, I have so much care upon me to find my daughter in food and clothes for her body, that I have no time to talk to her about her soul."

Farmer V—— once said to a minister, "Sir, you preach about faith, and say a great deal concerning it : pray what is faith?" The minister answered, "What is your idea of it?" He replied, "I suppose it to be the ten commandments."

A Mr. C. on a minister's mentioning to him, in his last sickness, the necessity of the Holy Ghost's influence, answered, "I suppose, Sir, that the Holy Ghost was a good man, who lived a great while ago."

Lady H. once asking a lady, "Whether she knew who it was that redeemed her?" received for answer, "Yes, Madam, I know very well who it was that redeemed me : it was Pontius Pilate."

Francis de Malherbe, a French poet, used to say, that when the poor promised him that they would pray to God for him, "that he did not believe they could have any great interest in heaven, since they were left in such a bad condition upon earth; and that he should be better pleased if the Duke de Luyne, or some other favourite, had made him the same promise."

An old woman of seventy years of age being inquired of by a Gospel minister concerning the state of her soul, and how she expected to be saved? replied, with a degree of warmth, "Not by this book (putting her hand upon the Bible, which lay on the table) but by my own heart, and the prayer-book."

An elderly woman having heard the doctrine of the new birth insisted on in a sermon from 2 Corinthians, v. 17. upon leaving the place of worship, was overheard to address herself with apparent seriousness, in words to this effect : "Well, this cannot be true ; for the wise man says, 'There is nothing new under the sun.'"

"Several persons of sixty years, and upwards," says Mr. Doolittle, "being asked concerning the three offices of Christ, could give no other account of them than this, That they were Father, Son, and Holy Ghost."

"I have heard of a witty parson," says Dr. Beattie, "who, having been dismissed for irregularities, used afterwards in conversation to say that he thanked God he was not cashiered for ignorance and insufficiency, but only for vice and immorality!"

A gentleman who had engaged a footman, in his service, on telling him that "morning and evening prayers were offered in the family, and that he hoped it would not be any objection to him," he replied, "No, Sir ; but I hope you will consider it in my wages."

Lewis IX. actually stopped a priest, who after having prayed for the health of his body, was beginning to implore heaven for his future welfare

—" Hold ! hold !" cried he, " you have gone far enough for once. Never be tiresome in your address to God Almighty. Stop now, and pray for my *soul another time.*"

A certain gentleman in France, having feasted high on sensual gratifications, said, " Let God Almighty give me all the good things in Paris, and secure me from the monster Death, and he may keep his heaven to himself and welcome."

Henry II. hearing Mentz, his chief city, was taken, used this blasphemous speech : " I shall never," said he, " love God any more, that suffered a city so dear to me to be taken from me."

W. Tindall, who made the first version of the Bible in English, once fell in company with a certain divine remarkable for his learning, with whom he disputed, and drove him so close, that at length the divine blasphemously cried out, " We had better be without God's laws than the Pope's."

In the reign of Edward VI. most of the priests in Scotland imagined the New Testament to be a composition of Luther's, and asserted that the Old alone was the word of God.

Caligula, the Roman Emperor, commanded that he should be worshipped as a god, and caused a temple to be erected for him. He built also his house in the capitol, that so he might dwell with Jupiter; but being angry that Jupiter was still preferred before him, he afterwards erected a temple in his palace, and would have had the statue of Jupiter Olympus in his form brought thither ; the ship, however, which was sent for it was broken in pieces by a thunderbolt. He used to sit in the middle of the images of the gods, and caused the most rare and costly fowls and birds to be sacrificed to him. He had also certain instruments made, whereby he imitated thunder and lightning; and when it really thundered, he used to cast stones towards heaven, saying,—" Either thou shalt kill me, or I will kill thee ;" with other blasphemies, which are not proper to mention in this work.

Xerxes having made a bridge of boats over the Hellespont, for the passage of his immense army from Asia into Europe, a tempest arose, and destroyed it; upon which he caused his men to give the sea three hundred stripes, and throw chains in it, to bind it to its good behaviour ; which office was performed, accompanied with these arrogant expressions : " Unruly water! thy lord has ordered thee this punishment : and, whether thou wilt or no, he is resolved to pass over thee."

A certain Italian having his enemy in his power, told him there was no possible way for him to save his life, unless he would immediately deny and renounce his Saviour. The timorous wretch, in hopes of mercy, did it; when the other forthwith stabbed him to the heart, saying —" That now he had a full and noble revenge, for he had killed at once both his body and soul."

The above are only individual instances of error and depravity ; but what shall we say when we consider the mass of mankind at large ? The inhabitants of the globe are computed to be upwards of eight hundred millions. Of these, four hundred and eighty-one millions are supposed to be Pagans ; one hundred and forty millions are Mahometans ; nine millions are Jews; only one hundred and seventy millions are called Christians. Of these only fifty millions are Protestants ; and of these, alas! how few are truly devoted to God !

INDOLENCE.

" No disposition so totally unfits a man for all the social offices and social enjoyments of life as indolence. An idle man is a mere blank in the creation, and lives to no purpose." He is his own tormentor; always full of wants and of complaints ; while his inactivity often proves fatal both to his body and his mind.

" The worst importunities, the most embarrassing perplexities of business, are softness and luxury, compared with the incessant cravings of vacancy, and the unsatisfactory expedient of idleness."

It was a law among the Athenians, " That those who had been brought up to no employ by their parents, should not be obliged to keep them if they came to want in their old age," which all other (legitimate) children were.

So uncommon, and so much out of fashion, is idleness in China, that it is recorded of one of the Emperors, that, seeing a man unemployed, he expressed his gret and his fears, that, on account of the man's idleness, some one of his subjects must be that day destitute of food.

" Augustus," says Flavel, " built an *Apragapolis*, a city void of business ; but I am sure God never erected any city, town, or family, to that end. If you be negligent, you cannot be innocent."

" Pray of what did your brother die ?" said the Marquis Spinola, one day, to Sir Horace Vere. " He died, Sir," replied he, " of having nothing to do." " Alas ! Sir," said Spinola, "that is enough to kill any general of us all." Montesquieu says, " We in general place idleness among the beatitudes of heaven ; it should rather, I think, be put amidst the tortures of hell. Austin calls it the burying a man alive."

Varia Servilius, descended of a Prætorian family, was remarkable for nothing but sloth and indolence, in which he grew old and odious, insomuch that it was commonly said by such as passed his house, *Hic Varia situs est*—Here lies Varia ! Thus speaking of him as a person not only dead, but buried to all intents and purposes of rational existence.

" If you ask me," says Lavater, " which is the real hereditary sin of human nature, do you imagine I shall answer, pride or luxury, or ambition or egotism ? No ; I shall say, *indolence.* He who conquers *indo-*

lence will conquer all the rest." If we do not agree altogether with this gentleman's opinion, it shows us, at least, what a great evil he supposed *indolence* to be.

" When I visited a country neighbour of mine (says Lord Clarendon) in the morning, I always found him in bed ; and when I came in the afternoon, he was asleep, and to most men besides myself was denied. Once walking with him, I doubted he was melancholy, and, by spending his time so much in bed, and so much alone, that there was something that troubled him ; otherwise that it could not be that a man upon whom God had poured so many blessings, should be so little contented as he appeared to be. To which he answered, ' that he thought himself the most happy man alive in a wife, who was all the comfort he could have in this world ; that he was at so much ease in his fortune, he did not wish it greater ; but he said he would deal freely with me, and tell me, if he were melancholy, (which he suspected himself of,) what was the true cause of it ; that he had somewhat *he knew not what to do with ; his time he knew not how to spend ;* which was the reason he loved his bed so much, and slept at other times, which he said he found did him no good in his health." Lord Clarendon adds, that the unhappy gentleman's melancholy daily increased with the agony of his thoughts, till he contracted those diseases which carried him off at the age of thirty-six.

How wretched must this disposition make the possessor of it ! Man was made for activity, and in the present state, indeed, much of his happiness seems to depend on it. When he becomes idle, he becomes miserable : both a plague to others, and a burden to himself. It is a saying among the Turks, that a "busy man is troubled with one devil, but the idle man with a thousand ;" and the Grand Seignior himself, we are told, is always taught some mechanical business.

INFIDELITY.

WHATEVER specious arguments infidels bring forward in support of their doctrines, there is one thing which seems very prominent in their characters ; I mean pride. They oppose their own reason to the facts of ages, the fulfilment of prophecy, the evidence of miracles, and the good sense of the wisest and best men who have ever lived.

" The sufficiency of human reason," says Young, " is the golden calf which these men set up to be worshipped ; and, in the frenzies of their extravagant devotion to it, they trample on venerable authority, strike at an oak with an osier, the doctrine of God's own planting, and the growth of ages, with the sudden and fortuitous shoots of imagination, abortive births of an hour. The human improvements on divine revelation may be compared to the profaning of the Holy Bible with the figure of Heathen idols under *Antiochus Epiphanes*; or, rather, to the proud *Roman* Emperor, who took the head from Jupiter's statue, and placed his own in its stead."

The elegant Saurin strikingly describes the folly and madness of such men : " What surprises me, what stumbles me, what frightens me, is to see a diminutive creature, a contemptible man, a little ray of light glimmering through a few feeble organs, controvert a point with the Supreme Being, oppose that Intelligence who setteth at the helm of the world, question what he affirms, dispute what he determines, appeal from his decision, and even after God hath given evidence, reject all doctrines that are beyond his capacity. Enter into thy nothingness, mortal creature ! What madness animates thee ? How darest thou pretend, thou who art but a point, thou whose essence is but an atom, to measure thyself with the Supreme Being, with Him whom the heaven of heavens cannot contain ?"

Men of infidel principles are sometimes as ignorant as they are impertinent. One of this sort was making himself merry in a large company at the expense of the Scriptures, and told his companions that he could prove the prophet of the Christians (as he called Christ) mistaken, even upon the most common subjects. After awakening the curiosity of the company, he thus gratified it. " Christ says that *old bottles* are not so strong as new, (alluding to Matt. ix. 17 ;) and therefore if new wine is put into *old bottles* it will break them. Now, don't every body know that old glass is just as strong as new ? for whoever heard that glass was the weaker for being old ?"

A clergyman in company, who had been made the butt of his wit, gently reproved the ignorance and folly of this witling, by asking him if he understood Greek. " Greek, Sir ! no, Sir ; but what has Greek to do with it ? A bottle is a bottle, whether it be in Greek or English ; every body knows that an old bottle is just as good and as strong as a new one." " Not quite, Sir," replied the other, " if they are made of leather or skins, as the fact was as to the bottles Christ speaks of, as the Greek name imports, and indeed it is so in many countries, even to this day, that people use skins by way of vessels to contain wine." On which side the laughter of the company turned is not very difficult to conceive. We may here learn that the knowledge of the original languages in which the Scriptures are written is of no small utility to a Christian minister.

Mr. Hobbes, the celebrated infidel, in bravado would sometimes speak very unbecoming things of God and his word. Yet when alone he was haunted with the most tormenting reflections, and would awake in great terror if his candle happened to go out in the night. He could never bear any discourse of death, and seemed to cast off all thought of it. Notwithstanding all his high pretensions to learning and philosophy, his uneasiness constrained him to confess, when he drew near to the grave, that "he was about to take a leap in the dark."

Even the hero of modern infidels, we are informed, when he came to die, was in the greatest horror. When the Doctor came, he exclaimed, "I am abandoned by God and man. Doctor, I will give you half of what I am worth, if you will give me six months life." The Doctor answered, "Sir, you cannot live six weeks." Voltaire replied, "Then I shall go to hell, and you will go with me!" and soon expired.

The late celebrated Mr. Gibbon, just before his death, confessed, that "when he considered all worldly things, they were all fleeting; when he looked back, they had been fleeting; and when he looked forward, *all was dark and doubtful.*" Surely no one can wish to be an infidel for the comfort of it!

Infidelity is not only shocking as to its nature, but every way injurious as to its tendency. The following instance is a confirmation of it. A servant who waited at the table of Mr. M. often hearing this subject brought forward, at last became as great an adept in these principles as his master; and being thoroughly convinced that for any of his misdeeds he should have no after account to make was resolved to profit by the doctrine, and made off with many things of value, particularly the plate. He was, however, so closely pursued, that he was brought back with his prey to his master's house, who examined him before some select friends. At first the man was sullen, and would answer no questions; but being urged to give a reason for his infamous behaviour, he resolutely said, "I had heard you so often talk of the impossibility of a future state, and that after death there was no reward for virtue, nor punishment for vice, that I was tempted to commit the robbery."— "Well, but, you rascal," replied Mallet, "had you no fear of the gallows?" "Sir," said the fellow, looking sternly at his master "what is that to you? If I had a mind to venture that you had removed my greatest terror: why should I fear the least?"

LEARNING.

While some pride themselves in their acquirements, and assume a great degree of consequence from their superiority of knowledge, there are others, who make it their business to depreciate learning, and think no respect due to, or felicity to arise from, intellectual attainments. But as ignorance is no honour, so knowledge is no disgrace to a rational creature. It is true, indeed, "that many parts of what is called learning resemble the man's horse, which had but two faults; he was hard to catch, and good for nothing when he was caught." But that knowledge which has the glory of the Divine Being, our own real improvement, and the good of others, for its object, should be sought by all; and we should disdain to be upon a level with those, "who, like brutes inclosed in a narrow circle of sensations, never aspire to improve their faculty of intelligence any farther than as its improvement is necessary to the sensual enjoyment of a few gross gratifications, in which all their felicity is contained."

Bishop Beveridge, at 18 years of age, wrote a Treatise on the Excellency and Use of Oriental Tongues, especially Hebrew, Chaldee, Syriac, Arabic, and Samaritan, with a Syriac Grammar.

Witsius made so rapid a progress in learning, that before he was fifteen years of age, he could not only speak and write the Latin language correctly, and with some degree of fluency, but also readily interpret the books of the Greek Testament, and the Orations of Isocrates, and render the Hebrew Commentaries of Samuel into Latin. At the same time giving the etymology of the original words, and assigning the reasons of the variations of the pointing grammatically.

It is said of John Picus, Prince of Mirandula, that such was his genius for learning languages, that he was master of two and twenty before he had seen so many years.

6

James Crichton, known by the appellation of the admirable Crichton, was born in Scotland. At the age of twenty years, he thought of improving himself by foreign travel; and having arrived at Paris, the desire of procuring the notice of its university, or the pride of making known his attainments, induced him to affix placards on the gates of its colleges, challenging the professors to dispute with him in all the branches of literature and the sciences in ten languages and either in prose or in verse. On the day appointed, three thousand auditors assembled. Fifty masters, who had laboriously prepared for the contest, proposed to him the most intricate questions, and he replied to them in the language they required with the happiest propriety of expression, with an acuteness that seemed superior to every difficulty, and with an erudition which appeared to have no bounds. Four celebrated doctors of the church then ventured to enter into disputation with him. He obviated every objection they could urge in opposition to him; he refuted every argument they advanced. A sentiment of terror mingled itself with their admiration of him. They conceived him to be an antichrist. This singular exibition continued from nine in the morning till six at night, and was closed by the President of the University, who, having expressed in the strongest terms of compliment the sense he entertained of his capacity and knowledge, advanced towards him, accompanied by four professors, and bestowed on him a diamond ring and a purse of gold.

It must not, however, be understood that the study of the sciences, or the acquisition of languages, always procure the literary adventurer the happiness he desires. Joseph Scaliger perfectly understood thirteen languages, was deeply versed in almost every branch of literature, and was perhaps one of the greatest scholars that any age has produced; yet he found so much perplexity, not in acquiring but in communicating his knowledge, that sometimes, like Nero, he wished he had never known his letters.

LONDON.

As London is the grand emporium of the world, and a place where there is every advantage, it is no wonder it should be the resort of all ranks of people. Its religious advantages, however, are not less than its political and commercial. Here the gospel is preached in all its purity, and vast multitudes flock to hear it. Here are lectures at all seasons to accommodate the people, and to leave the ignorant without excuse. Here are ministers of all denominations, and of various gifts, suited to the different sentiments, tastes, and experience of hearers. Here are public meetings to inspire with ardour, and social companies to instruct and establish the mind. Here are friendly societies and charitable institutions to excite generosity and move compassion. In this respect I look on London as superior to any city in the world, and wonder not at the partial attachment many possess to it. Nor is London less famous for learning. "The happiness of London," says Dr. Johnson, "is not to be conceived but by those who have resided in it. I will venture to say, there is more learning and science within the circumference of ten miles from where we sit, than in all the rest of the kingdom."

King James the First, willing to make a present to Dr. Donne, appointed him to wait on him at dinner the next day. His majesty being set down, before he ate any meat, said, "Dr. Donne, I have invited you to dinner, and though you sit not down with me, yet I will carve to you of a dish that I know you love. You love London well: I do, therefore, make you Dean of St. Paul's; take your meat home to your study, say grace, and much good may it do you."

Mr. C——, of S——n, being in company once with a neighbouring

minister, who had an invitation to go from the country to a church in London, and the conversation turned upon that subject, his neighbour said to him. " Brother C——, I see my call exceeding clear to leave B——, and go to London." Mr. C—— replied, " Ah, brother, London is a fine place; and as it is to go there, you can hear very quick; but if God had called you to go to poor Cranfield, he might have called long enough, I fear, before you would have heard him."

According to Justice Colquhoun's calculation, " There are in London about 502 places of worship: One cathedral, one abbey, 114 churches, 130 chapels and chapels of ease, 207 meetings and chapels for dissenters, 43 chapels for foreigners, and 6 synagogues. About 4050 public and private schools, including inns of court, colleges, &c. About eight societies for morals, ten societies for learning and arts, 122 asylums for indigent; about 17 asylums for sick and lame, 13 dispensaries, and 704 friendly societies. Charity distributed, 750,000*l.*per annum." This is a pleasing account; but the following, I think, we cannot read without feeling emotions both of sorrow and pity. " There are about 2500 persons committed for trial in one year. Annual depredations amount to about 2,100,000*l*. Eighteen prisons, 5204 alehouses, within the bills of mortality. Amount of coin counterfeited 200,000*l*. per annum. About 3000 receivers of stolen goods; about 50,000 prostitutes. About 10,000 servants at all times out of place : 20,000 rise every morning, without knowing how they are to subsist through the day."

LYING.

The practice of lying is so prevalent in the world, and appears under so many forms, that a firm adherence to truth in every thing is considered as a disagreeable singularity by many. Even they who are not guilty of open lies, are too often found in the shameful practice of equivocation. Let all such, however, remember, that lying lips are an abomination to the Lord, and that he who wilfully deceives his neighbour, either by his tongue or his conduct, is a being to be dreaded in society, and, while attempting to deceive others, he is actually imposing upon and will eventually deceive himself.

The following instance of Dr. Johnson's conduct in this respect, while it reflects honour on him, will reprove many who are living in this sin. It is said of him, that he would not allow his servants to say he was not at home, if he really was, (as it is too much the custom of many.) " A servant's strict regard for truth," said he, "must be weakened by such a practice. A philosopher may know that it is merely a form of denial ; but few servants are such distinguishers. If I accustom a servant to tell a lie for me, have I not reason to apprehend that he will tell many more for himself?"

A strict adherence to truth the Doctor considered as a sacred obligation, insomuch that, in relating the most minute anecdote, he would not allow himself the smallest addition to embellish his story. The late Mr. Tyers, who knew Dr Johnson intimately, observed, "that he always talked as if he was talking upon oath."

Herodotus tells us, in the first book of his history, that from the age of five years to that of twenty, the ancient Persians instructed their children only in three things ; viz. to manage a horse, to shoot dexterously with the bow, and *to speak the truth.* Which shows of how much importance they thought it to fix this virtuous habit on the mind of youth betimes.

The following awful account is related of a man, whose name shall be concealed, in tenderness to surviving relatives. He waited upon a magistrate near Hitchin, in the county of Hertford, and informed him that he had been stopped by a young gentleman of Hitchin, who had knocked him down, and searched his pockets, but, not finding any thing there, he suffered him to depart. The magistrate, astonished at this piece of intelligence, despatched a messenger to the young gentleman, ordering him to appear immediately and answer to the charge exhibited against him: the youth obeyed the summons, accompanied by his guardian and an intimate friend. Upon their arrival at the seat of justice, the accused and the accuser were confronted; when the magistrate hinted to the man, he was fearful that he had made the charge with no other view than that of extorting money, and bade him take care how he proceeded; exhorting him, in the most earnest and pathetic manner, to beware of the dreadful train of consequences attending perjury.

The man insisted upon making oath of what he had advanced: the oath was accordingly administered, and the business fully investigated, when the innocence of the young gentleman was established, he having by the most incontrovertible evidence, proved an *alibi*. The infamous wretch, finding his intentions thus frustrated, returned home much chagrined, and, meeting soon afterwards with one of his neighbours, he declared he had not sworn to any thing but the truth, calling God to witness the same in the most solemn manner, and wished, if it was not as he had said, his jaws might be locked, and that his flesh might rot upon his bones; when, terrible to relate! his jaws were instantly locked, and the use of the faculty he had so awfully perverted was denied him forever; and after lingering nearly a fortnight, he expired in the greatest agonies, his flesh literally rotting upon his bones!

MEMORY.

As a clear judgment and a fine genius are every way valuable, so a good memory is of considerable advantage. It is the storehouse of the soul, and the repository of intellectual wealth. It is the library of the mind which we carry about with us. It is, indeed, to be lamented, that it often retains useless lumber and insignificant ideas, but it will be the business of a wise man to *lay up* in it those treasures which, in due time, he can *lay out* with utility. Many rules have been given for strengthening the memory, such as clear apprehension, method in what we commit to memory, frequent review, repetition, writing it in clear characters, &c. These, if attended to, no doubt will be serviceable; for the memory, like the body, is improved by exercise. Happy is he who, in addition to a cultivated understanding, posesses the powers of retention and recollection. He has a source of entertainment within himself. He can either be employed in retirement, or be useful in society. He carries his wealth with him wherever he goes, and makes use of it whenever he pleases. Some of the following instances, as well as those under Precocity, may be thought, by many readers, apocryphal, but there does not appear to me any reason to doubt their authenticity.

Mr. Thomas Vincent had the whole New Testament and Psalms by heart. He took this pains, he often said, not knowing but they who took from him his pulpit, might, in time, demand his Bible also.

Henry de Mesmes had such a memory, that he could repeat Homer from one end to the other.

Anthony Magliabechi, born at Florence, was distinguished by his great memory and constant attention to study. A gentleman, by way of experiment, is said to have lent him a manuscript he was going to print; and coming, some time after it was returned, with a melancholy face, pretending to have lost it, he requested Magliabechi to recollect as much as he could of it; upon which he wrote down the whole verbatim exactly as he had read it.

Bishop Jewel had naturally a very strong memory, which he had greatly improved by art, so that he could exactly repeat whatever he wrote after once reading. While the bell was ringing, he committed to his memory a repetition sermon, and pronounced it without hesitation. He was a constant preacher; and, in his own sermons, his course was to write down only the heads, and meditate upon the rest while the bell was ringing to church. So firm was his memory, that he used to say, if he were to deliver a premeditated speech before a thousand auditors, shouting or fighting all the while, they would not put him out. John Hooper, Bishop of Gloucester, who was burnt in the reign of Queen Mary, once, to try him, wrote about forty Welsh and Irish words. Mr. Jewel, going a little while aside, and recollecting them in his memory, and reading them twice or thrice over, said them by heart, backward and forward, exactly in the same order they were set down. And another time he did the same by ten lines of Erasmus's paraphrase in English; the words of which being read sometimes confusedly without order, and sometimes in order, by the Lord Keeper Bacon, Mr. Jewel, thinking a while on them, presently repeated them again, backward and forward, in their right order, and in their wrong, just as they were read to him; and he taught his tutor, Mr. Parkhurst, the same art.

Jedediah Buxton, a poor illiterate English peasant, who died some years ago, was remarkable for his knowledge of the relative proportions of numbers, their powers and progressive denominations. To these objects he applied the whole force of his mind, and upon these his attention was so constantly rivetted, that he frequently took no notice of external objects, and, when he did, it was only with respect to their numbers. If any space of time was mentioned before him, he would soon after say, that it contained so many minutes; and if any distance, he would assign the number of hair-breadths in it, even when no question was asked him by the company.

Being required to multiply 456 by 378, he gave the product, by *mental arithmetic*, (for he could neither read nor write,) as soon as a person in company had completed it in the common way. Being requested to work it audibly, that his method might be known, he multiplies 456 first by 5, which produced 2280; this he again multiplied by 20, and found the product 45,600, which was the multiplicand multiplied by 100; this product he again multiplied by 3, which produced 136,800, the sum of the multiplicand multiplied by 300. It remained, therefore, to multiply this by 78, which he affected by multiplying 2280 (the product of the multiplicand multiplied by 5) by 15, 5 times 15 being 75; this product being 34,200, he added to 136,800, which was the multiplicand multiplied by 300; and this produced 171,000, which was 375 times 456. To complete his operation, therefore, he multiplied 456 by 3, which produced 1368; and having added this number to 171,000, he found the product of 456, multiplied by 378, to be 172,368.

By this it appears that Jedediah's method of arithmetic was entirely his own, and that he was so little acquainted with the common rules, as to multiply 456 first by 5, and the product by 20, to find what sum it would produce multiplied by 100; whereas, had he added two cyphers to the figures, he would have obtained the product all at once.

A person who heard of his astonishing performance, meeting with him accidentally, in order to try his calculating powers, proposed to him the following questions. Admit a field be 423 yards long, and 383 broad, what is the area? After the figures were read to him distinctly, he gave the true product, 162,009 yards, in the space of two minutes. The same person asked him how many acres the said field measured; and in eleven minutes he replied 33 acres, 1 rood,

35 perches, 20 yards and a quarter. He was then asked, how many barley-corns would reach 8 miles? In a minute and a half he answered, 1,520,640 barley-corns. He was likewise asked, Supposing the distance between York and London to be 204 miles, how many times will a coach wheel turn round in that space, allowing the circumference of the wheel to be 6 yards? In thirteen minutes he answered 59,840 times.

Being asked how long after the firing of one of the cannons at Retford the report might be heard at Haughton Park, the distance being 5 miles, and supposing the sound to move at the rate of 1142 feet in one second of time, he replied, after about a quarter of an hour, in 23 seconds, 7 thirds, and that 46 remained. He was then asked, Admit 3,584 brocoli plants are set in rows, four feet asunder, and the plants seven feet apart, in a rectangular plot of ground, how much land will these plants occupy? In near half an hour, he said, 2 acres, 1 rood, 8 perches and a half.

This extraordinary man would stride over a piece of land or a field, and tell the contents of it with as much exactness as if he had measured it by the chain. In this manner he measured the whole lordship of Elmeton, of some thousands of acres, belonging to Sir John Rhodes, and brought him the contents not only in acres, roods, and perches, but even in square inches.

After this, he reduced them for his own amusement into square hairbreadths, computing about 48 to each side of the inch; which produced such an incomprehensible number as appeared altogether astonishing.

The only objects of Jedediah's curiosity, next to figures, were the King and royal family; and his desire to see them was so strong, that, in the beginning of spring, 1754, he walked up to London for that purpose, but was obliged to return disappointed, as his Majesty had removed to Kensington, just as he arrived in town. He was, however, introduced to the Royal Society, whom he called the *Volk of the Siety Court*. The gentlemen who were then present asked him several questions in arithmetic, to prove his abilities, and dismissed him with a handsome gratuity.

During his residence in London, he was carried to see the tragedy of King Richard III. performed at Drury-lane playhouse; and it was expected that the novelty of every thing in this place, together with the splendour of the surrounding objects, would have fixed him in astonishment, or that his passion would in some degree have been roused by the action of the performers, even if he did not fully comprehend the dialogue. But his thoughts were otherwise employed. During the dances, his attention was engaged in reckoning the number of steps. After a fine piece of music, he declared that the innumerable sounds produced by the instruments, perplexed him beyond measure.— But he counted the words uttered by Mr. Garrick in the whole course of the entertainment, and affirmed that in this he had perfectly succeeded.

Born to no fortune, and brought up to no particular profession, J. Buxton supported himself by the labour of his hands; and though his talents, had they been properly cultivated, might have qualified him for acting a distinguished part on the theatre of life, he pursued "the noiseless tenor of his way," sufficiently contented if he could gratify the wants of nature, and procure a daily subsistence for himself and family. He died in 1778, being about 70 years of age. See his Life.

PARENTAL AFFECTION.

God hath wisely and kindly implanted in the breasts of parents a most ardent principle of affection towards their children. And, indeed, the various trials and difficulties of a family require more than ordinary regard to conduct it with propriety; to bear with patience whatever transpires, and to watch with constancy against every evil to which children are exposed.

Agesilaus, King of Sparta, was, of all mankind, one of the most tender and indulgent fathers to his children. It is reported of him, that when they were little he would play with them and divert himself and them with riding upon a stick, and that, having been surprised by a friend in that action, he desired him not to tell any body of it, till he himself was a father. Henry IV. of France, would have his children call him papa, or father, and not Sire, which was the new fashion introduced by Catherine De Medicis. He used frequently to join in their amusements; and one day, as he was going on all-fours with the Dauphin, his son, on his back, an ambassador suddenly entered the apartment, and surprised him in this attitude. The monarch, without moving from it, said to him, "Monsieur l'Ambassadeur, have you any children ?" "Yes, Sire," replied he. "Very well ; then I shall finish my race round my chamber."

History informs us, that a father went to the agents of a tyrant to endeavour to redeem his two sons, military men, who, with some other captives of war, were appointed to die. He offered as a ransom to surrender his own life and a large sum of money. The soldiers who had it in charge to put them to death, informed him that this equivalent would be accepted for one of his sons, and for one only, because they should be accountable for the execution of two persons ; he might therefore choose which he would redeem. Anxious to save even one of them thus, at the expense of his own life, he yet was utterly unable to decide which should die, by choosing the other to live ; and remained in the agony of his dilemma so long, that they were both slain.

It is said that when the famous Dr. Kennicott had taken orders, he came to officiate in his clerical capacity in his native town : when his father, who was parish clerk, proceeded to place the surplice on his shoulders a struggle ensued between the modesty of the son and the affection of the parent, who insisted on paying that respect to his son which he had been accustomed to show to other clergyman : to this filial obedience he was obliged to submit. A circumstance is added, that his mother had often declared she should never be able to support the joy of hearing her son preach, and that, on her attendance at the church for the first time, she was so overcome, as to be taken out in a state of temporary insensibility.

After all, we discover the greatest affection to our children by endeavouring to form their minds into a virtuous and religious mould ; when we tender to them suitable instruction, and above all, earnestly pray for them, that they may be preserved from the snare and danger of the present world and be taught to prepare for a better. "Parents," says Dr. Doddridge, "are greatly solicitous for the temporal happiness of their children. For this they labour and watch; for this they deny themselves many an enjoyment, and subject themselves to many an uneasy circumstance. But, alas ! where is the real friendship of all this, while the precious soul is neglected ? It brings to my mind the account which an ancient writer[*] gives of the old Carthaginians, which I can never recollect without great emotion. He is speaking of that diabolical custom, which so long prevailed amongst them, of offering their children to a detestable Idol, which was formed in such a manner, that an infant put into its hands, which were stretched out to receive it, would immediately fall into a gulph of fire. He adds a circumstance which one cannot mention without horror : that the mothers, who, with their own hands, presented the little innocents, thought it an unfortunate omen that the victim should be offered weeping ; and therefore used a great many fond artifices to divert it, that soothed by the kisses and caresses of a parent, it might smile in the dreadful moment in which it was to be given up to the idol. Such is their parental care and love, such their concern for the present ease and prosperi-

* "Minutius Felix."

ty of their children, who neglect their souls: a fond solicitude, that they may pass smiling into the hands of the destroyer."

"To give children good instruction and a bad example," says Archbishop Tillotson, "is but beckoning to them with the hand to show them the way to heaven, while we take them by the hand, and lead them to hell." The following will show an instance of spiritual affection:

Mr. P. Henry drew up a short form of the baptismal covenant, for the use of his children: it was this—

"I take God the Father to be my chief good and highest end.

"I take God the Son to be my Prince and Saviour.

"I take God the Holy Ghost to be my sanctifier, teacher, guide, and comforter.

"I take the word of God to be my rule in all my actions;

"And the people of God to be my people in all conditions.

"I do likewise devote and dedicate unto the Lord my whole self, all I am, all I have, and all I can do.

"And this I do deliberately, sincerely, freely, and for ever."

This he taught his children, and each of them solemnly repeated it every Lord's day evening, after they were catechised, he putting his *amen* to it, and sometimes adding, "So say and so do, and you are made for ever." He also took pains to lead them to understand it, and to persuade them to a free and cheerful consent to it. When they grew up, he made them all write it over severally with their own hands, and very solemnly set their names to it, which he told them he would keep by him, and it should be produced as a testimony against them if they should afterwards depart from God, and turn from following after him.

PERSECUTION.

PERSECUTION and intolerance are words at which my soul recoils; words which call up the most unpleasant ideas; which make me tremble when I consider the inexpressible depravity of the human mind, and how far it has been extended and manifested among mankind.

Of all the absurdities and impieties, that of persecution for difference of opinion is the most cruel and flagrant, nothing more unreasonable, nothing more abhorrent for the true genius of Christianity.

That a man should be indifferent as to what he believes, or suppose that all doctrines are alike, this would be a mark of an ignorant and impious mind. Every man is bound to search into the will of his Creator, so far as it is revealed; to study his obligations to him, and to be earnestly concerned for the promotion of his glory in the world. But to triumph over others, to attempt to rob them of their private judgment, or to persecute them in any way because they differ from us in *thought*, is the greatest disgrace to reason, religion, and humanity. It is also as useless as it is wicked. It may make hypocrites, but not christians. Attempts have been made to establish an exact uniformity of sentiment, but all in vain, so it must be, while variety characterises all the works, material and intellectual, of the Creator's hand. Racks, tortures, gibbets, fires, with all the instruments of cruelty, have been applied, but the mind has risen superior to all; yea, the very sanguinary method made use of have, instead of repressing, supported and strengthened the cause of truth, while it has injured that of the opposers. It was a true saying of the Emperor Maximilian II. that "Such princes as tyrannize over the consciences of men, attack the throne of the Supreme Being, and frequently lose the earth by interfering too much with heaven." The spirit of persecution has been too prevalent in every age, and almost in every party; nor has free toleration been rightly understood till within these few years. The accounts given us of the ten pagan persecutions; the successive and unheard of cruelties of the church of Rome, and, alas! the too great portion of this spirit among Protestants are enough to make humanity sicken at the thought. We, however, live in a time when this spirit begins to be treated as it should be. The dawn of truth, love, and intelligence, appears, and the glorious Sun of religious liberty sheds his benign influence, around us. May it never cease to shine, till the whole world be enlightened, and the spirit of intolerance and religious oppression be heard of no more! Amen.

Francis I. King of France, used to declare, "that if he thought the blood in his arm was tainted with the Lutheran heresy, he would have it cut off; and that he would not spare even his own children, if they entertained sentiments contrary to the Catholic Church."

Don Pedro, one of the Spanish Captains taken by Sir F. Drake, being examined before the Lords of the Privy Council, as to what was their design of invading us? replied, " To subdue the nation, and root it out."—" And what meant you," said the Lords, "to do with the Catholics?" " To send them good men," says he, " directly to heaven, and you heretics to hell."—" For what end were your whips of cord and wire?" "To whip you heretics to death."—" What would you have done with the young children." " They above seven years old should have gone the way their fathers went: the rest should have lived in perpetual bondage, branded in the forehead with the letter L. for Lutheran."

N. B. The instruments of torture above alluded to, as thumb screws, whips, &c. are still shewn among other curiosities in the Tower of London.

The history of the dreadful persecution of the Protestants under Charles IX. of France, needs not a place here; but one of the most horrid circumstances attending it was, that when the news of this event reached Rome, Pope Gregory XIII. instituted the most solemn rejoicing, giving thanks to Almighty God for this glorious victory!!! An instance that has no parallel even in hell.

What a different spirit did Lewis XII. of France manifest! When he was incited to persecute the Waldenses, he returned this truly great and noble reply: "God forbid that I should persecute any for being more religious than myself."

We cannot be sufficiently thankful for the liberty we now enjoy. How our forefathers suffered, history informs us. Of the pious and excellent Mr. Shaw, a friend writes, " I have known him to spend part of many days and nights too in religious exercises, when the times were so dangerous, that it would hazard an imprisonment to be worshipping God with five or six people like minded with himself. I have sometimes been in his company for a whole night together, when we have been obliged to steal to the place in the dark, and stop in the voice by clothing and fast closing the windows, till the first daybreak down a chimney has given us notice to be gone."

" I have," says one, " nine children, and my ambition is, to engage them to treat a spirit of intolerance as Hamilcar taught Hannibal to treat the old Roman spirit of universal dominion. The enthusiastic Carthaginian parent, going to offer a sacrifice to Jupiter for the success of an intended war, took with him his little son Hannibal, then only nine years of age, and eager to accompany his father, led him to the altar, made him lay his little hand on the sacrifice, and swear that he would never be in friendship with the Romans. We may sanctify this thought by transferring it to other objects; and while we sing in the church, Glory to God in the highest, vow perpetual peace with all mankind, and reject all weapons except those which are spiritual; we may, we must declare war against a spirit of intolerance, from generation to generation."

POVERTY.

THOUGH the blessings of life, and a competency of temporal favours, are every way desirable, yet they who are in a measure deprived of them, should remember that poverty in itself is no real disgrace, though considered as such by those whose minds are influenced by custom and prejudice more than truth and benevolence. It must be confessed, indeed, that a considerable part of mankind make themselves poor by their pride, extravagance, and dissipation ; yet I believe poverty is frequently an attendant on genius and piety ; since many of the most wise, able, and excellent characters have languished under the severity of want and distress.

Homer, poor and blind, resorted to the public places to recite his verses for a morsel of bread.

The illustrious Cardinal Bentivoglio, the ornament of Italy and of literature, languished in his old age in the most distressful poverty, and having sold his palace to satisfy his creditors, left nothing behind him but his reputation.

Our great Milton, as every one knows, sold his immortal work for 10l. to a bookseller, being too poor to undertake the printing of it on his own account.

It is said that Samuel Boyse, whose Poem on Creation ranks high in the scale of poetic excellence, was absolutely famished to death ; and was found dead in a garret, with a blanket thrown over his shoulder, and fastened by a skewer, with a pen in his hand. He was buried by the parish.

Louis De Boissi, a celebrated French writer, and incontestably one of the first geniuses France ever produced, wanted bread. While all France was ringing with plaudits on his uncommon talents, he was languishing at home with a wife and child under the pressures of the extremest poverty, yea, to such a degree, that he at last sunk into despondency, and absolutely gave himself, wife, and child, up to be starved in a solitary apartment ; and would actually have been so, had it not been for a friend who found them in that miserable state, where they had been for two or three days without bread.

Otway, a poet of the first class, is said to have died in want, or, as related by one of his biographers, by swallowing, after a long fast, a piece of bread which charity had supplied. He went out, as is reported, almost naked, in the rage of hunger, and, finding a gentleman in a neighbouring coffee-house, asked him for a shilling. The gentleman gave him a guinea, and Otway, going away, bought a roll, and was choaked with the first mouthful. " All this," says Dr. Johnson, " I hope is not true ;" but observes, " that indigence and its concomitants, sorrow and despondency, pressed hard upon him, has never been denied, whatever immediate cause might bring him to the grave."

The famous Dr. Goldsmith was so poor, that he travelled on foot most part of his tour on the Continent : when he approached any peasant's house, he played on the German flute, which sometimes procured him a lodging and subsistence for the next day.

The great Dr. Johnson, for some time after he had reared his fame on an adamantine base, was flattered by the great, and listened to by the learned, was not able to emerge from poverty and dependence. It is upon record that he was arrested for a paltry debt of five guineas, and was obliged to his friend Mr. S. Richardson for emancipation.

To these we might add a long list of men eminent for their piety, and singular for their zeal to promote the good of mankind ; yea, the illustrious Apostles and the Lord Jesus Christ himself were poor. Though our Saviour was a King, possessed of all possible glory and intelligence in himself, yet while here we find, " instead of a crown of gold he had a crown of thorns ; for a sceptre, a reed put in his hand in derision; for a throne, a cross; instead of palaces, not a place to lay his head in; instead of sumptuous feasts to others, oftentimes hungry and thirsty himself; instead of great attendants, a company of poor fishermen; instead of treasures to give them, not money enough to pay tribute without working a miracle; and the preferment offered them was to give each of them his cross to bear. In all things the reverse of worldly greatness from the first to the last; a manger for a cradle at his birth; not a place to lay his head sometimes in his life, nor a grave of his own at his death."—Maclaurin's Ser. on Gal. vi. 14.

PRAYER.

"WHAT," says Hervey, "can be so truly becoming a *dependant state* as to pay our adoring homage to the Author of all perfection, and profess our devoted allegiance to the Supreme Almighty Governor of the universe? Can there be a more sublime pleasure, than to dwell in fixed contemplation on the beauties of the eternal mind? Can there be a more *advantageous employ*, than to present our requests to the Father of mercies?" "Men (said our gracious Saviour) ought always to pray, and not to faint."

The old Duke of Bedford used to say, "I consider the prayers of God's Ministers and People as the best walls round my house."

The great Dr. Boerhaave acknowledged, that an hour spent every morning in private prayer and meditation gave him a spirit and vigour for the business of the day, and kept his temper active, patient and calm.

It is said of Colonel Gardiner, that he had always his two hours with God in a morning. If his regiment were to march at four, he would be up at two. Alas! we have few officers who think it their duty or honour to be found in prayer.

For authors to implore the blessings of the Diving Being on their writings, is considered as a species of enthusiasm by many; yet we find Dr. Johnson, who was never considered as an enthusiast, making use of the following prayer on the occasion of his writing one of his most celebrated publications:—"Almighty God, the giver of all good things, without whose help all labour is ineffectual, and without whose grace all wisdom is folly; grant, I beseech thee, that in this undertaking thy Holy Spirit may not be withheld from me but that I may promote thy glory, and the salvation of myself and others: grant this, O Lord, for the sake of thy Son Jesus Christ. Amen."

Dr. Doddridge used frequently to observe, that he never advanced well in human learning without prayer, and that he always made the most proficiency in his studies when he prayed with the greatest fervency.

It is related of Horshead, professor of medicine, that he joined devotion with the knowledge and practice of physic. He carefully prayed to God to bless his prescription, and published a form of prayer upon this subject.

"God" says Dr. Watts, "expects to be acknowledged in the common affairs of life, and he does as certainly expect it in the superior operations of the mind, and in the search of knowledge and truth." The very Greek Heathens, by the light of reason, were taught to say, Εκ Διος αρχομεσθα, and the Latins, "A Jove Principium Musæ." In works of learning he thought it neccessary to begin with God. Bishop Saunderson says, that study without prayer is atheism, as well as that prayer without study is presumption. And we are still more abundantly encouraged by the testimony of those who have acknowledged, from their own experience, that sincere prayer was no hinderance to their studies: they have gotten more knowledge sometimes upon their knees than by their labour in perusing a variety of authors; and they have left this observation for such as follow: Bene orasse est bene studuisse: Praying is the best studying.

F

Though the following instance of the praying Ince has often been read, and perhaps as often told, yet, as there *may* be some into whose hands this work may fall who have never read nor heard it, we shall here insert it. Not long after the year 1662, Mr. Grove, a gentleman of great opulence, whose seat was near Bird-bush, upon his wife's lying danger-ously ill, sent to his parish minister to pray with her. When the mes-senger came, he was just going out with the hounds, and sent word he would come when the hunt was over. At Mr. Grove's expressing much resentment against the minister, for choosing rather to follow his diver-sions than attend his wife under the circumstances in which she then lay, one of the servants said, " Sir, our shepherd, if you will send for him, can pray very well; we have often heard him at prayer in the field." Upon this he was immediately sent for : and Mr. Grove asking him "whe-ther he ever did or could pray ?" the shepherd fixed his eyes upon him, and, with peculiar seriousness in his countenance, replied, "God forbid, Sir, I should live one day without prayer." Hereupon he was desired to pray with the sick lady, which he did so pertinently to her case, with such fluency and fervency of devotion, as greatly to astonish the husband and all present. When they arose from their knees, the gentleman ad-dressed him to this effect : "Your language and manner discover you to be a very different person from what your present appearance indicates. I conjure you to inform who and what you are, and what were your views and situation in life before you came into my service." Whereupon he told him, "he was one of the minis-ters who had lately been ejected from the church, and that, having nothing of his own left, he was content, for a livelihood, to submit to the honest and peaceful employment of tending sheep." Upon hearing this, Mr. Grove said, " Then you shall be my shep-herd," and immediately erected a meeting-house on his own estate, in which Mr. Ince preached, and gath-ered a congregation of Dissenters.

While it is our duty personally to dedicate ourselves to God, our fami-lies also should not be neglected. But, alas ! how much degenerated are we in this respect? " In the days of our fathers," says good Bish-op Burnet, "when a person came early to the door of his neighbour, and desired to speak with the master of the house, it was as common a thing for the servants to tell him with freedom, ' My master is at prayer,' as it is now to say, ' My master is not up.' "

The following instance may teach us that family devotion may be attend-ed to even by those who are in digni-fied and public situations. Sir Thom-as Abney kept up regular prayer in his family during all the time he was Lord Mayor of London ; and in the evening of the day he entered on his office, he, without any notice, with-drew from the public assembly at Guildhall, after supper, went to his house there performed family wor-ship, and then returned to the com-pany.

PRECOCITY OF GENIUS.

While the constant labours and extensive researches of eminent men deserve our praise, the premature de-velopment of genius excites both our admiration and astonishment. To see juvenile years graced with all the beauties of science and learning, strikes the mind as a singular pheno-menon. Whether all human souls be equal, so that their powers are only expanded, or restrained accord-ing to corporeal organization, or whe-ther they are different in their own nature, may, perhaps, be a matter of much controversy. It is evident, however, that what has cost many the labour of years, have been almost the first thoughts of others possessed of an early and fruitful genius. A few instances are here selected, which will, perhaps, afford some degree of entertainment to the reader.

Blaise Pascal, one of the sublimest geniuses the world ever produced, was born at Clermont in Auvergne, in 1623. He never had any preceptor but his father. So great a turn had he for the mathematics, that he learned, or rather invented, geometry when but twelve years old ; for his father was unwilling to initiate him in that science early, for fear of its diverting him from the study of the languages. At sixteen he composed a curious mathematical piece. About nineteen he invented his machine of arithmetic, which has been much admired by the learned. He afterwards employed himself assiduously in making experiments according to the new philosophy, and particularly improved upon those of Toricellius. At the age of twenty-four, his mind took a different turn ; for, all at once, he became as great a devotee as any age has ever produced and gave himself up entirely to prayer and mortification.

Christian Henry Heinecken was born at Lubec, Feb. 6, 1721, and died there June 27, 1725, after having displayed the most amazing proofs of intellectual powers. He could talk at ten months old, and scarcely had completed his first year of life, when he already knew and recited the principal acts contained in the five books of Moses, with a number of verses on the creation ; at thirteen months, he knew the history of the Old Testament, and the new at fourteen ; in his thirteenth month, the history of the nations of antiquity, geography, anatomy, the use of maps, and nearly eight thousand Latin words. Before the end of his third year, he was well acquainted with the history of Denmark, and the genealogy of the crowned heads of Europe ; in his fourth year, he had learned the doctrines of divinity, with their proofs from the Bible, ecclesiastical history, the institutes, 200 hymns with their tunes, 80 psalms, entire chapters of the Old and New Testaments, 1500 verses and sentences from ancient Latin classics, almost the whole Orbis Pic-

tus of Comenius, whence he had derived all his knowledge of the Latin language ; arithmetic, the history of the European empires and kingdoms ; could point out in the maps whatever place he was asked for, or passed by in his journies ; and recite all the ancient and modern historical anecdotes relating to it. His stupendous memory caught and retained every word he was told ; his ever active imagination used, whatever he saw or heard, instantly to apply some examples or sentences from the Bible, geography, profane or ecclesiastical history, the Orbis Pictus, or from ancient classics. At the Court of Denmark, he delivered twelve speeches without once faultering ; and underwent public examination on a variety of subjects, especially the history of Denmark. He spoke German, Latin, French, and Low Dutch, and was exceedingly good-natured and well behaved, but of a most tender and delicate bodily constitution ; never ate any solid food, but chiefly subsisted on nurses' milk, not being weaned till within a very few months of his death, at which time he was not quite four years old. There is a dissertation on this child, published by M. Martini at Lubec, in 1730; where the author attempts to assign the natural causes for the astonishing capacity of this great man in embryo, who was just shown to the world, and snatched away.

John Lewis Candiac, a premature genius, was born at Candiac, in the diocese of Nismes, in France, in 1719. In the cradle he distinguished his letters; at thirteen months he knew them perfectly ; at three years of age he read Latin, either printed or in manuscript ; at four, he translated from that tongue ; at six, he read Greek and Hebrew, was master of the principles of arithmeitc, history, geography, heraldry, and the science of medals, and had read the best authors on almost every branch of literature. He died of a complication of disorders at Paris, 1726.

John Philip Baratiere was a most

7

extraordinary instance of the early and rapid exertion of mental faculties. This surprising genius was the son of Francis Baratiere, minister of the French Church at Schwoback, near Nuremberg, where he was born January 10, 1721. The French was his mother tongue, with some words of High Dutch; and by means of his father's insensibly talking Latin to him, it became as familiar to him as the rest; so that, without knowing the rules of grammar, he, at four years of age, talked French to his mother, Latin to his father, and High Dutch to the maid and neighbouring children, without mixing or confounding the respective languages. About the middle of his fifth year, he acquired Greek in like manner; so that in fifteen months he perfectly understood all the Greek books in the Old and New Testament, which he translated into Latin. When five years and eight months old, he entered upon Hebrew; and in three years more, was so expert in the Hebrew text, that, from a Bible without points, he could give the sense of the original in Latin or French, or translate, extempore, the Latin or French versions into Hebrew. He composed a dictionary of rare and difficult Hebrew words; and, about his tenth year, amused himself for twelve months with the Rabbinical writers. With these he intermixed a knowledge of the Chaldaic, Syriac, and Arabic, and acquired a taste for divinity and ecclesiastical antiquity, by studying the Greek fathers of the first four ages of the church. In the midst of these occupations, a pair of globes coming into his possession, he could, in eight or ten days, resolve all the problems on them; and in January, 1735, he devised his project for the discovery of the longitude, which he communicated to the Royal Society of London, and the Royal Academy of Sciences at Berlin. In June, 1731, he was matriculated in the University of Altorf; and at the close of 1732, he was presented by his father at the meeting of the Reformed

Churches of the circle of Franconia, who, astonished at his wonderful talents, admitted him to assist in the deliberations of the Synod; and to preserve the memory of so singular an event, it was registered in their acts. In 1734, the Margrave of Brandenburgh Anspach granted this young scholar a pension of fifty florins; and his father receiving a call to the French Church at Stettin, in Pomerania, young Baratiere was, on the journey, admitted Master of Arts. At Berlin, he was honoured with several conversations with the King of Prussia, and was received into the Royal Academy. Towards the close of his life, he acquired a considerable taste for medals, inscriptions, and antiquities; metaphysical inquiries, and experimental philosophy.— He wrote several essays and dissertations; made astronomical remarks and laborious calculations; took great pains towards a history of the heresies of the anti-trinitarians, and of the thirty years' war in Germany: his last publication, which appeared in 1740, was on the succession of the Bishops of Rome. The final work he engaged in, and for which he gathered large materials, was inquiries concerning the Egyptian Antiquities. But the substance of this blazing meteor was now almost exhausted; he was always weak and sickly, and died October the 5th, 1740, aged nineteen years, eight months and sixteen days. So true is it that " premature genius too rarely enjoys a long career. The acceleration of nature in the mental powers seems to hurry the progress of the animal economy, and to anticipate the regular close of temporal existence." Baratiere published eleven different pieces, and left 26 manuscripts on various subjects, the contents of which may be seen in his life, written by M. Formey, Professor of Philosophy at Berlin.

John Smeaton, born near Leeds, in 1724, was an eminent civil engineer. The strength of his understanding, and the originality of his genius, appeared at early age: his playthings were not the playthings of children, but the tools which men employ; and he appeared to have greater entertainment in seeing the men in the neighbourhood work, and in asking them questions, than in any thing else. One day he was seen (to the distress of his friends) on the top of his father's barn, fixing up something like a windmill; another time he attended some men fixing a pump at a neighbouring village, and, observing them cut off a piece of a bored pipe, he was so lucky as to procure it, and he actually made with it a working pump that raised water. This happened while he was in petticoats, and most likely before he attained his sixth year.

PREACHING.

"THE history of the pulpit," says one, " is curious and entertaining. It has spoken all languages, and in all sorts of style. It has partaken of all the customs of the schools, the theatres, and the courts of all the countries where it has been erected It has been a seat of wisdom, and a sink of nonsense. It has been filled by the best and the worst of men. It has proved in some hands a trumpet of sedition, and in others a source of peace and consolation; but on a fair balance, collected from authentic history, there would appear no proportion between the benefits and the mischiefs which mankind have derived from it; so much do the advantages of it preponderate! In a word, evangelical preaching has been, and yet continues to be, reputed foolishness; but it is real wisdom, a wisdom and a power by which it pleaseth God to save the souls of men."

The judicious Bishop Burnet prescribed a way to stop the progress of the puritan ministers, when complained against by some of the clergy for breaking into and preaching into their parochial charges. " Out-live, out-labour, out-preach them," said his Lordship.

Dr. Manton, having to preach before the Lord Mayor, the Court of Aldermen, &c. at St. Paul's, the Doctor chose a subject in which he had an opportunity of displaying his judgment and learning. He was heard with admiration and applause by the more intelligent part of the audience. But as he was returning from dinner with the Lord Mayor in the evening, a poor man following him, pulled him by the sleeve of his gown, and asked him, if he were the gentleman that preached before the Lord Mayor? He replied, " He was."—" Sir," says he, " I came with hopes of getting some good for my soul, but I was greatly disappointed, for I could not understand a great deal of what you said: you were quite above me." " Friend, if I did not give you a sermon, you have given me one; and by the grace of God, I will never play the fool to preach before my Lord Mayor in such a manner again."

There is nothing like simplicity in preaching. The Rev. Mr. Berridge, although long accustomed to the schools, was remarkably careful to preach with great plainness of speech, so much so, that, if possible, there might not be uttered a word but the meanest of his hearers might understand. On an occasion when the Rev. Mr. Romaine had been preaching at his church, after the service, the good vicar said, " Brother Romaine, your sermon was good, but my people cannot understand your language." Mr. Romaine, whose style was remarkably simple, could not recollect any expression in his sermon that could be above their comprehension, and therefore requested him to mention it. Mr. Berridge said, " You have endeavoured to prove that God is *Omniscient* and *Omnipotent;* but if you had said that God was almighty, and knew every thing, they would have understood you." Let young divines, especially those who are called to preach to plain and simple congregations, remember this.

There is too much affectation sometimes discovered even in giving out the text. The late Mr. Milner, of

Hull, used to tell of a divine whom he once heard, who, instead of announcing his text in the usual way, began with observing to his hearers, that "A very interesting caution which he meant to make the groundwork of the observations which he should then bring forward to them, was to be found on sacred record in the 12th verse of the 10th chapter of the apostle Paul's former letter to the church of Christ in the populous and polite city of Corinth."

Perhaps those sermons have the best effect which make our hearers out of love with themselves. When Father Massilon had preached his first advent at Versailles, Lewis XIV. said these remarkable words to him: "Father, I have heard many fine orators in my chapel, and have been much pleased with them; but as for you, always when I have heard you I have been very much displeased with myself."

Those who believe themselves called to the sacred work of the ministry, whether primates or curates, ought to be diligent in their work, and especially in preaching the gospel. A noted friar in Italy, famous for his learning and preaching, was commanded to preach before the Pope at a year of Jubilee; and, to be the better furnished, he repaired a good while before to Rome, to see the fashion of the conclave, to accommodate his sermon the better. When the day came he was to preach, having ended his prayer, he, looking a long time about, at last cried with a loud voice three times, "St. Peter was a fool! St. Peter was a fool! St. Peter was a fool!" Which words ended, he came out of the pulpit. Being after convented before the Pope, and asked why he so carried himself; he answered, "Surely, Holy Father, if a priest may go to heaven abounding in wealth, honour, and preferment, and live at ease, never or seldom to preach, then surely St. Peter was a fool, who took such a hard way in travelling, in fasting, in preaching, to go thither."

It is related of Dr. Guise, that he lost his eyesight whilst he was in prayer before sermon. Having finished prayer, he was consequently forced to preach without notes. As he was led out of the meeting after service was over, he could not help lamenting his sudden and total blindness. A good old gentlewoman, who heard him deplore his loss, answered him, "God be praised that your sight is gone: I never heard you preach so powerful a sermon in my life. Now we shall have no more notes: I wish, for my own part, that the Lord had taken away your eyesight twenty years ago, for your ministry would have been more useful by twenty degrees." Whatever may be said in favour of notes, the old gentlewoman, however, formed a strong argument against them from her feelings.

As collections are sometimes necessary to be made for charitable purposes and the support of the gospel, it devolves upon ministers more particularly to say something to excite the generosity of the auditory. Dr. Gill, it is said, preaching a charity sermon some years since, concluded thus: "Here are at present, I doubt not, persons of divided sentiments, some believing in free-will, and some in free-grace. Those of you who are free-willers, and merit-mongers, will give to this collection of course, for the sake of what you suppose you will get by it. Those of you, on the other hand, who expect salvation by grace alone, will contribute to the present charity out of love and gratitude to God. So, between free-will and free-grace, I hope we shall have a good collection." Though there be nothing, perhaps, reprehensible in the above, yet it were to be wished that some who undertake to plead the cause of charity and the gospel would do it with less effrontery, and not insult the understandings and feelings of the people, as is too much the case.

"I never preached a sermon," says the excellent Mr. Shepherd, "which did not cost me prayers and strong cries with tears in the composing of it. I never preached the sermon of which I had not first got good to my soul. I never went up to the pulpit, but as if going up to give account to God of my conduct."

MISTAKES AND SINGULARITIES OF PREACHERS.

A CERTAIN preacher having lost his fortune in the South Sea Scheme, 1719, and having occasion to mention the deliverance of the Israelites from Egypt, told his audience that Pharaoh and his host were all drowned in the South Sea. The less a minister interferes with the cares of this world, the better; the better both as to his personal happiness and public ministrations.

Many years ago, a Mr. Tavernour, of Water Eaton, in Oxfordshire, high sheriff of the county, came, it is said, in pure charity, not out of ostentation, and gave the scholars a sermon in St. Mary's Church, with his gold chain about his neck, and his sword by his side, and accosted them thus: " Arriving at the mount of St. Mary's, in the stony stage where I now stand, I have brought you some fine biscuits, baken in the oven of charity, and carefully conserved for the chickens of the church, the sparrows of the spirit, and the sweet swallows of salvation."—What an assemblage of images!

Dr. Sacheverell, in one of his speeches or sermons, made use of the following simile : " They concur like parallel lines, meeting in one common centre." The Doctor, one would think, must have been a sorry mathematician.

A Mr. Swinton, chaplain of the goal at Oxford, and also a frequent preacher before the Universities, was a learned man, but often thoughtless and absent. He once preached the condemnation sermon on repentance before the convicts on the preceding day of their execution. In the close he told his audience, that he should give them the remainder of what he had to say on the subject the next Lord's Day. A Doctor of Divinity,

and a plain matter of fact man, by way of offering an apology for Mr. S——, gravely remarked, "that he had probably preached the sermon before the University." "Yes, Sir," said Dr. Johnson, "but the University were not to be hanged the next morning."

An eminent man, who had been well bred, told his congregation at Whitehall, " that if they did not vouchsafe to give their lives a new turn, they must certainly go to a place which he did not think fit to name in that courtly audience." This was mincing the matter with a witness!

A Mr. Peters, in preaching on Ps. cvii. 7. told his audience that God's right way was a great way about. He then made a circumflex on the cushion, and said, that the Israelites were led " crinkledom cum crankledom."

Sprat the poet, and Burnet, were old rivals. On some public occasion, they both preached before the House of Commons. There prevailed, at that time, an indecent custom. When the preacher touched any favourite topic in a manner that delighted his auditory, their approbation was expressed by a loud hum, continued in proportion to their zeal or pleasure. When Burnet preached, part of his congregation hummed so loud and so long, that he sat down to enjoy it, and rubbed his face with his handkerchief. When Sprat preached, he likewise was honoured with the like animating hum; but he stretched out his hand to the congregation, and cried, " Peace, peace; I pray you, peace."

This humming practice brings to mind the custom prevalent in the fourth century. The preacher then promoted, yea sometimes exhorted, their hearers, as at stage plays, to testify their applause by shouting or clapping their hands. Such practices must have been very indecorous, and ill-suited both to the place, persons and subjects. Happy for us, such customs have sunk into oblivion.

The list of anecdotes, under this

article, might have been greatly enlarged; but it would, perhaps, be loss of time to enumerate every thing which ignorance and mistake have been the parents of.

ANECDOTES OF THOSE WHO READ THEIR SERMONS.

"It requires," says one, "a degree of courtesy to call this preaching, and seems to need no gifts but teeth and tongue, and hardly these, as many persons perform it." Bishop Wilkins observes, that "It will not be convenient for one that is a constant preacher to pen all his discourses, or to tie himself to phrases: when we have the matter and notion well digested, the expressions of it will easily follow." "By a slavish confinement to paper, and disuse of memory," says another, "a minister quite unqualifies himself to preach on any accidental occasion. He would do it if he had his notes; but neither the time, the nature of the occasion, nor even decency, will permit him to have them; and, therefore, loses that opportunity of serving the Lord. Yea, what if any disorder should affect his eyes in youth or old age? Will he preach Christ without his eyes, or, at least, without a pair of glasses? No; he will no longer draw a sickle in the harvest, though the Lord of the harvest should not deprive him of life, reason, tongue, or strength of body, but quit the field like a lazy coward, before he is called from it. Yea, farther; he is, on his ordinary occasions, equally liable to be useless. What if, by some unforeseen accident, he happened to drop his notes between his chamber and his church; or, by forgetfulness, leave them behind him? The misfortune would not only render him no minister for that week, but the very notion of his disappointment, occasioned by a culpable practice, would provoke the grief of some, and the mirth of others."

The author of this work, however, must beg leave to remark, that though he thus speaks against reading sermons, yet he is no advocate for *unstudied* ones; and upon particular occasions, some may find it convenient to read their discourses.

Mr. Heard having heard Dr. M—— preach, the Doctor afterwards asked him, how he liked his sermon? "Like it!" said Mr. H. "Why, Sir, I have liked it and admired it these twenty years." The Doctor stared. "Upon that shelf," added Mr. H. "you will find it verbatim. Mr. Boehm was an excellent preacher!" Mr. H. was a bookseller; and booksellers are sometimes dangerous hearers, when a preacher deals in borrowed sermons.

Three several clergymen, on three successive Sundays, delivered the very same discourse, on "Fall not out by the way," in the same church, and to the same congregation, not far from one of our Universities.

A late minister of —— read a discourse in his church, intended to excite his congregation to gratitude for an interval of fine weather, whilst at the very interval of reading it, the rain descended in torrents from the bursting clouds, with a violence sufficient to show the folly of being tied to notes.

They who read sermons composed by others, are very often led into mistakes. A German divine says, "One of these retailers of small ware, having picked up an homily composed some years before, when the plague was raging in the country, preached it to his congregation on the Lord's Day. Towards the close, having sharply reproved vice, he added, '*for these vices it is that God has visited you and your families with that cruel scourge the plague, which is now spreading every where in this town.*' At uttering these words, the people were all so thunderstruck, that the chief magistrate was obliged to go to the pulpit, and to ask him, '*For God's sake, Sir, pardon the interruption, and inform me where the plague is, that I may instantly endeavour to prevent its farther spreading!*' '*The plague, Sir?*' replied the preacher: '*I know nothing about the plague. Whether it is in the town or not, it is in my homily.*' "

A minister, not far from London, one day went to his place of worship, and happened, by neglect, to leave his notes on his closet table. A servant, who did not affect his master's *reading method*, fumbled them among some rubbish in the corner of the room, and went his way. The minister, missing his sermon, whispered the pew-opener to fetch it while he was praying: the man went, and searched for a full hour, but could not find it. The minister prayed all the time, with the avocation of some longing glances at the door for the pew-opener: when he prayed himself out of breath, and the people out of patience, he sat down wearied.— At length the man appeared, but no sermon: after some minutes' painful reflection, he rose up, and plainly told the congregation that the sermon was lost, and, therefore, they were to have none that day; but withal promised, if the sermon should be found, that he would cause it to be printed for their instruction, and never preach by notes again.

The following is not a bad portrait of one who entirely confines himself to his notes. " He lays open his performance at large in the face of the whole assembly, like a boy at school; he reads and blunders, and blunders and reads; he stands in the pulpit like a speaking statue, without life and motion; his eyes are fixed down to the space of a few square inches, as if he stared at a ghost; he hangs his head over his scroll, as if he were receiving sentence of death. If the poor drudge could look around him, he would see the half of his audience dozing over his dull repetition; not a soul affected, unless, perhaps, an old beggar gives a groan from a dark corner when he hears the sound. An honest countryman, happening to hear one of these paper geniuses preach, was asked by his wife, when he went home, how he liked the preacher. " Alas!" said he, " he was as poor a preacher as ever I saw, woman: he was just like a crow picking the corn; for he always put down his head for a pick, and then looked about to see if any person was coming near him."

Mr. Betterton being one day at dinner at his Grace's the Archbishop of Canterbury, his Grace expressed his astonishment that the representation of fables in their pieces should make more impression upon the mind, than that of truth in the sermons of the clergy: upon which Mr. Betterton, desiring leave to explain the reason of it, and obtaining it, on condition of preserving the respect due to religion, said, " May it please your Grace, it is because the clergy, in reading their sermons, pronounce them as if they were reading fables; and we, in acting our parts, and using them in a proper gesture, represent them like matters of fact." There is, undoubtedly, a considerable degree of weight in Mr. Betterton's observation: the want of life, earnestness, and energy, in the clergy, prevents their being attended to in the manner which could be wished, and greatly lessens the effect of the discourses.

ACTION OF PREACHERS.

AMONG many things which strengthen the prejudices of men against religion, is the awkward, irreverent, and slovenly manner of some (otherwise excellent and celebrated) ministers in the pulpit. While a man should certainly be on his guard, lest by an over-attention to his gesture, he convert the pulpit into a stage, merely to show how well he can perform, so he ought to be very cautious that he be not so indifferent and trifling as to excite the indignation of the auditory. If there be a place in creation where propriety of speech, solemnity of manner, and decency of action, be exhibited, surely the pulpit is the place. It is said of Dr. Doddridge, that in one of his diaries there was found an account of an admonition he had received from a friend, concerning an improper gesture in his public prayers, which seemed to denote a due want of reverence to God. Upon which he writes, "I would engrave this admonition upon my heart." A word to the wise is enough.

I once knew (says one) a pious and sensible young man, who, through a bad habit which he had unfortunately acquired, made so many *antics*, as the people termed them, in the pulpit, as to prejudice and grieve many. A very serious and sensible person, who constantly heard him, really thought he was afflicted with that species of paralysis termed St. Vitus's dance; and hearing some blame him, seriously entered on his defence, on the ground of its being a visitation of God.

MIMICKING PREACHERS.

I KNEW a young man of respectable talents, (says a good author,) who absolutely unfitted himself for public speaking by mimicking others. He was educated for the ministry, and was in every respect well qualified for the office; but having, without suspicion, frequently amused himself and others by imitating the tones and gestures of the most eminent preachers of the city where he lived, when he began to preach himself, he could not avoid falling into one or the other of those tones and manners which he had so often mimicked. This, as soon as it was perceived, threw the audience into a burst of laughter, and he was soon obliged to quit the profession altogether, for no other reason than he had thus spoiled himself by the talent of imitation. I may add, says this writer, in further support of this remark, that I have known no instance of one eminent for mimicking who did not, in time, make himself contemptible.

FAITHFULNESS.—FAITHFUL PREACHERS.

IT becomes all who are called to the sacred office of the ministry to be faithful in the discharge of the work committed to them. Nor is there any thing in this abhorrent from decency and respect : on the contrary, faithfulness *to* a people is the highest mark of concern *for* them.

The Bishop of Durham once requiring the famous Mr. Gilpin, upon his canonical obedience, to preach a visitation sermon, he found himself obliged to comply, though without any previous notice, and after the clergy were assembled. This prelate was a well-meaning but weak man, and wholly in the hands of his Chancellor. Mr. Gilpin thought this no unfavourable opportunity to open his Lordship's eyes, and induce him to exert himself where there was so great a reason for it; for private information had often been given him without success. Mr. Gilpin was now resolved, therefore, to venture upon a public application. In this spirit, before he concluded his sermon, turning towards the Bishop, he addressed him thus—"My discourse now, Reverend Father, must be directed to you. God hath exalted you to be Bishop of this diocese, and requireth an account of your government thereof. A reformation of all those matters which are amiss in the church is expected at your hands.— And, now, lest perhaps, while it is apparent that so many enormities are committed every where, your Lordship should make answer, that you had no notice of them given you, and that these things never came to your knowledge, [for this, it seems, was the Bishop's common apology to all complaints,] behold, I bring these things to your knowledge this day. Say not, then, that these crimes have been committed by the fault of others, without your knowledge; for, whatever either yourself should do in person, or suffer by your connivance to be done of others, is wholly your own. Therefore, in the presence of God, his angels, and men, I pronounce you to be the author of all these evils; yea, and in that strict day of general account I will be a witness to testify against you, that all these things have come to your knowledge by my means; and all these men shall bear witness thereof who have heard me speak unto you this day." This freedom alarmed every one: the Bishop, they said, had now got that advantage over him that had been long sought for. But when Mr. Gilpin, before he went home, went to pay his compliments to his Lordship, "Sir," said the Bishop, "I purpose to wait upon you home myself." This he accordingly did; and as soon as Mr. Gilpin had carried him into a parlour, the Bishop turned suddenly round, and seizing him eagerly by the hand, "Father Gilpin," says he, "I acknowledge you are fitter to be Bishop of Durham than I am to be parson of this church of your's. I ask forgiveness of past injuries. Forgive me, father: I know you have enemies; but, while I live Bishop of Durham, be secure; none of them shall cause you any farther trouble." Thus, "he that rebuketh a man, afterwards shall find more favour than he that flattereth with his tongue."

Lewis XII. of France, made war with the Protestants on the score of religion, and, at the head of his army, besieged the city of St. Jean D'Angely, which, after a considerable siege, capitulated upon very advantageous terms. While the King remained in this town, after the capitulation, Mr. Welch, the protestant minister, continued to preach as usual; but the King hearing of it, was much offended, and one day sent the Duke D'Espernon to order him out of the pulpit, and to bring him before him.— The Duke went with his guard, and, as soon as he entered the church where Mr. Welch was preaching, Mr. Welch desired the people to make way, and to set a seat, that the Duke might hear the word of the Lord. The Duke, instead of interrupting him, sat down, and heard him with great attention, till he had finished his discourse, and then told him he must go with him to the King: which Mr. Welch readily did.— When the Duke came to the King, the King asked him, "Why he brought not the minister, and why he did not interrupt him?" The Duke answered, "never man spake like this man; but that he had brought him with him." Whereupon, Mr. Welch was called into the King's presence, and upon his admission silently prayed to God for wisdom and assistance. The King asked him, "How he durst preach where he was, since it was against the law of France for any man to preach within the verge of his court?" Mr. Welch answered, "Sir, if you did right, you would come and hear me preach, and make all France hear me likewise: for (said he) I preach not as those men whom you hear: my preaching differs from theirs in these two points: first, I preach that you must be saved by the merits and death of Jesus Christ, and not by any merits or works of your own. Next, I preach, that, as you are King of France, you are under the authority and command of no man on earth. Those men (added he) whom you hear, subject you to the Pope of Rome; which I will never do." The King replied no more, but " Et bien vous etiez mon ministre: Well, well; you shall be my minister." Accordingly, he was favourably dismissed, and the King left the town in peace.

Knox, the Scotch reformer, said, "there was nothing in the pleasant face of a lady to affray him; assured the Queen of Scots, that, if there were any spark of the Spirit of God, yea, of honesty, or wisdom in her, she would not be offended with his affirming in his sermons, that the diversions of her court were diabolical crimes, evidences of impiety or insanity."

Dr. Hugh Latimer, one of the primitive reformers, was raised to the Bishopric of Worcester in the reign of Henry VIII. It was the custom of those times for each of the Bishops to make presents to the King on new-year's day. Bishop Latimer went with the rest of his brethren to make the usual offering; but, instead of a purse of gold, he presented the

King with a New Testament, in which was a leaf doubled down to this passage—" Whoremongers and adulterers God will judge."

Dr. Edmund Calamy was never known to be intimidated when he thought his duty was concerned. He dared to censure the conduct of Cromwell to his face. His grandson informs us, that he had General Monck for his auditor in his own church, soon after the Restoration; and that, having occasion to speak in his sermon of filthy lucre, he said : " Some men will betray three kingdoms for filthy lucre's sake," and immediately threw his handkerchief, which he usually waved up and down while he was preaching, towards the General's pew.

Baxter, it is said, discovered the same intrepidity when he reproved Cromwell, and expostulated with Charles II., as when he preached to a congregation of mechanics.

The late Mr. Whitefield, in a sermon he preached at Haworth,(for Mr. Grimshaw,) having spoken severely of those professors of the gospel, who, by their loose and evil conduct, caused the ways of truth to be evil spoken of, intimated his hope that it was not necessary to enlarge much upon that topic to the congregation before him, who had so long enjoyed the benefit of an able and faithful preacher, and he was willing to believe that their profiting appeared to all men.—This roused Mr. Grimshaw's spirit, and notwithstanding the great regard he had for the preacher, he stood up and interrupted him, saying, with a loud voice, " O, Sir! for God's sake do not speak so; I pray you, do not flatter them : I fear the greater part of them are going to hell with their eyes open."

Bishop Burnet is said to have remonstrated with King Charles II. in the following manner :—" The only mean of extricating yourself from the troubles which surround you is, to remove the crowd of giddy and guilty creatures that flutter about your court; for nothing hath so much tended to alienate the affections of your subjects, after the great loyalty and deliverances you have experienced, as the scandalous reports of your life and conversation, which, if you persist in, Divine vengeance will pursue you in this life, and render you for ever miserable in that which is to come." An address of a similar kind, to the same monarch, is to be found in the dedication of Barclay's Apology for the Quakers.

It is said of Mr. Whiston that he was remarkable for speaking the plainest truths on every occasion, and to persons of every degree. During the year 1725, when he, with Dr. Clarke, Dr. Berkeley, and others, had the honour to attend Queen Caroline on a certain day of every week, to talk of the progress of science, her Majesty one evening took occasion to pay him a just compliment on his truth and integrity, requesting that he would, with his usual plainness, point out to her any fault that he might have observed in her conduct. At first he begged to be excused, adding, that few persons could bear to have their faults plainly told to them, and least of all royal personages, who, from their elevation, are necessarily surrounded by flatterers, to whose lips truth is a stranger. Her Majesty replied, that he was to consider her not as a queen, but as a philosopher; and that philosophy is of very little use, if it cannot enable its professors to bear, without offence, truths necessary to their own improvement.—Upon this he told her, that the greatest fault which he had observed in her conduct was her indecent behaviour in the house of God, which he assured her had made very unfavourable impressions on the minds of many persons, who, coming to town from distant parts of the country, had gone to chapel to obtain a sight of her Majesty, the King, and the royal family. The Queen made no reply; but, in about six weeks afterwards, renewed her request, that Mr. Whiston would point out the most glaring improprieties in her conduct. To this, he answered, that he had laid down a maxim from which he could not deviate;—never to point out to any person more than one fault at a time, and never to give a second reproof till he had observed some good consequence to have arisen from the first. Much to the Queen's honour, she was pleased with this plain dealing, and continued to think favourably of Mr. Whiston.

ENCOURAGEMENT TO PREACHERS.

HE who is desirous of doing good, and, for that end, preaches explains, and enforces the truth, will feel no small degree of uneasiness, if he do not find his labours attended with some degree of success. It is not sufficient that he prays, studies, and labours, but his benevolent mind will be anxious to hear of some good effect. Let none, however, engaged in this sacred work, despair. Who can tell what the *net* contains while it is under water? Who can know the extent of his usefulness while in the present state? Let not any suppose he is useless, because *he himself* has not evidence of it. It is not always proper for ministers to know how far they have been successful. What God sees necessary for encouragement, we may expect; but for more than this, we must wait with patience until that day when the whole will be disclosed. In the mean time, ignorance of the event of our exertions, must not produce indifference and laxity in them. The two following anecdotes may afford encouragement to ministers:

A minister of the gospel was, about thirty years ago, called to the important work of preaching to his fellowsinners the unsearchable riches of Christ; but being extremely diffident of his abilities, and having preached for several years seemingly to little purpose, he came to a resolution to preach no more. Happening to be much straitened in his sermon, on a Lord's day afternoon, and drinking tea afterwards with some Christian friends, he hinted his intention to them, and declared that he could not preach even that same evening.— They represented the disappointment it must be to a large congregation, who were assembling together, as no other minister could possibly be procured then to supply his place, and, therefore, they begged he would try once more. He replied, that it was in vain to argue with him, for he was quite determined not to preach any more. Just at that instant, a person knocked at the door, and, being admitted, it proved to be a good old experienced Christian, who lived at a considerable distance, and she said she came on purpose to desire Mr. —— to preach that evening from a particular passage of scripture: she said she could not account for it, but she could not be happy without coming from home to desire it might be preached from that evening. Being asked what the text was, she said she could not tell where it was, but the words were these: "Then I said, I will speak no more in his name; but his word was as a fire shut up in my bones, and I was weary with forbearing, and I could not stay." This extraordinary circumstance so struck the preacher, that he submitted to preach from these words that evening: he experienced much liberty, and has continued ever since with wonderful success and comfort.

N. B. The good woman has often protested since, that she knew nothing of the minister's intention, or the debate about his preaching.

The late Rev. Mr. Warrow, of Manchester, a little before his death, was complaining to some of his people, that he had not been made the instrument of calling one soul to the knowledge of the truth for the last eight years of his ministry. He preached but two sermons after this, before the Lord called him to himself; and, soon after his death, between twenty and thirty persons proposed themselves as church members, who had been called under Mr. W.'s two last sermons. Let not ministers think their work is done, while they can preach another sermon, or speak another word.

FREQUENT AND USEFUL PREACHERS.

HOWEVER pleasant the acquisition of knowledge may be to ministers of the gospel, they must remember, that they are not called perpetually to "breathe the air of the study, and tread the dust of the schools," but to be laborious and active in the communication of truth to others. They are not to be as "sullen lamps, enlightening only themselves;" but as conspicuous suns, enlightening and animating all around them. He is the best minister, who joins with a pious mind, a benevolent and useful life.

It appears from a little account book, wherein Mr. Whitefield minuted the times and places of his ministerial labours, that he preached upwards of eighteen thousand sermons from the time of his ordination to that of his death.

In the first year of Dr. Cotton Mather's ministry, he had reason to believe, he was made the instrument of converting at least thirty souls. It was constantly one of his first thoughts in a morning, "What good may I do to-day?" He resolved this general question into many particulars. His question for the Lord's-day morning, constantly was—"What shall I do, as the pastor of a Church, for the good of the flock under my charge?" His question for Monday morning was, "What shall I do for the good of my own family?" in which he considered himself as a husband, a father, and a master. For Tuesday morning——"What good shall I do for relations abroad?"—Sometimes he changed this meditation for another—"What good shall I do to my enemies?" for it was his laudable ambition to be able to say, he did not know of any person in the world, who had done him any ill office, but he had done him a good one for it. His question for Wednesday morning was, "What shall I do for the churches of the Lord, and the

more general interests of religion in the world?"——His question for Thursday morning was, "What good may I do to the several societies to which I am related?" The question for Friday morning was, "What special objects of compassion, and subjects of affliction, may I take under my particular care, and what shall I do for them?" And his Saturday morning question, relating more immediately to himself, was, "What more have I to do for the interest of God in my own heart and life?"

The Rev. Mr. B. had nine children; two departed in their infancy; a son of twenty-two, and a daughter of thirty, died triumphantly in the faith of Christ, both of whom, with his surviving son and four daughters, he had the inexpressible pleasure of admitting into the communion of his church, every one of them being the fruit of his own ministry.

The Rev. Mr. Berridge, is said, in one year, to have been visited by a thousand different persons under serious impressions; and it has been computed, that under his own and the joint ministry of Mr. Hicks, about four thousand were awakened to a concern for their souls in the space of twelve months. Incredible as this may appear, it comes authenticated through a channel so respectable, that it would be illiberal to disbelieve it.

The Rev. Mr. Grimshaw was very laborious, faithful, and useful in his work. Without intermitting his stated services at home, he went much abroad. In a course of time, he established two circuits, which, with some occasional variations, he usually traced every week, alternately. One of these he often pleasantly called his idle week, because he seldom preached more than twelve or fourteen times. His sermons, in his working, or busy week, often exceeded the number of twenty-four, and sometimes amounted to thirty.

He once apologized for the length of his discourse to this effect: "If I were in some situations, I might not think it needful to speak so much; but many of my hearers who are wicked and careless are likewise very ignorant, and very slow of apprehension. If they do not understand me, I cannot hope to do them good; and when I think of the uncertainty of life, that perhaps it may be the last opportunity afforded, and that it is possible I may never see them again till I meet them in the great day, I know not how to be explicit enough. I endeavour to set the subject in a variety of lights; I express the same thoughts in different words, and can scarcely tell how to leave off, lest I should have omitted something, for the want of which my preaching and their hearing might prove in vain. And thus, though I fear I weary others, I am still unable to satisfy myself."

Though he often preached to great numbers, he was a no less attentive servant to a few. When any were willing to hear, he was ready to preach; and he often cheerfully walked miles in the winter, in storms of wind, rain, or snow, upon lonely unsheltered moors, to preach to a small company of poor, aged, decrepit people, in a cottage.

With the following description of a true preacher, we will conclude this article:

"Having imbibed the meek and lowly spirit of his Master, he will not be ambitious of saying *fine* things to win applause, but of saying *useful* things to win souls. Such a preacher will not come into the pulpit, as an actor comes upon the stage, to personate a feigned character, and to forget his real one, to utter sentiments or represent passions not his own. No; the man and the preacher are, in this case, one and the same. When he is in the pulpit, the man appears as well as the preacher; when he is out of it, the preacher appears as well as the man. In the pulpit he is the man, wound up to an higher tone; the man seen in a more solemn light of a serious character: out of it, he is the preacher unbent; the preacher seen in the softer light of ordinary human-

ity: or, it may be taken thus: in the pulpit, the serious character appears in him all pure and refulgent; out of it, mixed and shaded; but still it is the same serious character: the man of virtue, the man of piety, appears."—See Dr. Fordyce's Eloquence of the Pulpit.

PRIDE.

OF all the evil principles which belong to human nature, none, perhaps, is more prevalent than pride. There are some, however, who are more under its influence than others, "who think of nothing but themselves, and who imagine all the world thinks about them too; they suppose they are the subject of every conversation, and fancy every wheel which moves in society hath some relation to them. People of this sort are very desirous of knowing what is said of them; and, as they have no conception that any but glorious things are said of them, they are extremely solicitous to know them, and often put this question—"Who do men say that I am?'"

When one asked a philosopher what the great God was doing? he replied, "His whole employment is to lift up the humble and to cast down the proud." And indeed, there is no one sin which the Almighty seems more determined to punish than this. The examples of God's displeasure against it are most strikingly exhibited in the histories of Pharaoh, Hezekiah, Haman, Nebuchadnezzar, and Herod.

One day, when Alcibiades was boasting of his wealth, and the great estates in his possession (which generally blow up the pride of young people of quality,) Socrates carried him to a geographical map, and asked him to find Attica. It was so small, it could scarcely be discerned upon the draught; he found it, however, though with some difficulty; but upon being desired to point out his own estate there—"It is too small," says he, "to be distinguished in so little a space." "See, then," replied Socrates, "how much you are affected about an imperceptible point of land !" This reasoning might have been urged much farther still. For what was Attica compared to all Greece, Greece to Europe, Europe to the whole world, and the whole world itself to the vast extent of the infinite orbs which surround it ? What an insect, what a nothing, is the most powerful prince of the earth, in the midst of this abyss of bodies and immense spaces, and how little of it does he occupy !

When Pope Adrian VI. was advanced to the Pontifical Chair, he built a college at Louvain, and caused the following account of his rise and preferments to be inscribed over the gate : " *Trajectum plantavit, Louvanium rigavit, Cæsar incrementum dedit :* Utrecht planted, Louvain watered, the emperor gave the increase." Under which some impartial hand, to rebuke the ungodliness of the Pontiff, added, *Hic Deus nihil fecit :* In all this, God and his Providence had nothing to do."

Pride is not only an attendant in the busy and gay scenes of life, but predominant even in death. It is said of a prince, that he ordered these words to be engraved on his tomb; " I could do all things." But the very subject of information was a contradiction to the assertion.

Henry III. of France was so proud, that he set rails about his table, and affected the pomp of an Eastern king ; and yet so mean, that he often walked in procession with a beggarly brotherhood, with a string of beads on his hands, and a whip at his girdle

It was a strange and thoughtless expression of a very ingenious author —" Among all the millions of vices," says he, " that I inherit from Adam, I have escaped the first and father sin of pride ;" and attempts to prove it by asserting his humility, after many boasted instances of his learning and acquirements. It appears this man lived much abroad, and conversed but little at home. He knew much of the world, but was not acquainted with himself; and while he practised this vanity in so public a manner, he strongly denied that any belonged to him.

PROVIDENCE; PROVIDENCES.

It has been remarked, that he who duly observes Divine providences shall never want providences to observe ; and certainly it becomes us as rational creatures and true Christians, to contemplate the consummate wisdom and unbounded goodness of God in the various events which transpire. It is true there are many difficult texts in the book of Providence which we cannot easily elucidate ; but, even what we at *present* see, hear, and know, should lead us to admire Him who ordereth all things after the counsel of his own will ; and to wait with patience till the day arrive when the various leaves of this copious volume shall be unfolded to our view, and when we shall be constrained to say, " He hath done all things well."

Richard Boyle, (generally called the Great Earl of Cork,) it is said, outlived most of those who had known the meanness of his beginning ; but he delighted to remember it himself, and even took pains to preserve the memory of it to posterity in the motto which he always used, and which he caused to be placed on his tomb, viz. " *God's Providence is my inheritance.*" A noble motto truly !

The history of God's providence, as connected with the government of his church, affords matter both for admiration and thankfulness. " Who would have thought," says Saurin, " that King Henry VIII., a cruel and superstitious king, the greatest enemy the Reformation ever had ; he who by the fury of his arms, and by the productions of his pen, opposed this great work, refuting those whom he could not persecute, and persecuting those whom he could not refute ; who would have thought that this monarch should first serve the work he intended to subvert, clear the way for reformation, and, by shaking off the yoke of the Roman Pontiff, execute the plan of Providence, while he seemed to do nothing but satiate his voluptuousness and ambition?

'"Who would have thought, that the ambitious Clement,* to maintain some chimerical rights which the pride of the clergy had forged, and which the cowardice of the people, and the effeminacy of their princes, had granted; who would have believed, that this ambitious Pope, by hurling the thunders of the Vatican against this King, would have lost all England, and thus would have given the first stab to a tyranny which he intended to confirm.

"Who would have imagined, that Zuinglius would have had such amazing success among the people in the world the most inviolably attached to the customs of their predecessors; a people scrupulously retaining even the dress of their ancestors; a people, above all, so inimical to innovations in religion, that they will hardly bear a new explication of a passage of scripture, a new argument, or a modern critical remark; who would have supposed, that they could have been persuaded to embrace a religion diametrically opposite to that which they had imbibed with their mother's milk?

"Who would have believed, that Luther could have surmounted the obstacles that opposed the success of his preaching in Germany; and that the proud emperor, Charles V., who reckoned among his captives, pontiffs and kings, could not subdue one miserable monk?

"Who would have thought, that the barbarous tribunal of the inquisition, which had enslaved so many nations to superstition, should have been one of the principal causes of the reformation in the United Provinces?"

Queen Mary having dealt severely with the Protestants in England, about the latter end of her reign, signed a commission to take the same course with them in Ireland; and, to execute the same with greater force,

* Pope Clement VII.　G

she nominated Dr. Cole one of the commissioners. This Doctor, coming with the commission to Chester, on his journey, the Mayor of that city, hearing that her Majesty was sending a messenger into Ireland, and he being a churchman, waited on the Doctor, who, in discourse with the Mayor, took out of a cloak-bag a leather box, saying unto him, *Here is a commission that shall lash the heretics of Ireland,* calling the Protestants by that title. The good woman of the house, being well affected to the Protestant religion, and, also, having a brother, named John Edmonds, of the same, then a citizen in Dublin, was much troubled at the Doctor's words; but watching her convenient time, while the Mayor took his leave, and the Doctor complimented him down the stairs, she opened the box, took the commission out, and placed in lieu thereof a sheet of paper with a pack of cards wrapt up therein, the knave of clubs being faced uppermost. The Doctor, coming up to his chamber, and suspecting nothing of what had been done, put up the box as formerly. The next day, going to the water side, wind and weather serving him, he sailed towards Ireland, and landed on the 7th of October, 1558, at Dublin. When he arrived at the Castle, the Lord Fitz-Walter, being Lord Deputy, sent for him to come before him and the Privy Council. He came accordingly, and, after he had made a speech, relating upon what account he had come over, he presented the box to the Lord Deputy, who, causing it to be opened, that the secretary might read the commission, there was nothing, save a pack of cards, with the knave of clubs uppermost; which not only startled the Lord Deputy and Council, but the Doctor, who assured them he had a commission, but knew not how it was gone. Then the Lord Deputy made answer, "Let us have another commission, and we will shuffle the cards in the meanwhile." The Doctor, being troubled in his mind, went away, and returned into

England, and, coming into Court, obtained another commission: but, staying for the wind on the water side, news came to him that the Queen was dead, and thus God preserved the Protestants of Ireland.— Queen Elizabeth was so delighted with this story, which was related to her by Lord Fitz Walter, on his return to England, that she sent for Elizabeth Edmonds, whose husband's name was Mathershad, and gave her a pension of 40*l.* during her life.

There are some circumstances in the life of Mr. Oliver Heywood, who was a persecuted minister of the seventeenth century, which afford us pleasing ideas of the providential care of God towards his people. The following anecdote, says his biographer, is authentic. It is said, that his little stock of money was quite exhausted, the family provisions were entirely consumed, and Martha, a maid servant, who had lived in his family several years, and who often assisted them, could now lend no more assistance from the little savings of former days. Mr. Heywood still trusted, that God would provide, when he had nothing but the Divine promise to live upon. He said,

" When cruise and barrel both are dry,
" We still will trust in God Most High."

When the children began to be impatient for want of food, Mr. Heywood called his servant, and said to her, " Martha, take a basket, and go to Halifax; call upon Mr. N——, the shopkeeper, in Northgate, and tell him, I desire him to lend me five shillings: if he will be kind enough to do it, buy us some cheese, some bread, and such other little things as you know we most want: be as expeditious as you can in returning, for the poor children begin to be fretful for want of something to eat. Put on your hat and cloak, and the Lord give you good speed: in the mean time, we will offer up our requests to Him, who feedeth the young ravens when they cry, and who knows what we have need of before we ask him." Martha observed her master's direc-

tions; but when she came near the house where she was ordered to beg for the loan of five shillings, through timidity and bashfulness, her heart failed her. She passed by the door again and again, without having courage to go in and tell her errand. At length, Mr. N——, standing at his shop-door, and seeing Martha in the street, called her to him, and said, " Are you not Mr. Heywood's servant?" When she had, with an anxious heart, answered in the affirmative, he added, " I am glad I have this opportunity of seeing you: some friends at M——, have remitted to me five guineas for your master, and I was just thinking how I could contrive to send it." Martha burst into tears, and, for some time, could not utter a syllable. The necessities of the family, their trust in Providence, the seasonableness of the supply, and a variety of other ideas breaking in upon her mind at once, quite overpowered her. At length she told Mr. N—— upon what errand she came, but that she had not courage to ask him to lend her poor master money. The tradesman could not but be affected with the story, and told Martha to come to him when the like necessity should press upon them at any future time. She made haste to procure the necessary provisions, and, with a heart lightened of its burden, ran home to tell the success of her journey.

Though she had not been long absent, the hungry family had often looked wishfully out at the window for her arrival. When she knocked at her master's door, which now must be kept locked and barred, for fear of constables and bailiffs, it was presently opened; and the joy to see her was as great as when a fleet of ships arrive, laden with provisions, for the relief of a starving town, closely besieged by an enemy. The children danced round the maid, eager to look into the basket of eatables; the patient mother wiped her eyes; the father smiled, and said, " The Lord hath not forgotten to be gracious; his word is true from the beginning: the young lions do lack and suffer hunger, but they that seek the Lord, shall not want any good thing." Martha related every circumstance of her little expedition, as soon as tears of joy would permit her; and all partook of the homely fare, with a sweeter relish than the fastidious Roman nobles ever knew, when thousands of pounds were expended to furnish one repast. Had you been present while this pious family were eating their bread and cheese, and drinking pure water from the spring, you might, perhaps, have heard the good man thus addressing the wife of his bosom: "Did I not tell you, my dear, that God would surely provide for us? Why were you so fearful, O you of little faith? Our heavenly Father knoweth that we have need of these things. Jesus said to his disciples, When I sent you without purse or scrip, lacked ye any thing? And they said, Nothing, Lord."

The spirit of persecution raged so warmly against him, that this worthy man was under the necessity of taking leave of his dear family, and going he knew not whither. But the question was, how should he be equipped for his journey? He had a horse; but the little money that remained must be left for the support of the family, for whom Mr! Heywood was much more concerned than for myself. One winter's morning, when it was yet dark, the horse was saddled; and this good man, after bidding adieu to his affectionate wife, and saluting his children in their beds, set out, like Abraham when he left his father's house, not knowing whither he went. He moved silently along in by-ways for some time, for fear of being seen, till he had got out of the neighbourhood. Having not one farthing in his pocket to bear his travelling expenses, he committed himself to the protection of Providence. He determined at length to leave his horse at full liberty to go what way it would, and thus travelled on for a considera-

ble part of the day, till both man and beast stood in great need of refreshment. Towards evening, the horse bent its course to a farm house, a little out of the road. Mr. Heywood called at the door, and a clean decent woman came out to inquire what he wanted. "I have reason," said he, "to make an apology for giving you this trouble, being an entire stranger in these parts. My horse stands in need as well as myself of shelter and refreshment for the night: if you could any way make it convenient to furnish my horse with a little hay, and a stand under cover, and myself with a seat by your fire side, I ask no more." The good woman, a little surprised at his request, told him she would consult her husband.—After a few minutes, they both came to the door, and Mr. Heywood repeated his solicitation; but told them that he had no money to satisfy them for any trouble they might have on his account; yet he hoped God would reward them. They immediately desired him to alight; the master led the horse into the stable, and the mistress took the stranger into the house, invited him to sit down, stirred up the fire, and began to prepare him something to eat. Mr. Heywood told her, "that he was concerned to see her give herself so much trouble; that, being unable to make her any recompense, he did not request either a supper or a bed, but only that he might sit by the fire side till morning." The mistress assured him, "that for an act of hospitality she did no expect any reward, and that, though the accommodations her house would afford were but indifferent, he should be welcome to them, and therefore she hoped he would make himself easy." After supper, they all sat down before the fire, and the master of the house desired to know of the stranger, what countryman he was.—"I was born," said he, "in Lincolnshire, but I have a wife and family in the neighbourhood of Halifax." "That is a town," said the farmer, "where I have been; and

8*

some years ago I had a little acquaintance with several persons there. Pray do you know Mr. S——, and Mr. D——? and is old Mr. F. yet alive?" The stranger gave suitable answers to these and many other inquiries. At length the kind hostess asked him, "if he knew any thing of one Mr. Oliver Heywood, who was formerly a minister at some chapel not far from Halifax, but was now, for some account or other, forbidden to preach?" The stranger replied, "There is a great deal of noise and talk about that man: some speak well, others say every thing that is bad of him; for my own part, I can say little in his favour." "I believe," said the farmer, "he is of that sect which is every where spoken against; but, pray, do you personally know him? and what is it that inclines you to form such an indifferent opinion of his character?" "I do know something of him," said the stranger; "but as I do not choose to propagate an ill report of any one, if you please, we will talk on some other subject." After keeping the farmer and his wife in suspense for some time, who were a little uneasy at what he had said, he told them, "That he was the poor outcast of whom they had made so many kind inquiries." All was then surprise, and joy, and thankfulness, that a merciful Providence had brought him under their roof. The master of the house said, "Mr. Heywood, I am glad to see you here, having long had a sincere regard for you, from the favourable reports I have always heard of you. The night is not far spent. I have a few neighbours who love the gospel: if you will give us a word of exhortation, I will run and acquaint them. This is an obscure place, and, as your coming here is not known, I hope we shall have no interruption." Mr. Heywood consented; a small congregation was gathered; and he preached to them with that fervour, affection, and enlargement, which attending circumstances served to inspire. On this joyful occasion, a small collection was voluntarily made to help the poor traveller on his way.

There is hardly any article under which a greater fund of matter might be brought forward than under this of Providence. Indeed, the life of almost every individual presents us with some singular events relative to the dispensations of Providence. Most men, who have any sense of the Divine favour at all, have seen something or other remarkable in the course of their lives, which must lead them to adore the wise designs and kind interpositions of Him who governs the universe at large, and each inhabitant thereof in particular. But the above must suffice.

READING.

AMIDST the profusion of advantages we enjoy in the present state, that of the art of printing must not be considered as the least. Before this happy invention, it need not be said what difficulties were in the way to mental acquirements. This art is replete with a variety of pleasant and lasting effects, and though, like all other favours, abused by the vicious and profane, it will be considered by the pious and wise as a cause for great gratitude.

As to reading, the sacred oracles should occupy our attention, and be the subject of our study in preference to any other book whatever. Its sublime descriptions, historic relations, pure doctrines, and interesting sentiments, should not only be read but remembered by all.

In the reading of other books, the same object should be kept in view as in reading this; I mean the improvement of our minds and the rectitude of our conduct. Some, indeed, read only for amusement, and not for profit, and on this account it is that they prefer a novel to a book that is calculated for real instruction, not remembering that these works of imagination, while they tend to raise pleasing sensations, too often infuse the subtle poison of loose principles and baneful immorality.

There are others who seem to have

no taste for reading of any kind. Such we cannot expect to have enlarged minds or extensive knowledge; nor can they, I think, be the most happy part of the human race. "Sorrow," as one observes, "is a kind of rust of the soul which every new idea contributes in its passage to scour away. It is the putrefaction of stagnant life, and is remedied by exercise and motion." By reading, the mind is often refreshed, the powers exerted and enlivened, and the judgment informed. Men of sense and of religion have always delighted in it, and even amidst the bustle of the gay world, and in the brilliant career of heroism, men have retained a taste for reading. Alexander was very fond of reading. Whilst he was filling the world with the fame of victories, marking his progress by blood and slaughter, marching over smoking towns and ravaged provinces, and though hurried on by fresh ardour to new victories, yet he found time hang heavy upon him when he had no book.

Brutus spent among books all those moments which he could spare from the duties of his office: even the day before the celebrated battle of Pharsalia, which was about to decide the empire of the universe, he was busy in his tent, and employed till night in making an extract from Polybius.

Pliny, the Elder, while at his meals, made some one read to him; and, when he travelled, he had always a book and conveniences for writing along with him.

Petrarch was always low spirited when he did not read or write. That he might not lose time when he travelled, he wrote in all the inns where he stopped. One of his friends, the Bishop of Cavaillon, fearing that he would, by this ardour, injure his health, begged him one day to give him the key of his library. Petrarch consented, not knowing what he was going to do with it. The Bishop locked up his books, and forbade him to read or write for ten days. Petrarch obeyed, though with the greatest reluctance: but the first day appeared longer to him than a year; the second, he had a head-ache from morning to night, and the third he found himself, early in the morning, very feverish. The good Bishop, touched with his condition, restored him the key, and, at the same time, his health and spirits.

Alcibiades, meeting with a schoolmaster, who had none of Homer's works, could not forbear giving him a box on the ear, and treating him as an ignorant fellow, and one who could not make any other than ignorant scholars: "Must we not say the same," says Rollin, "of a professor who has no books?"

Valesius borrowed books of every body, and used to say, "He learned more from borrowed books than from his own; because, not having the same opportunity of reviewing them, he read them with more care."

Archbishop Ussher, suspecting that the Fathers had been misquoted by Stapleton, a Papist, took up a firm resolution, "That, in due time, (if God gave him life,) he would read all the Fathers, and trust none but his own eyes in searching out their sense:" which great work, he began at twenty years of age, and finished at thirty-eight; strictly confining himself to read such a portion every day, from which he suffered no occasion to divert him.

William King, the poet, at eighteen years of age, was elected to Christ's church, where he is said to have prosecuted his studies with so much intenseness and activity, that, before he was eight years standing, he had read over, and made remarks upon twenty-two thousand odd hundred books and manuscripts.

Pope says, "That from fourteen to twenty, he read only for amusement; from twenty to twenty-seven, for improvement and instruction:— that, in the first part of this time, he desired only to know; and, in the second, he endeavoured to judge."

Bishop Butler's abstruse work on the analogy of religion to human nature, was a favourite book with

Queen Caroline.——She told Mr. Sale, the orientalist, "That she read it every day at breakfast;" so light did her metaphysical mind make of that book, which Dr. Hoadly, Bishop of Winchester, said he could never look into without making his head ache.

There are some books which require peculiar attention in reading in order to understand them. A spruce macaroni was boasting, one day, that he had the most happy genius in the world. "Every thing," said he, "is easy to me! People call Euclid's elements a hard book; but I read it yesterday from beginning to end in a piece of the afternoon, between dinner and tea-time." "Read all Euclid," answered a gentleman present, "in one afternoon! How was that possible?" "Upon my honour, I did, and never read smoother reading in my life."—"Did you master all the demonstrations, and solve all the problems as you went?" "Demonstrations and problems! I suppose you mean the a's, and b's, and c's; and 1's, and 2's, and 3's; and the pictures of scratches, and scrawls? No, no; I skipt all they. I only read Euclid himself; and all Euclid I did read, and in one piece of the afternoon too."—Alas! how many such readers are there! Such are likely to get as much knowledge of the subject they read, as this young man did of geometry.

Those who have collected books, and whose good nature has prompted them to accommodate their friends with them, will feel the sting of an answer which a man of wit made to one who lamented the difficulty which he found in persuading his friends to return the volumes which he had lent them: "Sir," said he, "your acquaintance find, I suppose, that it is much more easy to retain the books themselves, than what is contained in them." I would just observe here, that nothing can be more mean and unkind, than to borrow books of persons, and to lose them, as is too frequently the case. If my friend gratifies my request in lending; if, by so doing, he saves me the expense of purchasing; or if, also, by the loan, I gain considerable information, or intellectual profit, it is base and ungrateful either to suffer the book to be injured, or not to return it. I give this as a hint to some who are more in the habit of *borrowing* than *returning* books.

"He who would read with pleasure," says Dr. Knox, "will attend to the times of the day, and the seasons of the year. The morning has been universally approved as the best time for study; the afternoon may be most advantageously spent in improving conversation. Those faculties which, before dinner, are capable of engaging in the acutest and sublimest disquisitions, are found, by general experience, to be comparatively dull and stupid after it." I know not how it is," said a celebrated writer, " but all my philosophy, in which I was so warmly engaged in the morning, appears like nonsense as soon as I have dined." Very hot weather is particularly unfavourable to reading. The months of July, August, and September, are by no means the seasons in which the fruits of the mind arrive at maturity.

"There are three capital mistakes," says one, "in regard to books. Some, through their own indolence, and others from a sincere belief of the vanity of human science, *read no book but the Bible.* But these good men do not consider that, for the same reasons, they ought not to preach sermons; for sermons are *libri, ore, vivaque voce, pronunciati:* The holy scriptures are *illustrated* by other writings. Others collect great quantities of books for *show,* and not for *service.* This is a vast parade, even unworthy of reproof. Others purchase large libraries, with a sincere design of reading all the books. But a very large library, is learned *luxury,* not *elegance;* much less *utility.*" Much reading, is no proof of much learning; fast readers are often desultory ones. Hence the reason some know so *little*, is because they *read* so much. The *helluo librorum*, and the true scholar, are two very different characters. Yet we are told of the famous Perkins, that he had the knack of quickly running through a folio, and entering entirely into the author's subject, while he appeared to be only skimming the surface; but then it must be remembered, that he was a man of uncommon quickness and penetration.

RETIREMENT.

HOWEVER pleasant and profitable society may be, there are certain moments when we should consider it our duty to retire from the world. " The great and the worthy, the pious and the virtuous," says a divine, " have ever been addicted to serious retirement. It is the characteristic of little and frivolous minds, to be wholly occupied with the vulgar objects of life. These fill up their desires, and supply all the entertainment which their coarse apprehensions can relish; but a more refined and enlarged mind, leaves the world behind it, feels a call for higher pleasures, and seeks them in retreat. The man of public spirit has recourse to it. in order to form plans for general good; the man of genius, in order to dwell on his favourite themes; the philosopher, to pursue his discoveries; and the saint to improve himself in divine things."

Similis, captain of the guards to Adrian, got leave to quit that emperor's service, and spent the last seven years of his life in rural retirement. At his death, he ordered the following inscription on his tomb: " Here lies Similis, who lived but seven years, though he died at sixty-seven." Our true age, and our real life, are to be dated from the time of our abstraction from the world, and of our conversion to God.

Sir John Mason, Privy Counsellor to Henry VIII., upon his death-bed, delivered himself to those about him to this purport: "I have seen five princes, and have been privy counsellor to four. I have seen the most remarkable things in foreign parts, and been present at most state transactions for thirty years together, and have learned this, after so many years experience, that seriousness is the greatest wisdom, temperance the best physician, and a good conscience the best estate; and were I to live my time over again, I would change the court for a cloister; my privy counsellor's bustles for an hermit's retirement; and the whole life I have lived in this palace for one hour's enjoyment of God in the Chapel: all things else forsake me, besides my God, my duty, my prayer."

It is said of a captain, of whom historians have taken more care to record the wisdom than the name, that he required the Emperor Charles V. to discharge him from his service. Charles asked the reason. The prudent soldier replied, "Because there ought to be a pause between the hurry of life and the day of death."

The great Emperor Charles V. towards the close of his life, retired to a monastery. He said that he had tasted more satisfaction in his solitude in one day than in all the triumphs of his former reigns; and that the sincere study, profession, and practice of the Christian religion had in it such joys and sweetnesses that courts are strangers to: and, in his retirement, we are told that he was particularly curious with regard to the construction of clocks and watches, and having found, after repeated trials, that he could not bring any two of them to go exactly alike, he reflected, it is said, with a mixture of surprise as well as regret on his own folly, in having bestowed so much time and labour in the more vain attempt of bringing mankind to precise uniformity of sentiment concerning the intricate and mysterious doctrines of religion.

Mr. Isaac Ambrose used to retire every year for a month into a little hut in a wood, where he shunned all society, and devoted himself to reli- gious contemplation; and of the fa mous Law it is said, that such was his love of retirement, that it was very seldom he passed more than two hours in the company of any person.

Retirement requires a mind enlarged and improved. He who has never been in the habit of reading and contemplation, will find it no relief, but a burden to him. A tradesman, who had acquired a large fortune in London, retired from business and went to live at Worcester. His mind being without its usual occupation, and having nothing else to supply its place, preyed upon itself, so that existence was a torment to him. At last he was seized with the stone, and a friend, who found him in one of his severest fits, having expressed his concern, " No, no, Sir," said he, "don't pity me ; what I now feel is ease, compared with that torture of mind from which it relieves me." What a pity it is, that they who think it so much their duty to cultivate their business, never think of cultivating their minds ! Such, when age or infirmity calls them to retirement, find nothing pleasing to reflect on, but are tired of life, and every thing proves a burden to them. A mind well informed is better than a pocket well stored.

Profitable as retirement is, it must be remembered that *all* our time is not to be spent in this way. An extreme is to be guarded against, or otherwise our retirement, perhaps, will be more injurious than useful to us. A gentleman of Brabant, it is said, lived five and twenty years without ever going out of his own house, entertaining himself with forming a magnificent cabinet of pictures and paintings. This gentleman might have done more good in the course of this twenty-five years, by mixing himself with society, than by all his collection of paintings and pictures.

"Although retirement is my dear delight," says Melmoth, " yet, upon some occasions, I think I have too much of it ; and I agree with Balzac, ' Que la solitude est certainement une belle chose, mais il y a plaisir d'avoir

quelqu'un a qui on puisse dire de tems en tems que la solitude est une belle chose.' ' Solitude is certainly a fine thing, but there is a pleasure in having some one whom we may tell, from time to time, that solitude is a fine thing :' " and besides,

> Thoughts shut up want air,
> And spoil like bales unopened to the sun.
> 'Tis converse qualifies for solitude,
> As exercise for salutary rest.
> YOUNG.

There is, perhaps, some truth in the following remark of Horace Walpole, Earl of Orford—"Few Englishmen, I have observed, can bear solitude without being hurt by it. Our climate makes us capricious, and we must rub off our roughness and humours against one another."

REVERENCE OF GOD, RELIGION, ETC.

HE who possesses no reverence for the Divine Being, who, while he believes in his existence, violates his laws and despises his authority, shows at once the depravity of his heart and the weakness of his reason ; and yet, alas ! how many such characters are there who view the great God as a tyrant, and consider him as an object whose service may be dispensed with ! Indeed, were we to form an idea of the Divine character by the respect paid to it by the generality, we should suppose him the greatest enemy instead of the best friend of mortals. To fear and serve God, however, is the voice of reason, wisdom, and religion. Let him, therefore, who wilfully lives in the neglect of his duty to God, remember, that he is a disgrace to himself, an enemy to his fellow creatures, and obnoxious to the Divine displeasure.

The sublime descriptions of Jehovah, as given in the sacred Scriptures, should impress our minds with the highest ideas of veneration and regard. An elegant writer justly observes, " Meditation on such a Being, so constantly and so wonderfully employed in promoting the good of his creatures, tends surely to crush every selfish and to enlarge every generous affection of the soul. It softens the heart into compassion, and expands it into benevolence, when we consider mankind as framed and supported by the same almighty power, and redeemed by the same goodness. The pride of knowledge, the splendour of conquest, and the pageantry of power, shrink into obscurity and insignificance, when we reflect on Him whom the heaven of heavens cannot contain. All the lurking impurities of our souls are seen with loathing, and all the secret crimes of our lives remembered with horror, while we consider that he trieth the very heart and reins, and that his eye seeth afar off. All the dark and tempestuous scenes of the world cease to alarm and depress us, adversity loses her sting, and prosperity assumes new and more delightful charms, when we consider that no event takes place without the appointment of our Maker."—White's Sermons.

The celebrated Linnæus, always testified in his conversation, writings, and actions, the greatest sense of God's omniscience; yea, he was so strongly impressed with the idea, that he wrote over the door of his library, "*Innocui vivite, numen ad est,*" "Live innocent, God is present."

The great Mr. Boyle had such a veneration of God, and such a sense of his presence, that he never mentioned the name of God without a pause and visible stop in his discourse. How different the conduct of these illustrious men to that of many who live in the constant violation of the third command! How shocking to the ears of a pious man, to hear the name of God so irreverently and unnecessarily used as it is! Let such as are guilty of the practice recollect what an awful account they must give in the great day of judgment. "The story is well known," says Mr. Scott, "of the person who invited a company of his friends that were accustomed to take the Lord's name in vain; and contrived to have all their discourse taken down, and

read to them. Now, if they could not endure to hear the words repeated which they had spoken during a few hours, how shall they bear to have all that they have uttered through a long course of years brought forth as evidence against them at the tribunal of God ?"

Let me here just drop a word to those who, while they profess attachment to religion, only injure it by their irregularity of character. I believe nothing gives infidels a greater reason to suspect the reality of religion, nothing furnishes skeptics with stronger arguments for their tenets, nothing makes the profane more contented in their course of impiety, than when they find those who profess superior sanctity no better than the world at large. Lord Rochester told Bishop Burnet, that "there was nothing that gave him and many others a more secret encouragement in their ill-ways, than that those who pretended to believe *lived* so, that they could not be thought to be in earnest." O ye professors who are marked for volatility of disposition and indecision of character, think what you are doing. Let not the sacred religion of Jesus be wounded in the house of his friends. If religion be nothing in your view, act honestly ; give up the name ; but if it be (as it surely is) divine, then let all your powers be employed in its defence, and your life one continued testimony of its excellence.

Many have mistaken the agitation of the passions for real religion. "We may easily conceive," says Dr. Stennet, "how a pleasing kind of sensation excited in the breast by a pathetic description of misery, particularly the sufferings of Christ, may be taken for religion. One of a compassionate disposition, but grossly ignorant, perhaps an Indian, hearing for the first time, in a Christian assembly, a striking description of our Saviour's last passion, melted into tears, and, after the service was over, eagerly besought the preacher to be ingenuous with him, and tell him whether the fact he had related was true, for he hoped in God that such a cruel deed could never have been perpetrated!"

Such was Mr. Hervey's strict piety, that he suffered no moment to go unimproved. When he was called down to tea, he used to bring his Hebrew Bible or Greek Testament with him; and would either speak upon one verse or upon several verses, as occasion offered. "This," says Mr. Romaine, "was generally an improving season. The glory of God is very seldom promoted at the tea-table; but it was at Mr. Hervey's. Drinking tea with him was like being at an ordinance; for it was sanctified by the word of God and prayer."

Discarded as religion is, there is nothing so well calculated to inspire the mind with hope, or possess it with real comfort. Riches, power, or human learning, cannot vie with vital godliness.—"*I would*," says Hugo Grotius, "*give all my learning and honour for the plain integrity of John Urick*," who was a religious poor man that spent eight hours of his time in prayer, eight in labour, and but eight in meals, sleep, and other necessaries. "This spiritual wisdom is the principal thing."

Secretary Walsingham, an eminent courtier and statesman in Queen Elizabeth's time, in his old age retired into privacy, in the country. Some of his former gay companions came to see him, and told him he was melancholy. "No," said he, "I am not melancholy; I am serious: and it is fit I should be so. Ah! my friends, while we laugh, all things are serious round about us. God is serious, who exerciseth patience towards us. Christ is serious, who shed his blood for us. The Holy Ghost is serious, in striving against the obstinacy of our hearts: the holy Scriptures bring to our ears the most serious things in the world; the holy Sacrament represents the most serious and awful matters; the whole creation is serious in serving God and us; all that

are in heaven and hell are serious! How then can we be gay?"

By this seriousness above-mentioned, we are, however, not to understand a gloominess of temper, or an absolute seclusion from society. There is a happy medium which religion teaches. "Human nature is not so miserable as that we should be always melancholy, nor so happy as that we should be always merry. A man should not live as if there were no God in the world; nor, at the same time, as if there were no men in it. Disgust with the world should never prevent our assisting the inhabitants of it; and our contempt of life should always be accompanied with charity for the living."

Religion, however, should be the grand business of life, and without it great names, conspicuous situations, sounding titles, and extensive riches, are all empty things. Let us then study how to live to God, to know ourselves, to improve our time. Let us not imagine that the finest genius, the greatest powers, the most consummate worldly wisdom, or any thing else, will be a substitute for real religion. "My heart has yearned (says M. Cecil) at marking a great man, wise in his generation, skilfully holding the reins of a vast enterprise, grasping with a mighty mind its various relations, and penetrating with an eagle's eye into—what? every thing but HIMSELF. A fallen spirit in a disordered world! Having a day of salvation, and that neglected! How natural was the dying language of such a one, when he cried out, ' *The battle is fought, the battle is fought*; *but the victory is lost for ever!*' "

"Alas! how many celebrated geniuses, how many deep philosophers, how many splendid conquerors, shall awake in eternity from their vain dreams of glory; each wishing he had been an ideot, or even a brute, that he might never have been eternally a wretch, responsible for talents and privileges neglected and abused!" —See Rev. Mr. Cecil's Sermon, entitled "The true Patriot."

SABBATH DAY.

"The Christian Sabbath," says Hervey, "is an inestimable privilege to the Church of Christ. It is a pledge of God's distinguishing love. It is a happy mean of building us up in the knowledge of establishing us in faith, and preparing us for our everlasting rest."

"The happiness of heaven (Henry observes) is the constant keeping of a sabbath. Heaven is called a *sabbath*, to make those that love sabbaths long for heaven, and to make those that long for heaven love sabbaths."

The Sabbath-day was anciently called *dies lucis*, the day of light. Also, *Regina dierum*, the Queen of Days. The primitive church had this day in high veneration : it was a great badge of their religion : for when the question was asked, " Keepest thou the Sabbath ?" the answer was made, " I am a Christian, and dare not omit the celebration of the Lord's day." That great man, Judge Hale, thus speaks of the Sabbath.— "I have," says he, "by long and sound experience, found that the due observance of this day, and of the duties of it, have been of singular comfort and advantage to me. The observance of this day hath ever had joined to it a blessing upon the rest of my time ; and the week that hath been so begun hath been blessed and prosperous to me ; and, on the other side, when I have been negligent of the duties of this day, the rest of the week has been unsuccessful and unhappy to my own secular employments; so that I could easily make an estimate of my successes the week following, by the manner of my passing of this day: and this I do not write lightly nor inconsiderately, but upon a long and sound observation and experience."

It was the frequent and almost constant custom of Mr. Grimshaw to leave his church while the psalm was singing, to see if any were absent from worship, and idling their time in the church yard, the street, or the ale-houses ; and many of those whom he so found he would drive into the church before him. " A friend of mine," says Mr. Newton, " passing a public-house in Haworth, on a Lord's day morning, saw several persons making their escape out of it, some jumping out of the lower windows, and some over a low wall : he was at first alarmed, fearing the house was on fire; but upon inquiring what was the cause of the commotion, he was told, ' that they saw the parson coming.' They were more afraid of their parson than a justice of peace. His reproofs were so authoritative, and yet so mild and friendly, that the stoutest sinners could not stand before him.

"One Lord's day, as a man was passing through Haworth, on horseback, his horse lost a shoe : He applied to a blacksmith, who told him, ' That he could not shoe a horse on the Lord's day, without the minister's leave.' They went together to Mr. Grimshaw, and the man satisfying him that he was really in haste, going for a midwife, Mr. Grimshaw permitted the blacksmith to shoe the horse, which otherwise he would not have done for double pay.

"He endeavoured, likewise, to suppress the generally prevailing custom in country places, during the summer, of walking in the fields on a Lord's day, between the services, or in the evening, in companies. He not only bore his testimony against it from the pulpit, but reconnoitered the fields in person, to detect and reprove the delinquents. One instance of this kind, which shows both his care of his people, and his great ascendency over them, and which is ascertained by the testimony of many witnesses, some of whom, I believe, are still living, I shall relate. There was a spot, at some distance from the village, to which many young people continued to resort: he had often warned them, in his preaching, against this custom, and, at last, he disguised himself one evening, that

9

he might not be known till he was near enough to discover who they were. He then spoke, and charged them not to move. He took down all their names with his pencil, and ordered them to attend him on a day and hour which he appointed. They all waited upon him accordingly, as punctually as if they had been served with a judge's warrant. When they came, he led them into a private room, where, after he had formed them into a circle, and commanded them to kneel down, he kneeled down in the midst of them, and prayed for them with much earnestness for a considerable time; and concluded the interview, when he rose up, by a close and affecting lecture. He never had occasion, afterwards, to repeat this friendly discipline. He entirely broke the custom, and the place has never been resorted to on a Sunday evening from that time to the present day."

Mr. Matthew Henry was particularly observant of the Sabbath day. It was somewhat singular, that the two last Sabbaths he spent on earth, God should direct him to a subject suitable to what he had appointed, and was so speedily to be performed for him. Those two Sabbaths, he was wholly taken up with the thought of that eternal Sabbath, and rest, which the spirits of just men enjoy in heaven. The last Sabbath but one, he preached from Heb. iv. 9. " There remaineth, therefore, a rest to the people of God ;" and the last of all from the first verse of the same chapter, " Let us, therefore, fear, lest, a promise being left us of entering into his rest, any of you should seem to come short of it."

It is said of the pious and learned Mr. Gouge, that as he forebore providing suppers on the eve before the Sabbath, that servants might not be kept up too late, so he would never suffer any servant to tarry at home, to dress any meat on the Lord's day for any friends, whether they were mean or great, few or many.

How many persons, who call themselves Christians, can reconcile their *Sunday proceedings*, with their consciences, or the word of God, I know not ! Whatever difference of sentiment there may be, as to the particular day, it is evident, there never has been any abrogation of the spirit, meaning, or end of the law, as to devoting the seventh part of our time to God. What, then, will they have to answer for, who set apart this day for travelling, visiting, feasting, and worldly amusements ? What an awful account many professors will have to give, who violate this day, by working, posting their books, keeping their servants from public worship, and buying things which might easily have been obtained on the preceding day ! Let all such remember, how incompatible this is with the law of God, and even the laws of the land.

All persons who profane the Lord's day, are liable to the following penalties; and it were to be wished, the magistrates would put these laws in execution with the utmost strictness.

By doing, or executing, any business, or work, of their *ordinary callings*, on the Lord's day, or any part thereof, (works of necessity and charity only excepted,) under which head of ordinary callings, is included *shaving on Sundays*, which is a most shameful and notorious custom.

By the 29th Car. II. cap. 7. Persons convicted hereof, by view of a Justice of the Peace, confession of the party, or witness, are to pay five shillings, or be put in the stocks two hours. Licensed houses besides *forfeit* their licenses.

By public crying, or exposing to sale, any wares, merchandise, &c.

By the same Act, it is forfeiture of goods so exposed to sale.

By idling, or wandering, in the time of divine service.

By the same Act, five shillings, or stocks two hours.

Ale-house keepers, vintners, innkeepers, permitting tippling in their houses.

By 1st Jac. I. cap. 9. If convicts of such permission, are to pay 10s; and if convicts of drunkenness, disabled to an ale-house for three years, by 21st Jac. I. cap. 7.

Shoemakers selling, or putting to sale any shoes, boots, &c., upon the Sabbath-day.

By 1st Jac. c. 22. s. 28. forfeit 3s. 4d. a pair, besides the value thereof.

SCRIPTURES.

" ALL scripture is given by inspiration of God, and is profitable for doctrine, for reproof, for correction, for instruction in righteousness."

The Bible is not only the oldest, but the best book in the world. The matter, the manner, the end, the harmony, the success of the Scriptures, together with their wonderful preservation, character of the penmen, and accomplishment of their predictions, should teach us their divine authority. Infidels may reject, skeptics may doubt, and the licentious may sneer; but no one who ever wished to take away this foundation stone, could produce any other equal to it, on which the structure of a pious mind, a solid hope, a comfortable state, or wise conduct, could be raised. A view of the heathen world, a sight of mankind at large, will evidently show how far the light of nature can carry men. Revelation only is the *sure word*, in the beautiful language of the Apostle, whereunto we do well to take heed as unto a light that shineth in a dark place.

" Read and revere the sacred page ; a page
" Which not the whole creation could produce,
" Which not the conflagration shall destroy,
" In nature's ruins not one letter lost."
Young.

A lady of suspected chastity, and who was tinctured with infidel principles, conversing with a minister of the gospel, objected to the scriptures, on account of their obscurity, and the great difficulty of understanding them. The minister wisely and smartly replied,—" *Why, madam, what can be easier to understand than the seventh commandment,* ' Thou shalt not commit adultery ?' "

" We had in our congregation," says one, " a poor aged widow, who could neither read the Scriptures, nor live without hearing them read ; so much instruction and pleasure did she derive from the oracles of God." She lived in a lone place, and the family where she lodged could not read; but there was one more cottage near, and in it a little boy, a shepherd's son, who could read ; but he, full of play, was not fond of reading the Bible. Necessity is the mother of invention. The old widow determined to rise one hour sooner in a morning, to spin one halfpenny more, to be expended in hiring the shepherd's boy to read to her every evening a chapter, to which he readily agreed.

Collins, the poet, it is said, travelled with no other book than an English Testament, such as children carry to school. When a friend took it into his hand, out of curiosity, to see what companion a man of letters had chosen, " I have but one book," said Collins, " but that is the best."— Happy would it be for poets, if they all were of the same mind.

The learned Salmasius said, when on his death-bed, " O! I have lost a world of time! If one year more were to be added to my life, it should be spent in reading David's Psalms, and Paul's Epistles."

It is not every man that chooses the Bible in preference to worldly emolument.——The following instance, however, is related of John Wesselus, one of the most learned men in the 15th century. His patron having been elected Pope, by the name of Sixtus IV., continued his favour to him, and offered him all kinds of preferment; but Wesselus desired only one copy of the Bible, in Hebrew and Greek, out of the Vatican library. The Pope thought this a very stupid request. " Why did you not," said he, " desire a mitre, or some such thing?" "Because I do not want one," replied Wesselus. His request was granted. The Bible, to a pious mind, is more to be desired than the greatest riches, or the most elevated and conspicuous situations in the world.

A worthy officer, not long since, assembled all his men in the cabin, and, stating the critical situation of his country, proposed to them the contribution of ten day's pay, as a free-will offering to the necessities of their country. This being cheerfully agreed to, he presented each of them with a Bible, desiring them to peruse it carefully, adding, " It will instruct you to fear God, honour the King, and love your country." Were every officer to do likewise, what good might we not expect?

A minister meeting with some sailors, who appeared to be serious, asked them if there were any more on board, who were of the same opinion with themselves? "Yes, Sir," said one of them, " there are several of us, when opportunity offers, meet for reading and prayer; and we hope there are six of us, who are truly changed, who were all vile sinners two years ago, but have been taught to love God by reading the Bible." What an encouragement is this to distribute Bibles among sailors, as well as others!

It has been supposed, that the Scriptures are read by the poor and illiterate only; and that there is nothing in them worthy the attention of the great, the wise, and the learned: but this is a mistake. It is their peculiar excellency, that they are calculated for the benefit of the most sagacious philosopher, as well as the most humble peasant.

There is no book in the world so admirably adapted to the capacities of all men as the Bible. It is so sublime in its language, so noble in its doctrine, yet plain in its precepts, and excellent in its end, that the man must be ignorant and depraved indeed, who lives without reading it.

Queen Elizabeth spent much of her time in reading the best writings of her own and former ages, yet she by no means neglected that best of books, the Bible; for proof of which, take her own words. " I walk," says she, "many times in the pleasant fields of the holy Scriptures, where I pluck up the goodlisome herbs of sentences by pruning, eat them by reading, digest them by musing, and lay them up at length in the high seat of memory, by gathering them together; so that, having tasted their sweetness, I may less perceive the bitterness of life."

Lord Rochester.—A comparison of the 53d chapter of Isaiah, with the account given in the four Evangelists, of the sufferings of Christ, became the instrument of convincing this witty and wicked Earl. It is said, that " Mr. Parsons, in order to his conviction, read to him the 53d chapter of Isaiah, and compared it with our Saviour's passion, that he might there see a prophecy concerning it, written many ages before it was done; which the Jews, that still blasphemed Christ, still kept in their hands as a book divinely inspired. The Earl told Bishop Burnet, that, as he heard it read, he felt an inward force upon him, which did so enlighten his mind, and convince him, that he could resist it no longer; for the words had an authority which did shoot like rays or beams in his mind: so that he was not only convinced by the reasoning he had about it, which satisfied his understanding, but by a power which did so effectually constrain him, that he did ever after as firmly believe in his Saviour, as if he had seen him in the clouds. He had it read so often to him, that he had got it by heart, and went through great part of it, in discourse with the Bishop, with a sort of heavenly pleasure, giving him his reflections upon it."—See Burnet's Life of the Earl of Rochester.

It is said of Sir Isaac Newton, that he did not confine himself only to natural religion, for he was thoroughly persuaded of the truth of revelation. And amidst the great variety of books which he had constantly before him, that which he studied with the greatest application, was *the Bible;* and he understood the nature and force of moral certainty, as well as he did that of a strict demonstration.

The famous Selden, one of the most eminent philosophers, and most learned men of his time, who had taken a diligent survey of antiquity, and what knowledge was considerable amongst Jews, Heathens, and Christians, and read as much, perhaps, as any man ever read, towards the end of his days declared to Archbishop Ussher, that notwithstanding he had been so laborious in his inquiries, and curious in his collections, and had possessed himself of a treasure of books and manuscripts, upon all ancient subjects, yet he could rest his soul on none, save *the Scriptures :* and, above all, that passage gave him the most satisfaction in Titus ii. 11 —14, " The Grace of God," &c.

Sir Christopher Hatton, a great statesman, a little before his death, advised his relations to be serious in searching after the will of God in his holy word ; "For," said he, "it is deservedly accounted a piece of excellent knowledge, to understand the laws of the land, and the customs of a man's country ; how much more to know the statutes of heaven, and the laws of eternity ; those immutable, and eternal laws of justice and righteousness ! To know the will and pleasure of the Great Monarch and Universal King! *I have seen an end of all perfection, but thy commandment is exceeding broad.* Whatever other knowledge a man may be endowed with, could he, by a vast and imperious mind, and a heart as large as the sand upon the sea shore, command all the knowledge of art and nature, of words and things, and yet not know the author of his being, and the preserver of his life, his sovereign and his judge, his surest refuge in trouble, his best friend or worst enemy, the support

of his life, and the hope of his death, his future happiness, and his portion for ever, he doth but go down to hell with a great deal of wisdom."

Mr. Locke, justly esteemed one of the greatest masters of reason, being asked, a little before his dissolution— " *What was the shortest and surest way for a young gentleman to attain a true knowledge of the Christian religion in the full and just extent of it ?*" made this memorable reply, " Let him study the holy scriptures, especially the New Testa. ment. Therein are contained the words of eternal life. It has God for its author, salvation for its end, and truth, without any mixture of error, for its matter."

In another place, he says, " The only way to attain a certain knowledge of the Christian religion in its full extent and purity, is the study of the holy scriptures."

Mr. Locke spent the last fifteen years of his life at Oates, in Essex, at the seat of Sir Francis Masham. " During this agreeable retirement, he applied himself especially to the study of the holy scriptures, and employed the last years of his life in hardly any thing else."

Sir William Jones' opinion of the Bible, was written on the last leaf of one belonging to him, in these strong terms : " I have regularly and attentively read these holy scriptures, and am of opinion, that this volume, independently of its divine origin, contains more sublimity and beauty, more pure morality, more important history, and finer strains of poetry and eloquence, than can be collected from all other books, in whatever age or language they may have been composed."

The honourable Robert Boyle is another instance. His whole life and fortune were spent in illustrating the beauties of the two grand volumes of Creation and Revelation. He has said every thing in favour of the Bible that language admits of. He calls it "*that matchless book,*" and has written a whole volume to

9*

illustrate its beauties. Nor was his admiration confined to mere words; for he was at the charge of a translation and impression of the four Gospels and Acts of the Apostles into the Malayan language, and this book he sent over all the East Indies. He was moreover at a considerable expense for an impression of the New Testament in the Turkish language. He also spent seven hundred pounds in an edition of the Irish Bible, which he ordered to be distributed in that country. He contributed largely also to the impressions both of the Welch Bible and of the Irish Bible, for the use of the Highlands in Scotland. He gave, during his life, 300 pounds towards propagating the Christian religion in America.

There is a wonderful depth in the scriptures: the more we study them, the more we shall be enamoured with and astonished at the beauties they contain. The learned Le Clerc tells us, that, while he was compiling his Harmony, he was so struck with admiration of the excellent discourses of Jesus, and so inflamed with the love of his most holy doctrine, that he thought he but just then began to be acquainted with what he scarcely ever laid out of his hands from his infancy.

We will conclude this article with the following anecdote of Oxenstein, Chancellor of Sweden. He was a person of the first quality, station, and ability, in his own country.— Being visited in his retreat from public business by Commissioner Whitlock, Ambassador from England to Queen Christiana, in the conclusion of their discourse, he said to the ambassador,—" I have seen much, and enjoyed much of this world, but I never knew how to live till now. I thank my good God, who has given me time to know Him, and to know myself. All the comfort I have, and which is more than the whole world can give, is feeling the good Spirit of God in my heart, and reading in this good book (holding up the Bible) that came from it." This enlightened and experienced man farther addressed the ambassador as follows :— "You are now in the prime of your age and vigour, and in great favour and business; but all this will leave you, and you will one day better understand and relish what I say to you; and then you will find, that there is more wisdom, truth, comfort, and pleasure, in retiring and turning your heart from the world to the good Spirit of God, and in reading the Bible, than in all the courts and favours of princes." "This I had, (says William Penn,) as near as I am able to remember, from the ambassador's own mouth, more than once. A very remarkable and edifying account, when we consider from whom it came, one of the greatest and wisest men of his age, while his understanding was as sound and vigorous as his experience and knowledge were great."

TRANSLATION OF THE SCRIPTURES.

WHEN Queen Elizabeth opened the prisons at her coming to the crown, one piously told her, that there were yet some good men left in the prison undelivered, and desired they might also partake of her princely favour; meaning the four Evangelists, and Paul, who had been denied to walk abroad in the English tongue, when her sister Mary swayed the sceptre. To this she answered,— "They should be asked whether they were willing to have their liberty;" which soon after appearing, they had, says an old divine, their gaol delivery; and have ever since had their liberty to speak to us in our own tongue at the assemblies of our public worship; yea, and to visit us in our private houses also.

Our English translation of the Bible was made in the time and by the appointment of James the First.— According to Fuller, the number of translators amounted to forty-seven. Every one of the company was to translate the whole parcel, and compare all together. These good and learned men entered on their work in the spring, 1607, and three years elapsed before the translation was finished.

Bugenhagius assisted Luther in the translation of the Bible into German, and kept the day on which it was finished annually a festival with his friends, calling it "The Feast of the Translation of the Bible;" and it certainly deserves a *red letter* more than half the saints in the calendar.

Soon after Tindale's New Testament was published, a royal proclamation was issued to prohibit the buying and reading such translation or translations. But this served to increase the public curiosity, and to occasion a more careful reading of what was deemed so obnoxious.— One step taken by the Bishop of London afforded some merriment to the Protestants. His Lordship thought that the best way to prevent these English New Testaments from circulation would be to buy up the whole impression, and therefore employed a Mr. Packington, who secretly favoured the reformation, then at Antwerp, for this purpose; assuring him, at the same time, that cost what they would, he would have them, and burn them at Paul's Cross. Upon this Packington applied himself to Tindale (who was then at Antwerp) and upon agreement the Bishop had the books, Packington great thanks, and Tindale all the money. This enabled Tindale instantly to publish a new and more correct edition, so that they came over thick and threefold into England; which occasioned great rage in the disappointed Bishop and his popish friends. One Constantine being soon after apprehended by Sir Thomas More, and being asked how Tindale and others subsisted abroad, readily answered, "That it was the Bishop of London who had been their chief supporter, for he bestowed a great deal of money upon them in the purchase of New Testaments, to burn them; and that upon

H

that cash they had subsisted till the sale of the second edition was received."

The following incident respecting the venerable Bede is worthy of remembrance. One of the last things he did was the translating of St. John's Gospel into English.— When death seized on him, one of his devout scholars, whom he used for his secretary or amanuensis, said to him, "My beloved master, there remains yet one sentence unwritten." "Write it then quickly," replied Bede; and, summoning all his spirits together, (like the last blaze of a candle going out,) he indited it, and expired.

Mark Hildesley, Bishop of Soder and Man, deserves to be here recorded as an example of diligence and activity in promoting the translation of the holy scriptures into the Manks language. His whole heart was set upon this work, and God greatly blessed him in it. On Saturday, 28th of November, 1772, he was crowned with the inexpressible happiness of receiving the last part of *the Bible Translation*, so long and so greatly the object of his ardent prayers: upon which occasion, according to his own repeated promise, he very emphatically sang, *Nunc, Domine Dimittis*, in the presence of his congratulating family. The next day, which was Advent Sunday, he officiated in his own chapel, and preached on the uncertainty of human life. In the evening he again called his family together, and resumed the subject. On the next day he was seized with a stroke of apoplexy, and in a few days afterwards calmly resigned a valuable existence, in the seventy-fourth year of his age. We ought to be particularly thankful to God when he spares the lives of his servants to finish those works which are of such importance and utility to mankind.

SLEEPING AND INATTENTION
IN THE HOUSE OF GOD.

WE may well ask whether such an inconsistency was ever seen in a Pagan temple or a Mahometan mosque. "He who sleeps in a place of worship," says one, "is as though he had been brought in for a corpse, and the preacher was preaching at his funeral." Upon this subject I cannot help transcribing what has been written by an eminent author.— "Constant sleepers," says he, "are public nuisances, and deserve to be whipped out of a religious assembly, to which they are a constant disgrace. There are some who have regularly attended a place of worship for seven years, twice a-day, and yet have not heard one whole sermon in all the time. These dreamers are a constant distress to their preachers. In regard to their *health*, would any but a stupid man choose such a place to sleep in? In respect to their *character*, what can be said for him, who *in his sleep makes mouths and wry faces, and exhibits strange postures; and sometimes snorts, starts, and talks in his sleep? Where is his *prudence*, when he gives occasion to malicious persons to suspect him of gluttony, drunkenness, laziness, and other usual causes of sleeping in the day time. Where is his *breeding*? He ought to respect the company: what an offensive rudeness to sit down and sleep before them! Above all, where is his *piety* and fear of God?"

"Where is your respect for your minister?" says another. "For six days he labours, and on the seventh he brings into the pulpit what he has in secret prepared. Unhappy man! Thy hearers tell thee to thy face, that thy labours for a week are not worthy their attention for an hour. Oh! how often has it been, that, when the faithful zealous man of God has had his heart warm with his subject, and has fondly thought each attendant's feelings were in unison with his own, that by your indecent yawning, your filthy snoring, or repeated nodding before his eyes, his pleasure hath yielded to surprise, his surprise to grief, and his grief to discouragement, until he has

not possessed sufficient fortitude to close the sentence he had begun; and a season which promised universal delight becomes, through your indolence, tormenting to the preacher, and unprofitable to attentive hearers."

As Mr. Nicoll, of Exeter, was once preaching, he saw several of the aldermen asleep, and thereupon sat down. Upon his silence, and the noise that presently arose in the church, they awoke, and stood up with the rest; upon which he arose, and said, "*The Sermon is not yet done; but now you are awake, I hope you will hearken more diligently,*" and then went on.

Aylmer, Bishop of London, in 1580, took a Hebrew Bible out of his pocket, and began to read it. This immediately awakened his hearers, who looked up to him, amazed, that he should entertain them so unprofitably; when, finding they were awake and very attentive, he proceeded in his sermon, after admonishing them how much it reflected on their good sense, that, in matters of mere novelty, and when they understood not a word, they should listen so heedfully, and yet be so regardless of points of the utmost importance.

It is said that Dr. South, one of the chaplains of Charles the Second, preaching on a certain day before the court, which was composed of the most profligate and dissipated men in the nation, perceived, in the middle of his discourse, that sleep had generally taken possession of his hearers. The doctor immediately stopped short, and, changing his tone of voice, called out to Lord Lauderdale three times. His Lordship standing up, "My Lord," says South, with great composure, "I am sorry to interrupt your repose, but I must beg of you that you will not snore quite so loud, lest you awaken his Majesty."

It is related of Dr. Young, that, as he was preaching in his turn at St. James's, he plainly perceived it was out of his power to command the attention of his audience. This so affected the feeling of the preacher, that he sat back in the pulpit, and burst into tears.—And of Bishop Abbot it is said, that once, on such an occasion, he took out his Testament, and read Greek.

The Bishop of Massilon, in the first sermon he ever preached, found the whole audience, upon his getting into the pulpit, in a disposition no way favourable to his intentions. Their nods, whispers, or drowsy behaviour, showed him that there was no great profit to be expected from his sowing in a soil so improper. However, he soon changed the disposition of his audience by his manner of beginning. "If," says he, "a cause the most important that could be conceived were to be tried at the bar before qualified judges; if this cause interested ourselves in particular; if the eyes of the whole kingdom were fixed upon the event; if the most eminent counsel were employed on both sides; and if we had heard from our infancy of this yet undetermined trial, would you not all sit with due attention, and warm expectation, to the pleadings on each side? Would not all your hopes and fears be hinged on the final decision? And yet, let me tell you, you have this moment a cause where not one nation, but all the world, are spectators: tried not before a fallible tribunal, but the awful throne of heaven; where not your temporal and transitory interests are the subject of debate, but your eternal happiness or misery; where the cause is still undetermined, but, perhaps, the very moment I am speaking, may fix the irrevocable decree that shall last for ever; and yet, notwithstanding all this, you can hardly sit with patience to hear the tidings of your own salvation. I plead the cause of heaven, and yet I am scarcely attended to." What an admirable address! O ye sleepy hearers, read it and reform.

SLANDER.

WHILE in the present state, we must prepare for and expect the at-tacks of slander and malevolence. If we are ever so poor and obscure, the tongue of calumny will find us out: or ever so wise and conspicuous, the spirit of invective will assault us. "Cherish good humour, (says one,) paint pleasure in your face, endeavour by your pleasing deportment to communicate happiness to all about you; be, if I may speak so, the life and soul of society; and it will be said you are not solid; you have the unworthy ambition of becoming the amusement of mankind. Put on an austere air; engrave on your countenance, if I may speak thus, the great truths that fill your soul; and you will be taxed with pharisaism and hypocrisy; it will be said that you put on a fair outside to render yourself venerable; but that under all this appearance very likely you conceal an impious, irreligious heart. Take a middle way; regulate your conduct by times and places; weep with them that weep, and rejoice with them that rejoice; and you will be accused of lukewarmness. Pick your company, confine yourself to a small circle, make it a law to speak freely only to a few select friends, who will bear with your weaknesses, and who know your good qualities; and you will be accused of pride and arrogance: it will be said that you think the rest of mankind unworthy of your company; and that you pretend wisdom and taste are excluded from all societies, except such as you deign to frequent. Go every where, and, in a spirit of the utmost condescension, converse with every individual of mankind; and it will be said that you are unsteady; a city, a province cannot satisfy you; you lay all the universe under contribution, and oblige the whole world to try to satiate your unbounded love of pleasure."

A Persian soldier, who was heard reviling Alexander the Great, was well admonished by his officer; "*Sir, you are paid to fight against Alexander, and not to rail at him.*" May we not say of mankind at large, that they are bound to pray for their enemies, and not to rail at them ?

Among the Romans there was a law, that if any servant who had been set free slandered his former master, the master might bring him into bondage again, and take from him all the favours he had bestowed on him.

Augustine had a distich written on his table, which intimated, that whoever attacked the character of the absent were to be excluded. Such a distich, in modern times, I think, would be very serviceable.

When any one was speaking ill of another, in the presence of Peter the Great, he at first listened to him attentively, and then interrupted him. "Is there not," said he, "a fair side also to the character of the person of whom you are speaking ? Come, tell me what good qualities you have remarked about him." One would think this monarch had learnt that precept—"Speak not evil one of another."

The famous Boerhaave was one not easily moved by detraction. He used to say, " The sparks of calumny will be presently extinct of themselves, unless you blow them." It was a good remark of another, that " the malice of ill tongues cast upon a good man is only like a mouthful of smoke blown upon a diamond, which, though it clouds its beauty for the present, yet it is easily rubbed off, and the gem restored, with little trouble to its owner."

The late Rev. Mr. Pearce, of Birmingham, was a man of an excellent spirit. It was a rule with him to discourage all evil speaking; nor would he approve of just censure, unless some good and necessary end were to be answered by it. Two of his distant friends being at his house together, one of them, during the absence of the other, suggested something to his disadvantage. He put a stop to the conversation by answering, "He is here: take him aside, and tell him of it by himself: you may do him good."

STUDY.

WHILE some are lost in dissipation and thoughtlessness, there are others whose minds are absorbed in diligent and laborious study. And, indeed, he who has no taste for intellectual pleasures, seems to be but a small remove from the animal tribes. He who cannot bear thinking, or at least has no disposition for investigation, but takes things merely from the report of others, or as they are imposed upon him by custom or prejudice, is a mere slave, and hardly can be wise. It is a remark, worthy of attention, that " *Thinking has been one of the least exerted privileges of cultivated humanity.*" It must be confessed there is too much truth in the observation. That all men think, is not denied; but, alas ! few think with propriety, few bend their thoughts to right objects, few divest themselves of the shackles of ignorance and custom : to be, however, intelligent, to be candid, to be useful, a man should give himself to application. In a word, he who would be happy in himself, respectable in society, and a blessing to the world, should industriously persevere in the study of those subjects which are calculated to enlarge the mind, meliorate the disposition, and promote the best interests of mankind.

Instances of intense Study, &c.

Demosthenes' application to study was surprising. To be the more removed from noise, and less subject to distraction, he caused a small chamber to be made for him under ground, in which he shut himself up sometime for whole months, shaving on purpose half his head and face, that he might not be in a condition to go abroad. It was there, by the light of a small lamp, he composed his admirable orations, which were said, by those who envied him, to smell of the oil, to imply that they were too elaborate. "It is plain," replied he, " your's did not cost you so much trouble." He rose very early in the morning, and used to say, that "he was sorry when any workman was at his business before him." He copied Thucydides' History eight times, with his own hand, in order to render the style of that great man familiar to him.

Adrian Turnebus, an illustrious French critic, was indefatigable in his application to study, insomuch that it was said of him, as it was of Budæus, that he spent some hours in study even on the day he was married.

Frederick Morel had so strong an attachment to study, that, when he was informed of his wife's being at the point of death, he would not lay down his pen till he had finished what he was upon; and when she was dead, as she was before they could prevail upon him to stir, he was only heard to reply coldly, "*I am very sorry ; she was a good woman.*"

Sir Isaac Newton, it is said, when he had any mathematical problems or solutions in his mind, would never quit the subject on any account. Dinner has been often three hours ready for him before he could be brought to table. His man often said of him, that, when he has been getting up of a morning, he has sometimes begun to dress, and with one leg in his breeches sat down again on the bed, where he has remained for hours before he has got his clothes on.

Mr. Abraham Sharp, the astronomer, through his love of study, was very irregular as to his meals, which he frequently took in the following manner : a little square hole, something like a window, made a communication between the room where he usually studied and another chamber in the house where a servant could enter ; and before this hole he had contrived a sliding-board ; the servant always placed his victuals in this hole, without speaking a word, or making the least noise ; and when he had a little leisure he visited his cupboard, to see what it contained to satisfy his hunger or thirst. But it often happened that the break-

fast, the dinner, and the supper remained untouched by him when the servant went to remove what was left; so deeply was he sometimes engaged in his calculations and solemn musings. It is related, that, at one time, after his provisions had been neglected for a long season, his family being uneasy, resolved to break in upon his retirement ; he complained, but with great mildness, that they had disconcerted his thoughts in a chain of calculations which had cost him intense application for three days successively. On an old oak table, where, for a long course of years, he used to write, cavities might easily be perceived, worn by the perpetual rubbing of his arms and elbows.

Such has been the pleasure arising from reading and study, that even the full prospect of death itself has not eradicated the love for it.

Of the famous Hooker it is related, that, notwithstanding his severe and lingering illness, he continued his studies to the last. He strove particularly to finish his Ecclesiastical Polity, and said often to a friend who visited him daily, that "he did not beg a long life of God for any other reason, but to live to finish the three remaining books of Polity ; and then, "Lord, let thy servant depart in peace," which was his usual expression. A few days before his death his house was robbed; of which having notice he asked "are my books and written papers safe?" And being answered that they were, "Then," said he, "it matters not, for no other loss can trouble me."

A singular circumstance is related of the illustrious Boerhaave, who kept feeling his pulse, the morning of his death, to see whether it would beat till a book he was eager to see was published. He read the book, and said, "Now the business of life is over."

When Gesner found his last hour approaching, he gave orders to be carried into his study, that he might meet death in a place which had been most agreeable to him all his life.

The progress of Old age in New Studies.

Cato, at eighty years of age, thought proper to learn Greek; and Plutarch, almost as late in life, Latin.

Henry Spelman, having neglected the sciences in his youth, cultivated them at fifty years, and became a proficient.

Fairfax, after having been general of the parliamentary forces, retired to Oxford to take his degrees in law.

Colbert, the famous French minister, almost at sixty returned to his Latin and law studies.

Tellier, the chancellor of France learnt logic merely for an amusement, to dispute with his grand-children.

Though the above instances are somewhat singular, yet young persons should beware of procrastination, and not lose the present moment in expectation of improving the future. Very few are capable of making any proficiency under the decrepitude of old age, and when they have been long accustomed to negligent habits. Great defects and indigested erudition have often characterised the οψιμαθεις, or "late learned."

Singular Methods of Study.

It is recorded of Anthony Magliabechi, that his attention was continually absorbed, day and night, among his books. An old cloak served him for a gown in the day, and for bed clothes at night. He had one straw chair for his table, and another for his bed, in which he generally remained fixed, in the midst of a heap of volumes and papers, until he was overpowered with sleep. With all this intense application to reading, his knowledge was well estimated in the observation applied to him, that he was a learned man among booksellers, and a bookseller among the learned.

John Williams, an English prelate, used to study in a particular way. He used to allot one month to a certain province, esteeming variety almost as refreshing as cessation from labour;

at the end of which, he would take up some other matter, and so on till he came round to his former courses. This method he observed, especially in his theological studies, and he found his account in it.

David Blondel, a Protestant minister, in the 17th century, had been esteemed one of those who had the greatest knowledge of ecclesiastical and civil history. He had a very singular way of studying : he lay on the ground, and had round about him the books which he wanted for the work he was about.

Descartes used to lie in bed sixteen hours every day, with the curtains drawn, and the windows shut. He imagined, that in that easy and undisturbed situation, he had more command over his mind, than when it was interrupted by external objects. And Malebranche used to meditate with his windows shut, as the light was a disturbance to him.

Mezerai, the famous historian, used to study and write by candlelight, even at noonday in summer; and, as if there had been no sun in the world, always waited upon his company to the door with a candle in his hand.

The famous Mr. Brindley, when any extraordinary difficulty occurred to him, in the execution of his works, generally retired to bed, and has been known to lie there one, two, or three days, till he had surmounted it. He would then get up and execute his design without any drawing, or model, for he had an extraordinary memory, and carried every thing in his head.

Anecdotes, including advice to Students.

He who would wish to make proficiency in any science, must give himself to study. Knowledge is not to be gained by wishing, nor acquired by dignity and wealth. Application is necessary both for prince and peasant. Many, in elevated situations, are very desirous of the honour, but averse to the labour, of intellectual attainments.

Euclid was asked, one day, by King Ptolemæus Lagus, "Whether there was not a shorter and easier way to the knowledge of geometry than that which he had laid down in his Elements?" He answered, that "there was, indeed, no royal road to geometry." In the same manner, when Alexander wanted to learn geometry by some easier and shorter method, he was told by his preceptor, that "he must here be content to travel the same road with others; for that all things of this nature were equally difficult to prince and people." We may apply this observation to learning in general. If we wish to enjoy the sweets, we must encounter the difficulties of acquisition. The student must not be always in the world, or living at his ease, if he wish to enlarge his mind, inform his judgment, or improve his powers; he must read, think, remember, compare, consult, and digest, in order to be wise and useful.

In respect to study, there are some necessary precautions to be attended to, both as to the body and the mind. Hence, a minister of the gospel used to give this advice to young students. 1. That they should not buy too many books, as that would hurt their pockets. 2. That they should not engage in any amorous pursuits, as that would hurt the mind; and, 3. That they should not sit up late at night, as that would injure their health.

Dr. Whitaker gave the following three rules to Mr. Boyce, when a student:—1. To study always standing. 2. Never to study close to a window. 3. Never to go to bed with his feet cold.

Night studies are very prejudicial to the constitution, and ought to be avoided by all who wish to prolong their lives, and to be useful in their day and generation. Thuanus tells us of Acidalius, that his excessive application to study, was the occasion of his untimely death; and that his sitting up at nights, brought upon him a distemper which carried him off in three days, at the age of twenty-eight. Lord Bacon greatly impaired his constitution by this; Hervey and Toplady the same; and, it is said of Dr. Owen, that he would have gladly exchanged all the learning he had gotten by night studies for the health he had lost thereby. "Nocturnal studies (says Dr. Knox,) too long and too closely continued, seldom fail to injure the eyes, and, together with them, the whole nervous system. They who are impelled by necessity to work by night and by day, must, indeed, submit with patience to their destiny; but that he who is master of his time, should chain himself down to a more exhausting toil than the labour of the galley slave, is a species of folly approaching to insanity. And, indeed, I know of nothing more likely to produce madness, than intemperate study, with want of exercise, want of air, and want of sleep. It will, after all, be but a poor comfort, to have gone through a whole library, and to have lost our eyes and our senses in the course of the laborious progress."

However fond of study, therefore, let the student pay some attention to health. It is said of Euripides, the tragedian, that he used to retire to a dark cave to compose his tragedies; and of Demosthenes, the Grecian orator, that he chose a place for study where nothing could be heard or seen; but, with all deference to such venerable names, we cannot help condemning their taste. A man may surely think to as good a purpose in an elegant apartment, as in a cave; and may have as happy conceptions where the all-cheering rays of the sun render the air wholesome, as in places where they never enter.

Charles V., during his celebrated solitude, sometimes cultivated the plants in his garden with his own hands, and sometimes rode out in the neighbourhood; and often relieved his mind in forming curious works of mechanism. Descartes spent the afternoon in the conversation of his friends, and in the cultivation of a

10

small garden. After having, in the morning, settled the place of a planet, in the evening he would amuse himself with watering a flower.— Barclay, in his leisure hours, was a florist. Balzac amused himself with making pastils. Peiresc found his amusements amongst his medals and his antiquarian curiosities. Rohault wandered from shop to shop to observe the mechanics labour. Cardinal de Richlieu, amongst all his great occupations, found a recreation in violent exercise, such as jumping, &c. It is said of the very laborious Mr. Poole, that his common rule was, while he was engaged in writing his famous Synopsis, to rise about three or four o'clock in the morning, and continue his studies till the afternoon was pretty far advanced, when he went abroad, and spent the evening at some friend's house, in cheerful conversation.

SUPERSTITION.

A JUDICIOUS history of superstition, it has been observed, would be a curious and entertaining work, and would exhibit the human character in a remarkable point of view. The general features of it have been the same in all ages; but it assumes certain peculiarities, according to the diversity of character of different nations. It gained admission into the science of medicine at an early period; it prevailed, also, in natural philosophy; and every one knows the prevalence it has had in the religious world.

Simeon, a Syrian Shepherd, after addicting himself to the senseless austerities of the monkish life, passed thirty-seven years standing on the top of five pillars, of six, twelve, twenty-two, thirty-six, and forty cubits high. Habit and exercise instructed him to maintain his situation without fear or giddiness, and successively to assume the different postures of devotion. He sometimes prayed in an erect attitude, with his outstretched arms in the figure of a cross; but his most familiar practice was that of bending his meagre skeleton from the forehead to the feet; and a curious spectator, after numbering twelve hundred and forty-four repetitions, at length desisted from the endless account. The progress of an ulcer in his thigh, might shorten, but it could not disturb, this *celestial* life; for he expired without descending from his column.

Charles V. as an expiation for his sins, gave himself discipline in secret, with such severity, that the whip of cords which he employed as the instrument of his punishment was found, after his decease, tinged with his blood. Nor was he satisfied with these acts of mortification. The timorous and distrustful solicitude which always accompanies superstition, still continued to disquiet him, and unabated by all that he had done, prompted him to aim at something extraordinary, at some new and singular act of piety, that would display his zeal, and merit the favour of heaven. The act on which he fixed was as wild and uncommon as any that superstition ever suggested to a disordered fancy. He resolved to celebrate his own obsequies before his death. He ordered his tomb to be erected in the chapel of the monastery. His domestics marched thither in funeral procession, with black tapers in their hands. He himself followed in his shroud. He was laid in his coffin with much solemnity. The service for the dead was chanted; and Charles joined in the prayer which was offered up for the rest of his soul, mingling his tears with those which his attendants shed, as if they had been celebrating a real funeral. The ceremony closed with sprinkling holy water on the coffin in the usual form; and, all the assistants retiring, the doors of the chapel were shut. Then Charles rose out of the coffin, and withdrew to his apartment, full of those awful sentiments which such a singular solemnity was calculated to inspire. But either the fatiguing length of the ceremony, or the impression which this image of death left upon his mind, affected him so much, that the next day he was seized with a fever. His feeble frame could not long resist its violence; and he expired soon after, aged 58 years, 6 months, and 21 days.

"I knew a Russian princess," says one, "who had always a large silver crucifix following her in a separate carriage, and which she usually placed in her bed-chamber. When any thing fortunate had happened to her in the course of the day, and she was satisfied with her admirers, she had lighted candles placed about the crucifix, and said to it in a familiar style, "See now, as you have been very good to day, you shall be treated well: you shall have candles all night; I will love you; I will pray to you." If, on the contrary, any thing occurred to vex this lady, she had the candles put out: forbade the servants to pay any homage to the poor image; and loaded it with reproaches and revilings." Although superstition is generally the mark of a weak mind, such is the infirmity of human nature, that we may find many instances of it among men of the most sublime genius and most enlightened minds. Socrates believed that he was guided by a demon. Lord Bacon believed in witchcraft; and relates that he was cured of warts by rubbing them with a piece of lard with the skin on, and then nailing it with the fat on the post of a chamber window facing the sun. Henry IV. one of the most illustrious of monarchs, was very uneasy before his assassination on account of some prophecies. The enlightened Cudworth defended prophecies in general, and called those who opposed the belief of witchcraft by the name of Atheists.

SWEARING AND PROFANITY.

THERE is nothing so low, vulgar, and wicked, as swearing, and it is surprising that men, who wish to be considered as wise and polite, should be found so much in the habit of it. It is not, however, peculiar to the in-ferior circles of life, but prevails among the great and honourable, so called. Wise and suitable reproofs of this sin have, however, had a good effect, as the following instances show:—

Mr. John Howe being at dinner with some persons of fashion, a gentleman expatiated largely in praise of Charles I. and made some disagreeable reflections upon others. Mr. Howe, observing that he mixed many horrid oaths with his discourse, took the liberty to say, that, in his humble opinion, he had omitted one great excellence in the character of that prince; which, when the gentleman pressed him to mention, and waited with impatience to hear it, he told him this: "*that he was never heard to swear an oath in common conversation.*" The gentleman took the reproof, and promised to break off the practice.

Another time he passed two persons of quality who were talking with great eagerness, and d———d each other repeatedly. Upon which, taking off his hat, he said to them, "I pray God save you both;" for which they both gave him their thanks.

At the time when the Conformity Bill was debated in Parliament, Mr. Howe passed a noble Lord in a chair in St. James's Park, who sent his footman to call him, desiring to speak with him on this subject. In the conversation speaking of the opponents of the dissenters, he said, "D—n these wretches, for they are mad." Mr. Howe, who was no stranger to the nobleman, expressed great satisfaction in the thought, that there is a God who governs the world, who will finally make retribution to all according to their present characters; "And he, my Lord, has declared, he will make a difference between him that sweareth and him that feareth an oath." The nobleman was struck with the hint, and said, "*I thank you, Sir, for your freedom. I take your meaning, and shall endeavour to make a good use of it.*" Mr. Howe, replied, " My lord, I have more reason to thank your lordship for saving me the most difficult part of a discourse, which is the *application*."

An Elector of Cologne (who was likewise an Archbishop) one day swearing profanely, asked a peasant, who seemed to wonder, what he was so surprised at ? " To hear an archbishop swear," answered the peasant, " I swear," replied the elector, " not as an archbishop, but as a prince." " But, my lord," said the peasant, " when the prince goes to the devil, what will become of the archbishop ?"

Prince Henry, son of King James I. being at a hunting match, the stag, almost spent, crossed a road where a butcher was passing with his dog. The stag was instantly killed by the dog ; at which the huntsmen were greatly offended, and endeavoured to irritate the prince against the butcher. But his highness answered coolly, " What, if the butcher's dog killed the stag, how could the butcher help it ?" They replied, that, if some princes had been so served, they would have sworn dreadfully. " Away," cried the prince ; " all the pleasure in the world is not worth an oath."

As Mr. Romaine was one day walking in the street with another gentleman, he heard a poor man call upon God to damn him. Mr. R. stopped, took out half-a-crown, and presenting it, said, " My friend, I will give you this if you will repeat that oath." The man started : "What ! Sir," said he, " do you think I will damn my soul for half-a-crown ?" Mr. R. answered, " As you did it just now for nothing, I could not suppose you would refuse to do it for a reward !" The poor creature, struck with this reproof, as Mr. R. intended he should be, replied, " God bless and reward you, Sir, whoever you are. I believe you have saved my soul : I hope I shall never swear again while I live."

The late Dr. Gifford, as he was once showing the British Museum to strangers, was very much vexed by the profane conversation of a young gentleman who was present. The doctor, taking an ancient copy of the Septuagint, and showing it to him, " O !" said the gentleman, " I can read this." " Well," said the doctor, "read that passage," pointing to the Third Command. Here the gentleman was so struck, that he immediately desisted from swearing.

Swearing, we find, is prohibited by the law of the land, as well as by the law of God. By the 19th G. II. c. 21, s. 1,4, 6,7, if any person shall profanely curse or swear, and be thereof convicted, on the oath of one witness, before one Justice of the Peace, or by confession ; every person so offending shall forfeit as followeth, viz. Every daylabourer, common soldier, sailor, or seaman, 1s. and every other person under the degree of a gentleman, 2s. and every person of or above the degree of a gentleman, 5s. And if he shall, after conviction, offend a second time, he shall forfeit double ; and for every other offence, after a second conviction, treble. And if he do not immediately pay down the sum so forfeited, he shall be sent to the house of correction. And if any Justice or Mayor shall wilfully and wittingly omit the performance of his duty in the execution of this Act, he shall forfeit 5l. And if any constable or other peace-officer shall omit the performance of his duty in the execution of this Act, he shall forfeit 40s.

TACITURNITY.

" He who knows not how to be silent, knows not how to speak," said Pittacus, "and he that hath knowledge, spareth his words," said Solomon ; that is, " He will be few of his words, as being afraid of speaking amiss. He that hath knowledge, and aims to do good with it, is careful, when he doth speak, to speak to the purpose, and, therefore, saith little, that he may take time to deliberate upon it. He spares his words, because they are better spared than ill-spent." [Henry.]

An ancient hermit, after he had

heard the first verse of the 39th Psalm, "I will take heed to my ways, that I offend not with my tongue," refused to hear the second, saying, "the first was lesson sufficient for him." The reader of this verse to him, asked him, many years after, "whether he had learned to reduce this lesson to practice?"—"Nineteen years," replied the hermit, "have I been trying, and have hardly attained the practice." In order to speak well, we must speak but little, remembering always the maxim of St. James,—"If any man seem to be religious, and bridleth not his tongue, this man's religion is vain." Plutarch says of Epaminondas, that no man knew more, and spake less than he did.

He was a wise philosopher who bound his scholars to a silence of five years, that they might not use their tongues till they knew how to govern them, nor speak till they had something to say.

Addison, who could write so agreeably on all subjects, is well known to have been given to taciturnity; and Dr. Johnson, with all his brilliant and masterly powers, could not be said to possess companionable *agrément.*

"It is astonishing," says Pavillon, "that among the numerous rules for teaching men to speak, there have been none hitherto laid down for teaching them to be silent. Yet this certainly requires most skill; since we are prompted by nature to speak, while silence is a species of restraint. How many are great talkers—or great orators, if that sounds better, compared with the silent? We have the art of saying much *on* a little, whereas we most want the art of saying much *in* a little. What is rhetoric, with all its boasted figures? An ignorant woman, agitated by strong passions, is as energetic as Cicero. It is true that she does not, like Cicero, know the names of the several figures of speech, which her emotion has employed; a mighty science, truly, after so laborious a stu-

dy as that of rhetoric! But the art of silence, is quite a different affair; it is not acquired by passion, but by vigilance and reason: and how much more difficult it is to comply with the precepts of the latter than the former, need hardly be urged.

"In ancient as well as in modern history, we every where meet with orators; nothing is more common than accounts of men who talked a great deal, and talked well; but the glorious character of a silent man has only, as it appears to me, been conferred on a single character. He, indeed, it must be confessed, acted up to it, and was at the head of one of the greatest designs ever executed. I mean William, Prince of Orange, who made such a formidable stand against Spain, and founded the Commonwealth of the United Provinces. Cardinal Granville, a Spanish statesman, well knew the importance of this person's taciturnity; for, receiving advice that Count Egmont and Count Horn, were both taken, he asked whether ' *the silent man,*' also, was apprehended; and, being answered in the negative, he replied— ' *Ah! then nothing is done.*'"

Howell, clerk to the most honourable Privy Council of King Charles the First, in his familiar letters, speaks thus in favour of silence :— "There is a saying, which carrieth no little weight with it, that 'Parvus amor loquitur, ingens stupet :'— 'Small love speaks, while great love stands astonished in silence.' The one keeps talking, while the other is struck dumb with amazement : like deep rivers, which, to the eye of the beholder, seem to stand still, while small, shallow rivulets, keep a noise; or, like empty casks, that make an obstreperous hollow sound, which they would not do, were they replenished, and full of substance."

A babbler, being at table with a number of persons, among whom was one of the seven sages of Greece, expressed his astonishment that a man so wise did not utter a single word. The sage instantly replied, "*A fool* cannot hold his tongue." "Take away from the conversations of the generality of persons, in most companies, their slanders against the absent, their shallow criticisms, their ignorant political opinions, and their barren witticisms against religion, and you will find, that, on a just calculation, those who speak the most, do not say more than those who keep a profound silence. It is for this reason, that a man of sense always prefers passing even for stupid, by his taciturnity, to the infamous talent of shining at the expense of religion, of the laws, of men of genius, and of his neighbours, to divert those who are falsely named great wits, or rejoice the hearts of men who want judgment, justice, and humanity."

INSTANCES OF GOOD TEMPERS AND FORGIVENESS.

NOTHING is more congenial to Christianity, than a spirit of forgiveness. Jesus Christ constantly inculcated and exemplified it; and his followers, in proportion as they are like him, will manifest the same spirit. There have been Alexanders and Cæsars, who have boasted of conquering the world, but, after all, never arrived to the honour of swaying the sceptre over themselves, but have continued resentful and rapacious, passionate and vicious, to the last. Christianity teaches us, however, to repress the rising passions, forgive the offending party, and to do good even to those who hate us. Happy is the man who lives under the influence of this spirit; for "he that is slow to anger, is better than the mighty ; and he that ruleth his spirit, than he that taketh a city."

"What great matter," said a heathen to a Christian, while he was beating him almost to death, "what great matter did Christ ever do for thee ?"—" Even this," said the Christian; "that I can forgive you, though you use me thus cruelly."

Sir Walter Raleigh, a man of known courage and honour, being very injuriously treated by a hot-headed rash youth, who next proceeded to challenge him, and, on his refusal, spit in his face, and that too in public, the knight, taking out his handkerchief with great calmness, made him only this reply: " Young man, if I could as easily wipe your blood from my conscience, as I can this injury from my face, I would this moment take away your life." The consequence was, that the youth, with a sudden and strong sense of his misbehaviour, fell on his knees, and begged forgiveness.

It was said of Archbishop Cranmer, that the way to have him one's friend, was to do him an unkindness. Of Archbishop Ussher, also, it is said, that he was of so sweet a temper, that he never was known to do an ill office to any one, or to be revenged of any who had injured him. Of Mr. Hervey, also, it is recorded, that he was never known to be in a passion. Of how few can this be said ! It would be well, however, could we learn to attain this victory over ourselves. It would not only produce happiness in our own minds, but bear an indelible impression on the minds of others. "For the tempers and lives of men," says Mr. Fuller, " are books for common people to read, and they will read them, though they should read nothing else."

Such was the sweet temper and amiable conduct of the Rev. Philip Henry, (father to the celebrated commentator,) that the people gave him the title of " Heavenly Henry ;" and by this title he was commonly known through all the country. He used to observe, that in almost every quarrel there was a fault on both sides ; and that generally they were most in fault that were most forward and clamorous in their complaints. To a woman who complained to him how bad a husband she had, and asked, (after a long complaint which he patiently heard) " what would you have me to do now ?" " Why, truly," he replied, " I would have you go home, and *be a better wife to him, and then you will find that he will be a better husband to you.*" Labouring to persuade one to forgive an injury that was done him, he argued thus: "*Are you not a Christian?*" and followed that argument so close, that at length he prevailed.

Sir Isaac Newton's temper, it is said, was so equable and mild, that no accident could disturb it; a remarkable instance of which is related as follows: Sir Isaac had a favourite little dog, which he called Diamond. Being one evening called out of his study into the next room, Diamond was left behind. When Sir Isaac returned, having been absent but a few minutes, he had the mortification to find that Diamond had overset a lighted candle among some papers, (the nearly finished labour of many years,) which soon were in flames, and almost consumed to ashes. This loss, as Sir Isaac was then very far advanced in years, was irretrievable; yet, without once striking the dog, he only rebuked him with this exclamation: "Oh, Diamond! Diamond! you little know the mischief you have done!"

The famous Dr. Boerhaave was once asked by a friend, who admired his patience under provocations, "Whether he knew what it was to be angry, and by what means he had so entirely suppressed that impetuous and ungovernable passion?" He answered, with the utmost frankness and sincerity, that "he was naturally quick of resentment, but that he had, by daily prayer and meditation, at length attained to this mastery over himself."

It is related of Dr. Hough, Bishop of Worcester, who was remarkable for the evenness of his temper, that having a good deal of company at his house, a gentleman present desired his lordship to show him a curious weather-glass, which the Bishop had lately purchased, and which cost him above thirty guineas. The servant was accordingly ordered to bring it; who in delivering it to the gentle-man, unfortunately let it fall, and broke it all to pieces. The company were all a little deranged from this accident, but particularly the gentleman who asked to see it, and who was making many apologies for the acci-dent. "*Be under no concern, my dear Sir!*" said the Bishop, smiling; "*I think it rather a lucky omen: we have hitherto had a dry season, and now I hope we shall have some rain; for I protest I do not remember ever to have seen the glass so low in my life.*"

The Duke of Marlborough possessed great command of temper, and never permitted it to be ruffled by little things, in which even the greatest men have been occasionally found unguarded. As he was one day riding with Commissary Marriot, it began to rain, and he called to his servant for his cloak. The servant not bringing it immediately, he called for it again. The servant, being embarrassed with the straps and buckles, did not come up to him. At last, it raining very hard, the Duke called to him again, and asked him what he was about, that he did not bring his cloak. "You may stay, Sir, (grumbles the fellow,) if it rains cats and dogs, till I can get at it." The Duke turned round to Marriot, and said, very coolly, "Now I would not be of that fellow's temper for all the world."

Dr. Goldsmith's impetuosity of temper was sometimes great, but this was corrected by a moment's reflection. His servants have been known, upon this occasion, purposely to throw themselves in his way, that they might profit by it immediately after; for he who had the good fortune to be reproved was certain of being rewarded for it.

The late Rev. Mr. Brewer, of Stepney, was a man remarkable for a peaceful temper. He had adopted certain maxims, by the constant observance of which he maintained, in all his civil, domestic, and sacred connexions, the utmost harmony, peace, and union; for he used to say, "*He was deaf, when he could hear; blind, when he could see; dumb, when he could speak; that he extinguished all the fires he could, and never kindled any."*

One cannot but reflect on the great advantages of such a disposition.—Men may call it weakness and effeminacy; but without it there is no real felicity. He who is determined to sacrifice every thing to his own passion and temper, and will never submit in the least to any of his fellow-creatures, will find it not only a barrier to his felicity, but a stain upon his character.

"Our state in this life resembles that of passengers in a crowded street: every one, pursuing the way in which business or pleasure leads him, meets with obstacles and interruptions from others bent upon the same errand. If all resolve to keep their road directly onward, without the least attention to others, neither yielding a little to let them pass, nor regulating their steps and motions in some correspondence with those of the rest, universal confusion must ensue, and none will be able to advance with tolerable speed. Whereas, if every one attends a little to the accommodation of his neighbour as well as his own, and complies with such rules as are laid down for the general advantage, all may proceed with reasonable convenience and expedition. In the march of life, no one's path lies so clear as not in some degree to cross another's; and if each be determined, with unyielding sturdiness, to keep his own line, it is impossible but he must both give and receive many a rude shock."

TEMPERANCE.

TEMPERANCE has been called the best physic. It is certainly conducive to health, and not only so, but to cheerfulness likewise. As intemperance clogs the body, wastes the property, and stupifies the mind, so temperance is fruitful of a variety of blessings and comforts unknown to the voluptuous.

It is said of Diogenes, that, meeting a young man who was going to a feast, he took him up in the street, and carried him home to his friends, as one who was running into imminent danger, had he not prevented him.

"What would that philosopher have said, had he been present (says Addison) at the gluttony of a modern meal? Would not he have thought the master of a family mad, and have begged his servants to have tied down his hands, had he seen him devour fowl, fish, and flesh; swallow oil and vinegar, wine and spices; throw down salads of twenty different herbs, sauces of an hundred ingredients, confections and fruits of numberless sweets and flavour?—What counter-ferments must such a medley of intemperance produce in the body! For my part, when I behold a fashionable table set out in all its magnificence, I fancy that I see gouts and dropsies, fevers and lethargies, with other innumerable distempers, lying in ambuscade among the dishes."

Lewis Cornaro, a Venetian of noble extraction, was memorable for having lived healthful and active to above 100 years of age, by a rigid course of temperance. In his youth he was of a weak constitution, and, by irregular indulgence, reduced himself, at about forty years of age, to the brink of the grave, under a complication of disorders; at which extremity he was told, that he had no other chance of his life, but by becoming sober and temperate. Being wise enough to adopt this wholesome counsel, he reduced himself to a regimen, of which there are very few examples. He allowed himself no more than twelve ounces of food and fourteen ounces of liquor each day, which became so habitual to him, that when he was about seventy years old, the experiment of adding two ounces to each, by the advice of his friends, had like to have proved fatal to him. At eighty-three he wrote a treatise, which has been translated into English, and often printed, entitled,

" Sure and certain Methods of attaining a long and healthful Life ;" in which he relates his own story, and extols temperance to a degree of enthusiasm. At length, the yolk of an egg became sufficient for a meal, and sometimes for two, until he died with much ease and composure.

" A knight of my acquaintance," says Dr. Cotton Mather, " visiting the famous Dr. Lower in his last sickness, asked him for the best advice he could give him, how to preserve his health and prolong his life ? The Doctor only answered him, " Do not eat too much." After some other discourse, the knight, not imagining that the Doctor had thoroughly answered his inquiry, repeated it. The Doctor thereupon only repeated his answer, " Why, did I not tell you, do not eat too much ?" and farther said not.

Sir Theodore Mayem,on his deathbed, gave this advice to a noble friend that asked his counsel for the preservation of health —" Be moderate in your diet, use much exercise and little physic."

Sully, the great statesman of France, kept up always at the table of Villebon, the frugality to which he had been accustomed in early life in the army. His table consisted of a few dishes dressed in the plainest and most simple manner. The courtiers reproached him often with the simplicity of his table. He used to reply, in the words of an ancient, " If the guests are men of sense, there is sufficient for them ; if they are not, I can very well dispense with their company."

TIME.

It is of the utmost consequence that we improve our time. " Never," says one, " delay till to-morrow, what reason and conscience tell you ought to be performed to-day. To-morrow is not your's, and, though you should live to enjoy it, you must not overload it with a burden not its own." " God (says another,) who is liberal and generous in all other gifts, teaches us,

by the wise economy of his Providence, how circumspect we ought to be in the right management of our time ; for he never gives us two moments together ; he gives us only the second as he takes away the first, and keeps the third in his hands, leaving us in an absolute uncertainty whether he will give it us or not."

Grotius used to take for his motto, " Hora ruit," to put himself in continual remembrance, that he should usefully employ that time which was flying away with extreme rapidity ; and yet, so great a sense had he of the non-improvement of it, that, with all his learning, when he came to die, he exclaimed, " I have wasted my life in incessant toil, and have done nothing."

Dr. Cotton Mather was so careful to redeem his time, that to prevent the tediousness of visits, he wrote over his study door, in capital letters —" BE SHORT."

Mr. Henry Jessey, a nonconformist minister, had the following motto put over his study door :

Amice quisquis huc ades,
Aut agito paucis aut abi,
Aut me laborantem adjuva.

" Whatever friend comes hither,
Despatch in brief, or go,
Or help me busied too." H. J.

Titus, the Roman Emperor, throughout the course of his whole life, called himself to an account every night for the actions of the past day ; and, as often as he found he had slipped any one day without doing good, he entered upon his diary this memorial, " Perdidi diem ;" I have lost a day. Thus may every man say, who suffers a day to pass without doing something for God, for his soul, or for his fellow-creatures.

" Take care of the pence, for the pounds will take care of themselves," was a very just and sensible reflection of old Mr. Loundes, the famous Secretary of the Treasury under William III., Anne, and George I. " I therefore recommend to you," says an author, " to take care of minutes, for hours will take care of themselves.

Be doing something or other all day long, and not neglect half hours and quarters of hours, which, at the year's end, amount to a great sum."

"An Italian philosopher," says Dr. Johnson, "expressed in his motto, that *time was his estate;* an estate, indeed, which will produce nothing without cultivation, but will always abundantly repay the labours of industry, and satisfy the most extensive desires, if no part of it be suffered to be wasted by negligence, to be overrun with noxious plants, or laid out for show rather than for use."

VANITY OF THE WORLD.

"THERE are few people in the word," says Saurin, "who do not form in their minds agreeable plans of happiness, made up of future flattering prospects, which have no foundation except in their own fancies. The disposition of mind, which is so general among mankind, is also one of the principal causes of their immoderate desire to live. Some have questioned whether any mortal were ever so happy as to choose to live his life over again, on condition of passing through all the events through which he had gone from his birth to his last hour. Without investigating this problem, I venture to affirm, that mankind would be much less attached to the world, if they did not flatter themselves with the hope of enjoying more pleasure than they had hitherto experienced. A child fancies, that, as soon as he arrives at a certain stature, he shall enjoy more pleasure than he had enjoyed in his childhood; and this is pardonable in a child. The youth persuades himself that men, who are what they call settled in the world, are incomparably more happy than young people can be at his age. While we think ourselves condemned to live single, solitude seems intolerable; and when we have associated ourselves with others, we regret the happy days we spent in the tranquillity of solitude. Thus we go on from fancy to fancy, and from one chimera to another, till death arrives,

subverts all our imaginary projects of happiness, and makes us know, by our own experience, what the experience of others might have fully taught us long before, that is, that the whole world is vanity; that every state, all ages, and all conditions, have inconveniences peculiar to themselves, and one which is common to them all; I mean, a character of disproportion to our hearts; so that, by changing our situation, we often do no more than change our kind of infelicity."

Nicholas Breakspear, who on his advancement to the popedom, assumed the name of Adrian IV. was, in the early part of his life, reduced to the necessity of submitting to servile offices for bread. He studied in France, where, though he laboured under the pressures of poverty, he made a wonderful progress in learning. One day, on an interview with an intimate friend, he told him, "That all the hardships of his life were nothing in comparison to the Papal Crown;" and speaking of the difficulties and sorrows he had experienced, he observed, "That he had been, as it were, strained through the alembic of affliction."

It was a pertinent discourse of Cineas, dissuading Pyrrhus, from undertaking a war against the Romans; "Sir," said he, "when you have conquered them, what will you do next?" "Then Sicily is near at hand, and easily to master."—"And what when you have conquered Sicily?" "Then we shall pass over to Africk, and take Carthage, which cannot long withstand us."—"When these are conquered, what will be your next attempt?" "Then," said Pyrrhus, "we will fall in upon Greece and Macedon, and recover what we have lost there."—"Well, when all are subdued, what fruit do you expect from all your victories?" "Then," said he, "we will sit down and enjoy ourselves."—"Sir," replied Cineas, "may we not do it now? Have you not already a kingdom of your own? And he that cannot enjoy himself with a kingdom, cannot with the whole world." Such are the designs of men, and so we may answer them. Most are projecting how they can get such an estate ; then how they may raise themselves to honour : and think that their advancement in both will bring them satisfaction. Alas! this will not do. Their desires will still run before them; and they may as well sit down content where they *are*, as where they *hope to be*.

Vetellius, an Emperor of Rome, was so luxurious, that at one supper he had upon his table two thousand fishes of different kinds, and seven thousand flying fowls. He was drawn through the streets of Rome with a halter about his neck, and was put to death.

Dioclesian found a crown so disagreeable, that he cast it off, and retired to a private life. And another said, from his own bitter experience, that if any man knew what cares and dangers were wrapt in a crown, he would not take it up if he saw it lie in the way before him. " The troubles of a whole nation," observes one, " concentre in the throne, and lodge themselves in the royal diadem; so that it may be but too truly said of every prince, that he wears a crown of thorns."

Charles V. Emperor of Germany, King of Spain, and Lord of the Netherlands, was born at Ghent in the year 1500. He is said to have fought sixty battles, in most of which he was victorious; to have obtained six triumphs; conquered four kingdoms; and to have added eight principalities to his dominions : an almost unparalleled instance of worldly prosperity and the greatness of human glory. But all these fruits of his ambition, and all the honours that attended him, could not yield him true and solid satisfaction. Reflecting on the evils and miseries which he had occasioned, and convinced of the emptiness of earthly magnificence, he became disgusted with all the splendor that surrounded

him, and thought it his duty to withdraw from it, and spend the rest of his days in religious retirement. Accordingly he voluntarily resigned all his dominions to his brother and son ; and after taking an affectionate and last farewell of his son, and a numerous retinue of princes and nobility, that respectfully attended him, he repaired to his chosen retreat, which was situated in a vale in Spain, of no great extent, watered by a small brook, and surrounded with rising grounds covered with lofty trees. A deep sense of his frail condition and great imperfection appears to have impressed his mind in this extraordinary resolution, and through the remainder of his life. As soon as he landed in Spain, he fell prostrate on the ground, and, considering himself now as dead to the world, he kissed the earth, and said,—" Naked came I out of my mother's womb, and naked I now return to thee, thou common mother of mankind!"

A remarkable instance of the unsatisfactory nature of all worldly prosperity is afforded by the Emperor Septimus Severus, " Omnia fui, et nihil expidit;" "I have been all things, and all is of little value," was his declaration, after having been raised from an humble station to the Imperial Throne of Rome and the Sovereignty of the World.

Eminence of situation is no proof of superior happiness : hence Pope Adrian VI. had this inscription put on his monument : " Here lies Adrian the Sixth, who was never so unhappy in any period of his life, as in that in which he was a Prince."

I am credibly informed, says Mr. Orton, in his Sermons on Old Age, that a person who had lately a large sum of money left to him to distribute in charity, had application made to him for a share of it from no less than thirty persons who had rode in their own coaches.

From the above circumstances we may learn to moderate our desires, and not to depend on any fascinating situation or earthly good, however

I

alluring : not, indeed, that we are to conclude that temporal blessings are to be undervalued, and that terren enjoyments are to be neglected altogether. "Nothing," as one observes, "except the grossest stupidity and ingratitude, can render us insensible to temporal prosperity, and to the external means of happiness, when Providence thinks fit to bestow them upon us. When our cup overflows with blessings, and we are surrounded with every thing which can render life not only comfortable but delightful, shall we, because imperfection is the indelible character of every worldly advantage, give way to melancholy and sorrow, or suffer such gloomy discontent to suppress and render vain every motive to gratitude and joy ? Forbid it reason— Forbid it religion." Let us then attend to the golden mean, neither to expect a heaven in this life, nor to make it a hell by our discontent, impatience, and folly. Let us not depend on futurity, nor " overlook present happiness, in the idle hope that some future period of life will afford us more complete satisfaction ; thus bartering the enjoyment of actual good for the empty shadow of vain expectation."

ANECDOTES OF YOUNG PERSONS AND CHILDREN.

" EARLY piety," says Henry, " it is to be hoped will be *eminent* piety. Those that are good betimes, are likely to be very good. He [Obadiah] that feared God from his youth, feared him greatly."

" Sentiments of piety and virtue," says Mr. Bryson, "cannot be impressed too early on the human mind. They are the origin of respectability in society, give relish to the innocent enjoyments of this life, and happily prepare for the fruition of consummate felicity in the life to come."

It is related of a Mr. Baily, minister of the Gospel in New-England, that from a child he knew the holy Scriptures, and from a child was wise unto salvation ; giving great and constant evidence of it by his habitual fear of God. There was one very remarkable effect of it. His father was a man of very licentious conversation. His mother one day took the child, and calling the family together, made him pray with them. His father coming to understand how the child had prayed with the family, it smote his soul with great conviction, and he became an altered man.

A child of six years of age, being introduced into company for his extraordinary abilities, was asked by a dignified clergyman, "Where God was," with the proffer of an orange. " Tell me (replied the boy) where he is not, and I will give you two."

Dr. Watts's inclination for learning made an early display of itself : it is reported of him that while he was very young, before he could speak plain, when he had any money given him, he would say to his mother, " A book, a book, buy a book." He began to learn Latin at four years old. When he was about seven or eight, he was desired by his mother to write her some lines, as was the custom with the other boys, after the school hours were over, for which she used to reward them with a farthing. The Doctor obeyed, and presented her with the following couplet—

" I write not for a farthing, but to try,
" How I your farthing writers can outvie."

At the age of 21 or 22, he composed great part of his Hymns. The following circumstance gave rise to his making of them : While he was at his father's, at Southampton, the hymns which were sung at the dissenting meeting there, were so little to the gust of Mr. Watts, that he could not forbear complaining of them to his father. His father bade him try what he could do to mend the matter. He did, and had such success in his first essay, that a second hymn was earnestly desired of him, and then a third, and fourth, &c. till in process of time there was such a number of them as to make up a volume.

The excellent Mr. John Shower, when quite a child, was observed constantly to retire to his closet for devotion, and to return in such a frame of mind, as indicated that he had been conversing with heaven.

The famous Mr. Joseph Alleine, when but a school boy, was very studious, and was always known by this character : " The lad that will not play."

Ecclesiastical history furnishes us with the following instance ; At Cæsarea, in Cappadocia, a child named Cyril, in a time of heavy persecution, called continually on the name of Jesus Christ, and neither threats nor blows could divert him from it. Many children of his own age persecuted him ; and his unnatural father, who was a heathen, turned him out of doors. At last they brought him before the criminal judge, who both threatened and entreated him ; but he said, " I rejoice to bear your reproaches : God will receive me ; I am glad that i am expelled out of our house ; I shall have a better mansion. I fear not death, because it will introduce me to a better life."

In the end he was condemned to the flames, with a full expectation that he would recant, and save his life ; but he persisted, saying, " Your fire and your sword are insignificant : I go to a better house, and more excellent riches ; despatch me presently, that I may enjoy them." They did so, and he suffered martyrdom amidst a throng of wondering spectators.

Emelia Geddie, of Hiltown, in Scotland, gave very early indications of an uncommon quickness of parts, and more uncommon seriousness and piety. The first thing remarked in her was, her disposition to make inquiries on the various objects around her, and the improvement she made upon the answers she received. " Ought we not (said she) to love that God who made all these things, and gave them to us ?" She had an early attachment to prayer, and an extraordinary gift in it ; insomuch, that at four years old she prayed in a society of experienced Christians, to which her mother had introduced her, to their great astonishment and edification.

A good man speaking to her one day of prayer, she said, " When I was a child, my mother taught me to pray ; but now the Lord teaches me." Being asked how she knew the Lord's teaching from that of her mother, her reply was, " The Lord makes me both to rejoice and weep ; he makes my heart glad, and gives me new words."

She even raised a little society of young ones like herself, who met for religious exercises, and made her their president. She persevered in a course of extraordinary piety till her death, which was very happy and religious, in her sixteenth year, 1681.

In the life of Mrs. Mary Terry we find the following account of her pious brother. He was a child that read much and thought much, and spent much of his time in walking and pondering by himself. He could never be found without some good book or other in his pocket, even when he was but little above five years old. He was constant to his retirements for secret duty. But that which deserves a particular remark, was a concern which this young child had, some time before he died, for the spiritual welfare of an aged faithful servant, that had been above forty years in the family, and who by weakness was confined to her chamber, having passed the seventieth year of her age. This little child, when not eight years old, would take delight to be with her, and of his own accord discourse of the things of God, and pray with her, in which, as that servant said, he would deliver himself pertinently, and in such an affecting manner, as was wonderful. He continued thus until she died, and was hereby no small help and comfort to that poor servant. Thus out of the mouths of babes and sucklings God perfects praise. He died in the tenth year of his age.

It is said of Dr. Conyers, that he appeared to have had serious impressions from his infancy; and is remembered to have retired at a certain time from his playfellows, when only five years of age, and to have run down a lane to say his prayers. He was very fond of going to church when a little boy; and if he happened to be at play when the bell tolled for any ordinary service of the day, no solicitation of his juvenile companions could restrain his attendance.

Duke Hamilton, from a child, was remarkably serious, and took delight in reading his Bible. When he was about nine years old, and playing about the room, the Duchess told Lady C. E., a relation, that she said to him, "Come, write me a few verses and I'll give you a crown." He sat down and took pen and paper, and in a few minutes produced the following lines :

As o'er the sea-beat shore I took my way,
I met an aged man, who bid me stay ;
"Be wise," said he, "and mark the path you
   go ;
This leads to heaven, and that to hell below ;
The way to life is difficult and steep ;
The broad and easy leads you to the deep."

THE ATHEIST CONVINCED.

THE famous astronomer Athanasius Kircher, having an acquaintance who denied the existence of a Supreme Being, took the following method to convince him of his error upon his own principles. Expecting him upon a visit, he procured a very handsome globe of the starry heavens, which, being placed in a corner of the room in which it could not escape his friend's observation, the latter seized the first occasion to ask from whence it came, and to whom it belonged. "Not to me," said Kircher, "nor was it ever *made by any person*, but came here by mere chance." "That," replied his skeptical friend, "is absolutely impossible : you surely jest." Kircher, however, seriously persisting in his assertion, took occasion to reason with his friend upon his own atheistical principles. "You will not," said he, "believe that this small body originated in *mere* chance; and yet you would contend that those heavenly bodies, of which it is only a faint and diminutive resemblance, came into existence without order and design." Pursuing this chain of reasoning, his friend was at first confounded, in the next place convinced, and ultimately joined in a cordial acknowledgment of the absurdity of denying the existence of a God.

The following account of the *Atheist's Creed* drawn up by Archbishop Tillotson, will show us how unreasonable, disinteresting, and uncomfortable, such a system must be. "The atheist believes that there is no God, nor possibly can be ; and consequently that the wise as well as unwise of all ages have been mistaken, except himself and a few more. He believes that either all the world have been frighted with an apparition of their own fancy, or that they have most unnaturally conspired together to cozen themselves ; or that this notion of a God is a trick of policy, though the greatest princes and politicians do not at this day know so much, nor have done time out of mind. He believes either that the heavens and the earth, and all things in them, had no original cause of their being, or else that they were made by chance, and happened, he knows not how, to be as they are ; and that in this last shuffling of matter, all things have, by great good fortune, fallen out as happily and as regularly, as if the greatest wisdom had contrived them ; but yet he is resolved to believe that there was no wisdom in the contrivance of them. He believes that matter of itself is utterly void of all sense, understanding, and liberty ; but, for all that, he is of opinion that the parts of matter may now and then happen to be so conveniently disposed as to have all these qualities, and most dexterously to perform all those fine and free operations which the ignorant attribute to spirits." Such is the atheist's creed, from whence we learn that he must be weak, credulous, and absurd.

Of all principles, that of atheism is the most incongruous to the nature of man, and the most inimical to true happiness. Without the belief of a God, and the hope of immortality, the miseries of human life would often be insupportable.

BIBLE VALUED.

WHAT an invaluable blessing is it to have the Bible in our own tongue! Our forefathers rejoiced when they were first favoured with the opportunity of reading it for themselves. We are told, that when Archbishop Cranmer's edition of the Bible was printed, in 1538, and fixed to a desk in all parochial churches, the ardour with which men flocked to read it was incredible. They who could, procured it; and they who could not, crowded to read it, or to hear it read in churches, where it was common to see little assemblies of mechanics meeting together for that purpose after the labour of the day. Many even learned to read in their old age, that they might have the pleasure of instructing themselves from the scriptures. Mr. Fox mentions two apprentices who joined each his little stock, and bought a Bible, which at every interval of leisure they read; but being afraid of their master, who was a zealous papist, they kept it under the straw of their bed.

By a law, however, in the 34th of Henry VIII. it was enacted, that no woman, except noblewomen and gentlewomen, might read to themselves alone, or to others, any texts of the Bible, &c. nor artificers, apprentices, journeymen, husbandmen, nor labourers, were to read the Bible or New Testament in English to themselves, or to any other person, privately or openly. With what pleasure ought we to reflect on our deliverance from those times of darkness, and that *now* we live in a land of Bibles, and in a time when they are circulating in almost every part of the world!

An exceedingly poor woman, whose life was not very consistent, used to speak against going to be examined by the minister before admission to the sacrament; yet at last, by the importunity of her husband, she was prevailed on to go. The minister, finding her grossly ignorant, discovered the great danger of it to her with so much mildness and sweetness, that she burst into tears, beseeching him to give her some directions in spiritual matters; which accordingly he did, and withal referred her to a neighbour that might read to her; and ever after she became eminent for piety, insomuch that she and her husband, being very poor, and not having any candles in the evening, she would fetch a handful of thatch from her house, and, kindling it, she would get her husband to make haste and read as much out of the Bible as he could while the blaze lasted, which she marked diligently, and with a great deal of care and joy.

It is recorded of our Edward VI. that, upon a certain occasion, a paper which was called for in the council chamber happened to be out of reach: the person concerned to produce it took a Bible that lay by, and standing upon it, reached down the paper. The king, observing what was done, ran himself to the place, and, taking the Bible in his hands, kissed it, and laid it up again. This circumstance, though trifling in itself, showed his majesty's great reverence and affection to that best of all books; and whose example is a striking reproof to those who suffer their Bibles to be covered with dust for months together, or throw them about as if they were of little value, or only a piece of useless lumber.

I have read of one, who, being a prisoner in a dark dungeon, when the light was brought to him for a little time to eat his diet, would pull out his Bible, and read a chapter, saying that he could find his mouth in the dark, but not read in the dark.

Robert, King of Sicily, thus said: "The holy books are dearer to me than my kingdom; and were I under any necessity of quitting one, it should be my diadem." And even the haughty Lewis XIV. sometimes read his Bible, and considered it as the finest of all books. Dr. Harris, in all his wills, always renewed this legacy:—Item, I bequeath to all my children, and to my children's children, to each of them, a Bible, with this inscription, "None but Christ." —A noble legacy, truly! If parents were to leave such a boon as this to all their children, with an earnest request that they should constantly read and study it, it might, under the divine blessing, be the means of enriching them more than if they left them thousands of gold and silver.

We are informed of Dr. Marryat, that after he was somewhat advanced in youth, having a strong memory, he thought it his duty to make it a secret repository of the words of divine revelation:

Accordingly "he treasured up," says one, "*a larger portion of the Scriptures* than, perhaps, any one besides, whom we have known, ever did: for there are some who can assure us they had the account immediately from himself,—that he has *committed to memory* not a few *whole books*, both of the *Old Testament* and the *New*. When he mentioned this, he named distinctly *Job, Psalms, Proverbs, Ecclesiastes, Isaiah*, and *Jeremiah*, with all the *minor Prophets:* and every one of *the Epistles* likewise in the *New Testament*, with the book of *the Revelation;* and that he might carefully retain the whole of what he had thus learnt, he declared, it was his practice to repeat them *memoriter* once a year.—The special reason or motive which he assigned for his entering upon this method deserves a particular notice. He began it in the younger part of life, when, being

under a deep sense of the evil of sin, and his mind sadly ignorant of God's way of salvation by the righteousness of the glorious Messiah, or being in the dark as to his own personal interest in it, he was sorely distressed with fears that hell must be his portion. At that time it was put into his heart, that, if he *must go to hell*, he would endeavour to carry with him as much of *the word of GOD* as possibly he could.—And it seems to me to have been a secret *latent principle* of the *fear* and *love* of God that established him in this purpose. For it looks as if he desired to have a supply of scripture materials for his mind to work upon, choosing it should ever be employed in recollecting and reflecting upon those records, that thereby, if possible, it might be kept from blaspheming God, like the rest of the spirits in the infernal prison."

The society which has been lately formed for the purpose of circulating the sacred scriptures through the British dominions, and other countries, whether Christian, Mahometan, or Pagan, we trust will be of incalculable benefit. A clergyman in Wales, gives us the following interesting account. "I cannot express, says he, "the joy I felt on receiving the information of a society being formed for supplying various nations of the world with Bibles. The Sunday Schools have occasioned more calls for Bibles, within these five years, than perhaps ever was known before among our poor people. The possession of a Bible, produces a feeling among them, which the possession of no one thing in the world besides, could produce. In many houses, they have but one Bible, for the use of a numerous family; of course, every one cannot obtain the free use of it at all vacant seasons, when they might read it; and frequently the young people, and the menial servants, who are debarred the use of it, are the most anxiously desirous for the reading of it. The last Oxford edition was bought up by them principally, in every parish were dispersed with the greatest avidity, and there was not half enough to answer the demand for them. I have seen some of them overcome with joy, and burst into tears of thankfulness, on their obtaining possession of a Bible, as their own property, and for their free use. Young females, in service, have walked thirty miles to me, with the only bare hope of obtaining a Bible each, and returned with more joy and thanksgiving than if they had obtained spoils. We, who have half a dozen Bibles by us, and are in circumstances to obtain as many more, know but little of the value those put upon *one*, who, before, were hardly permitted to look into a Bible once a week."

In the year 1272, the pay of a labouring man was three halfpence per day. In 1274, the price of a Bible, with a Commentary, fairly written, was thirty pounds. That precious volume, which may now be obtained, by many labourers, for one day's pay, would then have cost them more than thirteen years' labour to procure.

It is further worthy of remark, that, in the year 1240, the building of two arches of London bridge, cost twenty-five pounds, five pounds less than the value of a Bible!—How great are the privileges of British Christians! We now enjoy the blaze of gospel day : the lines are fallen to us in pleasant places, yea, we have a goodly heritage.

The Bible the best Book.

A society of gentlemen, most of whom had enjoyed a liberal education, and were persons of polished manners, but had unhappily imbibed infidel principles, used to assemble at each other's houses for the purpose of ridiculing the scriptures, and hardening one another in their unbelief. At last, they unanimously formed a resolution solemnly to burn the Bible, and so to be troubled no more with a book which was so hostile to their principles, and disquieting to their consciences. The day fixed upon arrived ; a large fire was prepared ; a Bible was laid on the table, and a flowing bowl ready to drink its dirge. For the execution of their plan, they fixed upon a young gentleman of high birth, brilliant vivacity, and elegance of manners. He undertook the task, and, after a few enlivening glasses, amidst the applauses of his jovial compeers, he approached the table, took up the Bible, and was walking leisurely forward to put it into the fire ; but, happening to give it a look, all at once he was seized with trembling ; paleness overspread his countenance, and he seemed convulsed. He returned to the table, and laying down the Bible, said, with a strong asseveration, "We will not burn *that* book till we get a *better*."

Soon after this, the same gay and lively young gentleman died, and, on his death-bed, was led to true repentance, deriving unshaken hopes of forgiveness, and of future blessedness, from that book he was once going to burn. He found it, indeed, the best book, not only for a living, but a dying hour."

BIGOTRY AND PREJUDICE.

NOTHING is more opposite to the spirit of Christianity, than bigotry. "This," as one observes, "arraigns, and condemns, and executes, all that do not bow down and worship the image of its idolatry. Possessing exclusive prerogative, it rejects every other claim. How many of the dead has it sentenced to eternal misery, who will shine for ever as stars in the kingdom of their Father! How many living characters does it reprobate as enemies to the cross of Christ, who are placing in it all their glory !"

A bigoted, "litigious Christian, if he be right in his opinions, (which is much to be doubted,) is wrong in his way of defending them : he keeps a doctrine, and breaks a commandment."

Wollaston, the learned author of the Religion of Nature Delineated, once asked a bigot, "How many sects he thought there might be in the world?" "Why," said he, "I can make no judgment; I never considered the question."——"Do you think," said Wollaston, "there may be a hundred?" "O yes, at least," cried the bigot.—"Why, then," replied the philosopher, "it is ninety-nine to one that you are in the wrong."

Few men were more bigoted or cruel than Archbishop Laud. He sharpened the spiritual sword, and drew it against all sorts of offenders, intending that the discipline of the Church should be felt as well as spoken of. There had not been such a crowd of business in the High Commission Court since the Reformation, nor so many large fines imposed, as under this prelate's administration. The fines, we are told, were assigned to the repairs of St. Paul's, which gave rise to an unlucky proverb, "that the Church was repaired with the sins of the people."

The following account of the conduct of a mother towards her son, shows us that bigotry has a tendency to eradicate even some of the best affections which the Almighty has planted in our nature for the wisest of purposes. The son had, it seems, from a principle of conscience, in opposition to his interest, renounced the religious system, in which he had been educated, for another which he deemed more consonant to truth.— When the mother was informed of the circumstance, she told him, that "she found it her duty, however severe the struggle, to alienate her affections from him, now he had rendered himself an enemy to God, by embracing such erroneous sentiments." It is said, that she was completely successful in these endeavours, and that the duty she enjoined upon herself was scrupulously performed during the remainder of her days.—What an affecting instance of perverted principles!

Such is the nature of bigotry, and such the evil of prejudice, that it insults the dead as well as the living.

Chillingworth's book, entitled, "The Religion of Protestants, a safe Way to Salvation," is acknowledged to be one of the most solid and rational defences of protestantism ever published. But such was Dr. Cheynell's prejudice against it, that, when Chillingworth was buried, he came to his grave with this book in his hand, and, after a short preamble to the people, in which he assured them how happy it would be for the kingdom if this book and all its fellows could be so buried, that they might never rise more, unless it were for a confutation, "Get thee gone," said he, "thou cursed book, which has seduced so many precious souls; get thee gone, thou corrupt, rotten book, earth to earth, dust to dust: get thee gone into the place of rottenness, that thou mayest rot with thy author, and see corruption."—Poor doctor! how feeble thy efforts; how ineffectual thy wishes! Protestantism yet lives and flourishes, and we have reason to believe it will live and extend itself in all directions; and, for this reason,—because it is the religion of the Bible, and the cause of truth. Enemies it may and will have, but, "being divine, it is incapable of being wounded, and will, in the issue, walk with a meek and god-like dignity over the graves of her opponents, and finally triumph in the complete blessedness of all her adherents."

We in general look for this spirit of bigotry and prejudice among the lower classes of society, and those whose minds have never been expanded by sound knowledge. But, alas! it is too prevalent among those who are considered as intelligent and learned. What shall we say to the following instances? Whiston would not go to hear Dr. Gill preach, merely because he was informed that the doctor had written a folio book on the Canticles. A wise reason indeed! Dr. Johnson, when he was at Edinburgh, although he was personally acquainted with the celebrated Dr. Robertson, declined going to hear him, because he would not be seen in a Presbyterian church.— Dr. Berkely, late prebendary of Canterbury, in his sermon on the 1st Tim. i. 15, declares that salvation is promised *only to the episcopal church;* and another modern divine, in a recent publication, devoutly *gives up all dissenters from episcopacy to the uncovenanted mercies of God.* Benign Jehovah, defend us from such illiberality!

At the funeral of Mr. G. when Mr. D. a clergyman, refused to walk in procession with Mr. B. a dissenting minister, a man of activity and spirit, the following pleasant circumstance happened. Mr. D. meeting the corpse, and finding Mr. B. walking before it, directed him to walk behind. Mr. B. not complying with this order, Mr. D. endeavoured to outwalk him; but Mr. B. being as nimble as he, kept up with him till the rector quickening his pace, they both fairly ran for it till they got to the church door. Mr. D. was so much offended, that, after the funeral, his pride and bigotry getting the better of every other consideration, he sent back the hatband and scarf, and even the pins that had been used on the occasion.

When Mr. Staunton preached a lecture on Lord's day afternoon, at ——, in Oxfordshire, his labours were so acceptable, that people flocked from all parts to hear him. This was not pleasing to the incumbent, who took the more time in reading prayers, that this novel lecturer might have the less time for preaching, and then left the church, but was followed by none but his clerk, whom he would not suffer to give out the psalm. Mr. S. had preached some time on that text—"Buy the truth, and sell it not;" upon which the incumbent, when he met any coming into the church, as he went out, would say, with a sneer—"What! are you going to buy the truth?" Poor creature, how it hurt him to see all the people going one way, while he and his clerk were going another!

An Irish earl related the following anecdote of his grandfather, when an insurrection of the papists was expected in Ireland. The earl's grandfather, conversing familiarly with one of his popish tenants, (a good kind of man so called, whom he had favoured,) told him that he was sure he would not have any hand in murdering him, should the papists prevail. "No,' said the farmer, "I never would hurt your lordship." "But," said the peer, "suppose the priest should tell you that it is the pope's order, and that it is for the good of the church?" "Oh, then," said the poor bigoted papist, "your lordship knows I could not disobey the pope's order." Such is the nature of implicit faith and the spirit of bigotry!!!

THE CAVILLER REPROVED.

A CERTAIN man went to a dervise, and proposed three questions. 1st. Why do they say that God is omnipresent? I do not see him in any place: show me where he is? 2dly. Why is man punished for crimes? since whatever he does proceeds from God: man has no free will, for he cannot do any thing contrary to the will of God; and if he had power, he would do every thing for his own good. 3dly. How can God punish Satan in hell fire, since he is formed of that element? and what impression can fire make on itself?

The dervise took up a large clod of earth and struck him on the head with it. The man went to the cadi, and said, "I proposed three questions to such a dervise, who flung such a clod of earth at me, as has made my head ache." The cadi, having sent for the dervise, asked—"Why did you throw a clod of earth at his head instead of answering his questions." The dervise replied—"The clod of earth was an answer to his speech. He says he has a pain in his head: let him show me where it is, and I will make God visible to him. And why does he exhibit a complaint to you against me? Whatever I did was the act of God : I did not strike him without the will of God ; and what power do I possess ? And, as he is compounded of earth, how can he suffer pain from that element?" The man was confounded, and the cadi highly pleased with the dervise's answer.

CONSTANCY.

THERE is something truly noble and praiseworthy in constancy. To be firm in the midst of opposition, to endure hardships without murmuring, and to persevere through every difficulty, is highly characteristic of the Christian spirit : such, however great their sufferings, shall not lose their reward. "Behold, we count them happy which endure : the spirit of glory and of God rests upon them. Their's, says the Saviour, is the kingdom of heaven."

When one of the kings of France solicited M. Bougier, who was a protestant, to conform to the Roman Catholic religion, promising him in return a commission, or a government, "Sire!" replied he, "if I could be persuaded to betray my God for a marshal's staff, I might be induced to betray my king for a bribe of much less value."

Under the reign of paganism, a Christian woman, notwithstanding her pregnancy, was condemned to die for her profession. The day before her execution she fell in labour, and crying out in her pangs, the jailer insulted her, saying, "If you make a noise to-day, how will you endure a violent death to-morrow ?" To which she replied, " To-day I suffer what is ordinary, and have only ordinary assistance ; to-morrow I am to suffer what is more than ordinary, and shall believe for more than ordinary assistance."—O, woman ! great was thy faith.

Sir William Askew, of Kelsay, in Lincolnshire, was blessed with several daughters. His second, named Ann, had received a genteel education, which, with an agreeable person and good understanding, rendered her a very proper person to be at the head of a family. Her father, regardless of his daughter's inclination and happiness, obliged her to marry a gentleman who had nothing to recommend him but his fortune, and who was a most bigoted papist. No sooner was he convinced of his wife's regard for the doctrines of the reformation from popery, than, by the instigation of the priests, he violently drove her from his house, though she had borne him two children, and her conduct was unexceptionable. Abandoned by her husband, she came up to London in order to procure a divorce, and to make herself known to that part of the court who either professed or were favourites of protestantism ; but as Henry VIII. with consent of parliament, had just enacted the law of the Six Articles, commonly called the Bloody Statute, she was cruelly betrayed by her own husband, and upon his information taken into custody, and examined concerning her faith. The act above mentioned denounced death against all those who should deny the doctrine of transubstantiation, or that the bread and wine made use of in the sacrament were not converted, after consecration, into the *real* body and blood of Christ ; or maintain the necessity of receiving the sacrament in both kinds ; or affirm that it was lawful for priests to marry ; that the vows of celibacy might be broken ; that private masses were of no avail ; and that auricular confession to a priest was not necessary to salvation. Upon these articles she was examined by the inquisitor, a priest, the Lord Mayor of London, and the Bishops' Chancellor, and to all their queries gave proper and pertinent answers ; but, not being such as they approved, she was sent back to prison, where she remained eleven days, to ruminate alone on her alarming situation, and was denied the small consolation of a friendly visit. The king's council being at Greenwich, she was once more examined by

Chancellor Wriothesley, Gardner, Bishop of Winchester, Dr. Cox, and Dr. Robinson; but, not being able to convince her of her supposed errors, she was sent to the Tower. It was strongly suspected that she was favoured by some ladies of high rank, and that she carried on a religious correspondence with the queen; so that the Chancellor Wriothesley, hoping that he might discover something that would afford matter of impeachment against that princess, the Earl of Hertford, or his countess, who all favoured the reformation, ordered her to be put to the rack; but her fortitude in suffering, and her resolution not to betray her friends, were proof against that diabolical invention. Not a groan, not a word could be extorted from her. The chancellor provoked with what he called her obstinacy, augmented her tortures with his own hands, and with unheard of violence; but her courage and constancy were invincible, and these barbarians gained nothing by their cruelties but everlasting disgrace and infamy. As soon as she was taken from the rack, she fainted away; but being recovered, she was condemned to the flames. Her bones were dislocated in such a manner, that they were forced to carry her in a chair to the place of execution. While she was at the stake, letters were brought her from the Lord Chancellor, offering her the king's pardon if she would recant; but she refused to look at them, telling the messenger, "that she came not thither to deny her Lord and Master." The same letters were also tendered to three other persons condemned to the same fate, and who, animated by her example, refused to accept them: whereupon the Lord Mayor commanded the fire to be kindled, and with savage ignorance cried out, *Fiat Justitia*—Let justice take its course. The fagots being lighted, she commended her soul, with the utmost composure, into the hands of her Maker, and, like the great Founder of the religion she professed, expired, praying for her murderers, July 16, 1546, about the twenty-fifth year of her age.

"I do not know," observes a good writer, "if all circumstances be considered, whether the history of this or any other nation can furnish a more illustrious example than this now related. To her father's will she sacrificed her own inclinations; to a husband, unworthy of her affections, she behaved with prudence, respect, and obedience. The secrets of her friends she preserved inviolable, even amidst the tortures of the rack. Her constancy in suffering, considering her age and sex, was equal, at least, if not superior, to any thing on record; and her piety was genuine and unaffected, of which she gave the most exalted proof, in dying a martyr for the cause of her religion and liberty of conscience. But who can read this example, and not lament and detest that spirit of cruelty and inhumanity which are imbibed and cherished in the church of Rome? a spirit repugnant to the feelings of nature, and directly opposite to the conduct and disposition of the Great Author of our religion, who came not to destroy men's lives, but to save them."

THE CONVERTED INNKEEPER.

WHEN the Rev. Mr. —— went to his living in the country, a very great audience collected from the neighbouring towns and villages, in one of which lived an old inn-keeper, who, having made free with his own tap, had well carbuncled his nose and face, which bore the visible marks of his profession. He had heard the report of the concourse at this church, as many went from his own town; but he always stoutly swore he would never be found among the fools who were running there: on hearing, however, of the particularly pleasing mode of singing at the church, his curiosity was a little excited, and he said he did not know but when next

P——n feast came, which was half way, he might go and hear the singing; but with some imprecation, that he would never hear a word of the sermon.

He lived about six miles distant, and, when P——n feast came, after dining with a party, instead of staying to drink, he came to the afternoon service, merely to hear the singing at the church, with a full resolution of keeping his vow, and excluding every word of the sermon.

He was a corpulent man, and, as it was a hot summer's day, he came in all of a perspiration, and having with difficulty found admission into a narrow open pew with a lid, as soon as the hymn before sermon was sung, which he heard with great attention, he leaned forward, and, fixing his elbows on the lid, secured both his ears against the sermon with his fore-fingers. He had not been in this position many minutes before the prayer finished, and the sermon commenced with an awful appeal to the consciences of the hearers, of the necessity of attending to the things which made for their everlasting peace; and the minister addressing them solemnly, "He that hath ears to hear, let him hear." Just the moment before these words were pronounced, a fly had fastened on the carbuncled nose of the inn-keeper, and, stinging him sharply, he drew one of his fingers from his ear, and struck off the painful visitant: at that very moment, the words "He that hath ears to hear, let him hear," pronounced with great solemnity, entered the ear that was opened, as a clap of thunder; it struck him with irresistible force: he kept his hand from returning to his ear, and, feeling an impression he had never known before, he presently withdrew the other finger, and hearkened with deep attention to the discourse which followed.

That day was the beginning of days to him; a change was produced upon him, which could not but be noticed by all his former companions.

He never, from that day, returned to any of his former practices, nor ever afterwards was he seen in liquor, nor heard to swear. He became truly serious, and for many years, went all weathers six miles to the church, where he first received the knowledge of divine things. After about eighteen years' faithful and close walk with God, he died rejoicing in the hope of that glory he now enjoys.

CRUELTY.

Nothing can be more contrary to nature, to reason, to religion, than cruelty. Hence an inhuman man is generally considered as a monster. Such monsters, however, have existed; and the heart almost bleeds at the recital of the cruel acts such have been guilty of. It teaches us, however, what human nature is when left to itself; not only treacherous above all things, but *desperately* wicked.

Commodus, the Roman emperor, when but twelve years old, gave a shocking instance of his cruelty, when, finding the water in which he bathed somewhat too warm, he commanded the person who attended the bath to be thrown into the furnace, nor was he satisfied till those who were about him pretended to put his order in execution. After his succession to the empire, he equalled, if he did not exceed in cruelty, Caligula, Domitian, and even Nero himself; playing, we may say, with the blood of his subjects and fellow-creatures, of whom he caused great numbers to be racked and butchered in his presence, merely for his diversion. Historians relate many instances of his cruelty. He caused one to be thrown to wild beasts for reading the life of Caligula, written by Suetonius; because that tyrant and he had been born on the same day of the month, and in many bad qualities resembled each other. Seeing one day a corpulent man pass by, he immediately cut him asunder; partly to try his strength, in which he excelled all men, and partly out of curiosity, as himself owned, to see his entrails drop out at once. He took pleasure in cutting off the feet and putting out the eyes of such as he met in his rambles through the city. Some he murdered because they were negligently dressed ; others because they seemed trimmed with too much nicety. He assumed the name and habit of Hercules, appearing publicly in a lion's skin, with a huge club in his hand, and ordering several persons, though not guilty of any crimes, to be disguised like monsters, that, by knocking out their brains, he might have a better claim to the title, *the great destroyer of monsters.* He, however, was destroyed in his turn : Martia, one of his concubines, whose death he had prepared, poisoned him ; but, as the poison did not quickly operate, he was strangled by a wrestler in the thirty-first year of his age.

In Italy, during the greater part of the sixteenth century, assassinations, murders, and even murders under trust, seem to have been almost familiar among the superior ranks of people. Cæsar Borgia invited four of the little princes in his neighbourhood, who all possessed sovereignties, and commanded armies of their own, to a friendly conference at Senigaglia, where, as soon as he arrived, he put them all to death.

History records but few characters more cruel than Charles IX. It is said, that when he observed several fugitive Huguenots about his palace, in the morning after the dreadful massacre of thirty thousands of their friends, he took a fowling-piece, and repeatedly fired at them. That this prince was naturally barbarous, we may learn from the following anecdote : One day, when he amused himself with rabbit-hunting, " Make them all come out," said he, " that I may have the pleasure of killing them all."

This sanguinary monarch died very wretched, for he expired bathed in his own blood which burst from his veins, and in his last moments, he exclaimed—" What blood !—what murders !—I know not where I am ! —how will all this end ?—what shall I do ?—I am lost for ever !—I know it !"

The late celebrated King of Prussia, intending to make, in the night, an important movement in his camp, which was in sight of the enemy, gave orders that by eight o'clock, all the lights in the camp should be put out, on pain of death. The moment that the time was past, he walked out himself to see whether all were dark. He found a light in the tent of a captain Zietern, which he entered just as the officer was folding up a letter. Zietern knew him, and instantly fell on his knees to entreat his mercy. The king asked to whom he had been writing ; he said it was a letter to his wife, which he had retained the candle these few minutes beyond the time in order to finish. The king coolly ordered, him to rise and write one line more which he should dictate. This line was, to inform his wife, without any explanation, that by such an hour the next day he should be a dead man. The letter was then sealed and despatched as it had been intended, and the next day the captain was executed.

The cruel Parent.

The Honourable Commodore Byron was an eye witness to the following shocking scene of brutal rage on the coasts of Patagonia. I shall present the reader with it in his own words.—" Here I must relate a little anecdote of our *Christian* cacique. He and his wife had gone off at some distance from the shore, in their canoe, when she dived for sea eggs ; but not meeting with great success, they returned a good deal out of humour. A little boy of theirs, about three years old, whom they appeared to be dotingly fond of, watching for his father and mother's return, ran into the surf to meet them. The father handed a basket of sea eggs to the child, which being too heavy for him to carry he let it fall ; upon which the father jumped out of the canoe, and, catching the boy up in his arms, dashed him with the utmost violence against the stones! The poor little creature lay motionless and bleeding, and in that condition was taken up by the mother, but died soon after. She appeared inconsolable for some time, but the brute his father showed little concern about it."

But we need not search the records of other countries for anecdotes of cruelty. Alas! England has been guilty in too many instances; we will only, however, select one: Alexander Leighton, a doctor of divinity, by desire of some of his friends, had written and published a book, entitled "Zion's Plea against Prelacy." It contained some warm, imprudent invectives against the prelates, and the conduct of those in power. Soon after the publication of the work, without an information upon oath, or legal proof who was the author, Leighton, as he was coming from church, was arrested by two high-commissioned pursuivants: they dragged him to the house of Laud, where he was kept till seven in the evening without food. Laud returning at this time in great pomp and state, with Corbit, Bishop of Oxford, he demanded to be heard. The haughty Laud did not deign to see him, but sent him to Newgate: he was clapped into irons, and confined in an uninhabitable apartment: where, notwithstanding the weather was cold, and the snow and rain beat in, there was no convenient place to make a fire. From Tuesday night to Thursday noon he was unsupplied with food, and in this wretched dwelling was kept fifteen weeks, without any friend, not even his wife being suffered to come near him. His own house was, in the mean time, rifled by the officers of the high commission court, his wife and children treated by these ruffians with great barbarity, himself denied a copy of the commitment, and the Sheriffs of London refused to bail him at his wife's petition. At the end of fifteen weeks he was served with a subpoena.

Heath, the Attorney General, on an assurance that he should come off well, extorted a confession from him that he was the author of the book: an information was immediately lodged against him in the Star Chamber by Heath. He confessed the writing of the book, but with no such intention as the information suggested. He pleaded that his aim was to remonstrate against certain grievances in church and state under which the people suffered, to the end that parliament might take them into consideration, and give such redress as might be for the honour of the king, the quiet of the people, and the peace of the church. This answer not being admitted as satisfactory, the following cruel sentence was by this tyrannical court pronounced against him, though sick and absent, viz.

"That he should pay a fine of ten thousand pounds to his majesty's use; and in respect that the defendant had heretofore entered into the ministry, and the court of Star Chamber did not use to inflict any corporeal or ignominious punishment upon any person so long as they continued in orders, the court referred him to the high commission, there to be degraded of his ministry; that done, for farther punishment and example to others, the delinquent to be brought to the pillory at Westminster (the court sitting,) and there whipped; after his whipping, to be set in the pillory for some convenient space; to have one of his ears cut off, his nose slit, and to be branded in the face with S. S. for a sower of sedition; then to be carried to the prison of the Fleet, and at some convenient time afterwards be carried to the pillory at Cheapside, upon a market day, to be there likewise whipped, then set in the pillory, have his other ear cut off; and then be carried back to the prison of the Fleet, there to remain during life, unless his majesty be graciously pleased to pardon him."

Such was the sentence; which, when it was pronounced, that inhuman wretch Bishop Laud pulled off his cap, and gave God thanks for it. This sentence was given at the end of Trinity term. It was not till Michaelmas term following after the degradation that it was put in execution.

On Friday, November the 16th, part of his sentence was put in execution in this manner : In the New Palace Yard at Westminster, in term time, he was severely whipped, then put in the pillory, where he had one of his ears cut off, one side of his nose slit, branded on the cheek with a red hot iron with the letters S. S. and afterwards carried back to the Fleet, to be kept in close custody. On that day sevennight, his sores upon his back, ears, nose, and face, not being cured, he was whipped again at the pillory in Cheapside, and there had the remainder of his sentence executed upon him, by cutting off the other ear, slitting the other side of the nose, and branding the other cheek. Dr. Leighton, in his own account of this horrid execution, adds, that the hangman was made half drunk, and enjoined to perform his office with ferocity ; that he stood, after receiving the punishment of the lash, almost two hours in the pillory, exposed to frost and snow, and then suffered the rest; that, being with these miseries disabled from walking, he was denied the benefit of a coach, and carried back to prison by water, to the farther endangering his life.

The treatment and prosecution of Dr. Leighton were notoriously illegal and inhuman. The judgment passed against him was by an arbitrary court, whose jurisdiction was unconstitutional, in a manner created by the crown, and cherished as a never failing engine of despotism. The tyranny it exerted outwent every example of former ages. It was the ready minister of vengeance to all who opposed the designs of Charles I. and entirely influenced in its conduct by the persecuting furious spirit of Laud. The sentence passed against the unhappy Leighton was directly contrary to the humane spirit of the British laws, and the single instance of such execrable barbarity would have disgraced the government of an absolute monarch.

Cruelty to Animals.

As cruelty should not be shown towards the human species, neither should it be indulged towards the animal tribes. "I ever thought," says Judge Hale, "that there is a certain degree of justice due from man to the creatures, as from man to man ; and that an excessive use of the creature's labour is an injustice for which he must account. I have therefore always esteemed it as a part of my duty, and it has always been my practice, to be merciful to my beasts ; and upon the same account I have declined any cruelty to any of God's creatures, and, as much as I could, prevented it in others as a tyranny. I have abhorred those sports that consist in torturing them ; and if any noxious creature must be destroyed, or creatures for food must be taken, it has been my practice to do it in a manner that may be with the least torture or cruelty ; ever remembering, that though God has given us a dominion over his creatures, yet it is under a law of justice, prudence, and moderation, otherwise we should become *tyrants* and not *lords* over God's creatures ; and therefore those things of this nature which others have practised as *recreations*, I have avoided as *sins*."

Children should be early prohibited from tormenting insects, lest it should degenerate into insensibility, and they become inattentive to every kind of suffering but their own. We find that the supreme court of judicature at Athens thought an instance of this sort not below its cognizance, and punished a boy for putting out the eyes of a poor bird that had unhappily fallen into his hands. And Mr. Locke informs us of a mother who permitted her children to have birds and insects, but rewarded or punished them as they treated them well or ill.

The following circumstance, it is said, occurred at Abo in Finland. A dog, who had been run over by a carriage, crawled to the door of a tanner in that town : the man's son, a boy fifteen years of age, first stoned, and then poured a vessel of boiling water upon the miserable animal. This act of diabolical cruelty was witnessed by one of the magistrates, who thought such barbarity deserved to be publicly noticed. He therefore informed the other magistrates, who unanimously agreed in condemning the boy to this punishment. He was imprisoned till the following market day ; then, in the presence of all the people, he was conducted to the place of execution by an officer of justice, who read to him his sentence—" Inhuman young man, because you did not assist an animal who implored your assistance by its cries, and who derives being from the same God who gave you life ; because you added to the torture of the agonizing beast, and murdered it, the council of this city have sentenced you to wear on your breast the name you deserve, and to receive fifty stripes." He then hung a black board round his neck, with this inscription, " A savage and inhuman young man," and, after inflicting upon him twenty-five stripes, he proceeded—" Inhuman young man, you have now felt a very small degree of the pain with which you tortured a helpless animal in its hour of death. As you wish for mercy from that God who created all that live, learn humanity for the future." He then executed the remainder of the sentence.

There is no doubt but cruelties often exercised may become so customary, as to render the heart insensible. I was once (says a writer) passing through *Moorfields* with a young lady aged about nine or ten years, born and educated in Portugal, but in the *Protestant* faith ; and, observing a large concourse of people assembled around a pile of faggots on fire, I expressed a curiosity to know the cause. She very composedly answered, " I suppose that it is nothing more than *that they are going to burn a Jew.*" Fortunately it was no other than roasting an ox upon some joyful occasion. What rendered this singularity the more striking, were the natural mildness and compassion of the young person's disposition.

THE CURATE RELIEVED.

A VIOLENT Welsh squire having taken offence at a poor curate who employed his leisure hours in mending clocks and watches, applied to the bishop of St. Asaph, with a formal complaint against him for impiously carrying on a trade, contrary to the statute. His lordship having heard the complaint, told the squire he might depend upon it that the strictest justice should be done in the case : accordingly the mechanic divine was sent for a few days after, when the bishop asked him " How he dared to disgrace his diocese by becoming a mender of clocks and watches?" The other, with all humility, answered, " To satisfy the wants of a wife and ten children." " That won't do with me," rejoined the prelate, " I'll inflict such a punishment upon you as shall make you leave off your pitiful trade, I promise you ;" and immediately calling in his secretary, ordered him to make out a presentation for the astonished curate to a living of at least one hundred and fifty pounds per annum.

CUSTOM AND HABIT.

WHATEVER be the cause, says Lord Kames, it is an established fact that we are much influenced by custom : it hath an effect upon our pleasures, upon our actions, and even upon our thoughts and sentiments. Habit makes no figure during the vivacity of youth ; in middle age it gains ground ; and in old age governs without control. In that period of life, generally speaking, we eat at a certain hour, take exercise at a certain hour, go to rest at a certain hour, all by the direction of habit ; nay, a particular seat, table, bed, comes to be essential : and a habit in any of these cannot be contradicted without uneasiness. "The mind," says Mr. Cogan, "frequently acquires a strong and invincible attachment to whatever has been familiar to it for any length of time. Habit, primarily introduced by accident or necessity, will inspire an affection for peculiarities which have the reverse of intrinsic merit to recommend them."

"I once attended," says the last mentioned author, "a prisoner of some distinction in one of the prisons of the metropolis, ill of a typhus fever, whose apartments were gloomy in the extreme, and surrounded with horrors; yet this prisoner assured me afterwards, that, upon his release, he quitted them with a degree of reluctance; custom had reconciled him to the twilight admitted through the thick barred grate, to the filthy spots and patches of his plastered walls, to the hardness of his bed, and even to confinement. He had his books, was visited by his friends, and was greatly amused and interested in the anecdotes of the place.

"An officer of the municipality at Leyden also informed the author of an instance, which marks yet more strongly the force of habit. A poor woman, who had for some misdemeanour been sentenced to confinement for a certain number of years, upon the expiration of the term, immediately applied to him for re-admission. She urged that all her worldly comforts were fled, and her only wish was to be indulged in those imparted by habit. She moreover threatened, that, if this could not be granted as a *favour*, she would commit some offence that should give her a *title* to be reinstated in the accustomed lodgings." Thus we see that custom is a catholicon for pain and distress.

The influence of custom is surprising also as to natural objects. What different ideas are formed in different nations concerning the beauty of the human shape and countenance! A fair complexion is a shocking deformity upon the coast of Guinea: thick lips

K

and a flat nose are a beauty. In some nations, long ears that hang down upon the shoulders are the objects of universal admiration. In China, if a lady's foot is so large as to be fit to walk upon, she is regarded as a monster of ugliness. Some of the savage nations in North America tie four boards round the heads of their children, and thus squeeze them, while the bones are tender and gristly, into a form that is almost square. Europeans are astonished at the absurd barbarity of this practice; but when they condemn those savages, they do not reflect that the ladies in Europe had, till within a few years, been endeavouring for nearly a century past to squeeze the roundness of their natural shape into a square form of the same kind; and that, notwithstanding the many distortions and diseases which this practice was known to occasion, custom had rendered it agreeable among some of the most civilized nations which perhaps the world ever beheld.

What influence has custom over dress, furniture, the arts, and even over moral sentiments! It requires, however, to be watched. It should never pervert our sentiments with regard to humanity and religion. To make custom an apology for what is unreasonable and irreligious, is making a bad use of it indeed.

DEISM, DEISTS.

Notwithstanding the repeated attacks of infidelity, the Christian has nothing to fear. "Not one in fifty, (says Mr. Bogue) of those who call themselves deists or atheists, understand the nature of the religion which they profess to reject. And are these creatures formidable antagonists who disbelieve what they do not understand, because they wish it not to be true? They are a dishonour to any sect. Besides, the alarm has far exceeded reality. I will venture to affirm, without fear or contradiction, that, from the birth of Christ to the present hour, there never was a country where one fifth part of the people were deists, or where one tenth part were atheists; nor a period of twelve years' continuance, when the civil government was under the influence of either one or the other, or when they persecuted the truth. Superstition has slaughtered more victims in a week than deism and atheism have since the hour that Christ expired upon the cross."

A gentleman was arguing with a deist on the absurdity of rejecting Christianity without examination.— He owned that he never knew a person examine the subject who did not afterwards embrace it; but excused himself from examining, under the plea that to do so was analogous to drinking brandy, which always produced intoxication. "Is it not honourable to Christianity (says the gentleman) to have enemies, who must give up the exercises of their reason before they reject it?"

The Unhappy Deists.

I knew, says one, a jurist and statesman by profession, well learned, and of good parts. He was so well read in the scriptures and divinity in general, that he might have passed for no ordinary theologian. He had, though a speculative unbeliever, maintained several theses with great success: on the other hand, he could, in his opinion, account for every appearance in nature from a theory of matter and motion; still, with all his belief and unbelief, he frankly confessed to me *that he was unhappy.* And, being then in a state of celibacy, farther acknowledged, that 'should he ever change his situation, he was determined never to suffer the secrets of his heart to transpire to his wife and children; that in all externals he would strictly conform to the church;' adding, as one of his philosophical and political reasons, that it was better to be comforted upon a false ground, than to live *without any consolation.*

The late Lord P——, after he turned deist, took every opportunity to show his contempt of religion.— The clergyman and parishioners of the place where his lordship's seat in Northamptonshire stood, usually passed in sight of the house, in their way to church. At the time of going and returning he generally ordered his children and servants into the hall, for the vile purpose of laughing at and ridiculing them. He pursued this course for some time; but at length, drew near the close of life. Upon his dying pillow his views were altered. He found, that, however his former sentiments might suit him in health, they could not support him in the hour of dissolution. When in the cold arms of death, the terrors of the Almighty were upon him. Painful remembrance brought to view ten thousand insults offered to that God, at whose bar he was shortly to stand; and, conscience strongly impressed with the solemnity of that day, he but too justly feared the God he had insulted would then spurn him to hell. With his mind thus agitated, he called to a person in the room, and desired him to go into the library, and fetch "the cursed book," meaning that which had made him a deist. He went, but returned, saying, "he could not find it." The nobleman then cried with vehemence, "that he must go again, and look till he found it; for he could not die till it was destroyed." The person, having at last found it, gave it into his hands. It was no sooner committed to him, than he tore it to pieces, with mingled horror and revenge, and committed it to the flames. Having thus taken vengeance on the instrument of his own ruin, he soon breathed his last.

The Deist confounded.

A deist on a visit to his friends, among other topics of conversation, was pleased to enlarge considerably on the sufficiency of reason, separate from Divine assistance, to guide us to happiness. To whom the relative present, who was a farmer, made the following reply: "Cousin, when you were about fourteen years of age, you were bound an apprentice to a ——, and having served the appointed time, you soon became a master, and have now continued in business about twelve years. I wish to know whether you could not prosecute your trade at this time to greater advantage than when you first embarked in it." The tradesman admitted that his experience in business was of considerable value to him; but asked, "What relation that had to the present topic of discourse?" The farmer answered, "You were come to the perfect use of your reason, and had been for a long time taught how to manage your trade; and if, therefore, your reason without experience was insufficient to preserve you from many errors, in so plain and easy a business as your's, how can you imagine that it should be sufficient, without any Divine assistance, to guide you to heaven?" The deist was nonplussed. How forcible are right words! Job, vi. 25.

It has often been a matter of wonder, that the principles and reasonings of infidels, though frequently accompanied with great natural and acquired abilities, are seldom known to make any impression on sober people. It is said of a gentleman lately deceased, who was eminent in the literary world, that in early life he drank deeply into the free-thinking scheme. He and one of his companions of the same turn of mind often carried on their conversations in the hearing of a religious but illiterate countryman. This gentleman afterwards becoming a serious Christian, was concerned for the countryman, lest his faith in the Christian religion should have been shaken. One day he took the liberty to ask him, whether what had been so frequently advanced in his hearing had not produced this effect upon him? "By no means," answered the countryman; "it never made the least impression upon me." "No impression upon you!" said the gentleman. "Why, you must know that we had read and thought on these things much more than you had any opportunity of doing." "O,

yes," said the other; "but I know also your manner of living; I knew that, to maintain such a course of conduct, you found it *necessary* to renounce Christianity."

If we look at the writings and conduct of the principal adversaries of Christianity, we shall form no very favourable opinion of their system as to its moral effects. "The morals of Rochester and Wharton," says one, "need no comment. Woolston was a gross blasphemer. Blount solicited his sister-in-law to marry him; and, being refused, shot himself. Tindal was originally a protestant, then turned papist, then protestant again, merely to suit the times; and was, at the same time, infamous for vice in general, and the total want of principle. He is said to have died with this prayer in his mouth: 'If there be a God, I desire that he may have mercy upon me.' Hobbes wrote his Leviathan to serve the cause of Charles I. but finding him fail of success, he turned it to the defence of Cromwell, and made a merit of this fact to the usurper, as Hobbes himself unblushingly declared to Lord Clarendon. Morgan had no regard for truth, as is evident from his numerous falsifications of scripture, as well as from the vile hypocrisy of professing himself a Christian in those very writings in which he labours to destroy Christianity. Voltaire, in a letter now remaining, requested his friend D'Alembert to tell for him a direct and palpable lie, by denying that he was the author of the Philosophical Dictionary. D'Alembert, in his answer, informed him that he had told the lie. Voltaire has, indeed, expressed his own moral character, perfectly, in the following words: 'Monsieur Abbe, I must be read; no matter whether I am believed or not.' He also solemnly professed to believe the Catholic religion; although, at the same time, he doubted the existence of a God. Hume died as a fool dieth. The day before, he spent in a pitiful and unaffected unconcern about this tremendous sub-

12*

ject; playing at whist, reading Lucian's Dialogues, and making silly attempts at wit, concerning his interview with Charon, the heathen ferryman at Hades."—See Dr. Dwight's excellent Discourses on the Nature and Danger of Infidel Philosophy, p. 45—47.

" Collins, though he had no belief in Christianity, yet qualified himself for civil office by partaking of the Lord's Supper; Shaftesbury did the same; and the same is done by hundreds of infidels to this day. Yet these are the men who are continually declaiming against the hypocrisy of priests!

" I shall conclude this catalogue with a brief abstract of the Confessions of J. J. Rousseau. After a good education in the Protestant religion, he was put apprentice. Finding the situation disagreeable to him, he felt a strong propensity to vice, inclining him to covet, dissemble, lie, and at length to steal; a propensity of which he was never able afterwards to divest himself. ' I have been a rogue,' says he, ' and am so still, sometimes, for trifles which I had rather take than ask for.'

" He abjured the Protestant religion, and entered the hospital of the Catechumens at Taurin, to be instructed in that of the Catholics: ' For which, in return,' says he, ' I was to receive subsistence. From this interested conversion,' he adds, ' nothing remained but the remembrance of my having been both a dupe and an apostate.'

" After this, he resided with a Madame De Warren, with whom ' he lived in the greatest possible familiarity.' This lady often suggested that there would be no justice in the Supreme Being, should he be strictly just to us; because, not having bestowed what was necessary to render us essentially good, it would be requiring more than he had given. She was, nevertheless, a very good Catholic, or pretended, at least, to be one, and certainly desired to be such. If there had been no Christian morality

established, Rousseau supposes she would have lived as though regulated by its principles. All her morality, however, was subordinate to the principles of M. Savel (who first seduced her from conjugal fidelity, by urging, in effect, that exposure was the only crime,) or rather she saw nothing in religion that contradicted them. Rousseau was far enough from being of this opinion, yet he confessed he dared not combat the arguments of the lady; nor is it supposable he could, as he appears to have acted on the same principles at the time.— ' Finding in her,' he adds, ' all those ideas I had occasion for to secure me from the fears of death, and its future consequences, I drew confidence and security from this source.'

" The writings of Port Royal, and those of the Oratory, made him half a Jansenist; and, notwithstanding all his confidence, their harsh theory sometimes alarmed him. A dread of hell, which, till then, he had never much apprehended, by little, and little disturbed his security; and, had not Madam De Warren tranquillized his soul, would, at length, have been too much for him. His confessor, also, a Jesuit, contributed all in his power to keep up his hopes.

" After this, he became familiar with another female, Theresa. He began by declaring to her, that he would never either abandon or marry her. Finding her pregnant with her first child, and hearing it observed, that he who had best filled the Foundling Hospital was always the most applauded, ' I said to myself,' quoth he, ' since it is the custom of the country, they who live here may adopt it. I cheerfully determined upon it without the least scruple; and the only one I had to overcome was that of Theresa, whom, with the greatest imaginable difficulty, I persuaded to comply.' The year following, a similar inconvenience was remedied by the same expedient; no more reflection on his part, nor approbation on that of the mother. ' She obliged with trembling. My fault,' says he, 'was great; but it was an error.'

"He resolved on settling at Geneva, and on going thither, and being mortified at his exclusion from the rights of a citizen, by the profession of a religion different from his forefathers, he determined openly for the latter. 'I thought,' says he, 'the gospel being the same for every Christian, and the only difference in religious opinions the result of the explanations given by men to that which they did not understand, it was the exclusive right of the sovereign power in every country to fix the mode of worship and these unintelligible opinions; and that, consequently, it was the duty of a citizen to admit the one, and conform to the other, in the manner prescribed by the law.' Accordingly, at Geneva, he renounced popery.

"After passing twenty years with Theresa, he made her his wife. He appears to have intrigued with a Madam De H——. Of his desires after that lady, he says, 'Guilty without remorse, I soon became so without measure.' Such, according to his own account, was the life of uprightness and honour, which was to expiate for a theft which he had committed when a young man, and laid it to a female servant, by which she lost her place and character. Such was Rousseau, the man whom the rulers of the French nation have delighted to honour, and who, for writing this account, had the vanity and presumption to expect the applause of his Creator. 'Whenever the last trumpet shall sound,' saith he, 'I will present myself before the Sovereign Judge, with this book in my hand, and loudly proclaim, Thus have I acted—these were my thoughts—such was I. Power Eternal! assemble round thy throne the innumerable throng of my fellow mortals! let them listen to my confessions, let them blush at my depravity, let them tremble at my sufferings; let each in his turn expose, with equal sincerity, the failings, the wanderings of his heart;

and, if he dare, aver I was better than that man.'"—So much for the morality of infidels!!!

DISCONTENT AND GRIEF.

"THE discontented man," says Dr. Stennett, "is ever restless and uneasy, dissatisfied with his station in life, his connexions, and almost every circumstance that happens to him. He is continually peevish and fretful, impatient of every injury he receives, and unduly impressed with every disappointment he suffers. He considers most other persons as happier than himself, and enjoys hardly any of the blessings of Providence with a calm and grateful mind. He forms to himself a thousand distressing fears concerning futurity, and makes his present condition unhappy, by anticipating the misery he may endure years to come."

If we examine the records of history; recollect what has happened within the circle of our own experience; consider with attention what has been the conduct of almost all the greatly unfortunate, either in private or public life, whom we may have either read of, or heard of, or remember; and we shall find that the misfortunes of by far the greater part of them, have arisen from their not knowing when they were well, when it was proper for them to sit still, and to be contented. The inscription upon the tombstone of the man who had endeavoured to mend a tolerable constitution by taking physic, "*I was well; I wished to be better: here I am*," may generally be applied with great justness to the distress of disappointed avarice and ambition.

"Men," says an elegant author, "are too often ingenious in making themselves miserable, by aggravating to their own fancy, beyond bounds, all the evils which they endure. They compare themselves with none but those whom they imagine to be more happy; and complain that upon them alone has fallen the whole load of human sorrows. 'I will restore your daughter again to life,' said an Eastern sage to a prince who grieved immoderately for the loss of a beloved child, 'provided you are able to engrave on her tomb the names of three persons who have never mourned.' The prince made inquiry after such persons, but found the inquiry vain, and was silent."

It is said of Mr. G——h, who, though simple, honest, humane, and generous, yet was so peevish and splenetic, that he would often leave a party of his convivial friends abruptly, in order to go home and brood over his misfortunes. How different a disposition was that of Mr. Samuel Medley, the grandfather of the late Mr. Medley, of Liverpool! This good man was particularly noted for his cheerfulness, and was a pleasing example of remarkable confidence in God, as it respected his providential dispensations; frequently saying, he could never fret five minutes in his life, let things look ever so dark.

THE DISGUISED AND DISSOLUTE CLERGYMAN RECLAIMED.

THE following account, as related by a clergyman, may be depended on as a fact:—

"Shortly after the return of the Duke of York from Holland, one of the regiments which had suffered very materially in the different engagements, was quartered in my parish. A private soldier called upon me one evening after divine service, with a request that I would explain a particular part of my discourse which he had just heard, expressing, at the same time, much interest in the general subject of it. I found him to be a very well-informed man, of distinguished piety, and much religious knowledge. His language and address, betrayed evident marks of strong natural sense, aided by an unusual acquaintance with the word of God, and the operations of his grace upon the heart.

"He frequently called upon me during the continuance of the regi-

ment in my neighbourhood, and every succeeding interview gave me fresh proofs of his religious attainments. At that time, he was the only man in the regiment who made any profession of religion, and, on that account, was ridiculed and despised by the greater part of his companions.

"At length, the regiment having nearly repaired, by fresh recruits, the loss sustained in Holland, was ordered to join a camp, then forming, for the purpose of collecting troops for the Egyptian expedition, under the command of Sir Ralph Abercromby. A few days before their departure, W——, (for that was his name,) brought with him another private of the same regiment, who had expressed a particular desire to speak with me, but of whom he knew very little, except that in some of the engagements in Holland, he had been observed voluntarily to seek danger, and needlessly to hazard his person, as if with a desperate resolution of ridding himself of life. On being introduced to me, alone, the stranger said, that he hoped I should excuse the liberty he had taken of coming to request that I would purchase a small parcel which he had brought, in order to enable him to supply himself with a few necessaries, preparatory to his voyage to Egypt, as he had no other means of raising a little money. He was a tall young man, of a dark sun-burned countenance, having something in his aspect, speech, and address, which struck me as being above his present appearance. On opening his parcel, which he did not do without some confusion, it proved to consist of some clergyman's bands, one or two religious books, and some manuscript sermons. 'Sir,' said he, 'you will hear with surprise, and I cannot mention it without some uneasiness, what I have for a long time concealed from every one around me, that I am in reality a brother clergyman, though now disguised in the habit of a common soldier. My father is a clergyman in Wales: he educated me himself for the Church, and procured me ordination, with a title to a curacy, at ——, in the county of W—— : my name is E——. I continued upon that cure three years, during which time, I am sorry to say, through much imprudence and inattention to the decorum which suited my character, I contracted several debts, which I had neither the means, nor the prospect of paying. Fearing disgrace and imprisonment, and knowing my father's inability to assist me, I quitted the town, and formed the resolution of enlisting as a soldier, which I shortly afterwards did, and was soon sent on the expedition to Holland, whence I lately returned. That you may have no doubts as to the truth of my story, which may possibly induce you to sympathize with a brother clergyman in distress, I will show you several letters and papers, which, when you have read, I trust you will give me credit for the truth of my relation.' He, also, wrote some sentences in my presence, which proved his hand-writing to be the same with that of the manuscript sermons he had requested me to purchase. On examining the letters, (some of which were from his father, expostulating with him on his extravagance,) and putting a variety of questions to him, I felt fully satisfied as to the truth of his story.

"I was greatly concerned at what he had related, and began to enter into a close and friendly expostulation with him, on the inconsistency of his present situation, with the sacred profession to which he was bound by ties the most indissoluble. I urged the duty of his endeavouring to return, if possible, to the discharge of his ministerial duties, with a mind influenced and improved by the experience of past hardships and misfortunes. As he did not appear disposed to follow this advice, I brought forward, with much earnestness, every argument which scripture or reason suggested to my mind on the subject, and begged that he would permit

me to endeavour to procure his discharge from the army, by a representation of his case to the Duke of York. Although he spoke to me with much civility, and thanked me for my advice, and the offer I had made, yet I was sorry to perceive a great reluctance on his part to avail himself of my counsel, and but little appearance of remorse for what had passed; he talked like a man weary of the world, who had no desire to continue in it, and no hope of sustaining a respectable character in it : it was plain, that no impression of a religious nature was made on his mind. The peculiarity of his situation, and the occasion of his coming, led him at the same time to pay attention to what I said. I entered into a long conversation with him on the nature and design of Christianity in general, as well as of the pastoral office in particular; examined him as to his views of the doctrines of the gospel, and explained my own to him very fully. I entreated him to take what I had said to him in good part, and urged him by every sacred consideration to act the part which it appeared to me his duty and interest to adopt. He said but little in reply; and almost declined saying any more. I, therefore, purchased his little parcel, gave him a couple of books, and dismissed him with a blessing, once more entreating him to lay to heart what I had said. In two days, the regiment went away; nor did I see either W——, or Mr. E——, before their departure.

"A circumstance of so singular a nature frequently occupied my thoughts afterwards; and whenever I wore the bands which I had purchased from Mr. E——, I felt an increased interest in his behalf. From that time, till the return of our troops from Egypt, I had no opportunity of hearing any thing respecting him, except that a clergyman of his name had certainly officiated at the town which he had specified a few years since : this I learned from a native of the place.

"Some time after, my old acquaintance W——— called upon me, and said he was just arrived from Egypt and had a great deal to say to me. With the same excellence of heart and head as he had testified on every former occasion, he entered into a clear and satisfactory account of the events of the Egyptian expedition; describing, in a very affecting manner, the outward hardships and dangers he had encountered, as well as the inward consolation and support which he had derived from the power of religion on his mind.

"I have now," continued he, "a story to relate, which I am certain you will feel a deep concern in. You, without doubt, remember that young clergyman, whom I brought to your house the year before last; the Rev. Mr. E———. At that time I knew but very little of him; he, however, shortly after we had left you, observed with some emotion, that what you said to him made more impression upon his mind than any thing he had ever heard in the course of his life: he then made me also acquainted with his history, to which I was before a stranger. From that day I was confined in the hospital with a fever, and did not see him again before our departure for Egypt. We embarked on board of different ships; it was not, therefore, till our arrival at Malta, that we met together. Mr. E——— took an immediate opportunity of saying: 'W———, I have long wished to see you; I want to tell you how greatly indebted I feel to that dear friend of your's at ———: I can never forget him; his words made a deep impression on my heart, and I trust, by the blessing of God, they will yet make a still deeper.

"I found, on conversing with him, that, since I saw him, he had become affected with a deep sense of his spiritual danger, and, by meditation and secret prayer during the voyage, had acquired much insight into religion. He showed strong marks of penitence, and gave a fa-vourable hope of an important change having taken place in his views and dispositions. I was also happy to find, that, on the re-assembling of the regiment after the voyage, among the recruits were a few very seriously disposed. Mr. E——— and myself soon formed a little religious society amongst them, which gradually increased to the number of twenty-four: we met as often as possible to read the Bible together, converse on the concerns of eternity, and unite in prayer to Almighty God for his blessing on our endeavours. We derived much benefit from these meetings. Mr. E———, in particular, expressed himself highly delighted by such a profitable mode of passing those hours which, in our line of life, are too generally devoted to drinking, debauchery, and profaneness. In his confidential conversations with me he frequently mentioned your name, and showed me the substance of your friendly advice to him, which he had from memory committed to paper.

"When we arrived on the coast of Africa, Mr. E——— and myself were in the same boat at the time of our landing at Aboukir. Throughout the whole of the tremendous fire, which for a considerable time the French artillery kept upon us, I observed great coolness and patient fortitude in his countenance. His deportment was very different from what I had seen when we served together in Holland. At that time, he always appeared desperate and careless; now, I thought I could perceive a courage blended with humility, which evidently proceeded from a much more exalted source. We both, by the mercy of God, escaped unhurt on that day. Our little society continued its meetings as regularly as the trying circumstances of our situation would permit. Mr. E——— was three or four times engaged with the enemy afterwards, and always behaved, both before and during the battle, with much steady, and I may call it godly, courage.

"On the evening preceding the 21st of March, our whole society met together. Mr. E—— said, in the presence of the rest, 'I cannot account for the strong impression which has seized my mind, that I shall not survive the event of to-morrow's engagement: no such pre-possession ever occupied my thoughts on any former occasion ; I feel, therefore, strongly affected by this : but, if it be thy will, O God! thy will be done.' We then united to-gether in prayer for him, for our-selves, and for all our brethren in arms ; beseeching God to prepare us for the awful trial, and give us grace either to meet death with joyful hope, or to receive his sparing mercy, if our lives should be preserved, with gratitude. Knowing the importance of the next day's battle, and the little chance we stood of all meeting again in this world, we embraced each other with peculiar attachment and mutual recommendation to the God of battle and the Preserver of souls. Oh, Sir, it was a happy but trying season to us! I saw Mr. E—— an hour before the horrors of that bloody day commenced. His words were, ' Pray earnestly for me ; and if I am killed, and you should be spared, give my last blessing to our worthy and dear friend at ——— : tell Mr. ———,' continued he, 'that I owe him more than words can repay. He first opened my heart to conviction, and God has blessed it to repentance ; through the unspeak-able mercies of Christ, I can die with comfort.'

"After the severe engagement which followed, wherein the brave Abercromby fell, according to agree-ment our little society met. Every life was spared except that of poor Mr. E——, whose head was taken off by a cannon ball at an early pe-riod of the action. Such was the will of God. Whilst, therefore, we returned hearty thanks for our pre-servation, we blessed God's goodness for sparing the life of our departed brother, till, by a lively exercise of faith and repentance, as we had every reason to trust, God had made him his own. I now also bless God that I have had this opportunity of seeing and relating to you a story which I know you rejoice to hear."

DOUBTS REMOVED.

A PERSON in a state of despon-dency once gave way to unbelief, so far as to question the whole truth of the Christian religion ; and even came to the resolution of giving up all as a delusion. In this state of mind he was returning home one night to his house near London : it was so dark, that he could not dis-cern a single object before him. It was in the very moment he was doubting if ever such a person as Christ existed at all, and had been crucified without the gates of Jeru-salem, when a man in his way fell right into his arms, and he felt his face against the beard of a Jew, who happened to be going to town. They mutually begged pardon, and depart-ed, and with the Jew went all his doubts for ever. "In the croaking of a Jew," said the late Mr. Ryland, "I hear as if the voice of Gabriel proclaimed from heaven, 'Jesus, the true Messiah, was crucified without the gates of Jerusalem.' "

In the life of Archbishop Ussher, we are told of a lady who had been wavering in her religion, that her doubts were removed by the occasion of a Jesuit's being unable to proceed in a disputation with the bishop, and leaving the place with shame.

Melancthon, going once upon some great service for the church of Christ, and having many doubts and fears about the success of his business, was greatly relieved by a company of poor women and children, whom he found praying together for the prosperity of the church.

Athenagoras, a famous Athenian philosopher in the second century, not only doubted of the truth of the Christian religion, but was deter-mined to write against it : however, upon an intimate inquiry into the facts on which it was supported, in the course of his collecting materials for his intended publication, he was convinced by the blaze of evidence in its favour, and turned his designed invective into an elaborate apology, which is still in being.

THE DUELLIST ALARMED.

The preaching of the late Rev. J. Scott having been made effectual to the production of a great change in a young lady, the daughter of a country gentleman, so that she could no longer join the family in their usual dissipations, and appeared to them as melancholy, or approaching to it ; her father, who was a very gay man, looking upon Mr. Scott as the sole cause of what he deemed his daughter's misfortune, became exceedingly enraged at him; so much so, that he actually lay in wait in order to shoot him. Mr. Scott being providentially apprised of it, was enabled to escape the danger. The diabolical design of the gentleman being thus defeated, he sent Mr. Scott a challenge. Mr. Scott might have availed himself of law, and prosecuted him ; but he took another method. He waited upon him at his house, was introduced to him in his parlour, and, with his characteristic boldness and intrepidity, thus addressed him :—"Sir, I hear that you have designed to shoot me, by which you would have been guilty of murder ; failing in this, you have sent me a challenge! And what a coward must you be, sir, to wish to engage with a blind man (alluding to his being short-sighted !) As you have given me the challenge, it is now my right to chose the time, the place, and the weapon ; I, therefore, appoint the present moment, sir, the place where we now are, and the sword for the weapon, to which I have been the most accustomed." The gentleman was evidently greatly terrified ; when Mr. Scott, having attained his end, produced a pocket Bible, and exclaimed, "This is my sword, sir ; the only weapon I wish to engage with." "Never," said Mr. Scott to a friend to whom he related this anecdote, "never was a poor careless sinner so delighted with the sight of a Bible before !"

Mr. Scott reasoned with the gentleman on the impropriety of his conduct, in treating him as he had done, for no other reason but because he had preached the truth. The result was, the gentleman took him by the hand, begged his pardon, expressed his sorrow for his conduct, and became afterwards very friendly to him.

EDUCATION.

LYCURGUS esteemed it one of the greatest duties of a legislator to form regulations for the education of the Spartan children. His grand maxim was, "That children were the property of the state, to which alone their education was to be entrusted." In their infancy the nurses were instructed to indulge them neither in their diet nor in those little froward humours which are so peculiar to that age ; to inure them to bear cold and fasting; to conquer their first fears, by accustoming them to solitude and darkness. Their diet and clothing were just sufficient to support nature, and defend them from the inclemency of the seasons. Their sports and exercises were such as contributed to render their limbs supple, and their bodies compact and firm. Their learning was sufficient for their occasions ; for Lycurgus admitted nothing but what was truly *useful.* They trained them up in the best of sciences—the principles of wisdom and virtue.

Agesilaus, King of Sparta, being asked what he thought most proper for boys to learn, answered, "What they ought to do when they come to be men." Thus useful, not extensive or ostentatious, learning is the best.

In the education of young persons, much is to be considered in respect to their teachers. As such ought to be possessed of ability, so they ought to be encouraged. "Pity it is," says the great Mr. Ascham, "that commonly more care is had, yea, and that among very wise men, to find out rather a cunning man for their horse, than a cunning man for their children. They say *nay* in one word, but they do so in deed; for to one they will gladly give a stipend of two hundred crowns by the year, and are loth to offer to the other two hundred shillings. God, that sitteth in heaven, laugheth their choice to scorn, and rewardeth their liberality as it should. For he suffereth them to have tame and well ordered horses, but wild and unfortunate children; and, therefore, in the end, they find more pleasure in their horse than comfort in their child."

The moral principle of children ought to be strictly attended to. They who write of Japan tell us that these people, though mere heathens, take such an effectual course in the education of their children, as to render a lie and breach of faith above all things odious to them; insomuch, that it is a very rare thing for any person among them to be taken in a lie, or found guilty of breach of faith. What a reproach is this to Christians! How culpable are they, whether tutors or parents, who even for once suffer a lie to pass unpunished or unreproved!

Plato, in several parts of his writings, lays down this great principle: That the end of the education and instruction of youth, as well as of government, is to make them better; and that whosoever departs from this rule, how meritorious soever he may otherwise appear to be in reality, does not deserve either the esteem or the approbation of the public. This judgment that great philosopher gave of one of the most illustrious citizens of Athens, who had long governed the republic with the highest reputation; who had filled the town with temples, theatres, statues, and public buildings, beautified it with the most famous monuments, and set it off with ornaments of gold; who had drawn into it whatever was curious in sculpture, painting, and architecture, and

13

had fixed in his works the model and rule of taste for all posterity.

"But," says Plato, "can they name one single man, citizen or foreigner, bond or free, beginning with his own children, whom Pericles made wiser or better by all his care?" He very judiciously observes, that his conduct, on the contrary, had caused the Athenians to degenerate from the virtues of their ancestors, and had rendered them idle, effeminate, babblers, busy-bodies, fond of extravagant expenses, and admirers of vanity and superfluity. From whence he concludes, that it was wrong to cry up his administration so excessively, since he deserved no more than a groom, who, undertaking the care of a fine horse, had taught him only to stumble and kick, to be hardmouthed, skittish, and vicious.—It is easy to apply this to education: it is of little consequence what we teach children, if we do not learn them to be *better*.

We should be careful what books we put into the hands of children. All publications tending to infidelity, looseness of character, vice, &c. ought to be proscribed. If the Athenian laws were so delicate, that they disgraced any one who showed an inquiring traveller the wrong road, what disgrace, among Christians, should attach to that tutor, parent, or author, who, when a youth is inquiring the road to genuine and useful knowledge, directs him to blasphemy and unbelief?

The effect of a good education, in a national point of view, is very important. The late celebrated Henry Fielding assured a person, that, during his long administration of justice in Bow Street, only six Scotchmen were brought before him. The remark did not proceed from any national partiality in the magistrate, but was produced by him in proof of the effect of a sober and religious education, among the lower ranks, on their morals and conduct.

From the tables of the celebrated Mr. Howard, it appears that in the whole of Scotland, whose population, at the time of his calculation, was estimated at one million six hundred thousand souls, only one hundred and thirty-four persons were convicted of capital crimes in a period of nineteen years, being, on the average, about seven in each year. In a subsequent table we are informed, that in the single circuit of Norfolk in England, including six counties, and containing not more, it is supposed, than eight hundred thousand persons, (being but one half of the population of Scotland,) no less than four hundred and thirty criminals were condemned to death in the space of twenty-three years; which is an annual average of nearly nineteen capital convicts, besides eight hundred and seventy-four sentenced to transportation.

THE EMPTY CHURCH.

WHERE the truth is not preached in its purity and simplicity, we do not find many hearers. A minister went one day to a certain church in the city to officiate for the lecturer. After a walk of two miles, he entered the church a few minutes before the time, and was surprised not to see an individual in the church, except the boy who was tolling the bell with the surplice on his arm. He went into the vestry, and was but just sat down, when a man in black opened the door, and walking up, addressed him with a very consequential air: "Pray, Sir, who may you be?" "Who am I?—Such a one: and am come to preach for your lecturer this afternoon."—"There was nobody here last Sunday," said this man; "and I see nobody to-day." Upon which, taking up his hat, he stalked off with dignity, saying, "Let us depart in peace;" and left the clergyman overwhelmed with indignation and astonishment. These things ought not so to be. On the Lord's day—in the midst of the city of London—in one of its most beautiful churches—not an individual attended for two successive sabbaths!—

They Ɐ⅂ⱢⱢNⱢ   e for effects so
awfu

T   XPOSITOR.
M   :t at Boston, in
Am   to his wonted
libe   ent of chocolate,
sug   v. Dr. B. with a
bill   ceptance of it as
a c‒‒‒‒‒‒ ‒‒ ‒‒‒ vi. 6, "Let him that is taught in the word, communicate unto him that teacheth in all good things." The Doctor, who was then confined by sickness, returned his compliments to Mr. W. thanked him for his excellent *family expositor*, and wished Mr. W. to give him a practical exposition of Matt. xxv. 36. "I was sick, and ye visited me."

THE PIOUS FARMERS.
The Farmer's Faith better than the Prelate's Disquisitions.

THE late King of Sweden was, it seems, under serious impressions for some time before his death. A peasant being once, on a particular occasion, admitted to his presence, the king, knowing him to be a person of singular piety, asked him, "What he took to be the true nature of faith?" The peasant entered deeply into the subject, and much to the king's comfort and satisfaction. The king at last, lying on his death bed, had a return of his doubts and fears as to the safety of his soul; and still the same question was perpetually in his mouth to those about him—"What is real faith?" His attendants advised him to send for the Archbishop of Upsal; who, coming to the king's bedside, began in a learned logical manner to enter into the scholastic definition of faith. The prelate's disquisition lasted an hour. When he had done, the king said, with much energy, "*All this is ingenious, but not comfortable; it is not what I want; nothing, after all, but the farmer's faith will do for me.*" So true is that observation, that religion is a plain thing; and indeed it wants no metaphysical subtilties, no critical disquisitions, no laborious reasonings, to set it in a clear light.

When the late Mr. Burgess was a boy, he went with a load of seed wheat to a farm-house some miles distant : on the road they met a wagoner, who asked where they were going. They told him; and he answered, " The Lord have mercy upon you, then, for you and your horses will be sadly taken care of." When they arrived at the house, the master came out, and said, " Well, my boys, you are safely arrived; come in and refresh yourselves: my men shall unload your wheat, and take care of your horses." This was accordingly done. When Mr. B was in the house, partaking of his hospitality, he thought certainly this man was one of those he had read of in the Bible, who were despised for their religion, being exceedingly surprised to find him act so contrary to the account he had heard; when, looking at the chimney-piece, he saw the following lines :

"I have no house-room for the cursed swearer,
"Nor any welcome for the false tale-bearer :
" The liar shall not in my presence dwell:
"Such guests as those are only fit for hell."

Mr. B. lived to be upwards of seventy, when he visited that same place, found the house new built, in the possession of a good man, and the same lines written over the new chimney-piece.

FASHION.

" The power of fashion (says Mr. Cogan, in his Treatise on the Passions) is an ideal influenza, that spreads with the utmost rapidity, infecting a whole community where it commenced ; sometimes extending to distant nations, and acquiring such strength in its progress, that nothing can resist its force. It does not possess the degree of merit attendant upon the excessive love of novelty, which always imagines the object to possess some degree of worth ; a circumstance, this, by no means essential to the influence of fashion, whose authority is, in general, derived from things known to be idle and insignificant. Fashion gives absolute sway to modes, forms, colours, &c. wantonly introduced by the whim of an individual, with whom the majority have not the most distant connexion ; concerning whom they are totally ignorant, unless circumstances and situations of notoriety should render their characters either *equivocal* or *unequivocal*. It is capable of instantaneously altering our opinion of the nature and qualities of things, without demanding any painful exertions of the understanding, or requiring the slow process of investigation. With the quickness of a magic wand, it in a moment subverts all those ideas of beauty, elegance, and propriety, we had before cherished. It makes us reject as odious, what we had lately contemplated as most desirable ; and raptures are inspired by qualities we had just considered as pernicious and deformed. Unwilling to renounce our title to rationality, unable to resist the power of fashion, we make every attempt to reconcile reason with absurdity : thus, in numberless instances, we attempt to vindicate to ourselves and others the novel affection."

Too much attention to fashionable dress certainly displays an imbecility of mind. Alphonsus, King of Arragon, used to wear no better apparel than the ordinary sort of his subjects did ; and, being advised by one to put on kingly apparel, he answered, " I had rather excel my subjects in my behaviour and authority, than in a diadem and purple garments."

Augustus Cæsar used to say, " that rich and gay clothing was either the ensign of pride, or the nurse of luxury." A very just sentiment.

Alexander Severus, when he came to be Emperor of Rome, sold all the precious stones which were in the palace, saying, "that they were not of any use to men." He wore very plain and ordinary apparel, saying, " that the empire consisted in virtue, not in bravery."

In the reign of W. Rufus, there

was a mode which prevailed throughout Europe, both among men and women, to give an enormous length to their shoes, to draw the toe to a sharp point, and to affix to it the figure of a bird's bill, or some such ornament which was turned upwards, and which was often sustained by gold or silver chains tied to the knee.

The ecclesiastics took exception at this ornament, which they said was an attempt to belie the scripture, where it is affirmed that no man can add to his stature; and they declaimed against it with great vehemence; nay, assembled some synods, who actually condemned it. But such was the power of fashion and custom, that though the clergy at that time could overturn thrones, and had sufficient authority to send above a million of men on their errand (crusades) to the deserts of Asia, they could not prevail against these long pointed shoes; and it actually maintained its ground, in opposition to all, for several centuries.

"It may be a sufficient censure of some fashions," observes Mr. Newton, "to say that they are ridiculous. Their chief effect is to disfigure the female form. And perhaps the inventors of them had no worse design than to make a trial, how far they could lead the passive unthinking *many* in the path of absurdity." Some fashions, which seem to have been at first designed to hide a personal deformity, have obtained a general prevalence with those who had no such deformity to hide. We are informed that Alexander had a wry neck, and therefore his courtiers carried their heads on one side, that they might appear to be in the king's fashion. We smile at this servility in people who lived in Macedonia twenty centuries before we were born; yet it is little less general among ourselves in the present day.

A lady once asked a minister, whether a person might not pay some attention to dress and the fashions without being proud. "Madam," replied the minister, "whenever you see the tail of the fox out of the hole, you may be sure the fox is there."

A certain minister lately paid a visit to a lady of his acquaintance who was newly married, and who was attired in the modern indecent fashion. After the usual compliments, he familiarly said, "I hope you have got a good husband, Madam." "Yes, Sir," replied she, "and a good man too,"—"I don't know what to say about his goodness," added the minister, rather bluntly; "for my Bible teaches me that a good man should clothe his wife, but he lets you go half naked."

The Man of Fashion.

"The external graces, the frivolous accomplishment of that impertinent and foolish thing called a man of fashion, are commonly more admired than the solid and masculine virtues of a warrior, a statesman, a philosopher, or a legislator. All the great and awful virtues, all the virtues which can fit either for the council, the senate, or the field, are, by the insolent and insignificant flatterers who commonly figure the most in such corrupted societies, held in the utmost contempt and derision. When the Duke of Sully was called upon by Lewis the Thirteenth to give his advice in some great emergency, he observed the favourites and courtiers whispering to one another, and smiling at his unfashionable appearance. 'Whenever your majesty's father,' said the old warrior and statesman, 'did me the honour to consult me, he ordered the buffoons of the court to retire into the anti-chamber.'"

FEMALES, ANECDOTES OF.

Learned Females.

LADIES have sometimes distinguished themselves as prodigies of learning. Many of the most eminent geniuses of the French nation have been of the female sex. Several of our countrywomen have also made a respectable figure in the republic of letters.

Queen Elizabeth, by a double translating of Greek without missing, every forenoon, and of Latin every afternoon, attained to such a perfect understanding in both tongues, and to such a ready utterance of Latin, and that with such judgment, as there were few in either of the universities, or elsewhere in England, that were comparable to her.

Of Lady Jane Gray it is said, that beside her skill in the Latin and Greek languages, she was acquainted with the Hebrew also; so as to be able to satisfy herself in both the originals.

Mary Cunitz, one of the greatest geniuses in the sixteenth century, was born in Silesia. She learned languages with amazing facility, and understood Polish, German, French, Italian, Latin, Greek, and Hebrew. She attained a knowledge of the sciences with equal ease; she was skilled in history, physic, poetry, painting, music, and playing upon instruments; and yet these were only an amusement. She more particularly applied herself to the mathematics, and especially to astronomy, which she made her principal study, and was ranked in the number of the most able astronomers of her time. Her astronomical tables acquired her a prodigious reputation.

Anna Maria Schurman was born in the year 1607. Her extraordinary genius discovered itself at six years of age, when she cut all sorts of figures in paper with her scissars, without a pattern. At eight she learned, in a few days, to draw flowers in a very agreeable manner. At ten, she took but three hours to learn embroidery. Afterwards she was taught music, vocal and instrumental, painting, sculpture, and engraving, in all which she succeeded admirably. She excelled in miniature painting, and in cutting portraits upon glass with a diamond. Hebrew, Greek, and Latin, were so familiar to her, that the most learned

men were astonished at it. She spoke French, Italian, and English, fluently. Her hand-writing, in almost all languages, was so inimitable, that the curious preserved specimens of it in their cabinets.

Constantia Grierson, born of poor parents in the county of Kilkenny, in Ireland, was one of the most learned women on record, though she died at the age of twenty-seven, in 1733. She was an excellent Greek and Latin scholar, and understood history, divinity, philosophy, and mathematics. She proved her skill in Latin, by her dedication of the Dublin edition of Tacitus to Lord Carteret, and by that of Terrence to his son; to whom she also addressed a Greek epigram.

Mary, Queen of Scots, at an early period, is said to have pronounced, with great applause, before the whole court, a Latin harangue, in which she proved that it was not unbecoming the fair sex to cultivate letters, and to acquire learning.—She applied also, with great success, to the study of the French, Italian, and Spanish, which she spoke not only with propriety, but with fluency and case.

Margaret, Dutchess of Newcastle, if not a learned, is known, at least, as a voluminous writer, for she extended her literary productions to the number of twelve folio volumes.

These instances are not selected to imply that a *learned education* ought to be given to females in general. They are sufficient, however, I think, to decide the controversy respecting the intellectual talents of women, compared with those of men; enough to prove that there are radical powers in the female sex as well as the male.

Females, however, would do well to embrace every opportunity of enlarging their minds with useful knowledge. Instead of losing time by perusing those works of imagination in which so many take delight, and by which so many are actually rendered dissolute, how much better

13*

to see them employed in studying the pages of history, of grammar, of morality, of useful literature in general, and of religion ! And here I cannot help recommending to my female readers Mrs. Hannah Moore's admirable Strictures on Education, "which (says Dr. Porteus, the late Bishop of London) present to the reader such a fund of good sense, of wholesome counsel, of sagacious observation, of a knowledge of the world and of the female heart, of high-toned morality and genuine christian piety ; and all this enlivened with such brilliancy of wit, such richness of imagery, such variety and felicity of allusion, such neatness and elegance of diction, as are not, I conceive, easily to be found so combined and blended together in any other work in the English language."—See the bishop's charge to his clergy in 1798, 1799.

Industrious Females.

I once knew a lady (observes one) noble by birth, but more noble by her virtues, who never sat idle in company, unless when compelled to it by the punctilio of ceremony, which she took care should happen as rarely as possible. Being a perfect mistress of her needle, and having an excellent taste in that as in many other things, her manner, whether at home or abroad with her friends, was to be constantly engaged in working something useful or something beautiful ; at the same time that she assisted in supporting the conversation with an attention and capacity which I have never seen exceeded. For the sake of variety and improvement when in her own house, some one of the company would often read aloud, while she and her female visitants were thus employed. I must add, that during an intimate acquaintance of several years, I do not remember ever to have seen her once driven to the polite necessity of either winning or losing money at play, and making her guests defray the expense of the entertainment.

What a happy simplicity prevailed in ancient times, when it was the custom for ladies, though of the greatest distinction, to employ themselves in useful and sometimes laborious works ! Every one knows what is told us in scripture to this purpose concerning Rebecca, Rachel, and several others. We read in Homer of princesses drawing themselves water from springs, and washing, with their own hands, the finest of the linen of their respective families. The sisters of Alexander the Great, who were the daughters of a powerful prince, employed themselves in making clothes for their brothers. The celebrated Lucretia used to spin in the midst of her female attendants. Among the Romans, no citizen of any note ever appeared in public in any garb but what was spun by his wife and daughters. It was a custom in the northern parts of the world, not many years ago, for the princesses who then sat upon the throne to prepare several of the dishes at every meal. The depravity of the age has, indeed, affixed to these customs an idea of meanness and contempt ; but, then, what has it substituted in the room of them ? A soft indolence, a stupid idleness, frivolous conversation, vain amusements, a strong passion for public shows, and a frantic love of gaming.

The habits of industry, says an elegant female writer, cannot be too early, too sedulously formed. Let not the sprightly and the brilliant reject industry as a plebian quality ; as a quality to be exercised only by those who have their bread to earn, or their fortune to make. It is the quality to which the immortal Newton modestly ascribed his own vast attainments ; who, when he was asked by what means he had been enabled to make that successful progress which struck mankind with wonder, replied, that it was not so much owing to any superior strength of genius, as to a habit of patient thinking, laborious attention, and close application. Industry is the sturdy and hard-working pioneer, who, by persevering labour, removes obstructions, overcomes difficulties, clears intricacies, and then facilitates the march and aids the victories of genius.

Useful Females.

It is said of the wife of the learned Budæus, that, so far from drawing him from his studies, she was sedulous to animate him when he languished. Ever at his side, and ever assiduous, ever with some useful book in her hand, she acknowledged herself to be a most happy woman. Budæus was not insensible of his singular felicity : he called her the faithful companion, not of his life only, but of his studies.

We owe, it is said, to the wife of Judge Croke, and her superiority of soul; we owe to the virtue of this woman, and her disregard of selfish considerations, in comparison of the honour and duty of her husband, the immortal decision in the case of *ship-money;* a decision which fixed one of the bulwarks of our constitution; a decision of more durable and certain worth than a thousand triumphs. She told her husband, who had resolved to give his opinion for this new claim of prerogative, that "She hoped he would do nothing against his conscience, for fear of any danger or prejudice to him or his family; and that she would be content to suffer want or any misery with him, rather than be an occasion for him to do or say any thing against his judgment or conscience."—Vide White-lock's Memorials, 25. Macauly, vol. xi. p. 226, 227.

We owe to the virtue of another admirable woman (Queen of Edward III.) that one of the most illustrious of kings did not, at the siege of Calais, eclipse the lustre of his conquest by a cruelty which would for ever have been a disgrace to our annals. The king, having turned the siege into a blockade, was greatly incensed at their obstinate resistance, which had detained him eleven months under their walls. At length, however, he consented to grant their lives to all the garrison and inhabitants, except six of the principal burgesses, who should deliver to him the keys of the city with ropes about their necks. When these terms were made known to the people of Calais, they were plunged in the deepest distress; and, after all the miseries they had suffered, they could not think without horror of giving up six of their fellow-citizens to cer tain death. In this extremity, when the whole people were drowned in tears, and uncertain what to do, Eustace De Pierre, one of the richest merchants in the place, stepped forth, and voluntarily offered himself to be one of these six devoted victims. His noble example was soon imitated by five others of the most wealthy citizens. These true patriots, barefooted and bareheaded, with ropes about their necks, were attended to the gates by the whole inhabitants, with tears, blessings, and prayers, for their safety. When they were brought into Edward's presence, they laid the keys of the city at his feet; and, falling on their knees, implored his mercy in such moving strains, that all the noble spectators melted into tears. The king's resentment was so strong for the many toils and losses he had suffered in this tedious siege, that he was in some danger of forgetting his usual humanity ; when the queen, falling upon her knees, before him, earnestly begged and obtained their lives. This great and good princess conducted these virtuous citizens, whose lives she had saved, to her own apartment, entertained them honourably, and dismissed them with presents.

It is said of Queen Mary II. that she ordered good books to be laid in the places of attendance, that persons might not be idle while they were in their turns of service. She gave her minutes of leisure to architecture and gardening; and since it *employed many* hands, she said, *she hoped it would be forgiven her.*

How peculiarly useful may females be in a domestic state! In many cases, observes one, the opinion of

L

the wife may be preferable to that of our own. Their judgment may be less clouded by interest ; they stand back from the objects ; we are too near ; they are cool and calm ; we, by being in the scene, are ruffled and inflamed. An eminent minister, a few years ago, in a publication, declared to the world, that he had never, in any particular business, acted contrary to the suggestions of his wife, without having reason afterwards to repent of it.

Let me press upon my fair readers to study plans of usefulness, both as to the body and the mind, so that their families, their neighbours, their friends, their country, may be the better for them. "While others are weightily engaged in catching a fashion, or adjusting a curl, let the object of your cultivation be the understanding, the memory, the will, the affections, the conscience. Let no part of this internal creation be unadorned ; let it sparkle with the diamonds of wisdom, of prudence, of humility, of gentleness. These ornaments alone will confer dignity, and prepare for usefulness."

It would be a pleasant summer amusement, says Mrs. H. Moore, for our young ladies of fortune, if they were to preside at such spinning feasts as are instituted at Nuneham, for the promotion of virtue and industry in their own sex. Pleasurable anniversaries of this kind would serve to combine in the minds of the poor two ideas which ought never to be separated, but which *they* are not very forward to unite,—that the great wish is to make them *happy* as well as good.

It would be a noble employment, observes the above mentioned authoress, and well becoming the tenderness of their sex, if ladies were to consider the superintendence of the poor as their immediate office. They are peculiarly fitted for it ; for, from their own habits of life, they are more intimately acquainted with domestic wants than the other sex ; and in certain instances of sickness and suffering peculiar to themselves they should be expected to have more sympathy, and they have obviously more leisure. There is a certain religious society distinguished by simplicity of dress, manners, and language, whose poor are, perhaps, taken better care of than any other ; and one reason may be, that they are immediately under the inspection of the women.

"Do you know," says an ingenious writer, "what we must admire in you ? It is not your dress : we could make a beast fine with trappings. It is not your abilities ; it would not be your abilities, if you had such powers as angels have ; for, indeed, what but a fine creature is Gabriel to us ? a fine speculation, more beautiful than the rainbow to look at ; but what is it to us ? What we admire, and what we ought to admire, in man, is that collection of fine feelings which make him a human creature, social and useful. Sympathy and fellow feeling, tenderness of heart and pity for the wretched, compassion for your neighbours, and reverence for your God, the melting eye, the soothing tone, the silver features, the ingenious devices, the rapid actions of a soul all penetrated with reason and religion, these are the qualities we admire in you. O, I love the soul that must and will do good, the kind creature that runs to the sick bed, I might rather say bedstead, of a poor neighbour, wipes away the moisture of a fever, smooths the clothes, beats up the pillow, fills the pitcher, sets it within reach, administers only a cup of cold water ; but in the true spirit of a disciple of Christ becomes a fellow worker with Christ in the administration of happiness to mankind. Peace be with that good soul ! She also must come in due time into the condition of her neighbour, and then may the Lord strengthen her upon the bed of languishing, and, by some kind hand like her own, make all her bed in her sickness."

A tribute of respect might be here

paid to celebrated pious women. The names of Parr, Russell, Rowe, Hope, Glenorchy, Huntingdon, Langham, Warwick, Hastings, Brooks, and a vast number of others, will not soon be forgotten. But for interesting accounts of these illustrious characters, see Gibbon's Memoirs of Pious Women, with additions, by the Rev. G. Jerment.

THE FOOL'S REPROOF.

THERE was a certain nobleman (says Bishop Hall) who kept a fool, to whom he one day gave a staff, with a charge to keep it till he should meet with one who was a greater fool than himself: not many years after, the nobleman fell sick, even unto death. The fool came to see him : his sick lord said to him, " I must shortly leave you."—" And whither are you going ?" said the fool. " Into another world," replied his lordship.— " And when will you come again ? Within a month ?" " No."—" Within a year ?" " No."—" When then ?" " Never."—"Never !" said the fool : " and what provision hast thou made for thy entertainment there whither thou goest ?" " None at all."— " No ?" said the fool, "none at all ! Here, then, take my staff; for, with all my folly, I am not guilty of any such folly as this."

FORBEARANCE AND KINDNESS.

" ALL that is great and good in the universe is on the side of clemency and mercy. If we look into the history of mankind, we shall find that in every age, those who have been respected as worthy, have been distinguished for this virtue. Revenge dwells in little minds : a noble and magnanimous spirit is superior to it. Collected within itself, it stands unmoved by the impotent assaults of our enemies ; and with generous pity, rather than with anger, looks down on their unworthy conduct. It has been truly said, that the greatest man on earth can no sooner commit an injury, than a good man can make himself greater by forgiving it.

Anger and revenge are uneasy passions ; " hence," says Seed, " it appears that the command of loving our enemies, which has been thought a hard saying, and impossible to be fulfilled, is really no more, when resolved into its first principles, than bidding us to be at peace with ourselves, which we cannot be, so long as we continue at enmity with others."

The heathens themselves saw the reasonableness of the spirit which we are now inculcating, and approved of it. It is said, concerning Julius Cæsar, that upon any provocation he would repeat the Roman alphabet before he suffered himself to speak, that he might be more just and calm in his resentments, and also that he could forget nothing but wrongs, and remember nothing but benefits.

It becomes a man, says the Emperor Antoninus, to love even those that offend him. A man hurts himself, says Epictetus, by injuring me ; and what then ? Shall I therefore hurt myself by injuring him ?—In benefits, says Seneca, it is a disgrace to be outdone ; in injuries, to get the better. Another heathen, when he was angry, with one by him, said, " I would beat thee ; but I am angry."

Philip, the King of Macedon, discovered great moderation, even when he was spoken to in shocking and injurious terms. At the close of an audience which he gave to some Athenian ambassadors who were come to complain of some act of hostility, he asked whether he could do them any service. " The greatest service thou couldst do us," said Demochares, " will be to hang thyself." Philip, though he perceived all the persons present were highly offended at these words, made the following answer, with the utmost calmness of temper : "Go ; tell your superiors, that those who dare make use of such insolent language are more haughty and less peaceably inclined than those who can forgive them."

It is recorded to the honour of Edward III. that one day, being laid down upon the bed, one of his domestics, who did not know that he was in the room, stole some money out of a chest he found open, which the king let him carry off without saying a word. Presently after the boy returned to make a second attempt. the king called out to him, without any violence of passion, "Sirrah, you had best be satisfied with what you have got; for if my chamberlain come and catch you, he will not only take away what you have stolen, but also whip you severely." The chamberlain coming in and missing the money, fell into a great rage; but the king calmly said to him, "Be content; the chest should not have been left open. The temptation was too strong for the poor youth: he wanted money more than we do, and there is still enough left for us."

There was one who did Sir Matthew Hale a great injury, who, coming afterwards to him for his advice in the settlement of his estate, he gave it very frankly to him, but would accept no fee for it; and thereby showed both that he could forgive as a Christian, and that he had the soul of a gentleman in him, not to take money of one who had wronged him so heinously. When he was asked by one how he could use a man so kindly who had wronged him so much, his answer was, he thanked God, he had learned to forget injuries.

Tiberius, the Roman emperor, at the beginning of his reign, acted, in most things, like a truly generous, good-natured, and clement prince. All slanderous reports, libels, and lampoons, upon him and his administration, he bore with extraordinary patience; saying, "That in a free state, the thoughts and tongues of every man ought to be free;" and, when the senate would have proceeded against some who had published libels against him, he would not consent to it, saying, "We have not time enough to attend to such trifles: if you once open a door to such in-

formations, you will be able to do nothing else; for, under that pretence, every man will revenge himself upon his enemies by accusing them to you." How noble was the conduct of this heathen! and what a reproof does his conduct afford to many who are professed Christians, and who have not learnt that apostolic lesson, "to be patient toward all men!"

Mr. Burkitt observes, in his Journal, that some persons would never have had a particular share in his prayers, but for the injuries they had done him. This reminds me of an exemplary passage concerning Mr. Lawrence's once going, with some of his sons, by the house of a gentleman that had been injurious to him: he gave a charge to his sons to this purpose, "That they should never think or speak amiss of that gentleman, for the sake of any thing he had done against him; but, whenever they went by his house, should lift up their hearts in prayer to God for him and his family." This good man had learnt to practice that admirable precept of our Lord, "Pray for them which despitefully use you and persecute you."

Of Mr. John Henderson, it is observed, that the oldest of his friends never beheld him otherwise than calm and collected: it was a state of mind he retained under all circumstances. During his residence at Oxford, a student of a neighbouring college, proud of his logical acquirements, was solicitous of a private disputation with the renowned Henderson: some mutual friends introduced him, and, having chosen his subject, they conversed for some time with equal candour and moderation; but Henderson's antagonist, perceiving his confutation inevitable, (forgetting the character of a gentleman, and with a resentment engendered by his former arrogance,) threw a full glass of wine *in his face*. Henderson, without altering his features, or changing his position, gently wiped his face, and then coolly replied,

' This, Sir, *is a digression: now for the argument.*"

A certain noble courtier being asked by what means he had continued so long in favour, replied, "By being thankful, and patiently enduring injuries."

A gentleman once went to Sir Eardley Wilmot, Knt. (late Lord Chief Justice of the Court of Common Pleas,) under the impression of great wrath and indignation, at a real injury he had received from a person high in the political world, and which he was meditating how to resent in the most effectual manner. After relating the particulars, he asked Sir Eardley, if he did not think it would be *manly* to resent it. "Yes," said the knight, "it will be *manly* to resent it, but it will be *God-like* to forgive it." The gentleman declared, that this had such an instantaneous effect upon him, that he came away quite a different man, and in a very different temper from that in which he went.

Mr. Cecil observes of the late ingenious artist, Bacon, that though he was naturally irritable, yet he was not at all vindictive : he was warm in his attachments, but more disposed to lament his wrongs than to resent them. "I do not recollect," says Mr. C., "any one in which I have observed so much natural irritability, tempered with such meekness and forbearance. The following instance will exemplify this remark. While Mr. Bacon was walking one day in Westminster Abbey, he observed a person standing before his principal work, who seemed to pride himself on his taste and skill in the arts, and who was exuberant in his remarks. "This monument of Chatham," said he to Mr. B. (whom it is evident he took for a stranger,) "is admirable upon the whole, but it has great defects." "I should be greatly obliged," said Mr. B., "if you would be so kind as to point them out to me."— "Why, here," said the critic ; "and there, do you not see ? Bad—very bad !" at the same time employing his stick upon the lower figures with a violence that was likely to injure the work. "But," said Mr. B., "I should be glad to be acquainted *why* the parts you touched, are bad?" He found, however, nothing determinate in the reply, but the same vague assertions repeated, and accompanied with the same violence. "I told Bacon," said he, "repeatedly of this, while the monument was forming: I pointed out other defects ; but I could not convince him." "What, then, you are personally acquainted with Bacon ?" said Mr. B. "O yes," replied the stranger, "I have been intimate with him for many years." Mr. B., instead of being roused to indignant anger, only said, "It is well for you, then," taking his leave of him, "that your friend, Bacon, is not now at your elbow ; for he would not have been pleased at seeing his work so roughly handled."

It happened, during a voyage from Pensacola to Cadiz, that a captain of infantry, who could not swim (one of the officers who had so basely trepanned Mr. Bowles, and was now accompanying him to old Spain,) fell overboard ; and, as his countrymen exhibited no great degree of celerity in hoisting out the boat, he was in the most imminent danger of being drowned. Mr. Bowles viewed the scene, and, as it may be easily supposed, was not unmoved at it. He now beheld an enemy, who had committed a flagrant breach of faith on one element, about to be sacrificed by another; but, at the same time, he saw a fellow creature struggling for existence, and the noble sentiments of a Pagan poet, not unworthy or inferior to any ever inculcated by a Christian sage, finally prevailed :

"Homo sum et nihil a me alienum puto."

Mr. Bowles, at that critical moment, happened to stand upon the poop, clothed in a Spanish dress, and, having determined on what he was to do, he instantly threw aside his gold-laced habit, and, leaping into the sea, swam towards the spot where his persecutor maintained a feeble and unequal struggle with the waves. Having come up with him, he lifted his head above the water, and addressed him thus in the Castilian language, within sight and hearing of the officers and ship's crew :— "Wretch! it is in my power either to leave you to your fate, or to precipitate you, at this very moment, to the bottom of the ocean ;—live, however, (added he, raising him up,) if life can be desirable to such a man as you, and from my hands!" Having spoken thus, he bore him towards the frigate, and helped to get him on board. This circumstance made a suitable impression on the minds of the spectators ; and, to the honour of the Spaniards, be it recorded, it was mentioned afterwards at Madrid with great eulogium and applause.

"Let nothing," says one, "be done too suddenly, or angrily : let us be men of thoughts. It was the habit of more than one holy man, not to give a reply to any important query before he had made a pause, and put up a silent ejaculation ; and a steady person used to stop another, inconsiderately hasty, with, ' Pray stay a little, and we shall have done the sooner.' "

The late Rev. Mr. Clarke, of Frome, was a man of peace. He was one day asked by a friend, "How he kept himself from being involved in quarrels ?" He answered, " By letting the angry person always have the quarrel to himself." This saying seems to have had some influence on some of the inhabitants of that town ; for, when a quarrel has been likely to ensue, they have said, "Come, let us remember old Mr. Clarke, and leave the angry man to quarrel by himself." If this maxim were followed, it would be a vast saving of expense, of comfort, and of honour, to thousands of the human race.

FORTITUDE, INTREPIDITY, AND CONTEMPT OF DEATH.

WHAT vast extremes characterize the mind of man! While some tremble at the shaking of a leaf, and die in the very thought of danger, others possess not only strength of mind sufficient to bear the difficulties of life, but shrink not at the very approach of death itself.

Anaxarchus, the philosopher, having sharply reproved Nicroceon, and being by him ordered to be beaten to death with iron mallets, said, "Strike, strike on : thou mayest break in pieces this vessel of Anaxarchus, but Anaxarchus himself thou canst not touch." So Socrates is reported to have cried out, when persecuted, "Amyntas and Meletus," said he, "can kill me, but they cannot *hurt* me."

When a handful of Spartans undertook to defend the pass of Thermopylæ against the whole army of Persia, so prodigious, it was reported, were the multitude of the Persians, that the very flight of their arrows would intercept the shining of the sun. "Then," said Dieneces, one of the Spartan leaders, " we shall have the advantage of fighting in the shade."

Just before the battle of Agincourt, news was brought to King Henry's camp, that the French were exceedingly numerous ; that they would bring into the field more than six times the number of the English troops ; to which the brave Captain Gam immediately replied, "Is it so ? Then there are enough to be cut in pieces, enough to be made prisoners, and enough to run away."

Sir Thomas More, some time Lord Chancellor of England, fell into disgrace with his sovereign, and was committed to the Tower : on which occasion, the Lieutenant of the Tower made an apology for the diet, lodging, and accommodations, as unsuitable to the dignity of so great a man. "No apology, Sir," replied the courtly prisoner : " I don't question but I shall like your accommodations very well ; and, if you once hear me complain, I give you free leave to turn me out of doors."

Sir John Lisle, a royalist in the civil wars, was sentenced to death after being taken prisoner at the seige of Colchester. This brave man, having tenderly embraced the corpse of Sir Charles Lucas, his departed friend, immediately presented himself to the soldiers, who stood ready for his execution. Thinking that they stood at too great a distance, he desired them to come nearer. One of them said, "I warrant you, Sir, we shall hit you." He replied, with a smile, "Friends, I have been nearer you when you have missed me."

When Sir Walter Raleigh was brought upon the scaffold to suffer death, he vindicated his conduct in a most eloquent and pathetic speech, and then, feeling the edge of the fatal instrument of death, observed, with a smile, "*It is a sharp medicine, but a sure remedy for all woes.*" Being asked which way he would lay himself on the block, he replied, "*So the heart be right, it is no matter which way the head lies.*"

Pierre Du Terrail, Chevalier De Bayard, being mortally wounded in retreating from the Imperialists, he placed himself under a tree, his face towards the enemy, saying, "As in life I always faced the enemy, so I would not in death turn my back upon them."

Richard I. King of England, having invested the Castle of Chalus, was shot in the shoulder with an arrow: an unskilful surgeon, endeavouring to extract the weapon, mangled the flesh in such a manner, that a gangrene ensued. The castle being taken, and perceiving he should not live, he ordered Bertram De Gourdon, who had shot the arrow, to be brought to his presence. Bertram being come, "What harm," said the king, "did I ever do to thee, that thou should'st kill me?" The other replied, with great magnanimity and courage, "You killed, with your own hand, my father and two of my brothers, and you likewise designed to have killed me. You may now satiate your revenge. I would cheerfully suffer all the torments that can be in-

flicted, were I sure of having delivered the world of a tyrant who filled it with blood and carnage." This bold and spirited answer struck Richard with remorse. He ordered the prisoner to be presented with one hundred shillings, and set at liberty; but one of the king's friends, like a true ruffian, ordered him to be flayed alive.

The following modern instance is extracted from a late French work, entitled, *Ecole Historique et Morale du Soldat.* A mine underneath one of the outworks of a citadel was entrusted to the charge of a sergeant and a few soldiers of the Piedmontese guards. Several companies of the enemy's troops had made themselves masters of this work, and the loss of the place would probably soon have followed, had they maintained their post in it. The mine was charged, and a single spark would blow them all into the air. The sergeant, with the greatest coolness, ordered the soldiers to retire, desiring them to request the king to take care of his wife and children; struck fire, set a match to the train, and sacrificed himself for his country.

Anne de Montmorency, a peer, marshal, and constable of France, being wounded at the battle of St. Dennis, a cordelier attempting to prepare him for death when he was covered with blood and wounds, he replied, in a firm and steady voice, "Do you think that a man who has lived nearly eighty years with honour, has not learned to die for a quarter of an hour?"

But of all the instances of fortitude and contempt of death, none are to be compared with those who have suffered in the cause of Christianity; for such is the peculiar excellency of the system, that its true adherents have not only thought it their honour to live under its influence, but their privilege to die for its defence. Martyrs, indeed, have been found in almost every cause: but none have ever been so signally supported, or have died so nobly, as the martyrs of

14

Christ. Some instances, perhaps, are found of their courting it, when they might have avoided it; but, in general, they have been men whose lives bore striking testimonies in favour of that truth which they sealed by their deaths. "Blessed are they," says our Lord, "who are persecuted for righteousness' sake, for theirs is the kingdom of heaven." They preferred truth to ease, liberty of conscience to hypocrisy, and the glory of their Master before the honour of man. They chose rather to suffer affliction than to enjoy the pleasures of sin, which were but for a season; esteeming the reproaches of Christ greater than the treasures of the world. Happy they, of whom the world was not worthy. Peace be with all them who are not ashamed to live nor afraid to die in the defence of Christianity!

We shall here select a few instances of Christian fortitude in the hour of death.

John Huss, when the chain was put about him at the stake, said, with a smiling countenance, "My Lord Jesus Christ was bound with a harder chain than this for my sake; and why should I be afraid of this old rusty one?" When the fagots were piled up to his very neck, the Duke of Bavaria was officious enough to desire him to abjure. "No," said Huss, "I never preached any doctrine of an evil tendency; and what I taught with my lips I now seal with my blood." He said to the executioner, "Are you going to burn a *goose*? In one century you will have a *swan* you can neither roast nor boil." If he were prophetic, he must have meant *Luther*, who had a swan for his arms. The flames were then applied to the fagots, when the martyr sung a hymn with so loud and cheerful a voice, that he was heard through all the cracklings of the combustibles and the noise of the multitude. At last his voice was short after he had uttered, "*Jesus Christ*, thou Son of the living God, have mercy upon me!" and he was consumed in a most miserable manner.

When the executioner went behind Jerom of Prague to set fire to the pile, "Come here," said the martyr, "and kindle it before my eyes; for if I dreaded such a sight, I should never have come to this place, when I had a free opportunity to escape." The fire was kindled, and he then sung a hymn, which was soon finished by the encircling flames.

Thomas Bilney suffered at Norwich in the year 1531, in the time of King Henry VIII. The night before he suffered he put his finger into the flame of a candle, as he had often done before, and answered, "I feel, by experience, that the fire is hot; yet I am persuaded by God's holy word, and by the experience of some spoken of in it, that in the flame they felt no heat, and in the fire no consumption; and I believe, that though the stubble of my body shall be wasted, yet my soul shall thereby be purged; and that, after short pain, joy unspeakable will follow."

As he was led forth to the place of execution, one of his friends spoke to him, praying to God to strengthen him, and to enable him patiently to endure his torments: to whom Mr. Bilney answered, with a quiet and pleasant countenance, "When the mariner undertakes a voyage, he is tossed on the billows of the troubled seas; yet in the midst of all, he beareth up his spirits with this consideration, that ere long he shall come into his quiet harbour: so," added he, "I am now sailing upon the troubled sea, but ere long my *ship* shall be in a quiet *harbour*: and I doubt not, but, through the grace of God, I shall endure the *storm*: only I would entreat you to help me with your prayers."

The officers then placed the fagots about him, and set fire to the reeds, which presently flamed up very high; the holy martyr, all the while, lifting up his hands towards heaven, sometimes calling upon *Jesus*, and sometimes saying, "*Credo*," i. e.

I believe. The wind being high, and blowing away the flame, he suffered a lingering death. At last, one of he officers beat out the staple to which the chain was fastened that supported his body, and so let it fall into the fire, where it was presently consumed.

John Lambert suffered in the year 1538. No man was used at the stake with more cruelty than this holy martyr. They burned him with a slow fire by inches; for if it kindled higher and stronger than they chose, they removed it away. When his legs were burnt off, and his thighs were mere stumps in the fire, they pitched his poor body upon pikes, and lacerated his broiling flesh with their halberts. But God was with him in the midst of the flame, and supported him in all the anguish of nature. Just before he expired, he lifted up such hands as he had, all flaming with fire, and cried out to the people with his dying voice, with these glorious words, " *None but Christ ! None but Christ !*" He was at last bent down into the fire and expired.

George Wishart, when brought to the stake, the executioner, upon his knees, said, " Sir, I pray you forgive me, for I am not the cause of your death." Wishart, calling him to him, kissed his cheeks, saying, "Lo ! here is a token that I forgive thee : my heart, do thine office." He was then tied to the stake, and the fire kindled. The captain of the castle, coming near him, bade him to be of good courage, and to beg for him the pardon of his sin ; to whom Wishart said, "This fire torments my body, but no whit abates my spirit." Then looking towards the cardinal, he said, "He who, in such state from that high place, feeds his eyes with my torments, within a few days shall be hanged out at that same window, to be seen with as much ignominy as he now leans there with pride:" and so his breath being stopped, he was consumed by the fire, near the castle of St. Andrew's, in the year 1546. This prophecy was fulfilled, when, after

the cardinal was slain, the provost raising the town, came to the castle gates, crying, " What have you done with my Lord Cardinal ? Where is my Lord Cardinal ?" To whom they within answered, " Return to your houses, for he hath received his reward, and will trouble the world no more :" but they still cried. " We will never depart till we see him." The *Leslies* then hung him out at that window, to show that he was dead : and so the people departed.

Mr. Lawrence Saunders, who was executed the 8th of February, 1555, when he came to the place, fell on the ground, and prayed ; and then arose, and took the stake in his arms to which he was to be chained, and kissed it, saying, " Welcome the cross of *Christ !* welcome everlasting life !"

Mr. John Bradford was taken into Smithfield with a strong guard of armed men. When he came to the place where he was to suffer, he fell on his face, and prayed; after which he took a fagot, and kissed it, and the stake likewise. Then, having put off his clothes, he stood by the stake, and lifting up his eyes and hands towards heaven, said,"*O England, England,* repent of thy sins ; beware of idolatry, beware of antichrists ; take heed they do not deceive you." Then he turned his face to John Leaf, a young man of about twenty years old, who suffered with him, and said, " Be of good comfort, brother, for we shall sup with the Lord this night." He then embraced the reeds, and said, " Straight is the gate, and narrow is the way, that leadeth to life eternal , and few there be that find it." After which he was fastened to the stake, and burnt, on the first of July, in the year of our Lord 1555. He ended his life like a lamb, without the least alteration of countenance, and in the prime of his days.

When Bishops *Latimer* and *Ridley,* who were burnt on the north side of Oxford, the 16th of October, 1555, were brought to the stake, *Latimer* lifted up his eyes with a sweet and amiable countenance, saying, "*Fidelis est Deus*," &c.: i. e. God is faithful, who will not suffer us to be tempted above that which we are able. When they were brought to the fire, on a spot of ground on the north of *Baliol College*, where, after an abusive sermon, being told by an officer that they might now make ready for the stake, Mr. *Latimer*, having thrown off his prison attire, appeared in a shroud prepared for the purpose; "And whereas before," says Mr. Fox, " he seemed a withered and crooked old man, he stood now bold, upright, as comely a father as one might lightly behold." Being thus ready, he recommended his soul to God, and delivered himself to the executioner, saying to the Bishop of London," We shall this day, brother, light such a candle in *England* as never shall be put out."

Philpot, when he was came into *Smithfield*, kneeled down, and said, " I will pay my vows in thee, O *Smithfield!*" Being come to the stake, he kissed it, and said, " Shall I disdain to suffer at this stake, when my Lord and Saviour refused not to suffer a most vile death upon the cross for me?" When he was bound to the stake, he repeated the hundred and sixth, seventh, and eighth *Psalms*, and prayed most fervently; till at length, in the midst of the flames, with great meekness and comfort, he gave up his spirit to God.

Archbishop Cranmer, who had recanted through fear of death, and finding, after all, that they were determined to burn him, when brought to the stake, held out his right hand, and said, " This is the hand that wrote, and therefore it shall first suffer punishment." Fire being applied to him, he stretched it out in the flame, and held it there unmoved, except that once he wiped his face with it, till it was consumed; crying with a loud voice, "This hand hath offended;" and often repeating, " This unworthy right hand!" At last, the fire getting up, he soon expired, never stirring nor crying out all the while : only keeping his eyes fixed to heaven, and repeating more than once, " Lord *Jesus*, receive my spirit!" He died in the sixty-seventh year of his age.

Monsieur Homel was pastor of the Protestant church at *Vivaretz*, in the Province of *Cevennes*, in *France*, and was with peculiar cruelty broken upon the wheel at *Tournon*, a city in the same province, October, 1683. The following account was written by an eye and ear witness, who declared he had trembled, and his hair stood upright, at the remembrance of it.

"I count myself happy," said this saint at his execution, "that I can die in my Master's quarrel. What, would my gracious Redeemer descend from heaven to earth, that I might ascend from earth to heaven? Would he undergo an ignominious death, that I might be possessed of a most blessed life? Verily, if, after all this, to prolong a frail and miserable life, I should lose that which is everlasting, should I not be a most ungrateful wretch to my GOD, and a most cruel opposer of my own happiness? No, no; the die is cast, and I am immoveable in my resolution. I breathe after that hour : O! when will that good hour come, that will put a period to my present miserable life, and give me the enjoyment of one which is infinitely blessed?— Farewell, my dear wife! I know your tears, your continual sighs, hinder bidding me adieu! Don't be troubled at this wheel upon which I must expire; 'tis to me a triumphal chariot which will carry me to heaven. I see heaven opened, and my sweet *Jesus* with his outstretched arms ready to receive me; for he is the divine spouse of my soul.

" I am leaving the world, in which is nothing but adversity, in order to get into heaven, and enjoy everlasting felicity. You shall come to me; I shall never come back to you! All that I recommend to you is, to educate our dear children in the fear of GOD, and to be careful that they swerve not from the way prescribed to them in the holy scriptures. I have bequeathed them a little formulary for their instruction, to the end, that, if ever they be brought into the like condition with myself, they may undergo it courageously, and be confident in the goodness of our GOD, who will send the divine Comforter to strengthen them in all their straits and distresses. Prepare them for suffering betimes, to the end that in the great day, when we shall appear before the judgment seat of *Christ*, we may be able to bespeak him, ' *Lord! here we are, and the children which thou hast graciously given us.*' Ah! I shall never have done. Ah! why am I hindered from departing? Farewell, my dear people, 'tis the last farewell I shall give you! Be steadfast; be fixed; and know that I never preached to you any thing but the pure truth of the gospel, the true way which leads to heaven."

Somebody telling him that he had spoke too much, "How!" said he, "have I spoke too much? I have spoken nothing but the very truth. I have neither spoken nor done any thing that is in the least injurious to the sacred majesty of our august monarch; but, on the contrary, I have always exhorted the people committed by the *Lord* to my charge to render those honours which are due to our king. I have taught them that our lives and fortunes are at his disposal, and that we are bound to employ them in defence of his estate and crown. But as for our consciences, we hold them of our GOD, and must keep them for him." Then his judges, turning from him, ordered the executioner to do his office; which thereupon he did, by breaking his arms and legs.

And it being then demanded, whether he would die a *Roman Catholic?* he answered, "How, my lords! had it been my design to have changed my religion, I would have done it before my bones had been thus broken to pieces: I wait only for the hour of my dissolution. Courage,

courage, O my soul! thou shall presently enjoy the delights of heaven. And as for thee, O my poor body, thou shalt be reduced to dust; but it is for this end, that thou mayest be raised a spiritual body. Thou shalt see things that never entered into the heart of man, and which are, in this life, impossible to be conceived."— Again, addressing himself to his wife, he said, "Farewell, once more, my well-beloved spouse! I am waiting for you: but know, though you see my bones broken to shivers, my soul is replenished with inexpressible joys."

Every limb, member, and bone of his body, were broken with the iron bar, forty hours before the executioner was permitted to strike him upon the breast with a stroke which they call *le coup de grace*, the blow of mercy; that death-stroke which put an end to all his miseries.

But our want of room will not permit us to enlarge. The reader may consult Fox's Book of Martyrs, and other publications of a similar kind.

Let us all learn to cherish a principle of fortitude. "It is one of the greatest of all military virtues, and was in high esteem among the old Romans, that the same word with them expresses both virtue and valour: and as every christian is in a militant state, and hath many enemies to conflict with, fortitude, therefore, stands in the foremost rank of the Christian virtues. ' Watch ye; stand fast in the faith; quit yourselves like men: be strong.' "

FRATERNAL LOVE.

IT has been an antiquated saying, that brothers and sisters hardly ever agree. I believe there is too much truth in the assertion. Exceptions, however, have been found, and brethren have dwelt together in unity. Where this takes place, it forms a pleasing scene; a scene peculiarly gratifying to the parents, every way beneficial to the children themselves, and productive of good to mankind at large. Learn ye, who are united by the ties of nature, to promote mutual harmony and fraternal affection, that ye may thus resemble those celestial beings who live, and shall live, in endless union and unspeakable felicity in the world above.

As one of the water-bearers at the fountain of the Fauxbourgs St. Germain, in Paris, was at his usual labours, in August, 1766, he was taken away by a gentleman in a splendid coach, who proved to be his own brother, and who, at the age of three years, had been carried to India, where he made a considerable fortune. On his return to France, he had made inquiry respecting his family; and hearing that he had only one brother alive, and that he was in the humble condition of a water-bearer, he sought him out, embraced him with great affection, and brought him to his house, where he gave him bills for upwards of a thousand crowns per annum.

The father of that eminent lawyer, Mr. Sergeant Glanvill, had a good estate, which he intended to settle on his eldest son; but he proving a vicious young man, and there being no hopes of his recovery, he devolved it upon the sergeant, who was his second son. Upon the father's death, the eldest, finding that what he had considered before as the mere threatenings of an angry old man, were now but too certain, became melancholy; which, by degrees, wrought in him so great a change, that what his father could not prevail in while he lived was now effected by the severity of his last will. His brother, observing this, invited him, together with many of his friends, to a feast; where, after other dishes had been served up, he ordered one which was covered to be set before his brother, and desired him to uncover it: upon his doing which, the company, no less than himself, were surprised to find it full of writings; and still more when the sergeant told them, "that he was now doing what he was sure his father would have done, had he lived to see the happy change which now they all saw in his bro-

ther; and therefore he freely restored to him the whole estate."

Timoleon, the Corinthian, is a noble pattern of fraternal love; for being in a battle with the Argives, and seeing his brother fall down dead with the wounds he had received, he instantly leaped over his dead body, and with his shield protected it from insult and plunder; and though sorely wounded in this generous enterprise, *he* would not, by any means, retreat to a place of safety, till he had seen the corpse carried off the field by his friends. How happy for Christians, would they imitate this heathen, and as tenderly screen from abuse and calumny the wounded reputation or dying honour of an absent or defenceless brother!

Mr. H——, an ingenious artist, being driven out of employment, and reduced to great distress, had no resource to apply to except that of an elder brother, who was in good circumstances. To him, therefore, he applied, and begged some little hovel to live in, and some small provision for his support. The brother melted into tears, and said, "You, my dear brother! you live in a hovel! You are a man; you are an honour to the family. I am nothing. You shall take this house and the estate, and I will be your guest, if you please." The brothers lived together, without it being distinguishable who was proprietor of the estate, till the death of the elder put the artist in possession of it.

Lord Ab——n's brother, who was a churchman, once solicited him to apply for a living which was vacant, and in the gift of the crown, worth 1000*l.* a year. Lord Ab——n's answer was as follows: "I never ask favours. Inclosed is a deed of annuity for 1000*l.* per annum."

In the month of September, 1801, W. T. M. Esq. departed this life, and, dying without a will, his large property, which was chiefly landed estate, devolved to his eldest son. By this circumstance, the eight younger children were unprovided for; but this gentleman, with a generosity seldom equalled, but which does honour to christianity, immediately made over to his younger brothers and sisters three considerable estates (it is said of the value of ten thousand pounds,) which were about two thirds of the whole property. This munificence is the more extraordinary, as he had a young and increasing family of his own. On a friend remonstrating with him on his conduct, his answer was, "I have enough; and am determined that all my brothers and sisters shall be satisfied."

THE FRIAR AND THE NIGHT WHISPER.

WHILE Mr. Welch was minister in one of the *French villages*, one evening, a popish friar, travelling through the country, because he could find no lodging in the whole village, addressed himself to Mr. Welch's house, begging the favour of a lodging for that night. The servants informed Mr. Welch, who readily consented; but as he had supped, and family worship was over, he did not see the friar, but retired to his room. After the friar had supped, the servant showed him to his chamber, between which and Mr. Welch's there was but a thin deal partition. After the friar's first sleep, he was surprised with hearing a constant whispering kind of noise, at which he was exceedingly frightened.

The next morning, as he walked in the fields, a countryman met him, and, because of his habit, saluted him, asking him "where he had lodged that night?" The friar answered, "with the *Hugonot* minister." The countryman asked him what entertainment he met with. The friar answered, "very bad; for," said he, "1 always imagined there were devils haunting these ministers' houses, and I am persuaded there was one with me this night; for I heard a continual whisper all the night, which

I believe was nothing else but the minister and the devil conversing together." The countryman told him he was much mistaken, and that it was only the minister at his night prayers. "O," says the friar, "does the minister pray any?" "Yes," said the countryman, "more than any man in *France;* and if you will stay another night with him, you may be satisfied." The friar returned to Mr. Welch's house, and, feigning indisposition, begged another night's lodging, which was granted him.

After a while, Mr. Welch came down, assembled the family, and, according to custom, first sung a psalm, then read a portion of scripture, which he briefly expounded, and then prayed in his usual fervent manner: to all which the friar was an astonished witness. At dinner the friar was very civilly entertained, Mr. Welch thinking best to forbear all questions and disputes for the present. In the evening, Mr. Welch had family worship, as in the morning, which occasioned still more wonder in the friar. After supper, they all retired, the friar longing to know what the night-whisper was. He laid awake till Mr. Welch's usual time of night for rising to pray; when, hearing the same whispering noise, he crept softly to Mr. Welch's door, and there heard not only the sound, but the words distinctly, and such communications between God and man as he knew not had been in the world. Upon this, the friar waited for Mr. Welch to come out of his chamber; when he told him, he had lived in darkness and ignorance till this time, but was now resolved to give himself up entirely to Mr. Welch's teaching, and declared himself a Protestant. Mr. Welch congratulated him upon his better understanding, and exceedingly encouraged him; and it is said that he lived and died a true Protestant. "This account I had," says his biographer, "from a very pious minister who was bred in Mr. Welch's house in France."

FRUGALITY AND CHARITY UNITED.

Two persons who were employed in collecting money for some public charity, knocked at the door of a certain gentleman, intending to solicit his donation. While waiting there, they overheard the master of the house severely reproving his servants for the waste of a small piece of candle. Judging, from this appearance of extreme parsimony, that he was a covetous man, one of them proposed that they should lose no more time in waiting there, but go on to another house ; the other person, however, thought it best to stay. At length they were introduced, when the gentleman, having read their case, immediately presented them with five guineas. The collectors, so agreeably disappointed, could not conceal their surprise ; which, being observed by the donor, he desired to know why they expressed so much wonder at the gift. " The reason, sir," said one of them, " is this : we happened to hear you severely blaming your servants for losing an inch of candle, and expected nothing from a person who we feared was so parsimonious." " Gentlemen," replied he, " it is true I am very exact in the economy of my affairs : I cannot endure the waste of any thing, however small its value ; and I do this, that I may save out of a moderate income something to give to God and religion."

" Let us be frugal," says one, " as to our dress, our time, our diet, our money." There is a certain skill, which our forefathers used to call a knack, an art of doing things ; and it is remarkably seen in many poor women's laying out the earnings of their husbands. Call it what we will, it is one of the highest qualifications of

The Poor Man's Wife,

and nothing contributes more to the ease of his living than this female accomplishment. How she reckons I cannot tell ; but she keeps out of debt, lives in cleanliness and plenty, and can always spare half a dozen turves to warm a cold sick neighbour's cordial. She says, " My husband's harvest wages clothe himself and children ; my gleaning pays the shoemaker ; the orchard pays my rent ; the garden does this, the flail procures that ; the children's spinning wheels yield so and so ;" and, good heart ! she crowns all by saying, " Bless the Lord, O my soul, and forget not all its benefits. He forgiveth all thine iniquties, and healeth all thy diseases. He redeemeth thy life from destruction, and crowneth thee with loving kindness and tender mercies. He satisfieth thy mouth with good things ; so that thy youth is renewed like the eagle. Bless the Lord, O my soul."

GLUTTONY, FEASTING, AND INTEMPERANCE.

Such is the intemperance of some, that, as the French proverb says, *They dig their graves with their teeth ;* while the kitchen is their shrine, the cook their priest, the table their altar, and their belly their god. Hence likewise it is said, that *meat also kills as many as the musket ; the board kills more than the sword.* Gluttony is irrational, indecent, dangerous, and sinful. It is the cause of other sins, and often tends to poverty, distress, and ruin.

There is, however, a morbid sort of gluttony, called *fames canina,* "dog-like appetite," which sometimes occurs, and renders the person seized with it an object of pity and of cure, as in all other diseases. But professed habitual gluttons may be reckoned amongst the monsters of nature, and deemed, in a manner, punishable, for endeavouring to bring a dearth or famine in the places where they live. For which reason, people think King James I. was in the right, when, a man being presented to him that could eat a whole sheep at one meal, he asked, " What he could do more than another man ?" and being answered, " He could not do so much," said, "Hang him, then, for it is unfit a man should live that eats so much as twenty men, and cannot do so much as one."

One of our Danish kings, named Hardikenute, was so great a glutton, that a historian calls him Bacca de Porco, "Swine's Mouth." His tables were covered four times a day with the most costly viands that either the air, sea, or land, could furnish; and, as he lived, he died; for, revelling and carousing at a wedding banquet at Lambeth, he fell down dead. His death was so welcome to his subjects, that they celebrated the day with sports and pastimes, calling it *Hock-tide*, which signifies scorn and contempt.

It is said that Heliogabulus, the Roman emperor, when he was near the sea, would eat no fish; in the midland, no flesh. Whole meals were made of the tongues of singing birds and peacocks, or of the brains of the most costly creatures. He used to say, that "that meat was not savoury whose sauce was not costly."

It was a sordid and brutish wish of Philoxenus, who wished that he had the throat of a crane, or vulture, that the pleasures of his taste might last the longer.

Cæsar, the son of Pope Alexander, was one of those who devoted himself to all kinds of intemperance. In daily breakfasts, dinners, and banquets, he spent five hundred crowns, not reckoning feasts, and extraordinary inventions; and, for parasites, buffoons, and jesters, he allowed yearly two thousand suits of clothes from his wardrobe.

Antipater, well said of Demadas, (a glutton grown old,) that nothing now was left but his belly and tongue; that all the man beside was gone.

Marriot, who was a lawyer at Gray's inn, piqued himself upon the brutal qualification of a voracious appetite, and a powerful digestive faculty; and deserves to be placed no higher in the scale of beings than a cormorant, or an ostrich. He increased his natural capacity for food by art and application; and had as much vanity in eating to excess, as any monk ever had in starving himself.

There are some who, though they cannot be called gluttons, yet seem as if they placed all their happiness in mere eating and drinking; making, as the Apostle says, a god of their belly, whose glory is in their shame, who mind earthly things. The following is a just delineation of such a character.——"Succus," says a spiritual writer, "will undertake no business that may hurry his spirits, or break in upon his hours of *eating* and *rest*. If he read, it shall only be for half an hour, because that is sufficient to amuse the spirits; and he will read something that will make him laugh, as rendering the body fitter for its food and rest. Or, if he has at any time a mind to indulge a grave thought, he always has recourse to a useful treatise upon the *Ancient Cookery*. He talks coolly and moderately upon all subjects, and is as fearful of falling into a passion, as of catching cold; being very positive that they are both equally injurious to the *stomach*. If ever you see him more hot than ordinary, it is upon some provoking occasion, when the dispute about cookery runs very high, or in the defence of some beloved dish, which has often made him happy. Succus is very loyal, and, as soon as ever he likes any wine, he drinks the king's health with all his heart. Nothing could put rebellious thoughts into his head, unless he should live to see a proclamation against eating of *pheasants' eggs*. All the hours that are not devoted either to repose or nourishment, are looked upon by Succus as waste or spare time : for this reason, he lodges near a coffee-house and a tavern, that when he rises in the morning, he may be near the news, and, when he parts at night, he may not have far to go to bed. In the morning, you always see him in the same place in the coffee-room; and, if he seems more attentively engaged than ordinary, it is because some criminal has broke out of Newgate, or somebody was robbed last night, but they cannot tell where. When he has learnt all that he can, he goes home to settle the matter with the barber's boy that comes to shave him.

"The next waste time that lays upon his hands, is from dinner to supper; and, if ever melancholy thoughts come into his head, it is at this time when he is often left to himself for an hour or more, and that after the greatest pleasure he knows is just over. He is afraid to sleep, because he has heard it is not healthful at that time; so that he is forced to refuse so welcome a guest.

"But he is soon relieved by a settled method of playing at cards, till it is time to think of some little nice matter for supper. After this, Succus takes his glass, talks of the excellency of the English constitution, and praises that minister most who keeps the best table.

"On Sunday night, you may sometimes hear him condemning the iniquity of the *town rakes;* and the bitterest thing that he says against them is this, that he verily believes some of them are so abandoned, as not to have a *regular meal,* or a sound night's sleep in a week.

"At eleven, Succus bids all good night, and parts in great friendship. He is presently in bed, and sleeps till it is time to go to the coffee-house next morning.

"If you were to live with Succus for a twelvemonth, this is all that you would see in his life, except a few curses and oaths that he uses as occasion offers.'' Such is the character of Succus; a character, it is to be feared, which suits too many of our modern gentlemen of pleasure.

GRATITUDE.

"Examples of ingratitude,'' Mr. Paley observes, "check and discourage voluntary beneficence : hence, the cultivation of a grateful temper, is a consideration of public importance. A second reason for cultiva-

ting in ourselves that temper, is, that the same principle which is touched with the kindness of a human benefactor, is capable of being affected by the Divine goodness, and of becoming, under the influence of that affection, a source of the purest and most exalted virtue. The love of God is the sublimest gratitude. It is a mistake, therefore, to imagine, that this virtue is omitted in the Scriptures; for every precept which commands us to love God, because he first loved us, presupposes the principle of gratitude, and directs it to its proper object.''

The following pleasing example of genuine gratitude, is extracted from Hackwell's Apol. l. 14. c. 10. p. 436. "Francis Frescobald, a Florentine merchant, descended of a noble family in Italy, had gained a plentiful fortune, of which he was liberal-handed to all in necessity; which being well known to others, though concealed by himself, a young stranger applied to him for charity.— Signior Frescobald, seeing something in his countenance more than ordinary, overlooked his tattered clothes, and compassionating his circumstances, asked him what he was, and of what country, 'I am,' answered the young man, 'a native of England; my name is Thomas Cromwell, and my father-in-law is a poor sheer-man. I left my country to seek my fortune; came with the French army that was routed at Gatylion, where I was page to a footman, and carried his pike and burgonet after him.' Frescobald, commiserating his necessities, and having a particular respect for the English nation, clothed him genteelly, took him into his house, till he had recovered strength by better diet, and, at his taking leave, mounted him on a good horse, with sixteen ducats of gold in his pockets.— Cromwell expressed his thankfulness in a very sensible manner, and returned by land towards England; where being arrived, he was preferred into the service of Cardinal Wolsey.

"After the Cardinal's death, he

worked himself so effectually into the favour of King Henry VIII. that his majesty made him a Baron, Viscount, Earl of Essex, and, at last, Lord Chancellor of England. In the mean time, Signior Frescobald, by repeated losses at sea and land, was reduced to poverty; and, calling to mind, without ever thinking of Cromwell, that some English merchants were indebted to him in the sum of fifteen thousand ducats, he came to London to procure payment.

"Travelling in pursuit of this affair, he fortunately met with the Lord Chancellor, as he was riding to Court; who, thinking him to be the same gentleman that had done him such great kindness in Italy, immediately alighted, embraced him, and, with tears of joy, asked him if he was not Signior Francis Frescobald, a Florentine merchant? 'Yes, sir,' said he, 'and your most humble servant.' 'My servant!' said the Chancellor; 'No; you are my special friend, that relieved me in my wants, laid the foundation of my greatness, and, as such, I receive you: and, since the affairs of my sovereign will not now permit a longer conference, I beg you will oblige me this day with your company at my house to dinner with me.'

"Signior Frescobald was surprised and astonished with admiration who this great man should be, that acknowledged such obligations, and so passionately expressed a kindness for him: but, contemplating awhile his mien, his voice, and carriage, he concluded it to be Cromwell, whom he had relieved at Florence; and, therefore, not a little overjoyed, went to his house, and attended his coming. His lordship came soon after, and immediately taking his friend by the hand, turned to the lord high admiral and other noblemen in his company, saying, 'Don't your lordships wonder that I am so glad to see this gentleman? This is he who first contributed to my advancement.' He then told them the whole story, and, holding him still by the hand, led him into

the dining-room, and placed him next himself at table. The company being gone, the Chancellor made use of this opportunity to know what affair had brought him to England. Frescobald, in a few words, gave him the true state of his circumstances; to which Cromwell replied, 'I am sorry for your misfortunes, and I will make them as easy to you as I can; but, because men ought to be just before they are kind, it is fit I should repay the debt I owe you.' Then, leading him to his closet, he locked the door, and opening a coffer, first took out sixteen ducats, delivering them to Frescobald, and said, 'My friend, here's the money you lent me at Florence, with ten pieces you laid out for my apparel, and ten more you paid for my horse; but considering that you are a merchant, and might have made some advantage by this money in the way of trade, take these four bags, in every one of which are four hundred ducats, and enjoy them as free gifts of your friend." These the modesty of Frescobald would have refused, but the other forced them upon him. He next caused him to give him the names of all his debtors, and the sums they owed; which account he transmitted to one of his servants, with a charge to find out the men, and oblige them to pay him in fifteen days, under the penalty of his displeasure; and the servant so well discharged his duty, that in a short time the entire sum was paid. All this time, Signior Frescobald lodged in the Chancellor's house, where he was entertained according to his merits, with repeated persuasions for his continuance in England, and an offer of the loan of sixty thousand ducats for four years, if he would trade here; but he desired to return to Florence, which he did, with extraordinary favours from the Lord Cromwell."

A very poor man, busied in planting and grafting an apple tree, was rudely interrupted by this interrogation:—"Why do you plant trees, who cannot hope to eat the fruit of them ?" 'He raised himself up, and, leaning upon his spade, replied, "Some one planted trees for me before I was born; and I have eaten the fruit : 1 now plant for others, that the memorial of my gratitude may exist when I am gone."

It is said that the first settlers of New-England met with many difficulties and hardships, as is generally the case when a civilized people attempt establishing themselves in a wilderness country. Being men of piety, they sought relief from heaven, by laying their wants and distresses before the Lord in frequent set days of fasting and prayer. Constant meditation and discourse on their difficulties kept their minds gloomy and discontented; and, like the children of Israel, there were many disposed to return to that Egypt which persecution had induced them to abandon. At length, when it was proposed in one of their assemblies to proclaim a fast, a farmer, of plain sense, rose and remarked, that the inconveniences they suffered, and concerning which they had so often wearied heaven with their complaints, were not so great as they might have expected, and were diminishing every day as the colony strengthened; that the earth began to reward their toil, and to furnish liberally for their subsistence ; that the seas and rivers were full of fish, the air sweet, the climate healthy, and, above all, that they were in the full enjoyment of their civil and religious liberty : he therefore thought that reflecting and conversing on these subjects would be more comfortable, as tending more to make them contented with their situation; and that it would be more becoming the gratitude they owed the Divine Being, if, instead of a fast, they should appoint a *thanksgiving.* His advice was taken, and, from that day to this, they have in every year observed circumstances of public felicity sufficient to furnish cause for a thanksgiving day, which is, therefore, constantly ordered and religiously observed.

THE HAPPY TENANT.

A pious clergyman in the diocese of Bishop Burnet, had frequently meditated on these words of our Lord, "Blessed are the meek, for they shall inherit the earth." He considered that the Author spake as man never spake, and he prayed earnestly that he might understand their full import. The providence of God answered his prayer by the following occurrence : One day, as he was meditating in the fields, he heard the voice of joy and praise from a neighbouring cottage : curiosity led him to the window, and he beheld the happy tenant, a poor woman, with the scanty provision of a cup of water and a piece of bread : her hands and eyes were lifted up to heaven, while with joyful gratitude she exclaimed, "What, all this, and Jesus Christ too!" This fact explained the text in its true signification : it taught him that a small thing the righteous hath is better than great riches of the ungodly.

HEARERS AND PUBLIC WORSHIP.

Bigoted Hearer.

A person meeting another returning after having heard a popular preacher, said to him, "Well, I hope you have been highly gratified." "Indeed, I have," replied the other. "I wish I could have prevailed on you to hear him : I am sure you would never have relished any other preacher afterwards." "Then," replied the wiser Christian, "I am determined I never will hear him, for I wish to hear such a preacher as will give me so high a relish and esteem for the word of God, that I shall receive it with greater eagerness and delight whenever it is delivered."

Humble Hearer

" A torch may be lighted by a candle, and a knife be sharpened by an unpolished stone ;" so Mr. Hildersham used to say, "that he never heard any faithful minister in his life, that he was so mean, but he could discover some gift in him that was wanting in himself, and could receive some profit by him."

The Practical Hearer.

A poor woman in the country went to hear a sermon, wherein, among other evil practices, the use of dishonest weights and measures was exposed. With this discourse she was much affected. The next day, when the minister, according to his custom, went among his hearers, and called upon the woman, he took occasion to ask her what she remembered of his sermon. The poor woman complained much of her bad memory, and said she had forgotten almost all that he delivered. "But one thing," said she, "I remembered; I remembered to burn my bushel."—A doer of the word cannot be a forgetful hearer.

Constant Hearer.

It is said of the late Countess of Burford, that though for the last few years of her life she had to ride almost constantly on horseback, upwards of sixteen miles, to and from the churches where she attended, yet neither frost, snow, rain, nor bad roads, were sufficient to detain her at home. How unlike the conduct of many, who suffer any trivial incident to keep them from the house of God!

Punctual Hearer.

A woman who always used to attend public worship with great punctuality, and took care to be always in time, was asked how it was she could always come so early; she answered, very wisely, "That it was part of her religion not to disturb the religion of others."

The late Hearer.

A minister, whom I well knew, observing that some of his people made a practice of coming in very late, and after a considerable part of the sermon was gone through, was determined that they should feel the force of a public reproof. One day, therefore, as they entered the place of worship at their usual late period, the minister, addressing his congre-gation, said, "But, my hearers, it is time for us now to conclude, for here are our friends just come to fetch us home." We may easily conjecture what the parties felt at this curious, but pointed address.

The deaf Woman a constant attendant.

"I have in my congregation," said a venerable minister of the gospel, "a worthy aged woman, who has for many years been so deaf as not to distinguish the loudest sound, and yet she is always one of the first in the meeting. On asking the reason of her constant attendance (as it was impossible for her to hear my voice,) she answered, 'Though I cannot hear you, I come to God's house because I love it, and would be found in his ways; and he gives me many a sweet thought upon the text, when it is pointed out to me: another reason is, because there I am in the best company, in the more immediate presence of God, and amongst his saints, the honourable of the earth. I am not satisfied with serving God in private: it is my duty and privilege to honour him regularly and constantly in public.'"—What a reproof this to those who have their hearing, and yet always come to a place of worship late, or not at all!

The fearful Christian turned courageous.

There was one Victorinus, famous in Rome for teaching rhetoric to the senators; this man in his old age was converted to Christianity, and came to Simplicianus (who was an eminent man) whispering softly in his ears these words, "*I am a Christian;*" but this holy man answered, "*I will not believe it, nor count thee so, till I see thee among the Christians in the church.*" At which he laughed, saying, "*Do, then, those walls make a Christian? Cannot I be such except I openly profess it, and let the world know the same?*" A while after, being more confirmed in the faith, and considering that, if he should thus continue ashamed of

Christ, Christ would be ashamed of him in the last day, he changed his note, and came to Simplicianus, saying, "*Let us go to the church; I will now in earnest be a Christian.*" And there, though a private profession of his faith might have been sufficient, yet he chose to make it openly, saying, "That he had openly professed rhetoric, which was not a matter of salvation; and why should he be afraid to own the word of God in the congregation of the faithful?

HIGHWAYMEN RECLAIMED.

A NOTORIOUS robber in Scotland, known by the name of John of the Score, happening to meet with a poor man travelling with two horses, forcibly took them both away, regardless of the entreaties of the distressed countryman, who, falling on his knees, begged him, *for Jesus Christ's sake*, to restore one of them, as the maintenance of his family depended on his horses.

The thief, having returned home, became from that day dull and melancholy, unable to rest at home, or pursue his depredations abroad; for which he could assign no cause but this, that the words which the poor man had uttered concerning *Jesus Christ* (which by the way, he was so ignorant as not to understand)laid like a heavy weight upon his spirit. Desiring, therefore, his sons to shift for themselves, and secretly restrained from attempting to escape or hide himself, he was apprehended by the ministers of justice, imprisoned in Edinburgh, tried, and condemned to die.

Being visited by the Reverend Mr. Blyth and a Mr. Cunningham, who had formerly known him, he was exhorted to consider his miserable and dangerous condition as a dying sinner, and to fly for refuge to *Jesus Christ.* Hearing that name, he suddenly cried out, "Oh! what word is that? for it has been my death! This is the word that has lain on my heart ever since the poor man mentioned it, so that I had no power to escape.

The minister took occasion to preach to him JESUS, as the only and all-sufficient Saviour. "But will he," said the relenting thief, "will he ever look upon me? will he ever show mercy to me, who would not, for his sake, show mercy to that poor man, and give him back his horses?"

After farther instruction, a real and most gracious change appeared in him, of which he discovered the most convincing evidence; he attained to a happy assurance of his interest in Christ; and, on the scaffold where he suffered, spoke so wonderfully of the Lord's dealings with him, as left a conviction on the spectators, and forced them to acknowledge a glorious truth and reality in the grace of God.

"It was my lot, a few years ago," says Dr. Lettsom, "to be attacked on the highway by a genteel-looking person, well mounted, who demanded my money, at the same time placing a pistol to my breast. I requested him to remove the pistol, which he instantly did: I saw his agitation, from whence I concluded he had not been habituated to this hazardous practice; and I added, that I had both gold and silver about me, which I freely gave him, but that I was sorry to see a young gentleman risk his life in so unbecoming a manner, which would probably soon terminate at the gallows: that, at the best, the casual pittance gained on the highway would afford but a precarious and temporary subsistence; but that, if I could serve him by a private assistance more becoming his appearance, he might further command my purse; and at the same time, I desired him to accept a card containing my address, and to call upon me, as he might trust to my word for his liberty and life. He accepted my address, but I observed his voice faltered. It was late at night, there was, however, sufficient starlight to enable me to perceive, as I leaned towards him on the window of my carriage, that his bosom was overwhelmed with conflicting passions.

At length, bending forward on his horse, and recovering the power of speech, he affectingly said, ' I thank you for your offer—American affairs have ruined me—I will, dear Sir, wait upon you.' Two weeks afterwards, a person entered my house, whom I immediately recognised to be this highwayman. ' I come,' said he, ' to communicate to you a matter that nearly concerns me, and I trust to your honour to keep it inviolable.' I told him that I recollected him, and I requested him to relate his history with candour, as the most effectual means of securing my services; and such was the narrative, as would have excited sympathy in every heart. His fortune had been spoiled on the American continent, and, after a long imprisonment, he escaped to this asylum of liberty, where, his resources failing, and perhaps with pride above the occupation of a sturdy beggar, he rashly ventured upon the most dreadful alternative of the highway, where in his second attempt, he met with me. I found that his narrative was literally true, which induced me to try various means of obviating his distresses. To the commissioners for relieving the American sufferers application was made, but fruitlessly : at length he attended at Windsor, and delivered a memorial to the Queen, briefly stating his sufferings, and the cause of them. Struck with his appearance, and pleased with his address, she graciously assured him of patronage, provided his pretensions should, on inquiry, be found justified. The result was, that, in a few days, she gave him a commission in the army ; and, by his public services, twice has his name appeared in the Gazette among the promotions. After some years employment in the service of his sovereign, this valuable officer fell a victim to the yellow fever in the West Indies."

"A second time I was attacked and robbed, and at the instant seized the criminal, whom I knew. He fell on his knees, returned the money he had taken from me, and prayed forgiveness. I told him that I could not commute felony ; he must instantly depart, and advised him to go to sea, and never suffer me to see him again. About two years afterwards, on visiting a person in the country, I met with this offender : upon inquiring into his situation, I found that he had since been married, and was become a respectable farmer."

Dr. Conder, during his residence at Cambridge, having taken a ride to Peterborough for the benefit of the air, on his return, he saw a gentleman in a private lane, at some distance, standing by his horse. As he approached, the supposed gentleman mounted, and, coming up to him, demanded his money. The doctor (then Mr. Conder) immediately recognised him as a former inhabitant of Cambridge, but thought it prudent to conceal his knowledge. Not satisfied with receiving all his cash, to the amount of several guineas, the highwayman asked him for his watch. This being a family piece, he pleaded hard to retain it : but the man persisting in a menacing tone in his demand, he surrendered it, though not without strong symptoms of reluctance.

The doctor was a man of tender sympathy. This amiable quality soon suppressed all concern for personal safety, and the property thus violently wrested from him ; and led him to commisserate an unhappy man, whose evil practices were leading him, in hasty strides, to the chambers of death, and to attempt to reclaim him. He immediately addressed him with great civility, inquired what way he was going, and proposed, if agreeable, to ride in company ; assuring him, at the same time, that he need not entertain the least fearful apprehension upon his account. His obliging manner won upon the highwayman, and opened the way to a familiar conversation.

During the robbery itself, the man, with all the assumed courage, could not conceal the agitation of his mind.

From this circumstance the doctor took occasion to suggest that his present mode of subsistence, separate from its moral turpitude, was both unwise and dangerous, as the small sums generally collected at one time in these adventures were inadequate to the risk, as they required the frequent exposure of his person, and must subject him to perpetual alarms. The robber urged the common plea of necessity. The doctor represented, that it was an unpleasant and commonly a fatal necessity, as it was not only a trespass upon the rights of society and the authority of God, but would subject him to a dreadful penalty in the life that now is, as well as in that which is to come. Here he entreated him to desist from these pernicious habits—urged him to repentance, assuring him that there was forgiveness, through Jesus Christ, for the most atrocious offenders; and that he did not doubt, if he implored direction from above, but Providence would so direct his way, as to enable him to "provide all things honest in the sight of all men."

This conversation appeared to make a deep impression; the immediate effect of which was, the robber took the watch, and returned it to him, saying "he conducted himself so much like a gentleman, that he could not think of retaining it." The doctor replied, that he greatly valued the watch, and received it with pleasure; but acknowledged that he had a higher object in view than the restoration of his property.

As they continued their discourse, he took the money out of his pocket, and tendered that also to the doctor, saying, that his conscience would not permit him to keep it. But the doctor absolutely refused receiving it, begging him not to consider it as forced from him, but as the gift of benevolence, to a necessitous man. At this instance of generosity he appeared additionally affected.

Coming nearer to Cambridge, the robber told him, that he was under a necessity of leaving him, and, on parting, wept considerably, saying, he hoped he should attend to his advice. He then took a cross-road, on the skirts of the town; but having previously committed other robberies in the neighbourhood, was almost immediately identified and seized. The doctor leisurely continued his ride, and, on his arrival at Cambridge, was greatly surprised to meet him in the street, in the custody of the persons who apprehended him. On his commitment to the castle, he sent for his spiritual monitor, who found him in very great distress. During his confinement, both before and after trial, he made him repeated visits, which were rendered eminently useful; and, at his execution, he had every reason to believe, he died a real convert.

A certain man, who having dissolutely spent all his estate, had only so much money left as would buy him a sword, which he did resolving to maintain himself by robbing on the highway. As he was passing by a church where a minister was preaching, he stepped in, and heard the sermon; when it pleased God to work so effectually upon him, that it changed his former resolution; and God so blessed his endeavours in his calling, that he maintained himself and family comfortably ever after.

HISTORY.

"WISDOM is the great end of history; it is designed to supply the want of experience. Though it enforce not its instruction with the same authority, yet it furnishes us with a greater variety of instruction than it is possible for experience to afford in the course of the longest life. Its object is to enlarge our views of the human character, and to give full exercise to our judgment on human affairs." This observation is just, as to history itself; but the many wilful mistakes, together with the prejudices of historians, have rendered it contemptible in the eyes of some men. Hence,

When Frederick the Great of

Prussia ordered his secretary to read to him, "What," said he, "shall I read? Will your majesty hear me read history?" "No, no," replied the king; "no history, there is no truth in history."

When Sir Robert Walpole's son Horace was about to read to him some historical piece, he stopped him short. "O do not read history," said the father, "for that I know must be false."

Charles V. had so little faith in historians, that when he had occasion to send for Sleidan's History, he used to say, "Bring me my liar."

These objections to history, however, are founded upon ignorance and prejudice. To suppose all history unworthy of our perusal, because some part of it may want sufficient authority, is highly absurd. A wise and judicious mind will make a proper discrimination between *historic relation* and those things which bear evident marks of *historic fact*. To a person possessing such a mind, history, no doubt, will be very profitable; it will tend to enlighten the understanding, mature the judgment, afford entertainment, and excite to action.

Cicero also has justly observed, that history is the light of ages, the depository of events, the faithful evidence of truth, the source of prudence and good counsel, and the rule of conduct and manners.

No set of men ought to be more accurate, more just to truth, and more divested of prejudice, than historians. "I reckon a lie in history," says Bishop Burnet, "to be a much greater sin than a lie in common discourse, as the one is like to be more lasting, and more generally known than the other."

"Some writers of history have, however, the effrontery to pretend to give us a detail of the debates of privy councils, and of the most secret conversations and cabals of courtiers, with as much formal precision as if they had been cabinet ministers in the courts of all the princes of the age concerning which they write, and as if nothing had been transacted or determined without their privacy; nor do they scruple to entertain us with a circumstantial account of a battle, a siege, or the operations of a whole campaign, with as much pretended accuracy as if they had taken the field with the army and accompanied every detachment employed on different services during the whole contest. Such narratives ought always to be suspected; generally speaking, they ought to be totally disregarded. Mr. Boswell relates, that Dr. Johnson used to say, 'We talk of history; but let us consider how little history, I mean real, authentic history, we have. It is not to be questioned but such kings reigned, such battles were fought, such cities were taken, and such countries conquered, as we find mentioned; but all the colouring of history is mere conjecture.' In this Dr. Johnson is most certainly right. It is only the outlines of history, the leading and important facts, which have been productive of great and conspicuous effects, which ought to attract our attention, excite our reflection, and hold a place in our remembrance."—See *Bigland's Letters on the Study and Use of Ancient and Modern History.*

HONESTY AND INTEGRITY.

Nouschervan, a Persian king, having been hunting, and desirous of eating some of the venison, in his field, several of the attendants went to a neighbouring village, and took away a quantity of salt, to season it. The king, suspecting how they had acted, ordered, that they should immediately go and pay for it; then, turning to his attendants, he said, "This is a small matter in itself, but a great one as it regards me; for a king ought ever to be just, because he is an example to his subjects; and, if he swerves in trifles, they will become dissolute. If I cannot make all my people just in the smallest things, I can, at least, show them, it is possible to be so."

1 *

Some years since, resided in a country village, a poor but worthy clergyman, who, with the small stipend of 40l. per annum, supported himself, a wife, and seven children. At one time, walking and meditating in the fields, in much distress, from the narrowness of his circumstances, he stumbled on a purse of gold.— Looking round, in vain, to find its owner, he carried it home to his wife, who advised him to employ, at least, a part of it in extricating them from their present difficulty: but he conscientiously refused, until he had used his utmost endeavours to find out its former proprietor, assuring her, *that honesty is always the best policy.* After a short time, it was owned by a gentleman who lived at some little distance, to whom the clergyman returned it, with no other reward than thanks. On the good man's return, his wife could not help reproaching the gentleman with ingratitude, and censuring the over-scrupulous honesty of her husband; but he only replied as before, *honesty is the best policy.* A few months after this, the curate received an invitation to dine with the aforesaid gentleman; who, after hospitably entertaining him, gave him the presentation to a living of 300l. per annum, to which he added a bill of 50l. for his present necessities. The curate, after making suitable acknowledgments to his benefactor, returned with joy to his wife and family, acquainting them with the happy change in his circumstances; and, adding, that he hoped she would now be convinced, that *honesty was the best policy;* to which she readily assented.

One day, when a vacant see was to be filled, the synod observed to the emperor, Peter the Great, that they had none but ignorant men to present to his majesty. "Well, then," replied the czar, "you have only to pitch upon the most *honest* man: he will be worth two *learned* ones."

Previously to Dr. Goldsmith's publishing his "Deserted Village," the bookseller had given him a note for one hundred guineas for the copy, which the Doctor mentioned a few hours after to one of his friends, who observed, it was a very great sum for so short a performance. "In truth," replied Goldsmith, "I think so too; I have not been easy since I received it; therefore, I will go back, and return him his note: which he absolutely did, and left it entirely to the bookseller to pay him according to the profits produced by the sale of the piece, which turned out very considerable.—Honesty is the best policy.

In a late war in Germany, a captain of cavalry was ordered out on a foraging party. He put himself at the head of his troop, and marched to the quarter assigned him. It was a solitary valley, in which hardly any thing but woods could be seen. In the midst of it, stood a little cottage; on perceiving it, he went up, and knocked at the door: out comes an ancient Hernouten, (better known in this country by the name of Moravian Brethren,) with a beard silvered by age. "Father," says the officer, "show me a field where I can set my troopers a foraging." "Presently," replied the Hernouten. The good old man walked before, and conducted them out of the valley. After a quarter of an hour's march, they found a fine field of barley. "There is the very thing we want," says the captain. "Have patience for a few minutes," replied his guide: "you shall be satisfied." They went on, and, at the distance of about a quarter of a league farther, they arrived at another field of barley. The troop immediately dismounted, cut down the grain, trussed it up, and remounted. The officer, upon this, says to his conductor, "Father, you have given yourself, and us, unnecessary trouble: the first field was much better than this." "Very true, sir," replied the good old man, "but it was not mine."—This stroke, (says my author, and that justly,) goes directly to the heart. I defy an Atheist to produce me any thing once to be compared with it. And, surely, he who does not feel his heart warmed by such an example of exalted virtue, has not yet acquired the first principles of moral taste.

Mr. Addison, in a letter to a friend, makes the following declaration.— "Believe me, when I assure you, I never did, nor ever will, on any pretence whatsoever, take more than the stated and customary fees of my office. I might keep the contrary practice concealed from the world, were I capable of it, but I could not from myself; and I hope I shall always fear the reproaches of my own heart, more than those of all mankind." This reflected great honour on Mr. Addison's integrity.

HONOUR.

TRUE honour, though it be a different principle from religion, yet is not contrary to it. Religion embraces virtue, as it is enjoined by the laws of God; honour, as it is graceful and ornamental to human nature. The religious man fears, the man of honour scorns to do an ill action. The latter considers vice as something that is beneath him, the other as something that is offensive to the Divine Being; the one as what is unbecoming, the other as what is forbidden.

But what mistaken notions have some men of honour! They establish any thing to themselves for a point of honour, although it is contrary both to the laws of God, and of their country. "Timogenes was a lively instance of one actuated by false honour. Timogenes would smile at a man's jest, who ridiculed his Maker, and, at the same time, run a man through the body that spoke ill of his friend. Timogenes would have scorned to have betrayed a secret that was entrusted with him, though the fate of his country depended upon the discovery of it.— Timogenes took away the life of a young fellow in a duel, for having spoken ill of Belinda, a lady whom he himself had seduced in her youth, and betrayed into want and ignominy. After having ruined several poor tradesmen's families, who had trusted him, he sold his estate to satisfy his creditors; but, like a man of honour, disposed of all the money he could make of it in paying off his *play* debts, or, to speak in his own language, his debts of honour."

Virtue and honour were deified among the ancient Greeks and Romans, and had a joint temple consecrated to them at Rome; but, afterwards, each of them had separate temples, which were so placed, that no one could enter the temple of honour, without passing through that of virtue; by which the Romans were continually put in mind, that virtue is the only direct path to true glory. Plutarch tells us, that the Romans, contrary to their usual custom, sacrificed to honour uncovered; perhaps to denote that, wherever honour is, it wants no covering, but shows itself open to the world. Dr. South observes, that princes may confer honours, or rather titles and names of honour; but they are a man's own actions which must make him truly honourable; and every man's life is the herald's office, from whence he must derive and fetch that which must blazon him to the world; honour being but the reflection of a man's own actions, shining bright in the face of all about him, and from thence rebounding upon himself.

The Spanish historians relate a memorable instance of honour and regard to truth. A Spanish cavalier, in a sudden quarrel, slew a Moorish gentleman, and fled. His pursuers soon lost sight of him, for he had, unperceived, thorwn himself over a garden wall. The owner, a Moor, happening to be in his garden, was addressed by the Spaniard, on his knees, who acquainted him with his case, and implored concealment. "Eat this," said the Moor, (giving him half a peach,) "you now know that you may confide in my protection." He then locked him up in his apartment, telling him that, as soon as it was night, he would provide for his escape to a place of greater safety. The Moor then went into his house, where he had just seated himself, when a great crowd, with loud lamentations, came to his gate, bringing the dead body of his son, who had just been killed by a Spaniard. When the shock of surprise was a little over, he learnt, from the description given, that the fatal deed was done by the very person then in his power. He mentioned this to no one, but, as soon as it was dark, retired to his garden, as if to grieve alone, giving orders that none should follow him. Then, accosting the Spaniard, he said, "Christian, the person you have killed is my son: his body is now in my house. You ought to suffer; but you have eaten with me, and I have given you my faith, which must not be broken." He then led the astonished Spaniard to his stables, mounted him on one of his fleetest horses, and said, "Fly far, while the night can cover you: you will be safe in the morning. You are, indeed, guilty of my son's blood; but God is just and good, and I thank him I am innocent of your's, and that my faith given is preserved."

This point of honour is most religiously observed by the Arabs and Saracens, from whom it was adopted by the Moors of Africa, and by them was brought into Spain. The following instance of Spanish honour may still dwell in the memory of many living, and deserves to be handed down to the latest posterity. In the year 1746, when we were in hot war with Spain, the *Elizabeth* of London, Captain William Edwards, coming through the gulf from Jamaica, richly laden, met with a most violent storm, in which the ship sprung a leak, that obliged them, for the saving of their lives, to run into the Havana, a Spanish port. The captain went on shore, and directly waited on the governor; told the occasion of his putting in, and that he surrendered the ship as a prize, and

himself and his men as prisoners of war, only requesting good quarter. "No, sir," replied the Spanish governor: if we had taken you in fair war at sea, or approaching our coast with hostile intentions, your ship would then have been a prize, and your people prisoners; but when, distressed by a tempest, you come into our ports for the safety of your lives, we, the enemies, being men, are bound as such, by the laws of humanity, to afford relief to distressed men who ask it of us. We cannot, even against our enemies, take advantage of an act of God: you have leave, therefore, to unload your ship, if that be necessary, to stop the leak; you may refit her here, and traffic so far as shall be necessary to pay the charges; you may then depart; and I will give you a pass, to be in force till you are beyond Bermuda. If after that you are taken, you will then be a lawful prize; but now you are only a stranger, and have a stranger's right to safety and protection."—The ship accordingly departed, and arrived safe in London.

A remarkable instance of the like honour is recorded of a poor unenlightened African negro, in Captain Snelgrave's account of his Voyage to Guinea. A New-England sloop, trading there in 1752, left a second mate, William Murray, sick on shore, and sailed without him. Murray was at the house of a black named Cudjoe, with whom he contracted an acquaintance during their trade. He recovered, and, the sloop being gone, he continued with this black friend till some other opportunity should offer of his getting home. In the mean time, a Dutch ship came into the road, and some of the blacks, coming on board her, were treacherously seized, and carried off as their slaves. The relations and friends, transported with sudden rage, ran into the house of Cudjoe, to take revenge by killing Murray. Cudjoe stopped them at the door, and demanded what they wanted. "The white men," said they, "have carried away our brothers and sons, and we will kill all white men. Give us the white man you have in your house, for we will kill him." "Nay," said Cudjoe : "the white men that carried away your relations are bad men : kill them when you can take them : but this white man is a good man, and you must not kill him." "But he is a white man," they cried, "and the white men are all bad men, and we will kill them all." "Nay," says he ; "you must not kill a man who has done no harm, only for being white. This man is my friend ; my house is his post ; I am his soldier, and must fight for him ; you must kill me before you can kill him. What good man will ever come again under my roof, if I let my floor be stained by a good man's blood ?" The negroes seeing his resolution, and being convinced by his discourse that they were wrong, went away ashamed. In a few days Murray ventured abroad again with his friend Cudjoe, when several of them took him by the hand, and told him "they were glad they had not killed him ; for he was a good (meaning innocent) man : their God would have been very angry, and would have spoiled their fishing."

HUMILITY.

THERE is nothing more characteristic of a true Christian than humility. "It is the first lesson that he learns in the school of Christ, and is the source of contentment and solid peace of mind. If he hear that any one has reviled him, he is ready to say with the philosopher, 'had he known me better, he would have said worse things of me than that.' The fiercest storms of adversity blow over him. Humility gives a pliancy to his mind, which saves it by yielding to the force it cannot resist ; like the weak and bending reed that weathers out the tempest that fells the tall and sturdy oak."

Aristippus and Æschines having quarrelled, Aristippus came to him, and said, "Æschines, shall we be friends ?" "Yes, sir," said he, "with all my heart." "But remember," saith Aristippus, "that I, being older than you, do make the first motion." "Yes," said the other : "and therefore I conclude you are the worthiest man ; for I began the strife, and you began the peace."

"Should any one," saith St. Augustine, "ask me concerning the Christian religion, and the people of it, I would answer, that the first, second, and third things therein, and all, is humility."

Ignatius was so humble, that he disdained not to learn of any. Gregory the Great was so exemplary in his humility, that though he was born of noble parents, yet he had so little respect to his descent, that he would often say, with tears in his eyes, "That all glory was miserable, if the owner of it did not seek after the glory of God." King Agathocles would be served in earthen vessels, to remind him of his father, who was a poor potter. Wellegis, Archbishop of Mentz, being a wheelwright's son, hung wheels and wheelwright's tools about his bedchamber, and wrote under them, in capital letters, "Wellegis, Wellegis, remember thy original."—"This is all I know," said a philosopher, "that I know nothing."

Bishop Ussher was so humble, that in practical subjects he would apply himself to the capacity of the poorest and weakest Christian that came to him for information and satisfaction of their doubts. He had high thoughts of others, and low thoughts of himself. Godly persons, however poor, had great power over him. He would visit them in their sickness, supply their wants, beg their prayers, and countenance their cause and persons.

It is recorded of the Rev. Mr. Fletcher, that he never thought any thing too mean but sin ; he looked on nothing else as beneath his character. If he overtook a poor man or woman on the road with a burden too heavy for them, he did not fail to offer his assistance to bear part of it ;

and he would not easy take a denial. This, indeed, he has frequently done.

In the evening of the day Sir Eardley Wilmot kissed hands on being appointed chief justice, one of his sons, a youth of seventeen, attended him to his bedside. "Now," said he; "my son, I will tell you a secret worth your knowing and remembering. The elevation I have met with in life, particularly this last instance of it, has not been owing to any superior merit or abilities, but to my *humility;* to my not having set up myself above others, and to a uniform endeavour to pass through life void of offence towards God and man."—Thus humility is the way to honour.

Few, it is said, have exceeded Dr. Doddridge in the exercise of humility, both with relation to God and man. With respect to God, it was apparent in the deepest expressions of concern for the defects of his improvements and his services; and with regard to man, it was manifested in his condescension to the meanest persons, in his behaviour to his pupils, and in the patience with which he submitted to the words of reproof. He was even highly thankful to his friends for pointing out to him what they judged to be amiss in his conduct. In a letter to Dr. Wood, of Norwich, he thus expresses himself; "Pity me, and pray for me, as you do in the midst of so many hurries. O my poor, poor attempts of service!—they shame me continually. My prayers, my sermons, my lectures, my books (in hand,) my letters, all daily shame me." Some have thought, that, though this was sincere, yet it was an excessive effusion. But to this it may be answered that instead of its being excessive, it is only a proof of his increasing knowledge, arising from light given to him; for, in proportion as we receive light and grace, so shall we be led to see the imperfection of every thing we do. It was this that influenced Job to say, "Behold, I am vile;" Isaiah, "Lo, I am undone;" and Paul, that he was the least of saints.

THE HUNTING PRELATE.

In what a deplorable state were the clergy in the tenth century! Both in the eastern and western provinces they were composed of a most worthless set of men, shamefully illiterate and stupid. We may form some notion of the Grecian patriarchs from the single examle of Theophylact. This *exemplary* prelate, who sold every ecclesiastical benefice as soon as it became vacant, had in his stable above two thousand hunting horses, which he fed with pig-nuts, pistachios, dates, dried grapes, figs steeped in the most exquisite wines; to all which he added the richest perfumery. One Holy Thursday, as he was celebrating high mass, his groom brought him the joyful news that one of his favourite mares had foaled; upon which he threw down the liturgy, left the church, and ran in raptures to the stable, where, having expressed his joy at the *grand* event, he returned to the altar to finish the divine service, which he had left interrupted during his absence.—I am afraid that we have too many hunting clergymen in our enlightened day.

POWER OF IMAGINATION.

It is difficult to give credit to every thing that has been said on this head; it is evident, however, that there have been many strange and extraordinary instances of the strength of imagination.

An old writer gives us the following instance. A man in a burning fever, leaning over his bedside, pointed with his finger to the chamber door, desiring those who were present to let him swim in that lake, and that he then should be cool. His physician humoured the conceit: the patient walked carefully about the room, seemed to feel the water gradually ascending to his neck, and, at length, having said that he felt himself cool and well, was found, in reality, to be so. Medical men acknowledge that imagination has much to do both in inducing and curing many disorders. ﹖ Many have imagined their limbs to be made of glass, of wax, &c. of enormous sizes, and of fantastical shapes; and others have even fancied themselves dead.

In the Memoirs of Count De Maurepas, we find an account of a most singular hypochondriac in the person of the Prince of Bourbon. He once imagined himself to be a *hare*, and would suffer no bell to be rung in his palace, lest the noise would drive him to the woods. At another time he fancied himself to be a *plant*, and, as he stood in the garden, insisted on being watered. He some time afterwards thought he was dead, and refused nourishment; for which, he said, he had no farther occasion. This whim would have proved fatal, if his friends had not contrived to disguise two persons who were introduced to him as his grandfather and Marshal Luxembourg; and who, after some conversation concerning the shades, invited him to dine with Marshal Turenne. Our hypochondriac followed them into a cellar, prepared for the purpose, where he made a hearty meal. While this turn of his disorder prevailed, he always dined in the cellar with some noble ghost. We are also informed that this strange malady did not incapacitate him for business, especially when his interest was concerned.— This account is drawn from the Appendix to the Monthly Review for December, 1792.

﹖ Fienus, who wrote upon this subject, relates a singular instance of one whose delusion represented his body so large, that he thought it impossible for him to get out of the room. The physician, fancying there could be no better way of rectifying his imagination than by letting him see that the thing could be done, ordered him to be carried out by force. Great was the struggle; and the patient no sooner saw himself at the outside of the door, than he fell into the same agonies of pain as if his bones had all been broken by being forced through a passage too little for him, and died immediately after.

Of the important effects arising from bodily labour when united with mental excitement, we have recorded a remarkable instance in the *Monitor et Preceptor* of Dr. Mead. "A young student at College became so deeply hypochondriac, that he proclaimed himself dead, and ordered the college bell to be tolled on the occasion of his death. In this he was indulged; but the man employed to execute the task appeared to the student to perform it so imperfectly, that he arose from his bed in a fury of passion, to toll the bell for his own departure. When he had finished, he retired to his bed in a state of profuse perspiration, and was from that moment alive and well."

Simon Brown, a dissenting minister, was born at Shepton Mallet, in Somersetshire, 1680. Grounded and excelling in grammatical learning, he early became qualified for the ministry, and actually began to preach before he was twenty. He was first called to be a pastor at Portsmouth, and afterwards removed to the Old Jewry, where he was admired and esteemed for a number of years. But the death of his wife and only son, which happened in 1723, affected him so as to deprive him of his reason; and he became from that time lost to himself, his family, and to the world: his congregation at the Old Jewry, in expectation of his recovery, delayed for some time to fill his post; yet, at length, all hopes were over, and Mr. Samuel Chandler was appointed to succeed him in 1725. This double misfortune affected him at first in a manner little different from distraction, but afterwards sunk him into a settled melancholy.

He quitted the duties of his function, and would not be persuaded to join in any act of worship, public or private. Being urged by his friends for a reason of this extraordinary change, at which they expressed the utmost grief and astonishment, he told them, after much importunity, that " he had fallen under the sensible displeasure of God, who had caused his rational soul gradually to perish, and left him only an animal life in common with brutes : that, though he retained the human shape, and the faculty of speaking in a manner that appeared to others rational, he had all the while no more notion of what he said than a parrot ; that it was, therefore, profane in him to pray, and incongruous to be present at the prayers of others ;" and, very consistently with this, he considered himself no more as a moral agent, or subject of either reward or punishment. In this way of thinking and talking he unalterably and obstinately persisted to the end of his life, though he afterwards suffered, and even requested, prayers to be made for him. Some time after his secession from the Old Jewry, he retired to Shepton Mallet, his native place ; and though in his retirement he was perpetually contending that his powers of reason and imagination were gone, yet he was as constantly exerting both with much activity and vigour. He amused himself sometimes with translating parts of the ancient Greek and Latin poets into English verse ; he composed little pieces for the use of children ; an English Grammar and Spelling Book ; an Abstract of the Scripture History, and a Collection of Tables, both in metre ; and with much learning he brought together, in a short compass, all the *Themata* of the Greek and Latin tongues, and also compiled a Dictionary to each of those works, in order to render the learning of both these languages more easy and compendious. Of these performances none have been made public; but what showed the strength and vigour of his understanding, while he was daily bemoaning the loss of it, were two works composed during the two last years of his life, in Defence of Christianity against Woolston and Tindal. He wrote an Answer to Woolston's Fifth Discourse on the Miracles of our Saviour, entitled, A fit rebuke for a ludicrous Infidel, with a Preface concerning the Prosecution of such writers by the civil Power. The preface contains a vigorous plea for liberty, and is strongly against prosecutions in matters of religion; and, in the Answer Woolston is as well managed as he was by any of his refuters, and more in his own way, too. His book against Tindal was called, A defence of the religion of Nature and the Christian Revelation, against the defective account of the one, and the exceptions against the other, in a book entitled, Christianity as Old as the Creation ; and it is allowed to be as good a one as that controversy produced. He intended to dedicate it to Queen Caroline ; but as the unhappy state of his mind appeared in the dedication, some of his friends very wisely suppressed it, as sure to defeat the use and intent of his work. The copy, however, is preserved, and, as it is a great curiosity, we here present it to the reader.

" Madam,

" Of all the extraordinary things that have been rendered to your royal hands since your first happy arrival in Britain, it may be boldly said what now bespeaks your majesty's acceptance is the chief. Not in itself, indeed : it is a trifle unworthy your exalted rank, and what will hardly prove an entertaining amusement to one of your majesty's deep penetration, exact judgment, and fine taste, but on account of the author, who is the first being of the kind, and yet without a name. He was once a man, and of some little name, but of no worth, as his present unparalleled case makes but too manifest ; for, by the immediate hand of an avenging God, his very thinking substance has, for more than seven years, been continually wasting away, till it is wholly perished out of him, if it be not utterly come to nothing. None, no not the least remembrance of its very ruins, remains ; not the shadow of an idea is left, nor any sense, so much as one single one, perfect or imperfect, whole or diminished, ever did appear to a mind within him, or was perceived by it. Such a present, from such a thing, however worthless in itself, may not be wholly unacceptable to your majesty, the author being such as history cannot parallel: and if the fact, which is real, and no fiction or wrong conceit, obtains credit, it must be recorded as the most memorable, and indeed astonishing, even in the reign of George II. that a tract, composed by such a thing, was presented to the illustrious Caroline; his royal consort needs not to be added. Fame, if I am not misinformed, will tell that with pleasure to all succeeding times. He has been informed, that your majesty's piety is as genuine and eminent as your excellent qualities are great and conspicuous. This can, indeed, be truly known to the Great Searcher of hearts only. He alone, who can look into them, can discern if they are sincere, and the main intention corresponds with the appearance: and your majesty cannot take it amiss, if such an author hints, that his secret approbation is of infinitely greater value than the commendation of men, who may be easily mistaken, and are two apt to flatter their superiors. But, if he has been told the truth, such a case as his will certainly strike your majesty with astonishment, and may raise that commisseration in your royal breast, which he has in vain endeavoured to excite in those of his friends, who, by the most unreasonable and ill-founded conceit in the world, have imagined that a thinking being could, for seven years together, live a stranger to its own powers, exercises, operations, and state, and to what the Great God has been doing in it and to it. If your majesty, in your most retired address to the King of kings, should think of so singular a case, you may, perhaps, make it your devout request, that the reign of your beloved sovereign and consort may be renowned to all posterity,

by the recovery of a soul now in the utmost ruin; the restoration of one utterly lost at present amongst men. And, should this case affect your royal breast, you will recommend it to the piety and prayers of all the truly devout who have the honour to be known to your majesty: many such, doubtless, there are, though courts are not usually the places where the devout resort, or where devotion reigns; and it is not improbable that multitudes of the pious throughout the land may take a case to heart, that, under your majesty's patronage, comes thus recommended. Could such a favour as this restoration be obtained from heaven by the prayers of your majesty, with what transport of gratitude would the recovered being throw himself at your majesty's feet, and, adoring the Divine Power and Grace, profess himself,

"Madam,
"Your Majesty's
"Most obliged and dutiful servant,
"SIMON BROWN."

A complication of distempers, contracted by his sedentary life (for he could not be prevailed on to refresh himself with air and exercise)brought on a mortification, which put a period to his labours and sorrows about the latter end of 1732. He was, unquestionably, a man of uncommon abilities and learning. His management of Woolston showed him to have also vivacity and wit; and, notwithstanding that strange conceit which possessed him, it is remarkable that he never appeared feeble nor absurd, except when the object of his frenzy was before him.

Many curious circumstances have been mentioned of Dr. Watts, respecting the strength of imagination; but as it does not appear that they are founded on any certainty, we shall entirely omit them here.

IMPLICIT FAITH.

THE Christian religion, says Dr. Campbell, has always been understood to require faith in its principles, and faith in principles requires some degree of knowledge or apprehension of those principles. But the schoolmen have devised an excellent succedaneum to supply the place of real belief, and this they have denominated *implicit faith,* an ingenious method of reconciling things incompatible; to believe every thing, and to know nothing. Implicit faith has been sometimes styled *fides carbonaria,* from the story of one who, examining an ignorant collier on his religious principles, asked him what it was that he believed. He answered, " I believe what the church believes." The other rejoined, " What, then, does the church believe?" He replied readily, " The church believes what I believe." The other, desirous, if possible, to bring him to particulars, once more resumed his inquiry. " Tell me, then, I pray you, what it is which you and the church *both* believe." The only answer the collier could give was, " Why, truly, Sir, the church and I *both*—believe the same thing."

THE INFIDEL ALARMED.

The late Samuel Forrester Bancroft, Esq., accompanied Mr. Isaac Weld, junior, in his travels through North America, and the two Canadas; a very interesting narrative of which is published. As they were traversing one of the extensive lakes of the northern states in a vessel, on board of which was Volney, celebrated, or, rather, notorious, for his atheistical principles, which he has so often avowed, a very heavy storm came on, insomuch that the vessel, which had struck repeatedly with great force, was expected to go down every instant; the mast having gone by the board, the helm quite ungovernable, and, consequently, the whole scene exhibiting confusion and horror.— There were many female as well as male passengers on board, but no one exhibited such strong marks of fearful despair as Volney; throwing himself on the deck, now imploring, now imprecating the captain, and remind-

ing him, that he had engaged to carry him safe to his destination, vainly threatening, in case any thing should happen. At last, however, as the probability of their being lost increased, this great mirror of nature, human or inhuman, began loading all the pockets of his coat, waistcoat, breeches, and every place he could think of, with dollars, to the amount of some hundreds; and thus, as he thought, was preparing to swim for his life, should the expected wreck take place. Mr. Bancroft remonstrated with him on the folly of such acts, saying, that he would sink like a piece of lead with so great a weight on him; and, at length, as he became so very noisy and unsteady as to impede the management of the ship, Mr. Bancroft pushed him down the hatchways. Volney soon came up again, having lightened himself of the dollars, and, in the agony of his mind, threw himself upon the deck, exclaiming, with uplifted hands and streaming eyes,—" *Oh, mon Dieu! mon Dieu!—que'st ce que je ferai! que'st ce que je ferai!*"—Oh, my God! my God! what shall I do! what shall I do!—This so surprised Bancroft, that, notwithstanding the moment did not very well accord with flashes of humour, yet he could not refrain from addressing—" *Eh! bien! Mons. Volney! vous avez donc un Dieu a present:*" Well, Mr. Volney! what—you have a God now! To which Volney replied, with the most trembling anxiety, " *Oh, oui! oui!*"—O yes! O yes! The ship, however, got safe; and Mr. Bancroft made every company which he went into, echo with this anecdote of Volney's acknowledgment of God. Volney, for a considerable time, was so hurt at his weakness, as he calls it, that he was ashamed of showing himself in company at Philadelphia, &c., but, afterwards, like a modern French philosopher, said, that those words escaped him in the instant of alarm, but had no meaning, and he again utterly renounced them.

THE INFIDEL CORRECTED.

A YOUNG gentleman, of moderate understanding, but of great vivacity, by dipping into many authors of the modish and freethinking turn, had acquired a little smattering of knowledge, just enough to make an Atheist, or a freethinker, but not a philosopher, or a man of sense. With these accomplishments, he went into the country to visit his father, who was a plain, rough, honest man, and wise, though not learned. The son, who took all opportunities to show his learning, began to establish a new religion in the family, and to enlarge the narrowness of their country notions; in which he succeeded so well, that he seduced the butler by his table talk, and staggered his eldest sister. The old gentleman began to be alarmed at the schisms that arose among his children, but did not yet believe his son's doctrine to be so pernicious as it really was, till one day, talking of his setting dog, the son said he did not question but Carlo was as immortal as any one of the family; and, in the heat of the argument, told his father, that, for his part, he expected to die like a dog. Upon which, the old man, starting up in a passion, cried out, "Then, sirrah, you shall live like one;" and, taking his cane in his hand, cudgelled him out of his system, and brought him to more serious reflections, and better studies. "I do not," continues Sir Richard Steele, from whom this story is taken, "mention the cudgelling part of the story with a design to engage the secular arm in matters of this nature; but certainly if it ever exerts itself in affairs of opinion and speculation, it ought to do it on such shallow and despicable pretenders to knowledge, who endeavour to give a man dark and uncomfortable prospects of his being, and to destroy those principles which are the support, happiness, and glory, of all public societies, as well as of private persons."

GRATITUDE.

"THERE is not any vice," says

N

South, "against which mankind have raised such a loud and universal outcry, as against ingratitude; a vice never mentioned, even by any heathen writer, but with peculiar detestation. An ungrateful man is a reproach to his creation; an exception from all the visible world: neither the heavens above, nor the earth beneath, afford any thing like him; and, therefore, if he would find his parallel, he must go to the region of darkness: for, besides himself, there is nothing but hell, that is receiving, and never restoring.

"Ingratitude is too base to return a kindness, and too proud to regard it; much like the tops of mountains, barren, indeed, but yet lofty: they produce nothing, they feed nobody, they clothe nobody, yet are high and stately, and look down upon all the world about them.

"Ingratitude is generally attended with hard-heartedness, a want of compassion. Thus, Nero sent an assassin to murder his own mother, and wished that mankind had but one head, that he might have the pleasure of cutting it off. And what an instance of ingratitude and cruelty have we in Tullia! Tullia was daughter of Servilius Tullius, sixth king of Rome; and, having married *Tarquinius Superbus*, and put him first upon killing her father, and then invading his throne, she came through the street where the body of her father lay, newly murdered, and wallowing in his blood: she commanded her trembling coachman to drive his chariot and horses over the body of her king and father, triumphantly, in the face of all Rome, who were looking upon her with astonishment and detestation."

In a little work, entitled *Friendly Cautions to Officers*, the following atrocious instance of ingratitude is related. An opulent city in the west of England, little used to have troops with them, had a regiment sent to be quartered. The principal inhabitants, and wealthiest merchants, glad to show their hospitality and attachment to their sovereign, took the first opportunity to get acquainted with the officers, inviting them to their houses, and showing every civility in their power. This was, truly, a desirable situation. A merchant, extremely easy in his circumstances, took so prodigious a liking to one officer in particular, that he gave him an apartment in his own house, and made him, in a manner, absolute master of it, the officer's friends being always welcome to his table.—— The merchant was a widower, and had only two favourite daughters: the officer, in so comfortable a station, cast his wanton eyes upon them, and, too fatally succeeding, ruined them both.——Dreadful return to the merchant's misplaced friendship!

The consequence of this ungenerous action was, that all officers ever after were shunned as a public nuisance, as a pest to society; nor have the inhabitants, perhaps, yet conquered their aversion to a red coat.

We read in Rapin's History, that during Monmouth's rebellion, in the reign of James II. a certain person, knowing the humane disposition of one Mrs. Gaunt, whose life was one continual exercise of beneficence, fled to her house, where he was concealed and maintained for some time. Hearing, however, of the proclamation which promised an indemnity and reward to those who discovered such as harboured the rebels, he betrayed his benefactress; and such was the spirit of justice and equity which prevailed among the ministers, that he was pardoned and recompensed for his treachery, while she was burnt alive for her charity.

The following instance is also to be found in the same history. Humphrey Bannister and his father were both servants to, and raised by, the Duke of Buckingham; who, being driven to abscond, by an unfortunate accident befalling the army he had raised against the usurper, Richard III., he, without footman or page, retired to Bannister's house, near Shrewsbury, as to a place where he had all the reason in the world to expect security. Bannister, however, upon the king's proclamation, promising 1000 pounds reward to him that should apprehend the duke, betrayed his master to John Merton, the High Sheriff of Shropshire, who sent him under a strong guard to Salisbury, where the king then was; and there, in the market-place, the duke was beheaded. But Divine vengeance pursued the traitor Bannister; for, demanding the 1000l. that was the price of his master's blood, King Richard refused to pay it, saying, "He that would be false to so good a master, ought not to be encouraged." He was afterwards hanged for manslaughter; his eldest son soon ran mad, and died in a hogsty; his second become deformed and lame; and his third son was drowned in a small puddle of water. His eldest daughter was pregnant by one of his carters; and his second was seized with a leprosy, whereof she died.

The following barbarous instances are from ancient history.

When Xerxes, King of Persia, was at Celene, a city of Phrygia, Pythius, a Lydian, who had his residence in that city, and, next to Xerxes, was the most opulent prince of those times, entertained him and his whole army with an incredible magnificence, and made him an offer of all his wealth towards defraying the expenses of his expedition.— Xerxes, surprised and charmed at so generous an offer, had the curiosity to inquire to what sum his riches amounted to. Pythius made answer, that, having the design of offering them to his service, he had taken an exact account of them, and that the silver he had by him amounted to 2,000 talents (about 255,000l. sterling,) and the gold to 4,000,000 of darics (about 1,700,000l. sterling,) wanting 7,000. All this money he offered him, telling him that his revenue was sufficient for the support of his household. Xerxes made him very hearty acknowledgments, and entered into a particular friendship with him, but declined accepting this present. The same prince, who had made such obliging offers to Xerxes, having desired a favour of him some time after, that out of his five sons, who served in the army, he would be pleased to leave him the eldest, in order to be a comfort to him in his old age, the king was so enraged at the proposal, though so reasonable in itself, that he caused his eldest son to be killed before the eyes of his father; giving the latter to understand, that it was a favour that he spared him and the rest of his children. Yet this is the same Xerxes who is so much admired for his humane reflection at the head of his numerous army, "That of so many thousand men, in one hundred years' time there would not be one remaining; on which account he could not forbear weeping at the uncertainty and instability of human things." He might have found another subject of reflection, which would have more justly merited his tears and affliction, had he turned his thoughts upon himself, and considered the reproaches he deserved for being the instrument of hastening the fatal term to millions of people, whom his cruel ambition was going to sacrifice in an unjust and an unnecessary war.

Basilius Macedo, the Emperor, exercising himself in hunting, a sport he took a great delight in, a great stag, running furiously against him, fastened one of the branches of his horns in the emperor's girdle, and, pulling him from his horse, dragged him a good distance to the imminent danger of his life; which a gentleman of his retinue perceiving, drew his sword and cut the emperor's girdle asunder, which disengaged him from the beast, with little or no hurt to his person. But observe what reward he had for his pains: "He was sentenced to lose his head, for putting his sword so near the body of the emperor," and suffered death accordingly.

The ungrateful Guest.

A certain soldier in the Macedonian army had, in many instances, distinguished himself by extraordinary acts of valour, and had received many marks of Philip's favour and approbation. On some occasion he embarked on board a vessel, which was wrecked by a violent storm, and he himself cast on the shore helpless and naked, and scarcely with the appearance of life. A Macedonian, whose lands were contiguous to the sea, came opportunely to be witness of his distress; and, with all humane and charitable tenderness, flew to the relief of the unhappy stranger. He bore him to his house, laid him in his own bed, revived, cherished, comforted, and for forty days supplied him freely with all the necessaries and conveniences which his languishing condition could require. The soldier, thus happily rescued from death, was incessant in the warmest expressions of gratitude to his benefactor, assured him of his interest with the king, and of his power and resolution of obtaining for him, from the royal bounty, the noble returns which such extraordinary benevolence had merited. He was now completely recovered, and his kind host supplied him with money to pursue his journey. In some time after, he presented himself before the king; he recounted his misfortunes, magnified his services: and this inhuman wretch, who had looked with an eye of envy on the possessions of the man who had preserved his life, was now so abandoned to all sense of gratitude, as to request that the king would bestow upon him the house and lands where he had been so tenderly and kindly entertained. Unhappily, Philip, without examination, inconsiderately and precipately granted his infamous request; and this soldier, now returned to his preserver, repaid his goodness by driving him from his settlement, and taking immediate possession of all the fruits of his honest industry. The poor man, stung with this instance of unparalleled ingratitude and insensibility, boldly determined, instead of submitting to his wrongs, to seek relief; and, in a letter addressed
16*

to Philip, represented his own and the soldier's conduct, in a lively and affecting manner. The king was instantly fired with indignation : he ordered that justice should be done without delay ; that the possessions should be immediately restored to the man whose charitable offices had been thus horribly repaid : and, having seized the soldier, caused these words to be branded on his forehead— *The Ungrateful Guest ;*—a character infamous in every age, and among all nations ; but particularly among the Greeks, who, from the earliest times, were most scrupulously observant of the laws of hospitality.

JUSTICE AND EQUITY.

CIVILIANS distinguish justice into two kinds : one they call communicative ; and this establishes fair dealing in the mutual commerce between man and man, and includes sincerity in our discourse, and integrity in our dealings. The effect of sincerity is mutual confidence, so necessary among the members of the same community ; and this mutual confidence is sustained and preserved by the integrity of our conduct. Distributive justice is that by which the differences of mankind are decided according to the rules of equity : the former is the justice of private individuals ; the latter, of princes and magistrates."

Chancellor Egerton, one morning, coming down stairs to go to Westminister Hall, observed these words written upon the wall before him : " Tanquam non reversurus," as if never to return, intimating how impartial he ought to be ; supposed to have been written there by some person who had that day an important cause to be tried, and feared oppression.

Sir Thomas More, when Lord Chancellor of England, was remarkable for his justice, and attention to the duties of his station. It is said, that the meanest claimant found ready access to him : no private affection could bias his judgment or influence his decree ; no opportunity was given for intrigue or interested solicitation ; and, after he had presided in the court of chancery for two years, such was his application to business, that one day, calling for the next cause, he was told there was not another then depending : a circumstance which he immediately ordered to be set down on record, and we suppose it will be allowed an unique of the kind.

Lord Bacon, in his Essays modern and civil, gives the following anecdote of Sir Thomas. A person who had a suit in chancery sent him two silver flagons, not doubting of the agreeableness of the present. On receiving them, he called one of his servants, and ordered him to fill those two vessels with the best wine in his cellar ; and, turning round to the servant who had presented them, " Tell your master," said the inflexible magistrate, " that, if he approves my wine, I beg he would not spare it ;" and returned the cups.

Lord Chief Justice Holt was one of the ablest and most upright Judges that ever presided in a court of justice. Such was the integrity and firmness of his mind, that he could never be brought to swerve in the least from what he esteemed to be law and justice. He was remarkably strenuous in nobly asserting, and as rigorously supporting, the liberties of the subject, to which he paid the greatest regard ; and would not even suffer a reflection, tending to depreciate them, to pass uncensured, or without a severe reprimand. He lost his place, as Recorder of London, for refusing to expound the law suitably to the king's designs. He asserted the law with such intrepidity, that he incurred, by turns, the indignation of both houses of parliament.

It is said of Mr. Jonas Hanway, that in his department of commissioner for victualling the navy, he was uncommonly assiduous and attentive, and kept the contractors and persons who had dealings with the office at a great distance. He would not even accept of a hare, or peasant, or the smallest present, from any of them; and when any were sent him, he always returned them; not in a morose manner, as if he affected the excess of disinterestedness, but with some mild answer; such as, "Mr. Hanway returns many thanks to Mr.—— for the present he intended him, but he has made it a rule not to accept any thing from any person engaged with the office: a rule which he hopes Mr.——'s good intentions will not expect him to break through."

It is recorded of Sir Matthew Hale, that, whenever he was convinced of the injustice of any cause, he would engage no farther in it than to explain to his client the grounds of that conviction. He abhorred the practice of misreciting evidences; quoting precedents or books falsely or unfairly, so as to deceive ignorant juries or inattentive judges; and that he adhered to the same scrupulous sincerity in his pleadings which he observed in the other transactions of his life. For he used to say, "it was as great a dishonour as a man was capable of, that, for a little money, he was to be hired to say or do otherwise than he thought."

This brings to mind the saying of Epaminondas, who, when great presents were sent to him, used to observe, "If the thing you desire be good, I will do it without any bribe, even because it is good: if it be not honest, I will not do it for all the goods in the world."

When he was once going his circuit, he understood that the Protector had ordered a jury to be returned for a trial in which he was more than ordinarily concerned. Upon this information, he examined the sheriff about it, who knew nothing of it, for he said that he referred all things to the under sheriff; and having next asked the under sheriff concerning it, he found the jury had been returned by order from Cromwell: upon which he showed the statute, that all juries ought to be returned by the sheriff or his lawful officer; and this not being done according to law, he dismissed the jury and would not try the cause. Upon which the Protector was highly displeased with him, and, at his return from the circuit, he told him, in anger, "that he was not fit to be a judge." To which all the answer he made was, "That it was very true."

Colonel Tatham, who practised law while in the Tennessee government, published, among others, the following rules:

"*Fiat Justitia!*

"Having adopted the above motto as early as I had the honour of admission to the bar, I have covenanted with myself that I will never knowingly depart from it, and on this foundation I have built a few maxims, which afford my reflections an unspeakable satisfaction.

"1st. I will practice law, because it offers me opportunities of being a more useful member of society.

"2dly. 1 will not turn a deaf ear to any man because his purse is empty.

"3dly. I will advise no man beyond my comprehension of his cause.

"4thly. I will bring none into law who my conscience tells me should be kept out of it.

"5thly. 1 will never be unmindful of the cause of humanity; and this comprehends the fatherless, widows, and bondages.

"6thly. I will be faithful to my client, but never so unfaithful to myself as to become a party in his crime.

"7thly. I will never acknowledge the omnipotence of legislation, or consider any acts to be law beyond the spirit of the constitution.

"8thly. No man's greatness shall elevate him above the justice due to my client.

"9thly. I will not consent to a compromise where I conceive a verdict essential to my client's future reputation or protection: for of this he cannot be a complete judge.

"10thly. I will advise the turbulent with candour: and, if they will go to law against my advice, they must pardon me for volunteering it against them.

" 11thly. I will acknowledge every man's right to manage his own cause if he pleases.

" The above are *my* rules of practice; and though I will not, at this critical juncture, promise to finish my business in person, but, if the *public* interest should require my removal from hence, I will do every thing in my power for those who like to employ me, and endeavour to leave them in proper hands if I should be absent.

(Signed) "WILLIAM TATHAM.
" Knoxville, March 21, 1793."

THE INFLEXIBLE JURYMAN.

IN the trial of the famous William Penn and William Mead, at the Old Baily, for an unlawful assembly in the open street, in contempt of the king's laws, &c. we find a striking instance of the inflexible justice of the jury. After the jury had withdrawn an hour and a half, the prisoners were brought to the bar to hear their verdict : eight of them came down agreed, but four remained above, to whom they used many unworthy threats, and in particular to Mr. *Bushel*, whom they charged with being the cause of the disagreement. At length, after withdrawing a second time, they agreed to bring them in *guilty of speaking in Gracechurch street*, which the court would not accept for a verdict, but, after many menaces, told them they should be locked up, without meat, drink, fire, or tobacco: nay, they should starve unless they brought in a proper verdict. *Wm. Penn* being at the bar, said, " *My jury ought not to be thus threatened. We were by force of arms kept out of our meeting-house, and met as near it as the soldiers would give us leave. We are a peaceable people, and cannot offer violence to any man.*" And, looking upon the jury, he said, " *You are Englishmen: mind your privilege; give not away your right.*" To which some of them answered,

" *Nor will we ever do it.*" Upon this they were shut up all night, without victuals or fire, nor so much as a chamber utensil, though desired. Next morning they brought in the same verdict : upon which they were threatened with the utmost resentments. The mayor said, *he would cut Bushel's throat as soon as he could.* The recorder said, " *he never knew the benefit of an inquisition till now ; and that the next sessions of parliament a law would be made, wherein those who would not conform should not have the benefit of the law.* The court having obliged the jury to withdraw again, they were kept without meat and drink till next morning, when they brought in the prisoners *not guilty ;* for which they were fined forty marks a man, and to be imprisoned till paid. The prisoners were also remanded to *Newgate,* for their fines in not pulling off their hats. The jury, after some time, were discharged by *habeas corpus,* returnable in the Common Pleas, where their commitment was judged illegal.—This was a noble stand for the liberty of the subject in very dangerous times, when neither law nor equity availed any thing.

The following will give us an idea of the inflexibility and decision of a single juryman in opposition to all the rest. Mr. ——, being on a jury in a trial of life and death, he was completely satisfied of the innocence of the prisoner ; all the other eleven were of the opposite opinion ; but he was resolved that a verdict of guilty should not be brought in. In the first place, he spent several hours in trying to convince them ; but found that he made no impression, and that he was fast exhausting the strength which was to be reserved for another mode of operation. He, therefore, calmly told them it should now be a trial who could endure confinement and famine the longest, and that they might be quite assured he would sooner die than release them at the expense of the prisoner's life. In this situation they spent about twenty-four hours, when, at length, they all acceded to his verdict of acquittal.

LIBERALITY OF SENTIMENT.

KINDNESS, liberality of sentiment, candour, charity, are expressions now exceedingly perverted. They become a sanctuary, in which the unprincipled, the erroneous, and the careless, too often take refuge. But let it be remembered that "that candour which regards all sentiments alike, and considers no error as destructive, is no virtue. It is the offspring of ignorance, of insensibility, and of cold indifference. The blind do not perceive the difference of colours; the dead never dispute; ice, as it congeals, aggregates all bodies within its reach, however heterogeneous their quality. Every virtue has certain bounds, and when it exceeds them it becomes a vice; for the last step of a virtue, and the first step of a vice, are contiguous. But, surely, it is no wildness of candour that leads us to give the liberty we take; that suffers a man to think for himself unawed, and that concludes he may be a follower of God, though he follows not with us."

Wickliffe's bones were dug up forty years after he was buried, and thrown into the river.—But it deserves to be recorded of Charles V. that he would not suffer Luther's bones to be touched, though he was an avowed enemy to him.—While Charles' troops were quartered at Wirtemberg, in 1547, which was one year after Luther's death, a soldier gave Luther's effigy, in the church of the castle, two stabs with his dagger; and the Spaniards earnestly desired that his tomb might be pulled down, and his bones dug up and burnt: but the emperor wisely answered, "I have nothing farther to do with Luther; he has henceforth another Judge, whose jurisdiction it is not lawful for me to usurp. Know that I make no war with the dead, but with the living, who still make war with me." He would not, therefore,

suffer his tomb to be demolished, and he forbade any attempt of that nature, upon pain of death.

Dr. H——, Bishop of W——, had observed, among his hearers, a poor man remarkably attentive, and made him some little presents. After a while, he missed his humble auditor, and, meeting him, said, "John, how is it that I do not see you in this aisle as usual?" John with some hesitation, replied, "My lord, I hope you will not be offended, and I will tell you the truth. I went the other day to hear the Methodists; and I understand their plain words so much better, that I have attended them ever since." The Bishop put his hand into his pocket, and gave him a guinea, with words to this effect; "God bless you! and go where you can receive the greatest profit to your soul."

When Archbishop Secker was laid on his couch with a broken thigh, and sensible of his approaching dissolution, Mr. Talbot, of Reading, who had lived in great intimacy with, and had received his preferment from him, visited him at Lambeth. Before they parted, "You will pray with me, Talbot," said the archbishop. Mr. Talbot rose, and went to look for a prayer book. "That is not what I want now," said the dying prelate: "kneel down by me, and pray for me in the way I know you are used to do." With which command Mr. Talbot readily complied, and prayed earnestly from his heart for his dying friend, whom he saw no more.

The archbishop's conduct, which he observed towards the several divisions and denominations of Christians in this kingdom, was such as showed his way of thinking to be truly liberal and catholic. He was sincerely desirous of cultivating a good understanding with the dissenters. He considered them, in general, as a conscientious and valuable class of men. With some of the most eminent of them, Watts, Doddridge, Leland, Chandler, Lardner, he maintained an intercourse of friendship or civility. By the most candid and considerate part of them he was highly reverenced and esteemed; and to such among them as needed help, he showed no less kindness and liberality than to those of his own communion.

What an honour did the comprehension bill, for relaxing the terms of conformity on behalf of the protestant dissenters, confer on the names of Dr. Wilkins, afterwards Bishop of Winchester, Lord Bridgman, Sir Matthew Hale, Tillotson, and Stillingfleet! The bill, however, was thrown out by the bishops; and though, afterwards, the scheme was revived, and again rejected, yet in what a striking point of view does it exhibit to us the liberty and candour of the excellent characters above named, as also of the king and queen, who expressed their desire of a union!

LUXURY.

THE Almighty is justly styled the Father of mercies. He opens his liberal hand, and is perpetually supplying the wants of his creatures. But how lamentable is it that his favours should be abused, and that those blessings, which should leave us to admire and adore him, become, through our depravity, the occasion of rendering ourselves like beasts! "Human life, we own, is full of troubles; and we are all tempted to alleviate them as much as we can, by freely enjoying the pleasurable moments which Providence thinks fit to allow us; and enjoy them we may: but if we would enjoy them safely, and enjoy them long, let us temper them with the fear of God. As soon as this is forgotten, the sound of the *harp* and *viol* is changed into the signal of death. The serpent comes forth from the roses where it had lain in ambush, and gives the fatal sting. Pleasure in moderation is the cordial, in excess it is the bane, of life."

Luxury, among the Romans, prevailed to such a degree, that several laws were made to suppress, or at least limit it. The extravagance of the table began about the time of the battle of Actium, and continued in great excess till the reign of Galba. Peacocks, cranes of Malta, nightingales, venison, wild and tame fowl, were considered as delicacies. A profusion of provisions was the reigning taste. Whole wild boars were often served up, and sometimes they were filled up with various small animals, and birds of different kinds: this dish they called the Trojan horse, in allusion to the wooden horse filled with soldiers. Fowls, and game of all sorts, were served up in whole pyramids, piled up in dishes as broad as moderate tables. Lucullus had a particular name for each apartment; and in whatever room he ordered his servants to prepare the entertainment, they knew by the direction the expense to which they were to go. When he supped in the Apollo, the expense was fixed at 50,000 drachmæ; that is, 1,250*l.* M. Antony provided eight boars for twelve guests. Vitellius had a large silver platter, said to to have cost a million of sesterces, called Minerva's Buckler. In this he blended together the livers of gilt heads, the brains of pheasants and peacocks, the tongues of phenicopters, and the milts of lampreys. Caligula served up to his guests pearls of great value dissolved in vinegar; the same was also done by Clodius, the son of Æsop, the tragedian. Apicius laid aside 90,000,000 of sesterces, besides a mighty revenue, for no other purpose but to be sacrificed to luxury: finding himself involved in debt, he looked over his account, and though he had the sum of 10,000,000 of sesterces still left, he poisoned himself, for fear of being starved to death.

The Roman laws to restrain luxury were *Lex Orchia, Fannia Didia, Licinia Cornelia,* and many others: but all these were too little; for as riches increased among them, so did sensuality.

What were the ideas of luxury entertained in England about two centuries ago, may be gathered from the following passage of Holinshed, who, in a discourse prefixed to his History, speaking of the increase of luxury, says, " Neither do I speak this in reproach of any man, God is my judge ; but to show that I do rejoice rather to see how God has blessed us with his good gifts, and to behold how that, in a time wherein all things are grown to the most excessive prices, we yet do find means to obtain and achieve such furniture as heretofore was impossible. There are old men yet dwelling in the village where I remain, which have noted three things to be marvellously altered so in England within their round remembrance ; one is, the multitude of chimneys lately erected, whereas, in their young days, there were not above two or three, if so many, in most uplandish towns of the realm (the religious houses and manor places of their lords always excepted, and, peradventure, some great parsonages) but each made his fire against a reredoss [skreen] in the hall where he dressed his meat, and where he dined. The second is, the great amendment of lodging : for, said they, our fathers, and we ourselves, have lain oft upon straw pallets covered only with a sheet, under coverlets made of a dog's waine or horharriots (to use their own terms) and a good log under their head instead of a bolster. If it were so that the father or good man of the house had a mattress or flock bed, and sheets, a sack of chaff to rest his head upon, he thought himself to be as well lodged as the lord of the town. So well were they contented, that pillows (said they) were thought meet only for women in childbed : as for servants, if they had any sheets above them, it was well ; for seldom had they any under their bodies to keep them from pricking straws, that ran oft through the canvass and their hardened hides. The third thing they tell of, is the exchange of treene [wooden] platters into pewter, and wooden spoons into silver or tin ; for so common were all sorts of treene vessels in old times, that a man should

hardly find four pieces of pewter (of which was one, peradventure, a salt) in a good farmer's house. Again, in times past, men were contented to dwell in houses builded of sallow, willow, &c. so that the use of oak was, in a manner, dedicated wholly unto churches, religious houses, princes' palaces, navigation, &c. But now willow, &c. are rejected, and nothing but oak any where regarded ; and, yet, see the change ; for when our houses were builded of willow, then had we oaken men ; but now, when our houses are come to be made of oak, our men are not only become willow, but a great many altogether of straw, which is a sore alteration. In these, the courage of the owner was a sufficient defence to keep the house in safety ; but now the assurance of the timber must defend the men from robbing. Now have we many chimneys, and yet our tenderlings complain of rheums, catarrhs, and poses ; then had we none but reredoses, and our heads did never ache. For as the smoke in those days was supposed to be a sufficient hardening for the timber of the house, so it was reputed a far better medicine to keep the good man and his family from the quacks or pose ; wherewith, as then, very few were acquainted. Again, our pewterers, in time past, employed the use of pewter only upon dishes and pots, and a few other trifles for service : whereas now they are grown into such exquisite cunning, that they can, in a manner, imitate by infusion any form or fashion, of cup, dish, salt, bowl, or goblet, which is made by the goldsmith's craft, though they be ever so curious, and very artificially forged. In some places beyond the sea, a garnish of good flat English pewter (I say flat, because dishes and platters in my time began to be made deep and like basins, and are, indeed, more convenient both for sauce and keeping the meat warm) is esteemed so precious, as the like number of vessels that are made of fine silver."

Particular instances of luxury in

eating, however, might be adduced from an earlier period, surpassing even the extravagance of the Romans. Thus, in the tenth year of the reign of Edward IV. 1470, George Nevill, brother to the Earl of Warwick, at his instalment into the archiepiscopal see of York, entertained most of the nobility and principal clergy, when his bill of fare was, 300 quarters of wheat, 350 tuns of ale, 104 tuns of wine, a pipe of spiced wine, 80 fat oxen, 6 wild bulls, 1004 wethers, 300 hogs, 300 calves, 3000 geese, 3000 capons, 300 pigs, 100 peacocks, 200 cranes, 200 kids, 2000 chickens, 4000 pigeons, 4000 rabbits, 204 bitterns, 4000 ducks, 200 pheasants, 500 partridges, 2000 woodcocks, 400 plovers, 100 curlews, 100 quails, 1000 egrets, 200 rees, 400 bucks, does, and roebucks, 1506 hot venison pasties, 4000 cold ditto, 1000 dishes of jelly, parted, 4000 dishes of jelly, plain, 4000 cold custards, 2000 hot custards, 300 pikes, 300 breams, 8 seals, 4 porpuses, 400 tarts. At this feast, the Earl of Warwick was steward, the Earl of Bedford, treasurer, and Lord Hastings comptroller, with many more noble officers; 1000 servitors, 62 cooks, 515 menial apparitors in the kitchen. But such was the fortune of the man, that, after this extreme prodigality, he died in the most abject but unpitied poverty, *vinctus jacuit in summa inopia.*

And as to dress, luxury in that article seems to have attained a great height long before Holinshed's time ; for, in the reign of Edward III. we find no fewer than seven sumptuary laws passed in one session of parliament to restrain it. It was enacted, that men servants of lords, as also of tradesmen and artizans, shall be content with one meal of fish or flesh every day, and the other meals daily shall be of milk, cheese, butter, and the like. Neither shall they use any ornaments of gold, silk, or embroidery ; nor their wives or daughters any veils above the price of twelve pence. Artisans and yeomen shall not wear cloth above the price of 40s. the whole piece (the finest being about 6l. per piece) nor the ornaments before named. Nor the women any veils of silk, but only those of thread made in England. Gentlemen under the degree of knights, not having 100l. yearly in land, shall not wear any cloth above 4 1-2 marks the whole piece. Neither shall they or their females use cloth of gold, silver, or embroidery, &c. But esquires having 200l. per annum or upwards of rent, may wear cloth of 5 marks the whole piece of cloth, and they and their females may also wear stuff of silk, silver ribbons, girdles, or furs. Merchants or citizen-burghers, and artificers or tradesmen, as well of London as elsewhere, who have goods and chattels of the clear value of 500l. and their females, may wear as is allowed to gentlemen and esquires of 100l. per annum. And merchant citizens and burgesses, worth above 1000l. in goods and chattels, may (and their females) wear the same as gentlemen of 200l. per annum. Knights of 200 marks yearly may wear cloth of six marks the piece, but no higher ; but no cloth of gold, nor furred with ermine : but all knights and ladies having above 400 marks yearly, up to 1000l. per annum, may wear as they please, ermine excepted ; and they may wear ornaments of pearl and precious stones for their heads only. Clerks having degrees in cathedrals, colleges, &c. may wear as knights and esquires of the same income. Ploughmen, carters, shepherds, and such like, not having 40s. value in goods or chattels, shall wear no sort of cloth but blankets and russet lawn of 12d. and shall wear girdles and belts ; and they shall only eat and drink suitable to their stations. And whosoever useth any other apparel than is prescribed in the above laws, shall forfeit the same.

THE MINISTER'S PRAYER-BOOK.

THE pastor of a congregation in

America, after many years' labour among his people, was supposed by some of them, to have declined much in his vigour and usefulness; in consequence of which, two gentlemen of the congregation waited upon him, and exhibited their complaints. The minister received them with much affection, and assured them, that he was equally sensible of his languor and little success, and that the cause had given him very great uneasiness. The gentlemen wished he would mention what he thought was the cause. Without hesitation, the minister replied, "The loss of my prayer-book." "Your prayer-book!" said one of the gentlemen, with surprise; "I never knew you used one." "Yes," replied the minister, "I have enjoyed the benefit of one for many years till lately, and I attribute my want of success to the loss of it. The prayers of my people were my prayer-book; and it has occasioned great grief to me, that they have laid it aside. Now, if you will return, and procure me the use of my prayer-book again, I doubt not that I shall preach much better, and that you will hear more profitably."——The gentlemen, conscious of their neglect, thanked the minister for the reproof, and wished him a good morning.

THE MISTAKEN DOCTOR.

A LADY being visited with a violent disorder, was under the necessity of applying for medical assistance. Her doctor, being a gentleman of great latitude in his religious sentiments, endeavoured, in the course of his attendance, to persuade his patient to adopt his creed, as well as to take his medicines. He frequently insisted, with a considerable degree of dogmatism, that *repentance* and *reformation* were all that either God or man could require of us, and that, consequently, there was no necessity for an atonement by the sufferings of the Son of God. As this was a doctrine the lady did not believe, she contented herself with following his medical prescriptions, without embracing his religious, or rather, irreligious creed. On her recovery, she forwarded a note to the doctor, desiring the favour of his company to tea, when it suited his convenience, and requested him to make out his bill. In a short time, he made his visit, and, the tea table being removed, she addressed him as follows: "My long illness has occasioned you a number of journeys, and, I suppose, doctor, you have procured my medicines at considerable expense." The doctor acknowledged, that "good drugs were not to be obtained but at a very high price." Upon which she replied, "I am extremely sorry that I have put you to so much .abour and expense, and also promise, that, on any future indisposition, I will never trouble you again. So you see that I both *repent* and *reform*, and that is all you require." The doctor immediately, shrugging up his shoulders, exclaimed, "That will not do for me."— *The words of the wise are as goads.* Ecc. xii. 11.

How many are there, like the above mentioned gentleman, who mistake on this grand point! but, as Bishop Porteus justly observes, (see his Sermons, vol. ii. p. 41,) "From whence do they learn, that repentance alone will obliterate the stains of past guilt; will undo every thing they have done amiss : will reinstate them in the favour of God; will make satisfaction to his insulted justice, and secure respect and obedience to his authority, as the moral governor of the world? Do the scriptures teach them this? No: they plainly tell us, that 'without shedding of blood, there is no remission of sins.' But, perhaps, they collect it from the very nature of the thing itself. Consider, then, what repentance is. It is nothing more than sorrow for what we have done amiss, and a resolution not to do it again. But can this annihilate what is past? Most assuredly it has no such power. Our former transgressions still remain uncancelled: they are recorded in the books of heaven, and it is not our future good deeds

17

can wipe them out. 'We may as well affirm,' says a learned divine, 'that our former obedience atones for our present sins, as that our present obedience makes amend for antecedent transgressions.'

"The ancient Pagans themselves did not entertain such notions as these. When they had offended their gods, they thought of nothing but oblations, expiations, lustrations, and animal sacrifices. This shows that they believed something else as necessary besides their own repentance and reformation. Nay, some of the greatest, and wisest, and best among them, declared, in express terms, 'that there was wanting some universal method of delivering men's souls, which no sect of philosophy had ever yet found out.'" [Porphyry.]

MODESTY.

"A JUST and reasonable modesty," says Addison, "sets off every great talent a man may be possessed of. It heightens all the virtues which it accompanies; like the shades in paintings, it raises and rounds every figure, and makes the colours more beautiful, though not so glaring as they would be without it. Modesty is not only an ornament, but a guard to virtue. It is a kind of quick and delicate feeling in the soul, which makes her shrink and withdraw herself from every thing that has danger in it.

"I have read somewhere," says he, "in the history of Greece, that the women of the country were seized with an unaccountable melancholy, which disposed several of them to make away with themselves. The senate, after having tried many expedients to prevent this self-murder, which was so frequent among them, published an edict, that, if any woman whatever, should lay violent hands upon herself, her corpse should be exposed naked in the street, and dragged about the city in the most public manner. This edict immediately put a stop to the practice which was before so common. We may see, in this instance, the strength of modesty which was able to overcome the violence of madness and despair."

Instances of modesty are to be found among the wise and learned, as well as others. The Rev. Mr. Hooker was a man so bashful and modest by natural disposition, that he was not able to outface his own pupils.

Mr. Thomas Gouge, though so great a man, never put any value upon himself, or hunted for applause from man; and this was very observable in him, that the charities which were procured chiefly by his interest and industry, where he had occasion to speak, or to give an account of them, he would rather impute it to any one that had but the least hand and part in the procuring of them, than assume any thing of it to himself. "Another instance of his modesty, (says Archbishop Tillotson,) was, that when he had quitted his living of St. Sepulchre's, upon some dissatisfaction about the terms of conformity, he willingly forbore preaching, saying, 'There was no need of him here in Lodon, where there were so many worthy ministers; and that he thought he might do as much, or more good, in another way, which could give no offence.'"

Modesty may be thought, by some, a barrier to preferment; but it is not always so; for as one observes, "there is a call upon mankind to value and esteem those who set a moderate price upon their own merit; and self-denial is frequently attended with unexpected blessings, which, in the end, abundantly recompense such losses as the modest seem to suffer in the ordinary occurrences of life." Dr. Sanderson was a man of great modesty, and, yet, purely by the dint of merit and modesty together, he made his way not only to considerable preferment in the church, but gained the estimation and affection of all parties.

Sir Matthew Hale, though a learned, was a very modest man. Soon after he was constituted Chief Baron of the Exchequer, he was knighted.

This is an honour usually conferred upon the chief judges; but Mr. Hale desired to avoid it, and therefore declined, for a considerable time, all opportunity of waiting on the king; which the lord chancellor observing, he sent for him upon business one day, when his majesty was at his house, and told his majesty, "There was his modest chief baron:" upon which he was unexpectedly knighted.

MURDERERS DISCOVERED.

FEW murderers escape without meeting with the awful punishment due to their crimes. Many strange stories, indeed, have been told of this kind, some of which, however, it must be confessed, stand on too good authority to be rejected. The following is translated from a respectable publication at Basle.

A person who worked in a brewery quarrelled with one of his fellow-workmen, and struck him in such a manner that he died upon the spot. No other person was witness to the deed. He then took the dead body, and threw it into a large fire under the boiling-vat, where it was in a short time so completely consumed that no traces of its existence remained. On the following day, when the man was missed, the murderer observed very coolly, that he had perceived his fellow-servant to have been intoxicated; and that he had probably fallen from a bridge which he had to cross in his way home, and been drowned. For the space of seven years after, no one entertained any suspicions of the real state of the fact. At the end of this period, the murderer was again employed in the same brewery. He was then induced to reflect on the singularity of the circumstance that his crime had remained so long concealed. Having retired one evening to rest, one of the other workmen who slept with him, hearing him say in his sleep, "It is now full seven years ago," asked him, "What was it you did seven years ago?"—"I put him," he replied, still speaking in his sleep,

"under the boiling-vat." As the affair was not entirely forgotten, it immediately occurred to the man that his bed-fellow must allude to the person who was missing about that time, and he accordingly gave information of what he had heard to a magistrate. The murderer was apprehended; and though at first he denied that he knew any thing of the matter, a confession of his crime at length obtained from him, for which he suffered condign punishment.

The following event lately happened in the neighbourhood of Frankfort-upon-the-Oder:—A woman, conceiving that her husband, who was a soldier in the Prussian service, had been killed at the battle of Jena, in 1806, married another man. It turned out that her husband had been only wounded, and taken prisoner by the French. A cure was soon effected; and he joined one of the Prussian regiments which entered into the pay of France. After serving three years in Spain, he was discharged, returned suddenly to his native country, and appeared greatly rejoiced to find his wife alive. She received him with every mark of affection, but did not avow the new matrimonial connexion she had formed. After partaking of some refreshment, he complained of being quite overcome with fatigue, and retired to rest. She immediately joined with her new husband to despatch the unwelcome visiter in his sleep; which they accomplished by strangling him, and put his body into a sack. About midnight, in conveying it to the Oder, the weight of the corpse burst the sack, and one of the legs hung out. The woman set about sewing up the rent, and in her hurry and confusion sewed in, at the same time, the skirts of her accomplices coat. Having reached the bank of the river, and making a great effort to precipitate his load as far into the stream as possible, he was dragged from the elevated ground he had chosen into the river, but contrived to keep his head above water for several minutes. The woman, not considering how important it was to keep silent, filled the air with her cries; and brought to the spot several peasants, who, at the hazard of their own lives, extricated the drowning man from his perilous situation, at the same time discovering the cause. The man and woman were charged with the crime, made a full confession, and were consigned to the officers of justice.

MUSIC.

NOTWITHSTANDING music has been prostituted to the worst of purposes, it is not, on that account, to be considered an evil. Wise and good men have found it a most pleasant relaxation from the anxiety of care, the toil of business, and the labour of study. Pope, Swift, and Johnson, indeed, deemed music so trivial an art, that it degraded human nature, and they treated its votaries as fools; but their ears, as has been observed, were so defective, that a totally blind person was as well qualified to decide critically on painting, as these great writers were with respect to music.

It was Luther's custom to amuse himself with his lute at dinner and supper: "music," said he, "is one of the fairest and most glorious gifts of God, to which Satan is a bitter enemy; for it removes from the heart the weight of sorrow and the fascination of evil thoughts. Music is a kind and gentle sort of discipline; it refines the passions, and improves the understanding. How is it," continued he, "that on profane subjects we have so many fine verses and elegant poems, whilst our religious poetry remains so languid and dull? Those who love music are gentle and honest in their tempers. I always loved music," added Luther, "and would not, for a great matter, be without the little skill which I possess in this art."

It is said that a traveller lately discovered, in a private house at Wirtemberg, many sheets of music in the hand-writing of Luther, and apparently of his own composition. We

have the authority of Handel, to attribute to him that sublime piece of church music, known in England as accompanying the 100th Psalm; and the same great man acknowledges, that he studied the compositions of Luther, and derived singular advantages from them.

Socrates, when far advanced in years, learned to play upon musical instruments.

The celebrated Bishop Berkely was so fond of it, that he always kept one or two exquisite performers to amuse his leisure hours.

It is said of the Rev. George Herbert, that his chief recreation was music; in which art he was a most excellent master, and composed many divine hymns and anthems, which he set or sung to his lute or viol. It is also observed, that Bishop Potter's recreation was usually vocal music; in which he himself always bore a part.

Dr. Cotton Mather thus writes to his son: " As for music, do as you please. If you fancy it, I do not forbid it; only do not, for the sake of it, alienate your time too much from those that are more important matters. It may be so, that you may serve your God the better for the refreshment of one that can play well upon an instrument. However, to accomplish yourself at regular singing, is a thing that will be of daily use to you. For I would not have a day pass you without singing, but so as, at the same time, to make a melody in your heart to the Lord; besides the part you may bear in *hymnis suavisonantis ecclesiæ;* In the sweet-sounding hymns of the church."

Bishop Beveridge observes, that, of all recreations, he found music to be the best, and especially when he played himself. "It calls in my spirits," says he, "composes my thoughts, delights my ear, recreates my mind, and so not only fits me for after-business, but fills my heart at the present with pure and useful thoughts."

"Music," says Dr. Knox, " is the most delightful soother of the wearied mind. The heart dances at the sound of the lyre; fresh spirits animate the veins; the clouds of dejection are dissipated, and the soul shines out once more, like the sun after a mist, in the blue expanse of æther."

"I have been informed," says the author of Fitzosborne's letters, "that one of the greatest lights of the present age never sits down to study till he has raised his imagination by the power of music. For this purpose he has a band of instruments near his library, which play till he finds himself elevated to a proper height; upon which he gives a signal, and they instantly cease."

Notwithstanding all that has been said above in favour of music, I cannot dismiss this article without observing, that even here we may run into an extreme. It appears to me, also, to be an error in many parents, who bring up their children to this, while things of a more important nature are neglected.

"Almost any ornamental acquirement," says Mrs. H. More, "is a good thing, when it is not the *best* thing a woman has; and talents are admirable when not made to stand proxy for virtues. I am intimately acquainted (she observes) with several ladies, who, excelling most of their sex in the art of music, but excelling them also in prudence and piety, find little leisure or temptation, amidst the delights and duties of a large and lovely family, for the exercise of this charming talent: they regret that so much of their own youth was wasted in acquiring an art which can be turned to so little account in married life, and are now conscientiously restricting their daughters in the portion of time allotted to its acquisition."

THE NEGLIGENT MINISTER REPROVED.

A CERTAIN minister, who was more busied in the pleasures of the chace than in superintending the souls of his flock, one day, meeting with little sport, proposed to entertain his companions at the expense of an inoffensive Quaker, whom he had often very rudely ridiculed, and who was then approaching them. Immediately he. rode up briskly to him, saying, "Obadiah, have you seen the hare?" "Why, neighbour, hast thou lost him?" said the Quaker.—"Lost him! yes, indeed!" "Then," replied he, "if I were the hare, I would run where I am sure thou couldst never find me." "Where the d—— is that?" said the blustering son of Nimrod. "Why, neighbour," answered the other, "I would run into thy study."

THE NEGRO PREACHER:
An Affecting Narrative.

In the Island of St. Thomas, in the West Indies, there was a negro, named Cornelius: he was enlightened about fifty years ago, and soon began to preach to his countrymen. He was blessed with considerable talents, and was able to speak and write the Creole, Dutch, Danish, German, and English languages. Till 1767 he was a slave. He first purchased the freedom of his wife, and then laboured hard to gain his own liberty; which, at last, he effected, after much entreaty, and the payment of a considerable sum. By degrees he was also enabled to purchase the emancipation of his six children. He learned the business of a mason so well, that he was appointed master mason to the royal buildings, and had the honour to lay the foundation stone of six Christian chapels for the use of the Moravian brethren. His gifts for preaching were good, and remarkably acceptable, not only to the negroes, but to many of the whites. He spent even whole nights in visiting the different plantations, yet was by no means puffed up, but ever retained the character of an humble servant of Christ. When death approached (which was in November, 1701) he sent for his family. His children and grand-children assembled round the bed of the sick parent;

he summoned up all his strength, sat up in the bed, uncovered his venerable head, adorned with locks as white as snow, and addressed them thus :

"I rejoice exceedingly, my dearly beloved children, to see you once more together before my departure; for I believe that my Lord and Saviour will soon come, and take your father home to himself. You know, my dear children, what my chief concern has been respecting you, as long as I was with you ; how frequently I have exhorted you, with tears, not to neglect the day of grace, but surrender yourselves, with soul and body, to your God and Redeemer; to follow him faithfully. Sometimes I have dealt strictly with you in matters which I believed would bring harm to your souls, and grieve the Spirit of God; and I have exerted my paternal authority, to prevent mischief; but it was all done out of love to you. However, it may have happened that I have been sometimes too severe : if this has been the case, I beg you, my dear children, to forgive me. O, forgive your poor dying father !"

Here he was obliged to stop, most of the children weeping and sobbing aloud. At last one of the daughters, recovering herself, said, "We, dear father, we alone have cause to ask forgiveness ; for we have often made your life heavy, and have been disobedient children." The rest joined in the same confession. The father then continued : "Well, my dear children, if you all have forgiven me, then attend to my last wish and dying request. Love one another : do not suffer any quarrels and disputes to rise among you after my decease. No, my children," raising his voice, "love one another cordially ; let each strive to show proofs of love to his brother or sister : nor suffer yourselves to be tempted by any thing to become proud, for by that you may even miss of your souls' salvation ; but pray our Saviour to grant you lovely minds and humble hearts. If you follow this advice of your father

my joy will be complete, when I shall once see you again in eternal bliss, and be able to say to our Saviour, Here, Lord, is thy poor unworthy Cornelius, and the children thou hast given me. I am sure our Saviour will not forsake you ; but I beseech you, do not forsake him."

His two sons and four daughters are employed as assistants in the mission. By them, he lived to see twelve grand-children and five great grand-children ; being about eighty-four years old. He was attended to the grave by a very large company of negro brethren and sisters, who, being all dressed in white, walked in solemn procession to the burial ground at New Hernhut.

What Christian can peruse this affecting narrative without blessing God, who to our sable brethren hath vouchsafed this abundant grace ! and who can refrain from blessing God, who excited the Moravian Church to these labours of love, and who hath so wonderfully succeeded their apostolic efforts ! Who that has tasted the Lord is gracious will refuse the aid of his heart, his hand, his purse, in promoting missionary exertions, so honoured of our God and Saviour!

THE PIOUS NEGROES.

"In one of my excursions," says one, "while I was in the province of New York, I was walking by myself over a considerable plantation, amused with its husbandry, and comparing it with that of my own country, till I came within a little distance of a middle-aged negro, who was tilling the ground. I felt a strong inclination, unusual with me, to converse with him. After asking him some little questions about his work, which he answered very sensibly, I wished him to tell me whether his state of slavery was not disagreeable to him, and whether he would not gladly exchange it for his liberty. "Massah," said he (looking seriously upon me) "I have wife and children ; my massah takes care of them and I have no care to provide any thing. I have a good massah, who teach me to read; and I read good book, that makes me happy."—"I am glad," replied I, "to hear you say so; and, pray, what is the good book you read?" "The Bible, massah; God's own good book." —"Do you understand, friend, as well as read this book? for many can read the words well who cannot get hold of the true and good sense." "O massah," says he, "I read the book much before I understand; but at last I felt pain in my heart: I found things in the book that cut me to pieces."—"Ay!" said I, "and what things were they?" "Why, massah, I found that I had bad heart, massah; a very bad heart indeed! I felt pain, that God would destroy me because I was wicked, and done nothing as I should do. God was holy, and I was very vile and naughty; so I could have nothing from him but fire and brimstone in hell." In short, he entered into a full account of his convictions of sin, which were, indeed, as deep and piercing as any I had ever heard of; and what scriptures came to his mind which he had read, that both probed him to the bottom of his sinful heart, and were made the means of light and comfort to his soul. I then inquired of him what ministry or means he made use of, and found that his master was a Quaker, a plain sort of man, who had taught his slaves to read, but who had not, however, conversed with this negro upon the state of his soul. I asked him, also, how he got comfort under all this trial. "O, massah," says he, "it was Christ gave me comfort by his dear word. He bade me come unto him, and he would give me rest; for I was very weary and heavy laden." And here he went through a line of the most precious texts in the Bible; showing me by his artless comment upon them as he went along, what great things God had done, in the course of some years, for his soul.

Some years since, a lady was on a visit to Mr. D——, of Trenton, in North America. One day, whilst at dinner, she observed to him that the negro servant who waited, appeared almost too old and infirm for service. He replied, notwithstanding his present appearance, it was not more than two years since he had purchased him from on board a ship; and at that time he did not appear more than thirty years of age, strong, healthy, and active; so much so, that he intended he should have worked in the field, but was under the necessity of changing his intention, from his great falling-off in strength, without any apparent reason, not having a day's illness to his knowledge, but that he had observed he had been exceedingly dejected till within a few months, in which he had been remarkably cheerful and happy. He told her also that he had been of great use to him in breaking him of the habit of swearing. His method was to stand opposite his master, whilst waiting at table; and every time he took his Maker's name in vain, the negro made a most profound bow, with great solemnity. His master asking him why he did so? he told him he never heard that great Name mentioned without his whole soul being filled with the greatest awe.—One day the lady was passing through the kitchen, and seeing none but him, she said, "What, old man, are there none but you here!" "Yes, Missa," said he, "there are a great many here besides me; but you cannot see them: they are angels!" He was so remarkably humble, that he would eat nothing but what he met in the plates, after the rest of the family had dined: and he removed his bed into the dog kennel, saying it was good enough for him to sleep in. Since the time he grew more cheerful, he was always singing (both the tunes and songs were of his own making;) and his chorus was always the same, which was this, "I shall be white, and I shall be happy!"

A merchant in Jamaica, of the Hebrew nation, had three negroes, very bad characters, who frequently got

O

drunk and robbed him. Observing a sudden change in their conduct, he inquired into the cause. One of the poor fellows replied, "Massa, God Almighty in a top!" He was answered, "Was not God Almighty in a top (that is *above*) when you got drunk and robbed me?" "Yes, Massa," he replied; "but we no *savy* then," (*savy* is to *know*.) He then asked them how they came to know. They answered, "Massa, we have been gona chapel, and preacher tell me so; and now we fraid to get drunk and rob like fore time. God will see, and he will be angry. Him see, him savy every thing."

The Jewish master was well pleased with the good effect of the Christian instructions; and recommended it to them to continue to go to chapel whenever there was preaching, and he would take care to pay the expense, as they had so much profited by what they had heard.

THE INTREPID NONCONFORMIST.

Mr. Hicks, who, at the restoration of Charles II. was ejected from from his living of Saltash, in Cornwall, was remarkable for his courage, faith, and intrepidity. One asking him, about that time, what he would do if he did not conform, having a family likely to be growing, his answer was, " Should I have as many children as that hen has chickens (pointing to one that had a good number of them,) I should not question but God would provide for them all."—He removed to Kingsbridge, in this county, where he had a meeting, and took all opportunities that offered for preaching ; but, for many years together, he met with a great deal of trouble, and was harassed by the bishop's court, so as to be obliged to hide himself; but his great spirit carried him through all with cheerfulness. An apparitor being once sent to him with a citation, was advised beforehand, by some that knew him, to take heed how he meddled with Mr. Hicks, for he was a stout man : he came, however, to his house,

and asked for him. Mr. Hicks, coming down with his cane in his hand, looked briskly upon him. The man told him that he came to inquire for one Mr. Hicks, gentleman. He replied, " I am John Hicks, minister of the gospel." The apparitor trembled, and seemed glad to get from him; and Mr. H. never heard more of him. In the year 1671 he published a pamphlet, entitled, *A sad Narrative of the Oppression of many honest People in Devon, &c. ;* in which he named the informers, justices, and others, who were guilty of illegal proceedings, and particularly Judge Rainsford. Though his name was not to the book, he was soon discovered to be the author, and two messengers were sent down to apprehend him, and bring him up to court. It happened, that upon the road, Mr. H. fell into the company of these very messengers, not having, at first, the least suspicion of them. He travelled the best part of a morning, and at last dined with them; and they talked with great freedom against one Mr. Hicks, as an ill man, and a great enemy to government. He bore with all their scurrilous language till dinner was over, and then, going to the stable to his horse (of which he was always tender,) he there gave them to understand that he was the person whom they had so much vilified ; and, to teach them better how to govern their tongues, took his cane, and corrected them till they begged his pardon : upon which he immediately took his horse, and rode to London. By the means of one whom he well knew (who was then a favourite at court,) he got to be introduced to the king's presence. The king told him that he had abused his ministers and the justices of the peace. He replied, " Oppression, may it please your Majesty, makes a wise man mad. The justices, beyond all law, have very much wronged your majesty's loyal subjects, the Nonconformists in the west." He instanced in several particulars, and spoke with such presence of mind and ingenuity, that the king heard him with patience, seemed affected, and promised that they should have no such cause of complaint for the future. Soon after this, the Dissenters had some favour shown them; and Mr. H. thereupon, came up with an address from a considerable number of gentlemen and others in the west, and presented it. The king received it very graciously, and asked him if he had not been as good as his word. An indulgence was granted, and liberty to build places of worship; and, by his majesty's favour, Mr. H. got back a third part of what the Dissenters in those parts had paid in on the conventicle act.

INFLUENCE OF THE PASSIONS.

THE powerful influence of the passions and affections upon the human frame is astonishing. How many instances are there upon record of sudden death having been occasioned by the hasty communication of joyful tidings! "Like a stroke of electricity," says Dr. Cogan, "indiscreetly directed, the violent percussion has probably produced a paralysis of the heart, by the excess of its stimulus."

Pliny informs us that Chilo, the Lacedemonian, died upon hearing that his son had gained a prize in the Olympic games.

Valerius Maximus tells us that Sophocles, in a contest of honour, died in consequence of a decision being pronounced in his favour.

Aulus Gellius mentions a remarkable instance of the effect of accumulated joy. Diagora had three sons, who were all crowned on the same day as victors; the one as a pugilist, the other as a wrestler, and the third in both capacities. The sons carried their father on their shoulders through an incredible number of spectators, who threw flowers by handfuls on him, and applauded his glory and good fortune. But, in the midst of all the congratulations of the populace, he died in the arms and embraces of his sons.

Livy also mentions an instance of an aged matron, who, while she was in the depth of distress, from the tidings of her son's having been slain in battle, died in his arms, in the excess of joy, upon his safe return.

The Italian historian, Guicciardini, tells us, that Leo X. died of a fever, occasioned by the agitation of his spirits on his receiving the joyful news of the capture of Milan, concerning which he had entertained much anxiety.

It is said of a nobleman in the reign of Henry the Eighth, that when a pardon was sent him a few hours before the time which was fixed for his execution, that, not expecting it, it so transported him, that he died for joy.

What an effect has grief also produced on the body! Excessive sorrow has been the cause of sudden death, of confirmed melancholy, loss of memory, imbecility of mind, of nervous fevers, of hypochondriac complaints, and the loss of appetite.

Plautius, looking on his dead wife, threw himself upon her dead body, and presently died.

"I knew a woman," says one, "who, upon only hearing of the death of one of her friends, shrieked out, and immediately fell down, and died."

The Duchess of Burgundy, a princess of the House of Savoy, (wife to the grandson of Lewis XIV.) one day said to her husband, "As the hour of my dissolution is now drawing near, and I know you will not be able to live without a wife, I should be glad to know whom it is your intention to marry." "I hope," said the duke, "that God will never inflict so severe a punishment on me, as to deprive me of you; but, should I experience such a misfortune, I should not, most certainly, think of taking a second wife, since, being unable to support your death, I should follow you in less than a week." The duke died of grief on the seventh day after the decease of the duchess.

Other passions also have a wonderful effect upon the body. " Thus *fear* is peculiarly dangerous in every species of contagion. It has instantaneously changed the complexion of wounds, and rendered them fatal. It has occasioned gangrenes, induration of the glands, and epilepsies. It has produced a permanent stupor on the brain, and the first horrors of the imagination have, in some cases, made too deep an impression to be effaced by the most favourable change of circumstances. Thus *anger* has produced inflammatory and bilious fevers, hæmorrhages, apoplexies, inflammation of the brain, and mania. Thus *terror* has caused attacks of catalepsies, epilepsies, and other spasmodic disorders. Thus *love* has excited inflammatory fevers, hysterics, hectics, and the rage of madness.

—It might be mentioned here, however, the good effects which sometimes have been produced by the passions. Thus *hope* enlivens and invigorates both mind and body; it diffuses a temperate vivacity over the system, directing a due degree of energy to every part. *Joy* has been a potent remedy in some diseases; and what has been said of hope is applicable to joy under its more moderate influence. *Love* has cured intermittents, and fortified the body against dangers, difficulties, and hardships, that appeared superior to human force. Thus, even *anger*, we are told, has cured agues, restored speech to the dumb, and for several days arrested the cold hand of death. *Fear* has been known to relieve excruciating fits of the gout, to have rendered maniacs calm and composed; and the effects of fear in affording temporary relief in the tooth-ache are universally known."

THE END.

ANECDOTES,

RELIGIOUS MORAL, AND ENTERTAINING,

BY THE

LATE REV. CHARLES BUCK,

Author of Theological Dictionary.

ALPHABETICALLY ARRANGED, AND INTERSPERSED WITH A VARIETY
OF USEFUL OBSERVATIONS.

WITH

A PREFACE,

BY ASHBEL GREEN, D. D.

SOME TIME PRESIDENT OF PRINCETON COLLEGE.

TWO VOLS. IN ONE

VOL. II.

Solid Ground Christian Books
Birmingham, Alabama USA

INDEX TO VOL. II.

2

2

ANECDOTES.

PATIENCE.

"No MAN, in any condition of life, can pass his days with tolerable comfort, without patience. It is of universal use. Without it, prosperity will be continually disturbed, and adversity will be clouded with double darkness. He who is without patience, will be uneasy and troublesome to all with whom he is connected, and will be more troublesome to himself than to any other. The loud complaint, the querulous temper, and fretful spirit, disgrace every character: we weaken thereby the sympathy of others, and estrange them from the offices of kindness and comfort. But to maintain a steady and unbroken mind, amidst all the shocks of adversity, forms the highest honour of man. Afflictions, supported by patience, and surmounted by fortitude, give the last finishing stroke to the heroic and the virtuous character. Thus the vale of tears becomes the theatre of human glory; that dark cloud presents the scene for all the beauties in the bow of virtue to appear. Moral grandeur, like the sun, is brighter in the day of the storm, and never is so truly sublime as when struggling through the darkness of an eclipse."

Pericles was of so patient a spirit, that he was hardly ever troubled with any thing that crossed him. There was a man who did nothing all the day, but rail at him in the market-place, before all the people, notwithstanding Pericles was a magistrate. Pericles, however, took no notice of it, but, despatching sundry cases of importance till night came, he went home with a sober pace. The man followed him all the way, defaming him as he went. Pericles, when he came home, it being dark, called his man, and desired him to get a torch, and light the fellow home.

Bishop Cowper's wife, it is said, was much afraid that the bishop would prejudice his health by over-much study. When he was compiling his famous dictionary, one day, in his absence, she got into his study, and took all the notes he had been for eight years gathering, and burned them; whereof, when she had acquainted him, he only said, "Woman, thou hast put me to eight years study more."

Such has been the patience of the Saints, that it has struck their very enemies with surprise. Thus, Bishop Bonner gave the following testimony to Cuthbert Sympson's patience. "I say unto you, that if he were not an heretic, he is a man of the greatest patience that ever came before me.——He has been thrice racked in one day in the Tower, and in my house he has felt some sorrow; yet I never saw his patience broken."

Mr. Rivet, a learned and pious divine, was an instance of extraordinary patience, under excrutiating pains, which he bore for many days. "You see," says he, "through the grace of God, I am not tired : I wait, I believe, I persevere. Patience is much better than knowledge. I am no more vexed with earthly cares; I have now no desire but after heavenly things. I have learnt more divinity in these ten days, than in fifty years before. This body is feeble, but the spirit is strong and enriched.—Far be it from me that I should murmur. How small are these pains in comparison of that grace, through which I bear, with a quiet mind, whatsoever it pleaseth God to lay upon me! The body, indeed, suffers, but the soul is comforted, and filled abundantly."

Great was the patience of Mr. Gouge, under the visiting hand of God, especially in his old age, when suffering painful maladies; though, by reason of the bitterness of his pains by the stone, he has been heard to groan, yet never to complain. He was never heard to call himself *great sufferer*, but great sinner. He would often say, " Soul, be silent; soul be patient: it is thy God and Father that thus ordereth thy estate. Thou art his clay; he may tread and trample on thee as it pleaseth him: thou hast deserved much more; it is enough that thou art kept out of hell. Though thy pain be grievous, yet it is tolerable: thy God affords some intermissions; he will turn it to thy good, and, at length, put an end to all. None of these can be expected in hell." In the greatest agonies, he would say, " Well, yet in all these, there is nothing of hell, or God's wrath."

See articles Constancy, Forbearance, and Submission.

THE SUCCESSFUL PEACE-MAKERS.

WHEN Mr. Welch accepted of the call to Ayr, he found the wickedness of the country, and their hatred to religion so great, that no one would let him a house, till Mr. John Stewart, an eminent Christian, and some time provost of Ayr, accommodated him with an apartment in his house, and was to him a very able friend. Mr. Welch first addressed himself to the arduous task of healing their divisions, uniting their factious parties, and putting an end to their daily battles, which were so desperate, that no one could walk in the street at daytime, without the most imminent danger of being wounded. His method was this: after he had put an helmet on his head, he would go between the parties of fighting-men,

already covered with blood; but he never took a sword, which convinced them that he came not to fight, but to make peace. When he had brought them, by little and little, to hear him speak, and to listen to his arguments against such brutish proceedings, he would order a table to be spread in the street, and, beginning with prayer, persuaded them to profess themselves friends, and to sit down, and to eat and drink together; which, when done, he would finish this labour of love with singing a psalm. Thus, by degrees, labouring among them in word and doctrine, (for he preached every day,) and setting them a good example, he brought them to be a peaceable and happy people; and he grew, at length, in such esteem among them, that they made him their counsellor, to settle all their differences and misunderstandings, and would take no step of importance in civil affairs, without his advice.

The famous Mr. Elliot, of New England, was a great enemy to all contention, and would ring a loud curfew bell wherever he saw the fires of animosity. When he heard any ministers complain, that such and such in their flocks were too difficult for them, the strain of his answer still was, " Brother, compass them; and learn the meaning of these three little words, bear, forbear, forgive." When there was laid before an assembly of ministers a bundle of papers, containing matters of difference between some people, which he would rather unite, with an amnesty upon all their former quarrels, he, with some imitation of Constantine, hastily threw the papers into the fire, before them all, and, with great zeal, said, " Brethren, wonder not at what I have done: I did it on my knees, this morning, before I came among you."

When Mr. Fletcher was at Trevecka, two of the students were bitterly prejudiced against each other. He took them into a room by themselves, reasoned with them, wept over them, and, at last, prevailed. Their hearts were broken; they were melted down; they fell upon each other's necks, and wept aloud.

"Blessed are the peace-makers, for they shall be called the children of God." These are valuable, honourable, and useful members of society. While others go about as incendiaries, to destroy the happiness and peace of mankind, by blowing up the fires of discord and contention, these, on the contrary, find the greatest pleasure in being the instruments of allaying animosities, quenching the flames of malignity, and promoting unity and concord among men.—Happy characters! Prosperity be with you; and may your numbers be increased, and the God of peace honour you, at last, with a crown of glory, and hold you up to an assembled world, as those who have greatly contributed to the happiness of the human race!

PERSECUTION OVERRULED.

THE ardent zeal of the famous Mr. Bradbury, formerly minister of the church in New Court, Carey-street, exposed him to the hatred of the Papists, who employed a person to take away his life. To make himself fully acquainted with Bradbury's person, the man frequently attended at places of worship where he preached, placed himself in the front of the gallery, with his countenance fixed on the preacher. It was scarcely possible, in such circumstances, wholly to avoid listening to what was said.— Mr. B.'s forcible manner of presenting divine truth to view, awakened the man's attention, entered his understanding, and became the means of changing his heart. He came to the preacher with trembling and confusion, told his affecting tale, gave evidence of his conversion, became a member of the church, and was, to the hour of his death, an ornament to the gospel which he professed.

THE PIOUS LABOURER.

A GENTLEMAN of very considerable fortune, but a stranger to either personal or family religion, one evening took a solitary walk through part of his grounds. He happened to come near to a mean hut, where a poor man lived with a numerous family, who earned their bread by daily labour. He heard a voice pretty loud and continued. Not knowing what it was, curiosity prompted him to listen. The man, who was piously disposed, happened to be at prayer with his family. So soon as he could distinguish the words, he heard him giving thanks with great affection to God for the goodness of his providence, in giving them food to eat, and raiment to put on, and in supplying them with what was necessary and comfortable in the present life. He was immediately struck with astonishment and confusion, and said to himself, "Does this poor man, who has nothing but the meanest fare, and that purchased by severe labour, give thanks to God for his goodness to himself and family; and I, who enjoy ease and honour, and every thing that is pleasant and desirable, have hardly ever bent my knee or made any acknowledgment to my Maker and Preserver!"

It pleased God that this providential occurrence proved the means of bringing him to a real and lasting sense of religion.

THE PIOUS PHILOSOPHERS.

MR. ROBERT HOOKE, the mathematician and philosopher, seldom received any remarkable benefit in life, or made any considerable discovery in nature, or invented any useful contrivance, or found out any difficult problem, without setting down his acknowledgment to God.—How amiable is Philosophy when she walks by the side of her eldest sister, Religion! Abraham Moivre was born at Vitri, in Champagne, A. D. 1667. At the revocation of the Edict of Nantes, he determined to flee into England, rather than abandon the religion of his fathers. Before he left France, he had begun the study of mathematics, and he perfected himself in that science in London. His success in such studies procured him a seat in the Royal Society in London, and in the Academy of Sciences at Paris. He could never endure any bold assertions or indecent witticisms against religion. A person one day thought to pay him a compliment, by observing that mathematicians were attached to no religion. He answered, " I show you, Sir, that I am a Christian, by forgiving the speech you have now made."

Religion is no enemy to sound philosophy, and sound philosophy is no enemy to religion. It is pleasant when we see them both go on hand in hand together ; and that they can do so, we need only bring to our remembrance such distinguished characters as Bacon, Newton, Boyle, Locke, Selden, Grotius, Addison, Boerhaave, Euler, &c. &c. &c.

The Philosopher despised.

Alembert, at his leaving college, found himself alone and unconnected with the world, and saught an asylum in the house of his nurse. Here he lived and studied for the space of forty years. His good nurse perceived his ardent activity, and heard him mentioned as the writer of many books ; but never took it into her head that he was a great man, and rather beheld him with a kind of compassion. "You will never," said she to him one day, " be any thing *but* a philosopher : and what is a philosopher ?—a fool, who toils and plagues himself during his life, that people may talk of him *when he is no more.*"

POPISH MIRACLES, MYSTERIES, RELICS, AND CEREMONIES.

THE following will give us some idea of the fallacy of miracles in the Romish church.

" St. Anthony is thought to have have had a great command over fire, and a power of destroying, by flashes of that element, those who incurred his displeasure. A certain monk of St. Anthony one day assembled his congregation under a tree where a magpie had built her nest, into which he had found means to convey a small box filled with gunpowder, and out of the box hung a long thin match that was to burn slowly, and was hidden among the leaves of the trees. As soon as the monk or his assistant had touched the match with a lighted coal, he began his sermon. In the mean while the magpie returned to her nest, and, finding in it a strange body which she could not remove, she fell into a passion, and began to scratch with her feet, and chatter most unmercifully. The friar affected to hear her without emotion, and continued his sermon with great composure ; only he would now and then lift up his eyes towards the top of the tree, as if he wanted to see what was the matter. At last, when he judged that the match was near reaching the gunpowder, he pretended to be quite out of patience ; he cursed the magpie, wished St. Anthony's fire might consume her, and went on again with his sermon. But he had scarcely pronounced two or three periods, when the match, on a sudden, produced its effect, and blew up the magpie with its nest ; which miracle wonderfully raised the character of the friar, and proved afterwards very beneficial to him and his convent."

Galbert, monk of Marchiennes, informs us of a strange act of devotion in his time, and which, indeed, is attested by several contemporary writers. When the Saints did not readily comply with the prayers of their votarists, they flogged their relics with rods, in a spirit of impatience, which they conceived were proper to make them bend into compliance.

When the Reformation was spread in Lithuania, Prince Radzivil was so affected that he went in person to visit the pope, and pay him all possible honours. His holiness, on this occasion, presented him with a box of precious relics. Having returned home, the report of this invaluable possession was spread; and, at length, some monks entreated permission to try the effects of these relics on a demoniac who had hitherto resisted every kind of exorcism. They were brought into the church with solemn pomp, deposited on the altar, and an innumerable crowd attended. After the usual conjurations, which were unsuccessful, they applied the relics. The demoniac instantly became well. The people cried out, *A miracle!* and the prince, lifting his hands and eyes to heaven, felt his faith confirmed. In this transport of pious joy, he observed that a young gentleman, who was keeper of this rich treasure of relics, smiled, and appeared, by his motions, to ridicule the miracle. The prince, with violent indignation, took our young keeper of the relics to task; who, on promise of pardon, gave the following secret intelligence concerning them:—He assured him, that, in travelling from Rome, he had lost the box of relics; and that, not daring to mention it, he had procured a similar one, which he had filled with the small bones of dogs and cats, and other trifles similar to what was lost. He hoped he might be forgiven for smiling, when he found that such a collection of rubbish was idolized with such pomp, and had even the virtue of expelling demons. It was by the assistance of this box that the prince discovered the great impositions of the monks and the demoniacs, and who afterwards became a zealous Lutheran.

The following account of the miracle of the liquefaction of the blood of St. Januarius is related by a respectable eye witness. "The grand procession on this occasion was composed of a numerous body of clergy, and an immense number of people of all ranks, headed by the Archbishop of Naples himself, who carried the phial containing the blood of the saint. A magnificent robe of velvet, richly embroidered, was thrown over the shoulders of the bust: a mitre refulgent with jewels,

P

was placed on its head. The arch bishop, with a solemn pace, and a look full of awe and veneration, approached, holding forth the sacred phial which contained the precious lump of blood: he addressed the saint in the humblest manner, fervently praying that he would graciously condescend to manifest his regard to his faithful votaries, the people of Naples, by the usual token of ordering that lump of his sacred blood to assume its natural and original form: in these prayers he was joined by the multitude around, particularly by the women. My curiosity prompted me to mingle with the multitude: I got, by degrees, very near the bust. Twenty minutes had already elapsed since the archbishop had been praying with all possible earnestness, and turning the phial around and around, without any effect. An old monk stood near the archbishop, and was at the utmost pains to instruct him how to handle, chafe, and rub the phial: he frequently took it into his own hand, but his manœuvres were as ineffectual as those of the archbishop. By this time the people had become noisy; the women were quite hoarse with praying; the monk continued his operations with increased zeal, and the archbishop was all over in a profuse sweat with vexation.—An acquaintance whispered, it might be prudent to retire. I directly took his hint, and joined the company I had left. An universal gloom overspread all their countenances. One very beautiful young lady cried and sobbed as if her heart had been ready to break. The passions of some ot the rabble without doors took a different turn: instead of sorrow, they were filled with rage and indignation at the saint's obduracy, and some went so far as to call him an *old, ungrateful, yellow-faced rascal.*—It was now almost dark, and, when least expected, the signal was given that the miracle was performed. The populace filled the air with repeated shouts of joy; a band of music began to play. *Te deum* was sung; couriers were despatched to the royal family (then at Portici) with the glad tidings; the young lady dried up her tears; the countenances of our company brightened in an instant; and they sat down to cards, without farther dread of eruptions, earthquakes, or pestilence."

The mysteries, as they were called, or representations of the Divine Being, the crucifixion, &c. were formerly very common in the church of Rome. They served as the amusement and instruction of the people: and so attractive were these gross exhibitions in the dark ages, that they formed one of the principal ornaments of the reception which was given to princes when they entered towns.

In the year 1437, when Conrad Bayer, Bishop of Metz, caused the mystery of the passion to be represented on the plain of Veximiel, near that city, *God* was *an old gentleman* named Mr. Nicholas Neufchatel, of Touraine, Curate of St. Victory of Metz, and who was very near expiring on the cross, had he not been timely assisted. He was so enfeebled, that it was agreed another priest should be placed on the cross the next day, to finish the representation of the person crucified, and which was done: at the same time, the said Mr. Nicholas, undertook to perform the resurrection, which, being a less difficult task, he did it, it is said, admirably well. Another priest, whose name was Mr. John De Nicey, Curate of Metrange, personated Judas; and he had liked to have been stifled while he hung upon the tree, for his neck was dislocated: this being at length luckily perceived, he was quickly cut down, and recovered.

The following account of the representation of the crucifixion, as given us by Mr. Whitfield, is curious. "In the church belonging to the convent of St. De Beato, at Lisbon, we had not," says Mr. W. "waited long before the curtain was drawn up: immediately upon a high scaffold, hung in the front with black baize, and behind with silk purple damask laced with gold, was exhibited to our view an image of the Lord Jesus at full length, crowned with thorns, and nailed on a cross, between two figures of like dimensions, representing the two thieves. At a little distance, on the right hand, was placed an image of the Virgin Mary, in plain long ruffles, and a kind of widow weeds. The veil was purple silk, and she had a wire glory round her head. At the foot of the cross lay, in a mournful pensive posture, a living man, dressed in woman's clothes, who personated Mary Magdalen; and not far off stood a young man in imitation of the beloved disciple. He was dressed in a loose green silk vesture, and bob-wig. His eyes were fixed on the cross, and his two hands a little extended. On each side, near the front of the stage, stood two sentinels in buff, with formidable caps and long beards; and, directly in the front, stood another yet more formidable, with a large target in his hand: we may suppose him to be the Roman centurion. To complete the scene, from behind the purple hangings came out about twenty little purple-vested winged boys, two by two, each bearing a lighted wax taper in his hand, and a crimson and gold cup on his head, At their entrance upon the stage, they gently bowed their heads to the spectators, then kneeled, and made obeisance first to the image on the cross, and then to that of the Virgin Mary. When risen, they bowed to each other, and then took their respective places over against one another, on steps assigned for them on the front of the stage. Opposite to this, at a few yards distance, stood a black friar in a pulpit hung in mourning. For a while he paused; and then, breaking silence, gradually lifted up his voice till it was extended to a pretty high pitch, though, I think, scarcely high enough for so large an auditory. After he had proceeded in his discourse about a quarter of an hour, a confused noise was heard near the front gate door ; and, turning my head, I saw four long-bearded men, two of which carried a ladder on their shoulders; and after them followed two more with large gilt dishes in their hands, full of linen, spices, &c.: these, as I imagined, were the representatives of Nicodemus and Joseph of Arimathea. On a signal given from the pulpit, they advanced towards the steps of the scaffold ; but, upon their first attempting to mount it, at the watchful centurion's nod, the observant soldiers made a pass at them, and presented the points of their javelins directly to their breasts. They are repulsed. Upon this, a letter from Pilate is produced : the centurion reads it, shakes his head, and (with looks that bespoke a forced compliance) beckons the sentinels to withdraw their arms. Leave being thus obtained, they ascend, and, having paid their homage by kneeling first to the image on the cross, and then to the Virgin Mary, they retired to the back of the stage. Still the preacher continued declaiming, or rather, as was said, explaining the mournful scene. Magdalen persists in wringing her hands, and variously expressing her personated sorrow ; whilst John (seemingly regardless of all besides) stood gazing on the crucified figure. By this time it was near three o'clock, and therefore proper for the scene to begin to close. The ladders are ascended ; the superscription and crown of thorns taken off ; long white rollers put round the arms of the image; and then the nails knocked out which fastened the hands and feet. Here Mary Magdalen looks most languishing, and John, if possible, stands more thunderstruck than before. The orator lifts up his voice, and almost all the hearers expressed concern by weeping, beating their breasts, and smiting their cheeks. At length, the body is gently let down ; Magdalen eyes it, and gradually rising, receives the feet into her wide-spread handkerchief; whilst John (who hitherto had stood motionless, like a statue) as the body came nearer the ground, with an eagerness that bespoke the intense affection of a sympathising friend, runs towards the cross, seizes the upper part of it into his clasping arms, and, with his disguised fellow mourner, helps to bear it away. Great preparations were made for its interment. It was wrapped in linen and spices, &c. and being laid upon a bier richly hung, was afterwards carried round the churchyard in grand procession. The image of the Virgin Mary was chief mourner ; and John and Magdalen, with a whole troop of friars with wax tapers in their hands, followed after. Determined to see the whole, I waited its return, and, in about a quarter of an hour, the corpse was brought in and deposited in an open sepulchre prepared for the purpose ; but not before a priest, accompanied by several of the same order, in splendid vestments, had perfumed it with incense, sung to, and kneeled before it. John and Magdalen attended the obsequies ; but the image of the Virgin Mary was carried away, and placed upon the front of the stage, in order to be kissed, adored, and worshipped by the people. This I saw them do with the utmost eagerness and reverence. And thus ended this Good Friday's tragi-comical, superstitious, idolatrous, droll. Surely, thought I, whilst attending on such a scene of mock devotion, if ever, now is the Lord Jesus crucified afresh : and I could then, and even now, think of no other plea for the poor beguiled devotees, than that which suffering Innocence put up himself for his enemies, when actually hanging upon the cross, viz. 'Father, forgive them, for they know not what they do.' "

It is said of William Esculquens, who was Capitoul of Toulouse, that, being in perfect health, he caused a solemn service to be held in the church of the Dominicans in that city, at which were present the capitouls, his colleagues, with a great number of others who were invited. The service consisted in the representation of his own burial. He was laid at length in a coffin, having his hands joined, and surrounded by forty lighted torches. The mass being ended, the incense was administered about the pretended corpse with the customary prayers. Nothing now remained but to put the body in the ground; but his zeal did not extend to that length. They proceeded, therefore, to lay him behind the great altar; from whence he took himself away shortly after. Afterwards, having quitted his shroud, for resuming his gown of capitoul, he returned home, accompanied by his colleagues and the rest of the company, whom he kept to dine with him.—What lengths will weakness and superstition carry men to!

POPULARITY.

THOUGH popularity, in some respects, is a desirable thing, yet it is not always a criterion of real ability; nor is it to be sought after with that avidity as if it were the foundation of happiness. It has been the occasion of ruin to many, and of distress to more. Those who have aimed at it have been generally left to disappointment and confusion.

When Phocion had made a speech which was applauded by the populace, he asked, "Have I not said some foolish thing?"

To a really wise man, the well weighed approbation of a single judicious character gives more heartfelt satisfaction than all the noisy applauses of ten thousand ignorant though enthusiastic admirers. We may say with Parmenides, who, upon reading a philosophical discourse before a public assembly at Athens, and observing that, except Plato, the whole company had left him, continued, notwithstanding, to read on, and said that Plato alone was audience sufficient for him.

Lord Mansfield, in his speech upon Wilke's trial, declared this sentiment: "I do not," says he, "affect to scorn the opinion of mankind. I wish earnestly for popularity; I will seek, and I will have popularity: that popularity which follows, and not that which is run after. It is not the applause of a day, it is not the huzzas of thousands, that can give a moment's satisfaction to a rational being; that man's mind, must, indeed, be a weak one, and his ambition of a most depraved sort, who can be captivated by such wretched allurements, or satisfied with such momentary gratifications."

"I would not," says Dr. Doddridge, "purchase that phantom, popularity, which is often owing to the very worst part of a man's character or performances, by any compliances beneath the dignity of a Christian minister."

The means which some use in order to obtain popularity, and by which they often get it, are sometimes exceedingly improper. "For instance," says Dr. Campbell, "those who court popular applause, and look upon it as the pinnacle of human glory to be blindly followed by the multitude, commonly recur to defamation, especially of superiors and brethren. I know a preacher, who, by this expedient alone, from being long the aversion of the populace, on account of his dulness, awkwardness, and coldness, all of a sudden became their idol."

The love of fame, as well as gain, must have been very strong in the following instance, related by Gurnall. "I have read of one," says he, "that offered his prince a great sum of money to have leave once or twice a day to come into his presence, and only say, 'God save your majesty.' The prince, wondering at this large offer for so small a favour, asked him what this would advantage him. 'O, Sir,' said he, 'this, though I have nothing else at your hands, will get me a name in the country for one that is a great favourite at court; and such an opinion will help me more, by the year's end, than I am out for the purpose.'"

THE PRAYING KINGS.

OF all the virtues which united in the character of Gustavus Adolphus, King of Sweden, that which crowned the whole was his exemplary piety. The following is related of him when he was once in his camp before Werben. He had been alone in the cabinet of his pavilion some hours together, and none of his attendants at these seasons durst interrupt him. At length, however, a favourite of his, having some important matter to tell him, came softly to the door, and, looking in, beheld the king very devoutly on his knees at prayer. Fearing to molest him in that exercise, he was about to withdraw his head, when the king espied him, and, bidding him come in, said, " Thou wonderest to see me in this posture, since I have so many thousands of subjects to pray for me; but I tell thee, that no man has more need to pray for himself than he, who, being to render an account of his actions to none but God, is for that reason more closely assaulted by the devil than all other men beside."

Henry IV. of France, uttered this prayer just before a battle, in which he obtained an entire victory : " O Lord of Hosts ! who canst see through the thickest veil, and closest disguise ; who viewest the bottom of my heart, and the deepest designs of my enemies ; who hast in thine hands, as well as before thine eyes, all the events which concern human life ; if thou knowest that my reign will promote thy glory and the safety of thy people, if thou knowest that I have no other ambition in my soul but to advance the honour of thy holy name and the good of this state ; favour, O great God ! the justice of my arms, and reduce all the rebels to acknowledge him whom thy sacred decrees and the order of a lawful succession have made their sovereign : but if thy good providence has ordered it otherwise, and thou seest that I should prove one of those kings whom thou givest in thine anger, take from me, O merciful God ! my life and my crown ; make me, this day, a sacrifice to thy will: let my death end the calamities of France, and let my blood be the last that is spilt in this quarrel."

EXTRAORDINARY PRAYERS.

THE following singular narrative has already appeared in print, but, as some of my readers may not have met with it, we here insert it.

" A few days ago," says one, " I happened to make one of a large company, in which, among other topics of conversation, our settlement in New Holland was discussed. We soon began to turn our thoughts to the unhappy convicts : various tales were told respecting them, but one in particular struck my notice as peculiarly uncommon.

" Rather more than five years have elapsed since John —— was apprehended for the commission of a capital crime : the action was proved against him to the clear conviction of the jurors, and he was accordingly condemned. The keeper of his prison, who in innumerable other instances had shown himself possessed of the warmest philanthropy, observing signs of great contrition in the prisoner, pitied him, and from pitying began to sympathise with his afflictions. He visited and discoursed with him ; but soon found that, although thirty years of age, he had but faint ideas of a Supreme Being, and fainter still about a future state. In this deplorable situation he appeared dreadfully alarmed at the near prospect of dissolution, and tortured almost to madness by gloomy apprehensions of misery after death. The benevolent keeper did all in his power to alleviate his present distress, and, in part, to dissipate his horrors ; assuring him that there was a good and gracious God above, who would look down upon him with compassion, and, if he repented, would most assuredly pardon all his past errors ;

that he himself (the keeper) would instantly go and fetch him a prayer book to help his religious meditations; and that he hoped to find him more composed at their next meeting. ' O, Sir !' exclaimed the poor distressed criminal, his eyes streaming with tears, 'I cannot read ; I never did read ; I never tried to read at all ! Oh ! I shall go to hell !' The keeper was inexpressibly shocked at this exclamation ; but, as the unhappy man had been respited during his majesty's pleasure, he promised him that he would himself soon instruct him to read ; meanwhile that he would daily discourse and pray with him. He immediately went out of the cell, and in a few minutes returned, bringing with him an alphabet, with each letter printed by itself on a card. He explained their uses ; and concluded with saying, that the English language, and several others, were nothing else but words formed by a different combination of these letters.

"The poor fellow sat still upon the floor for a few minutes, as if absorbed in contemplation ; at length, he took hold of the keeper's hand, and said with a sigh, ' Ah, Sir ! I am dull and stupid ; I shall never be able to learn.' Then suddenly, as if struck with an instantaneous lucky thought, he swept up all the letters into one heap, and, desiring his kind friend to kneel down with him, he looked at the ceiling, as towards heaven. ' Good God !' cried he, with his hands violently clasped together, ' you know what a blockhead I am, and that I never can learn this hard thing ; but you know also that you made every thing, and can look into our thoughts. Look into mine, and, as you are wiser than any man, do me a favour. Mr. —— says that these letters have all the English words in them : you know if he speaks truth. Take, I pray you, these cards, and make the best prayer you can for me ; then read it out to yourself, and think as if I made it, for I promise you I will try to be a good man ; only let me know what you have written, that I may be as good as my word.'

"After this singular supplication they both arose, and the convict felt himself more easy. Soon after a pardon was offered, on condition of his going to Botany Bay for fourteen years."

The following is an account of an illustrious commander and constable of France, as given by Brantome : " Every morning (says the historian,) whether he was at home or in the army, on a march or in camp, he never neglected to recite and hear his paternosters. But it was a saying among the soldiers, ' Take care of the *paternosters* of Monsieur the Constable :' for whilst he was muttering them over, he would throw in by way of parenthesis, as the occasion of discipline or war demanded, ' Hang me that fellow on the next tree—pass me that other through the pikes—bring me hither that man, and shoot him before my face—cut me in pieces all those rascals who are so audacious as to defend that steeple against the king—burn me that village—set fire to all the country for a quarter of a league round :' and all this he would do without the least interruption to his devotions."—Strange devotion truly ! !

The famous Mr. George Edwards, at the end of his Gleanings of Natural History, made use of this remarkable petition ; " My petition to God (if petitions to God are not presumptuous) is, that he would remove from me all desire of pursuing natural history, or any other study, and inspire me with as much knowledge of his divine nature as my imperfect state is capable of ; that I may conduct myself for the remainder of my days in a manner most agreeable to his will, which must consequently be most happy to myself. What my condition may be in futurity is known only to the wise Disposer of all things : yet my present desires are (perhaps vain and inconsistent with the nature of things,) that I may become an intelligent spirit, void of gross matter, gravity, and levity, and endowed with a voluntary motive power either to pierce infinitely into boundless ethereal space or into solid bodies ; to see and know how the parts of the great universe are connected with each other, and by what amazing mechanism they are put and kept in perpetual and regular motion. But (O vain and daring presumption of thought!) I most humbly submit my future existence to the supreme will of the One Omnipotent."

Dr. Dodd, in an oration delivered at the dedication of Freemasons' Hall, Great Queen-street, May 23, 1776, thus addressed the Deity: "Consummate Architect and wondrous Geometrician, direct us to make the blessed volume of thy instructive wisdom the never erring *square* to regulate our conduct ; the *compass*, within whose circle we shall ever walk with safety and peace ; the infallible *plumb-line*, and criterion of rectitude and truth."—These are figures quite in style for a freemason.

John Boys, D. D., Dean of Canterbury, gained great applause by turning the Lord's prayer into the following execration, when he preached at Paul's Cross on the 5th of November, in the reign of James I. " Our pope which art in Rome, cursed by thy name; perish may thy kingdom ; hindered may thy will be, as it is in heaven, so in earth. Give us this day our cup in the Lord's Supper ; and remit our moneys which we have given for thy indulgences, as we send them back unto thee ; and lead us not into heresy ; but free us from misery, for thine is the infernal pitch and sulphur, for ever and ever. Amen."

PRAYERS ANSWERED.

It is very true that prayer cannot inform the Deity ; cannot persuade, cannot alter the Divine Mind : but I am far from thinking that it is only "a natural and just tribute to the Deity, and an admirable method of cherishing the virtues of the religious life." I think something, yea, I think much, is due to the *efficacy* of prayer. Petition is an important branch of prayer ; but to offer petitions without any expectation of their being answered, is too vague and trifling an idea to deserve confutation. That the doctrine of the efficacy of prayer has been and may be abused, is granted ; but still this forms no solid objection. Prayer is a mean which God himself has instituted ; by which his wisdom thinks fit to convey blessings which would not have been given without praying for. The sacred scriptures not only abound with express precepts binding us to prayer, but afford a great number of signal instances of answers to prayer.

Luther, it is said, was able to prevail with God at his pleasure, and to obtain what he desired.

Mr. Edward Pearse lay for some time declining in a consumption; and, finding himself going off the stage, made it the matter of his hearty prayer to God, " that something of his might be useful after his decease ;" which prayer was remarkably answered in the signal success of his little book, which he styled " The Great Concern," which has gone through twenty-one editions. The prayers of a Bunyan, a Hervey, a Watts, a Doddridge, and a hundred others, have been answered in this respect.

In professor Frank's accounts of the footsteps of Divine Providence in raising and supporting the hospital for the reception and education of poor children, and for educating students in divinity, we have several pleasing instances of prayer being answered.

At one time, when all provision was gone, and their necessities great, he observes, " In the midst of all these pressing circumstances I found one comfort, which was a presence of mind in prayer joined with a confident dependance upon that Lord who heareth the young ravens when they cry. When prayer was over, and I was just sitting down at the table, I heard somebody knock at the

2

door ; which when I opened, there was an acquaintance of mine holding in his hand a letter, and a parcel of money wrapt up, which he presented to me. I found therein fifty crowns, which was sent a great way, and was soon followed with twenty crowns more.

" At another time, being in great straits, and all our provision spent, and the daily necessity of the poor calling for large supplies, I closely adhered in my mind to that saying, " Seek first the kingdom of God and his righteousness, and all these things shall be added unto you ;" avoiding temporal cares, and turning the whole bent of my soul to God ; and, when I was now laying out the last of the money, I said in my thoughts, " Lord ! look upon my necessity." Then going out of my chamber in order to repair to the college where I was to attend my public lecture, I unexpectedly found a student in my house that waited for my coming out, and presented me the sum of seventy crowns, that were sent from a place above two hundred English miles distant.

" Another time," continues he, " all our provision was spent : but, in addressing myself to the Lord, I found myself deeply affected with the fourth petition of the Lord's Prayer, *Give us this day our daily bread ;* and my thoughts were fixed in a more especial manner upon the words *this day*, because on the very same day we had great occasion for it. While I was yet praying, a friend of mine came before my door in a coach, and brought the sum of four hundred crowns.

" Another time I was in the deepest poverty, and what was more, I was urged by the importunity of most that were about me, calling for a supply to their pressing necessity. But, having cast my eye upon the Lord, I answered them plainly thus ; " Now ye come all to seek money of me, but I know of another Benefactor to go to," meaning the Lord. The word was scarcely out of my mouth, when a friend of mine, who was then just come off a journey, put seven pounds ten shillings and sixpence into my hand.—This is enough to put Infidelity out of countenance, and make her ashamed to show her head."

A lady, who had just set down to breakfast, had a strong impression upon her mind that she must instantly carry a loaf of bread to a poor man who lived about half a mile from her house, by the side of a common. Her husband wished her either to postpone taking the loaf of bread till after breakfast, or to send it by her servant : but she chose to take it herself instantly. As she approached the hut, she heard the sound of a human voice. Willing to hear what it was, she stepped softly, unperceived, to the door. She now heard the poor man praying, and, among other things, he said, " O Lord, help me ; Lord, thou wilt help me ; thy promise cannot fail ; and although my wife, self, and children, have no bread to eat, and it is now a whole day since we had any, I know thou wilt supply me, though thou shouldst again rain down manna from heaven." The lady could wait no longer ; she opened the door. " Yes," she replied ; " God has sent you relief. Take this loaf, and be encouraged to cast your care upon Him, who careth for you ; and when you ever want a loaf of bread, come to my house."

J. W. was employed in a large manufactory, the foreman of which took every opportunity to make him the butt of ridicule to his companions for his religion, and because he refused to join in their drinking parties and Sunday frolics. As they lived in the same house, the foreman one day heard him at prayer, and resolved to listen ; when to his great surprise, he found himself the subject of the young man's supplication, who was spreading his case of infidelity and hardness of heart before God, and supplicating earnestly for him that God would give him repentance unto salvation, and create in him a new heart, and put a right spirit within him. The foreman was deeply penetrated with what he heard. He had never entertained an idea of the power or nature of true prayer; he wondered at the eloquence and fervour with which his own unhappy case had been pleaded before God. "I never," said he to himself, "thus prayed to God for myself." The impression dwelt upon his mind. The next day, he took John aside. "I wish," said he, "John you would preach to me a little." John, who only thought his grave face was meant to turn the subject into ridicule, said, "Mr. M——, you know I am no preacher; I don't pretend to it."—"Nay," said Mr. M——, "I don't know how you can preach to-day; but I heard you yesterday make such a description of my state, as convinces me that you can do it very well, and I shall be much obliged to you to repeat it." "Ah!" says John, "'tis true I was at prayer, and did, indeed, Mr. M——, heartily pray for you."—"Very well," said the foreman; "pray say it over again, for I never heard any thing in my life which so deeply affected me." John did not wait for much entreaty: they kneeled down together, cried to the God of all Grace, and found acceptance. From that day they were bosom friends, went to the same place of worship, and frequently bowed their knees together with praise and thanksgivings. Their conversation adorned their profession, and the mocker became a confessor of the grace which he had so often abused and turned into ridicule!

THE HUMBLE PREACHER THE MOST USEFUL.

A VERY pious man being ordained minister in Fifeshire, some of his people left hearing him, and went to other churches in the neighbourhood. He, one day, meeting some of them, asked them whither they were going. They replied, that they were going to hear such a one of his brethren, as his own sermons did not edify them

so much. He said with great heartiness, "O yes; go always where your souls get most edification; and may God's blessing, and mine go with you." The people were so affected, that they resolved rather to trust their edification with the Lord than desert the ministry of such a holy and humble man. His gift of prayer was very excellent, though his sermons did not bear any marks of strong intellect: his success, however, in winning souls to Christ, and building them up in him, was great. Some of his brethren, one day, expressing their wonder how his ministrations did so much good, while theirs did so little, another made answer, "That his brother, living under a deep sense of his own weakness, by the force of fervent prayer brings all that he says warm from the heart of God through his own, so that it never cools till it enters the hearts of his hearers; whereas we, being conscious of our abilities, depend on them in composing our sermons: and hence the Lord gives so little countenance to them."

PREFERMENT.

IT has been observed, that nothing could form a more curious collection of memoirs, than anecdotes of preferment. Could the secret history of great men be traced, it would appear that merit is rarely the first step to advancement. It would much oftener be found to be owing to superficial qualifications, and even vices. Sir Christopher Hatton owed his preferment to his dancing. Queen Elizabeth, with all her sagacity, could not see the future Lord Chancellor in the fine dancer.

When Lord North, during the American war, sent to the Rev. Mr. Fletcher, of Medeley (who had written on the unfortunate American war in a manner that had pleased the minister) to know what he wanted, he sent him word that he wanted but one thing (which it was not in his lordship's power to give him) and that was—*more grace.* "Sit anima mea cum Fletchero."

There was a worthy minister whom the great Cranmer designed for preferment, and he gave this reason of his design : " He seeks nothing, he longs for nothing, he dreams about nothing, but Jesus Christ."

When Queen Elizabeth made an offer of the archbishoprick of Canterbury to the Rev. Mr. Whitehead, (a great scholar, and a most excellent professor of divinity) he excused himself to the queen by saying, he could live plentifully on the gospel without any preferment, and accordingly did so.

The famous Bernard Gilpin was offered the bishoprick of Carlisle, and was urged to accept it by the Earl of Bedford, Bishop Sandys, and others, with the most powerful motives ; but he desired to be excused, and in that resolution remained immoveable. His reasons were taken from the largeness of the dioceses, which he thought were too great for the inspection of one person ; for he was so strongly possessed of the duty of Bishops, and of the charge of souls that was committed to them, that he could never be persuaded to keep two livings, over both of which he could not have a personal inspection, and perform all the offices of a pastor ; he added farther, that he had so many friends and relations in those parts to gratify and connive at, that he could not continue an honest man, and be their bishop. But though Mr. Gilpin would not be a bishop, he supplied the place of one by preaching, by hospitality, by erecting schools, by taking care of the poor, and providing for destitute churches.

To the above we might add the names of Bates and Baxter in former times, and Balguy and Tucker in more modern times, who have all thought proper to decline the mitre, and, of course, the emoluments and dignities attached to it.

How different was the conduct of the above excellent characters to that of Hamilton ! When he was about to be made Bishop of Galloway, one objecting to him, that it went against his conscience (for he had sworn to the covenant) he said, " Such medicine as could not be chewed must be swallowed whole." Fine sentiment for a bishop, truly ! ! !

In the reign of the unfortunate monarch whose abdication put a period to the regal honours of the house of Stuart, Dr. Wallis was then Dean of Waterford, in Ireland, and, during the troubles of that unhappy country at that period, suffered greatly in his private fortune, from the strong attachment to the Protestant faith. After peace was restored, and our religion firmly established by the accession of King William, Dr. Wallis was presented at the court of London, as a gentleman who had well merited the royal patronage. The king had before heard the story of his sufferings, and therefore immediately, turning to the dean, desired him to choose any church preferment then vacant. Wallis (with all the modesty incident to men of real worth) after a due acknowledgment of the royal favour, requested the deanery of Derry. "How!" replied the king, in a transport of surprise, "ask the deanery when you must know the bishoprick of that very place is also vacant ?" " True, my liege," replied Wallis, " I do know it, but could not in honesty demand so great a benefice ; conscious there are many other gentlemen who have suffered more than myself, and deserved better at your majesty's hands ; I therefore presume to repeat my former request." It is needless to add his request was granted. They parted, the dean highly satisfied with his visit, and the king astonished at the noble instance of disinterestedness he had just been a witness of.—What a mind did that man possess ! how praise-worthy ! how laudable an example to all in the sacred office ! What a reproof to the greedy pluralists ! How few can lay their hand on their hearts, and say, with the Dean of Derry, " I am satisfied !"

What will not some do for the sake of preferment, and that even when they are already well provided for ? The shameful impropriety of pluralities is never thought of; conscience is sacrificed to interest ; the value of money, and not of souls, becomes the prime object in view. What would the primitive Christians have said of a modern divine, who is said to be the curate of ——, supposed to be worth annually 5000*l.*? He is sub-almoner to ———, rector of ———, prebendary of —— ——, prebendary of ———, prebendary of ———, archdeacon of ———, and dean of ———.

The late Bishop L—— was possessed, at the time of his decease, of ten or more different preferments. He was bishop—head of a college—prebend—rector—librarian, &c. &c. &c.

Bishop Burnet, in his charges to the clergy of his diocese, showed a great deal of disinterested integrity, by vehemently exclaiming against pluralities, as a most sacrilegious robbery. And, in his first visitation at Salisbury, he urged the authority of St. Bernard, who, being consulted by one of his followers whether he might accept of two benefices, replied—"And how will you be able to serve them both ?" "I intend," answered the priest, "to officiate in one of them by a deputy." "Will your deputy be damned for you too !" cried the saint. " Believe me, you may serve your cure by proxy, but you must be damned in person." This expression so affected Mr. Kelsey, a pious and worthy clergyman, then present, that he immediately resigned the rectory of Bemerton, in Berkshire, worth 200*l.* a year, which he held then with one of greater value.

Situations where we can do the most good are preferable to all others, however great the emoluments. Dr. T. Gouge used often to say, with pleasure, that he had two *livings* which he would not exchange for the greatest in England; viz.

Christ's Hospital, where he used to catechise the poor children ; and *Wales,* where he used to travel every year, and sometimes twice in the year, to spread knowledge, piety, and charity.

THE IGNORANT PRIEST

THE following anecdote will afford us a striking instance of the ignorance that existed before the Reformation ; at the same time it confirms the relation generally given of Archbishop Cranmer's forgiving spirit.

The archbishop's first wife, whom he married at Cambridge, lived at the Dolphin Inn, and, he often resorting thither on that account, the popish party had raised a story, that he was ostler of that inn, and never had the benefit of a learned education. This idle story a Yorkshire priest had with great confidence asserted in an alehouse which he used to frequent, railing at the archbishop, and saying that he had no more learning than a goose. Some of the parish, who had a respect for Cranmer's character, informed the Lord Cromwell of this, who immediately sent for the priest, and committed him to the Fleet Prison. When he had been there nine or ten weeks, he sent a relation of his to the archbishop to beg his pardon, and humbly sue to him for a discharge. The archbishop instantly sent for him, and, after a gentle reproof, asked the priest whether he knew him ; to which he answered, No. The archbishop expostulated with him, why he should, then, make so free with his character. The priest excused himself by his being in drink. But this, Cranmer told him, was a double fault, and then let him know, that if he had a mind to try what a scholar he was, he should have liberty to oppose him in whatever science he pleased. The priest humbly asked his pardon, and confessed himself to be very ignorant, and to understand nothing but his mother tongue. "No doubt," said Cranmer, "you are well versed in the English Bible, and can answer any questions out of that. Pray tell me who was David's father ?" The priest stood still awhile to consider, but at last told the archbishop he could not recollect his name. "Tell me, then," said Cranmer, "who was Solomon's father ?" The poor priest replied, that he had no skill in genealogies, and could not tell.—The archbishop then advised him to frequent alehouse less, and his study more; and admonished him not to accuse others for want of learning till he was master of some himself; discharged him out of custody, and sent him home to his cure.

THE WICKED PRIESTS.

IN a remote part of Ireland, (in the province of Connaught,) which is inhabited chiefly by Catholics, a Testament found its way. The Catholics, who resided at such a distance from their chapel that they could seldom attend mass, happened to hear that this book (being a *Douay* translation) was a *divine* book, paid some attention to it. In the perusal of it, they were joined by some Protestants; and both observed, that the evil treatment which our Saviour endured was from the priests, and that it was by their influence and malice he was put to death. This gave rise to a warm dispute between the Protestants and the Catholics, to which of their denominations these wicked priests belonged. The Catholics, however, were silenced by this argument: That the Protestant clergy were not *priests*, but *ministers ;* and that, as no denomination had priests but the Catholics, it must have been they who acted this cruel part. The Catholics, sore under the charge, reproached their priest, on his next visit, for this wicked deed of his order; which obliged the priest to take the trouble of making a sermon on the occasion, to convince his people that they were the *Jewish* and not the Catholic priests who crucified the Redeemer. Pleased at acquiring this important information, the Catholics still attended to their Testament;

but discovering in it what characters of holiness, moderation, and self-denial, christian teachers should possess, they began to be further troublesome to their priest ; to prevent which for the future, he banished even the *Douay* Testament out of the country !!

PRINTS.
Improper Prints in Books, &c.
ONE cannot but smile at the odd and curious representations given us of certain objects in some old books of devotion. The paintings of angels, devils, spirits, &c. must excite the risibility of any sensible man, and none but injudicious limners and sculptors could engage in such performances.—But it is still more ridiculous to attempt any figures of the Deity. Instead of enlarging, it must contract our ideas of Him, who is without body, parts, or passions. All attempts, also, to represent the Trinity by triangles, and a dove in the centre, &c. should be entirely left alone.

"I can easily understand and readily admire, as a strong poetical figure," says Dr. Knox, "the touching of Isaiah's hallowed lips with fire ; but I cannot admire the engraver's representation, in some Bibles, of an angel from heaven with a blacksmith's tongs, burning the poor prophet's lips with a live coal.

"The representation of Satan in many serious books is so ridiculous, that one would almost imagine the artist intended to laugh at the idea of such a being. Who can bear some prints of demoniacs, where the possessed are exhibited vomiting up little black devils with cloven feet and long tails? If artists thought such figures likely to excite or preserve devotion, they must have been as weak as their admirers.

"Few books have had a greater popularity than the works of Bishop Taylor: several of them are adorned with good plates by Fairthorne, but disgraced by others of a ridiculous kind. The frontispiece to the *Rules of Holy Dying* cannot but excite mirth even in those who do not habitually sit in the seat of the scorner. On one side is the statue of a clergyman in his canonicals, with the inscription on the base, *Mercurius Christianus.* In the clouds, opposite to him, is the figure of an old man with a flag in one hand and a crown in the other, in a sitting posture, intended to represent Jesus Christ. The reader will immediately see the absurdity of introducing *Mercurius* in the same picture with our Saviour. On the other side is represented, in a most childish manner, hell and the devil. Here the figures are shockingly deformed ; but they are calculated to strike terror into none but children and those who labour under the weakest superstition."

There is a commentary on the Revelations, in which is a frontispiece containing an enormous gigantic picture of Jesus Christ. The artist has literally copied Rev. i. 14, &c.—his head and his hairs are like a fleece of wool ; for eyes he has *flames of fire ;* his legs and feet are like pillars of brass ; and, that nothing should be wanting, he *has in his right hand seven stars,* and *out of his mouth* proceeds *many waters,* and a *sharp two edged sword.*

The prints inserted in the Common Prayer Books are of a kind which none but the ignorant and the vulgar can admire. The cut entitled, Jesus tempted by the Devil, is almost as ludicrous as if it had come from Hogarth or Bunbury. The devil has a crown and sceptre, a modern coat, apparently a pair of boots, and from his rump hangs a tail resembling what is called a pig-tail !

In one of the ancient books on devotion, an angel is represented crowning the Virgin Mary, and God the Father himself assisting at the ceremony. In a book of Natural History, the Supreme Being is represented as *reading* on the seventh day, when he rested from all his works.

In the book that Featly published against the Baptists there was a plate representative of the people against whom he wrote performing the ordinance of baptism. Ministers, the administrators, and both men and women the receivers of baptism, are represented as stark naked in a river, and the ministers are thrusting the people's heads down forward into the water :—such a sight which had never been seen since the world began.

John Heywood wrote a treatise called the "Spider and Fly." There are seventy-seven chapters in this work, at the beginning of each of which is the portrait of the author, either standing or sitting before a table with a book on it and a window near it, hung round with cobwebs, flies, and spiders.—What would the present age say of an author whose books should be so full of himself?

Bishop Burnet tells us, that before the Reformation it was usual in England to have pictures of the Trinity. God the Father was represented in the shape of an old man, with a triple crown, and rays about his head ! The Son, in another part of the picture, looked like a young man, with a single crown on his head, and a radiant countenance. The blessed Virgin was between them, in a sitting posture ; and the Holy Ghost under the appearance of a dove, spread his wings over her. The picture, he tells us, is still to be seen in a prayer book printed in the year 1526, according to the ceremonial of Salisbury. Skippon also tells us, that there is at Padua a representation of the Trinity, being the figure of an old man with three faces and three beards. Henry Sherfield, Esq. the Recorder of Sarum, was tried May 20, 1632, for taking down some painted glass out of one of the windows of St. Edmund's church in Salisbury, in which were seven pictures of God the Father in the form of a little old man in a blue and red coat, with a pouch by his side. One represents him creating the sun and moon with a pair of compasses ; others, as working on the business of the six day's creation; and, at last, he sits in an elbow chair at rest. Many simple people, at their going in and out of church, did reverence to this window, because, as they said, the Lord their God was there. These artists and devotees surely never took for their rule that passage, "God is a spirit, and they that worship him must worship him in spirit and truth."— John iv. 24.

Some of the prints in Quarle's Emblems are curious. One of them, on "O wretched man that I am! who shall deliver me from the body of this death?" represents a man sitting in a melancholy posture in a large skeleton. Another, on "O that my head were waters and mine eyes a fountain of tears," &c. exhibits a human figure with several spouts gushing from it, like the spouts of a fountain. "This reminds me," says one, "of an emblem which I have seen in a German author on Matthew vii. 3, in which are two men, one of whom has a beam almost as big as himself, with a pointed end sticking in his left eye, and the other has only a small mote sticking in his right."

PROFLIGATE SONS RECLAIMED.

THE following is related of the famous Mr. John Welsh. He was, it is said, a most hopeless and extravagant youth. He frequently played truant; and, at last, while very young, he left his studies and his father's house, and went and joined himself to the thieves on the *borders* of the then two kingdoms, who lived by robbery and plunder. After he had suffered many hardships among them, and like the prodigal in the gospel, began to be in great misery, and no man gave unto him, he took the prodigal's resolution to return home to his father's house. He made Dumfries in his way homeward, where lived a Mrs. Forsyth, his father's cousin: her he earnestly entreated to bring about a reconciliation for him with his father.

He had not been long with this lady before his father came, providentially, to visit her; to whom, after conversing a while, she said, "Cousin, have you heard any thing of your son John?" "Oh, cruel woman!" said the father, with great grief, "how can you mention his name to me? The first news I expect to hear of him, is, that he is hanged for a thief." She answered, "Many a profligate boy has become a virtuous man;" and endeavoured to comfort him, but in vain. At length, he asked her if she knew whether his lost son was yet living. She answered, "Yes, he was yet alive, and hoped he would make a better man than he was a boy;" at the same time she introduced him to his father. The youth came in weeping, and threw himself at his father's feet, beseeching him for Christ's sake to pardon his misbehaviour; earnestly, and with much apparent sincerity, promising future amendment. His father reproached and threatened him; but, upon the importunities of Mrs. Forsyth, he was persuaded to a reconciliation. He then besought his father to send him to college; saying, "That, if ever he misbehaved again, he would be content that his father should disclaim him for ever." His father granted him his request; and, after a little time spent there, not only a thorough reformation, but a saving conversion, took place in him; and he was so diligent a student, that, in much less time than could be expected, he went through all his necessary studies, and entered early into the ministry. He became one of the most extraordinary characters of the age.

A minister happening to be some time since at Edinburgh, was accosted very civilly by a young man in the street, with an apology for the liberty he was taking. "I think, Sir," said he, "I have heard you at ——." "You probably might, Sir; for I have sometimes ministered there."— "Do you remember," said he, "a note put up for an afflicted widow, begging the prayers of the congregation for the conversion of an ungodly son?" "I do very well remember such a circumstance."—"Sir," said he," I am the very person; and, wonderful to tell, the prayer was effectual. I was going on a frolic with some other abandoned young men, one Sunday, and, passing by the chapel, I was struck with its appearance, and we agreed to mingle with the crowd, and stop for a few minutes to laugh and mock at the preacher and people. We were but just entered the chapel, when you, Sir, read the note, requesting the prayers of the congregation for an afflicted widow's profligate son. I heard it with a sensation I cannot express. I was struck to the heart; and, though I had no idea that I was the very individual meant, I felt the bitterness expressed of a widow's heart, who had a child as wicked as I knew myself to be. My mind was instantly solemnized : I could not laugh. My attention was riveted on the preacher. I heard his prayer and sermon with an impression very different from what had carried me into the chapel. From that moment the gospel truths penetrated my heart : I joined the congregation, cried to God in Christ for mercy, and found peace in believing; became my mother's comfort, as I had long been her heavy cross, and, through grace, have ever since continued in the good ways of the Lord. An opening having lately been made for an advantageous settlement in my own country, I came hither with my excellent mother, and, for some time past, have endeavoured to dry up the widow's tears, which l had so often caused to flow, and to be the comfort and support of her age, as I had been the torment and affliction of her former days. We live together, in the enjoyment of every mercy, happy and thankful; and every day I acknowledge the kind hand of my Lord, that ever led me to the chapel."

THE PROFLIGATE TURNED MISER.

A YOUNG man, who in two or three years spent a large patrimony in profligate revels, was at last reduced to absolute want. He went one day out of his house with an intention to put an end to his life, but, wandering awhile almost unconsciously, he came to the brow of an eminence which overlooked what were lately his estates. Here he sat down, and remained fixed in thought a number of hours, at the end of which he sprang from the ground with a vehement exulting motion. He had formed his resolution, which was, that all these estates should be his again. He had formed his plan, too, which he instantly began to execute ; he walked hastily forward, determined to seize the very first opportunity, of however humble a kind, to gain any money, though it were ever so despicable a trifle, and resolved absolutely not to spend, if he could help it, a single farthing of whatever he might obtain. The first thing that drew his attention was a heap of coals shot out of carts on the pavement before a house : he offered himself to shovel or wheel them into the place where they were to be laid, and was employed ; he received a few pence for his labour, and then, in pursuance of the saving part of his plan, requested some small gratuity of meat and drink, which was given him ; he then looked out for the next thing that might chance to offer, and went with indefatigable industry through a succession of servile employments in different places of longer and shorter duration, still scrupulously avoiding as far as possible the expense of a penny. He promptly seized *every* opportunity which could advance his design without regarding the meanness of the employment, or the degradation of appearance : by this course he had gained after some time, money enough to purchase, in order to sell again, a few cattle, of which he had taken pains to understand the value. He speedily but cautiously turned his first gains into second advantages; retained without a single deviation his extreme parsimony; and thus advanced by degrees into larger transactions and incipient wealth. The final result was, that he more than recovered his lost possessions, and died an inveterate miser, worth sixty thousand pounds. —So strange and contradictory is the character of man!!

PROTESTANTS REPROVED.

"I REMEMBER," says Mr. Matthew Henry, "when I was a young man, coming up to London in the stage coach, in King James's time, there happened to be a gentleman in the company that then was not afraid to own himself a Jesuit: many renconters he and I had upon the road; and this was one; he was praising the custom, in popish countries, of keeping the church doors always open, for people to go in at any time to say their prayers. I told him that it looked too much like the practice of the Pharisees, that prayed in the synagogues, and did not agree with Christ's command, ' Thou, when thou prayest, enter not into the church with the doors open, but into thy closet, and shut thy doors.' When he was pressed with that argument, he replied with some vehemence, ' I believe you protestants say your prayers no where; for (said he) I have travelled a great deal in the coach in company with Protestants, have often laid in inns in the same room with them, and have carefully watched them, and could never perceive that any of them said their prayers, night or morning, but one, and he was a Presbyterian.' " Superstitious and self-righteous as the Papists are, they are very attentive to the form at least; while it is too true that many Protestants, so called, never pray at all. *Fas est doceri ab hoste.*

THE PUGILISTS.

A SERIOUS young man in the army, not having a place in the barracks in which he was quartered, wherein to pour out his soul unto God in secret, went one dark night into a large field, adjoining. Here he thought no eye could see, nor hear him, but God's; but He, " whose thoughts are not as our thoughts," ordained otherwise. Two ungodly men, belonging to the same regiment, in whose hearts enmity had long subsisted against each other, were resolved that night to end it (as they said) by a battle; being prevented at day-time, for fear of punishment. They chose the same field to fight as the other had chosen to pray. Now the field was very large, and they might have taken different ways; but they were led by Providence to the same spot where the young man was engaged in this delightful exercise. They were surprised at hearing, as they thought, a voice in the field at that time of night; and much more so when they drew nearer, and heard a man at prayer. They halted, and gave attention; and, wonderful to tell, the prayer had such an effect upon both, as to turn that enmity they before manifested against each other into love. They took each other instantly by the hand, and cordially confessed, that there remained no longer, in either of their breasts, hatred against each other.

PUNCTUALITY.

NOTHING begets confidence sooner than punctuality. In business, or religion, it is the true path to honour and respect, while it procures a felicity to the mind unknown to those who make promises only to break them, or suffer themselves to be so entangled in their concerns, as to be incapable of being their own masters. Whoever wishes to advance his own interest, and to secure the approbation of others, must be punctual.

"Punctuality," says Dr. Johnson, "is a quality which the interest of mankind requires to be diffused through all the ranks of life, but which many seem to consider as a vulgar and ignoble virtue, below the ambition of greatness, or attention of wit; scarcely requisite amongst men of gaiety and spirit, and sold at its highest rate when it is sacrificed to a frolic, or a jest."

It is said of Melancthon, that, when he made an appointment, he expected not only the hour, but the minute, to be fixed, that the day might not run out in the idleness of suspense.

Of Sir William Blackstone, we are informed, that in reading his lectures, it could not be remembered that he ever made his audience wait even a few minutes beyond the time appointed. Indeed, punctuality, in his opinion, was so much a virtue, that he could not bring himself to think perfectly well of any one who was notoriously defective in this practice.

The late Rev. Mr. Brewer, of Stepney, when a student, under the tuition of the Rev. Mr. Hubbard and Dr. Jennings, was always punctual in attending the lectures at the tutor's house; where the students, who then lodged and boarded in private families, were expected to assemble at set hours. One morning, the clock had struck seven, and all rose up for prayer; but the tutor looking round, and perceiving that Mr. Brewer was not yet come, paused awhile. Seeing him now enter the room, he thus addressed him: "Sir, the clock has struck, and we were ready to begin; but, as you were absent, we supposed it was too fast, and therefore waited." The clock was actually too fast by some minutes.

THE REFORMER AND THE QUAKER.

A country clergyman was boasting, in a large company, of the success he had met with in reforming his parishioners, on whom his labours, he said, had produced a wonderful change for the better. Being asked in what respect, he replied, that, when he came first among them, they were a set of unmannerly clowns, who paid him no more deference than they did to one another; did not so much as pull off their hat when they spoke to him, but bawled out as roughly and familiarly as though he was their equal; whereas, now, they never presumed to address him but cap in hand, and, in a submissive voice, made him the best bow when they

were at ten yards distance, and styled him *your reverence*, at every word. A Quaker, who had heard the whole patiently, made answer, "And so, friend, the upshot of this reformation, of which thou hast so much carnal glorying, is, that thou hast taught thy people to worship thyself."

THE USEFUL REPROOF.

Mr. Henry Staples, a holy minister of the seventeenth century, had a remarkable talent for religious conversation. Wherever he visited, he used to drop some useful word, and, even on the road, he would often speak to strangers concerning the affairs of their souls. Having occasion to attend the assizes, at Molingar, in Ireland, a profane butcher occupied a stall just under his window at the inn. Mr. Staples, hearing him swear, opened the casement, reproved him, and shut it again. The butcher, continuing to multiply his oaths, Mr. Staples set the window open, that he might more readily continue his reproofs, which, at first, he received with all imaginable contempt. At length, however, Mr. Staples observed that the butcher, whenever he dropt an oath, looked up to see whether Mr. Staples noticed it. This encouraged him to persist in his reproofs, which he did to good purpose; for, not only a present reformation took place, but the man was led into serious reflection on his ways, and a change was produced. Some time after, when Mr. Staples came that way, he paid him the greatest respect, confessed his past folly, and thanked him for his kind reproof. To another person, he said, "This good man has saved my soul from hell!"

RESPECT TO WISE AND GREAT MEN.

The peculiar excellencies of great men, certainly deserve our admiration; and, it is much better to see merit rewarded by the tribute of praise, than to behold it the occasion of envy, as is too frequently the case. We should be cautious, however, of running into an extreme ; for, while we justly acknowledge the talents of the wise, we should carefully avoid the incense of flattery. The view of great qualities, and the remembrance of distinguished characters, will always be grateful to a wise and good man ; but he must not forget, that all the excellencies of mortals are only a few emanations from Him who is the fountain of all life, light, and perfection.

Such was the esteem in which Virgil was held, that one hundred thousand Romans rose up when he came into the theatre ; showing him the same respect as they did Cæsar himself.

Sir Isaac Newton was so esteemed, that the Marquis de l'Hopital, one of the greatest mathematicians of the age, said to the English who visited him, " Does Mr. Newton eat, drink, or sleep, like other men ? I represent him to myself as a celestial genius, entirely disengaged from matter."

Such was the respect paid to Shakspeare by the public in general, that when the mulberry tree planted upon his estate by his own hands was cut down, not many years ago, the wood, being converted to several domestic uses, was all eagerly bought at a high price, and each single piece treasured up by its purchaser, as a precious memorial of the planter.

Bishop Atterbury having heard much of Dr. Berkley, wished to see him ; accordingly he was introduced by the Earl of Berkley. After some time, Dr. Berkley quitted the room ; on which Lord Berkley said to the Bishop, " Does my cousin answer your Lordship's expectations ?" The bishop, lifting up his hands in astonishment, replied, " So much understanding, so much knowledge, so much innocence, and such humility, I did not think had been the portion of any but angels, till I saw this gentleman."

Pope sums up his character in one line. After mentioning some particular virtues that distinguished other prelates, he ascribes

"To Berkley every virtue under Heaven."

Such were the accomplishments, wit, learning, judgment, elocution, (together with a graceful person,) and behaviour, of that eminent divine William Cartwright, that Bishop Fell paid him this encomium, " that he was the utmost that man could come to."

Scarcely any man was ever more honoured, alive as well as dead, than Livy, the Roman historian. Pliny the younger relates, that a native gentleman travelled from Gades, in the extremest parts of Spain, to see Livy ; and though Rome abounded with more stupendous and curious spectacles than any city in the world, yet he immediately returned : as if, after having seen Livy, nothing farther could be worthy of his notice.

Several persons who had read Justus Lipsius' works, in Sarmatia, made a voyage into the Low Countries on purpose to see him.

The first time that the celebrated Abbadie heard Saurin preach, he exclaimed, " Is it an angel, or a man !"

Mr. Locke thus speaks of Dr. Pococke : " I can say of him what few men can say of any friend of their's, nor I of any other of my acquaintance ; that I don't remember I ever saw in him any one action that I did or could in my own mind blame, or thought amiss in him."

Some years ago, a traveller passing through Clermont wished to see the country house of the famous Bishop Massilon, in which he used to spend the greatest part of the year. He applied to an old vicar, who, since the death of the bishop, had never ventured to return to that country house, where he who inhabited it was no longer to be found. He consented, however, to gratify the desire of the traveller, notwithstanding the profound grief he expected to suffer in revisiting a place so dear to his remembrance. They accordingly set out together ; and the vicar pointed out every particular place to the stranger. "There," said he, with tears in his eyes, "is the valley in which the excellent prelate used to walk with us. There is the arbour in which he used to sit and read. This is the garden he took pleasure in cultivating with his own hands." Then they entered the house ; and, when they came to the room where Massilon died, "This," said the vicar, "is the place where we lost him!" and as he pronounced these words, he fainted.—The ashes of Titus, or of Marcus Aurelius, might have envied such a tribute of regard and affection.

Dr. Knox, in his Christian Philosophy, bears the following respectable testimony to the character of Dr. Watts. "For my own part, I cannot but think this good man approached as nearly to Christian perfection as any mortal ever did in this sublunary state ; and therefore I consider him as a better interpreter of the Christian doctrine than the most learned critics, who, proud of their reason and their learning, despised or neglected the very life and soul of Christianity, the living everlasting gospel, the supernatural operation of divine grace."

This article might be greatly enlarged by the names of Luther, Calvin, Erasmus, Spanheim, Ussher, &c. &c. but we shall conclude with the following.

A lady, who was a zealous admirer of that great philanthropist Mr. Howard, eager to behold and converse with so celebrated a man, called several times at his house before she could meet with him ; and, when she did gain admittance, her appearance was so little prepossessing, that the mind of Howard could not divert itself of a certain dread of assassination. Her amazing height, her *tout ensemble* was so extremely masculine, that the idea of a man disguised in woman's clothes instantly occurred, and he hastily rang his bell, and by a look commanded his servant to wait. His fears were, however, groundless ; for the good woman, after having sufficiently wearied his patience with an enthusiastic and bombastic display of the vast veneration in which she held his labours in the cause of humanity, very quietly took her leave, declaring *she could now die in peace.*

RESTITUTION.

OUR repentance cannot be very sincere where there is no restitution made to others whom we have injured. "If it be a sin to take that which is another man's from him by fraud or violence, it is the same, continued and repeated, to detain and keep it from him." "If we do not restore," says St. Augustine, "that which we have injuriously detained from another, our repentance is not real, but feigned and hypocritical."

Mr. Samuel Fairclough, at thirteen years of age, hearing his godfather, Mr. Samuel Ward, preaching of Restitution, from the instance of Zaccheus, and oft repeating that the sin was not forgiven unless what was taken was restored, was so touched with remorse for the robbing of an orchard, that, after a restless night, he went to a companion of his, and told him that he was going to Mr. Jude, the owner, to carry him twelve pence for his three penny-worth of pears, of which he had wronged him. His companion, fearing a whipping from his master, answered, "Thou talkest like a fool, Sam, for God will forgive us ten times sooner than old Jude will forgive us once." But Sam, being of another mind, went to Jude's house, confessed the injury, and offered the money. Jude pardoned him ; but would take no money. This grieved him more ; upon which he made application to his spiritual father, Mr. Ward, and opened to him the whole state of his mind, who received and treated him with great kindness and attention.

Mr. Richard Alleine, of Batcome, in Somersetshire, published an excellent treatise in defence of evangelical, experimental, practical religion, entitled, "Vindiciæ Pictatis." It was printed in four parts, but they may sometimes be met with all bound together in one thick 12mo. volume. A man in Yorkshire saw this book at a sale, coveted it, and stole it : but upon taking it home, and reading it, it proved the means of his conversion ; upon which he honestly took it back to the original owner, one Thomas Sawley, at Wood End, in Yorkshire, acknowledging his crime in stealing it ; but blessing God, who had over-ruled it to the salvation of his soul.

Mr. Burrough's, in a sermon on Ps. xvii. 14, hath these words : "These hands of mine had once *that* given to them, to be a means to convey ; to restore that which was taken wrongfully fifty years before. The wrong was fifty years ago : and after fifty years the conscience of the man troubles him, and he comes to bring, to restore that wrong, and desires it may be conveyed to such a place where he had done the wrong." [The reader will forgive the style of the author.]

A servant woman, in whom her master placed great confidence for her honesty, but who had robbed him, at various times, to a considerable amount, was awakened under the ministry of Mr. Pomfret. Some years after, Mr. Pomfret, in a discourse, was insisting upon restitution as a necessary branch of repentance ; upon which she brought the money to Mr. Pomfret, acknowledging what she had done, who immediately returned it to the gentleman's son, saying, "Sir, you see the good effects of the word of God!"

A certain minister in Warwickshire, preaching upon the eighth commandment, observed, in the conclusion of his discourse, that restitution was necessary in case of former dishonesty. The sermon, it seems, produced some good effect; for it obliged a man who had been active in a riot twenty years before to make restitution. The following is a copy of the letter which was found in the house of a cheese-factor, inclosing six shillings, and which had been privately put under the door.

"Mr.———,   April.

"Some years ago, I stole a cheese from you, when you lost a many, by a rude mob, which cheese might be worth three or four shillings; but I have gave you six, which you ought to have. Going to —— Meeting, there I heard a man preach, 'Thou shalt not steal ·' he reasoned so from it, that made me do this, which is your right : this was the 24th of April, which I heard him preach."

Let those who are conscious of dishonest actions in the days of their ignorance learn from hence to go and do likewise : and let preachers learn, from this circumstance, not to be afraid of preaching against particular sins, merely because they may be called legal.

RETRACTIONS AND ACKNOW-
LEDGEMENT OF FAULTS.

I CONSIDER this article of importance, as it exhibits to us the genuine spirit of Christianity, which teaches us to confess our faults, and likewise places before us examples of humility worthy of our imitation. It is hard to say, I have done wrong ; but, where we are culpable, our religion requires it, and it is more honourable to confess than to conceal, and show an obstinate spirit.

Lewis Du Moulin, doctor of physic, being in his last sickness visited by Dr. Burnet, and admonished of the foul language used in his books against Dr. Stillingfleet, Dean of St. Paul's ; Dr. Durel, Dean of Windsor ; Dr. Patrick, Dean of Peterborough, &c. desired Dr. Burnet to ask them pardon in his name ; and, when he spake of the Dean of St. Paul's, he expressed much sorrow, and shed some tears, and, upon their motion, signed the following recantation.

"As for my books, in which I mixed many personal reflections, I am

now sensible I vented too much of my own passion and bitterness; and therefore I disclaim all that is personal in them, and am heartily sorry for every thing I have written to the defaming of any person. I humbly beg God, and all those whom I have so wronged, pardon for *Jesus Christ's* sake; and am resolved, if God shall spare my life, never to meddle more with such personal things; and do earnestly exhort all people, as a dying man, that they will study more love and mutual forbearance in their differences, and will avoid all bitter and uncharitable reflections on one another's persons. And, as I earnestly pray those worthy men of the church of *England* to have charity and tenderness for the dissenters from them, so I beg of the dissenters that they would have a due regard and respect to those of the church of *England*, of whom I say now, let my soul be with theirs; and that all true protestants among us may heartily unite and concur in the defence and preservation of the holy reformed religion, now by the mercy of God, settled among us. And that men of all sides may, according to St. Paul's rule, *cease to bite and devour one another, lest we be destroyed one of another;* and that, whereunto we have already attained, we may walk by the same rule; hoping that, if any man is otherwise minded in some lesser things, God shall either reveal that to them, or mercifully forgive it through *Jesus Christ;* into whose hand I commend my spirit, and desire to appear before God in and through him, who gave himself for me: and therefore do now study to learn of him to be meek and lowly in heart, and to love all the brethren, as he loved me.
" This, in sincerity of heart, I sign,
"LEWIS DU MOULIN."
Mr. Howe had a particular intimacy with Dr. Tillotson (afterwards archbishop.) The doctor preached a sermon at court on Joshua xxiv. 15. in which he asserted that "no man is obliged to preach against the

religion of a country, though a false one, unless he has the power of working miracles." King *Charles* slept most of the time. When the sermon was over, a certain nobleman said to him, "It's a pity your majesty slept, for we have had the rarest piece of *Hobbism* that ever you heard in your life." " Odds fish," said the king, "he shall print it then;" and immediately called the Lord Chamberlain to give his command to the doctor to do it. When it came from the press, the doctor, as was usual with him, sent it as a present to Mr. *Howe;* who, on the perusal, was grieved to find a sentiment which had so ill a tendency, and drew up a long letter, in which he freely expostulated with the doctor for giving such a wound to the reformation, and carried it himself. The doctor, upon the sight of it, moved for a little journey into the country, that they might talk the matter over without interruption. Mr. *Howe* enlarged on the contents of the letter as they travelled in the chariot. The good doctor at length wept, and said this was the most unhappy thing that had befallen him for a long time; owned that what he had asserted was not to be maintained, and urged, in his excuse, that he had but little notice of preaching that day, and none of printing the sermon.

While Mr. F. was one day interring a corpse, he was suddenly interrupted in his duty by a voice of execration and blasphemy. Instantly, with a look of holy indignation, he turned to that part of the multitude whence the voice appeared to proceed; and singling out, as he supposed, the guilty person, he publicly rebuked her in terms as severe as the nature of the offence demanded. After the service was concluded, he received information that his rebuke had been improperly directed; when he immediately recalled the people, who were then dispersing from the grave, and, pointing to the person whom he had unwittingly injured, he expressed the utmost concern at having confounded the innocent with the guilty, and declared that, as his error was public, so he desired publicly to solicit the pardon of the offended party.

A minister often attending Mr. Romaine's preaching at St. Dunstan's, heard him throw out very severe things against the dissenters, which he thought not justifiable. He determined to wait on him for an explanation. He did so accordingly; and, having made his observations and complaints, Mr. R. replied, "I do not want to have any thing to say to you Sir." "If you will hear me, Sir," added the other, "I will tell you my name: I must, Sir, acquaint you with my profession; I am a protestant dissenting minister." "Sir," said Mr. Romaine, "I neither wish to know your name nor your profession." Upon which Mr. T—— bowed, and took his leave. Some time after, Mr. Romaine, to the great surprise of his hearer and reprover, returned the visit, and, after the usual salutation, "Well, Mr. T——, I am not come to renounce my principles: I have not changed my sentiments; I will not give up my preference to the church of England; but I am come as a Christian, to make some apology. I think my behaviour to you, Sir, the other day, was not becoming, nor such as it should have been," &c. They then shook hands, and parted good friends.

RICHES.

WHAT immense pains are men at in order to acquire riches! and when they are attained, alas! what little consolation do they afford! "Power and riches," says one, "are enormous and operose machines, contrived to produce a few trifling conveniences to the body, consisting of springs the most nice and delicate, which must be kept in order with the most anxious attention, and which, in spite of all our care, are ready every moment to burst into pieces, and to crush in their ruins their unfortunate possessor. They are immense fabrics, which it requires the labour of a life to raise; which threaten every moment to overwhelm the person that dwells in them, and which, while they stand, though they may save him from smaller inconveniences, can protect him from none of the severer inclemencies of the season. They keep off the summer shower, not the winter storm; but leave him always as much, and sometimes more, exposed than before, to anxiety, to fear, and to sorrow, to diseases, to danger, and to death."

Aartgen, a painter of merit, became so distinguished, that the celebrated Francis Floris went to Leyden out of mere curiosity to see him. He found him inhabiting a poor half-ruined hut, and in a very mean style of living. He solicited him to go to Antwerp, promising him wealth and rank suitable to his merit: but Aartgen refused, declaring that he found more sweets in his poverty than others did in their riches.

Abdalonymus, of the royal family of Sidon, and descended from King Cinyras, was contented to live in obscurity, and get his subsistence by cultivating a garden, while Strato was in possession of the crown of Sidon. Alexander the Great, having deposed Strato, inquired whether any of the race of Cinyras was living, that he might set him on the throne. It was generally thought that the whole race was extinct; but at last, Abdalonymus was thought of, and mentioned to Alexander, who immediately ordered some of his soldiers to fetch him. They found the good man at work, happy in his poverty, and entirely a stranger to the noise of arms, with which all Asia was at that time disturbed; and they could scarcely persuade him that they were in earnest. Alexander was convinced of his high descent by the dignity that appeared in his person, but was desirous of learning from him in what manner he bore his poverty. "I wish," said Abdalonymus, "I may bear my new condition as well. These hands have supplied my necessities; I have had nothing, and I have wanted nothing."—Thus we see that a contented mind is a continual feast, while the abundance of the rich will not suffer them to sleep.

Epaminondas, though one of the greatest men Greece ever produced, and who obtained many great and admirable victories, yet was such a contemner of riches, that, when he died, he left not enough to discharge the expenses of his funeral.

Paulus Æmilius, when he had conquered Perseus, disdained to cast his eyes upon the immense riches which were found in his treasury; and only permitted his sons, who were fond of learning, to take the books of that king's library.

Policrates bestowed five talents for a gift upon one Anacrisa, who for two nights after was so troubled with care how to keep them, and how to bestow them, that he carried them back again to Policrates, saying, "They were not worth the pains he had already taken for them."

Luther was remarkable for his contempt of riches, though few men had a greater opportunity of obtaining them. The Elector of Saxony offered him the produce of a mine at Sneberg; but he nobly refused it, lest it should prove an injury to him. His enemies were no strangers to this self-denial. When one of the popes asked a certain cardinal why they did not stop that man's mouth with silver and gold, his Eminence replied, "That *German beast* regards not money." In one of his epistles, Luther says, "I have received one hundred guilders from Taubereim, and Schartts has given me fifty; so that I begin to fear lest God should reward me in *this* life. But I declare I will not be satisfied with it. What have I to do with so much money? I gave half of it to P. Priorus, and made the man glad."

"The taste of real glory and real greatness," says Rollin, "declines more and more amongst us every day. New raised families, intoxicated with their sudden increase of fortune, and whose extravagant expenses are insufficient to exhaust the immense treasures they have heaped up, lead us to work upon nothing as truly great and valuable but wealth, and that in abundance; so that not only poverty, but a moderate income, is considered as an insupportable shame; and all merit and honour are made to consist in the magnificence of buildings, furniture, equipage, and tables.

"How different from this bad taste are the instances we meet with in ancient history! We there see dictators and consuls brought from the plough! How low in appearance! Yet those hands, grown hard by labouring in the field, supported the tottering state, and saved the commonwealth. Far from taking pains to grow rich, they refused the gold that was offered them, and found it more agreeable to command over those who had it, than to possess it themselves. Many of their greatest men, as Aristides among the Greeks, who had the management of the public treasures of Greece for several years; Valerius Publicolas, Menenius Agrippa, and many others, among the Romans, did not leave wherewithal to bury them when they died: in such honour was poverty among them, and so despised were riches. We see a venerable old man, distinguished by several triumphs, feeding in a chimney corner upon the garden-stuff his own hands had planted and gathered. They had no great skill in disposing of entertainments; but, in return, they knew how to conquer their enemies in war, and to govern their citizens in peace. Magnificent in their temples and public buildings, and declared enemies of luxury in private persons, they contented themselves with moderate houses, which they adorned with the spoils of their enemies, and not of their countrymen.

"Augustus, who had raised the Roman empire to a higher pitch of grandeur than ever it had attained before, and who, upon sight of the pompous buildings he made in Rome, could vain-gloriously but truly boast, that he should leave a city all marble, which he found all brick ; this Augustus, during a long reign of more than forty years, departed not one tittle from the ancient simplicity of his ancestors. His palaces, whether in town or country, were exceedingly plain ; and his constant furniture was such as the luxury of private persons would soon after have been ashamed of. He lay always in the same apartment, without changing it, as others did, according to the seasons ; and his clothes were seldom any other than such as the Empress Livia, or his sister Octavia had spun for him."

Crœsus was very rich, but being taken captive, was condemned to be burnt to death. When the funeral pile was erected, and Crœsus laid on it, preparatory to the execution of the sentence, he was observed to exclaim, emphatically, " O Solon, Solon !" which induced Cyrus to inquire into the cause of the ejaculation. Accordingly he was informed, that Crœsus, in his prosperity, having displayed his treasures to Solon the famous Athenian philosopher, demanded of him, whether he did not esteem him happy from the possession of such riches. To which the wise man calmly replied, " that no man could be pronounced happy as long as he lived, as the most prosperous could not possibly foresee what would happen to him before his death ;" and that Crœsus, now feeling the force of this remark, therefore expressed his conviction, by invoking the name of his sagacious monitor. This circumstance wrought so effectually on Cyrus's feelings, and inspired him with such sympathetic compassion for Crœsus, that he ordered him to be taken from the pile, and not only spared his life, but made an ample provision for his support, and afterwards consulted him on the most important occasions.—Such are the vicissitudes incident to human life !

Some will do any thing to obtain wealth. Conscience is stifled, laws violated, character injured, for the sake of worldly interest. But how noble is the contrary disposition, when we are enabled to deny ourselves, and to rise superior to an inordinate desire after it ! The following instance gives us a true picture of disinterestedness and true greatness. A poor man, who was door-keeper to a boarding-house in Milan, found a purse with two hundred crowns in it. The man who had lost it, informed by a public advertisement, came to the house, and, giving good proof that the purse belonged to him, the door-keeper restored it to him. The owner, full of joy and gratitude, offered his benefactor twenty crowns, which the other absolutely refused. He then came down to ten, and afterwards to five ; but, finding him inexorable, he throws his purse upon the ground, and in an angry tone, " I have lost nothing," says he, " nothing at all, if you refuse to accept of any thing." The door-keeper then accepted of five crowns, which he immediately distributed among the poor.

There cannot be a greater mistake than to suppose riches can make a man happy. How often do they inflate with pride, fill with anxiety, and expose to danger ! " I wonder," said Lucretia Gonzaga to a gentleman, " that you, who are a learned man, and so well acquainted with the affairs of this world, should yet be so strangely vexed at being poor, as though you did not know that a poor man's life is like sailing near the coast ; whereas that of a rich man does not differ from the condition of those who are in the main sea. The former can easily throw a cable on the shore, and bring the ship safe into the harbour ; whereas the latter cannot do it without difficulty."

A gentleman of vast fortune, (ten thousand pounds a year,) sent for a friend to Pall Mall, being very indisposed, to settle some affairs ; and while they were together, he walked to the window, and observed a chimney-sweeper's boy with his sack passing by. His friend was surprised to see the tears burst from his eyes; and, clasping his hands, with an oath he swore, "Now would I give every shilling I am worth in the world to change beings with that little sweep!"

"Though riches," says Dr. Johnson, "often prompt extravagant hopes and fallacious appearances, there are purposes to which a wise man may be delighted to apply them. They may, by a rational distribution to those who want them, ease the pains of helpless disease, still the throbs of restless anxiety, relieve innocence from oppression, and raise imbecility to cheerfulness and vigour."

"Our estate," says one, "is as much the gift of God as our *eyes* or our *hands*, and is no more to be buried, or thrown away at pleasure, than we are to put out our eyes, and throw away our limbs, as we please. If a man had *eyes*, and *hands*, and *feet*, that he could give to those that wanted them; if he should either lock them up in a *chest*, or please himself with some *needless* or *ridiculous* use of them, instead of giving them to his brethren that were *blind* and *lame*, should we not justly reckon him an inhuman wretch? If he should rather choose to amuse himself with *furnishing* his house with those things, than to entitle himself to an eternal reward, by giving them to those that wanted *eyes* and *hands*, might we not justly reckon him mad?

"Now *money* has very much the nature of *eyes* and *feet*, if we either lock it up in *chests*, or waste it in *needless* and *ridiculous* expenses upon ourselves, whilst the poor and distressed want it for their *necessary* uses. If we consume it in the *ridiculous ornaments* of apparel, whilst others are starving in *nakedness*, we are not far from the cruelty of him that chooses rather to adorn his house with the *hands* and *eyes*, than to give them to those that want them. If we choose to indulge ourselves in such expensive enjoyments as have

no *real use* in them, such as satisfy no *real want*, rather than by disposing of our money well, we are guilty of his madness, that rather chooses to lock up *eyes* and *hands*, than to make himself for ever blessed, by giving them to those that want them.

"For after we have satisfied our own *sober* and *reasonable* wants, all the rest of our money is but like *spare eyes* or *hands*: it is something that we cannot keep to ourselves without being *foolish* in the use of it; something that can only be used well by giving it to those that want it."

RIDICULE.

"If the talent of ridicule," says Mr. Addison, "were employed to laugh men out of vice and folly, it might be of some use in the world; but, instead of this, we find it is generally made use of to laugh men out of virtue and good sense, by attacking every thing that is serious and solemn, decent and praiseworthy, in human life."

If ever a vein of ridicule be necessary, I think it is here, where just argument can have no effect.

Some Jesuits once, in company with Mons. Boileau, asserted, according to the principles of that society, that *attrition* was only necessary, and that we were not obliged to love God. It was to no purpose to unravel their fallacies. They showed themselves inviolably attached to their error; when Mr. Boileau, starting up, cried, "Oh! how prettily will it sound in the day of judgment, when our Lord shall say to his elect, *Come you, ye well beloved of my Father;* for you never loved me in your life, but always forbad that I should be beloved, and constantly opposed those heretics who were for obliging Christians to love me: and you, on the contrary, Go to the Devil and his angels; you, the accursed of my Father; for you have loved me with your whole heart, and have solicited and urged every body else to love me." This raillery struck the opponents dumb, and bore down that opposition which the most cogent arguments could not quell.

" If a handsome opportunity presents itself," says one, "it may not be amiss to deal with an opinionative fellow, as Bishop Bramhall did with the popish missionary. When his antagonist would obstinately maintain whatever he had rashly advanced, the bishop drove the disputant up into so narrow a corner, that he was forced to affirm that *eating* was *drinking*, and *drinking* was *eating*, in a material or bodily sense. This assertion was so big with palpable absurdities, that he needed no greater trophy if he could get under the *Jesuit's* hand what he declared with his tongue ; which being desired, was by the other, in his heat and shame, to seem to retreat, as readily granted. But upon cooler thoughts," says my author, " finding, perhaps, after the contest was over, that he could not quench his thirst with a piece of bread, he reflected so sadly on the dishonour he had suffered, that not being able to digest it, in ten days' time he died.

THE RIGHTEOUS REVERED.

HOWEVER a depraved heart may rise in enmity against those who are truly religious, yet their amiable temper, great prudence, and just deportment, strike the mind of others with such peculiar force, as to extort from them both confessions and respect not a little extraordinary. The Earl of Rochester acknowledged, that, even in the midst of his wild paroxysms, he had a secret veneration for a good man.

The venerable and famous missionary Swartz, had acquired such a character among the heathen, that, when among a barbarous and lawless banditti, he was suffered to pass with his catechumen through contending parties of them unsuspected and unmolested. They said, " Let him alone —let him pass—he is a man of God !" This apostle of our own day has saved the inhabitants of a fort from perishing by famine, when the neighbouring heathen have refused to supply it with provision on any other assurance than that of his word. Even that tyrant, Hyder Ally, while he refused to negotiate in a certain treaty with others, said, " Send me Swartz ; send me the Christian Missionary," said this Mahometan ; " I will treat with him, for him only can I trust."

Another fact, relative to this great man, is worth mentioning. When the late Rajah of Tanjore was dying, and desired to commit his adopted son, the present Rajah, to this missionary, and with him, of course, the care of his dominions, the Christian, after the example of his Master, was not dazzled by the kingdoms of this world, nor the glory of them. He persuaded the dying prince to place the government of his son and his affairs in other hands. But a greater honour was reserved for him, which he *could* not refuse; namely, that at his death, the present Rajah shed a flood of tears over his body, mourned deeply while attending his funeral, and has written to England for a monument, which he intends to erect at Tanjore to the memory of his virtues.

These anecdotes show us, better than a thousand arguments, the importance of character, and the propriety of the apostle's exhortation, " Walk in wisdom towards them that are without."

Mr. Erskine (father of the famous Ralph and Ebenezer Erskine) was on his passage across the Firth of Forth, between Leith and Kinghorn when he found himself in the midst of very ungodly company, who were passengers with him in the same vessel. It grieved him exceedingly to hear the name of the great God perpetually profaned ; the good old man was, at length, so affected, that he could bear it no longer, but, rising suddenly from his seat, and taking hold of the mast, he uncovered his head, waved his hat in the air, and cried aloud, " Hallo, hallo, hallo !" as if he had seen some object at a distance. The company was struck, and all was silence and attention. He then, with great solemnity, pronounced the third commandment; "*Thou shalt not take the name of the Lord thy God in vain, for the Lord will not hold him guiltless that taketh his name in vain.*" He then quitted the mast, covered his head, and sat down. At first the giddy company began to elbow each other; then to titter; at last they broke out into a loud laugh. In a little time their conversation became as bad or worse than ever. Above all the rest, eminent in wickedness, was a lady who sat just opposite Mr. Erskine, who took a malignant pleasure in repeating the sacred name almost every sentence, accompanied with smiles of derision and contempt, designed to mortify this man of God.

The long suffering and infinitely merciful Father of the Universe seldom interposes, even in such flagrant instances of profanity as this: but here was an exception; when what *hearing* his word could not, *terror* soon effected. They proceeded on their voyage till they came between the islands and the Highlands on the other side, when a storm suddenly arose, the sea began to swell, and the heavens, becoming black with clouds, seemed to threaten vengeance upon the guilty crew. This change of circumstances produced a visible alteration in their conduct and countenances. The tempest raged; the danger was imminent; the skipper, no longer able to hold the helm, pronounced their doom to be certain and immediate death; when the lady, whose gaiety was now turned into the terrors of death, sprang across the boat, clasped her arms around Mr. Erskine's neck, and cried aloud, " If I die, Sir, I will die with you !"

It pleased an indulgent God, however, to spare them : they weathered the storm, and reached the wished-for shore in safety. There was no more swearing at that time. Their contempt was converted into deep respect ; and when the company separa-

ted, it was with serious faces, and low bows to good Mr. Erskine.

THE SCOLD CONVERTED.

THE late Rev. Mr. W. relates the following circumstance, in one of his journals. " Wednesday 9th, I rode over to a neighbouring town, to wait on a justice of the peace, a man of candour and understanding, before whom I was informed their angry neighbours had carried a whole wagon load of these new heretics (the Methodists.) But when he asked what they had done, there was a deep silence, for that was a point their conductors had forgot ! At length one said, " Why, they pretend to be better than other people ; and besides, they pray from morning to night." Mr. S. asked, " But have they done nothing besides ?" " Yes, Sir," said an old man; " an't please your worship, they have *converted* my wife. Till she went among them, she had such a tongue, and now she is as quiet as a lamb !" " Carry them back, carry them back," replied the justice, " and let them convert all the scolds in the town."

SCRIPTURE MISAPPLIED AND IRREVERENTLY USED.

To pervert, misapply, or irreverently use the sacred scripture, whether in the pulpit or in conversation, is an evil highly reprehensible. It leads to an improper familiarity with the scripture, furnishes an argument for the infidel, and is a proof either of our ignorance, error, levity, or malignity. The sacred volume ought always to be treated with the greatest reverence; and whether we preach from it, or converse about it, it ought to be with the greatest seriousness and care.

As it respects conversation, take the following example. " A person wishing to inform another he is alluded to, announces, in scripture language, " Thou art the man;" or, in excusing the attendance of a man lately married, that " He has married

a wife, and therefore cannot come."
Another tells us, " I have found my
sheep which was lost;" and I have
heard a person, upon a piece of business taking a more favourable turn
than expected, rebuke another jocose-
ly in the words of our Lord, " O, thou
of little faith, wherefore didst thou
doubt ?" which was followed by a
laugh ! I have also heard, and not in
a single instance, persons fond of
smoking tobacco invite others to have
with them "a burnt offering."

A man in the island of Jersey,
who was a notorious drunkard, would
often drink half a pint of neat Hol-
lands at a time, and with these words
in his mouth: " Be not drunk with
wine, wherein is excess, but be filled
with the *spirit*." On other occasions,
when drinking off a small glass, he
would profanely quote these words:
" *Take heed that ye despise not one
of these little ones.*"

As it respects the misapplication
of scripture in the pulpit we have too
many instances.

The following passage is found in
a sermon preached by a protestant
clergyman, at Bow Church, before
the Society for Reformation of Manners. " As for those that dropped in
by chance, or came out of custom or
curiosity, or to *spy out our liberty
that we have in the Lord*, or it may
be, they knew not why themselves,
they have the same freedom here, as
in the devil's chapel, to stay as few
or as many acts as they please; and
when they have heard as much as
serves their turn, or something they
do not like, or think it may be change
or dinner time, they are free to be
gone; and, as they came unsent and
unlooked for, so they may *depart not
desired ;* and the only remark I shall
make is, *that they went out from us,
but they were not of us ; for if they
had been of us, they would no doubt
have continued with us.*"

The typical parts have often been
abused. Thus, according to some,
the snuffers signify sound arguments,
faithful admonitions, and dreadful
excommunications. The *grate of*

net-work shows the rich usefulness
of Jesus Christ for justification. The
tree thrown into the waters, to
sweeten them, is Jesus Christ;
and we are told, that in countries
where the waters are venemous,
when the beasts come to drink, they
all wait for the unicorn, that so he
might first put in his horn, the virtue
of which expels the venemous corruption which was in the waters before, and then they all drink of the
same. O! so should the Lord's people wait in the waters of affliction
upon Christ, their *spiritual unicorn,*
who putteth *down his* long *horn of
grace* to sweeten, &c. See Worden's
Types, ch. 9. 23, 25. " Types
should," says one, " be handled cautiously and soberly, and always under the immediate direction of the
New Testament writers. A man is
always safe when he follows these
guides."

No book has been taken more liberties with than that of the Canticles.

A grave commentator thus allego-
rises. " Solomon's *bed* is the church;
the *sixty valiant men about it* are the
six working days of the week, and
the ten commandments ; the *thread
of scarlet* is a confession of faith in
the doctrince of the Trinity and
the death of Christ. *My beloved put
in his hand by the hole ;* that is,
Thomas put his hand into the side
of Christ." This devout rhapsody
the holy man calls heavenly food;
and he advises his readers to live
upon it with the lips of cogitations
and the teeth of admiration.—*Phi-
lon. Carpath epise in Cantic. interp.
apud Bibliot Patrum,* tom. I.

A man who allows his fancy to
play with scripture may make any
thing of it. The following parallel,
delivered in a sermon at St. Paul's,
in London, before the gentlemen of
Nottinghamshire, on the day of their
yearly feast, is curious.

The town of Nottingham doth run
parallel with *Jerusalem.* Was Jerusalem set upon precipitous hills ?
and is not Nottingham also ? And

as the mountains stood round about Jerusalem, do they not so about Nottingham? And as there were two famous ascents in Jerusalem, is it not so in Nottingham? I need not tell you that the soul of man is a precious thing, and the loss thereof sad in any country; yet, methinks, in the agueish parts of Kent and Essex, where I have seen, sometimes, a whole parish sick together, the souls that miscarry thence seem but to go from purgatory to hell. But those that perish out of Nottinghamshire go from heaven to hell. When a soul miscarries out of Nottinghamshire, methinks in melancholy visions, I see the infernals flocking about it, and saying, " Art thou come from those pleasant mountains to these Stygian lakes?" &c.—Was it worth a man's while to come, as the preacher tells his auditors he did, " twenty-four miles in *slabby* weather," to preach such stuff as this?

A certain preacher took for his text Acts xx. 15. *Paul went a-foot to Assos ;* and expatiated on the humility of trudging *a-foot*, after the apostle's example. Unluckily for this declaimer, the word πεζευειν does not signify to go a-foot; it means to go by land: and he might as well have preached on the *infirmities* of good men, and have proved that St. Paul was *timorous* of sailing.

It would be easy to transcribe more instances of this kind, but I suppose the reader is already tired with the above.

I shall only stop to express my grief that men whose business it is to inform others, should be so ignorant themselves; that they who pretend to *illuminate*, should *darken*. Such characters who substitute fancy for genius, and contemptible singularities for extraordinary powers, give but little evidence, in my opinion, of their being called to the sacred work of the ministry. And yet, alas! how many of those miserable preachers have we, with whom multitudes, as miserable as themselves, are carried away!

SERVANTS.

Sobriety, activity, fidelity, submission, patience, punctuality, sincerity, and obedience to their masters, are required of servants: but it is religion which will make them shine. This will enable them not merely to fill up, but to adorn their stations. This will sweeten all their toils, produce contentment in the place which Providence hath allotted them, and teach them to look forward to that happy period, when they shall be elevated to those honours which are immortal, and those glories which shall never fade.

The Faithful Servants.

At the recent banishment of the famous Barthelemy, it is said, his servant Le Tellier came running up, just as his master was getting into the carriage, with an order from the Directory permitting him to accompany his master. He delivered it to Angereau, who, having read, said, " You are determined, then, to share the fate of these men who are lost for ever? Whatever events await them, be assured they will never return." " My mind is made up," answered Le Tellier; " I shall be but too happy to share the misfortunes of my master."—" Well, then," replied Angereau ; " go, fanatic, and perish with him :" at the same time adding, " Soldiers, let this man be watched as closely as those miscreants." Le Tellier threw himself on his knees before his master, who was but too happy at this awful moment to press so affectionate a friend to his bosom. " This worthy fellow," say they, " has constantly shown the same courage and attachment, and we have always treated and considered him as one of our companions."

A Portuguese slave, who had fled into the woods to enjoy the liberty which was his natural right, having heard that his old master was arrested and likely to be condemned for a capital crime, came into the court of justice, assumed the guilt of the fact, suffered himself to be imprisoned,.

brought false though judicial proofs of his crime, and was executed in stead of his beloved master. Though we must condemn this conduct as an unjustifiable sacrifice of truth and of his own life, yet we cannot but admire the affection, greatness, generosity, and gratitude of mind here displayed.

A gentleman of respectability, Dr. L——, was lately confined for some time in the King's Bench prison; while his fortune, involved in a chancery suit, was unjustly withheld from him. During this distressing period he was obliged, by poverty, to tell his negro servant that, however repugnant to his feelings, they must part, his pecuniary difficulties being now such, that he was unable to provide himself with the necessaries of life. The negro replied, with affectionate warmth, "*No, massa, we will never part: many a year have you kept me, and now I will keep you.*" Accordingly he went out to work as a day labourer, and at the end of every week faithfully brought his earnings to his master; which proved sufficient for the support of both of them, until the recent decision of the chancery suit, by which the doctor obtained an award of thirty thousand pounds. Very much to the doctor's honour, he has settled a handsome annuity for life on this faithful and affectionate negro.

The following declaration, made in a court of justice, ought to be well considered by unfaithful and wicked servants :—

At a late trial at the Old Bailey of a man who had robbed his master, whose extreme lenity induced him to desist from prosecuting to conviction, although a bill of indictment had been found, the judge remarked, "*I would have servants know, when they are convicted of abusing the confidence reposed in them, which in many cases is unlimited, that it is a rule with his majesty never to extend mercy to them.*"

Servants should be honest, diligent, and civil, if it be only out of respect to themselves. Who is not struck with the answer of that slave, which history records, who, standing among others for sale, and being asked by a purchaser, "Wilt thou be faithful if I buy thee?" replied, "Yes; *whether you buy me or not.*"

Religious Servants.

"I have often been encouraged," says one, "when from the pulpit I have met a servant's attention, when I have seen them listening to a profitable remark while waiting in the parlour. I have been pleased to meet them at a bookseller's, inquiring for some instructive publication; and have been ready to say, upon such an occasion, 'Happy is the man (whatever be his station) that getteth understanding; for she is a tree of life to them that lay hold upon her.'"—Prov. iii. 13, 18.

The servants of Lord —— were greatly impressed, and evidently reformed, under the preaching of the gospel at ——. His lordship being one day on the promenade, was jeered by some of the company upon the revolution which had taken place among his servants by a change of their religion. The noble lord replied, "As to the change of their religion, or what their religious sentiments are, I cannot tell; but one thing I know, that, since they have changed their religion, they have been much better servants, and shall meet with no opposition from me."—How happy is it when our good conduct puts to silence the ignorance of foolish speakers!

A very interesting anecdote is related by a gentleman, who lately visited the north of Ireland, of the influence which the religion of *a servant maid* had upon a whole family in that country. "The family (he says) were dissenters; but dissenter, in many parts of Ireland, is but another name for an Arian or Socinian. The poor girl was much ridiculed for her religion by the young ladies, but did not render evil for evil; on the contrary, she would allow them to laugh at her, and then mildly reason with them. She made it her study to be attentive and useful to them; took opportunities to speak to them about religion; and would offer to read the sacred scriptures to them when they went to bed. They commonly fell asleep, and that in a little time, under the sound; but she was not discouraged.—Having exemplified Christianity in her life, Providence sent a fever to remove her to a better state. The young ladies were not permitted to see her during her illness; but they heard of her behaviour, which did not lessen the impression which her previous conduct had made upon them. Soon after, the two elder began to make a profession of real religion: the little leaven spread; and now all the *nine* young ladies appear truly pious. Nor is religion, in this highly favoured family, confined to them; other means were employed by God in producing this great change; but one of the two, who first became serious, informed me, that she chiefly ascribed it to the life and death of the servant maid."

Old Robert.

J. B——n, Esq. had a servant of the name of Robert Pasfield, better known by the name of *Old Robert*, who was a father in his family to the rest of his servants. He was utterly unlearned, being unable either to write or to read, yet of so strong a memory, as to become a kind of index to the family to call to mind whatever had been lost in the hearing of the word. This he did by means of a girdle of his own invention, upon which all the books and chapters of the Bible were divided into spaces: the chapters were marked by a long point or thong, and the verses by knots. By the help of this instrument he attained to an admirable faculty of repeating what he had been hearing, to the astonishment of many and the edifying of all. He had an excellent gift in prayer, and great fluency in religious conversation. He was, therefore, in high esteem in the family till the day of his death, when he was nearly four-

score years of age. His master attended him in some of his last moments.

"Some years ago," says a good writer, "I became acquainted with a servant whom I shall call Lucius; one who, knowing the human heart in its deceitfulness and depravity, stood before his God like the publican smiting upon his breast; but before his master he stood with an integrity and diligence which his master had long observed, and which at length gained his entire confidence. Lord —— thought and talked of Christianity like many more who have it yet to learn, but he was constrained to admire its effects in his servant Lucius. He saw in him evident marks of the fear of God, the consolations of the gospel, the truth it enjoins, and the devotion it inspires. But while he beheld all this as a singular matter of fact, maintained and exercised in a house like his, he was equally struck in observing that Lucius was one of the most humble and attentive of his domestics, and no less eminent as a servant, than as a saint. The unbelieving lord continued, while he lived, to advance and vindicate the Christian servant, and, dying, bequeathed a solid testimony of his virtues. To Lucius the servants also looked as to a common friend or brother: he instructed them, he assisted them, he reconciled them; he was their example; and if there were any more foolish and profligate than the rest, he had the honour of their reproach. I need only to add, that I mention this fact, as well as the former, to show how honourable a part such servants sustain in society: to show that true religion is the same in every age; to exhibit the fruits of genuine Christianity wherever it is found; and to encourage servants to higher aims than they usually entertain."

"Lydia," continues the same author, "is the servant of a small family, whose mistress I lately visited after a long illness. 'Sir,' said she, 'the girl who has just left the room is

4*

a greater comfort to me than I can express. She watches me with the affection of a daughter, and the care of a nurse. When my complaints make me peevish, she contrives something to soothe me. I often observe her taking pains to discover what would add to my comfort, and often am presented with the things I wish for, before I can express it in words. I live without suspicion, for I perceive her to be conscientious even to scrupulosity: my chief complaint is, that she takes so much care of me, that I cannot make her take sufficient care of herself.'—I have observed, said I, her attention at church, as well as when waiting upon you.

"'My servant,' continued she, 'is a Christian, and, in my late distress, afforded me her prayers, as well as her tears. Her parents were too poor to give her any education; but she has taught herself to read, and frequently reads the Scriptures to me. Now and then, while she is reading, her heart is too full to be quite silent on the passage; and then she drops an expression or two, accompanied with such simplicity and meaning, as bring to my mind those words, *I thank thee, O Father, Lord of heaven and earth, that thou hast hid these things from the wise and prudent, and hast revealed them unto babes.* In short, I esteem her one of the most valuable gifts I ever received from an indulgent Providence, and never could have supposed, that so much of my comfort depended on the faithfulness and care of a poor servant.'

"After saying some things to encourage this worthy girl, as I passed her in going away, I could not help saying, also, to myself, How much better do these retired virtues deserve recording, than those splendid mischiefs which historians call up all their eloquence to adorn!"

THE SMITH TURNED PREACHER.

A SMITH, with his leather apron on, came to Archbishop Ussher, en-treating his Grace to ordain him.—The good bishop looked on him with a smiling, (not a disdainful,) countenance, and asked him what he was? "A blacksmith," said he.—"Hast thou any learning?" said the bishop. "No other but my mother tongue," said the smith.—"Canst thou answer gainsayers?" continued the bishop: "dost thou not know this kingdom of Ireland is filled with priests and jesuits?" The smith replied, that if his Grace would examine him, he would answer him according to his ability. Whereupon, the bishop tried him as to several points of divinity; in which the smith gave him satisfaction,. to his great admiration. The bishop asked him what parish he lived in? He told him, and that the minister of the place was very sickly, and seldom preached.—— "Well," said the bishop, "I see thou hast good natural parts; I will write to the minister to let thee have his notes to preach;" which, as soon as the smith received, he got a gown and mounted the pulpit. The bishop sent one of his chaplains to hear him. The chaplain acquainted his Grace that he delivered all by memory with great affection and pathos. The bishop thought, within himself, that this man might do some good; so sent for him, and not only ordained him, but gave him a living of 80l. per annum. In that parish, there were about fifty families, whereof thirty were Papists, and about twenty Protestants. The smith, by his good preaching and living, in a year or two, made strange alterations; so that, in a short time, about thirty of the families were Protestants, and about twenty Papists.

SOLDIERS.
The Praying Soldier.

DURING the late unhappy commotions in Ireland, a private soldier in the army of Lord Cornwallis, was daily observed to be absent from his quarters, and from the company of his fellow-soldiers. He began to be suspected of withdrawing himself, for the purpose of holding intercourse with the rebels, and, on this suspicion, probably increased by the malice of his wicked comrades, he was tried by a court-martial, and condemned to die. The marquis, hearing of this, wished to examine the minutes of the trial; and, not being satisfied, sent for the man to converse with him. Upon being interrogated, the prisoner solemnly disavowed every treasonable practice, or intention, declared his sincere attachment to his sovereign, and his readiness to live and die in his service:—he affirmed, that the real cause of his frequent absence was, that he might obtain a place of retirement, for the purpose of private prayer, for which his lordship knew he had no opportunity among his profane comrades, who had become his enemies merely on account of his profession of religion. He said he had made this defence on his trial, but the officers thought it so improbable, that they paid no attention to it. The marquis, in order to satisfy himself as to the truth of his defence, observed, that, if so, he must have acquired some considerable aptness in this exercise. The poor man replied, that, as to ability, he had nothing to boast of. The marquis then insisted on his kneeling down, and praying aloud before him; which he did, and poured forth his soul before God with such copiousness, fluency, and ardour, that the marquis took him by the hand, and said, he was satisfied, that no man could pray in that manner who did not live in the habit of intercourse with his God. He not only revoked the sentence, but received him into his peculiar favour, placing him among his personal attendants, and the way to promotion.

On reading the above, every serious mind will be led to reflect on the remarkable intervention of Providence in behalf of this man of prayer; for this is the most prominent feature in the Christian character. He could not live without prayer, though he thereby exposed himself to the suspicion and hatred of his associates,

R

and even endangered his life; but that God, whom, like Daniel, he served, knew how to deliver him in the perilous hour; and, not only heard his prayers, but made the exercise of this duty itself the mean of his deliverance.—O, how does this reproach those who live without prayer, though they have every opportunity for retirement, unseen, and unsuspected!

This anecdote, also, does real honour to the character of the illustrious marquis, and to the British nation, who can boast of commanders warmly attached to that religion and piety which so many, in the present day, treat with contemptuous scorn.

The Reformed Soldier.

A soldier, not long since, becoming visibly religious, met with no little railing, both from his comrades and his officers. He was the servant of one of the latter. At length, his master asked him, "Richard, what good has your religion done you?" The soldier made this discreet answer: "Sir, before I was religious, I used to get drunk; now I am sober. I used to neglect your business; now I perform it diligently." The officer was silenced, and seemed to be satisfied. For so is the will of God, that, with *well-doing*, ye may put to silence the ignorance of foolish men. 1 Peter ii. 15.

THE POOR STUDENT IN DANGER.

BISHOP HORNE, when a student, was very desirous of purchasing the Hebrew Concordance, of Marius de Calasio; but, not knowing how to purchase it out of his allowance, or to ask his father, in plain terms, to make him a present of it, he told him the following story, and left the moral of it to speak for itself.

In the last age, when Bishop Walton's Polyglot was first published, there was at Cambridge, a Mr. Edwards, passionately fond of Oriental learning, who afterwards went by the name of Rabbi Edwards: he was a good man, and a good scholar; but, being rather young in the University, and not very rich, Walton's great work was far above his pocket. Nevertheless, not being able to sleep well without it, he sold his bed and some of his furniture, and made the purchase: in consequence of which, he was obliged to sleep in a large chest, originally made to hold his clothes. But getting into his chest one night rather incautiously, the lid of it, which had a bolt with a spring, fell down upon him, and locked him in past recovery; and there he lay well nigh smothered to death. In the morning, Edwards, who was always an exact man, not appearing, it was wondered what had become of him; till, at last, his bed-maker, or the person who, in better time, *had been his bed-maker*, being alarmed, went to his chambers time enough to release him; and, the accident getting air, came to the ears of his friends, who soon redeemed his bed for him. This story, Mr. Horne told his father; and it had the desired effect.

His father immediately sent him the money; for which he returned him abundant thanks, promising to repay him in the only possible way, viz. that of using the books to the best advantage They were, without question, diligently turned over while he worked at his Commentary on the Psalms, and yielded him no small assistance.

SUBMISSION TO GOD'S WILL.

HOWEVER dark and mysterious the dispensations of Divine Providence may appear to us, it becomes us to resign ourselves to the sovereign pleasure of Him who worketh all things after the counsel of his own will. Let us consider how little we know of the Divine plans. " A Providence occurs," says one; " it strikes us, we endeavour to explain it—but are we certain that we have seized the true meaning? Perhaps what we take as an end may be only the way; what we take as the whole may be only a part; what we deprecate may be a blessing, and what we sup-

plicate may be a curse; what appears confusion may be the tendencies of order; and what looks like the disasters of Providence may be the preparation of its triumph." It is not for us sinful mortals, however tried, either to dictate or to be impatient. Besides, it is only for us to look back, and we shall see the darkness gradually dispersing, and fresh and increasing light thrown on those events which appeared at first so mysterious.

There was a good woman, who, when she was ill, being asked whether she was willing to live or die, answered, "Which God pleaseth." But, said one that stood by, " If God should refer it to you, which would you choose?" " Truly," said she, " if God should refer it to me, I would even refer it to him again."

A gentleman meeting with a shepherd in a misty morning, asked him what weather it would be.—" It will be," said the shepherd, "what weather pleaseth me;" and being asked to express his meaning, said, " Sir, it shall be what weather pleaseth God; and what weather pleaseth God, pleaseth me."

" I see God will have all my heart, and he shall have it," was a fine reflection made by a lady when news was brought of two children drowned, whom she loved very much.

How few can say as Mauritius the Emperor did! When he saw his wife and children slain before his eyes by the traitor Phocas, he said, "Righteous art thou, O Lord, and upright are thy judgments."

"It is a dangerous thing to provoke God by obstinate grief, lest a worse thing come upon us. Where one tear falls upon the account of complying with God's will, a multitude fall in consequence of having our own will. Not only the miseries of this life, but of the life to come, are owing to this unresigned self-will. It may be written on many a tomb, " Here lies the body of N. N. because he would have his own will."

" Let us, therefore, learn to cultivate this spirit of submission to God. Let us consider what a reproach an impatient disposition is to us as Christians; as if God with all his perfections, and heaven with all its glories, were nothing: no; nothing to that child, that husband, that wife, that estate. I have seen a grief so stubborn and savage, as to prove insensible to all the principles and prospects that could be mentioned."

In such cases we fall short of many excellent heathens. We are outdone by those with whom we are ashamed to be compared, considering all things. Some of them had noble sentiments under the loss of estates, relations, or friends. Zeno lost all in a shipwreck; he protested it was the best voyage he ever made in his life, because it proved the occasion of betaking himself to the study of virtue and philosophy. Seneca says, he enjoyed his relations as one that was to lose them; and lost them as one who had them still in possession.

A Spartan woman had five sons in the army on the day of battle. When a soldier came running from the camp to the city to bring tidings, she, waiting at the gate to hear his report, asked, *What news?* Says the messenger, *Thy five sons are slain. You fool*, says she, *I did not ask after them. How goes it in the field of battle?* *Why*, says the messenger, *we have gained the victory;* Sparta *is safe. Then let us be thankful*, says she, *to the gods*, for our deliverance and continued freedom!—Seneca speaks to God in such language as this: "I only want to know your will: as soon as I know what that is, I am always of the same mind. I do not say you have taken from me; that looks as if I were unwilling; but that you have accepted from me; which I am ready to offer."

THE SUBMISSIVE WIFE.

A MARRIED woman was called effectually by Divine grace, and became an exemplary Christian; but her husband was a lover of pleasure and of sin. When spending an evening, as usual, with his jovial companions, at a tavern, the conversation happened to turn on the excellencies and faults of their wives, the husband just mentioned gave the highest encomiums of his wife, saying she was all that was excellent, only she was a d——d methodist. "Notwithstanding which," said he, "such is her command of her temper, that were I to take you, gentlemen, home with me at midnight, and order her to rise and get you a supper, she would be all submission and cheerfulness." The company looking upon this merely as a brag, dared him to make the experiment by a considerable wager. The bargain was made, and about midnight the company adjourned, as proposed. Being admitted, "Where is your mistress?" said the husband to the maid servant who sat up for him. "She is gone to bed, Sir." "Call her up," said he. "Tell her I have brought some friends home with me, and desire she would get up, and prepare them a supper." The good woman obeyed the unreasonable summons; dressed, came down, and received the company with perfect civility; told them she happened to have some chickens ready for the spit, and that supper should be got as soon as possible. The supper was accordingly served up; when she performed the honours of the table with as much cheerfulness as if she had expected company at a proper season.

After supper, the guests could not refrain from expressing their astonishment. One of them particularly, more sober than the rest, thus addressed himself to the lady: "Madam," said he, "your civility fills us all with surprise. Our unreasonable visit is in consequence of a wager, which we have certainly lost. As you are a very religious person, and cannot approve of our conduct, give me leave to ask, what can possibly induce you to behave with so much kindness to us?" "Sir," replied she, "when I married, my husband and myself were both in a carnal state.

It has pleased God to call me out of that dangerous condition. My husband continues in it. I tremble for his future state. Were he to die as he is, he must be miserable for ever; I think it, therefore, my duty to render his present existence as comfortable as possible."

This wise and faithful reply affected the whole company. It left an impression of great use on the husband's mind. " Do you, my dear," said he, " really think I should be eternally miserable? I thank you for the warning. By the grace of God, I will change my conduct." From that time he became another man, a serious Christian, and consequently a good husband.

" Married Christians, especially you who have unconverted partners, receive the admonition intended by this pleasing anecdote. Pray and labour for their conversion, for ' What knowest thou, O wife! whether thou shalt save thy husband? Or how knowest thou, O man! whether thou shalt save thy wife?'" 1 Cor. vii. 16.

THE REFORMED WIFE.

A MAN once came to the late Mr. Scott, of Matlock, complaining of his wife. He said she was so exceedingly ill-tempered, and she studiously tormented him in such a variety of ways, that she was the great burden of his life ; and, notwithstanding all the kind methods he had used to reduce her to a better disposition, she was not at all improved, but grew continually worse and worse. Mr. Scott exhorted him to try what a redoubled affection and kindness would do; observing to him that the command of Christ to husbands was, "to love their wives," and *that* " even as Christ loved the Church."

This advice did not appear to satisfy the man ; and he went away much dejected, resolving, however, if possible, to follow it ; since, though it had not hitherto succeeded, he could not but consider it as founded on the word of God. He accordingly increased his attention ; and, as an instance of his kindness, the next Saturday evening brought to his wife his whole week's wages, and, with an affectionate smile, threw them into her lap, begging her entire disposal of them. This would not succeed; she threw the wages in a volley (accompanied with many bitter execrations) at his head ; and afterwards continued in the practice of every spiteful and malicious trick that she could devise, or (according to the poor man's own conclusion) that Satan himself could suggest, to make his life miserable.

Some years elapsed, during which he sustained, as patiently as he could, this base and undutiful treatment, when Providence favoured him with another interview with his kind friend and father, Mr. Scott. This happened most opportunely, at a time when a neighbour had been telling him a recipe for the cure of refractory wives ; and, as a strong recommendation, mentioned that he had tried it on his own wife with the happiest effects. He therefore came to Mr. Scott with a countenance bespeaking a considerable degree of confidence, which led Mr. Scott, at first, to hope that his former advice had proved successful ; but he was undeceived, by being informed that, through the extremely vicious disposition of the woman, it had operated in a direction, and to a degree, precisely the reverse of what was expected from it. Upon being asked, why then he smiled and looked so pleasantly, he said, he believed he had really found out a remedy, which, if it should meet Mr. Scott's approbation, would not fail of effecting a cure ; for it had been tried by a neighbour of his on a wife, who, though she had been in all respects as bad as his, was, by one application only, become one of the most obedient and affectionate creatures living. " And what is this excellent remedy?" said Mr. Scott. " Why, Sir, it is a good horse-whipping ! You hear, Sir, what good effects have been produced : do you think I may venture to try it?"

Mr. Scott replied, " I read, my friend, nothing about husbands horsewhipping their wives in the Bible, but just the reverse ; namely, love, which I before recommended ; and can by no means alter the word of God : and doubt not, if you persevere, it will be attended with a happy result ;" accompanying his advice with exhortations to more earnest prayer. The man, though he left Mr. Scott both with a mind and countenance very different from those with which he came, resolved to follow his direction, for his esteem of him was very great ; and Providence calling Mr. Scott some time after to preach at Birmingham, his old friend, who then resided there, came into the vestry to him after he had done, and with a countenance expressive of ex, alted happiness, took him by the hand, and said, that he should have reason to bless God to eternity for the advice he had given him ; and that he had not been induced, by his weak importunities, to alter or relax it ; adding that his wife, who then stood smiling approbation by his side, was not only become a converted woman, through a blessing on his kind attentions to her, but was one of the most affectionate and dutiful of wives.

THE SWEARERS REPROVED.

In a family at Shelton lived Mr. G. a person much given to swearing. Mrs. F. being a good woman, had a girl about four years old that was remarkably attentive to every thing of a religious nature. The child would often remark, with great horror of mind, to her mother, how Mr. G. swore, and would wish to reprove him ; but for some time durst not. One time she said to her mother, " Does Mr. G. say our Father ?" (a term by which she called her prayers.) Mrs. F. would not tell. She then said, "I will watch, and, if he does, I will tell him of swearing so."

She did watch him, and saw him say his prayers privately in bed. Soon after this, she heard him swear bitterly ; upon which she said to him, " Did not you say Our Father this morning ? How dare you swear ! Do you think he will be your Father if you swear ?" He answered not a word, but seemed amazed, as well he might. He did not live long after this ; but he was never heard to swear again. So true is that Scripture, " Out of the mouths of babes and sucklings hast thou ordained praise."

A Persian, humble servant of the sun,
Who, though devout, yet bigotry had none ;
Hearing a lawyer, grave in his address,
With adjurations every word impress,
Suppos'd the man a bishop, or at least—
God's name so much upon his lips—a priest ;
Bow'd at the close with all his graceful airs,
And begg'd an interest in his frequent prayers. *Cowper.*

Two gentlemen having called at a coffee house in the city, and drank a bottle together, when about to part, both insisted on paying. One put a seven-shilling piece on the table, and swore dreadfully that his friend should be at no expense ; the other jocularly said, " That seven-shilling piece is a bad one," on which the other swore still faster. The master of the house, hearing what passed, came forward and said, if they would allow him to examine the money, he would tell them whether or not it was good. Returning soon after, he, in the most polite manner, laid the piece before them on a card printed as follows :

It chills my blood to hear the blest Supreme
Rudely appeal'd to on each trifling theme.
Maintain your rank, vulgarity despise ;
To swear is neither brave, polite, nor wise.
You would not swear upon a bed of death :
Reflect ; your Maker *now* could stop your breath.

The gentlemen read it, and he who had sworn, owned " He was justly and properly reproved, and would in future be more guarded in his expressions."

For more instances, see volume I.

The Swearer Punished.

Some years ago T. G. who lived in the parish of *Sedgley*, near *Wolverhampton*, having lost a considerable sum by a match at cock-fighting, to which practice he was notoriously addicted, swore, in the most horrid manner, that he would never fight another cock as long as he lived; frequently calling upon God to damn his soul to all eternity if he did, and, with dreadful imprecations, wishing the devil might fetch him if ever he made another bet.

It is not to be wondered at if resolutions so impiously formed should be broken : for a while, however, they were observed ; but he continued to indulge himself in every other abomination to which his depraved heart inclined him. But, about two years afterwards, Satan, whose willing servant he was, inspired him with a violent desire to attend a cocking at *Wolverhampton ;* and he complied with the temptation. When he came to the place, he stood up as in defiance of heaven, and cried, "I hold four to three on such a cock."— "Four what ?" said one of his companions in iniquity. "Four shillings," replied he.—"I'll lay," said the other. Upon which they confirmed the wager, and, as his custom was, he threw down his hat, and put his hand in his pocket for the money ; when, awful to relate, he instantly fell a ghastly corpse to the ground. Terrified at his sudden death, some who were present for ever after desisted from this infamous sport ; but others, hardened in iniquity, proceeded in the barbarous diversion, as soon as the dead body was removed from the spot.

This melancholy circumstance happened on a Thursday. On the Sabbath following, when a number of his relations and neighbours were conveying his body to the grave, a dog, that belonged to one of the company, happened to run under the coffin, (which was carried, I suppose, underhand, by napkins, or on a bier,) and was struck to all appearance dead : but being again recovered and let loose, ran a second time under the coffin, and was taken up actually dead, to the great astonishment of the company. Those who conveyed the corpse were so terrified, that they durst not, for the present, proceed to the churchyard, but proposed to leave the body on the spot; at length, however, resuming their courage, they conveyed him to the grave.

" *The fear of the wicked shall come upon him ;*" and " *Who ever hardened himself against God, and prospered ?*" By such signal interpositions of Divine Providence, the Lord shows he hath not forsaken the earth. May "many," who read or "hear" these lines, "fear, and turn to the Lord !"

SUPERSTITIOUS RITES.

THE following accounts will afford us an idea of the awful and miserable state of poor wretched heathens:

" As I was returning from Calcutta," says Mr. Carey, " I saw the *Sahamocon*, or a woman burning herself with the corpse of her husband, for the first time in my life. We were near the village of Noya Serai (Rennel, in his chart of the Hoogly river, spells it Niaserai.) As it was evening, we got out of the boat to walk, when we saw a number of people assembled on the river side. I asked them for what they were met, and they told me, to burn the body of a dead man. I inquired, whether his wife would die with him. They answered, 'yes;' and pointed to the woman. She was standing by the pile, which was made of large billets of wood, about two feet and a half high, four feet long, and two wide; on the top of which lay the dead body of her husband. Her nearest relation stood by her; and near her was a small basket of sweetmeats, called *kivy.* I asked them, whether this was the woman's choice, or whether she were brought to it by any improper influences. They answered, that it was perfectly voluntary. I talked till reasoning was of no use; and then began to exclaim, with all my might, against what they were doing; telling them that it was a shocking murder! They told me, it was a great act of holiness; and added, in a very surly manner, that, if I did not like to see it, I might go farther off; and desired me to go. I told them that I would not go; that I was determined to stay and see the murder; and that I should certainly bear witness of it at the tribunal of God. I exhorted the woman not to throw away her life; to fear nothing, for no evil would follow her refusing to burn. But she, in the calmest manner, mounted the pile, and danced on it, with her hands extended, as if in the utmost tranquillity of spirit. Previous to her mounting the pile, the relation, whose office it was to set fire to it, led her six times round it, at two intervals; that is, thrice at each circumambulation. As she went round, she scattered the sweetmeats above mentioned among the people, who picked them up, and ate them as very holy things. This being ended, and she having mounted the pile, and danced as above mentioned (which appeared only designed to show us her contempt of death, and to prove to us that her dying was voluntary) she then lay down by the corpse, and put one arm under its neck, and the other over it; when a quantity of dry cocoa leaves, and other substances, were heaped over them to a considerable height, and then *ghee*, or melted preserved butter, poured on the top. Two bamboos were then put over them, and held fast down, and fire put to the pile, which immediately blazed very fiercely, owing to the dry and combustible materials of which it was composed. No sooner was the fire kindled, than all the people set up a great shout, 'Hurre Bol!' 'Hurre Bol!' which is a common shout of joy, and an invocation of Hurree, the wife of Hur or Seeb. It was impossible to have heard the woman, had she groaned, or even cried aloud,

on account of the mad noise of the people; and it was impossible for her to stir or struggle, on account of the bamboos, which are held down upon them like the levers of a press. We made much objection to their using these bamboos, and insisted that it was using force to prevent the woman getting up when the fire burned her; but they declared it was only done to keep the pile from falling down. We could not bear to see more, but left them; exclaiming loudly against the murder, and full of horror at what we had seen."

What a dreadful custom! yet it is said that many thousands of such victims perish annually in the East Indies.

"This evening," says Mr. Ward, "we went to see a man rise from his grave who had been buried a month! A great crowd was collected, and every one waiting with impatience to see the resurrection. Brother Carey had some conversation with one of the Musselmans, who asked, upon his denying the divine mission of Mahommed, what was to become of Musselmans and Hindoos. Brother Carey expressed his fears that they would all be lost. The man seemed as if he would have torn him in pieces. At length, when the new moon appeared, the top of the grave was opened, and the man came forth, apparently unaltered by his confinement. He bowed with his head to the ground several times at the foot of a plantain tree, which, I suppose, he had planted on going into the grave, and upon which he also poured water. It was necessary that he should see the new moon immediately on coming forth from his confinement. Many crowded round him, and put out their hands for a gift, which all who asked obtained, and which, as far as I could see, consisted merely of particles of dust. Several persons brought presents, and it was probable a goat was offered in sacrifice after we were gone. This subterraneous abode was cut very deep, and divided into three or four rooms;

one to sit in, another to sleep in, &c. It was covered over with mats and soil, and the only opening into it was a hole at one end, two or three inches in diameter; through which he was supplied with milk and fruits by a man who waited on him, and who had a hut by the side of the grave. This is a Musselman's custom; and they say it has an allusion to the flight of their prophet. Perhaps it would not be continued, but that it is a qualification for receiving lands or offerings to canonized saints among them. Many persons in this country have built places like raised tombs, in a hole of the centre of which a lamp is kept burning in the night: these are consecrated to some saint, and the person who tends the lamp has whatever is given or left to the place. Passengers make their *salem*, and throw down a few *cowries* as they pass. In the above cave, some ground had been left to the place, and the man could succeed to it only by burying himself a month."

The following account of sacrificing aged persons and children to the Ganges, where they are devoured by sharks, is very affecting. These sacrifices are of two descriptions; first, of aged persons of both sexes, which are voluntary; and of children, which, of course, are involuntary. The fixed periods for the performance of those rites are at the full moons in November and January. The custom of sacrificing children arises from superstitious vows made by the parents, who, when apprehensive of not having issue, promised, in the event of their having five children, to devote the fifth to the Ganges.

"The island of Sagar, where these inhuman rites are administered, is held to be peculiarly sacred, from its being considered as the termination of the Ganges; and the junction of that river with the sea, is denominated, *The Place of Sacrifice.*

"So lately as November, 1801, some European seamen belonging to the pilot service of Bengal being on shore on the island, were witnesses to this horrid ceremony. The information they gave before one of the justices of the peace for Calcutta was on oath to the following effect:

"That, on going on shore, they saw the entrails of a human body floating on the water, and at the same time a great number of the natives assembled on the beach; as near as they could guess, about three thousand: that on asking a Fakeer, why so many of the natives were put into the water, he answered, that the Head Fakeer had ordered them to go into the water to be devoured by sharks, for the prosperity of their respective families; that they saw eleven men, women, and boys, thus destroyed: and it further appeared, by other incontestable evidence, that the victims destroyed in November amounted to thirty-nine; and, moreover, that a boy about twelve years old, who had been thrown into the river, having saved himself by swimming, a Gosayne endeavoured to extend his protection to him; but, singular and unnatural as it may appear, he was again seized, and committed to destruction by his own parents!!!"

How ought the recital of these dreadful customs to cherish in us a love for our own country, and gratitude for that gospel which is the glory of it! and how ought it to rouse us to the most ardent concern for the diffusion of gospel light where there is so much darkness! What a cold, yea, what a barbarous heart must that be, which would ask, 'What have Christians to do with this?' and how criminal those who refuse to lend a helping hand to so noble a work!

SUPERSTITION EXPOSED.

WHEN the celebrated John Knox went to Glasgow, he was informed that the great bell in the church there had the power of striking any heretic dead who presumed to touch it. He was requested to go and try it. He declined going up into the steeple, but, it is said, he requested it might be taken down and brought into the street, and he would venture to touch it. It was accordingly done, and he brought it to the test in the most public manner. The bell being laid in the street, he said it should either kill him, or he kill it; and for that purpose he provided a number of men with great hammers. He stood over it, and uttered the most severe sentiments he could against the Pope and church of Rome, as being the great Antichrist, and the whore of Babylon, as well as against the abominable doctrine it taught, and the wickedness of its priests. When the superstitious multitude should have witnessed this vile heretic drop down dead, he suddenly ordered his men to break the bell in pieces.—Thus was the imposture justly detected, and the Protestant faith confirmed and increased.

A Neapolitan shepherd came in anguish to his priest, "Father, have mercy on a miserable sinner. It is the holy season of Lent; and, while I was busy at work, some whey spurting from the cheese-press flew into my mouth, and, wretched man! I swallowed it. Free my distressed conscience from its agonies, by absolving me from my guilt!"—"Have you no other sins to confess?" said his spiritual guide. "No; I do not know that I have committed any other."—"There are," said the priest, "many robberies and murders from time to time committed on your mountains, and I have reason to believe you are one of the persons concerned in them." "Yes," he replied, "I am; but these are never accounted a crime; it is a thing practised by us all, and there needs no confession on that account."—Was not this straining at a gnat and swallowing a camel with a witness? yet many act little better than this man.

THE YOUTH RESTORED.

A young gentleman being reproved by his mother for being religious, he made her this answer: "I am resolved by all means to save my soul."

Some time after, he fell into a lukewarm state, during which time he was sick and nigh unto death. One night he dreamed that he saw himself summoned before God's angry throne, and from thence hurried into a place of torments; where, seeing his mother full of scorn, she upbraided him with his former answer, "why he did not save his soul by all means." This was so much impressed on his mind when he awoke, that, under God, it became the mean of his returning again to him: and, when any asked him the reason why he became again religious, he gave no other answer than this: "*If I could not in my dream endure my mother's upbraiding my folly and lukewarmness, how shall I be able to suffer that God should call me to an account in the last day, and the angels reproach my lukewarmness, and the devils aggravate my sins, and all the saints of God deride my follies and hypocrisies?*"

ADVERSITY SANCTIFIED.

AFFLICTION, as one observes, is of great advantage to the young. It humbles their pride, convinces them of their dependance on God, and that to him they owe all they have. It corrects extravagant expectations, restrains from sensual indulgences, and sometimes becomes the means of conversion to God.

A young man, who had been long confined with a diseased limb, and was near his dissolution, was attended by a friend, who requested that the wound might be uncovered. When this was done, "There," said the young man, "there it is, and a precious treasure it has been to me; it saved me from the folly and vanity of youth; it made me cleave to God as my only portion, and to eternal glory as my only hope; and I think it hath now brought me very near to my Father's house." Let not the young, then, imagine that a state of prosperity is always the best for them. Adversity, when sanctified, invigorates the mind, inures to hardships, teaches to sympathise with others; whereas prosperous situations in life enervate the mind, and may be compared to those countries where the sun shines with a scorching heat, and where nature pours all the necessaries, nay, the luxuries of life, in the greatest profusion, at man's feet. Happy they who, in early life, are enabled to devote themselves to the service of God; for should they be called to bear the yoke of affliction, they shall then feel resigned to the divine will, and acknowledge he doth all things well!

Afflictions, under the divine blessing, are rendered peculiarly profitable to believers. Hence many can join the Psalmist, Psa. cxix. 71, in saying, "It is good to be afflicted." It was the saying of a German divine, in his sickness, "In this disease I have learned how great God is, and what the evil of sin is; I never knew to what purpose God was before, nor what sin meant, till now." The Jews, under all the thunderings of the prophets, retained their idols, but after their Babylonish captivity no idols were found amongst them. Manasseh's chain was more profitable to him than his crown. When Tiribazus was arrested, he drew his sword, and defended himself; but when they told him that they came to take him to the king, he willingly yielded. So, though a saint may at first be a little impatient, yet when he is reminded that his afflictions are to bring him nearer to God, he yields, and kisses the rod. When Munster lay sick, and his friends asked him how he did, he pointed to his sores and ulcers, and said, "These are God's gems and jewels, wherewith he decketh his best friends, and to me they are more precious than all the gold and silver in the world."—"I think," said a celebrated minister, "that I have seldom had very sweet days, except when I have met with afflictions one way or other; yet the Lord deals so tenderly with me in my afflictions, that indeed I think

the strokes, as it were, go nearer *his* heart than *mine*."

The dispensations of divine Providence, though sometimes apparently severe, yet are all founded in wisdom and goodness. Manasseh, Nebuchadnezzar, Hezekiah, Job, David, Paul, and many others, have found their afflictions useful. Many have had reason to be thankful for their sickness, losses, poverty, disappointments. Winceslaus, King of Bohemia, after the defeat and flight of his army, being himself taken captive by the enemy, was asked how he did. His answer was,—"Never better. While I had all my army about me, I could find but little time to think on God; whereas now, being stripped of all earthly dependance, I think on God alone, and betake myself wholly to his providence."

May we not say, as Themistocles once did, "I had been undone, if I had not been undone?" Trouble makes way for the word to come to the conscience. David speaks of his affliction in higher terms than he did of his crown, Psa. cxix. 71. One said in affliction, "Strike on, strike on, strike on, Lord, for now I begin to know that I am a child of thine;" or, as the great Pascal said under affliction, "Now I begin to be a Christian." Pascal died August 19, 1662.

APPLAUSE DANGEROUS.

"THAT they be not high minded," was the charge Timothy was to give those who abounded in riches. But there are other characters besides the wealthy to whom it is applicable. For instance: it is a lamentable fact, that however desirable popularity may be in some respects, it has often been the occasion of a man's ruin. Those who are constantly receiving the applause of their fellow-creatures, stand, therefore, in particular need of the above-mentioned caution.

Draco was a celebrated lawgiver of Athens. His popularity, it is said, was uncommon; but the attention and kindness of his admirers proved fatal to him. Appearing in a public assembly, he was received with repeated applauses, and the people, according to the custom of the Athenians, showed their respect to their lawgiver, by throwing garments upon him. This was done in such profusion, that Draco was soon hid under them, and smothered by the too great veneration of his citizens. Thus the flatteries of some, and the applause of others, may become the occasion of much evil, by so inspiring us with pride, and filling us with self-complacency, as either to relax the exertion of intellect, or make us suppose that we are such a superior order of beings as gradually to excite the contempt of others, and finally to change our popularity into disgust. Let us, then, keep a vigilant eye, not on our enemies only, but on our friends, since a man's life may be equally destroyed by a profusion of that which is sweet and pleasant, as by that which is rank and poisonous.

APPROBATION.

MAN is a creature of feeling as well as intellect, and while he is directed by the one, he is often moved by the other. The following instance will show how the approbation and kindness of others affect the human mind.

The admirers of the celebrated composer Haydn, who were exceedingly numerous, were very desirous of testifying their regard to him in his old age, in a public manner, by performing the Creation, one of Haydn's chief works. The room contained about one thousand five hundred persons, and was full two hours before he arrived. As soon as it was known that he was coming, the eagerness of the audience could scarcely be contained. Some of the first rank waited to receive him. The illustrious old man was borne on a chair to the place reserved for him, amidst the acclamations of an enthusiastic audience. Such was the effect of the scene, that, oppressed at once with joy and infirmity, with a faltering voice he exclaimed, "This

is more than I have ever felt: let me die now, and be received among the blessed in another world!"

When the performance was ended, he was taken out with the same triumph as he entered. He raised his arms, as it were, to leave his blessing on the assembly, and just two months and a half afterwards he expired, in his seventy-sixth year.

If Haydn was so deeply affected at the kindness of his friends, and thought there was nothing worth living for after this, how much more may the Christian rejoice in the approbation of his Lord, and, enjoying an interest in Christ, may willingly leave this world, to be with the blessed above!

THE ATHEIST'S CONCLUSION.

DIAGORUS saw a servant of his stealing from him, and upon his denial of the theft, brought him before a statue of Jupiter thundering, and constrained him to adjure Jupiter, for the honour of his Deity, and of justice and fidelity, to strike him dead at his feet with thunder if he were guilty of the fact: and after three times repeating the dreadful oath, he went away untouched, without harm. Upon the sight of this, Diagorus cried out, as in the poet,

*. . . . . Audis
Jupiter hæc, nec labra moves cum mittere
vocem
Debueras vel marmoreus, vel ahœneus?*

Dost hear
This, Jove, nor movest thy lips, when fit it
were
Thy brass or marble spoke?

And whereas he should have been convinced that a statue could not be a God, he impiously concluded that God was nothing but a statue; and from that time was hardened in irreclaimable atheism. So another atheist reports of some Romans, that they successfully deceived by false oaths, even in the most sacred temple, in the presence of their supreme Deity, the repugnant avenger of purity; and because vengeance did not immediately overtake guilt, he acknowledges no other God but the world and nature, unconcerned in the governing of human affairs.

Extorted confessions from Atheists.

Sharp afflictions will awaken the apprehensions of a God in the most stupified consciences, and inspire them with new life and motion, and make them breathe out humble supplications for mercy and help to the Deity whom they denied before. Of this we have numerous instances ; I will produce some that were signal.

It is recorded by Æschylus, that the Persian messenger, in his narrative to the king of the overthrow of his army by the Grecians, related, that those gallants who, before the fight, in the midst of their cups and bravery, denied God and Providence, as secure of victory, yet afterwards, when furiously pursued by the ene my, they came to the river Strymon, which was frozen and began to thaw, when, upon their knees, they mournfully implored the favour of God that the ice might hold and give them a safe passage over from their pursuers.

Nature in extremities has irresistible workings, and the inbred notions of the Deity, though long suppressed by imperious lusts, will then rise up in men's souls. Tullus Hostilius is another example, who disdained to express submission to God by acts of worship, as a thing unbecoming his royal state ; but when his stubborn, fierce mind was broken in his diseased body, he used all the servile rites of superstition, and commanded the people to join with him, thinking, by his flattering devotions, to appease the incensed Deity.

Bion, the philosopher, was a declared atheist, till struck with a mortal disease, and then, as a false witness on the rack, confessed the truth, and addressed himself by prayers and vows to God for his recovery. Egregious folly, as the historian observes, to think that God would be bribed by his gifts, and was or not according to his fancy ! And thus it happens to many like him. As a lamp near expiring shines more clearly, so con-

science, burning dimly for a time, gives a dying blaze, and discovers HIM who is able to save and to destroy.

But how just were it to deal with them as Herofilus with Diodorus Cronus, a wrangler, that vexed the philosophers by urging a captious argument against the possibility of mo- tion ! For thus he argued : a stone, or whatever else, in moving itself, is either where it is, or where it is not ; if where it is, it moves not ; if where it is not, then it will be in any place but where it is. While this disputing humour continued, he one day fell and displaced his shoulder, and sent in haste for Herofilus, of excellent skill in surgery. But he, desirous first to cure his brain, and then his shoulder, told him, that his art was needless in that case ; " for, according to your own opinion, this bone, in the dislocation, either was where it was, or where it was not, and, to assert either, makes the displacing of it equally impossible : therefore, it is in vain to reduce it to the place from whence it was never parted." And thus he kept him wearing out, with pain and rage, till he declared himself convinced of the vanity of his irrefutable argument. Now, if, according to the impiety of atheists, there be no God, why do they invoke him in their adversities ? If there be, why do they deny him in their prosperity ? There can be no other reason assigned but this, that in their state of health, their minds are clouded with blind folly ; in sickness they are serious, and recover the judgment of nature. As it is ordinarily with distracted persons, that in the approaches of death, their reason returns, because the brain, distempered by an excess of heat, when the spirits are wasted, at last is reduced to a convenient temper.

FILIAL AFFECTION.

PERO was a daughter of Cimon, remarkable for her filial affection.— When her father had been sent to prison, where his judges had con- demned him to starve, she supported his life by giving him the milk of her breasts, as to her own child.

ADVICE.

THOMAS PORTER, a plain and simple man, whom Dr. Doddridge mentions, in his Memoirs of Colonel Gardiner, that he was very deficient in natural things, yet he enjoyed the gift of a vast retention, both of scripture phrases and scripture places; and had an aptness of applying suitable texts in a wonderful, though he pointed them out in an awkward manner. Two young persons, whose intentions were to be married in a short time, applied to him, acquainting him with their circumstances, and requesting a text; he immediately pointed them to Psalm xlvi. 10.— " Be still, and know that I am God," &c., as altogether suitable to their case. The parties were quite at a loss how to apply this to their intentions, and replied, that he must be mistaken, asking for another; but Thomas insisted on it, he had no other for them. The parties retired; but Providence soon explained that scripture, for, within a few days, by a sudden illness, one of the parties died, and the survivor was left to learn the needful lesson of submission to HIS will, who does as it pleases him in heaven or earth.

Paternal Advice.

A GENTLEMAN had two children, the one a daughter, who was very plain in her person, the other a son, who was a great beauty. One day, as they were playing together, they saw their faces in a looking-glass; upon which, the boy was so charmed with his beauty, that he extolled it mightily to his sister, who felt these praises as so many reflections on her own features. She accordingly acquainted her father with the affair, and complained of her brother's rudeness to her. Upon this, the old gentleman, instead of being angry, took his children on his knees, and, embracing them both with the greatest tenderness, gave them the following advice : " I would have you both look

at yourselves in the glass every day; you, my son, that you may be reminded never to dishonour the beauty of your face, by the deformity of your actions; and you, my daughter, that you may take care to hide the defect of beauty in your person, by the superior lustre of a virtuous and amiable conduct."

OLD AGE.

THE more advanced the true Christian is in years, the nearer he approaches his home; the more desirous is he to enjoy the presence of his God, and to be conformed to him.

As Julianus said, that when he had one foot in the grave, he would have the other in the school; so, though an old disciple hath one foot in the grave, yet he will have the other in Christ's school, that he may still be learning more of his love and grace. It is this only, he knows, will prepare him for every danger, bear him up under every infirmity, and excite his confidence to the end.

Confidius, a senator of Rome, told Cæsar, boldly, that the senators durst not come to council for fear of his soldiers; he replied, " Why, then, dost thou go to the senate ?" He answered, " Because my age takes away my fear." So, none more courageous in evil days, than aged Christians, who have long experienced the power of divine grace.

Vespasian, the Roman emperor, was so tired with the pomp of his triumph, that in the triumphant way, he often reproached himself, that, being an old man, he was engaged in such an empty and tedious show.

THE CHILD'S ADMONITION;
OR, THE LADY REPROVED.

IT is well to be corrected, even by a child. A noble lady says, (Mr. W—— told me,) that when she was weeping, on account of one of her children's death, her little daughter came innocently to her one day, and said, "Mamma, is God Almighty dead, that you cry so?" The lady, blushing, said, "No."——She then said, "Madam, will you lend me your glove?" She lent it her accordingly; and, after that, asking for it again; upon which, the child said— "Now, you have taken the glove from me, shall I cry, because you have taken away your own glove? And shall you cry because God has taken away my sister?"

ANECDOTE OF MR. ANDERSON.

MR. DAVID ANDERSON, once minister of Walton-upon-Thames, fearing the return of popery, went with his wife and five small children, to reside at Middleburg, in Zealand.— After a time, he was reduced to the greatest distress, but was restrained by modesty from making his case known. One morning, however, after he had been at prayer with his family, when they were all in tears together, because his children asked bread for breakfast, and he had none to give them, the bell rang, and Mrs. Anderson found a person at the door, who gave her a paper containing forty pieces of gold, which, he said, a gentleman had sent her. Soon after, a countryman brought a horse-load of provisions, but neither of the messengers would say from whom they were sent. Afterwards, money was regularly conveyed to Mr. Anderson to pay his rent, and ten pounds sterling every quarter, yet to the day of his death, he never discovered who was his benefactor. But Mr. John Quick, pastor of the English church at Middleburg, in 1681, was told by M. de Kening, a magistrate, that he carried the money to Mr. Anderson, being then apprentice to Myn-Heer de Hoste, a pious merchant of that place; who, observing a grave English minister, apparently in want, and dejected, privately inquired into his circumstances; and, with all possible secrecy, made him those remittances, saying, "God forbid that any of Christ's ambassadors should be strangers, and in distress, and we neglect to assist them!"

BIBLE ANECDOTES,
And happy effects of distributing the Bible.

THE Rev. Mr. Ramftler, of Fulneck, mentioned the case of a Hottentot who had been a despiser of every thing good, and, from his vicious habits and gross conduct, a terror to all decent persons. One day, returning home intoxicated, he had to swim across a deep river, but being disabled by the liquor, he laid himself down and slept off its effects. When he awoke he was impressed with a sense of his awful state; for he had often been warned. Under these convictions, he was much distressed to know how to pray. He went to his master, a Dutchman, to consult with him, but his master gave him no encouragement. A sense of his wickedness increased, and he had no one near him to direct him. Occasionally, however, he was admitted with the family at the time of prayer. The portion of Scripture which was one day read by the master, was the parable of the Pharisee and publican. While the prayer of the Pharisee was read, the poor Hottentot thought within himself, "this is a *good* man; here is nothing for me;" but when his master came to the prayer of the Publican, God be merciful to me a sinner—"this suits me," he cried; "now I know *how* to pray!" With this prayer he immediately retired, and prayed night and day for two days, and then found peace. Full of joy and gratitude, he went into the fields, and as he had no one to whom he could speak, he exclaimed, "*Ye hills, ye rocks, ye trees, ye rivers*, hear what God has done for my soul!—he has been merciful to me, a sinner."

The Rev. Mr. Newton, of Wakefield, speaking in favour of Bible Associations, mentioned a circumstance which took place in one of the Associations at the west end of London. The persons who had undertaken to solicit subscriptions called on the master of an alehouse, who refused to subscribe. They proceeded to state some of the benefits of the Associations, and the great want of Bibles ; but still he refused. They then asked his reason. He replied, " They do harm." "How so ?" "Why since the poor have subscribed to your Association they have not frequented my house so much as they did." " But they still will come to you for what they want." " True ; but before they used to come on Sunday evenings, and smoke their pipes, but now they stay at home and read their Bibles—I will therefore have nothing to say to you." The friends of the Bible, however, still persevered, saying, "Those who read their Bibles, there find written, '*Owe no man any thing ;*' they therefore learn to pay for what they have."

"Ah! ah! I never thought of that," cried he ; "it is better, then, I find, to sell less, than to have *many bad debts ;*" and with this he immediately subscribed.

At a late meeting of the Aberdeen Auxiliary Bible Society, the following pleasing anecdote was related by the Rev. Mr. Grant, of Orkney, who was an eye-witness of the scene. " Last year," said he, "a vessel for Stockholm, in Sweden, was driven upon our coast in a tremendous gale, and became a total wreck, so situated that no human aid could possibly be administered for the preservation of the crew. In a short time after the vessel struck she went in pieces. The spectators on shore beheld with pungent grief the awful situation of those on board ; but those on shore could render no assistance. All on board perished except one man, and he, driven by the merciless waves upon a piece of the wreck, entwined amongst the ropes attached to the mast. *Half naked and half drowned* he reached the shore, and was disengaged by those on shore from his heart-rending situation. As soon as they rescued him, astonishment filled their minds by observing a small parcel, tied firmly round his waist with a handkerchief. Some conclud-ed it was his money ; others it was the ship's papers ; and others said it was his watch. The handkerchief was unloosed, and, to their surprise and astonishment, it was his Bible—a Bible given to the lad's father from the British and Foreign Bible Society. Upon the blank leaf was a prayer written, that the Lord might make the present gift the means of saving his son's soul. Upon the other blank leaf was an account how the Bible came into the old man's hands ; and that gratitude to the British and Foreign Bible Society which inspires the heart of every Christian, was undisguisedly written by the old man. The request was that the son should make it the man of his counsel, and that he could not allow his son to depart from home without giving him the best pledge of his love—a Bible, although that gift deprived the other parts of the family. The Bible bore evident marks of being often read with tears.

When Mr. Chamberlaine, one of the Missionaries in India, was travelling a route he had been some time before, he called at a village where he had left a Testament ; what was the effect? That single Testament had been attended with a divine power, so that they loaded his horse with their idol gods.

Bible, Admonitions of.

Among the Lacedæmonians, there was a law that none should inform his neighbour of any evil that had befallen him ; but every man should be left to find it out in process of time. How many ministers and people act as if such a law existed in Britain ! They dare not tell, and are unwilling to be told, that "the wages of sin is death," and that the wrath of God abideth on every unbeliever. But the law of God's house is exactly the reverse of that we have mentioned. "Son of man," saith the Lord, "I have made thee a watchman unto the house of Israel," &c. &c.

Bible, Attachment to.

One thing which evidently distinguishes the Christian from other characters, is his attachment to the Bible. Some have been ready to part with all rather than with the Scriptures. We read of one that gave a load of hay for only a leaf of one of the Epistles. The famous Boyle, who died 30th December, 1691, said, speaking of the Scriptures, "I prefer a sprig of the tree of life to a whole wood of bay." Judge Hale, that ornament of his profession and country, said that "if he did not honour God's word by reading a portion of it every morning, things went not well with him all the day." Robert, King of Sicily, said, "the holy books are dearer to me than my kingdom, and were I under any necessity of quitting one it should be my diadem." M. De Rentz, a French nobleman, used to read three chapters a day with his head uncovered and on his bended knees. And such is the love of every Christian to the sacred volume, that they esteem it, as Job says, "more than their necessary food."

THE PRAYING BOY.

A GENTLEMAN was not long since called upon to visit a dying female. On entering the humble cottage where she dwelt, he heard, in an adjoining room, an infant voice. He listened, and found that it was the child of the poor dying woman engaged in prayer. "O Lord, bless my poor mother," cried the little boy, "and prepare her to die! O God, I thank thee that I have been sent to a Sunday school, and there have been taught to read my Bible : and there I learn that 'when my father and mother forsake me, thou wilt take me up!'—This comforts me now that my poor mother is going to leave me ; may it comfort her, and may she go to heaven—and may I go there too! O Lord Jesus, pity a poor child! and pity my poor dear mother ; and help me to say, Thy will be done." He

ceased ; and the visiter, opening the door, approached the bedside of the poor woman. "Your child has been praying with you," said he ; "I have listened to his prayer." "Yes," said she, making an effort to rise ; "he is a dear child.—Thank God he has been sent to a Sunday school : I cannot read myself, but he can ; and he has read the Bible to me, and I hope I have reason to bless God for it.—Yes, I have learned from him that I am a sinner : I have heard from him of Jesus Christ ; and I do—yes, I do, as a poor sinner, put my trust in him. I hope he will preserve me. I hope he has forgiven me!—I am going to die, but I am not afraid ; my dear child has been the means of saving my soul.—O how thankful am I that he was sent to a Sunday school!"

The Forgiving Boy.

In a school at Youghal, an instance lately occurred, in the master's accidental absence, of one boy being provoked to strike another. On hearing the complaint the master determined on punishing the culprit, when the aggrieved boy entreated pardon for the offender. On being asked why he would interpose to prevent a just example, he said, "I was reading in the New Testament lately, that Jesus Christ said we should forgive our enemies, and I wish to forgive him, and I beg he may not be punished for my sake." This Christian plea was too powerful to be resisted. The offender was pardoned, and the parent of the poor boy was highly pleased at the circumstance.

Caffre Boy.

A Caffre boy, twelve years old, was asked whether he did not repent having come to Guadenthall, (the missionary settlement of the Moravian brethren.) He answered in the negative. The missionary observing—"but in the Caffre country you had meat in plenty, and excellent milk, and here you cannot get it ;" he replied, "that is very true ; but

I wish to become a child of God, and I hear in this place how I may attain it; but, in my own country, I hear nothing of it; therefore I rejoice that I am come hither, and am satisfied with any thing."

Young reader, learn from this poor African boy how to prize your privileges in England, and to be thankful for you food, however plain.

The Extraordinary Boys.

A child, under eight years of age, has lately been exhibited at Spring Gardens, possessed of wonderful powers for performing arithmetical operations. His name is Zerah Colburn, and he was born at Cabut, in Vermont, in the United States of America, on the 1st of September, 1804. About two years ago, being at that time not six years of age, he first began to show his wonderful powers of calculation. His father, who had not given him any other instruction than such as is to obtained at a small school, was surprised to hear him repeating one day the products of several numbers. The news of this infant prodigy soon circulated through the neighbourhood, and the father was encouraged to undertake the tour of the United States, and finally to visit London, where they arrived on the 12th of May, 1812. He determines, with the greatest facility and despatch, the exact number of minutes or seconds in any given period of time. He tells the exact product arising from the multiplication of any number, consisting of two, three, or four figures; or any number consisting of six or seven places of figures, being proposed, he will determine, with expedition and ease, all the factors of which it is composed. This singular faculty consequently extends to the extraction of the square and cube roots of the number proposed; and likewise to the means of determining whether it be a prime number. At a meeting of friends, this child raised the number eight progressively to the sixteenth power, and in naming the last result, 881,474,976,710,656, he was

S

right in every figure. He was asked the square root of 106929, and before the number could be written down he answered 327. He was then required to name the cube root of 268,336,125, and, with equal facility and promptness, replied 645. One of the party requested him to name the factors which produced the number 247483, which he immediately did by mentioning the two numbers 941 and 263; which indeed are the only two numbers that will produce it.

Another of them proposed 171395, and he named the following factors as the only ones that would produce it, viz. 5×34279, 7×24485, 59×2905, 83×2063, 35×4897, 295×581, and 413×415.

He was then asked to give the factors of 36083, but he immediately replied that it had none, which, in fact, was the case, as 36083 is a prime number. One gentleman asked him how many minutes there were in forty-eight years; and before the question could be written down, he replied 25,228,800, and instantly added, that the number of seconds in the same period was 1,513,728,000. In one case he was asked to tell the square of 4395; he at first hesitated, but, when he applied himself to it, he said it was 19,316,020. On being questioned as to the cause of his hesitation he replied that he did not like to multiply four figures by four figures; "but," said he, "I found out another way; I multiplied 293 by 293, and then multiplied this product by the number 15, which produced the same result." On another occasion, the Duke of Gloucester asked him the product of 21,734 multiplied by 543; he instantly replied 11,801,562: but upon some remarks being made, the child said he had, in his own mind multiplied 65202 by 181. Although, in the first instance, it is evident that 4395 is equal to 293×15, and consequently that $(4395)^2 = (293)^2 \times (15)^2$; and that in the second case, 543 is equal to 181×3, and, consequently, that $21734 \times (181 + 3) = (21734 \times 3) \times 181$; yet it is remarkable that this combination should be immediately perceived by the child. Perhaps this child possesses an intuitive knowledge of some important properties of numbers ; and although he is incapable at present of giving any satisfactory account of the state of his mind, or of communicating to others the knowledge which it is so evident he does possess ; yet there is reason to believe that, when his mind is more cultivated, he will be able to divulge the mode by which he operates, and to point out some new principles of calculation. With this view a number of gentlemen have taken the child under their patronage, and have formed themselves into a committee for the purpose of superintending his education.

George Bidder, the wonderful calculating boy, was introduced, on Thursday, April the 6th, 1815, to her Majesty and the Princesses, by the Bishop of Salisbury, before whom he exhibited his surprising talents. Of these talents we cannot speak in terms sufficiently strong to express our wonder and admiration. It would be vain to attempt to account for them upon any of the known principles by which calculation is performed. We can testify to the rapidity and precision of his answers in many questions of considerable intricacy. The following were, among others, proposed to him by Messrs. Knight :—

What number multiplied by itself will produce 36,372,961 ?—A. 6031. Answered in eighty seconds.

How many minutes in forty-nine years ?—A. 25,754,400. Answered in two seconds.

Multiply 4698 by 4698 ?—Ans. 22,071,204.

From 3,287,625, sub. 2,343,756.—A. 943,869.

Multiply 5 eight times by itself ?—A. 1,953,125.

THE BACKSLIDER.

A serious Christian once asked a great backslider, whether he really had found more satisfaction in the indulgence of his lusts, and the full swing of carnal pleasure, than he before had done in the profession of the gospel, and in the hours he had formerly spent for God. He honestly replied he had not; and that so far from being happy, he was never untormented, except in a state of intoxicated dissipation. It pleased God, to restore him again, but not without such bitterness of soul as all the mad pleasures he had pursued were but a poor compensation to him for.

BENEVOLENCE.

A curate of Mr. C.'s has honourably recorded an instance both of his benevolence and his manners. In the year 1785, this gentleman was afflicted with a nervous fever, which brought considerable trouble and expense to his vicar in supplying his church. During his illness, besides the tenderness and sympathy with which he was treated in other respects, he continued to receive his full salary. To use his own words, " another quarter was ended with still less service done than the former. The like beneficence was exercised." The curate, confounded at such repeated and uninterrupted generosity, exclaimed, " Dear sir, I have no demand upon you for this sum of money: I cannot receive it; I have only done duty for a few weeks, and how much trouble and expense have I put you to by my illness !" With a tender smile, and a noble dignity of spirit becoming his natural and spiritual birth, Mr. C. replied, " Take that which is thine own: did not I agree with thee for a penny ?"

Such was the amiable character of our adorable Saviour, that he did not sit in the chair of ease till objects presented thmeselves to his notice; but he sought them out. He travelled not for the sake of curiosity, of discovery, of fashion. His journeys were all journeys of benevolence, and nothing could prevent him from prosecuting his design of mercy and love. Who are they that resemble him ? What shall we say to a Paul who was instant in season and out of season? What shall we say to the faithful missionaries, who leaving their native country, have gone to the ends of the earth, to carry the tidings of salvation to miserable heathens? What shall we say to a Howard, "whose activity carried him over half the globe to enter the dwellings of the wretched; to examine debts, and wants, and diseases; to endure loathsome sights and smells; to give time, and thought, and lands, and money," to the sick, the wretched and the captive? What shall we say to a Clarkson, who travelled in search of evidence, in order to abolish the slave trade, more than thirty-five thousand miles, which is nearly once and a half the circumference of the globe? These illustrious characters need no monument to perpetuate their fame. While memory holds a seat in the breast of mortals, their benevolence, their activity, their compassion shall be remembered; and when the universe shall fall, and time expire, they shall be had in everlasting remembrance in a better world.

A lady who was an intimate friend of the late Dr. Leechman, pressed him one day to change his open carriage for a close one: he walked several times up and down the room without returning any answer; "I hear you thinking," said she, "shall I be so vain as to set up a fine riage?"—"No," said he, "I wa thinking whether the difference in the tax, &c. would not give more comfort to a certain family, than I could enjoy from that convenience myself."

Benevolent Lady.

Extraordinary instances of liberality ought to be recorded, to show not merely the benevolence of the individual, but by way of example to others who have it in their power to do good. A minister being in London with a case from the country, solicited a mite from a lady. After hearing the particulars of the case, she gave him five pounds, presenting

him, at the same time, with another note of the same value to be distributed among the poor of his flock, and a two pound note for a suffering individual. He was preparing to return suitable thanks, when he was prevented by the lady desiring him to accept of a ten pound note for his wife. Such benevolence from a stranger, such unexpected favour, so overpowered his feelings, that he could only express his acknowledgments by grateful flowing tears. The benevolent lady then crowned the whole, by saying, "Sir, the distribution of my little donations will occasion you some trouble, to compensate which, permit me to beg your acceptance of this trifle." Upon examination, he found it to be another five-pound note. The sensation of the good man at the close of this interview can be much better conceived than expressed.

The benevolent Daughter rewarded.

"The duty," says one, "of trusting the promises and providence of God in giving to the poor, even when one's circumstances are moderate and precarious, especially on urgent occasions, and the still higher duty of relieving parents in distress, as far as children have it in their power, seem to be generally acknowledged: yet it is to be feared, that few so entirely rely on the promises of God on this subject, as to risk much in obeying his plain commands; and those who do, are often censured by their brethren as imprudent. It is to be feared also, that to expect any remarkable interposition of Providence in case of poverty occasioned by such conduct, however consonant to the divine precepts, would scarcely be exempted from the charge of enthusiasm. I have, however, known several instances, in which these promises of scripture have been *literally* understood, relied on, and fulfilled, even beyond expectation. A female servant, who was past the prime of her life, in an inferior station, but much respected for her well-known piety and integrity, had saved a little money from her wages, which, as her health was evidently on the decline, and there was reason to think she could not long support the fatigues of her situation, would probably soon be required for her own relief. Thus circumstanced, she heard that her aged parents, by unavoidable calamity, were reduced to extreme indigence, and, at the same time, she had reason to fear they were strangers to the comforts of true religion. She accordingly obtained leave to visit them; and making the best use of the opportunity, both shared her little with them, and used her utmost endeavours to make them acquainted with the consolations and supports of the Gospel, which she did apparently with some success. She was afterwards remonstrated with by a religious acquaintance, who observed, that, in all probability, she would herself soon stand in need of all the little she had laid by. But to this she replied, that she could not think it her duty to see her aged parents pining in want, while she had more than was needful for her present use, and that she trusted God would find her some friend if he saw good to disable her for service.

According to her faith, so it proved to her. She continued to assist her parents till their death: soon after which event, she was entirely deprived of health, as to be utterly incapable of labour. But when nothing but a workhouse was in prospect for her, God, in a wonderful manner, raised her up friends where she least expected them. For years she was very comfortably supported in a way she could never have conceived, and circumstances were at length so ordered, that her maintenance to the end of life was almost as much ensured, as any thing can be in this perishing uncertain world. So remarkably hath God verified his gracious word—" Trust in the Lord and do good, so shalt thou dwell in the land, and verily thou shalt be fed." Ps. xxxvii. 3.

THE BRAND PLUCKED OUT OF THE FIRE.

A PLAIN countryman, who was effectually called by divine grace under a sermon from Zech. ch. iii. ver. 2. was some time afterwards accosted by a quondam companion of his drunken fits, and strongly solicited to accompany him to the alehouse. But the good man strongly resisted all his arguments, saying, "I am a brand plucked out of the fire." His old companion not understanding this, he explained it thus: " Look ye," said he; " there is a great difference between a brand and a green stick : if a spark flies upon a brand, that has been partly burnt, it will soon catch fire again ; but it is not so with a green stick. I tell you I am that brand plucked out of the fire, and I dare not enter into the way of temptation for fear of being set on fire again." Let us imitate the conduct of this good man, in keeping out of the way of danger ; thus shall we enjoy peace, and preserve a conscience void of offence.

THE BOASTER REPROVED.

EURIPIDES was slow in composing, and laboured with difficulty, from which circumstance a foolish and malevolent poet once observed that he had written a hundred verses in three days, while Euripides had only written three. " True," says Euripides; " but there is this difference between your poetry and mine—yours will expire in three days, but mine shall live for ages to come." Thus we often find, that what is of rapid growth, soonest comes to decay. It has been found true also, sometimes in a moral sense, that those who have made the greatest profession, and seemed to have outstripped all others in their zeal, have, in time of temptation, fallen away : while the deliberate, the cautious, the humble, have held on their way.

BRITAIN ONCE IDOLATROUS.

BRITISH Christians ought to recollect, that their ancestors were once blind adolaters, serving dumb idols. An ancient writer, Dr. Plaifere, in a sermon preached before the University, at Cambridge, in the year 1573, says, before the preaching of the gospel of Christ, no church here existed, but the temple of an idol; no priesthood but that of paganism; no God but the sun, the moon, or some hideous image. To the cruel rites of the druidical worship succeeded the abominations of the Roman idolatry. In Scotland stood the temple of Mars; in Cornwall, the temple of Mercury; in Bangor, the temple of Minerva; at Malden, the temple of Victoria; in Bath, the temple of Apollo; at Leicester, the temple of Janus; at York, where St. Peter's now stands, the temple of Bellona; in London, on the site of St. Paul's Cathedral, the temple of Diana; at Westminster, where the Abbey rears its venerable pile, a temple of Apollo. But,

Wonders of grace to God belong,
Repeat his mercies in your song.

Now our country is blest with thousands of Christian churches, and multitudes of gospel ministers. The land is full of Bibles; and British Christians, sensible of their privileges, are strenuously engaged in diffusing the light of divine truth among the benighted nations. What hath God wrought?

THE TWO BROTHERS.

Horrible Rencontre.

" We were conducted by the captain of the Pizarro to the governor of the province, Don Vincente Emparan, to present to him the passports which had been given us by the first secretary of state. He received us with that frankness, and that noble simplicity, which, as at all times, characterised the Biscayan nation. Before he was named governor of Portobello and Cumana, he had distinguished himself as a captain of a vessel in the royal navy. His name recalls to mind one of the most extraordinary and distressing events recorded in the history of maritime wars. At the time of the last rupture between Spain and England, two brothers of M. D'Emparan fought during a whole night before the port of Cadiz, taking each other's ship for an enemy's. The battle was so terrible, that both vessels were sunk nearly at the same time. A very small part of the crew were saved; and the two brothers had the misfortune to recognize each other a little before they expired."

THE BREAD OF LIFE TO BE VALUED.

In a famine which prevailed on board of a ship at sea, one of the passengers said to another, "My friend, four thousand pounds are owing to me in France, which I should gladly relinquish for a loaf of bread and a glass of wine." How much more precious is the bread of life which can save the soul; and how those are to be pitied where there is a famine of the word of the Lord! Happy are they who are favoured with this inestimable blessing; and what exertions should they not make to bestow it on others!

CRUELTIES.

About the year 1796, the following most shocking and atrocious murder, under the name of *Suhumurunu*, * was perpetrated at Mujilupoor, about a day's journey south from Calcutta. Vaucharamu, a Bramin of the above place dying, his wife went to be burnt with the body; all the previous ceremonies were performed; she was fastened on the pile, and the fire kindled. The funeral pile was by the side of some brushwood, and near a river. It was a late hour when the pile was lighted, and was a very dark, rainy night. When the fire began to scorch this poor woman, she contrived to disengage herself from the dead body, and crept from under the pile, and hid herself among the brushwood; In a little

* Suhu, *with*,—murunu, *death*.

time it was discovered that only one body was on the pile. The relations immediately took the alarm, and began to hunt for the poor wretch who had made her escape. After they had found her, the son dragged her forth, and insisted upon her throwing herself upon the pile again, or that she should drown or hang herself. She pleaded for her life at the hands of her own son, and declared that she could not embrace so horrid a death. But she pleaded in vain; the son urged that he should lose his, and that therefore he would die or she should. Unable to persuade her to hang or drown herself, the son and the others then tied her hands and feet, and threw her on the funeral pile, where she quickly perished.

This was noticed in the House of Commons, in answer to an opposing statement, which asserted the "filial piety" of the Hindoos.

Burning a Leper to death at Cutwa.

" Last week I witnessed the burning of a poor leper. A pit, about ten cubits in depth, was dug, and a fire placed at the bottom of it. The poor man rolled himself into it, but instantly, on feeling the fire, begged to be taken out, and struggled hard for that purpose. His mother and sister, however, thrust him in again; and thus a man, who, to all appearance, might have survived some years longer, was cruelly burnt to death. I find that the practice is not uncommon in these parts."

The practice of diseased persons, and especially of those heavily afflicted with the leprosy, drowning themselves, is very common, and is recommended in the writings of the Hindoos. This poor wretch died with the notion that by thus purifying his body in the fire, he should receive a happy transmigration into a healthful body ; whereas, if he had died by the disease, he would, after four births, have appeared on earth a leper again !

Lately a Hindoo carpenter was drowned because he had the leprosy.

He was carried from one of the *ghauts* at *Alum-gunj*, in a boat, in the presence of a large assembly of people, and when, in deep water, put overboard. Two large earthen pots, one filled with sand, the other with barley, were fastened to his shoulders. The man sunk, but after some time floated on the surface of the water. The people in the boat rowed after him, and took him up, but made sure work of it the second time.

The same man informed me, that about two years ago, at a village about two miles from hence, a woman was burnt, after an attempt to escape from the flames ! The friends of the deceased husband were very poor, and could not afford to procure wood for the funeral pile. They, however, collected a quantity of palmyra leaves for the purpose ; and the living woman with the dead body, were, as usual, put into the midst of the heap; The fire was kindled, and the woman's clothes consumed ; but she struggled and got out of the flames, and attempted to run away, entreating her pursuers to spare her life, but, alas ! entreated in vain ; she was seized and destroyed ! !

The mode of burning the dead in this neighbourhood differs from that which I have seen in Bengal. Instead of wood, which I suppose is much dearer than in Bengal, they get a few bundles of long grass, such as poor people use for building their houses, and after placing the body on a kind of stage about a foot and a half from the ground, with some of the grass over and some under it, they set fire to the heap, let it flame for a minute or two perhaps, and then quench it, and throw the singed body in the river.

This ceremony I have several times witnessed, and the persons employed appeared to be as much diverted with the act of kindling and extinguishing the flames, as the boys in England are at bonfires in fields in the country.

Cruelty and Ignorance.

Albutius, a prince of Celtiberia, to

whom Scipio restored his wife, was a sordid man, father to Canidia. He beat his servants before they were guilty of any offence, "lest," said he, " I should have no time to punish them when they offend."

Herod, who massacred the male children at Bethlehem, in hopes that he might destroy the Saviour of mankind, died in exquisite torments, eaten of worms, at the age of seventy-one. He was remarkable for his cruelty. As he knew that the day of his death would become a day of mirth and festivity, he ordered the most illustrious of his servants to be confined and murdered the very moment that he expired, that every eye in the kingdom should seem to shed tears at his death.

Happily, however, his sanguinary commands were not carried into effect.

The reciting of instances of cruelty cannot be pleasant to a reader's feelings; only it tends to show us what human nature is when left to itself. Ptolemy IV. successively sacrificed to his avarice his mother, his wife, his sister, and his brother. Thus we see that the bonds of nature are no barriers against insatiable cruelty.

Nabis, a cruel tyrant of Lacedæmon, when he had exercised every art in plundering the citizens in Sparta, made a statue which, in resemblance, was like his wife, and was clothed in the most magnificent apparel, and whenever any one refused to deliver up his riches, the tyrant led him to the statue, which immediately, by means of secret springs, seized him in its arms, and tormented him in the most excruciating manner with bearded points and prickles hid under its clothes.

As the souls of men are of infinite value ; as through ignorance and depravity, they are exposed to the most imminent danger, how absolutely necessary is it for ministers to be faithful, plain, and zealous in the discharge of the commission entrusted to their hands ! Nothing is more despicable than the affectation of learning, wit, or eloquence, when souls are perishing for lack of knowledge. It is recorded, as an instance of the cruel temper of Nero, that in a general famine, when many perished by hunger, that he ordered a ship should come from Egypt (the granary of Italy) laden with sand for the use of wrestlers. In such an extremity to provide only for delight, that there might be spectacles in the theatre, when the city of Rome was affected with such misery as to melt the heart of any but a Nero, was most barbarous cruelty ;—but how much more cruel is he whose preparations for the pulpit, are only as chaff or sand, while the bread of life is kept out of sight, and many are ready to perish with hunger !

THE HINDOO'S CONFESSION.

WHEN one of the converted Hindoos came to be baptized he made this confession. He said he had been for years searching for a way of happiness in Poojahs, (holy places in the river, &c.) but all in vain ; but when he heard the word of Christ he could not rest. He sat up a whole night in distress of mind. He had great fears about his sins. When asked how he lost them, he said, " They went away in thinking on Christ." Thus we shall never get rid of our fear in any other way than by thinking on Christ, thinking on his atoning sacrifice, his finished righteousness, his great love, his free promise, his willingness to save. It was this that made another Hindoo say, when he was asked how he hoped to be saved, "I am a sinner, I have nothing to give to God ; but if a rich man become a poor man's surety, he may trust in him : thus I place my trust in Christ Jesus." Distressed Christian, you may firmly rely on the Saviour, he will never disappoint your fear ! Is he not able to save to the uttermost ; and will he condemn you ?

THE BLIND CONTROVERSIALISTS.

In our inquiries after truth, and defence of it, it ill becomes us to manifest a bigoted, petulant disposition. We may, with all our zeal, be mistaken.

A certain philanthropist, observing some poor blind men, very humanely furnished each of them with a staff to help them on their way ; but they, instead of thanking him, availing themselves of the aid thus afforded them, and assisting each other in the use of it, quickly fell into disputes respecting its breadth, length, and thickness, till being unable to adopt the same conclusion, and equally unwilling to agree to differ on the subject, forgetting the end for which the staff was bestowed, and the purpose to which it should be applied. In the heat of their contention, they actually employed it as a cudgel, with which they beat one another most unmercifully.   Thus angry controversialists too often use the Bible : that which was given them for their support, they convert into an instrument of discord and disputation.

THE COBLER.

A cobler at Leyden, who used to attend the public disputations held at the academy, was once asked if he understood Latin ?   "No," replied the mechanic ; "but I know who is wrong in the argument."   " How ?" replied his friend.   " Why, by seeing who is angry first."

THE WOODEN CHALICE.

Nothing can be more awful than when the ministers of the sanctuary degenerate and become idle and licentious : when they are ambitious for rich livings, great connexions, and the approbation of men, rather than to lay themselves out for the benefit of society, or the glory of God.   In proportion, however, as any church or churches become allied to the world, we find this to be the case. Hence primitive times most likely had the superiority as to simplicity, fidelity, and apostolic zeal.   One of the martyrs was asked the question, if he would receive the sacrament, provided it was administered to him in a wooden chalice ?   To which he answered, " The time was, when there were wooden cups and golden priests ; but, now," says he ;   " they are golden cups and wooden priests." In the first days they were more humble than now, and content with wooden vessels ; but the ministers were gold in regard to grace and godliness.   Let us bear this in mind, and earnestly entreat the great Head of the church, to increase the number of those who shall be simple in their manner, evangelical in their principles, laborious in their exertions, and devoted in their lives, that the work may prosper, and the word of the Lord have free course and be glorified.

CONVERSIONS.

W. B. had lived a dissolute life for nearly forty years.   He was notorious for drinking and Sabbathbreaking, and his general deportment was so abandoned, that he was wicked even to a proverb.   On Saturday evening, March 4, 1789, he attended a funeral at the parish-church, and, from the place of interment, he immediately betook himself to a publichouse, where he became so intoxicated, that it was with some difficulty he was enabled to reach his own habitation.   No sooner was he laid down upon his bed, and composed to sleep, than the words of Eliphaz were verified in his experience : " In thoughts from the visions of the night, when deep sleep falleth upon man, fear came upon me, and trembling, which made all my bones to shake."— For he dreamed a frightful dream :— he thought he saw a serpent of the hydra kind, with nine heads, ready to seize him ; whatever way he turned, a head presented itself ; nor could he by all the methods he devised, extricate himself from the baneful monster.   He awoke in great distress and perturbation.—Though it was but a dream, it made a strong impression upon his mind, and he was afraid that it portended some future evil. The next morning, one of the members of our meeting, as he was going to the house of God, observed him in a pensive posture, and asked him if he would go with him and hear a sermon on the old serpent. The sound of the word serpent, arrested his attention, and excited his curiosity to hear what I had to say upon such a subject. But for this expression, probably, the poor man had remained unmoved. Why the person used it, he could not tell, nor why he invited him to accompany him that morning, a thing which he had never done before, though they both lived under the same roof, but HE could tell who, in the days of his flesh, "must needs go through Samaria," and whose providences are always in coincidence with the purposes of his grace. As soon as prayer was ended, I preached from Gen. iii. 13, 14, and 15. "And the Lord God said unto the woman, what is this that thou hast done ; and the woman said, the serpent beguiled me, and I did eat. And the Lord God said unto the serpent, because thou hast done this, thou art cursed above all cattle, and above every beast of the field : upon thy belly shalt thou go, and dust shalt thou eat all the days of thy life ; and I will put enmity between thee and the woman, and between thy seed and her seed ; it shall bruise thy head, and thou shalt bruise his heel." As I was explaining who that serpent was, and the methods he took to beguile sinners, the Lord opened the poor man's eyes, and the word had free course, and was glorified. From that moment, he gave every demonstration of a real change of heart. About four or five months, he continued in the pangs of the new birth. The anguish of his soul was great indeed: he perceived the number of his sins, and felt the weight of his guilt. For some time, he was tempted to despair—I may say, to put an end to his existence ; but, while he was musing on his wretched condi-

tion, these words were applied as a sovereign remedy to his afflicted soul : " Believe on the Lord Jesus Christ, and thou shalt be saved." This ad ministered all that joy and comfort he stood in need of. Now he was enabled to believe, that Christ was as willing to forgive, as he was mighty to redeem : the burden of his guilt dropped from his mind as Pilgrim's did at the sight of the cross, and immediately he rejoiced with joy unspeakable and full of glory. I was with him a little while after, and, with a heart overflowing with gratitude to God, he showed me the place of his Bethel visit, where the Lord had opened to him his bleeding heart, and manifested his forgiving love. The whole neighbourhood allow him to be a converted man. The most wicked person in the place, will attest the truth of his conversion. He seems to be, as the apostle expresses it, a living epistle of Christ, seen and read of all men.

It is said of a Mr. T., and three of his associates, that, to enliven the company, they once undertook to mimic a celebrated preacher. The proposition was highly gratifying to all the parties present, and a wager agreed upon, to inspire each individual with a desire of excelling in this impious attempt. That their jovial auditors might adjudge the prize to the most adroit performer, it was concluded that each should open the Bible, and hold forth from the first text that should present itself to his eye. Accordingly, three in their turn, mounted the table, and entertained their wicked companions, at the expense of every thing sacred. When they had exhausted their little stock of buffoonery, it devolved on Mr. T. to close this very irreverent scene. Much elated, and confident of success, he exclaimed, as he ascended the table, " I shall beat you all !" But oh! the stupendous depth of divine mercy ! Who would have conceived, that a gracious Providence should have presided over such an assembly, and that this should be the time of heavenly love to one of the most outrageous mockers.

Mr. T., when the Bible was handed to him, had not the slightest preconception what part of the Scripture he should make the subject of his banter. However, by the guidance of an unerring Providence, it opened at the following remarkable passage, Luke xiii. 3: "Except ye repent, ye shall all likewise perish." No sooner had he uttered the words, than his mind was affected in a very extraordinary manner. The sharpest pangs of conviction now seized him, and conscience denounced tremendous vengeance upon his soul. In a moment, he was favoured with a clear view of his subject, and divided his discourse more like a divine, who had been accustomed to speak on portions of Scripture, than like one who never so much as thought on religious topics, except for the purpose of ridicule. He found no deficiency of matter, no want of utterance; and we have frequently heard him declare, "If ever I preached in my life by the assistance of the Spirit of God, it was at that time." The impression that the subject made upon his own mind, had such an effect upon his manner, that the most ignorant and profane could not but perceive, that what he had spoken, was with the greatest sincerity.

Carraciolus, an Italian marquis, and nephew to Pope Paul V. was converted by Peter Martyr's reading the first epistle of the Corinthians. The 53d chapter of Isaiah, was one mean of the conviction and conversion of the famous wit, Lord Rochester.

The blind Man converted by his Grandchild reading the Bible to him.

Although the Supreme Being could accomplish the work of conversion without the use of means, yet he is generally pleased to work by them. One of the principal of these, is his own word; sometimes by the preaching, and sometimes by the reading of it. A clergyman, in Ireland, met with a poor blind man, between ninety and a hundred years of age, and addressed him by remarking, that he was a very old man. He answered, "Aye;" and, after a short pause, he said, "it is well for me that I lived to be old; but it (with a low voice) was bad for Solomon." The clergyman asked him what reason he had to say that. He answered, "if Solomon had died when he was young, he would have been one of the greatest men in the world; but if I had died when I was young, I should have gone to hell. Solomon lived to disgrace himself; I have lived to obtain glory." After he had expressed his dependance on the blood of Christ for salvation, and acknowledged that it was by the Holy Ghost he came to the knowledge of divine things, the clergyman asked him, whether he had heard any person speak of those things: he said, "no;" then how he came to the knowledge of the Bible texts he had quoted?—He said, "that about five years before, having become blind, and desirous to prepare his soul, he caused a grandchild of his, that could read, to procure a Bible, which he made him read to him constantly; and that, through reading the Bible, the Lord opening his heart, made him feel his love," and then broke out into many expressions of praise! What a strong argument is this, first, to instruct the ignorant to read, and then to use the most vigorous exertions to circulate the sacred Scriptures among them! Who can calculate on the blessed effects!

When I was a child, between nine and twelve years old, I used to think it was a very good thing to go to church, which I did once every Sunday, but seldom more, spending the other part of my Sabbath in play, &c. but when I came home, and lay down on my bed of a night, there used to be a sting of conscience upon me, that I ought to be better, and serve God more, which made a little impression upon me for the night, but it was over in the morning; yet sometimes it followed me so that I made a resolution to be better, which I tried and wrote some prayers to read, of a night; but when I came to be with my companions again, it was all wore off; and I left off saying my prayers, and gave myself up to my companions again, and thus I went on from time to time; but one time, in particular, when in a great deal of trouble about my mother's affairs, and it came to my mind that I had been doing wrong, then it particularly struck me, that Christ came to die for me as a sinner, as well as any one; and that he did not die for me alone, but for all: which thought gave me comfort, till at last I came up to London. How I used to go to church once a day, and thought that that was enough, and so spent the rest of the day in going to tea-gardens, &c.: also to plays, &c. in the week days; but, as Providence would have it, I happened to catch hold of a companion who was a serious young man, and on the 20th August, 1786, as we were walking together, we happened to fall into a serious discourse, in talking of the joy of heaven, and the pains of hell which must befall them that are disobedient. I began to think that I had been hitherto going on in a wicked life, and that it was best for me to begin to work out my salvation, while I had the time, &c. continued; and that as I had found myself to be a wretchedly wicked sinner, I thought it was not too soon to come to him whose blood cleanses from all sin, which impression bore continually upon my mind; nevertheless, I thought it no harm to go to plays, &c. till I had heard ministers read the word of God; then I learnt that I must leave all for Christ; till at last, it worked so upon my mind, that I found to follow Christ was the best gain, and that if I still followed the pleasures of life, I could not serve Christ. From this time I found very little love to the world, and more to Christ: so I renounced all companions but him who was

made useful to me, and we met together of an evening to expound the Scriptures one to another: by which means, and by going often to hear ministers, I found myself, as it were, established in Christianity, had more and more a sense of my sin, and of the mercy of Christ in forgiving them; thus I went on, and sometimes I thought I should like to go into the ministry, though at the same time, I did not know what it was to be a minister.

Ananda Rayer's Conversion.

The account of Ananda Rayer's conversion is given by the Rev. Dr. John, the aged missionary at Tranquebar, in a letter to Mr. Desgranges. This Brahmin applied (as many Brahmins and other Hindoos constantly do) to an older Brahmin, of some fame for sanctity, to know " what he should do that he might be saved?" The old Brahmin told him that " he must repeat a certain prayer four lack of times;"—that is four hundred thousand times. This he performed in a pagoda, in six months, and added many painful ceremonies, but finding no comfort or peace from these external rites, he went to a Romish priest, and asked him if he knew what was the true religion? The priest gave him some Christian books in the Telinga language; and, after a long investigation of Christianity, the inquiring Hindoo had no doubt remaining on his mind, that " Christ was the Saviour of the world." But he was not satisfied with the Romish worship in many points; he disliked the adoration of images and other superstitions: and having heard from the priests themselves, that the protestant Christians at Tanjore and Tranquebar professed to have a pure faith, and had got the Bible translated, and worshipped no images, he visited Dr. John, and the other Missionaries at Tranquebar, where he remained four months, conversing, says Dr. John, " almost every day with me," and examining the holy Scriptures. He soon acquired the Tamul language (which has affinity with the Telinga) that he might read the Tamul translation; and he finally became a member of the protestant church. The Missionaries at Vizagapatam being in want of a learned Telinga scholar, to assist them in a translation of the Scriptures into the Telinga language, Dr. John recommended Ananda Rayer; "for he was averse," says he, " to undertake any worldly employment, and had a great desire to be useful to his brethren of the Telinga nation." The reverend Missionary concludes thus: " what Jesus Christ hath required of his followers, this man hath literally done : he hath left father, mother, sisters, and. brothers, and houses, and lands, for the gospel's sake."

Conversion of a Griqua, or South African.

A Griqua, named *Jacob Cloote,* had been the promoter of much evil; a ringleader among the young people in drunkenness and lewdness, every decent person was both ashamed and afraid of him. He seemed to have been given up to wickedness, and every means which had been tried to reclaim him was in vain. Mr. Campbell can tell you how he troubled us just before he left us. He stood charged with such grossly immortal conduct, that it was judged necessary to compel him to live near us, that we might check his proceedings; but he set us at defiance. For some time he raged and threatened to revenge himself. But, blessed be God! it seems that his heart is changed. He began now and then to come to the church. Brother Jantz and I took every opportunity to convince him of his danger. At first he showed great enmity; but one day he heard us and gave us no answer. We observed him a little affected. He then began to call on us, and, by degrees, to open his mind to us. This was soon known. Those who feared God were a little afraid of him, and his companions began to

ridicule him. But we perceived that he was humbled: his distress of mind became great; he attended closely at all our meetings, he endured the ridicule of his companions with patience, and declared his intention to do all he could to reclaim those whom he had been the means of debauching. He now speaks very humbly of himself, and abhors his former conduct. His conversion appears to have been the means of the conversion of others. One *Mannel Mannel,* a very great enemy, and a mocker at God's word, has been convinced, and is now seeking the Lord Jesus. *Andrie Hendric* is another who was of the same stamp as *Jacob Cloote,* and equal with him in all sinful practices. He was one of those who took the letters which Mr. Campbell sent away while here. Upon his return he said—" it is as if I was come back into a new world; every one is now speaking of Jesus." He is now walking humbly before God, and many more are inquiring.

Some years ago, a young man of the city of Norwich, about eighteen years of age, was walking, one morning, with a party of other young men, who had all agreed for that day to make holiday. The first object that attracted their attention, was an old woman who pretended to tell fortunes; they immediately employed her to tell theirs: and, that they might fully qualify her for their undertaking, first made her thoroughly intoxicated with spirituous liquor. The young man, of whom mention was first made, who was informed, among other things, that he would live to a very old age, and see his children, grand-children, and great grand-children growing up around him, though he had assisted in qualifying the old woman for the fraud by intoxicating her, yet he had credulity enough to be struck with those parts of her predictions which related to himself. " And so," quoth he, when alone, "I am to live to see children, grand-children, and great grand-children! At that age I must be a burden to the young people. What shall I do? There is no way for an old man to render himself more agreeable to youth than by sitting and telling them pleasant and profitable stories. I will then," thought he, "during my youth, endeavour to store my mind with all kinds of knowledge. I will see and hear, and note down every thing that is rare and wonderful, that I may sit, when incapable of other employment, and entertain my descendants. Thus shall my company be rendered pleasant, and I shall be respected rather than neglected in old age. Let me see; what can I acquire first? O! here is a famous methodist preacher, Whitfield; he is to preach, they say, to-night; I will go and hear him."

From these strange motives the young man declared he went to see Mr. Whitfield. He preached that evening from Matt. iii. 7. "But when he saw many of the Pharisees and Sadducees come to his baptism, he said unto them, O generation of vipers, who hath warned you to flee from the wrath to come?" "Mr. Whitfield," said the young man, "described the Sadducean character: this did not touch me. I thought myself as good a Christian as any man in England. From this he went to that of the Pharisees. He described their exterior decency, but observed that the poison of the viper rankled in their hearts. This rather shook me. At length, in the course of his sermon, he abruptly broke off, paused for a few moments, then burst into a flood of tears; lifted up his hands and eyes, and exclaimed, 'O, my hearers! the wrath's to come, the wrath's to come.'

"These words sunk deep into my heart, like lead in the waters. I wept, and, when the sermon was ended, retired alone. For days and weeks I could think of little else. Those awful words would follow me wherever I went—'the wrath's to come, the wrath's to come!'" The issue was, that the young man, soon after, made a public profession of religion, and in a little time became a very considerable preacher.

INFLUENCE OF CHRISTIANITY.

THE primitive Christians endured the fiery trial with insuperable constancy: and the most powerful argument that inspired their courage, despising life and death, was that Christ was their leader in those terrible conflicts; he was their spectator, when they encountered wild beasts and fiercer tyrants for the defence of his truth and glory of his name; and while they were suffering for him, he was preparing immortal crowns for them. This St. Cyprian, in his pastoral letters to the Christians in Africa, represents with such powerful eloquence, that kindled in their breasts a love to Christ *stronger than death.*

Basil affirms that the primitive saints showed so much comfort and courage, so much heroic zeal and constancy, that many of the heathens turned Christians. Lactantius boasts of the fortitude of the martyrs in his time.

"Our children and women (not to speak of men) do in silence overcome their tormentors, and the fire cannot so much as fetch a sigh from them." Hegesippus reports an observation of Antoninus the emperor, viz., that the Christians were always most courageous and confident in earthquakes, while his own heathen soldiers were, on such occasions, most fearful and dispirited. The suffering saint may be assaulted and troubled, but can never be conquered: he may lose his head, but cannot lose his crown, which the righteous Lord hath laid up for him.

Christianity Exemplified.

Christianity is not only a system of truth but of peace. Pliny the younger was obligated to bear his testimony to this. He presided over Pontus and Bithynia, in the office and with the power of proconsul. By his humanity, the persecution which had been begun against the

Christians of his province was stopped; for he solemnly declared to the emperor Trajan, that the followers of Christ were a meek and inoffensive sect of men; that their morals were pure and innocent; that they were free from all crimes, and that they voluntarily bound themselves, by the most solemn oaths, to abstain from vice and to relinquish every sinful pursuit. What can be a more charming exposition of the words of the apostle, 1 Peter ii. 12., than this testimony? How well it is to explain and illustrate the Scriptures by the purity of our conduct!

MELANCHOLY INSTANCE OF FEMALE CONSTANCY AND TENDERNESS.

A YOUNG lady of a good family and handsome fortune, had, for some time, extremely loved, and been equally beloved, by Mr. James Dawson, one of those unhappy gentlemen who suffered at Kennington Common for high treason; and had he been acquitted, or after condemnation found the royal mercy, the day of his enlargement was to have been that of their marriage.

I will not prolong the narrative by any repetition of what she suffered on sentence being passed upon him; none excepting those utterly incapable of feeling any soft or generous emotions, but may conceive her agonies; besides, the sad catastrophe will be sufficient to convince you of their sincerity. Not all the persuasions of her kindred could prevent her from going to the place of execution; she was determined to see the last of a person so dear to her, and accordingly followed the sledges in a hackney-coach, accompanied by a gentleman nearly related to her, and one female friend. She got near enough to see the fire kindled, which was to consume that heart she knew so much devoted to her, and all the other dreadful preparations for his fate, without being guilty of any one of those extravagancies her friends had

apprehended; but when all was over, and she found that he was no more, she drew her head back into the coach, and crying out—" My dear, I follow thee! Lord Jesus receive both our souls together!" fell on the neck of her companion, and expired in the very moment she was speaking.

CHASTITY.

WHEN Appius Claudius, the decemvir, became enamoured of Virginia, and her father had heard of his violent proceedings and intentions, he arrived at the place to which his daughter was removed, and demanded to see her; and when his request was granted, he snatched a knife and plunged it into Virginia's breast, exclaiming—" This is all, my dearest daughter, I can give thee to preserve thy chastity from the lust and violence of a tyrant!" However unjustifiable this might be, to take away the life of his child, it showed his great abhorrence of the act of unchastity, at least in his own daughter.

CHARITY.

THOUGH charity to the poor will not entitle us to the heavenly inheritance, as some imagine, yet it is a duty binding on all who have it in their power. Nor can those who are contracted, illiberal, and close, give any proof of their loving God while they have no charity to their brother. He who seeth his brother have need, and shutteth up the bowels of compassion for him, how dwelleth the love of God in him? In proportion as we feel the effects of divine grace, and are conformed to the conduct of the Saviour, we shall be desirous of doing good. The Rev. Mr. A. was so charitable, that he would have but five teeth in his rake in harvest time, that there might be more left for the gleaners; so that a boy has often gleaned half a bushel of barley a-day in his field. He always sold his grain cheaper to the poor than the market price. He employed a great many poor people in planting the common hedges with plumbs, cherries, and other fruit-trees, for the supply of the poor, and of travellers. At Christmas, he gave every poor parishioner a peck of corn. Of him it might be truly said, "When the ear heard him it blessed him; when the eye saw him it gave witness to him; because he delivered the poor that cried, and the fatherless, and them that had none to help them."

Some of the brethren belonging to the Rev. Mr. L.'s church at Portsea, were in the habit of ushering in the morning of the Lord's day by meeting in the vestry for social prayer, exhortation, and conference on some portion of scripture alternately. At one of these conference meetings, the text led to charity, when one of the brethren made the following comment on the text:—"I shall say nothing more than this; we have been talking of charity—it would be good to put it in exercise. Here is our brother E. F. goes to his work every morning this cold weather without a great coat, and here is my shilling towards buying him one." The good men took the hint, and the poor man was enabled to purchase the necessary article the next day. How much better would it be if many who are so violent to prove their orthodoxy would be as zealous in maintaining good works: for what doth it profit, though a man *say* he hath faith, and have not works: can faith save him?

Pretensions to Goodness false, unless founded in real Charity.

Let not any one, however, intrench himself in the supposed security of surrounding goodness. Let not any take comfort that he lives in an age of charity, if he himself be not charitable. We are not benevolent by contact or infection, or by breathing an atmosphere of charity. Yet who has not heard persons exultingly boast of this noble characteristic of the age, who are by no means remarkable for contributing their own contingent towards establishing its character? Probably many a man

gloried in the valour of his country, and exulted in the pride of being an Englishman, after the battles of Trafalgar and Salamanca, who, had he been sent into the action, would have been shot for cowardice.

Who has not seen the ready eye discharge its kindly showers at a tale of wo, and the frugal sentimentalist comfort himself that his tears had paid more cheaply the debt of benevolence, for which his purse had been solicited?

The author, many years ago, made one in a party of friends; an expected guest, who was rather late, at length came in: she was in great agitation, having been detained on the road by a dreadful fire in the neighbourhood. The poor family, who were gone to bed, had been with difficulty awakened. The mother had escaped by throwing herself from a two pair of stairs window into the street. She then recollected, that, in her extreme terror, she had left her child behind in bed. To the astonishment of all present, she instantly rushed back through the flames, and, to the general joy, soon appeared with the child alive in her arms. While she was expressing her gratitude, the light of the lamp fell on its face, and she perceived, to her inexpressible horror, that she had saved the child of another woman—her own had perished. It may be imagined what were the feelings of the company. A subscription was instantly begun. Almost every one had liberally contributed, when a nobleman, who could have bought the whole party, turning to the writer of these pages, said, "Madam, I will give you"—every expecting eye was turned to the peer, knowing him to be unused to the giving mood; the person addressed, joyfully held out her hand, but drew it back on his saying—"I will give you this affecting incident for the subject of your next tragedy."*

* Hannah More's Christian Morals, page 194, 195, &c.

DEATHS.

On Monday, 22d October, 1787, in Kevin-street, Dublin, a man laid a wager with another person, that he would drink a half pint full of strong spirits of whiskey, without taking it from his lip, upon which he attempted to drink off the liquor, but before he could finish it, he fell on the floor in convulsion, and immediately expired. See how men, to show their own bravery, ruin themselves ; but how awful must it be to be cut off in the very act of wickedness !

On Monday, 29th October, 1787, a farmer's apprentice, at Penzance, in Cornwall, hearing the hounds in pursuit after a hare, unharnessed a horse, and joined the chase ; but the hare running near a pit, the lad, following too rashly, fell in ; he was taken out, but expired in three hours afterwards. Let this be a warning to young people not to follow rashly after the things and pleasures of this world, lest they fall into the pit of destruction !

About the beginning of last month, a prodigious quantity of rain that fell on the mountains of Sacca, in the village of Sanguessa, in Spain, occasioned so terrible an inundation, that out of four hundred houses, which composed the village, one only is remaining ; two thousand souls were buried under the waters, which rose fourteen feet higher than they generally do. Oh, consider the judgments of God against sin ; and how awful it must be to have so many lives taken away, and perhaps very few prepared to die !

On Thursday morning, 8th November, 1787, at two o'clock, a most dreadful fire broke out in Chandler-street, Powis-street, in Berkley-street, Berkley-square, which entirely consumed the same. A woman, who lodged in the house, was burnt to death, as she was much in liquor when she went to bed. Oh, how unawares doth death come, when it is little thought of ! But how careful ought we to be of sinning against God, lest the sting of death come and destroy us with an utter destruction, and catch us in the very act of sin !

On Thursday, November 15th, 1787, as Mr. Trembles, farrier, of Newington Causeway, was speaking to a gentleman on horseback at his own door, he fell down suddenly and expired. Oh, how uncertain is the time of death, and how little do we think of it even when it is so near us. What a watchful eye and a prepared heart then ought we to keep, since we know not the day nor the hour of our departure from this earth, either to eternal happiness or misery.

Two awful instances of sudden death happened near Bridlington, on Friday, 16th November, 1787. That evening, about seven o'clock, Thomas Harrison left Bridlington in order to go to the quay, and was found dead by the road-side about ten at night. Several persons being called to convey the body home, one John Lewis got out of bed to assist, but as soon as he came to the place where the deceased was lying, he suddenly dropped down and instantly expired. Oh, how sudden doth death catch away even them that are in health ! Let this be a warning to all, how uncertain the time of death ! But it must be awful for them that are caught away in the twinkling of an eye, before they have time to prepare for eternity ; therefore prepare to meet your God.

28th November, 1787. Wednesday s'ennight, as Mr. H., merchant in Lancaster, was walking with Mr. S———t, he dropped down and died instantly. One would think that this is enough to alarm men of the uncertainty of life.

Lately, as some men were lounging on the sea-coast of Hapisburgh, instead of attending the important duties of the Sabbath, they observed a large fish, which having been bruised against the rocks by the dashing of the waves, was left in the shallow water, by the retreat of the tide. One of the persons swore that he would go and fetch it to land, and stripped himself accordingly. He reached the fish, and returning with it, his companions threw a rope for his assistance; but he vowed, with horrid imprecations on himself, that he would bring it as he first proposed, safe to land himself. Scarcely had he uttered the words, when he fell a lifeless corpse, his body floating on the water. Let this be a warning to all that keep not God's Sabbath; for, see his judgment upon such; but, what is more awful, is to be cut off with such horrid imprecations in his mouth against himself. Oh, where must such appear, when God shall say, "Arise, ye dead, and come to judgment!"

On Friday, 28th December, 1787, being Christmas week, the dead body of a man, who had perished through the inclemency of the weather, was found near Otham's Corner, between Westham and Hailsham, in the county of Sussex. The deceased had been to the latter place, and was returning home to Westham, where he had a little farm of his own; but, being overtaken by liquor, he was unable to proceed, and, falling down, he, in some little time afterward, perished. Oh, see the fruit of drunkenness, and profaning those days, which ought to be set apart for the service and commemoration of our Lord and Saviour Jesus Christ, who will come at the last day to judge those who pay no regard to him, and profane those days in which we ought to commemorate his goodness.

One of the ancients, standing by Cæsar's tomb, wept and cried out, "Where is now the flourishing beauty of Cæsar? What is become of his magnificence? Where are the armies now? Where the honours of Cæsar? Where are now the victories, the triumphs, and trophies of Cæsar?"——Happy the Christian: when *he* dies, he goes to live with Christ. He rises above the world to perfect unfading honour and happiness. Reader, seek those honours and treasures which are to be found in Christ, and in the pursuit and practice of true godliness.——Thy

dwelling on earth, may be mean, and thy grave unnoticed; but thou shalt have a mansion in the skies, while in the most important and pleasing sense, thy name shall be had in everlasting remembrance.

Notwithstanding that the living know they must die, yet how unconcerned are the generality of mankind as to the interest of their immortal souls! How lamentable to reflect, that this is generally delayed to the last!

It is related of Philip, King of the Macedonians, that while one was pleading before him, he dropped asleep, and, waking on a sudden, passed sentence against the righteous cause: upon this, the injured person cried out, "I appeal." The king, with indignation, asked, "To whom?" He replied, "From yourself sleeping to yourself waking;" and had the judgment reversed that was against him. "Thus," says Dr. Bates, "in matters of eternal moment, if there be an appeal from the sleeping to the waking thoughts of men, when death opens their eyes to see the dross of false treasures, and the glory of the true, what a change would it make in their minds, affections, and actions! But oh, folly and misery! they do but superficially consider things, till constrained, when it is too late." It was the sad exclamation of one upon his dying bed, "I had provided, in the course of my life, for every thing but death, and now I must die, though entirely unprepared for it." How different is the condition of the true Christian! He, as Mr. Henry remarks, "shall enter the harbour of eternal rest; not like a shipwrecked mariner, cleaving to some broken plank, and hardly escaping the raging waves, but like some stately vessel, with all her sails expanded, riding before a prosperous gale."

It was the chief design of the philosophers, by principles of reason, to fortify themselves against all frightful accidents, and, with a masculine mind, with an ardent and generous spirit, to encounter this inevitable

T

evil. When one of them was threatened by the Emperor Antigonus with present death, he boldly replied, "Threaten this to your dissolute courtiers, who are softened and melted by sensual pleasures, and easily receptive of terrible impressions; not to a philosopher, to whom death is contemptible in any appearance."— This was a piece of affected bravery; for Pagan philosophy could never furnish them with armour of proof against the dart of our last enemy. But the gospel, assuring us that death is an entrance into immortality, makes that to be the reality of a Christian that was a vain boast of the philosophers.

As all Christ's actings towards, for, and in his people, are free, so *they* move and act towards Christ freely: they hear, they pray, they wait, they weep, they work, they watch, freely and willingly: that spirit of grace and holiness, that is in them, makes them run with delight in all religious duties. It is reported of Socrates, that when the tyrant threatened him with death, he answered, "he was willing." "Nay, then," said the tyrant, "you shall live against your will." To which, he replied, " Whatever you do with me, it shall be my will." If nature, a little raised and refined, will enable a man to do this, will not grace enable him to do as much, yea, infinitely more?

Solon, when near his end, being visited by some friends, who were speaking softly of a point of philosophy, was, by the sound of wisdom, awakened from the sleep of death, that was just seizing on him; and, opening his eyes, and raising his head to give attention, was asked the reason of it? He answered, "That when I understand what you are discoursing of, I may die." Such was his delight in knowledge, that a little of it made his agony insensible. But here are many imperfections that lessen this intellectual pleasure, which shall cease in heaven. Here the acquisition of knowledge is often with the expense of health; the flower of the spirits, necessary for natural operations, is wasted by intense thought. How often are the learned sickly?— As the flint, when it is struck, gives not a spark without consuming itself, so knowledge is obtained by studies that waste our faint, sensitive faculties. But *then*, our knowledge shall be a free emanation from the spring of truth, without our labour and pains. Here, we learn by circuit, and discern by comparing things; our ignorance is dispelled by a gradual succession of light; but there, universal knowledge shall be infused in a moment. Here, after all our labour and toil, how little knowledge do we gain? Every question is a labyrinth, out of which the nimblest and most searching minds cannot extricate themselves.

An infidel writer, of the present day, advises his disciples to think of dying as little as possible. He tells them that dying is at best a humiliating, uncomfortable business, and, therefore, instructs them to live well, and die as they can.—Blessed be God, our religion teaches us another lesson: it directs us to live well; but does not leave us, at last, to "die as we can."

Happiness of Believers in Death.

Although the souls of believers, immediately upon their separation, are received into heaven, and, during the sleep of death, enjoy admirable visions of glory, yet their blessedness is imperfect, in comparison with that excellent degree which shall be enjoyed at the resurrection. As the Roman generals, after a complete conquest, first entered the city privately, and, having license of the senate, made their triumphal entry with all the magnificence and splendour becoming the greatness of their victories; so, after a faithful Christian *hath fought the good fight*, and is come off more than a conqueror, he enters privately into the celestial city; but when the body is raised to immortality, he shall then, in the company, and with the acclamations of the holy angels, have a glorious entry into it.

The following are part of the words of an eminent man, when dying of one of the most painful diseases known among men:—"It is long since I turned from corruptible things, and clave to those which are laid up in heaven. My God, my soul thirsteth for thee as the parched ground. When shall I present myself before the face of God? All delay seems long to me till Christ come; for whom, notwithstanding, I wait without impatience. Through the grace of God I am not tired. I wait, I believe, I persevere; patience is much better than knowledge.— Though it delay my joy, it sets me on the way to it. The sense of divine love increaseth in me every moment. My pains are tolerable, but my joy is inestimable. I have now no desires but after heavenly things. Oh, what a library I have now in my God, in whom are hid all the treasures of wisdom and knowledge! I shall no more know in part, but be filled with the knowledge of God, as the sea is covered with waters. I have learned more divinity, in these ten days, than I did in fifty years before. My dying work is a conflict; but yet it is sweet, because of the consolations of the Spirit of God which abound with me. My soul, thou hast striven enough; rest now in God thy Saviour; time passeth, and we pass away with it; but I am confirmed and strengthened by the grace of God every hour. My body suffers, but my soul is abundantly comforted. The Lord is my shepherd; I shall want nothing. His rod and his staff shall lead me safely through this short valley of the shadow of death. The sharper my pains are, I am the nearer to my deliverance; I have no more to do but to give up my soul into the hands of God. As for me, my meat is to do the will of God, and happily to run out the course of my life. I am refreshed with holy and heavenly food. 'Death is swallowed up in victory. Thanks be to God, who hath given us the victory through our Lord Jesus Christ.' My strength fails me more and more; but my soul is strong and joyful."—His wife having perceived the near appearance of death in him, bade him "farewell;" saying, "Dear heart, enter cheerfully into life everlasting." He replied, "Yes, yes, I go to my God, and your God. We are all gainers. I go before you, and you shall follow. We shall be caught up together to meet the Lord in the air, and so shall we be for ever with the Lord. I am ready, I am ready. Come, Lord Jesus, open, open the gate to thy servant!"

Prov. xiv. 32. *But the righteous hath hope in his death.*

On Tuesday afternoon, Mr. H. S. Golding, feeling the approaches of death, broke out in these rapturous expressions:—"I find now it is no delusion! My hopes are well founded! Eye hath not seen, nor ear heard, neither hath it entered into the heart of man to conceive the glory I shall shortly partake of! Read your Bible! I shall read mine no more!—no more need it!" When his brother said to him, "You seem to enjoy foretastes of heaven: "Oh," replied he, "this is no longer a foretaste—this is heaven! I not only feel the climate, but I breathe the fine ambrosial air of heaven, and soon shall enjoy the company! Can this be dying? This body seems no longer to belong to the soul; it appears only as a curtain that covers it; and soon I shall drop this curtain, and be set at liberty!" Then putting his hand to his breast, he exclaimed, "I rejoice to feel these bones give way!" repeating it, "I rejoice to feel these bones give way; as it tells me I shall shortly be with my God in glory!"

The last words which he was heard to utter were, "Glory, glory, glory!" He died on the Lord's day, April 17th, 1808, in the twenty-fourth year of his age.

Remarkable Death.

A man that was addicted to a very reprobate course of life, going one Sunday morning to buy a game-cock for fighting, was met in the way to meeting by a good man, who asked him where he was going. He related the whole to him, and, after much entreaty, was prevailed on to go with him to the meeting, where it pleased God to convince him of his misery. On the Monday morning he went to his work, where he was beset by the rest of the colliers, who swore at him, told him he was going mad, and upbraided him by saying, that before a month was at an end he would swear as bad as ever. Upon hearing this, he kneeled down before them all, and earnestly prayed that God would sooner take him out of the world than suffer him to blaspheme his holy name; whereupon he died immediately ; and the person who was the instrument of bringing him to a knowledge of the truth died in a few days afterwards.

Deaths remarkable, and Presentiment of it.

Though we are not bound to believe every idle story propagated by the weak and superstitious, yet it must be confessed there have been singular monitions and very remarkable events which have preceded the death of some men, the testimonies for which we cannot reasonably refect. The following, I believe, are attested by indubitable evidence.

The pious Mr. Ambrose had a very strong impulse on his mind, of the approach of death, and took a formal leave of his friends, at their houses, a little before his departure; and the last night of his life he sent his discourse concerning angels to the press. The next day he shut himself up in his parlour, where, to the great surprise and regret of all who saw him, he was found just expiring.

Dr. Willet, in his epistle dedicatory prefixed to his Hexapla upon Exodus, has this expression : "It is most honourable for a soldier to die fighting, and for a bishop or pastor praying; and if my merciful God shall vouchsafe to grant me my request, my earnest desire is, that in writing and commenting upon some part of the scriptures, I may finish my days." This request was granted him, for he was called hence as he was composing a commentary upon Leviticus.

Remarkable Presentiment of Death.

In a certain village lived a peasant, quiet, unaffected, and unnoticed. Poor himself, he married a poor girl ; they brought nothing together but affectionate hearts and industrious hands. However, by unwearied labour, they acquired a comfortable livelihood, and brought up their children in good habits like their own. At length his strength failed, though he was little more than fifty ; and he often said he should not live long. One morning, when he was as well as usual, he thus addressed his family :—" I shall soon finish my course : in nine days I shall be in heaven. How was I obliged, last night, to force my way through hosts! but at last I got safe. I heard the angels sing, and joined them. Oh, it sounded gloriously ! They said to me, in nine days you will be with us!"

On the evening of that very day, he was seized with his last illness. On the ninth day he saw the sun rise, thanked God for having brought him so far through life ; and spent the day in prayer and in conversation with his wife and children. In the evening, when the sun went down, he was sitting at the window, and said to his wife, " when the sun is quite down, I will lay myself down also." He did so ; praying for his wife and family: they stood around his bed. He asked for a glass of water ;—drank ;—gave to each his hand, and his blessing. He then exclaimed, " Naked came I out of my mother's womb, and naked shall I return thither. The Lord gave, the Lord hath taken away, blessed be the name of the Lord."

With these words he resigned his spirit.

His excellent wife survived him many years (I knew her personally, says our correspondent,) and his children prosper.

Victory over Death.

We read of a certain Cappadocian whom a viper had bitten, and when it had sucked his blood, the reptile itself died, from the effects of the venomous blood. But Christ (being life essential) prevailed over death and swallowed it up in victory, as the serpent of Moses swallowed up the other serpents, or as the fire swalloweth the fuel that is cast upon it; yea, by death he destroyed him that had the power of death, the devil; whose practice it was to kill men with death. Rev. ii. 23. This is the second death.

DECISION OF CHARACTER.

THE Christian must maintain the conflict under every disadvantage, and that even to the last; or otherwise he will come to his grave not covered with glory, but with shame. At the famous battle at Thermopylæ, the three hundred Spartans, who alone had refused to abandon the scene of action, withstood the enemy with such vigour, that they were obliged to retire wearied and conquered during three successive days; till the enemy suddenly falling upon their rear crushed them to pieces. Only one escaped of the three hundred; he returned home, where he was treated with insult and reproaches, for flying ingloriously from a battle in which his brave companions, with their royal leader, Leonidas, perished. Thus what reproaches will attend the man who deserts the field of action, and draws back in that cause which of all others is the most glorious and important? "My soul," saith Jehovah, "shall have no pleasure in him."

When Socrates was on his trial, his judges expected submission from him. Lysias, one of the most distinguished orators of his age, composed an oration, in a laboured and pathetic style, which he offered to Socrates, to be pronounced as his defence in the presence of his judges. Socrates read it, but, after he had praised the eloquence and animation of the whole, he rejected it, as neither manly nor expressive of fortitude; and, comparing it to Sicyonian shoes, which, though fitting, were proofs of effeminacy, he observed, that a philosopher ought to be conspicuous for magnanimity and for firmness of soul. But how much more the Christian!

How many might have risen to great preferments if they had complied upon base terms! When Basil was promised great things, if he would but subscribe to the Arian heresy, he refused them with scorn and contempt. When Hormisdas, a Persian nobleman, was divested of all his honours, on account of his religion, and afterward restored again, and offered greater advancements if he would renounce it, he answered, "If you think I will deny my Christ for these things, take them back again."

Happy are they who can adopt the language of the Psalms, and, from experience of the divine Presence, can say, "Whom have I in heaven but thee?—and there is none upon earth I desire beside thee." How many, however, are there so dejected as to imagine that they cannot appropriate this language to themselves! Some truly pious persons, because they have felt, on certain occasions, their passions most lively with regard to earthly objects, conclude that they love them more than the blessed Redeemer; but this is not a certain means of deciding, as religion is of a spiritual nature, and shows itself more in solid effects than forcible emotions. When the ambassadors of a certain nation came to the Romans, offering to be their allies, and were refused, "Then," said they, "if we cannot be your allies, we will be your subjects; we will not be your enemies." Trembling believer, what say you to this? Is the question asked, Who is on the Lord's side? will you dare say you are not? Rather will you not say, " Lord, I will be thine! I will not live for the world; I will not be my own. If I am not admitted as a friend, I will be a servant. If I enjoy not thy peculiar presence, I will not, I cannot be thine enemy. Though thou slay me, I will trust in thee."

DEMOCRITUS.

WE may learn a lesson here from a heathen philosopher.

It is said of Democritus, that he continually laughed at the follies and vanities of mankind, who distract themselves with care, and are at once a prey to hope and to anxiety. He told Darius, who was inconsolable for the loss of his wife, that he would raise her from the dead, if he could find three persons who had gone through life without adversity, whose names he might engrave on the queen's monument. The king's inquiry to find such persons proved unavailing, and the philosopher in some manner soothed the sorrow of his sovereign. If a heathen could both dictate and practice submission, what ought not a Christian to do?

DEPRAVITY.

A PERSON was tried and convicted of murder. The evidence was clear against him. He persisted, however, in his innocence; but begged to have the sacrament. This was refused him, on the ground of his pleading innocent against such clear evidence. He then confessed his guilt; and the sacrament was accordingly administered to him. "Now," says he, "I did not commit the murder; I have received the sacrament; I don't care for any of you."

DIGNITY OF THE CHRISTIAN.

THEODOSIUS, the Christian emperor, said that he esteemed it a greater dignity to be a child of God, and a member of his church, than to be at the head of an empire. And that he enjoyed this inestimable privilege seems evident, if we believe historians, who say that though he was the sole master of the whole Roman empire, the master of the world, yet he did not discover any thing of that pride and arrogance which too often disgrace those who are elevated to distinguished situations. It was his wish to treat his subjects as himself was treated when a private man and a dependant.

THE AWFUL DECEPTION.

IT is reported of king Canute, that he promised to make him the highest man in England who should kill King Edmond Ironside, his competitor; and that when one had done it, and expected his reward, he commanded him to be hanged on the highest tower in London. So Satan and his emissaries promise poor souls that such and such opinions and notions shall advance them; but, in the end, they shall find the promised glory turned into ignominy, and the promised heaven become a hell.

THE DAUGHTER'S PORTION
TRANSFERRED.

MR. RODGERS often related little anecdotes concerning the unexpected repulses, on the one hand, and the agreeable surprises, on the other, which occurred in the course of his begging season.

One of the latter class shall serve as a specimen. Mr. Rodgers, attended by an officer of the church, called one morning at the house of an excellent woman, a widow, who had recently lost, by death, a pious and beloved daughter. As her circumstances were narrow, little was expected from her.

Indeed, they called upon her chiefly to testify their respect, and to avoid the imputation of either forgetting her person, or despising her mite. To their great surprise, however, when their errand was made known, she presented to them with much promptness and cordiality, a sum which, for her, was very large—so large, indeed, that they felt and expressed some scruples about accepting it. She put an end to their scruples by saying, with much decision, " You must take it all : I had laid it up as a portion for my daughter ; and I am determined that HE who has my daughter shall have her portion too."

THE DEITY.

WE have a great example of modesty and judgment in the case before us of Simonides. Hiero, tyrant of Sicily, asked him what God was ? The philosopher, a learned and wise man, answered, " that it was not a question which could be immediately resolved, and demanded a day to consider it." Hiero then desired an answer, but Simonides asked two days more to think of it ; and as often as called upon, required double the time to give in his answer. At which Hiero wondering asked the reason of such delays : " Because," says he, " the longer I consider it, the more obscure it appears to me."

DISINTERESTEDNESS.

IT is reported of Pompey, that during the time of a great dearth in Rome, he procured a quantity of corn in foreign ports, and shipped it for that city ; but the mariners, meeting a tremendous storm, reluctantly performed their duty, on account of the danger, when Pompey, as an example, exerted himself, saying, " Better a few of us perish, than that Rome should not be relieved !" This was public spirit, and a proof of that disposition which seeks not her own.

Pittacus was considered as one of the wise men of Greece. His disinterestedness gained him many admirers, and when the Mitylenians wished to reward his public service by presenting him with an immense tract of territory, he refused to accept more land than what should be contained within the distance to which he could throw a javelin.

DREAM.

A MINISTER of the gospel, for some time after his entrance upon the sacred ministry, was frequently harassed with fears, that he could not be able to proceed in his work. One week, in particular, through the whole of which he could not bring his mind to fix for any time upon any subject, he turned over his Bible and concordance from day to day and supplicated the Throne of Grace. At times he seemed to have an insight into a passage of Scripture, but could not long pursue any meditation before he found himself almost obliged to give it up, through embarrassment and perplexity. In this unhappy state he continued till very late on the Saturday night, when he retired to his bed, almost in despair of being able to appear in the pulpit on the following day ; nor did he expect to sleep, the anxiety he felt was so great : but, contrary to his expectations, he soon went to rest ; and, before he awoke, he dreamed that he went to a parish church, where, in former days, he had statedly attended, and that with unspeakable pleasure, upon the ministry of the Rev. Mr. Venn. After the prayers were over, with tears of joy he beheld his dear minister ascend the pulpit, who, after a short, but comprehensive and animated extemporary prayer, took for his text Matt. viii. 2.—" Lord, if thou wilt, thou canst make me clean." After a very striking introduction, in which he exhibited the sense of the passage in the clearest point of view, he took occasion from thence, and that in a manner almost peculiar to himself, to point out the uncleanliness, pollution, and impurities of fallen man, together with the ability and willingness of the Lord Jesus Christ to make him clean, and also the poor sinner's earnest solicitude for the benefit, when once he becomes sensible of his absolute need thereof. At the conclusion of the service, the minister awoke from his sleep, surprised to find himself in bed, but very much refreshed by his sleep, and still more by his dream. He could not doubt of an invisible agency over the human mind, both by night and by day, when men wake and when they sleep. He thought he retained in his mind all that in his sleep he had heard; and found himself happy in being thus provided with what he so very much wanted—a subject whereon to discourse that day to his people. It served him for the whole day, which was a comfortable one to himself, and a time of refreshing to many of his flock.

A person (in whose history there is something very remarkable) had been kidnapped, when he was ten years old, and brought from his native place to Tranquebar, whither his mother followed, seeking him every where for several days, but in vain. At length being told that the mission church was dedicated to the one true God, she made a vow, that if he would restore her son to her within ten days, they would both become his servants. Accordingly, she found him within the time, but, unmindful of her promise, offered a sacrifice to an idol, and returned into her own country. Being reproved, however, in a dream, for having neglected to fulfil her vow, when she awoke she told the matter to her son, and, without conferring with her other relations, immediately returned to Tranquebar, where, after proper instruction, she was baptized, together with her son and one of her sisters; after which she ministered many years in the church, teaching the catechism in private houses.

Philip, having been baptized, was further instructed in the town school, served one of the missionaries for some time, and being thought able to be a schoolmaster, was entrusted with that office. After this he was employed as a catechist, and having shown himself faithful in that station, they trust he will make a good country priest. There were present at his ordination, the governor, and other European gentlemen, and a great many Christians belonging to their town and country congregations. Two reverend ministers of the Danish church, named Zion, assisted on the occasion, together with the country priests.

OLD DISCIPLES.

It was the saying of an old disciple upon his dying bed, " He is come! he is come (meaning the Lord) with a great reward for a little work!" Agrippa having suffered imprisonment for wishing Caius emperor, the first thing Caius did, when he came to the empire, was to prefer Agrippa to a kingdom; he gave him also a chain of gold, as heavy as the chain of iron that was upon him in prison. And will not Christ richly reward all his suffering saints? Surely he will: Christ will at last pay a Christian for every prayer he hath made, for every sermon he hath heard, for every tear he hath shed, for every morsel he hath given, for every burthen he hath borne, for every battle he hath fought, for every enemy he hath slain, and for every temptation that he hath overcome.

Cyrus, in a great expedition against his enemies, the better to encourage his soldiers to fight, in an oration he made at the head of his army, promised, upon the victory, to make every foot-soldier a horseman, and every horseman a commander, and that no officer that did valiantly should be unrewarded. But what are Cyrus' rewards to the rewards that Christ, our general, promises to his disciples!

An old disciple hath a crown in his eye, a pardon in his bosom, and a Christ in his arms; and therefore may sweetly sing out with old Simeon, " Lord, now let thy servant depart in peace." As Hilary said to his soul, " Soul, thou hast served Christ these seventy years, and art thou afraid of death? Go out, soul, go out!"

" Many a day," said old Cowper, " have I sought death with tears, not out of impatience, distrust, or perturbation, but because I am weary of sin, and fearful to fall into it." Nazianzen called upon the king of terrors, "Devour me, devour me!" And Austin, when old, could say, "Shall I die ever? Yes; why then, Lord, if ever, why not now, why not now?" So when Modestus, the emperor's lieutenant threatened to kill Basil, he answered, "If that be all, I fear not; yea, your master cannot more please me, than in sending me unto my heavenly Father, to whom I now live, and to whom I desire to hasten." It was the saying of an ancient minister a little before his death, "I cannot say I have so lived that I should not be afraid to die; but this I can say, I have so learned Christ, that I am not afraid to die."

DELAYS DANGEROUS.

THE following passage in the life of Thomas Lord Lyttleton, is related nearly in his own words:—" I have had some serious conversations with my father; and, one evening, he concluded by recommending it to me to address Heaven to have mercy upon me, and to join my own prayers to his constant and paternal ones for my reformation. These expressions, with his preceding counsels, and his affecting delivery of them, had such an effect upon me, that I had bent the stubborn sinews of my knees— when it occurred to me that my devotions might be seen through the key-hole. This drew me from my pious attitude; and having secured this aperture, I thought it would not be a useless precaution to let down the window-curtains also; but, during the performance of that ceremony, some lively music, which struck up in the street, caught my attention, and gave a sudden flirt to all my devout ideas; so I girded on my sword and went to the theatre, where the entertainments soon put me out of humour with praying, and into humour with myself."

ENMITY OVERCOME BY LOVE.

WE read in our own chronicles that Edmund, surnamed Ironside, (in whom England was blessed,) and Canute, the first Danish King, after many encounters and equal fights, at length embraced a present agreement, which was made by parting England between them both, and confirmed by oath and sacrament, putting on each other's apparel and arms, as a ceremony to express the atonement or reconciliation of their minds, as if they had transferred their persons to each other; Canute became Edmund, and Edmund, Canute. Even such an exchange, I may say, of apparel is there betwixt Christ and the pardoned sinner, &c. Christ puts upon his church his own comeliness, decks his bride with his own jewels, as Isaac did Rebecca; clothes her with needle-work, and makes her more glorious within than Esther even was in all her beauty and bravery; rejoiceth over her as the bridegroom over his bride; yea, he is ravished in his love to her, with one of his eyes lifted up to him in prayer and meditation, with one chain of her neck, that chain of his own graces in her.

EVIL OVERCOME BY GOOD.

MR. DEERING, a puritan minister, being once at a public dinner, a gallant young man on the opposite side of the table, who, besides other vain discourse, broke out into profane swearing, for which Mr. Deering gravely and sharply reproved him. The young man, taking this as an affront, immediately threw a glass of beer in his face. Mr. Deering took no notice of the insult; but wiped his face and continued eating as before. The young gentleman presently renewed his profane conversation, and Mr. Deering reproved him as before,—upon which, with more rage and violence, he flung another glass of beer in his face. Mr. Deering continued unmoved, still showing his zeal for the glory of God, by bearing the insult with Christian meekness and humble silence. This so astonished the young gentleman, that he rose from the table, fell on his knees, and asked Mr. Deering's pardon; and declared, that if any of the company offered him similar insults, he would stab them with his sword.—Here was practically verified the New Testament maxim—"be not overcome of evil, but overcome evil with good." Rom. xii. 21.

ENVY.

XANTIPPUS, the Lacedæmonian general, assisted the Carthaginians in the first Punic war. He defeated the Romans, and took the celebrated Regulus prisoner.

Such signal services deserved to be rewarded ; but the Carthaginians looked with envious jealousy upon Xantippus, and he retired to Corinth, after he had saved them from destruction. Some say that the Carthaginians ordered him to be assassinated, and his body to be thrown into the sea as he was returning home ; while others say that they had prepared a leaky ship to convey him to Corinth, which he artfully avoided.

EXPOSITORS DESPISED.

A CERTAIN divine being asked what he thought of a passage of Scripture, immediately gave his sense of it ; and on the querist replying, "I believe, Sir, expositors differ from you," he warmly answered, "Don't tell me about expositors ; I know the sense I have given to be the true one, for the Holy Spirit has taught me." A silencing argument this ! Who could reply to it ?

THE FAMILY EXPOSITOR.

MR. W. a merchant of Boston, in America, according to his wonted liberality, sent a present of chocolate, sugar, &c. to the Rev. Dr. B. with a billet desiring his acceptance of it as a comment on Gal. vi. 6.— "Let him that is taught in the word, communicate unto him that teacheth in all *good things.*" The doctor, who was then confined by sickness, returned his compliments to Mr. W. thanked him for his excellent *Family Expositor*, and wished Mr. W. to give him a practical exposition of Matt. xxv. 36.—"I was sick and ye visited me."

THE FOOLISH EMPEROR.

IT is recorded, as the unparalleled folly of Nero, that when he was ready to cut his own throat to avoid the fury of the multitude, he broke forth into great expressions of sorrow, that such a proficient in music as he was should die. It was not the loss of the Roman empire that so much troubled him, as that so much skill in music must die with him. He valued himself more as a fiddler, than as an emperor. Thus carnal men, with a folly infinitely more prodigious when death is near, are not so much affected with the loss of a crown of glory and the kingdom of heaven, as with their leaving this world and its vanities. This makes death intolerably bitter.

EVIL.—THE APPEARANCE OF IT TO BE AVOIDED.

SOCRATES speaks of two young men that flung away their belts, when, being in an idol's temple, the lustrating waters fell upon them ; "detesting," saith the historian, "the garments spotted with the flesh ;" and will you play and toy with the occasions of sin ? The Lord forbid !

Livia counselled her husband Augustus, not only not to do wrong, but not to seem to do so.

Cæsar would not search Pompey's cabinet, lest he should find new matter of revenge.

Plato mounted upon his horse, and judging himself a little moved with pride, presently dismounted lest he should be overtaken with loftiness in riding.

Theseus is said to have cut off his golden locks, lest his enemies should take advantage of him by seizing hold of them.

GOOD EXAMPLES NEGLECTED.

THE Rhodians and Lydians enacted laws, that those sons which followed not their fathers in their virtues but imitated vicious examples, should be disinherited and their lands given to the most virtuous of that race not admitting any impious heir to inherit ; and do you think that God will not disinherit all those of heaven and happiness, who follow vicious examples ? Assuredly he will.

Precepts instruct us what things are our duty, but examples assure us that they are practicable. They resemble a clear stream, wherein we may not only discover our spots, but wash them off. When we see men like ourselves, who are united to frail flesh, and in the same condition with us, commanding their passions, overcoming the most glorious and glittering temptations, we are encouraged in our spiritual welfare.

Examples, by a secret and lively incentive, urge us to imitation. The Romans kept in their houses pictures of their progenitors, to animate their spirits, and stimulate them to follow the precedents set before them. We are sensibly affected by the visible practice of saints, which reproaches our defects, and obliges us to the same care and zeal, more than by laws, though both · holy and good. Now the example of Christ is most proper to form us for holiness ; it being absolutely perfect, and accommodated to our present state.

When Seneca received the message of death from Nero, he heard it with firmness, and even with joy. He wished to dispose of his possessions as he pleased, but this was refused, and when he heard it, he turned to his friends who were weeping at his melancholy fate, and told them, that since he could not leave them what he believed to be his own, he would leave them at least "his own life for an example !" An innocent conduct which they might imitate, and by which they might acquire immortal fame. Happy are they, who if they can leave nothing else to posterity, can leave them a good example ! This has sometimes proved a legacy more enriching and useful than the best bequest of untold wealth, or the most valuable treasures.

EXTORTION PUNISHED.

Silanus, the son of Manlius Torquatus, was accused of extortion in the management of the province of Macedonia. The father himself desired to hear the complaints laid against his son ; and after he had spent two days in examining the charges of the Macedonians, he pronounced, on the third day, his son guilty of extortion, and unworthy to be called a citizen of Rome, and also banished him from his presence. "An extortioner," says the apostle, "cannot enter into the kingdom of God ;" as he gives no proof of that change of heart, and that holiness, "without which no man shall see the Lord."

LOVE TO ENEMIES.

Such is the nature of Christianity, that it teaches us to forgive injuries, and to be merciful to those who have injured us. A few years since, a person of considerable property had part of a fence broken down, and taken off his premises. On an investigation, the offender was known, who after some time, was sent for : on his arrival, he was placed in a room, where every thing desirable was sent for his refreshment. The good man of the house repeatedly desired him to partake plentifully, at the close of which, he steps softly to him, and with a gentle voice, says, "My friend, I hope after this, you will not carry away my fence any more." It had its desired effect. Let the injured learn to make the word of God their guide. ·

Such is the delightful tendency of the religion of Christ, that were this principle but acted on, what a world of peace and harmony should we behold ! But, alas ! men are too much disposed to revenge and retaliation—to oppose and injure one another. We find but few instances like the following. Abuh Hanifah, a most celebrated doctor among the orthodox Mussulmans, having causelessly received a malicious and violent blow on the face, spoke thus to him who struck him : " I could return you injury for the injury you have done me, but I will not. I could also inform against you to the caliph, but I will not be an informer. I could, in my prayer of addresses to God, represent the outrage done me, but I will forbear that. In fine, I could, at the day of judgment, desire God to revenge it; but far be it from me : nay, should that terrible day arrive at this very moment, and could my intercession then prevail, I would not desire to enter paradise without you." How noble an instance of a calm, serene, and forgiving mind ! How happy would it be for all Christians, and how honourable to the name of Jesus, were there more frequent exercises of this grace of forgiveness like this wise and virtuous Mahometan ; and, more especially like him, who, upon the cross, prayed, "Father, forgive them ; for they know not what they do."

How will some of the heathens condemn Christians, both as to the rule and practice of this duty ! for, whereas it is esteemed to be the character of pusillanimity or stupidity to bear frequent and great injuries unrevenged. One of their poets mixed this counsel, among other rules of morality :—" That man is arrived at an heroic pitch of goodness, who is instructed, in a dispassionate manner, to bear great injuries." And when Phocion, who had deserved so highly of the Athenians, was unjustly condemned to die, his son attending him to receive his last commands immediately before his death, he charged him never to revenge it on the Athenians.

The Rev. J. Brown, of Haddington, seems to have possessed this among his other qualities. At his outset, as an author, he was reviled from the pulpit and the press. On this occasion he remarks, " I reckon myself so much the more effectually obliged, by Christian love, to contribute my utmost endeavours towards the advancement of their welfare, spiritual and temporal ; and am resolved, through grace, to discharge these obligations as Providence shall give opportunity for the same. Let them do to, or with me what they will ; may their pardon be redemption, through the blood of Jesus, even the forgiveness of sins according to the riches of his grace ! and let them call me what they please, may the Lord call them the holy ones, the redeemed of the Lord sought out and not forsaken !"

Such was the command of Christ to his disciples, and such is the genius of the Christian religion ; anger and revenge are to give way to love and a forgiving spirit. Nor are we without many instances of this being carried into effect. It was the common saying of one with regard to his enemies, " Let us pray for them." Another, in his last sickness, declared "that from his heart he forgave his enemies, and should rejoice to meet those in heaven who had treated him as if he were not fit to live on earth." The same disposition, it is well known, shown very conspicuously in Cranmer.

The late celebrated Dr. Franck, of Halle, in Saxony, received two letters while sitting at dinner. Having read the first, which was replete with the most severe censure, expressed in language extremely abusive, he was so far from being incensed at it, that he appeared unusually cheerful, and immediately prayed for his poor blind adversary, that the Lord would illuminate his soul with the light of his Holy Spirit. But when he had read the second letter, he laid it aside with every mark of grief and displeasure, having been too much flattered and exalted therein by one of his friends. Such is the proper conduct of a real Christian, who possesses true humility and a pure conscience : he would rather be unjustly censured than exalted above measure.

" Having in my youth notions of severe piety," says a celebrated Persian writer, " I used to rise in the night to watch, pray, and read the Koran. One night, wholly engaged in these exercises, my father, a man of practical virtue, awoke while I was reading; Behold (said I to him) thy other children are lost in irreligious slumber, while I alone wake to praise God! 'Son of my soul,' he answered, 'it is better to sleep than wake to remark the faults of thy brethren.'"

God is infinitely gracious, and, in the dispensations of his mercy, has set us an example how to forgive others who have at any time injured or offended us. When he pardons an offender, he does it fully. "Having forgiven you all trespasses;'"— "I freely forgave thee all that debt;"— "Their sins and their iniquities will I remember no more." This example we must imitate. If we do not forgive others, we must not expect to be forgiven ourselves. This was once urged upon a dying man, who had lived in malice for some time past. He was told that he could not be saved if he did not forgive the offender. "Then," said he, "if I die, I will forgive him!" It is to be feared that too many feel the same disposition with that dying man, though they do not express themselves so openly.

EVASION SOMETIMES PARDONABLE.

In the short, but inglorious reign of James the Second, when Popery was making rapid strides to power, the king had his agents and emissaries in every part of the kingdom, to harass, vex, and weary the Protestants into a compliance with the measures he was endeavouring to bring about; and where persuasion and threats had no effect, sometimes force and violence were had recourse to. One of his agents, with a party of soldiers (rather ruffians, I should say,) went out on a Sabbath morning to "hunt down the Protestants," as they termed it; they met a young woman, a servant-maid, running along the road, early in the morning, without either shoes or stockings.

The captain of this band asked her where she was going, so early in the morning, and what was the urgency of the business that made her run so fast. She told him that she had learned that her elder brother was dead, and she was going to receive her share of the riches he had bequeathed to her, as well as to her other brothers and sisters; and she was afraid she should be too late. The commander was so well pleased with her answer, that he gave her half a crown to buy a pair of shoes, and also wished her success: but if he had known the real business she was going on, which was to a sacrament, he would most probably have prevented her from going that day to the place where she hoped to receive durable riches.

EXPERIENCE.

LASSUS is reckoned by some, as one of the wise men of Greece. He was noted more particularly for the laconic answer he gave to a man who asked him what could best render life pleasant and comfortable. He replied, in one word—"EXPERIENCE."

"I never," said Luther, "knew the meaning of God's word till I was afflicted."

"I well know now," says Cecil, "what it is to have preached from a text which I did not so much as understand, till it was thoroughly opened to me by experience."

LOVE OF FAME.

THEMISTOCLES, when a very young man, was observed, soon after the famous battle of Marathon, in which Miltiades obtained so much glory, to be much alone, very pensive, unwilling to attend the usual entertainments, and even to watch whole nights. Being asked by some of his friends what was the cause of all this, he answered, "The trophies of Miltiades will not suffer me to sleep." Thus fired with a love of glory, in a few years, he became the first man in Greece.

Young Christians, faith presents to your view far greater glories than Greece could bestow on her most successful heroes. The perishing honours of Miltiades and Themistocles are not worthy to be compared with the glory that shall be revealed. Could they forego all the pleasures of youth to have their names enrolled in the records of fame?—And cannot you, by the help of Almighty grace, become a good soldier of Jesus Christ; in the hope of obtaining a crown of glory that shall never fade.

ISLE OF FRANCE.

"In no one did I see the least appearance of religion," says Mr. Thompson, the Missionary speaking of this island, "except in a native of India, who, as we returned to the beach to go on board, in a most graceful manner, begged to be excused from assisting us to the boat, pointing to his turban, to indicate that his religion forbade him to work on that day. Our captain, to try him, offered him a great present; but without avail." Shame on many professors of Christianity!

FORGETFULNESS OVERRULED.

The Rev. Mr. N. one Sabbath morning, opened his Bible to mark the passage he had been studying through the week, and from which he intended to deliver a discourse that day; but, to his great surprise, he could not find the passage; for neither words nor text could he recollect. He endeavoured to recall the subject to memory; and made it a matter of prayer; but all to no effect. While thinking how he should be confounded before the congregation, another passage darted into his mind with peculiar energy. He accordingly preached from it; and, during the discourse, he observed a person, apparently in a clerical habit, enter the place, and after having heard a little, seemed bathed in tears, and never raised his head through the whole of the service. Mr. N. never had more liberty in preaching. In the evening, this person called on Mr. N. took him by the hand, saying his purse was at his service for the sermon, and added, "Two or three years ago, I heard you, in such a place, preach upon a subject, and ever since I have been under the spirit of conviction and bondage. This day I took my horse and rode to hear you; and, blessed be God, he has now given me to see him as my reconciled God and Father in Christ Jesus, and has also given me to enjoy that liberty wherewith he makes his people free." "After some interesting conversation, we both," says Mr. N. "begun to see the good hand of God in this matter, and his good providence in determining me, in such a remarkable manner, to preach upon a subject I had never before prepared, and which he had accompanied with such a powerful efficacy. To me it was one of my best days, and one which both by him and me will be remembered through a joyful eternity."

THE POWER OF FAITH.

The following anecdote may perhaps illustrate the promise—"as thy day is, so shall thy strength be." Deut. xxxiii. 25. Under the reign of paganism, a Christian, notwithstanding her pregnancy, was condemned to die for her profession. The day before her execution she fell into labour, and, crying out in her pangs, the gaoler insulted her, saying, "If you make a noise to-day, how will you endure a violent death to-morrow?" To this she replied, "To-day I suffer what is ordinary, and have only ordinary assistance; to-morrow I am to suffer what is more than ordinary, and shall hope for more than ordinary assistance."—Oh! woman, great was thy faith!

FRIENDSHIP.

When one desired to see Alexander's treasure, he told his servant to show him not his gold and silver, but his friends.

Volumnius, a Roman, had a wonderful friendship for Lucullus, whom Mark Antony put to death. His great lamentations were the cause of his being dragged to the triumvir, from whom he demanded to be conducted to the body of his friend, and there to be put to death. His request was readily granted.

Friendship is undoubtedly one of the greatest blessings we can enjoy. It is justly said, that it doubles our pleasures, and divides our sorrows. It gives a brighter sunshine to the incidents of life, and enlightens the gloom of its darker hours. What an instance of it have we in Pythias!

When Damon had been condemned to death by Dionysius, he obtained from the tyrant leave to go and settle his domestic affairs, on promise of returning at a stated hour to the place of execution. Pythias pledged himself to undergo the punishment which was to be inflicted on Damon, should he not return in time, and he consequently delivered himself into the hands of the tyrant. Damon, however, returned at the appointed moment, and Dionysius was so struck with the fidelity of these two friends, that he remitted the punishment, and entreated them to permit him to share their friendship, and enjoy their confidence.

FORTITUDE.

Anaxarchus was a philosopher of Abdera, one of the followers of Democritus, and the friend of Alexander. When that monarch had been wounded in a battle, the philosopher pointed to the wound, adding, that it was human blood, not the blood of a god. The freedom of Anaxarchus offended Nicrocreon, and, after Alexander's death, the tyrant, in revenge, seized the philosopher, and pounded him in a stone mortar with iron hammers. He bore this with much resignation, and exclaimed, "Pound the body of Anaxarchus, for thou dost not pound his soul!" Upon this, Nicrocreon threatened to cut out his tongue, when Anaxarchus bit it off with his teeth, and spat it into the tyrant's face.

FEMALE FORTITUDE, AND THE PERSECUTOR DISAPPOINTED.

A pious woman used to say she would never want, because her God would supply her every need. In a time of persecution, she was taken before an unjust judge for attending a conventicle, as they styled her offence. The judge, on seeing her, rejoiced over her, and tauntingly said, "I have often wished to have you in my power, and now I shall send you to prison, and then how will you be fed?" She replied, "if it be my heavenly Father's pleasure, I shall be fed from your table:"—and that was literally the case; for the judge's wife, being present at her examination, and being greatly struck with the good woman's firmness, took care to send her victuals from her table, so that she was comfortably supplied all the while she was in confinement: and in this she found her reward; for the Lord was pleased to work on her soul to her real conversion.

THE TRUE GOD.

The heathens, it is said, confined their gods to certain places; some to this city, and some to that; some to the hills, and some to the plains; some to the sea, and others to the land. Thus it is said, that the same night in which Alexander the Great was born, the temple of Diana, at Ephesus, was burnt to the ground; and the heathens gave this as a reason for it—because Diana was absent from the temple, being gone to assist at the birth of Alexander; implying that their goddess was so confined to one place, that she could not attend to what was doing elsewhere. Such were the miserable conceits of the heathens! But our God is Jehovah, omniscient and omnipresent! He is the God of the hills, as well as of the valleys; of the sea, as well as of the dry land: he is as truly present in the lowest depth, as in the highest heavens! Let us, then, trust in him; for he is a refuge for us, and a very present help in time of trouble!

8*

GOD ALL-SUFFICIENT.

IN the Church's extremity, when her conspiring enemies are great in number and power, faith raises the drooping spirits. "If God be for us, who shall be against us?" When Antigonus was ready to engage in a sea-fight with Ptolemy's armada, and the pilot cried out, "How many are they more than we!" the courageous king replied, "'Tis true, if you count their numbers, they surpass us; but, for how many do you value me?" Our God is all-sufficient, against all the combined forces of earth and hell. We are, therefore, commanded to cast all our care on him; for he careth for us.

JUSTICE OF GOD.

DIOGENES seeing Harpalus, a thief, go on prosperously, was tempted to exclaim, "Surely God hath cast off the government of the world, and regards not how things proceed here below!" But we know that God will have a day of assize to vindicate his justice; and he will let sinners know, that long forbearance is not forgiveness!

PROVIDENCE OF GOD.

MR. C. WINTER observes, that in a time when he was destitute, and knew not where to look for a supply, he received a letter, of which the following is a copy, and which he kept, as he said, to record the kind providence of the Lord:—

"*Dear and Rev. Sir,*

"I enclose you twenty pounds, as I suppose your purse may be low. I commend you to the grace and love of Jesus: may he long shine upon you, and bless you!

"My dear friend,

"Yours, affectionately,

"J. THORNTON."

Theophilus Gale, being on his way to London, was alarmed with the sight of the city in flames. He had left his papers in the possession of a friend, whose house he soon found to be involved in the general calamity, and he bitterly lamented, that the labours of many years were lost. But he was delighted with the grateful tidings, that his desk had been thrown into the cart, as an article just sufficient to make up the load, and that his treasure was safe. To this circumstance, the world is indebted for the publication of his learned work, entitled, "The Court of the Gentiles."

Bunyan was twice snatched, when in imminent danger of being drowned: and once, when he was a soldier in the civil wars, he was drawn out to stand as a sentinel, at the siege of Leicester; but another having requested, for certain reasons, to take his turn, was shot through the head, and thus was Bunyan preserved!

The providence of God, which triumphed over the persecutors of his servants, by rendering their rage the means of establishing the oppressed Puritans, in a land which should in future become an asylum for the persecuted, demands our grateful adoration.

GOD HONOURED BY IMPLICIT CONFIDENCE IN HIS MERCY AND GOODNESS.

ALEXANDER the Great had a famous, but indigent philosopher, in his court. This adept in science was once particularly straitened in his circumstances. To whom alone should he apply, but to his patron, the conqueror of the world? His request was no sooner made than granted. Alexander gave him a commission to receive of his treasurer whatever he wanted. He immediately demanded, in his sovereign's name, ten thousand pounds. The treasurer, surprised at so large a demand, refused to comply; but waited upon the king, and represented to him the affair, adding, withal, how unreasonable he thought the petition, and how exorbitant the sum.— Alexander heard him with patience: but, as soon as he had ended his remonstrance, replied, "Let the money be instantly paid; I am delighted with this philosopher's way of thinking; he has done me a singular honour: by the largeness of his request, he shows the high idea he has conceived both of my superior wealth, and my royal munificence."

Thus let us honour what the inspired penman styles *the marvellous loving-kindness of* JEHOVAH. From the King, *whose name is the* Lord *of hosts*, let us expect, I say, not what corresponds with our low models of generosity; I say, not what we suppose proportioned to our fancied deserts, but what is suitable to the unknown magnificence of his name, and the unbounded benevolence of his heart. Let us expect such divinely rich blessings as surpass all created power, and all human apprehension. Then we shall no longer be afraid assuredly to trust that gracious declaration, " *Jesus Christ is made of God unto us, both wisdom and righteousness, and sanctification and redemption.*" Jesus Christ hath given himself for us, and has thus laid a ground of confidence and trust for us in all the blessings of his purchase, from the pardon of our daily offences, even to the possession of eternal life in glory. " He that spared not his own Son, but delivered him up for us all, how shall he not with him also freely give us all things." Rom. viii. 32.

OMNISCIENCE OF GOD.

No silence, no solitude, nor darkness itself, can hide the designs and actions of the wicked, nor the sufferings of his people, from the all-piercing eye of God. How many millions of inhabitants are in the world; how different their conditions and circumstances, ebbing or flowing; but are all actually and distinctly known to God! Without his universal and infallible knowledge, it were impossible that God should govern the world, and judge it. Torquatus Manlius, a Roman of noble birth, though blind through age, was chosen consul and general, to rule the state and the

army; but no arguments, no entreaties, could persuade him to consent to it. He answered, that it was absolutely absurd, that the lives and estates of others should be committed to *his* providence and protection, who must necessarily manage all things by the eyes of others. The perfection of God's knowledge fully qualifies him to govern the world, and is the foundation of trust in him. " Not a sparrow falls to the ground without his permission, and the very hairs of our head are all numbered with him." —" He that planted the eye, shall he not see? he that formed the ear, shall he not hear? he that teacheth man wisdom, shall not he understand?" Ps. xciv. 9, 10.

THE WORKS OF GOD PREFERRED TO THE WORKS OF ART.

THE works of God in creation form a fine field of contemplation to a serious and reflecting mind. Blind indeed must he be who does not discern the wisdom, power, and goodness of the Almighty in the various objects around him! Yet this is the case with many. Were we to see a man placed in a beautiful museum, choosing rather to gaze at pebbles and stones than at the variegated objects before him, we should pity him. Yet how many are so lost in sensuality and folly, as never to behold with admiration and gratitude the beautiful system which they inhabit! It is not thus, however, with the wise and the righteous?—to them "the heavens declare the glory of God, and the firmament showeth his handy work."

A gentleman being invited by an honourable personage to see a stately building erected by Sir Christopher Hatton, he desired to be excused, and to sit still, looking on a flower which he held in his hand—" For," said he, " I see more of God in this flower, than in all the beautiful edifices in the world."

GOD'S GREATEST WORK IS THAT OF REDEMPTION.

ABOVE all his other works, the

U

giving of his Son to be a sacrifice for sin, is an incomparable demonstration how much God delights in the salvation of men. And since he has been at such an infinite expense to open the kingdom of heaven to all believers, to set before them, as the object of hope, a kingdom of unchangeable glory, infinitely transcending the earthly paradise that was forfeited by sin, we have the strongest assurance that he desires the felicity of his creatures. And how awful must be the guilt and misery of those persons who know that Christ has opened heaven by his blood, yet put away the glad tidings from them, and refuse to enter into it! When Brutus, that noble Roman general, intimated to a philosopher his desire of restoring Rome to liberty, the latter replied that the action would be glorious indeed, but that so many servile spirits tamely stooped under tyranny, that they were not worthy a man of virtue and courage should hazard himself to recover that for them which they so lightly esteemed. The redemption of mankind is, without controversy, the master-piece of God's works; it is that wherein all his attributes appear in their excellent glory. Yet how monstrous is the ingratitude of those who wretchedly neglect the great salvation, which the Son of God purchased by a life of sorrow, and a death of infinite suffering!

And did the holy and the just,
  The Sovereign of the skies,
Stoop down to wretchedness and dust,
  That guilty worms might rise?

Yes, the Redeemer left his throne,
  His radiant throne on high,
Surprising mercy! love unknown!
  To suffer, bleed, and die!

He took the dying traitor's place,
  And suffered in his stead;
For man, (O miracle of grace!)
  For man, the Saviour bled!

Dear Lord, what heavenly wonders dwell
  In thy atoning blood!
By this are sinners snatched from hell,
  And rebels brought to God.

MERCY OF GOD.

SUCH is the wonderful clemency of that God against whom we have all sinned! How little do his creatures resemble him! If we are offended, how hard is it to forgive! and if we do forgive, it is, perhaps, not without upbraiding for the fault. When the Quadi had offended the Emperor Valentinian, he punished them with great severity; and when these indigent people came to implore his mercy, he treated them with great contempt, and upbraided them with every mark of resentment. He spoke with such vehemence that he broke a blood vessel, and fell lifeless on the ground. What an unspeakable privilege is it for man, that he has to do with one that *delighteth in mercy*, and who, though he will not acquit the wicked, will most assuredly pardon the penitent and contrite! "Let, then, the wicked forsake his way, and the unrighteous man his thoughts; and let him return unto the Lord, who will have mercy upon him; and to our God, who will *multiply pardons* towards him." Is. lv. 7.

GOD'S WISDOM AND GOODNESS DISPLAYED IN THE OCEAN.

WHILE the sea, by means of its innumerable inhabitants, affords food to man in one part of the earth, where there is a deficiency of wood, it also supplies him with fuel. We are told by Mr. Crantz, in his History of Greenland, "that the great Founder of nature has denied this frigid rocky region the growth of trees, he hath bid the streams of the ocean to convey to its shores a great deal of wood, which, accordingly, comes floating thither, and lodges itself between the islands. Were it not for this, we Europeans should have no wood to burn; and the poor Greenlanders (who, it is true, do not use wood, but train-oil, for burning) would, however, have no wood to roof their houses, to erect their tents, to build their boats, and shaft their arrows, by which they must procure their maintenance." It is difficult to decide where the timber grows; but, wherever it may be produced, its arrival in this dismal part of the earth is an astonishing proof of the care of our Father who is in heaven, over the humblest of his children on earth.

Another important purpose answered by the sea, is the supply of the clouds with vapour. According to the calculation of Dr. Halley, every ten square inches of water yields, in summer, between the time of sun-rise and sun-set, a cubic inch of water; every square mile, 6914 tons. Thus the water poured into the sea by rivers, ascends to the clouds in the form of vapour, and these clouds being conveyed overland by the wind (which much more frequently blows from the sea than in a contrary direction) returns to the earth in the form of rain.

By means of the sea those who are skilled in the art of navigation are able to keep up a communication between distant countries; the blessings of commerce are thus extended, and the knowledge of the glorious gospel communicated to "isles afar off."

GOD THE ONLY OBJECT OF RELIGIOUS WORSHIP.

GOD is infinite in all possible perfections: all-sufficient to make us completely and eternally happy; HE disdains to have any competitor, and requires to be supreme in our esteem and affections. The reason of this is so evident by divine and natural light, that it is needless to spend many words about it. It is an observation of St. Austin's "that it was a rule among the heathens, that a wise man should worship all their deities." The Romans were so insatiable in idolatry, that they sent to foreign countries to bring the gods of several nations to Rome; an unpolished stone, a tame serpent, or whatever was reputed a deity, they received with great solemnity and reverence. But the true God had no temple, no worship in Rome, where there was a Pantheon dedicated to the honour of the false gods. The reason he gives for it is, "that the true God, who alone has divine excellencies and divine empire will be worshipped alone, and strictly forbids the assumption of any into his throne." To adore any besides HIM, is infinitely provoking to HIS dread Majesty.

SUBMISSION TO GOD.

IT is no less our interest than our duty to keep the mind in an habitual frame of submission. "Adam," says Dr. Hammond, "after his expulsion, was a greater slave in the wilderness than he had been in the enclosure." If the barbarian ambassador came expressly to the Romans to negotiate, on the part of his country, for permission to be their servants, declaring that a voluntary submission, even to a foreign power, was preferable to a wild and disorderly freedom, well may the Christian triumph in the peace and security to be attained by an unreserved submission to HIM who is emphatically called *the God of order.*

It is incumbent on us at all times to be resigned to the will of God. To live or to die, if it be *his* pleasure, it ought to be our's. Yet a Christian, with a hope full of immortality, cannot feel it as a matter of indifference, when he reflects on the glory of the celestial world. Pyrrho, a skeptical philosopher, showed great insensibility in every thing, and declared, that life and death were the same thing. His disciples hearing this, asked him why he did not hurry himself out of the world? "Because," said he, "there is no difference between life and death." A Christian, however, can say that however desirable life may be, yet *to be with Christ is far better.*

In a fretful state of mind, we are apt to dispute with Providence, and an imagination of innocence kindles discontent. Of this impatience, some even of the best moral heathens were guilty. Titus and Germanicus charged the gods with their untimely and, in their apprehension, undeserved deaths; but the due sense of sin will humble and quiet the mind under sufferings; it directs us to consecrate our sorrows, and to turn the flowing stream into the channel of repentance. "Be still, and know that I am God."—"I was dumb: I opened not my mouth, because thou didst it." "Why should a living man complain—a man, for the punishment of his sins?"

If smiling mercy crown our lives,
  Its praises shall be spread ;
And we'll adore the justice too,
  That strikes our comforts dead.

Peace, all our angry passions then ;
  Let each rebellious sigh
Be silent at *his* sovereign will,
  And every murmur die.

GENEROSITY UNITED WITH PARSIMONY.

Mr. Whitefield, in a sermon at the tabernacle, related the following anecdote, which has so good a tendency, that the insertion of it in this work may contribute to the promotion both of frugality and generosity, qualities that may reciprocally assist each other:—"Two persons, who were employed in collecting money for some public charity, knocked at the door of a certain gentleman, intending to solicit his donation. While waiting there, they overheard the master of the house severely reproving his servant for the waste of a small piece of candle. Judging from this appearance of extreme parsimony that he was a covetous man, one of them proposed that they should lose no more time in waiting there, but go on to another house. The other person, however, thought it best to stay. At length they were introduced, when the gentleman, having read their case, immediately presented them with five guineas. The collectors, so agreeably disappointed, could not conceal their surprise, which being observed by the donor, he desired to know why they expressed so much

wonder at the gift. 'The reason, sir,' said one of them, "is this : we happened to hear you severely blaming your servants for losing an inch of candle, and expected nothing from a person who, we feared, was so parsimonious.' 'Gentlemen,' replied he, 'it is true I am very exact in the economy of my affairs; I cannot endure the waste of any thing, however small its value; and I do this that I may save, out of a moderate income, something to give to God and religion.'"

The moral is obvious. Masters and mistresses of families, suffer no extravagance! Spare unnecessary expense! Spare, that you may have to spend for God; and you, servants, avoid profusion and waste! Think not your masters covetous, because careful; it becomes both them and you to be careful, that there may be somewhat "to give to him that needeth."

A GRENADIER'S LIFE SAVED BY THE BIBLE.

Lately died at Blynhill, in Staffordshire, in his eightieth year, John Brotherton, labourer, a native of that parish. During eighteen years of his youth he faithfully served his country in the grenadier company of the thirty-seventh regiment, and fought with that corps in the battle of Minden. Immediately on leaving his native cottage to enter the army, Brotherton took with him a small Bible, determined to make it the constant companion of his marches, Previous to an engagement, he put the book upon his breast, between his coat and waistcoat, a practice to which he once owed the preservation of his life. In an action fought in Germany, while the thirty-seventh regiment was engaged in close quarters with the enemy, he received a thrust from a bayonet, directed against his breast; and the point of the weapon, after piercing his belt and coat pressed through the cover of the Bible, and perforated fifty-two of the leaves. This book now remains in possession of one of his brothers.

But to how many has the Bible been the means, not only of preserving the body, but saving the soul! Happy for us to live in a day when this divine Book is rapidly circulating through the universe!

THE CONDESCENDING GENERAL.

A CERTAIN general happened to observe a common soldier, distinguishing himself, on the day of battle, with unusual activity and courage. Determined to reward merit whereever it was found, he advanced the brave plebeian to a captain's post. The latter had not long enjoyed the honour before he came to his benefactor, and, with a dejected countenance, begged leave to resign his commission. The general, surprised at such an unexpected request, asked him the reason, " Your officers," said the petitioner, "being gentlemen of family and education, think it beneath them to associate or converse with a rustic. So that now I am abandoned on every side; and am less happy since my preferment than I was before this instance of your highness's favour." "Is that the cause of your uneasiness?" inquired the general. "Then it shall be, redressed, and that very speedily. To-morrow I shall review the army, and to-morow your business shall be done." Accordingly, when the troops were drawn up, and expected every moment to begin their exercise, the general called the young hero from the ranks, leaned his hand upon his shoulder, and, in this familiar and endearing position, walked with him through all the lines. The stratagem had its desired effect. After such a signal and public token of the prince's regard, the officers were emulous of his acquaintance, and courted rather than shunned his company.

We may apply this to the case of many poor Christians. Will not the favour of the blessed Jesus give us as great a distinction and as high a recommendation in the heavenly world? Will not the angelic hosts respect and honour those persons who appear washed in his blood, clothed with his righteousness, and wearing the most illustrious token of his love that he himself could possibly give?

In these tokens of his love may we be found! Then shall we meet one another with courage and comfort at the great tribunal with honour and joy amidst the angels of light, with everlasting exultation and rapture around the throne of God and the Lamb!

THE GOOD GOVERNOR.

PETER the Great frequently surprised the magistrates by his unexpected presence in the cities of the empire. Having arrived, without previous notice, at Olonez, he went first to the regency, and inquired of the governor how many suits there were depending in the court of chancery. "None, sire," replied the governor. "None! how happens that?" "Why," replied the governor, " I endeavour to prevent lawsuits, and, by conciliating the parties, I act in such a manner that no traces of difference remain in the archives. If I am wrong, your indulgence will excuse me." " I wish," replied the czar, that all governors would act upon the same principles. Go on; God and your sovereign are equally satisfied."

GOOD BROUGHT OUT OF EVIL.

HE that was rival to Crassus, when he stood candidate for command of the legion in the Parthian war, was greatly concerned that he missed the dignity; but he saw himself blessed that he escaped the death and the dishonour of the overthrow when the news of it arrived at Rome. The gentleman at Marseilles cursed his stars that he was absent when the ship proceeded to sea, that had long waited for a wind; but he gave thanks to providence that blessed him with the cross, when he knew that the ship perished in the voyage and all the men were drowned. And even these virgins and barren women in Jerusalem that longed to become glad mothers, and for want of children would not be comforted, yet, when Titus sacked the city, found the words of Jesus true, " Blessed is the womb that never bare, and the paps that never gave suck."

THE TOKEN FOR GOOD.

NOTHING is more natural to an awakened mind than a desire to know whether his sins be forgiven ; but how often does he doubt ! The holiness of that God against whom he hath sinned, and the view he has of the guilt and magnitude of his transgression, produce much fear and anxiety lest he should not be the object of pardoning mercy. History informs us that when a man had offended Augustus, the emperor, to show his greatness of mind, declared he pardoned him. But the poor creature, who expected only destruction, astonished beyond measure, and fearing the declaration was too good to be true, in all the simplicity of nature instantly desired his majesty to give him some present as a proof that he had really forgiven him. Thus anxious is the awakened sinner ! Such a free and full forgiveness, after all his heinous provocation, seems incredible ; he therefore desires, " a token for good," that he may know that he has passed from death unto life, and that all his sins are forgiven. Such tokens God is pleased to give, in hearing his prayer, in exciting his affection, in weaning him from the world, in sanctifying his afflictions, in humbling his pride, in granting his Holy Spirit, in keeping him from sin, and giving him an earnest of the better world.

INSTABILITY OF HUMAN GREATNESS.

THE great king of Babylon was brought to see the vanity of trusting to human power ; and to acknowledge that the MOST HIGH, who ruleth in the heavens above and in the earth beneath, is the only object in whom even kings ought to confide. But Nebuchadnezzar has not been the only one who has made this confession. The progress of the great king Alp Arslan was retarded by the governor of Berzem ; and Joseph the Carizman presumed to defend his fortress against all the powers of the East. When he was produced a captive in the royal tent, the sultan, instead of praising his valour, severely reproached his obstinate folly, and the insolent replies of the rebel provoked a sentence, that he should be fastened to four stakes and left to expire in that painful situation. At this command, the desperate Carizmian, drawing a dagger, rushed headlong towards the throne : the guards raised their battle-axes ; their zeal was checked by Alp Arslan, the most skilful archer of the age ; he drew his bow, but his foot slipped—the arrow glanced aside, and he received in his breast the dagger of Joseph, who was instantly cut in pieces. The wound was mortal, and the Turkish prince bequeathed a dying admonition to the pride of kings. " In my youth," said Alp Arslan, " I was advised by a sage to humble myself before my God, to distrust my own strength, and never to despise the most contemptible enemy. I have neglected these lessons, and my neglect has been deservedly punished. Yesterday from an eminence I beheld the numbers, the discipline, and the spirit of my armies ; the earth seemed to tremble under my feet ; and I said in my heart, surely thou art the king of the world, the greatest and most invincible of warriors. These armies are no longer mine ; and in the confidence of my personal strength, I now fall into the hands of an assassin."

Demetrius Phalereus, a disciple of Theophrastus, gained such an influence over the Athenians, by his eloquence and the purity of his manners, that he was elected a decemvir, B. C. 317. He so embellished the city, and rendered himself so popular by his munificence, that the Athenians raised three hundred and sixty brazen statues to his honour. Yet, in the midst of all this popularity, his enemies excited a sedition against him; he was condemned to death; and all his statues were thrown down, after having been invested with the sovereign power for ten years.

Consider the most remarkable examples which history has recorded of rare talents, and rare fortune, united for the accomplishment of some illustrious end. What are they, if read aright, but so many lessons of humility? Philip, the father of Alexander the Great, was by far the most accomplished hero of his age. His birth was noble, his person graceful and dignified; his understanding of that rare class in which depth and facility are equally united, at once elegant and comprehensive, and embellished with all the learning that Greece in her best æra could supply; his achievements in arms were great and brilliant, and his success was almost unvaried. It was Philip's chief ambition to live to future ages; and, that the triumph of his glory might be permanent, he was anxious to embody it in the literature and eloquence of Athens. For this end he was content to pardon alike her insults and injuries, and courted with unwearied assiduity the acquaintance of the most considerable members of her commonwealth. But the eloquence of a single man defeated all his hopes. Demosthenes was his enemy; and that profligate demagogue has been able, by his matchless genius, to brand with unmerited infamy, during more than two thousand years the illustrious prince who vanquished and spared him.

If the ancient world produced any person more deserving of admiration than Philip, it was probably his son. It was Alexander's ambition to found a mighty empire, which should embrace both the eastern and western hemisphere, and to foster under one parent and protecting shade the com-

merce, learning, arts, and legislation of the world. The greatness of his design could be measured only by the extensive genius which conceived it, and his success was equal to both. In the very prime of youth, he overthrew the most potent kingdom of Asia : he selected the position and laid the foundation of a city, which for a thousand years drew into its bosom the wealth of three continents; he carried his victorious arms into the heart of India, and having fixed and fortified his eastern frontier, returned to Babylon to prepare for extending his conquests in the west. There, as he was retiring early to rest, he passed by a chamber where some of his young officers and friends were banqueting; and, in a thoughtless moment, for he was by habit very temperate, he accepted an invitation to join their carousals. The rest who does not know? In a few days he was laid in his grave; and in a few years, the great empire of which he thought to have laid the foundation so deep that it should have stood for ages, was broken in pieces, and the fragments dispersed to the four winds of heaven!

I will mention but one example more, and that, like the two former, of the most vulgar notoriety. Cæsar desired to be master of the world. By devoting thirty years of his life to a single object, by the exercise of the most unrivalled talents, and the perpetration of unexampled crimes, he seemed to have effected his purpose. He was declared dictator. And how long did he enjoy his elevation? The ability which had raised him so high, failed him when only a small portion of it was necessary to sustain him in his guilty eminence. He had fought his way to empire, at the head of legions who were devoted to him, and he had not the prudence to retain a mere body-guard to preserve what he had won. He had sustained a character for moderation, during a long series of years, with consummate skill and hypocrisy; and when nothing but the language of moderation was necessary to secure his popularity, he forgot to use it ; and provoked a people who were jealous of the name of liberty, though they had surrendered the substance, by an avarice of silly titles. He had delivered himself repeatedly from the most complicated and overwhelming distresses, by his matchless sagacity and courage, and he was ruined at last by foolishly overlooking an irregular, ill-concerted conspiracy, which a child might have discovered. He had lived in the midst of a thousand dangers in the field, and he fell by the hands of assassins.

These instances, and numberless others, which are less striking only because they are less notorious, have been cited by the moralists of every age, and, after a few serious comments, dismissed with a sigh over the vanity of earthly glory. They prove, indeed, its vanity beyond controversy; but they prove, also, much more. They express in large and striking characters, that hapless uncertainty which attends upon every scheme of earthly policy.   What is true of great things, is true of small. Private life has its Philips, and Alexanders, and Cæsars, without number, who are striving with unwearied diligence for the attainment of a commanding reputation, or brilliant establishments, or ascendancy of station. The mere moralist can do little more than condemn their folly, and weep over it; but the Christian may surely be taught, by such example, a lesson of far higher wisdom, and, touched with a sense of his own weakness, may learn to resign himself, without regret and without fear, into the hands of his beneficent Creator.

HEAVEN.

When Anaxagoras was accused of not studying politics for his country's good, he replied, " I have a very great care of my country," pointing up to heaven. So a Christian looks upon heaven as his country, and considers himself as a stranger and pilgrim here on earth ; nor will his heavenly-mindedness detract from his patriotism, for *he* is the best friend to order and happiness on earth whose affections are most set on things in heaven.

The idolatrous temple of Diana was so bright and splendid, that the door-keeper always cried to them that entered in, "Take heed to your eyes." But what faculties of vision must we have to behold the glory of the Temple above! If it is said that the righteous themselves shall shine forth as the sun, what will be the splendour of the Eternal Throne? What a delightful change from this world of darkness and imperfection to that where all shall be light and glory! Happy those who are made meet to be partakers of this inheritance of the saints in light!

It was said of Tully, when he was banished from Italy, and of Demosthenes, when he was banished from Athens, that they wept every time they looked towards their own country ; and is it strange that a believer should mourn every time he looks heaven-ward?

A distinguished character, in a neighbouring nation, had an extraordinary mark of distinction and honour sent him by his prince as he lay on his death-bed. "Alas!" said he, looking coldly upon it, "this is a mighty fine thing in this country ; but I am just going to a country where it will be of no service to me."

DECEITFULNESS OF THE HEART.

The beginning of Nero's reign was marked by acts of the greatest kindness and condescension—by affability, complaisance, and popularity. The object of his administration seemed to be the good of his people ; and, when he was desired to sign his name to a list of malefactors that were to be executed, he exclaimed, *"I wish to heaven I could not write!"* He was an enemy to flattery ; and when the senate had liberally commended the wisdom of his government, Nero desired them to keep their praises till he deserved them. Yet this was the wretch who assassinated his mother, who set fire to Rome, and destroyed multitudes of men, women, and children, and then threw the odium of that dreadful action on the Christians. The cruelties he exercised towards them were beyond description, while he seemed to be the only one who enjoyed the tragical spectacle. " The heart is deceitful above all things, and desperately wicked ; who can know it ?"

HONESTY THE BEST POLICY.

THE following instance of honesty may be properly read, and recommended to the children in the Sunday schools :—A nobleman, lately travelling in Scotland was asked for alms in the high-street of Edinburgh, by a little ragged boy : he said he had no change : upon which the boy offered to procure it. His lordship, in order to get rid of his importunity, gave him a piece of silver, which the boy conceiving was to be changed, ran off for the purpose. On his return, not finding his benefactor, who he expected would have waited, he watched for several days in the place where he had received the money, pursuing his occupation. At length the nobleman happening again to pass that way, he accosted him, and put the change he had procured into his hand, counting it with great exactness. His lordship was so pleased with the boy's honesty, that he has placed him at school, and means to provide for him.

HARDSHIPS MUST BE ENDURED.

IT is well when we can acquire this habit of the soul so useful in carrying us through the various scenes of human life. The Greeks and the Romans considered contempt of pleasure, endurance of pain, and neglect of life, as eminent qualities of a man, and a principal subject of discipline. Scævola held his arm in the fire to shake the soul of Porsenna. The savage inures his body to the torture, that in the hour of trial he may exult over his enemy. Even the Mussulman tears his flesh, and comes in gaily streaming with blood, to win the object of his affections. What then may not a Christian be willing to suffer, engaged in a cause so noble, and having an object in view so grand ? If God be his friend, the Saviour his guide, and heaven his end, what has he to fear, even under the greatest difficulties ? Never was a holy courage more eminently exemplified than in the Apostle Paul ; and never could any mortal utter these words with greater propriety, " *I endure all things !*"

HOMAGE PAID TO WORTH.

PINDAR, the celebrated poet, was a native of Thebes and flourished about five hundred years B. C. His fellow-citizens erected a monument to him ; and when Alexander the Great attacked Thebes, he gave express orders to his soldiers to spare the house and family of this pre-eminent bard. The Lacedæmonians had done the same before this period ; for, when they ravaged Bœotia, and burnt the capital, the following words were written upon the door of the poet :— " Forbear to burn this house ; it was the dwelling of Pindar."

At the time our illustrious countryman, Captain Cook, was exploring the South Pacific Ocean, and blessing the nations of Europe by his discoveries, England and France were at war with each other ; but so sensible were the French Government of the benefits that might be expected to result from the labours of the English circumnavigator, that they issued strict orders to the commanders of all their ships of war, not to molest him, or any person belonging to the expedition, should they fall in with them on the ocean.

Xerxes, when he destroyed all the temples in Greece, caused the temple of Diana to be preserved, on account of its beautiful structure : so, when the destroying angel is sent forth to execute his commission, the souls who bear the divine image and who are the temples of the living God, shall be spared.

John Sobieski, king of Poland, &c. was justly famous for having raised the siege of Vienna when that city was invested by the Turks in the year 1683.

Such was the admiration of Charles XII. for this illustrious prince, that, touched with enthusiasm, he wept as he stood over his tomb at Cracow, and exclaimed, " *So great a king ought never to have died.*"

HYPOCRISY.

HYPOCRISY, though it may be concealed for a time, will sooner or later discover itself. It is often with difficulty that the hypocrite can preserve his mask entire, and, when detected, to what shame and disgrace is he reduced. When Fescenia perfumed her breath, that she might not smell of wine, she condemned the crime of drunkenness, but grew ridiculous when the wine broke through the cloud of a tender perfume, and the breath of a lozenge. " And that indeed is the reward of a hypocrite : his laborious arts of concealment furnish all the world with declaration and severity against the crime which himself condemns with his caution."

INSTABILITY.

XERXES crowned his footmen in the morning, and beheaded them in the evening of the same day ; and Andromecus, the Greek emperor, crowned his admiral in the morning, and then took of his head in the afternoon. Roffensis had a cardinal's hat sent to him, but his head was cut off before it came to hand ! Most say of their crowns, as a certain king said of his, " Oh crown ! more noble than happy !" It was a just complaint which long ago was made against the heathen gods, *O faciles dare summa Deos eademque tueri difficiles !* They could give their favourites great gifts, but they could not maintain them in the possession of them.

IGNORANCE.

A KNOWLEDGE of the operations of nature is often of vast importance in carrying on great enterprizes. When Alexander the Great's admiral, Nearchus, and his men, first saw the flux and reflux of the sea, at the mouth of the river Indus, the phenomenon appeared to them a prodigy by which the gods testified the displeasure of heaven against the enterprize in which they were then embarked. And when Cæsar's army, on their landing on the coast of Britain, saw the sea ebbing and retiring from their ships, they took it for a stratagem of their enemies, gave themselves up for lost, and were so frightened and confounded, that the courage and conduct of their great commander could scarcely prevent their overthrow.

INTEMPERANCE.

IT is related of Alexis the poet, that from every season of the year he drew arguments to furnish a new title to his intemperance : the spring, he said, required liberal drinking in sign of joy for the revolution of nature ; the summer to temper our heat and refresh our thirst ; it was due to autumn because it is dedicated to the vintage ; and winter required it to expel the cold, which would otherwise congeal the blood and spirits. Thus he pleaded for the allowance of his excess. And so men, in the several ages of life that are correspondent to the seasons of the year, frame some excuses to delay repentance, and give some colour to their rebellion against God, who commands us to hear his voice *to day*, obediently and immediately, upon no less penalty than being excluded from his blessed rest for ever. Heb. iv. 7, 8.

INTOXICATION.

BY one of the laws of Pittacus, one of the seven wise men of Greece, every fault committed by a man when intoxicated was deemed to deserve double punishment.

THE INQUISITION.

THE late admiral Pye having been on a visit to Southampton, and the gentleman under whose roof he resided having observed an unusual intimacy between him and his secretary, inquired into the degree of their relationship, as he wished to pay him suitable attention. The admiral informed him that they were not related, but their intimacy arose from a singular circumstance, which, by his permission, he would relate. The admiral said, when he was a captain he was cruising in the Mediterranean. While on that station, he received a letter from shore, stating that the unhappy author of the letter was, by birth, an Englishman; that having been a voyage to spain, he was enticed, while there, to become a Papist, and in process of time was made a member of the inquisition; that there he witnessed the abominable wickedness and barbarities of the inquisitors. His heart recoiled at having embraced a religion so horribly cruel, and so repugnant to the nature of God; that he was stung with remorse, to think if his parents knew *what* and *where* he was, their hearts would break with grief; that he was resolved to escape if he (the captain) would send a boat on shore at such a time and place; but begged secrecy, since, if his intentions were discovered, he should be immediately assassinated. The captain returned for answer that he could not with propriety send a boat, but if he could devise any means to come on board, he would receive him as a British subject, and protect him. He did so; but being missed, there was soon raised a hue and cry, and he was followed to the ship.

A holy inquisitor demanded him, but he was refused. Another, in the name of his *holiness the Pope*, claimed him; but the captain did not know him or any other master but his own sovereign, King George. At length a third *holy brother* approached. The young man recognized him at a distance, and, in ter-

ror, ran to the captain, entreating him not to be deceived by him, for he was the most *false, wicked,* and *cruel* monster in all the inquisition. He was introduced, the young man being present, and to obtain his object began with the bitterest accusations against him; then he turned to the most fulsome flatteries of the captain, and, lastly, offered him a sum of money to resign him. The captain treated him with apparent attention, said his offer was very handsome, and if what he affirmed were true, the person in question was unworthy of the English name or of his protection. The holy brother was elated; he thought his errand was accomplished. While drawing his purse-strings, the captain inquired what punishment would be inflicted upon him. He replied, that it was uncertain, but as his offences were atrocious, it was likely that his punishment would be exemplary. The captain asked if he thought he would be burnt in a *dry pan.* He replied, that must be determined by the *holy inquisition,* but it was not improbable.

The captain then ordered the great copper to be heated, but no water to be put in. All this while the young man stood trembling; his cheeks resembled death, he expected to become an unhappy victim to avarice and superstition. The cook soon announced that the orders were executed. " Then I command you to take this fellow," pointing to the inquisitor, "and *fry him alive* in the copper." This unexpected command thunder-struck the holy father. Alarmed for himself, he rose to be gone. The cook began to bundle him away. "O good captain! good captain! spare, spare me, spare me!" " Have him away !" replied the captain. "Oh no, my good captain !" " Have him away ! I'll teach him to attempt to bribe a *British commander* to sacrifice the life of an *Englishman,* to gratify a herd of bloody men." Down the inquisitor fell upon his knees, offering him all his money, and promising never to return if he would let him begone. When the captain had sufficiently alarmed him, he dismissed him, warning him never to come again on such an errand. What must be the reverse of feelings in the young man, to find himself thus happily delivered? He fell upon his knees, in a flood of tears, before the captain, and poured out a thousand blessings upon his brave and noble deliverer. " This," said the admiral to the gentleman, " is the circumstance that began our acquaintance. I then took him to be my servant—he served me from affection ; mutual attachment ensued; and it has inviolably subsisted and increased to this day." Christian reader, such, and infinitely stronger, should be the attachment to Jesus Christ, who has delivered thee from eternal flames, and that at the expense of his own life !

INSTRUCTION PREFERRED TO FLATTERY.

PETER the Great caused many foreign books to be translated into the Russian language, and among others, " Puffendorf's Introduction to the State of Europe." A monk, to whom the translation of this book was committed, presented it some time after to the emperor, who turning over the leaves, changed countenance at one particular chapter, and addressing the monk with an indignant air, " Fool," said he, " what did I order thee to do ? Is this a true translation ?" Then referring to the original, he pointed out a paragraph in which the author had spoken with great asperity of the Russians, and which the translator had omitted. " Go instantly," said he, " and execute my orders rigidly : it is not to flatter my subjects that I have this book translated and printed, but to *instruct* and reform them."

SPIRITUAL JOY.

SPIRITUAL joy purifies and fortifies the soul against the ensnaring and corrupting allurements of the world. *The joy of the Lord is their strength ;* that, of which he is the author and object, is productive and preservative of the vigour of the soul, to resist the charms of the world. It is said of Orpheus, when he passed by the syrens, who, by their charming voices, subdued men to sleep and then destroyed them, that he played on his harp, and the sweet sound made him despise their singing, and prevented the danger. The fable is fitly moralized. Joy in the Lord is our portion, and that infinite sweetness that is in communion with him makes such an impression upon the soul, that the ensnaring and destructive pleasures of the world are abhorred in comparison with them. That firm peace and pure joy, *passes the understanding*, our most comprehensive faculty ; whereas all the pleasures of the world do not satisfy our senses.

INEBRIETY.

A VENERABLE clergyman once assured the author, that he had never done so much mischief as by the best sermon he had ever preached—it was against the sin of drunkenness. It happened to be an offence to which none of his auditors were addicted. After it was over, some of them expressed no small triumph at their own secure state, from a consciousness of being free from the vice which had been so well exposed ; and, as if the exercise of no virtue but the one opposite to the sin in question had been necessary, they went home exulting in their own superior goodness.

THE WEEPING INDIANS.

WHILE men remain in an unconverted state, they feel no sorrow for their multitudinous transgressions, and are insensible of the danger to which they are exposed; but when once divine grace touches the heart, they possess different feelings : no longer can they behold sin as a light and trivial thing—no longer can they think of Christ with unconcern : they mourn over their past conduct, and weep on the reflections of God's forbearance and compassion. "Whenever I saw a man shed tears," said an Indian, "I used to doubt his being a man. I would not have wept, if my enemies had even cut the flesh from my bones; so hard was my heart at that time: that I now weep is of God, who has softened the hardness of my heart." Another Indian relates that he had made thirteen notches in a piece of wood, by way of memorandum that he had been thirteen Sundays at Lichtenau to hear the word of God; and that when he considered how often he had heard of his Redeemer, and looked at the notches in the wood, he could not help weeping, although he endeavoured to conceal his tears.

VINDICTIVE JUSTICE.

SUCH is the misery to which all men are reduced by sin; the justice of God is eternal, inflexible and infinite, and cannot be dispensed with; nor can the law of God be broken without punishment being inflicted. It is said that the Greeks had so offended Darius, that a servant, every evening, by his order, repeated these words: "Remember, O king, to punish the Athenians!" Thus justice calls for punishment on all mankind, "as all have sinned and come short of the glory of God." But how delightful the thought that all who believe in him shall be delivered from this curse, through Him who was made a curse for us!

MINISTERIAL JOY.

DIAGORAS, when he saw his three sons crowned in one day at the Olympic games as victors, died with excess of joy while he was embracing them. What will be the joy of ministers to see those to whom they have been instrumental in conversion, all crowned in one day with an everlasting diadem of bliss which shall never fade away! How should the thought of this support them under their present trials; stimulate them to vigorous exertions in the best of all possible causes; and teach them to bear with patience any reproaches, so that they may but become the means of saving precious and immortal souls!

FALLIBILITY OF HUMAN JUDGMENT.

A GENTLEMAN died possessed of a considerable fortune, which he left to his daughter, appointing his brother to be her guardian, and the executor of his will; and if the young lady, who was then about eighteen, happened to die unmarried, or, if married, without children, her fortune was to go to her guardian and his kin. Notwithstanding the objections of her other relations, the uncle took her to his house near Epping Forest, whence she afterwards disappeared; and, on inquiry being made, it was proved that she went out with her uncle one day, and that he returned without her. He was, in consequence, taken into custody; and on examination, acknowledged that he did go out with her, and said that she found means to loiter behind as they were returning home, and therefore he knew not where she was, or what was become of her. This account, however, being thought improbable, he was detained in custody; when it was discovered that the young lady had been addressed by a gentleman, who, a few days before she was missing, set out on a pretended journey to the North, she having declared that she would marry him on his return; and that her uncle having often expressed great disapprobation of the match, she had frequently reproached him with unkindness and an abuse of his power. A woman was also produced, who swore, that on the day on which they went out, as she was coming through the forest about eleven o'clock in the forenoon, she heard a woman say, "Don't kill me, uncle! don't kill me!" and hearing the report of a gun immediately after, she made off as fast as possible, but could not be easy in her mind until she had told what had happened. Upon this evidence the gentleman was condemned and executed ; and, in about ten days after his execution, the lady came home, and declared, that having previously agreed to go off with the gentleman, he had given out that he was going to the North, but that he had waited at a small house near the forest, where horses were ready for himself and her, as well as two servants who were also on horseback ; that as she walked with her uncle, he reproached her for persisting in her resolution ; and after much altercation, she said, with some warmth, " *I have set my heart upon it : if I do not marry him it will be my death ! and don't kill me, uncle ! don't kill me !*"—That just as she had uttered these words, a man shot a wood-pigeon ; and that coming near the appointed place, she let her uncle go on ; and, her suitor being ready, she mounted her horse and rode off to lodgings near Windsor, where they were married the same day ; and, in about a week, went on a journey of pleasure to France, whence they were then returned.

DR. JOHNSON.

A YOUNG gentleman, to whom the late Dr. Johnson was godfather, called to see him a very short time before his death. In the course of conversation, the doctor asked him what books he read ; the young man replied, " The books, sir, which you have given me." Dr. Johnson, summoning up all his strength, and with a piercing eye fixed upon the youth, exclaimed, with the utmost energy, " Sam, Sam, read the Bible : all the books that are worth reading have their foundation and their merits there."

THE JUDGMENT DAY.

JEROME used to say, that it seemed to him as if the trumpet of the last day was always sounding in his ears, saying, " Arise, ye dead, and come to judgment." The generality, however, think but little of this awful and important period. A Christian king of Hungary, being very sad and pensive, his brother, who was a gay courtier, was desirous of knowing the cause of his sadness. " Oh, brother," said the king, " I have been a great sinner against God, and know not how to die, or how to appear before God in judgment !" His brother, making a jest of it, said, " These are but melancholy thoughts." The king made no reply ; but it was the custom of the country, that if the executioner came and sounded a trumpet before any man's door, he was presently led to execution. The king, in the dead of night, sent the executioner to sound the trumpet before his brother's door ; who hearing it, and seeing the messenger of death, sprang into the king's presence, beseeching to know in what he had offended. " Alas ! brother," said the king, " you have never offended me. And is the sight of my executioner so dreadful, and shall not I who have greatly offended, fear to be brought before the judgment seat of Christ ?"

ADVANTAGE OF INSTRUCTION.

AT a Conductor's Meeting lately held in the city of Bristol, where the teachers were requested to bring a few of those who had been rescued from a state of the greatest ignorance, who were permitted to tell their own unvarnished tale, a woman said she had reason above most to thank God for adult schools. Her husband had been the terror of the neighbourhood ; the tyrant of his family ; a drunkard, a sabbath-breaker, a blasphemer ; an injurious person, who cared not for his own household, but spent his wages at the ale-house—seldom came home until midnight ; drunk, quarrelsome, destructive of all her domestic comforts—he, by degrees, began to reform ; came home earlier, less intoxicated, and at length sober. She dared not ask the cause ; until he one day told her he had been *learning to read at an adult school.* He could read his Bible ; and, in that blessed book, he saw the odious picture of his former self held up to reprobation as fit only for the burning : he was determined to reform ; he dreaded eternal punishment : asked her to go to a woman's adult school, and learn also : she did ; she could now read her Bible : it was their mutual delight : that house, which was of late a *little hell*, had become a Bethel. Where blasphemy lately reigned, prayer and praise resounded. Every morning and night her three children were placed hand in hand between them; and "behold he prayed." His home, his children, his fire-side, were his delight.

INTERCESSION.

WE are informed by a certain historian, of two brothers, one of whom, for capital crimes, was condemned to die ; but upon the appearance of the other, who had lost an arm in the successful defence of his country, on the presentation of the remaining stump, the judges were so affected with a grateful recollection of his past services, as freely, for his sake, to pardon his guilty brother.

Thus our divine Redeemer, appearing " on the throne as a Lamb that had been slain," Rev. v. 6, " with scars of honour in His flesh, and triumph in His eyes," silently but powerfully reminds His heavenly Father of his bitter sufferings, and the important design of them ; even the eternal salvation of His people : nor does He thus appear in vain.

ANECDOTE OF THE KING AT HIS CORONATION.

AFTER the anointing was over in the Abbey, and the crown put upon the king's head, with great shouting, the two archbishops came to hand him down from the throne to receive the sacrament. He told them he would not go to the Lord's Supper and partake of that ordinance with the crown upon his head ; for he looked upon himself, when appearing before the King of kings, in no other character but as a humble Christian! —these were his very words. The bishops replied, that, although there was no precedent for this, it should be complied with. Immediately he put off his crown and laid it aside ; he then desired the same should be done with respect to the queen. It was answered that her crown was so pinned on her head that it could not easily be taken off ; to which the king replied, " Well, let it be reckoned a part of her dress, and in no other light." When I saw and heard this, says one, it warmed my heart to him : and I could not help thinking there would be something good found about him towards the Lord God of Israel.

Among other reasons for remembering the king in our prayers, Mr. A. mentions that he was a man of prayer himself ;—and adds, " I myself have heard, from good authority, that after a former restoration from that grievous malady under which he now labours, the king observed to a bishop, with whom he was in the habit of free conversation, that there had not a day passed in which he was not enabled to lift up his heart to God.

THE ROASTING JACK.

HIS Majesty riding from Windsor, one day in the month of July, 1779, was overtaken by a violent storm of rain ; and being separated from his company, he made towards a farmhouse, or rather a cottage, belonging to a man named Stiles, near Stoke. Here he alighted, and going into the house, found a girl turning a goose, which was hanging before the fire by a string. The king desired the girl to put his horse into the shed, which she consented to do ; at the same time requesting him to mind the goose. While she was gone the farmer entered, and great was his surprise to see the king, whom he knew, so employed. He, however, had the presence of mind to relieve his Majesty without appearing embarrassed ; and, on the return of his daughter, he went to rub down the horse. His Majesty, with his wonted good nature, conversed on this mode of cookery, and the advantages of a jack: soon after which the weather clearing up, he mounted and rode away. When he was gone, the farmer perceived a paper on the shelf, and, having opened it, found in it five guineas, with these words written in pencil, " *To buy a Jack.*"

SELF-KNOWLEDGE.

SELF-KNOWLEDGE was considered, even by the heathens, as so indispensably necessary, that it was a motto engraved on one of their temples, " *Know thyself!*" Thus they made the stones cry out of the wall to every one who entered, that, without this important acquisition, he was a vain worshipper.

SOUND KNOWLEDGE HUMILIATING.

MENEDEMUS was wont to say that the young boys that went to Athens, the first year were wise men; the second, philosophers; the third, orators; and the fourth were but plebeians, and understood nothing but their own ignorance.

Is not this often the case with young Christians and students? At first, with a little smattering of knowledge, they think themselves wise; but, as they proceed to climb the mount of knowledge, they find prospects open to their view of which they had formed no conception; and, overwhelmed with the view of the great and mighty objects before them, conclude, at last, that they know nothing as they ought to know.

THE TWO KNIGHTS; OR, ZEAL, TO BE DISCRIMINATED AND EXAMINED.

MANY things must concur before we can be allowed to determine whether zeal be a virtue or a vice. Those who are contending for the one or the other will be in the situation of the two knights, who meeting on a cross-road, were on the point of fighting about the colour of a cross that was suspended between them. One insisted it was gold; the other maintained it was silver. The duel was prevented by the interference of a passenger who desired them to change their positions. Both crossed over to the opposite sides; found the cross was gold on one side, and silver on the other. Each then acknowledged his opponent to be right.

THE HAPPY LAND.

As a gentleman, eminent for his happy mode of introducing religious conversation among young people, was one day going, in the stage-coach, to his country-house at Hampstead, he was accosted by a young man, who was his only companion, in the following terms:—" Sickness, sir, is a very uncomfortable thing: I have been running almost all over London to find out a physician to attend my sister, who is sick at Hampstead; but I am now so fatigued that I am compelled to take the stage." " Yes, sir," replied the gentleman, " sickness is a very uncomfortable thing; but I know a land in which there is no sickness!" " Do you, indeed?" rejoined the young man; " pray, where is it? I have travelled all round the world, and never heard of that land yet!"

" One of our old Hottentots," says Mr. Read, the missionary, was taken very ill the other day: when I visited him he said, ' This is the message of death!—I will now go and see the other country, where I have never been, but which I long to see!—I am weary of every thing here—I commit too much sin here—I wish to be free from it!—I cannot understand things well here, and you cannot understand me: the Lord hath spoken much to me, but I cannot explain it.' "

VICISSITUDES OF LIFE.

THE history of the world is the

history of human vicissitudes. The transition from wealth and property, to poverty and adversity, has been found to be very short and sudden. Hence it was the custom of the Roman triumphs that a slave should be placed behind the chariot, to remind the conqueror of the instability of earthly grandeur, and the infirmities of human nature.

LOVE AND FEAR UNITED.

Though it be true that love casteth out fear, and that there is a holy familiarity with, and confidence in God, yet there is a fear of reverence, in respect to God's perfections, arising from the knowledge of his excellency, which will continue even in heaven itself, when guilt will be done away; and, perhaps, then we shall have the most reverential awe of God. Hence a person of eminent holiness, when dying, was filled with great fears and tremblings. "I wonder," said one to him, "that you who know God do so fear him!" To which he answered, "If I knew him more, I should fear him more." It is not, then, incompatible with holy joy. It is said the churches "walked in the fear of God, and in the comfort of the Holy Ghost." Acts, ix. 13. There we see an union of fear and joy!

THE LORD'S NAME TAKEN IN VAIN.

In consequence of Bibles being sent on board his Majesty's ships of war, by the society formed for that purpose, Captain Cornwallis was very zealous to carry the laudable designs of the society into effect. In order to prevent profane swearing and the improper use of God's name among the ship's crew, he had a book to every mess, in which to insert each offender's name. For the first offence he was to forfeit a day's grog to the mess; for the second two days': for the third not only a week, but to suffer corporal punishment.

To these rules the captain made himself liable except to the punishment. Looking over the books, which

V

he did every morning when at sea, he found his own name inserted, sent for the informer, and inquired what he had said, and who was near when he used improper language on deck. Being told the chaplain was at his elbow, he called for the rev. gentleman, asked if he recollected hearing him say the preceding day, "By G—." He replied in the affirmative, but did not think it came within the meaning of the rules. The captain observed it was certainly an irreverent use of the sacred name, for which you should have reproved me, and your neglect is as bad as the crime.

You shall be punished for neglect of duty, and he shall be rewarded with a guinea. This had a pleasing effect on the crew, who were mustered to hear their captain's confession, their chaplain's reproof, and, we trust, the reward of their brother tar. Would to God the day were come when all captains of ships would do likewise! for the wickedness of many ships obviously requires such regulations.

It is said, that the late Rev. John Brown, of Haddington, when passing the Frith at Forth, between Leith and the Kinghorn, had for a fellow-passenger one who appeared to be a Highland nobleman. Mr. Brown observed, with much grief, that he frequently took the name of God in vain; but suspecting that to reprove him in the presence of the other passengers might lead only to irritate him, he forbore saying any thing until he reached the opposite shore. After landing, Mr. Brown observing the nobleman walking alone, stepped up to him, "Sir, I was sorry to hear you swearing while on your passage. You know it is written, 'Thou shalt not take the name of the Lord thy God in vain.'" On this the nobleman lifting his hat and bowing to Mr. Brown, made the following reply: "Sir, I return you thanks for the reproof you have now given me, and shall endeavour to attend to it in future; but," added he, "had you said this to me while in the boat, I believe I should have run you through with my sword."

LABOUR.

It was a custom of the Parthians not to give their children any meat in the morning before they saw the sweat on their faces from some labour. "I apprehend," says one, "there is not a more miserable, as well as a more worthless being, than a young man of fortune, who has nothing to do but to find new ways of doing nothing."

Indolence is injurious both to the body and the mind; whereas labour and exercise are profitable, and conducive to health and cheerfulness. When Cyrus conducted Lysander, the famous Lacedæmonian general, through his gardens, Lysander was struck at the charming prospect; and still more on finding that the plan and order of all were drawn by Cyrus himself, and many of the trees planted with his own hands. "What!" said Lysander, viewing him from head to foot, "is it possible, with these purple robes and splendid vestments, those strings of jewels and bracelets of gold, that you could play the gardener, and employ your royal hands in planting trees?" "Does that surprise you?" said Cyrus. "I protest, with the utmost sincerity, that when my health admits, I never sit down to table without having made myself sweat with some fatigue or other, either in military exercise, rural labour, or some toilsome employment, to which I apply with pleasure and without sparing myself." This was setting an example of industry worthy of imitation. The rich and the great would find far more true happiness in this way, than sitting at ease or indulging in luxury.

I knew an enthusiast, who thought it a temptation to work, and that it was his duty to pray all day: the consequence was, he was left to starve.

The greatest part of mankind are busily employed, but, alas! it is doing nothing; nothing conducive to their real happiness or the glory of HIM who made them. We labour in the fire for very vanity, while we neglect the awful and important scenes which must open to our view. "I told you of one," said a minister, "who ruined himself by beautifying a seat which did not belong to him, and you wondered at his folly; but the moral is better worth considering than the fact: for this is true of us all; when we waste our substance in forming scenes of grandeur and pleasure upon this earth, we are but beautifying what does not belong to us, and must soon be left behind. Let us labour therefore for that which shall not prove transient or inefficient. Let us seek that house not made with hands, eternal in the heavens."

SELF-LOVE.

Men look into the enchanting glass of their own fancies, and are vainly enamoured with the false reflection of their excellencies. Self-love hinders the sight of those imperfections which, discovered, would lessen the liberal esteem of themselves. The soul is a more obscure object to its eye, than the most distant star in the heavens. Seneca tells of some that had a strange infirmity in their eyes, so that wherever they turned, they encountered the visible moving image of themselves. Of which he gives this reason: "It proceeds from the weakness of the optic faculty, that for want of spirits derived from the brain, cannot penetrate through the diaphonous air, to see objects; but every part of the air is a reflecting glass of themselves." That which he conjectured to be the cause of the natural infirmity, is most true of the moral, the subject of our discourse. It is from the weakness of the mind that the judicative faculty does not discover the worth of others, but sees only a man's self, as singular in perfections, and none superior, or equal, or near him. A proud man will take occasion from any advantage to foment pride. Some from the perfections of the body, beauty, or strength ; some from the circumstance of their condition, riches, or honour ; and every one thinks himself sufficiently furnished with understanding.

LYING.

WHEN Denades, the orator, addressed himself to the Athenians, "I call all the gods and goddesses to witness," said he, "the truth of what I shall say ;" the Athenians, often abused by his impudent lies, presently interrupted him, by exclaiming, "And we call all the gods and goddesses to witness that we will not believe you."

Lying Punished.

One day there happened a tremendous storm of lightning and thunder, as Archbishop Leighton was going from Glasgow to Dunblane. He was descried, when at a distance, by two men of bad character. They had not courage to rob him ; but wishing to fall on some method of extorting money from him, one said, "I will lie down by the way-side as if I were dead, and you shall inform the archbishop that I was killed by the lightning, and beg money of him to bury me." When the archbishop arrived at the spot, the wicked wretch told him the fabricated story. He sympathised with the survivor, gave him money, and proceeded on his journey. But when the man returned to his companion, he found him really lifeless ! Immediately he began to exclaim aloud, " Oh, sir, he is dead ! Oh, sir, he is dead !" On this, the archbishop discovering the fraud, left the man with this important reflection : " It is a dangerous thing to trifle with the judgments of God."

THE DIVINE LAW MAGNIFIED.

THE story of Zeleucus, prince of the Locrians, is well known. To show his abhorrence of adultery, and his determination to execute the law he had enacted, condemning the adul-

terer to the loss of both his eyes ; and at the same time, to evince his love to his son, who had committed that crime, he willingly submitted to lose one of his own eyes, and ordered, at the same time, one of his son's to be put out ! Now what adulterer could hope to escape, when power was vested in a man whom neither self-love, nor natural affection in its greatest force, could induce to dispense with the law, or relax the rigour of its sentence ? So in God's way of saving sinners, the language both of the Father and the Son is manifestly, and most emphatically, "Let the law be magnified and be made honourable in the sight of the whole universe."

LIBERALITY REWARDED.

THE religion of the Bible is the religion of humanity. While it teaches us to adore and reverence the great Lord of the universe, it also inculcates compassion and attention to his creatures. Some, it is true, place all their religion in acts of charity to the poor, and imagine this will be a substitute for every thing else. Let us beware of running to the opposite extreme ; and because we cannot merit heaven by our beneficence, therefore never display any. The precepts and the promises relative to charity in the sacred volume, are very prominent and numerous. " It is more blessed to give than to receive ;" and few, we believe, have ever been the poorer, on the whole, for their liberality. Tiberius the Second was very famous for his bounty to the poor ; insomuch that his wife was wont to blame him for it ; and speaking to him once how he wasted his treasure that way, he told her, "He should never want money, so long as, in obedience to Christ's command, he supplied the necessities of the poor." Soon after this, under a marble table, which was taken up, he found a great treasure ; and news was also brought him of the death of one Narsus, a very rich man, who had left his whole estate to him.

LUXURY.

THE historian upbraids the Roman luxury, that with so much cost and hazard they should send to foreign parts for trees that were beautiful, but barren, and produced a shadow only without fruit. With greater reason we may wonder, that men should, with the expense of their precious hours, purchase barren curiosities which are unprofitable to their last end. How can a condemned criminal, who is in suspense between life and death, attend to study the secrets of nature and art, when all his thoughts are taken up how to prevent the execution of his sentence? And it is no less than a prodigy of madness that men who have but a short and uncertain space allowed them to escape the wrath to come, should rack their brains in studying things impertinent to salvation, and neglect the knowledge of a Redeemer?

Luxury and worldly pleasures have not only proved fatal to individuals, but to whole communities. Scaurus was celebrated for the large theatre he built at Rome, during his edileship. This theatre would contain 30,000 spectators, was supported by 360 columns of marble, thirty-eight feet in height, and adorned with 3,000 brazen statues. But this splendid edifice, according to Pliny, proved more fatal to the manners and the simplicity of the Romans than the proscriptions and wars of Sylla had done to the inhabitants of the city.

The luxury of Capua destroyed the bravest army which Italy ever saw, flushed with conquest, and commanded by Hannibal. The moment Capua was taken, the walls of Carthage trembled. They caught the infection, and grew fond of pleasure, which rendered them effeminate, and of course an easy prey to their enemies.

BENEVOLENT MERCHANT.

AUGUSTINE accounted nothing his own that he did not communicate to others. The bee stores her hive out of all sorts of flowers for the common benefit. It is a base and unworthy spirit, that induces a man to make himself the centre of all his actions. The very heathen could say, that a man's country, and his friends, and others, challenge a great part of him. And indeed, the best way of doing ourselves good, is by doing good to others; the best way to gather is to scatter.

The story of Pyrrhus, a merchant of Ithica, is memorable. Espying at sea an aged captive in a pirate's ship, he took compassion on him, redeemed him, and bought his articles of merchandize which the pirates had taken from him, consisting of several barrels of pitch. The old man perceiving that it was not for any good service he could render him, nor for the sake of gaining his commodity, but merely out of benevolence and pity that Pyrrhus had done this, discovered to him a great mass of treasure hidden in the pitch, by means of which the merchant in a short time became immensely rich, and thus was the word verified to him—"He that soweth liberally, shall also reap liberally."

MEEKNESS.

"A MEEK man," says Mr. Henry, "escapes many of those perplexities, those woes, and sorrows, and wounds without cause, which he that is passionate, provoking, and revengeful, brings upon his own head." An instance of this, I remember, Mr. Baxter gives in his book on Patience, to the following effect: "Once as he was going along the streets of London, a hectoring rude fellow jostled him; he went on his way, and took no notice of it; but the same man affronting the next person he met, in a similar manner, he drew his sword, and demanded satisfaction, on which mischief ensued. The two goats that met upon the narrow bridge, were both in danger had they quarrelled, but they were both preserved by the condescension of one that lay down, and let the other go over him. It is the evil tendency of passion that it turns our friends into enemies; but it is the excellency of meekness that it converts our enemies into friends, which is an effectual way of conquering them."

THE IRRITATED MAGISTRATE.

MAGISTRATES are, in the Scriptures, designated gods; and if such be their title what ought to be their conduct? God hath set them in the chair of justice and lent them his name. When the rude soldiers saw the senators at Rome sitting gravely in their robes, they looked upon them as gods; but as soon as one of them became irritated, and showed his temper, they took them for men. Thus it will be with all magistrates: as long as they act with dignity, justice, gravity, and equity, they will be honoured as gods; but if once they discover the fears, prejudices, and partialities of men, they will grow into contempt even with their friends. Claudius was at first a just judge, but his wife and servants ruined his principles.

THE POOR BIRD, OR THE JUVENILE MOURNER.

" WHAT occasions that melancholy look?" said I, to one of my young favourites, one morning. He turned away his face, to hide a tear that was ready to start from his eye. His brother answered for him.—" Mother is very angry with him," said he, " because he would not say his prayers last night; and he cried all day, because a sparrow died of which he was fond." The little mourner hastily turned round, and looking at me, exclaimed, "I could not say *thy will be done*, because of my poor bird." I took him by the hand, and pointing to his school-fellows, " Mark this observation," said I, " from the youngest present, only six years old; for it explains the nature of prayer, of which perhaps some of you are ignorant. Many persons repeat words, who never prayed in their lives. My dear boy, I am very glad to find you

were afraid to say to God what you could not say *truly* from your heart; but you may beg of him to give you submission to his will!"

THE MOURNER.

HERACLITUS passed his time in a solitary manner, and received the appellation of the obscure philosopher, and the mourner, from his constant custom of weeping at the follies, frailties, and vicissitudes of human affairs. Did Christians only feel as they ought, how many mourners should we have! Alas! how is God insulted, his name blasphemed, his commands disobeyed, and yet men are but little concerned for his honour, and the promotion of his glory in the world.

Mourning may be excessive.

Although nature may be allowed to feel, when providence calls away those who are the objects of our affection; yet if they die in the Lord, excessive sorrow for the loss we sustain is highly discreditable to our principles as Christians, who are looking forward to a blessed immortality. Chrysostom, speaking on this subject, and reflecting on the custom of those times, when at funeral solemnities, a train of mourning women attended the corpse, tearing their hair and their faces, and crying with all the expression of desperate sorrow, he thus exclaims: " Ah! Christian faith, and the religion that was triumphant over its enemies, in so many battles and victories, by the bloody death of the martyrs, how art thou insulted by the practice of those who profess thee in words! Is not this to be sorrowful, as those who have no hope? Are these the affections, the expressions of one that believes in the blessedness of immortal life? What will the heathens say? How will they be induced to believe the promises of Christ to his servants, of a glorious kingdom, when those who are so in title, behave themselves as if they had no steadfast faith in them?"

MARRIAGE.

AMONG the ancients, when persons were newly married they put a yoke upon their necks, or chains about their arms, to show that they were to be one, closely united, and drawing equally together in all the concerns of life.

The finest allegorical representation of the marriage union which I have met with, is that of an antique gem representing the marriage of Cupid and Psyche, in the collection of the duke of Marlborough : it may be seen also among Baron Stock's gems, and casts or copies of it in various other collections.

1st. Both are represented as winged, to show the alacrity with which the husband and wife should help, comfort, and support each other ; preventing, as much as possible, the intimation of a wish or want on either side, by fulfilling it before it can be expressed.

2d. Both are veiled, to show that modesty is an inseparable attendant on pure matrimonial connections.

3d. Hymen, or marriage, goes before them with a lighted torch, leading them by a chain, of which each has hold, to show that they are united together, and are bound to each other, and that they are led to this by the pure flame of love, which at the same instant both enlightens and warms them.

4th. This chain is not iron or brass (to intimate that the marriage-union is a state of thraldom or slavery) but it is a chain of pearls ; to show that the union is precious, delightful, and beautiful.

5th. They hold a dove, the emblem of conjugal fidelity, which they appear to embrace affectionately, to show that they are faithful to each other, not merely through duty, but by affection, and that this fidelity contributes to the happiness of their lives.

6th. A winged Cupid, or love, is represented as having gone before them, preparing the nuptial feast ; to intimate that active affections, warm and cordial love, are to them a continual source of comfort and enjoyment ; and that this is the entertainment they are to meet with at every step of their affectionate lives.

7th. Another Cupid, or genius of love, comes behind, and places on their heads a basket of ripe fruits, to intimate, that a matrimonial union of this kind will generally be blest with children, who shall be as pleasing to all their senses, as ripe and delicious fruits are to the smell and taste.

8th. The genius of love that follows them has his wings shrivelled up, or the feathers all curled, so as to render them utterly unfit for flight ; to intimate, that love is to abide with them, that there is to be no separation in affection, but that they are to continue to love one another with pure and fervent affection : thus love begins and continues this sacred union, which death alone can dissolve ; for God hath yoked them together.

A finer, or more expressive set of emblems has never, I believe, been produced, even by modern refined taste and ingenuity. This group of emblematical figures is engraved upon an onyx by Tryphon, an ancient Grecian artist. A fine drawing was made of it by Cipriani, and it has been engraved both by Bartolozzi and Sherwin.

The conjugal union, as it was ordained of God, so it is honoured by him, and therefore not to be despised ; yet, as strangers and pilgrims here on earth, it becomes us not to make an idol of domestic happiness. The time will come when a separation must take place, and how soon is only known to Him who is the sovereign disposer of all events. It is therefore well to stand resigned to the will of God. The Jews had a custom at their wedding feasts, for the married couple to drink out of the same glass together, and then to break it in pieces ; teaching them, by that emblem, that whatever felicity they expected together, their lives, upon which it all depended, were frail and brittle as glass. No sooner joined but they were warned to prepare for separation: so, in our form of matrimony, the clause, "until death do us part," is a memento to the same purpose. "It is as much my duty," says Dr. Grosvenor, "to pray that I may be willing and able to part with any dearest comforts in life in a right manner, as to pray for their continuance. We are apt to be most earnest for their continuance, as if it were a greater thing for God to please us, than for us to please Him." Happy are they who can say in the time of bereavement,

And should'st thou take them all away,
  Yet would I not repine:
Before they were possessed by me,
  They were entirely thine!

The celebration of marriage is different in different nations. In too many instances, however, it has been a scene of dissipation and licentiousness. The nuptials of Alexander were celebrated with uncommon splendour; no less than nine thousand persons attended, yet with all the gaiety, to each of these persons Alexander gave a golden cup to be offered to the gods. If a heathen, on such an occasion, did not forget his religion, superstitious as it was, what a reflection to professing Christians to make such a day a day of sinful festivity, instead of dedicating themselves to God and imploring his blessing.

MELANCHOLY REMOVED.

"CONSTANT riding," says Dr.Guyse, "is the best friend to health, and has been experienced by many, in circumstances of a low, gloomy, distressed and hurrying state of the spirits, to be of vast advantage. I have heard of, and I think know the gentleman, who was brought to so very low and melancholy a cast of mind, that he could not be persuaded, for many months together, that he was capable of going out of his room. At length, however, by an artful stratagem, he was told that his disorder was indeed incurable by any physician in England, but that there was one at Edinburgh, who, could he but get to him, would certainly cure him. After much difficulty, he was prevailed upon to attempt a journey thither, to have the advice of that physician, though he fancied it was impossible for him to ride so much as three or four miles in a day. But the servant that attended him was charged to drill him forward; and accordingly, by many persuasions, he prevailed upon him to ride three or four, and gradually more miles; till after some time he could make a tolerable day's journey. When he reached Edinburgh, he was told that the doctor was lately gone to the North of Scotland; and resolving not to lose his labour, he went thither also; but when he arrived there he found there was no such person as he was directed to inquire after. However, though he found not the man, he found the remedy; for, riding about six hundred miles thither, and as many back again, he became as well and comfortable as ever he had been in his life before.

THE HAPPY MEETING OF FATHER AND SON.

IN all the restless ardour of approaching manhood, impatient of restraint, a son, at the time when his father was in the high noon of life, left the paternal house, and went to seek in foreign climes the liberty and happiness which his heated imagination had painted. Tossed from one country to another, he was detained far beyond his intended period. In one of the unforeseen revolutions of the changing world, the father also was driven into foreign parts; and, by an unseen hand, the course of both was so directed, that the parent and his son met together in an obscure village in Italy. They knew not each other. The young man had lost the virgin bloom of youth with which he quitted his father's house, and having ripened into full manhood, discovered the stronger lines of expression, which had been heightened by the influence of the weather and the vicissitudes of his condition. The father having turned the brow of the hill of life, and meeting with unexpected reverses in his declining years, soon began to bear the deep furrows and the hoary hairs of age. Thus mutually altered, and separated for many years, which had been crowded with various scenes, there remained but little that could discover their near relation. Yet when the aged man entered the son's house, he involuntarily rose, and showed a more than ordinary repect to a person in whom he saw so much to venerate; whilst the father felt a new and peculiar pleasure in receiving the attention of so agreeable a stranger. They spake, and they readily replied, for the sake of hearing again the sound of each other's voice. The father's bowels yearned, the son's heart spake, and their lips could not keep silence. " Are you a native of Italy?" said the father. "No, sir," the son replied; " I perceive you also are a foreigner." This led on to further questions, and these produced more interesting information, till at length, hearing his own name mentioned, the son cried out, " My father!"—"My son! my son!" exclaimed the parent, and fell on his neck and embraced him. What a tender and affecting scene was this! Who that had been present, but must have been dissolved into tears? But while we are affected with such a relation as this, can we forget Him, who after all our transgressions and wanderings, still recognises us as his children, ready to forgive all our follies; and to receive us into his arms? Blessed God, may thy compassion bind my heart to thee that I may wander no more!

THE RICH MAN CONFOUNDED.

To be enabled to appropriate the Saviour as our wisdom, righteous-

ness, sanctification, and redemption, is of all enjoyments the greatest. The possession of wealth, talents, power, and fame, all sink to nothing when compared with this. The poorest, the most obscure, therefore, with this, is infinitely more happy than the most elevated without it. A gentleman one day took an acquaintance of his upon the leads of his house to show him the extent of his possession :—waving his hand about, " There," says he, "that is my estate." Then pointing to a great distance on one side—"Do you see that farm?" " Yes." " Well that is mine." Pointing again to the other side—"Do you see that house?" " Yes." " That also belongs to me." " Then," said his friend, " do you see that little village out yonder?" " Yes." " Well, there lives a poor woman in that village, who can say more than all this." "Aye! what can she say?" " Why, she can say, 'Christ is mine.'" He looked confounded, and said no more.

THE MILKWOMAN, OR UNJUST GAIN.

A certain person, who came to be a captain, or master of a vessel at sea, had two hundred pounds in gold, which he kept in a purse, that he was every now and then opening to look upon and count, after which he would lay it every night under his pillow, when he went to bed, for safety. A monkey that was in the ship, seeing this, took an opportunity when the master was absent, to lift up the pillow, and take the purse, with which he ran up to the top of the mast. When there, he opened the purse, took out piece by piece, turning them about, looking at them, then threw them down into the water, pleasing himself by the imitation. At length the captain spied him, and, of course, was much concerned ; but what to do he knew not : if he should shoot the creature, the purse would fall with him into the sea ; or if he should send up any hastily to fright him, it would be so too. He therefore got a person to go up gently round about the ropes, and when he came within reach, without disturbing the creature, he caught hold of the purse-strings, and brought it to the owner, who on counting it, found one half the sum was gone. On this he mustered the crew together, and thus addressed them: "My mates and fellow seamen," said he, "you see what has befallen me. My mother was a milk-woman in London, and I observed when I was a boy, how she was wont, when she came home with her pail, to put water into it, and by that means she saved these two hundred pounds, and gave them me ; and now one of them, or thereabouts, is thrown into the sea. Mark the just and righteous dealing of God to her son ; that which was water is gone to the water, and that which was pure gain only remains."

THE MAUSOLEUM.

WHEN Mausolus, a king of Caria, died, his wife was so disconsolate that she drank up his ashes, and erected one of the grandest and noblest monuments of antiquity to perpetuate his memory. The famous monument, which passed for one of the seven wonders of the world, was called *Mausoleum*, and from it all other magnificent sepulchres and tombs have received the same name. The expenses of the edifice were immense, and when Anaxagoras the philosopher saw it, he exclaimed, "How much money changed into stones !" But thus we may say of many persons, that they part with what is valuable for that which is comparatively of no value. They gain, indeed, a portion of this world, but in the pursuit neglect to seek a portion of the next.

A SOUND MIND A RARE THING.

A PERFECTLY just and sound mind is a rare and invaluable gift. It is given but to few, and a very small number of those few escape the bias of some predilection, perhaps occa-

sionally operating, and none are at all times perfectly free. "I once saw," says Mr. Cecil, "this subject forcibly illustrated. A watchmaker told me, that a gentleman had put an exquisite watch into his hands, that went irregularly. It was as perfect a piece of work as was ever made. He took it to pieces and put it together again twenty times. No manner of defect was to be discovered, and yet the watch went intolerably. At last it struck him, that possibly the balance-wheel might have been near a magnet. On applying a needle to it, he found his suspicion true. The steel-work in the other parts of the watch had a perpetual influence on its motions, and the watch went as well as possible with a new wheel." If the soundest mind be magnetized by any predilection, it must act irregularly.

THE MINISTER CONVERTED BY GOING TO THE FAIR.

VARIOUS are the ways in which God is pleased to bring his people to the knowledge of himself. Sometimes it is by stated ordinances, and sometimes by means apparently insignificant. "A scrap of paper," says Flavel, "coming to view, has been used as an occasion of conversion." This was the case of a minister in Wales, who had two livings, and cared little for either. Being at a fair, he bought something at a pedlar's standing, who rent off a leaf of Mr. Perkin's Catechism to wrap it in, and reading a line or two in it, it proved the means of his conversion.

MOTHERS CAN DO GREAT THINGS.

A CLERGYMAN, now fulfilling the duties of his office punctually, ardently, and faithfully, was asked, when examined by the bishop's chaplain, whether he had made divinity his study ? He replied he had not particularly ; "but," said he, "my mother taught me the Scripture." "Ah !" said the chaplain, "mothers can do great things !" The young man was examined with respect to the extent of his knowledge, was approved, ordained, and appointed to preach before the bishop.

Mothers may perceive how necessary and useful are their pious instructions, and be encouraged, while their husbands are busily engaged in providing for their families the meat that perisheth, to be diligent in bringing up their offspring in the knowledge of the Scriptures, as the mother of Timothy did. This anecdote may also lead reflecting parents to consider what ought to be the education of their daughters that they may become such mothers; for on the education of daughters depends the future welfare, not only of families, but of our country.

The excellent mother alluded to in the above anecdote, wrote as follows to another of her sons, on hearing of the birth of his eldest child :—" Give him an education that his life may be useful; teach him religion, that his death may be happy !"

MISSIONARY ANECDOTES.

A LETTER from the Rev. G. R. Nylander, the missionary who is placed among the Bulloms, dated July 4th, 1814, will throw some light on the degrading nature of the African superstitions. " How great the ignorance and superstitions of the Bulloms are," says he, " struck me very much, when I saw a crowd of people assembled, offering sacrifices to a cannon-ball and three decanter stoppers, recommending themselves and their children to the favour of that evil spirit of whom the ball and stoppers were the representatives. They say, like the Roman Catholics of their pictures, that when they address the ball and glass stoppers, they speak not to them, but to the devil that lives in the bush (woods.)

" They sometimes pray to God, as they say; but even that is done with superstition. I saw an old man at prayers, solemnly kneeling down before his house, with a brass pan before him wherein he had laid some pieces of gold, two rams' horns, a piece of iron, and two swords. He said he had been praying to God; and as God did not require any sacrifices of him, he laid those things down before God, and asked him to bless him and all his people.

" We have lately been making a monthly subscription for the relief of the poor starving natives hereabouts, (at Agra,) whose case is indeed very deplorable on account of the great scarcity of grain; many have died for hunger in the streets of Agra. We daily find here and there one starved to death. We were coming home one evening lately, through the wheat bazaar, and in the midst of the sellers of wheat and other grain, lay a poor man who had just breathed his last among the heaps of the grain. He had picked up a few husks of peas and grain, which it appeared he had been attempting to eat, but was too far gone. Not a single man in the bazaar would give this poor creature one handful of wheat to save his life !

" This is not the only instance of the hardness of heart of this people; they have no more feeling for the poor than if they were dogs. They show no mercy nor pity. Our plan for a subscription was begun at one of our prayer meetings. We collected, by way of donation, about sixty rupees. The Rev. Mr. Corrie has since obtained a subscription to a considerable amount, which he serves out to the poor every morning."

An old Chinese went one day to a missionary who was in the village, to represent to him the extreme desire he had of building a church there. " Your zeal is laudable," said the missionary to him, " but we have not now the means of defraying so great an expense." " I aspire to do it myself," replied the villager. The missionary, accustomed to see him for many years lead a very poor life, believed him not to be in a situation to accomplish what he proposed. He again praised his good intentions, representing to him the extent of the village, consequently the large size of a suitable building, and his incompetency to so great a work. "Excuse me," replied he; "I believe myself able to do what I propose." "But do you know," said the missionary, "that two thousand crowns, at least, are necessary for such an undertaking?" "I have them all ready," returned he; "and if I had not, I should not thus have importuned you." The missionary was much charmed at learning that this good man, whom he had thought very poor, was possessed of so much, and that he wished to employ it so usefully; nor was he less surprised when having the curiosity to ask him how he had been able to procure this sum, he ingenuously answered, "that for forty years, since he had conceived this design, he had retrenched from his food and clothes all that was not absolutely necessary, that he might have the consolation, before he died, of leaving in his village a house erected to the honour of the true God." Is not this a hint to many British Christians? How many are there now sitting under the sound of the gospel, and enjoying its glorious privileges, to whom some obscure town or dark village gave birth, but to which they have never once thought of sending the glad tidings of salvation? Let them, if possible, emulate the example of this inhabitant of China.

Mr. Carey, jun. riding out one afternoon to visit his patients, and passing by the place of public execution, saw two men suffering the punishment of crucifixion. At that time they had not long been nailed up. After Mr. C. had continued a spectator about half an hour, an order, procured by a Ceylon poengee, arrived for the release of one of them, who was immediately taken down. Moved by the sufferings and cries of the other, (a young man,) and understanding that he had committed no great offence, Mr. C. determined to use his interest with the viceroy in his behalf; and was so happy, after much entreaty, as to succeed. The poor sufferer, after enduring his torture about six hours, was at length unspiked, taken down, and brought home to the mission-house. How forcibly did the wounds of his hands and feet remind me of Him, "who suffered, the just for the unjust, that he might bring us to God!" Mr. C. dressed his wounds, and hopes soon to effect a cure. Oh, that this great deliverance from an untimely death, may lead to the greater deliverance of his soul from spiritual death!

The frame used for the infliction of this punishment is thus constructed: A board is placed on the ground, upon which the criminal stands, and to which his feet are nailed. Another board is placed at a proper height, for his head and shoulders to rest against; to which his hands, being extended, are nailed also. Other boards are fixed upright at the back; to which, in various parts, the body is made fast with ropes. The frame, which is of considerable extent, and always kept standing, is also used for inflicting other kinds of torture yet more terrible. Merciful Saviour! hasten thy visit to this part of the earth, so full of the habitations of cruelty!

The cross, as an engine of torture, was what various eastern nations used in putting such criminals to death as they thought were deserving of this dishonourable punishment; and particularly those against whom they meant to express their resentment, or on whom they poured more than ordinary contempt. It was long in use among the Romans, but was employed in putting to death only such of their malefactors as were slaves. It was laid aside when Christianity became the established religion of the empire, out of respect to Christ, who died upon the cross. Nay, that instrument of punishment was afterwards superstitiously revered by the Christians; a figure of it was interwoven in their banners of war, and was carried with pride in the van of their hostile legions, as a pledge of conquest and triumph. In the days of Christ, the death of the cross was considered as the most disgraceful that could be inflicted. To this death he was condemned by the sentence of Pilate, who was constrained to this act of injustice by the clamorous entreaties of the Jews; and, from the manner in which it was inflicted, it must have been shameful, lingering, and painful. After the criminal was scourged, his body was stretched naked on the cross, fixed to it with iron pins, by the hands and feet, (the most nervous part of the body, consequently, the most susceptible of pain,) the cross was then raised up, fixed in the ground, and the body kept hanging on it till life had expired. Though, for the most part, the Romans were so compassionate as to strangle the criminals before they were transfixed on the cross, to shorten the agonies of dying, no such lenity was shown to Him who was crucified the King of the Jews. This kind of death which Christ suffered, from the view now given of it, the manner in which the Romans inflicted it, must have been in the extreme painful and ignominious. But Christ endured the cross, despising the shame, a phrase descriptive of the patience and meekness with which he endured his suffering, and of holy contempt of all the reproaches cast upon him in his last moments.

Mr. Thom and others, visited a missionary settlement in Africa, and, early one morning, they conversed with three women, by an interpreter, on religious subjects. While they were speaking, another woman, from a hut near them, came behind, and listened with tears. She was dressed in sheep-skins, and held her young child in her arms. We asked her what made her weep? She replied, "I weep because I am such an unworthy creature; you have come from a far country to see us, but I hope to be saved by Jesus Christ." Her attitude, language, and tears, affected us all. Mr. T. thus proceeds:—

"When we asked a Namaqua woman to what country she belonged, she said, "I belong to Christ's country. It was the Saviour who brought me here to be instructed. I wish him to have more of my heart." She desired us to present her affectionate remembrance to all the Christian people of Britain. Now appeared to me the beauty of the following passage: "Ethiopia shall stretch out her hands unto God." As a Christian, I felt my heart one with theirs, and valued that communion of spirit which knows no distinction of colour, education, or country; and, as a Christian minister, I felt pity and love for immortal souls, and a more vigorous desire to spend my life in whatever way God shall see fit.

The Missionary Money-box.

A few weeks since, a trading vessel, laden with corn, from Cardigan, in Wales, was taken in the Channel by an American privateer. When the captain went into the cabin to survey his prize, he espied a little box, with a hole in the top, similar to that which tradesmen have in their counters, through which they drop their money; and at the sight of it he seemed a little surprised, and said to the Welch captain, "What is this?" pointing to the box with his stick. "Oh," said the honest Cambrian, "'tis all over now."—"What?" asked the American. "Why the truth is," replied the Welch captain, "that I and my poor fellows have been accustomed every Monday to drop a penny each into that box, for the purpose of sending out missionaries *to preach the gospel to the heathen*, but it is all over now!" "Ah!" said the American, "that is very good;" and after pausing a few minutes, he said, "Captain, I'll not hurt a hair of your head, nor touch your vessel." The pious Welchman was accordingly allowed to pursue his voyage unmolested.

When Mr. Giles Holloway was leaving *Tappanuli*, and settling his accounts with the natives, he expostulated with a battaman, who had been dilatory in his payments. "I would," says the man, "have been here sooner, but my *pangulu* (superior officer) was detected with my wife. He was condemned, and I staid to eat my share of him; the ceremony took us up three days, and it was only last night that we finished him." Mr. Miller was present at this conversation, and the man spoke with perfect seriousness. A native of the Island of Nias, who had stabbed a battaman in a fit of frenzy at *Battangtara* river, near *Tappanuli Bay*, and endeavoured to make his escape, was, upon the alarm being given, seized at six in the morning, and before eleven, without any judicial process, was tied to a stake, cut in pieces with the utmost eagerness, while yet alive, and eaten upon the spot, partly broiled, but mostly raw. His head was buried under that of the man whom he had murdered. This happened in Dec. 1780, when Mr. William Smith had charge of the settlement. A *raja* was fined by Mr. Bradley for having caused a prisoner to be eaten too close to the company's settlement; (and it should have been remarked, that these feasts are never suffered to take place within-inside of their own *kampongs*.) Mr. Alexander Hall made a charge in his public accounts of a sum paid to a *raja*, as an inducement to him to spare a man whom he had been preparing for a victim : and it is, in fact, this commendable discouragement of the practice by our government, that occasions it being so rare a sight to Europeans, in a country where there are no travellers for curiosity, and where the servants of the company, having appearances to maintain, cannot, by their presence as idle spectators, give a sanction to proceedings which it is their duty to discourage, although their influence is not sufficient to prevent them.

The Scripture account of the extreme heat of the climate of Nineveh, is well illustrated in the ingenious Mr. Campbell's Travels over land to India, p. 130.

It was early in the evening, when the pointed turrets of the city of Mosul opened on our view, and communicated no very unpleasant sensations to my heart. I found myself on Scripture ground, and could not help feeling some portion of the pride of the traveller, when I reflected that I was now within sight of Nineveh, renowned in Holy Writ. The city is seated in a very barren, sandy plain, on the banks of the river Tigris. The external view of the town is much in its favour, being encompassed with walls of solid stones, over which the steeples, or minarets of other lofty buildings, are seen with increased effect. Here I first saw a caravan encamped, halting on its march from the Gulf of Persia to Armenia; and it certainly made a most noble appearance, filling the eye with a multitude of grand objects, all uniting to form one magnificent whole. But though the outside be so beautiful, the inside is most detestable. The heat is so intense, that, in the middle of the day there is no stirring out ; and even at night, the walls of the houses are so heated by the days sun, as to produce a disagreeable heat to the body, at a foot, or even a yard distance from them. However, I entered it with spirits, because I considered it as the last stage of the worst of my pilgrimage ; but, alas! I was disappointed in my expectation, for the Tigris was dried up by the intensity of the heat and an unusually long drought, and I was obliged to take the matter with a patient shrug, and accommodate my mind with a journey on horseback, which, though not so long as that I had already made, was likely to be equally dangerous ; and which therefore demanded a full exertion of fortitude and resolution.

"It was still the hot season of the year, and we were to travel through that country, over which the horrid wind I have before mentioned sweeps its consuming blasts. It is called by the Turks *samiel*, is mentioned by holy Job, under the name of the east wind, and extends its ravages all the way from the extreme end of the Gulf of Cambaya up to Mosul. It carries along with it flakes of fire like threads of silk; instantly strikes dead those that breathe it, and consumes them inwardly to ashes, the flesh soon becoming black as a coal, and dropping off the bones. Philosophers consider it a kind of electric fire, proceeding from the sulphureous or nitreous exhalations, which are kindled by the agitations of the winds. The only possible means of escape from its fatal effects is to fall flat on the ground, and thereby prevent the drawing it in: to do this, however, it is necessary first to see it, which is not always practicable.

" The ordinary heat of the climate is extremely dangerous to the blood and lungs, and even to the skin, which blisters and peels from the flesh, affecting the eyes so much that travellers are obliged to wear a transparent covering over them to keep off the heat."

A West Indian planter being surprised to see some of his produce in safety, which might have been stolen with impunity, asked a negro watchman, " How is it that this has not been stolen, seeing you are all thieves ?" He was answered, " *No, massa ; the negurs who go to prayers never teeve !*" This simple reply so affected the planter, who had been much prejudiced against the methodists, that he immediately sent for Mr. Baxter, the missionary at Antigua, to instruct the slaves on his estate.

A few years since an act was passed by the legislature of Jamaica, prohibiting the missionaries from instructing the Negro slaves, and receiving them into their houses or chapels. Accordingly, they dare not suffer any slave to attend their places of worship. Frequently, however, while men of free condition entered to hear preaching, the slaves *crowded about the doors*, which the act forbad them to enter, with looks of the most expressive sorrow, and words of the most penetrating eloquence,— " Massa, me no go to heaven now.—White men keep black men from serving God.—Black man got no soul.—Nobody teach black man now." If ever the words of Sterne had a meaning, " I heard his chains, and the iron entered into my soul," it must have been on such an occasion as this.

Some people have had doubts respecting the depth and soundness of Christian experience among the negroes. Allow me to furnish a single instance from a multitude which might be recited. Soon after Mr. Gilbert began to preach, one Judy Athol went to hear him, " because," as she expressed herself, " oder negurs go. De word reach my heart." She instantly parted with all her jewels, bracelets, fine muslins, and lace, and never desired them again. She entertained the preachers many years at her house, and truly adorned her Christian profession. Such was the confidence reposed in her, on account of her exemplary character, that Mrs. A., upon whose estate she lived, requested her to become her housekeeper. But Judy declined the offer, alleging as a reason, that she could not then entertain her preachers, nor attend so constantly the means of grace. " After I had been some time on the island, Judy was taken ill. When her last moments were at hand, she despatched a messenger for me, with a request that I would visit her in her affliction. I gladly consented ; thinking it a favourable opportunity of ascertaining the real state of Judy's mind, and the nature of her future prospects. Being introduced to the dying saint, I said, ' Now, Judy, you have often told us how good your dear master Jesus has been to you. You were then in good health, but now you are dying, how is it with you now ?' Pausing a few minutes, she replied, ' O Massa ! my Massa Jesus always been good since I knew him: but now I dying, it all glory, glory.' In such a triumph died Judy Athol !"

At Bukapuram, in the Northern Circars, a child, only eight years old, who had been educated in Christianity, was ridiculed on account of his religion, by some heathens older than himself. In reply he repeated what he had been taught respecting God. "Show us your God," said the heathens. "I cannot do that," answered the child, "but I can show *yours* to you." Taking up a stone, and daubing it with some resemblance of a human face, he placed it very gravely upon the ground, and pushed it towards them with his foot—"There," says he, "is such a God as you worship." But to whom will you liken me ; or what likeness will ye compare unto me, saith the Lord? I am Jehovah, and besides me there is no God.—A just God, and yet a Saviour !

Kristno, a converted Hindoo, made the following observation in a conversation he had with some others, and which is a fine illustration of Ephesians, ch. ii. ver. 18—22. " The Hindoos," said he, " when they have built a new house, consider it unclean and untenantable till they have performed an offering, and then they take up their abode in it. So God ; he does not dwell in earthly temples, however magnificent ; his residence is in the heart. But how shall he dwell with man ? The sacrifice of Christ must be offered : then the house, the heart, in which this sacrifice is received, becomes the habitation of God through the spirit." Excellent divinity ! How truly wise are those whom God teaches !

A ship in distress, somewhere near the Swin, was descried by some fishermen, who immediately went to assist and relieve the crew, whom they took on board their smack. On her going down (for she sunk,) one of her crew jumped on board, and rushed into the cabin, at the risk of his life, to fetch something he had forgotten ; but great was their surprise when they found this precious treasure a BIBLE!

A missionary being once in company with some baptized Greenlanders, expressed his wonder how they could formerly lead such a senseless life, void of all reflection. Upon this one of them answered as follows :— " It is true we were ignorant heathens, and knew nothing of a God or a Saviour ; and indeed who should tell us of him till you came? But thou must not imagine that no Greenlander thinks about these things. I myself have often thought a kajah (a canoe or boat,) with all its tackle and implements, does not grow into existence of itself, but must be made by the labour and ingenuity of man ; and one that does not understand it would directly spoil it. Now the meanest bird has far more skill displayed in its structure than the best *kajah*, and no man can make a bird. But there is still far greater art shown in the formation of a man, than of any other creature. Who was it that made him ? I bethought me he proceeded from his parents, and they from their parents ; but some must have been first parents : whence did they come ? Common report informs me they grew out of the earth. But if so, why does it not still happen that men grow out of the earth ? And from whence did this same earth itself, the sea, the sun, the moon, and stars, arise into existence ? Certainly there must be some Being who made all these things ; a Being that always was, and can never cease to be. He must be inexpressibly more mighty, knowing, and wise, than the wisest man. He must be very good too ; for every thing that is made is good, useful, and necessary for us. Ah ! did I but know him, how would I love him, and honour him ! But who has seen him ?— who has conversed with him ? None of us poor men. Yet there may be men too, who know something of him. Oh ! could I but speak with them ! Therefore," said he, "as soon as ever I heard you speak of this great Being, I believed it directly with all my heart, because I had so long desired to hear it."

This testimony was confirmed by the others, with more or less attendant circumstances. As, for instance, they superadded, "A man is made quite different from the beasts. The brutes have no understanding, but they serve for food to each other, and all for the use of man. But man has an intelligent soul, is subject to no creature in the world; and yet man is afraid of the future state. There must be a Great Spirit that has the dominion over us. Oh! did we but know him! Oh! had we but him for our friend!"

The first preachers of Christianity were itinerants. And it must be owned, that however useful settled pastors may be, that itinerating, when undertaken by proper characters, is a most effectual way of spreading the gospel. Some who have been more attached to philosophy than religion, have greatly opposed it; but they forget that their great master, Socrates, set an example of itinerant teaching; for he had no particular place where to deliver his lectures; but as the good of his countrymen, and the reformation of their corrupted morals, and not the aggregation of riches, were the objects of his study, he was present every where, and drew the attention of his auditors, either in the groves of Academus, the Lyceum, or on the banks of Ilissus. Thus, too, did a greater than Socrates go about doing good. He taught the most sublime truths, inculcated the most suitable precepts; and delivered the most important instructions wherever he went. To him all places were alike; on the sea or on the land; in the house of Zaccheus, or the family of Lazarus; in the splendid temple, or the humble cottage; in the crowded assembly, or among the select few, his object was the same—the glory of God, and the happiness of man. "Blessed Saviour! may thy gospel be freely preached unto all nations; and the knowledge of thy truth be diffused throughout the universe! Amen."

Mr. Melville Horne, in his sermon before the Society for Missions to Africa and the East, thus applies the text, Luke xi. 27. Meditation on the wonders of the cross, familiarized and wrought by the Holy Spirit into the temper of our minds, would spread the spirit of mission far and wide among the clergy and laity. Our very women would catch the sacred fire, and glory in the welfare of the cross.—Christian matrons! from whose endeared and endearing lips we first heard of the wondrous babe of Bethlehem, and were taught to bend our knee to Jesus;—ye who first taught these eagles how to soar, will ye now check their flight in the midst of heaven? "I am weary," said the ambitious Cornelia, "of being called Scipio's daughter. Do something, my sons, to style me the mother of the Gracchi!" And what more laudable can inspire you, than to be the mother of the missionaries, confessors, and martyrs of Jesus?—Generations yet unborn shall call you blessed. The churches of Asia and Africa, when they make grateful mention of their founders, will say, "Blessed be the womb which bare them, and the breasts which they have suckled!"

Immolation on the Funeral Pile.—Extracted from a Letter from Mr. More, dated Digah, September 13, 1813.

"Yesterday, about half-past eleven, immediately after our morning worship, a native came to inform me, that a woman was burning with her husband in a garden nearly adjoining ours. Lieutenant P. and myself instantly ran off to the place, which was about a hundred and fifty yards from our native school-room, and about the same distance from the officer's residence who at present commands the station. By the time we arrived, the bodies were nearly consumed. Lieutenant Gilmore afterwards informed Lieutenant P. that himself and Dr. Thornton were spectators of the horrid scene. The persons who superintended the fire, throwing on it clarified butter, and keeping it up with long poles, exhibited all the appearance of determined murderers; while a vast concourse of spectators manifested great demonstrations of joy, assisted by the horrid clang of the instruments used on such occasions. The scene was calculated to strike the mind with inconceivable horror. The deceased was about sixteen years of age, and the wife about twelve. They were the son and daughter-in-law of Mootiram, a dealer in sugar, of whom we have purchased that article since our residence at Digah. I saw the unhappy father on the spot, and conversed with him on the evil of his conduct in this affair. His appearance indicated much distress; but he did not attempt to vindicate his conduct, further than by saying that the girl was determined, and he could not prevent it."

Account of a horrible Immolation in the neighbourhood of Serampore.

" Towards the close of 1813, Rammohun Sena, a clerk in the Serampore printing-office, saw three women burnt to death in a pit at Vidya-vatee. When the blaze had ascended to a great height, the women leaped into the pit, amidst the sounds of music and the shouts of the surrounding multitude, and were instantly covered by the burning combustibles.— They were the wives of a Telinga rajah, who had left his family at this place while he went on a pilgrimage to Benares, where he died. Taking some trifle, which had been the rajah's, with them into the fire they thus perished. At the time they plunged into the flaming pit, they had on a profusion of gold ornaments. Vidya-vatee is about three miles north of Serampore."

The Rut'ho Festival.

" On the second day of June the bathing of the image of Jugunnat'ha took place, of which god the village of Muhesha, adjoining Sérampore,

W

has a celebrated image. The landing-places on this occasion are crowded with bathers, expecting great advantages from ablutions performed on this auspicious day. At the appointed hour, the god is brought out of the temple in the arms of five or six stout brahmuns (this is the case at Muhesha,) and carried to a brick elevation at a short distance, where the god is drawn up by a cord round his neck, and placed on a seat. The brahmuns wait the arrival of the land-owner, and then perform the ceremony of ablution, repeating the proper formulas : the water is poured on the head of the god from the sacred conch through a cylinder having a thousand perforations. During the act of bathing, ten thousand spectators are seen at once in the act of homage, some with hands raised to the head, others prostrating themselves, and others stretching their arms towards heaven; after which they retire and the god is carried back to the temple.

" On the 19th, the same god was drawn up by the neck, and placed in his monstrous car, and then dragged by the crowd about a quarter of a mile, where the car remains for eight days for the mob to gaze at, while the god himself is carried in the arms of men to a neighbouring temple on a visit to his nephew, Radha-Bullubba. This year on account of the heavy rains, the people were comparatively few, and the car stuck fast in the mud, when some of the crowd began to attribute this disaster to the prayers of the native Christians. At length the brahmuns hit upon a lucky expedient ; they brought out Radha-Bullubba, and as soon as Jugunnat'ha saw his nephew, the car rolled on without further obstruction, assisted by the enthusiasm of the mob, who, equally with the god, felt pleased with the sight of this new miracle, which they had not sense enough to attribute to their own increased efforts.

" On the 28th, the god returned to his temple in the same order as he came out, and here the festival closed.

" A great fair is held at this festival, and lotteries, gaming and every obscenity is practised in the precincts of the temple which contains the god. The proprietors of these two temples realize annually not less than two thousand rupees.

" At the total wane of the moon, in this month, the image of Jugunnat'ha is exhibited, after having been newly painted, when numbers go to the temple with offerings. For fourteen days preceding, the god remains in a state of uncleanness, having been touched by a shoodra painter, and during this time is neither fed nor worshipped."

Account of the Churuk, or Swinging Festival.

" In May, 1813, this abominable festival was held, according to the annual custom, on the last day of the Hindoo year. There were fewer gibbet-posts erected at Serampore, but amongst the swingers was one female. A man fell from a stage thirty cubits high and broke his back ; and another fell from the swinging-post, but was not much hurt. Some days after the first swinging certain natives revived the cermonies.

As Mr. Ward was passing through Calcutta, at this last period, he saw several Hindoos hanging by the heels over a slow fire, as an act of devotion. Several Hindoos employed in the printing office applied, this year, to Mr. Ward, for protection, to escape being dragged into these pretendedly voluntary practices. It seems that the landlords of the poor, and other men of property, insist upon certain of their tenants and dependants engaging in these practices, and that they expect, and compel by actual force, multitudes every year to join the companies of sunyasees in parading the streets, piercing their sides, tongues, &c. To avoid this compulsion, many poor young men leave their houses and hide themselves ; but they are sure of being beaten if caught, or of having their huts pulled down. The influence and power of the rich have a great effect on the multitude in most of the idolatrous festivals: when the lands and riches of the country were in fewer hands, this influence carried all before it: but it is still very widely felt in compelling dependants to assist in public shows, and to contribute towards the expense of splendid ceremonies. Through divine goodness, however, the influence of commerce, the more general diffusion of wealth, and the intercourse of Europeans, are raising the Hindoos from this state of abject dependence on their spiritual tyrants ; and thus providential events are operating with the gospel to produce a happy change on the great mass of the population, especially in the more enlightened parts of Bengal.

NATURE'S LIGHT INSUFFICIENT, AND REVELATION NECESSARY.

SIN not only introduced misery, but ignorance into the world. Man knows nothing as he ought to know. Left to himself he gropes in the dark, and can neither find the way to happiness nor heaven. Nay, as one observes, " ask the wisest of men, and they will confess the weakness of reason, that after all its attainments, it falls infinitely short of perfection, and is far from being commensurate to truth, or the nature of things." The most extraordinary geniuses have spent their whole lives in unwearied diligence, and yet never attained true wisdom. Pythagoras, till the fiftieth year of his age, was a scholar under the greatest masters in the world. Democritus spent no less than fourscore years in hard study. Plato attended the lectures of Socrates, Archytas, and Eurytas, for forty years, and Aristotle laboured more than twenty years under Plato. Here were persons of the most solid judgment and vast capacity, with invincible study and application, and assisted with the labours of all preceding ages, and yet fell infinitely short of truth. How necessary, then, is divine revelation, to point out to us the right path? This is the only guide on which we can depend. And how thankful should we be, that unto us is this invaluable blessing given! Let us prove our gratitude by becoming the instruments of communicating it to others.

OMNISCIENCE OF GOD.

THE omniscience of God, as a modern writer observes, is a source of pleasing reflection to a good man : under the struggle he maintains with his corruption; under the reproaches of enemies, or the suspicions of friends; under trouble; and when at a throne of grace imploring his blessing. But how useful may this reflection be as a check to sin, and as a motive to virtue? One of the heathen philosophers, therefore, recommended it to his pupils, as the best means to induce and enable them to behave worthily, to imagine that some very distinguished character was always looking upon them. But what was the eye of a Cato to the eye of God? Who would not approve themselves unto him?

Oh may these thoughts possess my breast,
Where'er I rove, where'er I rest;
Nor let my weaker passions dare
Consent to sin, for God is there!

DR. OWEN.

A Mr. DAVIES, being under religious impressions, felt much inclined to open his mind to Dr. Owen. In the course of conversation, Dr. Owen said, " Young man, pray in what manner do you think to go to God?" Mr. Davies answered, " Through the Mediator, sir;" to which the Doctor replied, " That is easily said; but I assure you, it is another thing to go to God through the Mediator, than many who make use of the expression are aware of. I myself preached some years, while I had but very little, if any, acquaintance with access to God through Christ, until the Lord was pleased to visit me

with a sore affliction, by which I was brought to the brink of the grave, and under which my mind was filled with horror; but God was graciously pleased to relieve my soul by a powerful application of Ps. cxxx. 4. ' But there is a forgiveness with thee, that thou mayest be feared.' From this text I received special light, peace, and comfort, in drawing near to God through the Mediator; and on this text I preached immediately after my recovery." Perhaps to this exercise of mind we owe his excellent Exposition of that Psalm.

THE CONVERTED OSTLER.

WHO can calculate the happy effects often produced by public preaching? A man who was engaged as helper in the livery-stables of a horse-dealer in Surrey, was of so profligate a turn, and his language and general conversation so blasphemous, as to become disgusting to his fellow-servants, who objected to sleep in the same room with him, and requested their employer to remove him to another part of the house, which he complied with. Returning one day from an errand he had been sent upon, he was; induced to go into a place of divine worship, during the time of service; and such was the impression made upon his mind by the discourse of the preacher, that, on his return home, he intimated to his master an intention to leave his service, unless he consented to allow him three days in each week to devote a part of them to religious public duty; adding, that he had found a Master whose wages far exceeded what he received from him. His diligent and faithful discharge of the duty entrusted to him rendering him a faithful servant, the master readily consented to his proposition, and from that period a reformation was visible in his conduct : abandoning a vicious and depraved course of life, he became the admonisher of his fellow-servants, and showing them an example of what they ought to be, demonstrated that he was not " ashamed of the gospel

11*

of Christ, for it is the power of God unto salvation to every one that believeth."

PRAYER.

LET the main desires of the afflicted be for divine grace, which is never more necessary and useful than in time of trouble, that they may glorify God, and obtain their eminent end, the salvation of their souls by them. We are often very ardent in our prayers for trivial things, neglecting such as are most necessary and important; as if a prisoner loaded with irons should passionately entreat that his chains might be gilded, not loosed. How many spend their zealous affections in praying for temporal things, wherein their happiness does not consist! One of the reasons why God heaps upon rebellious sinners the good things of this life, is to teach us how despicable they are in his account—things, as it were, to be thrown away, while he oftens denies the petitions of his servants ooncerning temporal things. When Pelopidas interceded with Epaminondas, the wise governor of the Thebans, for the freedom of a base fellow, who for some crime was committed to prison, he denied his request, but he presently released him on the application of a vile and despicable person, assigning this reason, that it was a favour not worthy the dignity of Pelopidas, but suitable enough to the quality of the other petitioner.

THE PRAYERS OF THE WICKED ANSWERED TO THEIR DESTRUCTION.

PLUTARCH reports, that the Tyrians tied their gods with chains, because certain persons dreamt that Apollo said he would leave their city and go to the party of Alexander, who then besieged the town. And Apollodorus tells us of some that tied the image of Saturn with bands of wool upon his feet. So, says Bishop Saylor, some think that God is tied to their feet, and bound to be of their side and the interest of their opinion; and they think he can never go the

enemy's party so long as they charm him with certain forms of words or disguises of their own; and then all the success they have, and all the evil councils that are prosperous, all the mischiefs they do, and all the ambitious designs which succeed, they reckon upon the account of their prayers; and well they may, for their prayers are sins, and their desires are evil. Some prayers are answered to the destruction of the petitioner. Nero's mother prayed passionately that her son might be emperor. Her prayer was answered; but Nero murdered her. Julian the apostate prayed and sacrificed, and inquired of demons, and all that he might oppose the camp of Christ. He was heard too, in that he caused much blood of the Christians to flow; but the effect of his prayer was, that he lived and died a professed enemy to Christ. The righteous too have sometimes discovered much infirmity in their prayers. See Luke ix. 49 to 54, and Mat. xx. 21. They have not received, because they have asked amiss. God has sometimes answered the prayer of a wicked man to his ruin; but he will not thus deal with his people. He knoweth their necessities; and as a father pitieth his children, so he pitieth them that fear Him. Let us not then be disconcerted. If he answer not our supplication, it is for wise ends. Let us always take his word for our rule, his promise for our encouragement, and persevere, knowing that he hath said he will withhold no good thing from them who walk uprightly.

EJACULATORY PRAYER.

We have in Scripture very remarkable instances of the success which has attended *ejaculatory prayer*.—Observe Nehemiah; he stands before Ahasuerus, apprehensive of the monarch's displeasure, yet desirous to solicit him in behalf of Jerusalem. To be delivered from his fears, and to obtain his desires, what method does he use? The mean and servile arts of flattery? No; but the manly and devout expedient of prayer. " I prayed," says the patriot, "to God, to the God of Heaven." We cannot suppose that he fell on his knees, or spoke with his lips, while he continued in the royal presence ; but he darted up his soul in silent supplication. That supplication "pierced the clouds," reached the Eternal throne, and returned not again till a blessing was sent ; such as totally averted the wrath which was dreaded, and procured favour and assistance much beyond what he expected.

When David heard that Ahithophel, the ablest politician in his kingdom, had revolted to Absalom, sensible what a loss his affairs had sustained, and what an advantage the rebellious party had acquired, he betook himself to his God. He waited not for an opportunity of retirement ; but instantly, and upon the spot, cried, " *O Lord, I pray thee, turn the counsel of Ahithophel into foolishness !*"—A *short* address, but very efficacious. He who disappointeth the devices of the crafty sent a spirit of infatuation among the rebels, and inclined them to reject the advice of that subtle statesman ; and that false step brought upon their horrid enterprise the ruin it deserved, and chagrined the wretched traitor even to rage, frenzy, and suicide.

Amyntor, at a memorable period of his life, was under great distress of conscience, and harassed by violent temptations. He made his case known to an experienced friend, who said, " *Amyntor, you do not pray.*" Surprised at this, he replied, "I pray, if such a thing be possible, too much. I can hardly tell how many times in the day I bow my knee to God ; almost to the omission of my other duties, and the neglect of my necessary studies." " You mistake my meaning, dear Amyntor ; I do not refer you to the ceremony of the knee, but to the devotion of the *heart*, which neglects not any business, but intermingles prayer with *all* ; which in every place looks unto the Lord ; and on every occasion lifts up an indigent,

longing soul for the supply of his grace. This (added he, and spoke with a peculiar emphasis) *this* is the prayer which all the devils in hell cannot withstand." This, I would further observe, is the prayer which brings down somewhat of heaven into the heart ; in which I would myself desire to abound ; and would earnestly recommend to all my acquaintances and readers.

THE PRAYERS OF THE RIGHTEOUS ANSWERED TO THEIR SALVATION.

THE Almighty not only hears and answers the prayers of his people, but gives them more than they ask. When the philosopher asked a penny of Antigonus, he told him it was too little for a king to give ; when he asked a talent, he told him it was too much for a philosopher to receive. But the Giver of every good and perfect gift opens his liberal hand and bestows blessings of all kinds upon the sinful sons of men. It is true, indeed, that he bestows his favours in his own way and time. He denies us in one thing, that he may give us another of greater importance. Plato gave Diogenes a great vessel of wine when he asked but a little. The cynic thanked him, but said, " Thou neither answerest to the question thou art asked, nor givest according as thou art desired ; for when interrogated, how many are two and two ? thou answerest twenty." So says Bishop Taylor, it is with God and us, in the intercourse of our prayers. We pray for health, and he gives us, it may be, a sickness that comes into eternal life. We pray for necessary support for our persons and families, and he gives us more than we need. We beg for a removal of present sadness, and he gives us a cheerful spirit, a peaceful conscience, and a joy in God as an antepast of eternal rejoicings in the kingdom of God.

FAMILY PRAYER.

ALL who were acquainted with

Mr. Rees unite in testifying that they never knew a minister who excelled so much in the gift and spirit of prayer. Many, doubtless, will have reason to bless God for ever for an opportunity of joining him in this heavenly exercise. A pious man and woman of his acquaintance had an only son, whose name was Thomas; who, to the great grief of the parents, began to turn out wild. Mr. Rees went to lodge at the house, and the father and mother, with many tears, informed him of the ungodliness of their son. The following morning, before the family prayer, Mr. Rees took hold of the young man's hand, and spoke very seriously and affectionately to him respecting his salvation. In family worship he prayed for him with great enlargement, and, amongst others, used the following expression:—"O Lord, say to *this Thomas*, 'be not faithless but believing.'" The words, to use his own expression, entered his heart like a sword, and a permanent change was effected : he soon became a church member, and was an ornament to his Christian profession till death. A minister of the gospel, in the principality, son of an old friend of Mr. Rees, has frequently related the following anecdote, which I shall give in his own words. "When Mr. Rees was on a visit at Llanbrynmair, after he had gone to reside at Mynidd-bach, he called at my father's house on a certain day, about noon, a few weeks after the death of my mother. After some conversation with my father, he desired to have my family together ; he sat down in an elbow-chair, called the children (seven in number) to him, one by one, beginning at the eldest ; with great affection took the hand of each, asked his name, and spoke a few words according to the child's age. After reading a chapter, and explaining some parts of it, he kneeled down and prayed, enlarging particularly for each individual in the family, mentioning the names of such as had Scripture names. Though

at that time I was only eleven years of age, an impression was made upon my mind, which time can never fully erase." I believe the above may be considered as a fair specimen of Mr. Rees's general manner of visiting his friends. His custom in praying in families was to mention the names of such in the family as had scripture names; and he was scarcely pleased if his friends called their children by any other. Perhaps it would not be prudent for many ministers to attempt to imitate Mr. Rees in this ; but by reason of his very uncommon gifts, he could do it with such propriety and gravity, that it was scarcely possible the most inconsiderate person could remain unaffected. Mr. Rees used his best endeavours that none of his people should live without family worship. He was once endeavouring to prevail with a young professor to begin to pray in his family. The person said he had a great desire of engaging in this work, but he feared he had not sufficient gifts to pray publicly. Mr. Rees said he would write him a prayer if he would promise to use it. He said he certainly would. The prayer was composed, and the man devoutly used it for some time, both morning and evening; but on one occasion, as he was reading his prayer, the candle went out; notwithstanding which, the good man proceeded with great comfort and enlargement : and he found no need of a written prayer ever after.

PRAYER AND PLAY.

IN the spring season at Bath, in the year 1760, subscription books were opened for prayers at the abbey, and gaming at the rooms. At the close of the first day, the number of subscribers for prayers were *twelve*—and for gaming *sixty-seven !* The following lines were written on the occasion :—

The church and rooms the other day,
Open'd their books for prayer and play
The Priest got *twelve*, Hoyle *sixty-seven*
How great the odds for Hell 'gainst heaven

PUNISHMENTS.

Punishments practised by the Burmans, communicated by a Gentleman resident there.

"EVERY species of punishment of which the human mind can possibly conceive, is continually practised in this country. The nature and degree of the punishment depends entirely upon the whim and caprice of the ruling power, who issues the mandate. However, there are some punishments more common than others ; but these again vary both in degree and kind, according to the crime, and the character and sex of the criminal, except a departure from the general rule be made from anger or revenge, which is not unfrequently the case.

" The following are some which frequently occur, and may be divided into three classes—capital, severe, and trivial punishments.

" Among the first class may be placed beheading, crucifying, starvation, ripping open the body, sawing, piercing through, starving to death, flogging upon the breasts to death, scorching to death by the rays of the sun, blowing up with gunpowder or other combustible materials, pouring hot lead down the throat, scalding to death by plunging into hot oil, shooting with fire-arms, or arrows, spearing to death, squeezing to death by pressing a nut of the betel-tree between two bamboos, on each temple until the eyes and brains start out of the head, drowning, beating on the head to death with a large cudgel, giving to wild beasts, and roasting on a slow or quick fire.

"Severe punishments are such as cutting off the hands, feet, ears, nose, tongue, &c. extracting the eyes, flogging upon the breast, tying the arms with a thin cord till it cuts down to the bone, hanging up by the heels, hanging up by the tips of the fingers, exposing to the rays of the sun, and banishment into forests, from which it is almost impossible to escape.

" Among trivial punishments may be reckoned flogging, marking crime in legible characters upon the face or breast of the criminal, and condemning him to perform the office of public executioner for life, squeezing the legs or arms between two bamboos, confinement in the stocks, with the legs extended as far as possible. Such punishment as hanging, shooting, exposing in the pillory, burning the hands, condemning to a long confinement, and hard labour, are seldom practised ; banishment is not often heard of.

"It often happens that several of the severe or trivial punishments abovementioned are inflicted on a criminal previous to his being finally executed. Instances not unfrequently occur that a person, after being nailed by the hands and feet to a cross, has most of his members amputated, one by one, before he receives his mortal wound. Sometimes the punishment, though small in its kind, is continued as long as life remains ; and frequently so many various punishments of trivial nature are inflicted that death is the inevitable consequence ; united together they form capital punishments, severe in the extreme, and horrid to reflect upon ; and yet these are the most common.

" Frequently the innocent suffer with the guilty; as a wife for the fault of her husband, and children for the crime of their parents ; even a whole family is extirpated for the fault of a single individual, and servants are cut off for the crimes of their masters. These kinds of punishment, however, seldom occur but from sudden anger or revenge, except in the case of deserters and persons guilty of treason.

" When a person of royal extraction is to receive a capital punishment, it is generally done by drowning. In the first place the person is tied hands and feet, then sewed up in a red bag, which again is sometimes put into a jar, and thus the culprit is put into the water with a weight sufficient to sink him. This practice is resorted to because it is reckoned a sin to spill royal blood.

" Women, comparatively speaking, are seldom the subjects of capital punishment ; when an instance of this kind occurs, it is generally for some very flagrant crime. When they are executed, it is generally done by knocking their brains out with a large cudgel ; but sometimes they are ripped open, or blown up, or given to a tiger or some other wild beast.

" The bodies of criminals are always exposed to public view for three days, after which they are shovelled into a hole and covered with earth, not being permitted the honour of being burnt.

" Criminal causes are frequently tried by ordeal before judgment is passed.

" I will now just relate what punishments have been inflicted merely in the town of Rangoon since my residence in this country, a period of not more than four years. I witnessed the execution of some of the criminals, and the others I saw immediately after.

" One man had boiling lead poured down his throat, which immediately burst out from his neck, and various other parts of his body.

" Four or five persons, after being nailed through their hands and feet to a scaffold, had first their tongues cut out, then their mouths slit open from ear to ear, then their ears cut off, and finally their bodies ripped open.

" Six people were crucified. Their hands and feet were nailed to a scaffold ; their eyes were then extracted with a blunt hook ; and in this condition they were left to expire ; two died in the course of four days ; the rest were liberated, but died of mortification the sixth or seventh day.

" Four other persons were crucified ; but instead of being nailed, they were tied with their hands and feet stretched at full length in an erect posture. In this position they were to remain till death, and food was given them in order to prolong their miserable existence. In these kinds of punishment, the legs and feet of the criminals swell and mortify at the expiration of three or four days. Some are said to live in this state for a fortnight, and expire at last from fatigue and mortification. The four persons I saw were liberated at the end of three or four days.

" Another man had a large bamboo run through his body, which killed him instantly.

" Two people had their bodies ripped up, sufficient to admit of the protrusion of a small part of the intestines ; and, after being secured by cords in an erect posture upon bamboo rafters, with the hands and feet at full stretch, were set adrift in the river to float up and down with the tide for public inspection.

" I do not exactly recollect how many have been beheaded, but there must have been upwards of twenty.

" One man was sawn from the shoulder-bone downwards, till his bowels gushed out.

" One woman was beat to death with a large cudgel.

" Two persons were simply crucified, and almost immediately liberated.

" Five persons, consisting of a man, his wife, (far advanced in pregnancy,) his child about five years of age, and two other men, were led to the place of execution ; the men were sentenced to be crucified and opened, and the women and child were to be stretched upon the ground and opened. Every thing was prepared, and the executioner was standing by ready to perform his bloody office, and even boasting that he was able to perform it neatly, but a reprieve arriving, the execution was prevented.

" Several amputations of hands and feet have taken place : some died from loss of blood, but the greater part survived.

" These are most of the punishments I have seen or heard of during my residence at Rangoon ; but many other instances happened while I was occasionally absent, of which I have not given a relation. As for the crimes for which these punishments were inflicted, some appeared to deserve death, others were of a trivial nature, and some of the victims were completely innocent."

PATIENCE.

AN eminent and popular minister of the gospel of Christ had been very successful in his preaching, but it pleased God to visit him with affliction, and he lay on his couch for several years. A young man who officiated for him during his illness, one day called to see him, and was bold enough to ask him if he did not consider his illness a visitation of divine displeasure, seeing he lay so entirely useless? The venerable saint meekly replied, "Young man, my patience shall speak louder than thy preaching."

Tertullian, writing of the excellency of patience, and reflecting upon himself how opposite his fiery nature was to that virtue, became deeply affected with grief and shame, and drew up his own arraignment and process for his impatience.

PROMISES AND PREACHING NOT ALWAYS EFFECTUAL.

DIONYSIUS of Sicily, being extremely delighted with a minstrel that sung well, and played admirably on the harp, promised to give him a great reward. This so encouraged the man that it made him play still better; but when the music was done, and the man waited for the fulfilment of the promise, the king dismissed him empty, telling him that he should carry away as much of the promised reward as himself did of the music, and that he had paid him sufficiently with the pleasure of the promise for the pleasure of the music; both their ears had been equally delighted, and the profits *just none at all!* So it is with many people hearing sermons: they admire the preacher, and he pleases their ear; but neither of them get any good. The hearer forgets the ser-

mon, and the preacher is little profited by unmeaning applause, while what he has said is not reduced to practice.

PREACHING.

"IF we would preach to purpose," says an old author, "we must bring our hearts as well as heads into the pulpit, and our lives must be consistent with our doctrines, or we shall undo by the one what we attempt to do by the other. It is said of Æneas Sylvius (afterwards called Pope Pius Secundus,) that what Sylvius did, Pius undid !"

The wonderful Change produced by Preaching.

Mr. John Livingstone, chaplain to the countess of Wigton, aged twenty-seven, was appointed to preach to a very large company that had been assembled to join in celebrating the Lord's Supper. After very great discouragement in his own mind, he came to the place appointed, and preached in the open air from Ezek. xxxvi. 25, 26. When he was about to conclude, a heavy shower coming on, caused great confusion in so large an assembly, which gave him an occasion of addressing them to the following effect : "If a few drops of rain so discompose you, how would you be confused and filled with horror and despair, if God should deal with you as you have deserved ? and thus he will deal with all the finally impenitent. God might justly rain fire and brimstone upon you, as he did upon Sodom and Gomorrah. The Son of God, by tabernacling in our nature, and obeying and suffering in it, is the only refuge and covert from the storm of divine wrath due to our sins. His merits and mediation are the alone shelter from that storm ; and none but penitent believers have the benefit of it." Upon these topics he enlarged in a very pathetic strain for above an hour, with many earnest exhortations and warnings, and with pressing entreaties and persuasions.

It is attested by an author of good

credit, with great confidence, that near five hundred persons had at that time a discernible change wrought upon them, the most of whom proved afterwards lively Christians. Among other remarkable instances, the following is recorded:

Three young gentlemen from Glasgow, who were on a journey to Edinburgh, to join in the diversions of that city, stopped at Shotts, to breakfast, and from curiosity, were induced to attend on the preaching. When they returned, several circumstances indicated that their minds were deeply impressed by what they had heard.

They did not, however, speak to one another explicitly on the subject, but proceeded on their journey, yet, when they came to Edinburgh, they had no inclination to the diversion of the place, but after two days they returned home, still observing the same reserve as to what passed in their minds. After this they were retired, and seldom went abroad; at length one of them visited his companion, and informed him of the change which had taken place in his views and purposes in consequence of the sermon; and the other as frankly owned to him the concern that he was brought under at the same time. They then went together to the third, whom they found impressed in a similar manner; and so their purposed association in pursuit of worldly pleasures was changed for fellowship in prayer and religious exercises; and their practice was suited to their profession as long as they lived; so that they were eminently useful; and some of them were spared to an advanced age, a blessing to that neighbourhood.

PERSEVERANCE.

THERE is nothing in religion insuperable to the love of God and of our souls. Love is not cold and idle, but ardent and active in pursuit of its object. There are many proofs that resolute diligence will overcome great obstacles to the designs of men. Demosthenes, the Athenian, was the most unqualified for an orator of a thousand; his breath was so short, that he could not speak out a full sentence; his voice and pronounciation were so harsh, and his action so ungraceful and offensive to the most delicate senses, the eye and ear, that the first time he spoke in a public assembly, he was entertained with derision, and the second with disdain, from the people; yet, by unwearied industry and exercise, he corrected his defects, and became the most eloquent and perfect orator that ever flourished in Greece. Now can there be any height so difficult in religion but which a strong resolution joined with consequent endeavours, and the supernatural assistance of the Holy Spirit, will gradually attain.

Whoever wishes to obtain the victory must not be discouraged by violent opposition. It is reported of Alexander, that when surrounded by his enemies and sorely wounded, he still maintained his fortitude, and fought upon his knees. Spartacus did the same, covering himself with his buckler in one hand, and using his sword with the other. So the Christian, however wounded, must still persevere, fighting to the end the good fight of faith, that he may lay hold on eternal life.

An able seaman, says Mr. Cecil, once said to me, "In fierce storms, we have but one resource, we keep the ship in a certain position; we cannot act in any way but this; we fix her head to the wind, and in this way we weather the storm." This is a picture of the Christian; he endeavours to put himself in a certain position. My hope and help are in God; he is faithful. The man who has learnt this piece of heavenly navigation shall weather the storms of time and of eternity."

Thus, under the most discouraging circumstances, we must persevere, casting all our care on HIM who careth for us.

PERSECUTION.

THE history of the Waldenses affords us many shocking instances of barbarity on the part of their Catholic persecutors. Daniel Moudon, elder of the church of Rora, in Piedmont, after seeing his two sons beheaded, the wife and child of the one, and the two children of the other, massacred, was compelled to carry the heads of his sons upon his shoulders, to walk two hours barefooted, and was afterwards hanged.

About fifteen thousand men, women, and children, who had thrown themselves on the duke's clemency, were confined for about nine months, in fourteen castles in Piedmont, with a scanty allowance of unwholesome bread and water. They lay on bricks or rotten straw, and in such crowds that the air was infected ; eight thousand died in consequence of these barbarities. Most of the survivors were permitted to return to Switzerland, after threatenings and allurements had been tried, for the most part in vain, to induce them to forsake their religion. Those who did apostatize, did not regain their possessions, but were conveyed to a distant province. In many cases, however, the children were not permitted to accompany their parents to Switzerland, but were taken away and dispersed in Piedmont. Their pastors were also removed from them, and eighty men were forced to work in chains for three years in the citadel of Turin. Even those who were allowed to seek refuge in Switzerland endured great hardships. They were made to travel in the severest weather. Numbers died on the way, whom their friends were not even permitted to remain and bury. Women were seen lying in the snow with their infants still in their arms. Many expired at the very gates of Geneva. These wretched exiles, while they remained in Switzerland, were supported by the charitable contributions of the English and Dutch. Most of them afterwards obtained grounds in Wirtemberg, Durlach,

Hesse Darmstadt, and Hanau, where they established fourteen churches, and where seven ministers and schoolmasters were supported by King William. See *Jones's History of the Waldenses, for a particular account of these interesting people.*

PARADOX.

" As sorrowful, yet always rejoicing." This is indeed a paradox; but the following letter is an admirable exemplification of it :—

"Dear brother, and fellow labourer, " This is to inform you, I am sick, yet in the sweet enjoyment of the best of health ; to let you know I am very low, yet surprisingly exalted; that I am exceedingly weak, yet stronger by far than the world, Satan, death, or hell ; that I can hardly walk alone, and yet am able to travel to heaven in one day ; that I stagger through weakness, yet have more props to support myself, than heaven or earth ; that my pains have been violent, yet I have felt nothing ; that I am as happy as any soul can contain, and yet craving after more ; that Satan has often looked at me, but dared not speak to me, either good or bad ; that I am as poor as a church mouse, and yet my estate increases daily ; that I have lost my appetite, and yet feed daily on marrow and fatness, with wines well refined ; that I am wasted sadly, and yet thrive like a cedar of Lebanon ; that I am nothing but a bag of bones, yet flourish like the palm-tree ; that I have been occupied in great waters, and have gained much by trading : that I have been in the furnace, but none heated it but my matchless Lord. I have put my hand on the cockatrice' den, but he dared not come out ; I have played on the hole of the asp, without one sting on my fingers ; that I laid down with the lion, but arose with the lamb ; that I have been preaching every day, yet have not seen a pulpit this week ; that my soul loves Jesus, because he loves me ; that I brought nothing into this world, but shall carry Christ out ;

that heaven is eternally mine, but I am not my own; that my soul loveth S. and I know he loveth me. Go on, S. we shall at last reach the third heavens, as sure as there is a God."

W. H.

PARENTAL DUTY AND AUTHORITY.

THE superiors in the family must preserve order and tranquillity in it. The fire of discord turns a house into a little hell, full of the tormenting passions, sorrow and anguish, disdain and despite, malice and envy, that blast the most flourishing families. But when religion that is pure and peaceable governs the house, it turns it into a paradise, where the God of peace dwells and delights, and dispenses the most precious fruits of his favour. Wisdom and watchfulness are requisite to maintain a harmonious agreement in families, wherein are persons of different and contrary tempers. Some are of such unnatural dispositions that they love jars and dissensions, as some plants thrive on the top of the Alps, where they are continually exposed to storms. There is such an irregularity in the dispositions of some, that between those persons there is fierce hatred where entire love is due. The discord between brothers is deeply wounding and hardly curable. The reason of it is evident, for where by the law of nature, the dearest love is required and expected, the not obtaining it is so injurious and provoking, that the hatred in one is equal to the love to which the other does not correspond. The Spartan magistrates, celebrated for their wisdom and justice, being informed of frequent quarrels between two brothers, likely to end in bloody contentions, they sent for their father, and punished him, as more culpable and guilty, in not timely correcting them. Ruling wisdom in the father of the family, so as to conciliate love with respect, severity mixed with sweetness (which rarely meet) is necessary to prevent or compose dissensions in those little commonwealths

PEEVISHNESS.

I HAVE heard of a good woman, something inclined to passion, that used to say, "I must strive against peevishness, while I am young, or else what will become of me when I am old?"

PRACTICE TO BE PREFERRED TO HEARING.

IT is doubtless a privilege to be favoured with opportunities of hearing the word; but yet of how little avail is it, unless we practise what we hear? Some are always hearing, but little or no good effects are evident on their temper and life. "A person," says Mr. Erskine, "who had been to public worship, having returned home, perhaps somewhat sooner than usual, was asked by another of the family who had not been there, 'Is all done?' 'No,' replied he, 'all is *said*, but all is *not done*.'"

THE TRIUMPH OF PIETY;
Or, the Impious Books Destroyed.

SOME years before the revolution, a lady, who was a bookseller at Paris, attracted by the reputation of Father Beauvegard, an eloquent preacher, went to the church of Notre Dame to hear him. His discourse was particularly levelled against irreligious books; and the lady had cause enough to reproach herself on that score, having been in the habit of selling many publications which were contrary to good manners and to religion. Interest had blinded her, as it does many others in the same line of business; but, penetrated by the sermon, she could no longer dissimulate that impious and licentious books are a dreadful source of poison to the heart: and she was compelled to acknowledge that those who print, or sell, or contribute to circulate them in any way whatever, are so many public poisoners, whom God will one day call to an account for the evils they occasion. Impressed with these sentiments, she went to the preacher, and with tears in her eyes, said to him, "You have rendered me a great service, by giving me to see how culpable I have been in selling many impious books; and I entreat you to finish the good work you have begun, by taking the trouble to come to my warehouse to examine all the books which are in it, and to put aside all those which may be injurious to morals or religion. Whatever it cost me, I am determined to make the sacrifice. I had rather be deprived of a part of my property, than consent to lose my soul." Accordingly, Father Beauvegard paid her a visit the next day, to examine her books. When he had separated the good from the bad, she took the latter, and in his presence cast them one after another into a great fire she had taken care to provide.

The price of the works thus consumed, amounted, it is said, to about six thousand livres. She made the sacrifice without regret; and from that time endeavoured to sell no books but what might tend to counteract the evil done by others. Perhaps every one will admire this example, but few, we fear, will go and do likewise.

PRIDE.

DEMETRIUS, one of Alexander's successors, was either so proud and disdainful as not to allow those who had any affairs to transact with him the liberty of speech, or else he treated them with so much rudeness as obliged them to quit his presence with disgust. He suffered the Athenian ambassadors to wait two whole years before he gave them audience. How unlike is the conduct of God to that of such a man! He not only commands, but invites us to come into his presence, and promises us all things necessary for our real good. Let us then go boldly to his throne, seeing he giveth liberally, and upbraideth not.

Pride is an evil that puts men upon all manner of evil. Accius, the poet, though he was a dwarf, yet would be pictured tall of stature. Psaphon, a proud Libyan, would needs be a god; and having caught some birds, he taught them to speak and prattle, "the great god Psaphon."

Proud Simon, in Lucian, having got a little wealth, changed his name from Simon to Simonides, because there were so many beggars of his kin; and set the house on fire wherein he was born, because nobody should point at it.

THE NEW PRECEPT;
Or, the Eleventh Commandment.

THE eminent archbishop Ussher, being once on a visit in Scotland, heard a great deal of the piety and devotion of the famous Mr. Samuel Rutherford, who, he understood, spent whole nights in prayer, especially before the Sabbath. The bishop wished much to witness such extraordinary down-pouring of the Spirit; but was utterly at a loss how to accomplish his design. At length it came into his mind to dress himself like a pauper; and on a Saturday evening, when turning dark, he called at Mr. Rutherford's house, and asked if he could get quarters for a night, since he could go to no other house at so late an hour for that purpose. Mr. Rutherford consented to give the poor man a bed for a night, and desired him to sit down in the kitchen, which he did cheerfully. Mrs. Rutherford, according to custom on Saturday evening, that her servants might be prepared for the Sabbath, called them together and examined them. In the course of examination that evening, she asked the stranger how many commandments there were? To which he answered eleven. Upon receiving this answer, she replied, "What a shame is it for you! a man with gray hairs, living in a Christian country, not to know how many commandments there are! There is not a child of six years old in this parish but could answer this question properly." She troubled the poor man no more, thinking him so very ignorant; but lamented his condition to her servants ; and after giving him some supper, desired a servant to show him up stairs to a bed in a garret. This was the very situation in which he desired to be placed, that he might hear Mr. Rutherford at his secret devotion. However, he was disappointed ; for that night that good man went to bed, but did not fall asleep for some hours. The stranger did not go to bed, but sat listening, always hoping to hear Mr. Rutherford at prayer ; and at length concluding, that all the family were asleep, the bishop thought if he had been disappointed of hearing another offering up his desires to God at the throne of grace, he would embrace the opportunity himself, and poured out his heart to God with so much liberty and enlargement, that Mr. Rutherford, immediately below, overheard ; and getting up, put on his clothes. Should this have awakened Mrs. Rutherford, she could have suspected nothing of his design, seeing he rose commonly every day at three o'clock in the morning; and if she could have heard one at prayer afterwards, she would naturally have concluded it was her husband. Mr. Rutherford went up stairs, and stood waiting at the garret door till the bishop concluded his devotion ; upon which he knocked gently at the door, and the other opened it with surprise, thinking none were witnesses to his devotion. Mr. Rutherford took him by the hand, saying, " Sir, I am persuaded you can be none other than archbishop Ussher; and you must certainly preach for me to-day, being now Sabbath morning." The bishop confessed who he was ; and after telling Mr. Rutherford what induced him to take such a step, said he would preach for him on condition that he would not discover who he was. Happy union of souls, although of different persuasions ! yet not marvellous ; God makes but two distinctions among mankind, the righteous and the wicked.

Mr. Rutherford furnished the bishop with a suit of his own clothes,

and early in the morning he went out to the fields ; the other followed him and brought him in as a strange minister passing by, who had promised to preach for him. Mrs. Rutherford found that the poor man had gone away before any of the family were out of bed.' After domestic worship and breakfast, the family went to the kirk, and the bishop had for his text (John xiii. 34.) "A new commandment I give unto you, that ye love one another ;" a suitable subject for the occasion. In the course of his sermon, he observed that this might be reckoned the eleventh commandment : upon which Mrs. Rutherford said to herself, "that is the answer the poor man gave me last night ;" and looking up to the pulpit, said, "It cannot be possible that this is he !" After public worship, the strange minister and Mr. Rutherford spent the evening in mutual satisfaction ; and early on Monday morning the former went away in the dress he came in, and was not discovered.

POPERY.

THE following document was issued by the Pope against a person for renouncing the errors of the church of Rome, in 1758 :—

The Pope's curse, bell, book, and candle, on a heretic at Hampreston.

"By the authority of the blessed Virgin Mary, of St. Peter and Paul, and of the holy saints, we excommunicate, we utterly curse and ban, commit and deliver to the devil of hell, Henry Goldney, of Hampreston, in the county of Dorset, an infamous heretic, that hath, in spite of God and St. Peter, whose church this is, in spite of all holy saints, and in spite of our holy father the pope, (God's vicar here on earth,) and of the reverend and worshipful the canons, masters, priests, jesuits, and clerks of our holy church, committed the heinous crimes of sacrilege with the images of our holy saints, and forsaken our most holy religion, and continues in heresy, blasphemy, and corrupt lust. Excommunicated be he finally, and delivered over to the devil as a perpetual malefactor and schismatic. Accursed be he, and given soul and body to the devil to be buffeted. Cursed be' he in all holy cities and towns, in fields, and ways, in houses and out of houses, and in all other places, standing, lying, or rising, walking, running, waking, sleeping, eating, drinking, and whatsoever he does besides. We separate him from the threshold; from all the good prayers of the church; from the participation of holy mass; from all sacraments, chapels, and altars; from holy bread and holy water; from all the merits of our holy priests and religious men, and from all their cloisters; from all their pardons, privileges, grants, and immunities, all the holy fathers (popes of Rome) have granted to them; and we give him over utterly to the power of the devil; and we pray to our Lady, and St. Peter and Paul, and all holy saints, that all the senses of his body may fail him, and that he may have no feeling, except he come openly to our beloved priest at Stapehill, in time of mass, within thirty days from the third time of pronouncing hereof by our dear priest there, and confess his heinous, heretical, and blasphemous crimes, and by true repentance make satisfaction to our Lady, St. Peter, and the worshipful company of our holy church of Rome, and suffer himself to be buffeted, scourged, and spit upon, as our said dear priest, in his goodness, holiness, and sanctity shall direct and prescribe. Given under the seal of our holy church at Rome, the tenth day of August, in the year of our Lord Christ, one thousand seven hundred and fifty-eight, and in the first year of our pontificate. C. R."

"8th of October, 1758, pronounced the first time.

"15th of ditto, pronounced the second time.

"22d of ditto, pronounced the third time."

PROFANENESS REPROVED.

A FEW years ago, one of the stages which ply between two principal cities was filled with a group which could never have been drawn together by mutual choice. In the company was a young man of social temper, affable manners, and considerable information. His accent was barely sufficient to show that the English was not his native tongue, and a very slight peculiarity in the pronunciation of the *th*, ascertained him to be a Hollander. He had early entered into the military life; had borne both a Dutch and French commission; had seen real service, had travelled, was master of the English language, and evinced by his deportment that he was no stranger to the society of gentlemen. He had, however in a very high degree, a fault too common among military men, and too absurd to find an advocate among men of sense—he swore profanely and incessantly. While the horses were changing, a gentleman, who sat on the same seat with him, took him by the arm, and requested the favour of his company in a short walk. When they were so far retired as not to be overheard, the former observed, "Although I have not the honour of your acquaintance, I perceive, sir, that your habits and feelings are those of a gentleman; and that nothing can be more repugnant to your wishes than giving unnecessary pain to any one of your company." He started, and replied, "Most certainly, sir; I hope I have committed no offence of that sort!"

"You will pardon me," replied the other, "for pointing out an instance in which you have not altogether avoided it."

"Sir," said he, "I shall be much your debtor for so friendly an act: for, upon my honour, I cannot conjecture in what I have transgressed."

"If you, sir," continued the former, "had a very dear friend, to whom you were under unspeakable obligations,

12*

should you not be deeply wounded by any disrespect to him, or even by hearing his name introduced, and used with a frequency of repetition and a levity of air incompatible with the regard due to his character ?"

" Undoubtedly, and I should not permit it ; but I know not that I am chargeable with indecorum to any of your friends."

" Sir, my God is my best friend, to whom I am under infinite obligations. I think you must recollect that you have very frequently, since we commenced our journey, taken his name in vain. *This* has given to me, and to others of the company, excruciating pain." "Sir," answered he, with a very ingenuous emphasis, " I *have* done wrong. I confess the impropriety. I am ashamed of a practice which I am sensible has no excuse ; but I have imperceptibly fallen into it ; and I really swear without being conscious that I do so. I will endeavour to abstain from it in future, and as you are next me on the seat, I shall thank you to touch my elbow as often as I trespass."

This was agreed upon. The horns sounded, and the travellers resumed their places. In the space of four or five miles, the officer's elbow was jogged every few seconds. He always coloured, but bowed and received the hint without the least symptom of displeasure, and in a few miles more so mastered his propensity to swearing, that not an oath was heard from his lips for the rest, which was the greater part of the journey.

SCRIPTURE PROPHECY.

How wonderfully is Scripture explained by facts. The Arabians, the descendants of Ishmael, continue to this day enemies to the rest of the world, and are both robbers by land and pirates by sea. As they have been such enemies to mankind, no wonder mankind have been enemies to them, and that several attempts should have been made to extirpate them. They are spread over a vast country, thirteen hundred miles in length, and twelve hundred in breadth. Notwithstanding the opposition they have met with, they have from first to last maintained their independence, no conqueror has subdued them ; they still dwell in the presence of all their brethren, and in the presence of all their enemies.—What a striking proof is this of the truth of Scripture prophecy ! As Bishop Newton observes, men and manners change with times. How have the modern Italians degenerated from the courage and virtue of the old Romans ! How are the French and English polished and refined from the barbarians of the ancient Gauls and Britons ! but these people have continued the same with little or no variation !

THE PLOUGHMAN'S OPINION ; OR THE DIFFICULTY OF SELF-DENIAL.

In the parish where Mr. Hervey preached, when he was of Arminian sentiments, there resided a ploughman, who usually attended the ministry of the late Dr. Doddridge. Mr. Hervey being advised by his physician, for the benefit of his health, to follow the plough, in order to smell the fresh earth, frequently accompanied the ploughman in his rural avocation. One morning the following conversation passed :—

Mr. Hervey. My friend, I understand you can speak the language of Canaan.

Ploughman. A little, Sir.

Mr. H. Then I will propose you a question :—What do you think is the hardest thing in religion ?

Plough. I am a poor illiterate man, and you, sir, are a minister :—I beg leave to return the question.

Mr. H. Then I conceive the hardest thing in religion is to renounce *sinful flesh.*

Plough. I do not think so, sir.

Mr. H. Then will you give me your opinion.

Plough. Why, sir, the hardest thing in religion is to deny *righteous- self.* You know I do not come to hear you preach ; but go every sabbath with my family to Northampton to hear Dr. Doddridge. We rise early in the morning, and have prayer before we set out, in which I find pleasure ;—walking there and back, I find pleasure ;—under the sermon, I find pleasure ;—when at the Lord's table, I find pleasure ;—we read a portion of the Scripture, and go to prayer in the evening, in which I find pleasure ; but to this moment I find it the hardest thing to deny *righteous-self*.

This simple recital of the poor man so affected Mr. Hervey, that it proved a blessing to his soul, and the plough-man henceforth became his bosom friend.

PROCRASTINATION DANGEROUS.

It is reported of Thales, one of the Grecian sages, that being urged by his mother to alter his condition in life, he told her at first that it was too soon ; and afterwards when she urged him again, he told her it was too late. So says an old divine, "effectual vocation is an espousal to Christ." All the time of our life God is urging this upon us ; his ministers are still working for Christ ; if now we say it is too soon, for aught we know, the very next moment our sun may set, and then God will say it is too late. They who are never contracted to Christ on earth, shall never be united to Him in heaven.

How justly will the wilful neglect of salvation, so long and so compassionately offered to sinners, render the divine mercy inexorable to their prayers and tears at last. When a Roman gentleman, who was wont to revel in the night and sleep in the day, having wasted a great estate by luxury, petitioned the Emperor Tiberius to relieve his poverty, he was dismissed with this upbraiding answer, *Sero experrectus es*,—you are risen too late. He never opened his eyes to see his condition till it was past remedy. This is the sad case of many that waste the seasons of grace, and are careless of their

duty till upon the point of perishing, and then address themselves to God for his favour and pardon ; but are justly rejected with the reproaches of their obstinate neglect of salvation in the time of their lives. I doubt not that some are wonderfully converted and saved at last ; but these special mercies are like our Saviour's miraculous healing of the two blind persons as he was passing on that way, when great numbers of the blind remained uncured. We read a prodigious story in the Book of Kings, that a captain and his fifty men commanded Elias to come to the king, and immediately a tempest of lightning destroyed them. Now, who would think that another captain and his fifty men should be so desperate, having the ashes and relics of those miserable carcasses before their eyes, as to make the same citation to the prophet ? Yet they did, and provoked the justice of heaven to consume them. And this madness is exemplified in thousands every day ; for notwithstanding they see sinners like themselves cut off in their evil ways, they continue unreformed, as if they were fearless of hell—as if resolved to secure their own damnation.

THE PHILOSOPHER AND THE POOR WEAVERS.

Chilo, one of the Greek wise men, when he was at the point of death, called his friends to him, and said, he could find nothing to repent of in all his past life : not one fault, except in a single instance, leaning a little too favourably to a friend in judgment.

A few years ago two pious weavers were conversing together, and complaining of the trouble which they found from vain and evil thoughts in the solemn duties of religion. Another person of the same business overheard them, and, rushing forth, said, " I always thought you two vile hypocrites ; but now I know it from your own confession. For my part, I never had such vain and wicked thoughts in my life." One of the

X

men took a piece of money out of his pocket and put it into his hand, adding, "This shall be yours, if after you come from the church the next time, you can say you had not one vain thought there." In a few days he came saying, "Here take back your money, for I had not been five minutes in the church before I began to think how many looms could be set up in it."

POVERTY.

POVERTY is always better than profaneness. A poor man who is honest and good, stands on a far more elevated scale than the most opulent man who is base and impious. Yet poverty is not desirable, as it exposes to many inconveniences.

We cannot, however, easily account for the singularities of men. That which many think to be evil, others imagine to be good. What some avoid as unpleasant, others seek as beneficial. Thus, for instance, riches in general are sought after with avidity, yet poverty has been courted by some.

Tubero, a Roman consul, son-in-law of Paulus, the conqueror of Perseus, is celebrated for his poverty, in which he seemed to glory, as well as the rest of his family. Sixteen of the Tuberos, with their wives and children, lived in a small house, and maintained themselves with the produce of a little field, which they cultivated with their own hands! But how many thousands of Christians have endured poverty, rather than comply with the world! Here, indeed, is a holy singularity. The riches of this world become contemptible, if they impede our progress in the way to heaven. Rather let me be poor and obedient to the will of God, than to possess all the wealth of the universe and forget Him!

THE PHILISTINE'S HEAD;
Or, the Infidel reproved.

A GAY young spark, of a deistical turn, travelling in a stage coach to London, forced his sentiments on the company, by attempting to ridicule the Scriptures; and among other topics, made himself merry with the story of David and Goliath, strongly urging the impossibility of a youth, like David, being able to throw a stone with sufficient force to sink it into the giant's forehead. On this he appealed to the company, and in particular to a grave gentleman of the denomination called Quakers, who sat silent in one corner of the carriage. "Indeed, friend," replied he, "I do not think it at all improbable, if the Philistine's *head was as soft as thine.*"

PUN.

Puns are not wit, but many of them are strikingly pleasing. The dose of puns ought to be limited, according to the constitution to whom they are addressed; for some there are who cannot endure punning in a great degree. The best pun ever uttered, was made by a most learned man—"What," said he, "is M-A-JEST-Y, when deprived of the externals?"

PREFERMENT NO SECURITY AGAINST PAIN.

I BELIEVE the learned bishop of London, Dr. Lowth, upon whom Mr. Cadogan used frequently to call, did not question the sincerity of his declaration on the following occasion: The bishop had long been confined with the gout, and said, as he sat in pain, "Ah! Mr. Cadogan, see what a poor thing it is to be a bishop of London." "Truly, my lord," replied Mr. Cadogan, "I always thought it was a very poor thing to be a bishop of London, if a man possessed nothing better." It may be remarked, that such a reply came with a better grace, as it came from one who, in all probability, might have obtained a bishopric had he made it his object.

PLURALITIES.

AN Abbé, who had no preferment, exclaiming one day to Boileau against pluralities, said, " Is it possible that the people you named, who have the reputation of being very learned men, and are such in reality, should be mistaken in their opinions? Unless these would absolutely oppose the doctrine laid down by the apostles and the decisions of councils, must they not be obliged to confess, that the holding several livings at the same time is sinful? I myself am in holy orders ; and, be it said without vanity, of one of the best families in Touraine. It becomes a man of high birth to endeavour to make a figure suitable to it ; yet I protest to you, that if I can get an abbey, the yearly income of which is only a thousand crowns, my ambition will be satisfied ; and be assured that nothing shall tempt me to alter my resolution." Some time after this, an abbey of seven thousand crowns a year being vacant, his brother desired it for him, and was gratified in his request. The winter following, he got another of still greater value : and a third being vacant, he solicited very strongly for this also, and obtained it. Boileau, hearing of these preferments, went and paid his friend a visit. " M. l'Abbé," said he, " where is now that season of innocence and candour, in which you declared that pluralists hazarded their souls greatly ?"—" Ah, good Boileau," replied the Abbé, " did you but know how much pluralities contribute towards living well."—" I am in no doubt of that," replied Boileau ; " but of what service are they, good Abbé, towards *dying well?*" The above anecdote originally appeared in a book printed in Paris in 1698, and was translated into English by Mr. Lockman, the translator of the " Travels of the Jesuits."

DANGER OF POPULARITY.

PSAMMETICUS was a king of Egypt. He was one of the twelve princes who shared the kingdom among themselves ; but, as he was more popular than the rest, he was banished from his dominions, and re-tired into the marshes near the seashore.

TRUE PHILOSOPHY.

IT is recorded of Stilpo the philosopher, that when his city was destroyed, with his wife and children, and he alone escaped from the fire, being asked whether he had lost any thing, he replied, " All my treasures are with me—justice, virtue, temperance, prudence, and this inviolable principle, not to esteem any thing as my proper good that can be taken from me." His mind was erect and steadfast under the ruins of his country.

RESTRAINING POWER.

SUCH is the depravity of human nature, that were it not for the restraining power of the Almighty, the world would be reduced to the greatest distress and misery. It was a strange and barbarous custom among the Persians, that upon the death of the emperor, for five days the empire was left without government. And, as upon removing the stone from the fabulous cave of Æolus, the winds broke out in their fury, so by taking away the authority of the laws, license was given to all species of wickedness and the kingdom thrown into the utmost confusion. All were in arms, some to commit injuries, others to revenge them ; the chastity of none was secure, nor the estates of any safe, unless defended ; the bridle of fear was taken off ; there was no wickedness that was not boldly committed. But when the new king was proclaimed, all things were immediately reduced to order, that the advantage of government might be set off by this experimental confusion and mischief of anarchy. Now, if God, as one observes, left this perverted world, and Satan the prince of it, one day to their rage against his people, did he not shut it with doors and bars, it would be like the deluge overwhelming all, and not a remnant of the saints would be left.

142 RELIGIOUS, MORAL, AND

THE BARREN PROFESSORS REPROVED.

"WHAT do ye more than others?" is a very important inquiry for the Christian to consider. The sublime doctrines, holy precepts, delightful promises, and bright prospects of the Christian religion, all tend to excite to diligence and activity. Yet how many who call themselves Christians are outdone in many things, even by heathens! These things ought not so to be. An atheist being asked by a professor of Christianity, how he could quiet his conscience in so desperate a state, replied, " as much am I astonished as yourself, that, believing the Christian religion to be true, you can quiet your conscience in living so much like the world. Did I believe what you profess, I should think no care, no diligence, no zeal enough." Reader, dost *thou* believe?—then show thy faith by thy works.

PROVIDENCE ACKNOWLEDGED;
Or, the Great Emperor's Confession.

"THE bare light of nature," saith Dr. Barrow, "hath discerned, that were it not for such matters as these to spend a man's care and pains upon, this world would be a lamentable place to live in. There was, for instance, an emperor, great and mighty as ever wielded sceptre upon earth, whose excellent virtue coupled with wisdom (inferior, perhaps, to none that any man ever, without special inspiration, had been endowed with,) and which qualified him with great advantage to examine and to judge aright of things here; who, notwithstanding all the conveniences which his royal estate and well settled prosperity might afford, and of which he had had the fullest experience, nevertheless thus expressed himself: "What doth it concern me to live in a world without a God, or void of Providence?" To govern the greatest empire that ever was in the deepest calm; to enjoy the largest affluence of wealth or splendour, of re-

spect, or of pleasure; to be loved, to be dreaded, to be served, to be adored by so many nations; to have the whole civil world obsequious to his will and nod; all these things seemed vain and idle, not worthy of a man's regard, reflection, or choice, if there were no God to worship, no providence to observe, no piety to be exercised. So little worth a wise man's regard, common sense hath adjudged it to live without religion. Learn hence how extreme is the folly of atheism.

DIVINE PRESERVATION DURING SLEEP.

"I THINK," says Mr. Hervey, "it is referable only to a superintending and watchful Providence that we are not hurried into the most pernicious actions, when our imagination is heated, and our reason stupified by dreams. We have sometimes heard of persons who, walking in their sleep, have thrown themselves headlong from a window and been dashed to death on the pebbles. And whence is it that such disastrous accidents are only related as pieces of news, not experienced by ourselves or our families? Were our minds more sober in their operations, or more circumspect in their regards? No, verily; nothing could be more wild than their excursions; and none could be more inattentive to their own welfare. Therefore, if *we have laid us down and slept in peace,* it was because the Lord vouchsafed us the sweet refreshment: if *we rose again* in safety, it was because the Lord sustained us with his unremitted protection.

"Will the candid reader excuse me, if I add a short story, or rather a matter of fact, suitable to the preceding remark? Two persons who had been hunting together in the day, slept together the following night. One of them was renewing the pursuit in his dream; and, having run the whole circle of the chase, came, at last, to the fall of the stag

Upon this, he cries out with a determined ardour, *I'll kill him! I'll kill him!* and immediately feels for the knife which he carried in his pocket. His companion happening to be awake, and observing what passed, leaped from the bed. Being secure from danger, and the moon shining into the room, he stood to view the event; when, to his inexpressible surprise the infatuated sportsman gave several deadly stabs in the very place where a moment before the throat and the life of his friend lay. This I mention as a proof that nothing hinders us, even from being assassins of *others*, or murderers of ourselves, amidst the mad sallies of sleep, only the *preventing care* of our heavenly Father."

THE UNHAPPY QUARREL.

EPIPHANIUS relates, that Milesius and Peter, bishops of Alexandria, both confessors of the orthodox religion, and both condemned to suffer, being together in prison, upon a small difference fell into so great a dispute, that they drew a partition between each other in the prison, and would not hold communion in the same worship of Christ, for which, notwithstanding, they both suffered. How lamentable is it, when Christians agree in the grand and essential points, they should dispute and quarrel so much with each other about things of minor importance!

THE THREE QUESTIONS.

PAUL directs Christians to *examine* themselves whether they be in the faith, and to prove their ownselves, to know whether or not they are reprobates.

The precept is double, to show the necessity and difficulty of the work; to show that it is not a superficial, but serious examination which will enable a man to know whether he hath faith or not. Climacus reports that the ancients used to keep, in a little book, a memorial of what they did during the day. But oh! how few there are in these times that keep a diary of God's mercies, of spiritual experiences, and of their own infirmities! Seneca mentions a heathen, who every night asked himself three questions: What evil hast thou cured this day? What vice hast thou withstood this day? In what respect art thou made better this day? And shall not Christians take pains to find out what God hath done, and is doing in their hearts? Strict self-examination is the way to put an end to all your wranglings, and to put you' in possession of a heaven on earth.

THE QUAKER'S WATCH.

A PERSON of the denomination of Quakers, once took his watch to the maker, with the following words:— "Friend, I have once more brought my erroneous watch, which wants thy friendly care and protection: the last time he was at thy school, he was no ways benefitted by thy instruction. I find, by the index of his tongue, that he tells false, and that his motions are waving and unsettled, which makes me believe he is not right in the inward man; I mean the main spring. I would have thee improve him, with thy adjusting tool of truth, that if possible, thou mayest drive him from the error of his ways. Imagining his body to be foul, and the whole mass corrupted, purge him with thy cleansing stick, from all pollution, so that he may vibrate and circulate according to truth. I will board him with thee a few days, and pay thee when thou requirest it. In thy late bill, thou chargest me with the one eighth of a pound sterling, which I will pay thee also. Friend, when thou correctest him, do it without passion; lest, by severity, thou drivest him to destruction. I would have thee let him visit the sun's motion, and learn him his true calculation table, and equation; and when thou findest him conformable to that, send him home with a just bill of moderation, and it shall be faithfully remitted to thee by thy true friend."

RELIGION A SOURCE OF CONSOLATION.

Dr. Grosvenor's first wife was a most devout and amiable woman; the Sunday after her death, the doctor expressed himself from the pulpit, in the following manner :—I have had an irreparable loss, and no man can feel a loss of this consequence more sensibly than myself; but the cross of a dying Jesus is my support. I fly from *one* death for refuge to *another*." How much superior was the refuge and happiness of the Christian divine to those of the heathen philosopher, Pliny the younger, who says that, in similar distress, study was his only relief! *Itaque et infirmitate uxoris et meorum periculo, quorundam vero etium morte, turbatus, ad unicum deloris levamentum studia confugio.* Lib. viii. Ep. 19.

RELIGION.

There is, says Bishop Taylor, an universal crust of hypocrisy, that covers the face of the greatest part of mankind ; but true religion is open in its articles, honest in its prosecutions, just in its conduct, innocent when it is accused, ignorant of falsehood, sure in its truth, simple in its sayings, and, (as Julius Capitolinus said of the emperor Verus) it is *morum simplicium, et quæ adumbrare nihil possit.* It covers indeed a multitude of sins, by curing them, and obtaining pardon for them ; but it can dissemble nothing of itself : it cannot tell or do a lie ; but it can become a sacrifice : a good man can quit his life, but never his integrity.

Some time ago, a soldier was brought under concern for the interest of his soul, and becoming visibly religious, met with no little railing both from his comrades and officers. He was the servant of one of the latter. At length his master asked him,—" Richard, what good has your religion done you ?" The soldier made this discreet answer : " Sir, before 1 was religious, I used to get drunk ; now I am sober. I used to

neglect your business, now I perform it diligently." The officer was silenced, and seemed to be satisfied. Here we see the excellency of real religion ; it teaches us to deny all ungodliness, and to live soberly, righteously, and godly in this present world. Honesty, diligence, sobriety, quietness, are among its happy fruits. Its ways are ways of pleasantness and paths of peace.

Religion valued.

Ælian reports of one Nicostratus, that being a skilful artificer, and finding a curious piece of art, he was so much taken with it that a spectator, beholding him very intent in viewing the workmanship, asked him what pleasure he could take in gazing so long upon such an object ; He answered, " Hadst thou my eyes, thou wouldst be as much ravished as I am." So may we say of carnal persons :— had they the hearts and dispositions of believers, they would be as much delighted with all means of communion with God, as *they* are, and account that *their* privilege which now they esteem their vexation.

Religion not a mere external Ceremony.

" Labour," says Mr. Jackson, in the Morning Exercises, " to know and understand well, and often remember, wherein consists the life of true and real religion. There are so many things in the world that pretend to be religion, yet less deserve that name than the picture of a man, deserves the name of a man, that it is an easy mistake to nourish an enemy to religion, instead of religion, unless we be serious and cautious, and more apt to regard the characters which the Scriptures give of real religion, than hasty to take up the forms and fancies of men instead of religion. I have read of a French lady, who observing the glorious pomp and splendour of a popish procession, cried out How fine a religion is ours in comparison of the Hugonots ! A speech suiting her age and quality ; but in deed if religion did consist in such things, the question I have in hand would fall to the ground, for there could then be no exercise of religion among those who would not admit of such pompous solemnities."

Religion, Effect of.

At ———, in Yorkshire, after a handsome collection on the preceding evening had been made for the Missionary Society, a poor man, whose wages are about twenty-eight shillings per week, brought the next morning, at breakfast-time, a donation of twenty guineas. The friends hesitated to receive it ; doubting whether it was consistent with duty to his family and the world to contribute such a sum : when he answered to the following effect:—" Before I knew the grace of our Lord, I was a poor drunkard. I never could save a shilling., My family were in beggary and rags ;— but since it has pleased God to renew me by his grace, we have been industrious and frugal ; we have not spent many idle shillings : and we have been enabled to put something into the bank; and this I freely offer to the blessed cause of our Lord and Saviour." This was the second donation of this same poor man, to the same amount !

Advantages of Religion.

Freedom and felicity are inseparable : servitude is the fatal concomitant of vice. When a philosopher was asked what advantage he obtained by the study of philosophy, he replied, this among others, that if all the laws were cancelled, a philosopher would live as uniformly, according to the rules of decency and honesty, as before. Of the real Christian, it may be truly said, that were he destitute of the restraint of penal laws, he would, both from choice and judgment, be holy in all manner of conversation and godliness.

The truth of Religion proved by its Effects.

The Romans had a law, that every

one should, wherever he went, wear a badge of his trade in his hat, or outward vestment, that he might be known. Thus the Christian is never to lay aside the badge of his holy profession ; but to let his light shine and adorn the doctrines of God his Saviour in all things.

REPENTANCE.

REPENTANCE is absolutely essential to the Christian character. Hence Tertullian said, " I am born for nothing but repentance." Yet he is certainly the happiest man whose life has not been stained with enormous crimes. To make work for repentance, to use a common expression, is not to be commended, however safe we may be at last. And therefore Demosthenes acted wisely, who, when tempted to unlawful pleasures, and finding the price was no less than three hundred pounds of British money, said that he would not buy a repentance at so dear a price. Alas ! how many act a contrary part to the orator ; and by their prodigality, and love of the world, lay a foundation for bitter remorse and heavy suffering !

The Emperor Sigismund having made fair promises, in a sore fit of sickness, of amendment of life, asked Theodoricus, archbishop of Collon, how he might know whether his repentance was sincere, who replied,— " If you are as careful to perform in your health, as you are forward to promise in your sickness, you may safely draw that inference."

Though true repentance be never too late, yet late repentance is seldom true. Millions are now in hell, who have pleased themselves with the thoughts of after-repentance. The Lord hath made a promise to late repentance ; but where hath he made a promise of late repentance ? Yea, what can be more just and equal, than that such should seek and not find, who might have found but would not seek ; and that he should shut his ears against their late prayers, who have stopt their ears against his early calls ? The ancient warriors would not accept an old man into their army, as being unfit for service ; and dost thou think God will accept of thy dry bones, when Satan hath sucked out all the marrow ? What lord, what master, would take such into their service, as have all their days served their enemies ; and is it reasonable to expect that God should do it ? The Circassians, a kind of mongrel Christians, are said to divide their life between sin and devotion, dedicating their youth to rapine and their old age to repentance ; if this be thy case, reader, I would not be in thy place for ten thousand worlds !

I have read of a certain great man, that was admonished in his sickness to repent : but he refused to do it yet ; for if he should recover, his companions would laugh at him ; but growing worse and worse in point of health, his friends pressed him again to repent, but he then told them it was too late, *Qui jam judicatus sum et condemnatus ;* " for now," said he, " I am judged and condemned."

RETREAT DREADED, AND PERSEVERANCE ENCOURAGED.

GONSALVO protested to his soldiers, showing them Naples, that he had rather die one foot forwards, than have his life secured by one foot of retreat. " Shall such a man as I am, flee ?" said the undaunted Nehemiah. He will courageously venture life and limb, rather than by one foot of retreat, discredit his profession with the reproach of fearfulness. It was a brave and magnanimous speech of Luther, when dangers from opposers threatened him and his associates; " Come," said he, " let us sing the 46th Psalm, and let them do their worst." When Polycarp was fourscore and six years old, he suffered martyrdom courageously, resolutely and undauntedly. When one of the ancient martyrs was very much threatened by his persecutors, he replied, " There is nothing of things

visible that I fear; I will stand to my profession of the name of Christ, and contend earnestly for the faith once delivered to saints come on what will."

RETIREMENT.

RETIREMENT is assuredly favourable to the advancement of the best ends of our being. There the soul has freer means of examining into its own state and its dependence upon God. It has more unobstructed leisure for enjoying with its Maker, communion, sweet communion, large, and high. It has ampler means for reiterating the consecration of its powers and faculties to Him who gave them, than it could easily find in those broken snatches and uncertain intervals which busier scenes afford. But then we must be brought into a state and condition to reap benefit from retreat. The paralytic might as reasonably expect to remove his disease, by changing his position, as the discontented to allay the unruly motions of a distempered mind, merely by retiring into the country.

A great statesman, whom many of us remember, after having long filled a high official situation with honour and ability, began at length impatiently to look forward to the happy period when he should be exonerated from the toils of office. He pathetically lamented the incessant interruptions which distracted him even in the intervals of public business. He repeatedly expressed to a friend how ardently he longed to be discharged from the oppressive weight of his situation, and to consecrate his remaining days to repose and literature. At length, one of those revolutions in party, which so many desire, and by which so few are satisfied, transferred him to the scene of his wishes. He flew to his rural seat, but he soon found that the sources to which he had so long looked, failed in their power of conferring the promised enjoyment; his ample park yielded him no gratification, but what it had yielded him in town, without the present drawback; there he had partaken of its venison, without the incumbrance of its solitude. His hamadryads, having no dispatches to present and no votes to offer, soon grew insipid. The stillness of retreat became insupportable; and he frankly declared to the friend above alluded to, that such was to him the blank of life, that the only relief he ever felt, was to hear a rap at the door. Though he had before gladly snatched the little leisure of a hurried life for reading, yet when life became all leisure, books had lost their power to interest. Study could not fill a mind long kept on the stretch by great concerns, in which he himself had been a prime mover. The history of other times could not animate a spirit habitually quickened by a strong personal interest in actual events. There is a quality in our nature strongly indicative, that we were formed for active and useful purposes. These, though of a calmer kind, may be still pursued in retirement under the influence of the holy principle, powerful enough to fill the heart which fancies itself emptied of the world. Religion is that motive yet quieting principle, which alone delivers a man from perturbation in the world and inanity in retirement; without it, he will in one case be hurried into impetuosity, or in the other be sunk into stagnation. But religion long neglected, "will not come when you do call for it." Perhaps the noble person did not call.

REPROOF.

FEW things are, as one observes, more difficult than to administer reproof properly; but while the professed servants of God sometimes need reproof, the avowed servants of Satan need it much more frequently, and on different grounds. One day, a person being in the room of a poor aged Christian woman, and lamenting a want of firmness to reprove the abandoned when travelling, and, as an excuse, having recourse to that passage, "Give not that which is holy unto the dogs, neither cast your pearls before swine," she seriously and hastily replied, "O, sir! keen and just reproofs are no pearls; were you to talk to a wicked coachman respecting the love of God shed abroad in the heart by the Holy Ghost, and the pleasures of communion with God, you would cast pearls before swine, but not in reproving sin."

THE ROBBER DISARMED BY CHARITY.

A PIOUS lady of Montpelire, who devoted the greater part of her property to the relief of objects in distress, one day passing through a little wood, accompanied by her servant, was stopped by a man who presented a pistol to her, demanding her money or her life. The good lady, without being terrified, looked on him with an air of kindness, and said, "Ah! my friend, you must be reduced to extremity, since you are determined to take a part which both draws on you the wrath of God, and exposes you continually to all the rigours of human justice. I wish I had wherewith to supply your wants, and extricate you from the dangerous situation in which you are; but I have, alas! only eighteen francs, which I have taken for my journey, and I offer you them with all my heart."

The highwayman, looking upon her attentively, before he would take the money, wished to know who she was; and when she told him, "Wretch that I am," said he, throwing himself at her feet, "I have many times experienced your bounty, and have never been denied relief when I have sought it of you; and I was now upon the point of injuring you! Ah! believe me, my good lady, I did not know you, or I should not have molested you; for though I have given but too great a proof that I am a robber, yet I am not a monster,— which I must be to injure a person so charitable as you are. Go on, then; keep your money, and I will myself escort you out of the wood; and if any one come to attack you, I will defend you at the hazard of my life."

The lady was exceedingly affected, and endeavoured to represent to him his danger, and to urge motives of honour and religion to induce him to quit so dreadful a way of life; and promising to do more for him another time, she again offered the eighteen francs; but knowing that she wanted them for her journey, he would not accept them; till at last she prevailed on him to take nine of them, which she threw to him on going out of the wood.

DIVINE REALITIES NEGLECTED.

How many, like Felix, tremble, and are affected while hearing the word, but soon neglect or forget what they hear? " I have somewhere," says one, "read of an excellent preacher, who described the awful solemnities of the final judgment with such pathetic strains of eloquence, and in a manner so moving, that some of his audience burst forth into loud exclamations, as if the Judge himself had appeared, announcing the decisive sentence. In the height of the commotion, the preacher bade them restrain their tears and cries, for he had one thing more to add, the most astonishing of all. It was this; that within a quarter of an hour, the impression of those great events which they now felt, would vanish, and they would return home unaffected by them to those sensible objects that commonly engrossed their attention." Alas! this is too frequently the case; and that even with the best. "My soul," said David, "cleaveth unto the dust;" we may therefore well add, " quicken thou me according to thy word."

CLERICAL RESIDENCE.

CLERICAL residence is certainly the grand turning point of clerical usefulness. Without residing upon his cure of souls, the best man living cannot do his duty. The question once asked by the brethren of David may be fairly put to the conscience of every non-resident clergyman,— "With whom hast thou left those few sheep in the wilderness?" It will not be denied, that the most solemn oaths have been taken, and the most sacred promises made; and yet the minister of God, the very character who should be ready to explain the nature of an oath, and show the tendency of a promise to others, is breaking these engagements himself. The lamp which should illumine the sanctuary, is rarely seen within its walls. To compare great things with small: as a country squire, I keep a flock of sheep; no matter whether the Merino or the South Down. I am curious in my wool, and pride myself upon my superior mutton. My shepherd once said to me, 'Please your honour, I can have a cottage, with a nice bit of garden, in the next village; I will be sure to come early, and go home late; may I live there?' 'Certainly not, my good man,' said I, 'if you wish to continue in my service. I will give you a small cottage in my own field; but you want a garden: if the place suits you, live in it; but if not, leave the employment, and choose for yourself.' Now, sir, if my shepherd must be on the spot, to attend to his sheep, to watch over them, to administer medicine, to enlarge the fold, and change the pasture—how much more in a spiritual sense? Our Lord is said to have had compassion on the multitude, because they were as sheep having no shepherd. I fear that there are many such multitudes in the present day.

SAYINGS OF THE MARTYRS PREVIOUS TO THEIR EXECUTIONS.

DR. Huss, when the chain was put about him at the stake, said with a smiling countenance, "My Lord Jesus Christ was bound with a harder chain than this for my sake; and why should I be ashamed of this old rusty one?"

Jerom of Prague, observing the executioners about to set fire to the wood behind his back, cried out,

"Bring thy torch hither! Perform thy office before my face. Had I feared death I might have avoided it."

John Lambert, just before he expired, lifted up such hands as he had, all flaming with fire, and cried out to the people with his dying voice in these words, "None but Christ! none but Christ!"

George Wishart, at the stake, said, "This fire torments my body, but no whit abates my spirits."

Laurence Sanders, when he came to the place of execution, fell to the ground and prayed ; and then arose and took the stake in his arms to which he was to be chained, and kissed it, saying, "Welcome the cross of Christ! welcome everlasting life!"

Robert Ferrar said, (after a person had been talking to him of the severity and painfulness of the kind of death which he was to undergo) "If you see me once to stir, while I suffer the pains of burning, then give no credit to the truth of those doctrines for which I die ;" and by the grace of God he was enabled to make good this assertion.

John Bradford turning his face to John Leaf, a young man about twenty years old, who suffered with him, said, "Be of good comfort, brother, for we shall sup with the Lord this night :" he then embraced the reeds, and repeated the 7th ch. Matt., 13th verse.

Bishop Latimer, at his execution, said to Bishop Ridley, who suffered with him, "We shall this day, brother, light such a candle in England as shall never be put out!"

Bishop Ridley said to the smith, as he was knocking in the staple which held the chain, "Good man, knock it in hard, for the flesh will have its course."

John Philpot, when he was come into Smithfield, kneeled down and said, "I will pay my vows in thee, O Smithfield!" Being come to the stake, he kissed it, and said, "Shall I disdain to suffer at this stake, when my Lord and Saviour refused not to suffer a most vile death upon the cross for me ?"

Archbishop Cranmer, who signed the popish tenets only through fear of death, at his execution said, "This is the hand that wrote, and therefore it shall first suffer punishment." Fire being applied to him, he stretched out his right hand into the flame till it was consumed, crying with a loud voice, "This hand hath offended," and often repeating, "This unworthy right hand!"

That was a Christian expression of one of the martyrs to his persecutors—"You take a life from me that I cannot keep, and bestow a life upon me that I cannot lose, which is as if you should rob me of counters and furnish me with gold."

Ignatius, in his Epistle to the persecutors of the church, gloried, saying, "The wild beasts may grind me as corn between their teeth, but I shall by that become as choice bread in the hand of my God."

It is reported of Hooper, the martyr, that when he was going to suffer, a certain person addressed him, saying, "O sir, take care of yourself, for life is sweet and death is bitter." "Ah, I know that," replied he ; "but the life to come is full of more sweetness than this mortal life ; and the death to come is full of more bitterness than this uncommon death."

When Herod and Nicetes attempted to turn Polycarp from the faith, by insinuating that there was no evil in calling Cæsar lord, and offering sacrifices to him, he replied, that he had served Jesus Christ for many years, and had always found him a good master; that he should therefore submit himself to all the tortures they should inflict, rather than deny him ; and when he was threatened to be burnt, he replied to the proconsul, "Thou threatenest me with a fire that burns for an hour, and then dies, but art ignorant of the fire of the future judgment, and eternal damnation reserved for the ungodly. But why do you make delays? Order what punishment you think fit."

It is recorded concerning one of the martyrs, that when he was going to the stake, a nobleman besought him in a compassionate manner to take care of his soul ;—"So I will," he replied, "for I give my body to be burnt rather than have my soul defiled."

SABBATH DAY.

A YOUNG man who had been employed in a gentleman's garden in Suffolk, had a strong inclination to try his fortune near the metropolis. Accordingly he came to London, and soon got into a situation at the west end of the town, where he, in a few years, acquired so much property that he took some ground and entered into business for himself. He had been brought up in a religious manner, and in the strict observance of the sabbath ; but the love of the world now so far got the ascendency as to induce him to violate that sacred day, by selling various articles which his garden produced. Providence, however, frowned upon him, so that his prospects of great gain proved delusive. By some unaccountable means, he failed of success in all his schemes, and in a short time became a bankrupt. His sister, a pious young woman, who kept his house, told him her apprehensions, that the cause of his misfortunes was the profanation of the sabbath, and strongly urged him to begin business again upon a small scale, offering to lend him all she had (which was but thirty shillings) to buy a few necessary articles, upon this condition, that he should sell nothing on the Lord's Day, but to devote it wholly to religion ; in which case, she told him he might hope for a divine blessing. He agreed to take her advice ; and he soon experienced the wisdom of it ; for he quickly began to find his business wonderfully to prosper ; and, in a few years, rose to such affluence as to purchase the ground he had hired ; and to be able to communicate largely of his substance, for the honour of God, and for the good of many.

The Sabbath observed ; or, Nothing got by Sinning.

Many well–disposed people are under strong temptations to neglect the due observation of the sabbath day. A large family, the little time they have to spare on the week-days, the poverty of their circumstances, all operate as powerful incentives to appropriate this day to affairs which are not lawful, forgetting that they who serve God have too good a master to leave them to want and wretchedness. "I remonstrated," says one, "with a poor old woman who kept open her shop on Sundays ; I had reason to believe she was pious, though guilty of this sin. She acknowledged it was wrong, and that conscience often reproved her, but pleaded that she was a poor infirm old widow, without any support excepting that which she derived from her shop ; that her business on the week days would not maintain her ; and that she took as much money on the sabbath as on the other six days together. I told her nothing was gained by sin, nor any thing lost by obedience ; that she had trusted God with her eternal concerns, and surely might trust him with her temporal ; and that he had promised to provide for his people ; but, by breaking the sabbath, she took her affairs out of his hands ; no wonder therefore if she suffered distress. She acknowledged the truth of my remarks, and determined to shut the shop on the Lord's Day, which she accordingly did. Some time afterwards, I asked her whether she was poorer since she left off selling on Sundays. 'No,' said she, 'God has shown me, blessed be his holy name ! that he can provide for me abundantly :—there is *nothing got by sinning !*'"

SANCTIFICATION.

A FRIEND of Archbishop Usher repeatedly urged him to write his thoughts on sanctification, which at length he engaged to do ; but a considerable time elapsing, the performance of his promise was importunately claimed. The bishop replied to this purpose :—" I have not written, and yet I cannot charge myself with a breach of promise ; for I began to write, but when I came to treat of the new creature which God formeth by his Spirit in every regenerate soul, I found so little of it wrought in myself, that I could speak of it only as parrots, or by rote, without the knowledge of what I might have expressed, and therefore I durst not presume to proceed any further upon it." Upon this his friend stood amazed, to hear such a humble confession from so gracious, holy, and eminent a person. The bishop then added, " I must tell you, we do not well understand what sanctification and the new creature are. It is no less than for a man to be brought to an entire resignation of his own will to the will of God, and to live in the offering up of his soul continually in the flames of love as a whole burnt offering to Christ ; and oh! how many who profess Christianity are unacquainted experimentally with this great work upon their souls !"

SCRIPTURES.

LUTHER said he would not take all the world for one leaf of THE BIBLE. " To apply ourselves to the writings of the wisest heathens," says Dr. Bates, " in order to our happiness, and to neglect the Scriptures, is to be guilty of worse folly than the barbarous Indians at Mexico, who, though their woods abounded with wax, the labour of the bees, yet only made use of brands that afforded a little light with a great deal of smoke."

The sacred oracles are not only the fountains of truth ; but in them we discover the path of life. The knowledge and practice of these form the true Christian ; and such, in the last day, who have known and kept the word of God, shall escape that punishment to which *they* shall be exposed who have neglected and despised

it. In the Peloponnesian war, when the Athenian army was defeated in Sicily, and the prisoners were ordered to be put to death, such of them as could repeat any verses of Euripides were saved, out of respect to that poet, who was a citizen of Athens. So shall they be delivered from punishment who have hid God's word in their hearts ; and made it the constant rule of their lives ; and that for *his* sake, and through HIM who was delivered for our offences and raised again for our justification.

Search then diligently the word of eternal life, enrich and ennoble as it is with the chain, and the accomplishment of its prophecies,—with the splendour of its miracles ; with the attestation of its martyrs ; the consistency of its doctrines ; the importance of its facts ; the plenitude of its precepts ; the treasury of its promises ; the irradiations of the Spirit ; the abundance of its consolations ; the peace it bestows ; the blessedness it announces ; the proportion of its parts ; the symmetry of the whole ; altogether presenting such a fund of instruction to the mind, of light to the path, of document to the conduct, of satisfaction to the heart, as demonstrably prove it to be the instrument of God for the salvation of man.

SCRUPLES SOMETIMES UNNECESSARY.

" UNTO the pure," says the apostle to Titus, " all things are pure."

" I recollect the sense," says Saurin, " which a celebrated bishop in the Isle of Cyprus gave these words in the first ages of the church. I speak of Spiridion. A traveller exhausted with the fatigue of his journey waited upon him on a day which the church had set apart for fasting. Spiridion instantly ordered some refreshment for him, and invited him, by his own example, to eat. " No, I must not eat," said the stranger, " because I am a Christian." " And because you are a Christian," replied the bishop to him, " you may eat without scruple, agreeably to the decision of an apostle, *unto the pure all things are pure."* We cannot be ignorant of the shameful abuse which some have made of this maxim. We know some have extended it even to the most essential articles of positive law, which no one can violate without sin. We know particularly the insolence with which some place themselves in the list of those *pure* persons of whom the apostle speaks, although their gross ignorance and novel dignity may justly place them in the opposite class. But the abuse of a maxim ought not to prevent the lawful use of it. There are some things which are criminal or lawful according to the degree of knowledge and holiness of him who performs them. *Unto the pure all things are pure.* Would you then know how far to carry your scruples in regard to some steps? Examine sincerely and with rectitude to what degree you are *pure* in this respect. I mean, examine sincerely and uprightly, whether you be so far advanced in Christianity, as not to endanger your faith and holiness by this step.

THE UNPROFITABLE SERVANT.

"Know ye not," saith the apostle, "that the unrighteous cannot inherit the kingdom of God?" This is an awful declaration; but there is another class, who though not found among the profligate part of mankind, yet may be justly styled unprofitable servants. Birth and education, constitution and connection, necessity of character and love of gain, and many such things, are sufficient to produce a worldly decency of living. Now as this class do not act from principles of religion, they certainly have no right to the rewards of it. There was a law in Rome, that those who in a storm forsook the ship, should forfeit the property therein; and the ship and lading should belong entirely to those who staid in it. In a dangerous tempest, all the mariners forsook the ship, except only one sick passenger, who by reason of his disease, was unable to get out and escape. So it happened the ship came safe to port. The sick man kept possession, and claimed the benefit of the law; but it was agreed that the sick man was not within the reason of the law; for the reason of making it was to give encouragement to such as should venture their lives to save the vessel; but this was a merit which he could never pretend to, who neither staid in the ship upon that account, nor contributed any thing to its preservation. "Many persons," as one observes, "are in the condition of this man; though decent in their conduct, yet they can claim nothing under Christianity as a law, because they never acted on the reason of it."

Faithful Servants.

Mycytheus was a servant of Anaxalus, tyrant of Rhegium. He was entrusted with the care of the kingdom and of the children of the deceased prince, and he exercised his power with such fidelity and moderation, that he acquired the esteem of all the citizens, and at last restored the kingdom to his master's children, when come to years of maturity, and retired to peace and solitude with a small portion.

Panopion, a Roman, was saved from death, by the uncommon fidelity of his servant. When the assassins came to murder him, as being proscribed, the servant exchanged clothes with his master, and let him escape by the back-door. He afterwards went into his master's bed, and suffered himself to be killed as if he were Panopion himself.

Servant converted.

Mrs. ———— would often converse with her servants on the concerns of their souls, and administer reproof with mildness, encouragement, or tenderness, as their state required. The servant living with her at the time of her death, remarked with tears, "That she little thought when she entered the family, that her master would have proved her spiritual father, and her dear mistress her spiritual nurse," but so it was.

SCOFFERS REPROVED.

A SCOFFING infidel of considerable abilities, being once in company with a person of weak intellects, but a real Christian; and supposing, no doubt, that he should obtain an easy triumph, and display his ungodly wit, put the following question to him: " I understand, sir, that you expect to go to heaven when you die ; can you tell me what sort of a place heaven is ?" " Yes, sir," replied the Christian ; " *Heaven is a prepared place for a prepared people ;* and if your soul is not prepared for it, with all your boasted wisdom, you will never enter there."

For vain applause transgress not Scripture rules:
A witty sinner is the worst of fools.

Another of the same insolent tribe, once accosted a poor but pious woman, by saying, " So, I find you are one of those fools who believe in the Bible !"—" Yes," said she, " and with good reason, while so many infidels exist to prove the truth of its testimony, that *in every age there will be a generation of fools like you to blaspheme it !*"

Infidels pride themselves in appearing to be very witty at the expense of revelation. They are not, however, always successful in their attempts; for the Scripture, which is adapted to every case, hath provided a shield which rebuts the pointed arrow of their inveterate enemies.

The following is very laconic, but worthy to be observed :—A rake went into a church, and tried to decoy a girl by saying, " Why do you attend to such stuff as these Scriptures ?"—" Because," said she, " they tell me that in the last days there shall come such scoffers as you !" Well said, truly ! !

WORTH OF THE SOUL.

THE soul of man is of infinite value ; it is awful to recollect the state to which it is reduced by sin. Ignorant, depraved, rebellious, it is exposed to the wrath of an offended God. It may, however, under the divine fa-

vour, be recovered; and he who is the instrument of its recovery may be considered as having the highest honour conferred upon him. But how few are there who are striving in this great work ! persons in general, forgetting all others, seem to live only for themselves.

Seneca says, " I would so live as if I knew I received my being only for the benefit of others." And can any pleasure be equal to that of doing good ? When one was about to construct a lighthouse, he was asked, what was his object. " My object," said he, " is to give light and to save life." Thus should we all shine as lights in the world, that we may be the instruments of saving souls from death, and hiding a multitude of sins. " I never had a sight of my soul," says the emperor Aurelius, " and yet I have a great value for it, because it is discoverable by its operations; and by my constant experience of the power of God, I have a proof of his being, and a reason for my veneration."

How just is it that the soul should have the pre-eminence in all respects above the body. The one is the fading offspring of the earth, the other of a heavenly extraction, and incorruptible in its nature. When Pherecides, the Assyrian, first taught among the Grecians the doctrine of the soul's immortality, his discourse so prevailed on Pythagoras of Samos, that it changed him from an athleta into a philosopher. He that before wholly attended upon his body to make it excel in strength or agility, that he might contend victoriously in the Olympic games, then made it his business to improve and advance his soul in knowledge and virtue. And if the glimmering appearances of this great truth were so powerful upon him, how much more should the clear and certain discoveries of it be operative to make us chiefly regard the interest of our immortal part !

It was said of Caligula, *nec servum meliorem, nec deteriorem Dominum ;* while a subject none more obedient, but when advanced to the throne, he became the reproach of the empire, and plague of the world. So, while the body obeys the sanctity and sovereignty of the mind, it is an awful instrument; but if it usurp the government, the spirit is depressed in the most ignominious captivity, and man becomes like the beasts that perish.

The Loss of the Soul.

"The vanity of the purchase, and the value of the loss," says Dr. Bates, "is such, that no man, conscious of his immortality in the next state, but must acknowledge that he is an infinite loser, and prodigious fool, that gains the world by the loss of his soul. It is said of the ancient Germans, that in their commerce with the Romans, receiving silver for their amber, that has no virtue but to draw straws to it, they were amazed at the price. And certainly the great tempter cannot but wonder at the foolish exchange that men make, in giving their immortal souls to him for perishing vanities; and having this scornful advantage will much more upbraid them hereafter, than ever he allured them here."

Hence it was a good saying of one to a great lord upon his showing him his stately house and pleasant gardens; "Sir, you had need make sure of heaven, or else when you die, you will be a very good loser." Yes, and "what shall it profit a man if he gain the whole world and lose his own soul?"

ANECDOTE OF SOCRATES.

WHEN the disciples of Socrates brought rich presents to him, as proofs of their regard and affection, there was one who said, "I am poor, and having no property, I give you all I have, I give myself up unto you." Socrates answered, "Thou couldst not have brought me a more acceptable present. I receive the gift, and will restore thee back to thyself, better than when I received thee." You cannot carry any offer-

ing to Christ, so pleasing as yourself He is your sole master. Socrates was but as a glimmering taper amidst surrounding darkness : Christ is the great sun of righteousness. He will teach you freely and save you fully. You must, however, give yourself to him, not for a few years only, but for ever. If you continue in his word, and keep his covenant now, you shall hereafter dwell in his immediate presence, in the mansions of unsullied glory.

SUNDAY SCHOOL ANECDOTES.

A PIOUS minister being called, a few years ago, to preach a sermon for the benefit of the Sunday school in Northamptonshire, was led in his discourse to insist much on the necessity of being clothed with the Redeemer's robe of righteousness, as the only means by which men could be delivered from all that misery which awaited them as sinful creatures. While he was thus speaking, a violent storm of thunder and lightning came on, accompanied with hail and rain. The lightning struck a tree in the church-yard, shivered in pieces, and drove a part of it through one of the church windows. Alarmed at the circumstance, the congregation began to fly in all directions, seeking for refuge where it was the least likely to be found. The minister from this awful scene, took occasion to entreat them to remain in the house of God; reminding them, that if they were protected from their sins by the righteousness of the Lord Jesus Christ, let storms, thunder, and lightning, tempest, or even death itself come, they were perfectly safe.

In pursuing the discourse, his attention was attracted to one of the Sunday school girls, who was standing near the pulpit; and who was so peculiarly affected, that an impression came upon his mind, he had been the instrument of communicating some substantial good to the child. Thus impressed, he made it a point to call at the parent's house the next day and after the customary salutations, he was told by her mother that the child had been that day disappointed, as she had expected to go to the fair, but that a circumstance had occurred which would prevent her. "What! my dear," said the minister, "are you fond of going to the fair?" The child immediately replied, "Oh no, sir; I don't want to go to the fair. I now only want to be clothed in that robe of righteousness which you were speaking of yesterday: and that I may see Jesus Christ."

Struck with this delightful observation, the good man entered into conversation with the dear child; found her mind so sensibly wrought upon, that he had every reason to hope and believe a divine work had been begun upon her heart. He left her, intending to repeat his visit the next day; but he had scarcely reached his home before a messenger arrived to inform him, that this dear child of God had been found by her parent dead in the garden! So quickly did the Lord call her to his glory.

Oh, that all the young persons who read this, may seek for salvation through the Redeemer's righteousness! This alone will enable them, at the last day, to appear before the throne of Immanuel with joy; and, with this dear child, to sing eternal praises to HIM, who hath loved them, and washed them from their sins in his own precious blood!

SCHOOLS NEED REFORM.

"I MIGHT recite," says Cotton Mather, "the complaint of Austin, 'that little boys are taught in the schools the filthy actions of the Pagan gods; or the complaint of Luther, 'that our schools are pagan rather than Christian;' I might mention what a late author says, 'I knew an aged and eminent schoolmaster, who, after keeping a school about fifty years, said, with a sad countenance, that it was a great trouble to him, that he had spent so much time in reading pagan authors to his scholars.' It will be a happy circumstance when our schools shall be purged, and only such authors read as are at least inoffensive and harmless."

VOLUNTARY SLAVERY.

IT was the cruel and crafty advice offered to the Athenians, to keep the subdued inhabitants of Egina from rebelling, to cut off their thumbs, that they might be incapable of managing a spear, and by war obtaining a victorious rescue from their tyranny, yet be fit to pull the oar in the gallies. It is an emblem of Satan's dealing with his slaves; for, by the pleasures of sin, their hearts are weak, disabled from vigorous and holy resolutions to resist his power; they cannot make use of the armour of God for their defence: and their lusts are strong, they are patient of his drudgery, constant at the oar, and faithful to their chains. "In meekness, instructing those that oppose themselves: if God peradventure may give them repentance to the acknowledgment of the truth, and that they may recover themselves out of the snare of the devil, by whom *they are taken captive at his will*." 2 Tim. ii. 26.

THE CONSCIENTIOUS SOLDIERS.

SUCH was the fidelity and perseverance of the eminent prophet Daniel, that a quiet conscience was more to him than a smiling king; and in this we do well to follow his example, and never to break the laws of God to obey the commandments of men. When Alexander was rebuilding the temple of Belus, he ordered the Jewish soldiers who were in his army to work as the rest had done; but they could not be prevailed upon to give their assistance, and excused themselves with saying, that as idolatry was forbidden by the tenets of their religion, they therefore were not allowed to assist in building of a temple designed for idolatrous worship, and accordingly not one lent a hand on this occasion. They were punished for disobedience, but all to no purpose : so that at last, Al-

Y

exander, admiring their perseverance, discharged and sent them home. "This delicate resolution of the Jews," as one observes, "is a lesson to many Christians, as it teaches them, that they are not allowed to join or assist in the commission of an action that is contrary to the law of God."

The Dying Soldiers, and the Negro's Remark.

It is the character of the unregenerate, that "they live without hope and without God in the world." Of the sacred Scriptures they are ignorant; for divine ordinances they feel no regard; and to prayer they are utter strangers. But is this the case among a people who profess Christianity, and who have been baptised in the name of the Father, Son, and Holy Ghost? Alas! the natives of England, many of them, have not only been the promoters of vice at home, but set examples of it abroad, which the very heathens have been ashamed of. Some of our English soldiers were quartered on a settlement in Africa, where the climate was hot and unwholesome. They attended no place of worship, nor had any clergyman with them. While they were in this situation, a fatal distemper broke out among them, and carried them off daily. A poor negro, who was witness to the case, and probably of their conduct, made this observation upon it: "The English never speak to God Almighty—God Almighty never speaks to them; so the devil comes to fetch them away." Were this poor negro in England, however, we could introduce him to *some* who do *speak to God Almighty;* and that not only for themselves, but on behalf of the tribes of Africa, as well as the poor benighted pagans in other parts of the world.

SLEEPING DURING PUBLIC WORSHIP.

The habit of sleeping in a place of worship is every way disgraceful to the person himself; an offence to God; a discouragement to the preacher. Vespasian, when consul, accompanied Nero into Greece; but he offended the emperor by falling asleep while he repeated one of his poetical compositions. How much more may the Supreme Governor of heaven and earth be offended, in beholding his creatures careless when he calls their attention to the most important of all subjects, the interests of their immortal souls!

SIN THE HEIGHT OF FOLLY.

A serious Christian once asked a great backslider, whether he really had found more satisfaction in the indulgence of his lusts, and the full swing of carnal pleasure, than he before had done in the profession of the gospel, and in the hours he had formerly spent for God. He honestly replied, *he had not:* and that so far from being happy, he was not even untormented, except in a state of intoxicated dissipation. It pleased God to restore him again, but not without such bitterness of soul, as all the mad pleasures he had pursued were but a poor compensation to him for.

To what a wretched state does sin reduce men; that they must commit one sin in order to banish the reflection of the effects of another!

"It is recorded of Marius," says Dr. Bates, "that after his overthrow by Sylla, he was always in consternation, as if he heard the sound of the trumpets, and the noise of the victorious army pursuing him. And his fears were no longer quiet than whilst charmed with wine or sleep; he therefore was continually drunk, that he might forget himself, his enemy, and his danger." Thus men make a pitiful shift to forget their latter end; and whilst they are following either secular affairs or sensual pleasures, are unconcerned for what is to be hereafter.

STOICISM.

The Stoics' universal recipe for the cure of affliction was to change their opinions of them, and esteem them not real evils. Thus Possidonius, (so much commended by Tully,) who for many years was under torturing diseases, and survived a continual death, being visited by Pompey, at Rhodes, he entertained him with a philosophical discourse, and when his pains were most acute, he said, *Nihil agis dolor, quanquam sis molestus, nunquam te esse confitebor malum*—" in vain dost thou assault me, pain ; though thou art troublesome, thou shalt never force me to confess thou art an evil." But the folly of this boasting is visible : for though he might appear with a cheerful countenance in the paroxysm of his disease, to commend his philosophy, like a mountebank that swallows poison to put off his drugs, yet the reality of his grief was evident : his sense was overcome, though his tongue remained a stoic. If words could charm the sense not to feel pain, or compose the mind not to resent afflictions, it would be a relief to give soft titles to them. But since it is not fancy that makes them hard to bear, but their contrariety to nature, it is no relief to represent them otherwise than they are. All those subtle notions vanish when sensible impressions confute them.

THE SOVEREIGNTY OF GOD.

NOTHING can be more true than that God is infinitely wise, merciful, and good, and yet that he has permitted guilt and misery to enter the world, when it is evident his power could have prevented it. To attempt, therefore, to explain and reconcile the decrees of God with the agency of men, the analogy between God and an earthly parent will not always hold. I remember, says one, a gentleman once said to me, " Would you, if you were God, create any being to misery ?" My answer was, " When I am God I will tell you." It is not proper, therefore, to set up the human passions as a kind of standard and model from which God himself must form his estimate of right and wrong.

THE GRATEFUL SOVEREIGNS.

AN eye-witness related the following anecdote :—When the field-marshal Prince Schwartzenberg observed the defeat of the French, after the three days fighting at Leipsic, he was anxious to convey the tidings himself to his sovereign, who, together with the emperor of Russia and the king of Prussia, were stationed on a height about two miles from the field of battle. The field-marshal galloped at full speed, and saluting the emperor with his sword, said, " Your Majesty, the battle is at an end ; the enemy is beaten at all points,—they fly !—the victory is ours !" The emperor raised his eyes to heaven, and a tear was his answer; but his majesty dismounting, and having deposited his hat and sword on the ground, fell on his knees, and aloud returned his thanks to God. This example was followed by the two other monarchs, who, having also kneeled, said, "Brother, the Lord is with you !" At the same instant, all the officers in attendance, as well as the guard, kneeled down, and for several minutes a dead silence reigned ; after which more than a hundred voices cried, " The Lord is with us !" The sight of the three crowned heads, accompanied by a great number of distinguished warriors, kneeling under the canopy of heaven, and, with tears, praising the God of battles, was most affecting.

SOCIETY.

THAT man is formed for society there can be no doubt. The conduct of mankind is a practical exposition of the various passages of Scripture which refer to this point. " Man is born in society," says Montesquieu, "and there he remains." " The track of a Laplander on the snowy shore," says Ferguson, "gives joy to the lonely mariner; and the mute signs of cordiality and kindness which are made to him, awaken the memory of pleasures which he felt in society." A writer of a voyage to the North, after describing a scene of this sort, says, " We were extremely pleased to converse with men ; since in thirteen months we had seen no human creature." The wailings of the infant and the language of the adult when alone, the lively joys of the one and the cheerfulness of the other upon the return of company, are a sufficient proof of its solid foundation in the frame of our nature. As to the moral and spiritual advantages of society and union they are innumerable.

SIMPLICITY IN INSTRUCTION THE BEST MEANS TO ACCOMPLISH ITS DESIGN.

OUR heavenly Instructor, in order to accommodate his parables to the capacities of his audience, adopted the broad line of instruction conveyed under a few strong features of general parallel, a few leading points of obvious coincidence, without attending to petty exactnesses, or stooping to trivial niceties of correspondence. We are not, therefore, to hunt after minute resemblances, nor to cavil at slight discrepancies. We should rather imitate his example, by confining our illustration to the more important circumstances of likeness, instead of raising such as are insignificant into undue distinction. This critical elaboration, this amplifying mode, which ramifies a general idea into all the minutiæ of parallel, would only serve to divert the attention, and split it into so many divisions that the main object would be lost sight of.

The author once heard a sermon, which had for its text, " Ye are the salt of the earth." The preacher, a really good man, but wanting discretion, not contented with a simple application of the figure,—instead of a general allusion to the powerfully penetrating and correcting nature of this mineral; instead of observing that salt was used in all the ancient sacrifices,—indulged himself in a wide range, chemical and culinary, of all the properties of salt, devoting a se-

parate head to each quality. A long discussion on its antiseptic properties, its solution and neutralization, led to rather a luxurious exhibition of the relishes it communicates to various viands. On the whole, the discourse seemed better adapted for an audience composed of the authors of the Pharmacopeia, or a society of cooks, than for a plain untechnical congregation.

MOTIVES TO SUBMISSION DRAWN FROM THE EXAMPLE OF THOSE WHO PRECEDED US.

THE consideration that others before us have suffered in the cause of causes, should be a source of happiness under all our opposition. Phocion, the celebrated Athenian, though a man of great virtue, was condemned to death. He received the indignities of the people with uncommon composure, and when one of his friends lamented his fate, Phocion exclaimed, " This is no more than what I expected ; this treatment the most illustrious citizens of Athens have received before me ;" and, as he submitted to his fate, he prayed for the prosperity of Athens, and bade his friends to tell his son Phocus not to remember the indignities which his father had received from the Athenians.

THE SWADDLERS.

ONCE, as the Rev. J. Edwards was riding to a town where he was to preach, he was joined by a gentleman travelling to the same place who desired his company. Mr. E. took the first opportunity of introducing religious discourse, upon which his companion said, "I think, sir, by your manner of talking, you must be a *swaddler*." "I am, sir," replied Mr. E. The traveller expressed his surprise, and said, you appear to be a man of sense, and I am amazed that such a person can be a *swaddler ;* for I understand that the whole sect maintain this uncharitable tenet, that none but *swaddlers* can be saved." —" Sir," said Mr. E. "that is very true; we do maintain it; and if you will do me the honour of coming to hear me at such a place this evening, I think I can prove the point to your perfect satisfaction. On which the stranger declared he thought it impossible. This gave occasion for Mr. E. to display one of the principal traits in his character. When the hour arrived, the gentleman being present, he read the text—Ezek. xvi. 4 : " Thou wast not swaddled at all," &c. From which, by accommodation, he particularly investigated the miserable state of man by nature, who, after all his attempts to cover himself with a righteousness of his own, is not *swaddled at all*—not clothed, but as exposed as ever. After this, in his own energetic style, he insisted on the necessity of the Saviour's righteousness, for the justification of guilty sinners. The traveller was much pleased with the ingenuity of the thought; and afterwards came to Mr. E., saying, " You have indeed proved your point; and I join with you in the belief, *that none but swaddlers can be saved.*"

SUPERSTITION ; OR THE WONDERFUL CANDLE.

THE following instance from Weld's Travels in Canada, shows the ignorance and superstition in which some of the Canadians are immersed. " On the evening before we reached Quebec," says Mr. Weld, " we stopped at the village of St. Augustin Calvaire, and after having strolled about for some time, returned to the farm-house where we had taken up our quarters for the night. The people had cooked some fish, that had just been caught, while we had been walking about, and every thing being ready on our return, we sat down to supper by the light of a lamp which was suspended from the ceiling. The glimmering light, however, that it afforded, scarcely enabling us to see what was on the table, we complained of it to the man of the house, and the lamp was in consequence trimmed ; it was replenished with oil ; taken down and set on the table; still the light was very bad. " Sacra Dieu !" exclaimed he, " but you shall not eat your fish in the dark," so saying, he stepped aside to a small cupboard, took out a candle, and having lighted it, placed it beside us. All was going on well, when the wife, who had been absent for a few minutes, suddenly returning, poured forth a volley of the most terrible execrations against her poor husband, for having presumed to have acted as he had done. Unable to answer a single word, the fellow stood aghast, ignorant of what he had done to offend her: we were quite at a loss also to know what could give rise to such a sudden storm ; the wife, however, snatched up the candle, and hastily extinguishing it, addressed us in a plaintive tone of voice, and explained the whole affair. It was the holy candle—" La chandelle benite," which her giddy husband had set on the table; it had been consecrated at a neighbouring church, and supposing there should be a tempest at any time, with thunder and lightning ever so terrible, yet if the candle were but kept burning, while it lasted, the house, the barn, and every thing else belonging to it, were to be secured from danger. If any of the family happened to be sick, the candle was to be lighted, and they were instantly to recover. It had been given to her that morning by the priest of the village, with an assurance that it possessed the miraculous power of preserving the family from harm, and she was confident that what he told her was true. To have contradicted the poor woman would have been useless; for the sake of our ears, however, we endeavoured to pacify her, and that being accomplished, we sat down to supper, and even made the most of our fish in the dark."

SUPERSTITION.

AIUS LOCUTUS was the name of a god among the Romans, who was deified on this occasion · M. Ceditus, a plebeian, informed the tribunes that, passing through the new street in the night, he heard a voice more than human, near the temple of Vesta, which gave the Romans notice that the Gauls were coming against Rome ; but this information being neglected on account of the meanness of the person, they suffered very much from that invasion ; wherefore, to expiate the offence, they erected a temple in the new street to this fancied deity, by the advice of Camillus their deliverer.

We may occasionally derive lessons of instruction, even from the superstitions of the heathen. Here was a supposed information from heaven slighted, and slighted because of the meanness of the reporter of it. Public miseries ensued ; and when these were at length surmounted, a penitent disposition is displayed, and divine honour paid to the fancied being whose counsel had been neglected.

How often have *we* refused to hear HIM that speaketh from heaven ! " we would none of his counsel, and despised his reproof!" and how often have we severely suffered by our unbelief! " Christians, let the heathens reprove you and teach you penitence: and henceforth pay double honour to your heavenly Teacher, your true *Aius Locutus.*"

THE HAPPY TURN.

THERE is no condition in this life so mean, and none so high, but it is subject to change; so that it becomes a wise man to foresee and prepare for it, that he may neither in prosperity be lifted up, nor in adversity be cast down ; but depend on the grace and conduct of God, in all the vicissitudes of providence. " The prudent man foreseeth the evil, and hideth himself, but the simple pass on and are punished." A certain gentlewoman having sunk into a melancholy state of mind, got a wheel, a little pretty wheel, that she could hang at her girdle, and put into her lap, and usually employed herself in spinning hour after hour and day after day.

Coming one day upon her at work— " Oh!" said she, " *blessed be God that hath sent me this turn.*" They call their spinning-wheels in that country *turns*. I perceived the diversion of that innocent employment had worn off her trouble. That expression of hers made such an impression on my mind at the time, that I cannot but remember it since for the relief of others. Let that man or woman that is now afflicted and disconsolate, and who think they shall never have joy more, take heart from this narration, for time may come when God will also send them their turn.

TEMPTATION.

THE Christian may sometimes be brought so low through temptation and desertion, as to imagine he must at last be cast away. Of Mr. G. it is said, that he lay languishing in distress of mind for five years ; during which he took no comfort in meat or drink, nor any pleasure in life ; being under a sense of some backsliding, he was distressed as if he had been in the deepest pit of hell. If he ate his food, it was not from any appetite, but with a view to defer his damnation, thinking within himself that he must needs be lost so soon as his breath was out of his body. Yet after all this he was set at liberty, received great consolation, and afterward lived altogether a heavenly life. Let not the tempted believer then despond, nor the returning backslider fear lest he should be rejected ; for thus saith Jehovah, " I will heal their backslidings, I will love them freely, for mine anger is turned away from them."

TYRANTS NEVER HAPPY.

WE know that when, in Henry the Eighth or Edward the Sixth's day, some great men pulled down churches and built palaces, and robbed religion of its just encouragements and advantages ; the men that did it were sacrilegious ; and we find also that God hath been punishing that great sin ever since ; and hath displayed to so many generations of men, to three or four descents of children, that those men could not be esteemed happy in their great fortunes against whom God was so angry that he would show his displeasure for a hundred years together. When Herod had killed the babes of Bethlehem, it was seven years before God called him to an account : but he that looks upon the end of that man, would rather choose the fate of the oppressed babes than of the prevailing and triumphing tyrant. It was forty years before God punished the Jews, for the execrable murder committed upon the person of their KING, the Holy Jesus ; and it was so long that when it did happen, many men attributed it to their killing St. James, their bishop, and seemed to forget the greater crime. We are to stand to the truth of God's word, not to the event of things ; because God hath given us a rule, but hath left the judgment to himself; and we die so quickly (and God measures all things by the standard of eternity, for one thousand years with God are but as one day) that we are not competent to measure the times of God's account and the returns of judgment. We are dead before the arrow comes ;— but the man escapes not unless his soul can die, or that God cannot punish him. Such is their fate. They spend their days in plenty and in a moment descend into hell. In the mean time they drink, and forget their sorrow ; but they are condemned ;— they have drank their hemlock ; only the poison does not yet operate : the bait is in their mouths, and they are sportive, but the hook hath stuck their nostrils, and they shall never escape the ruin. And let none call the man fortunate, merely because his execution was deferred for a few days, when the very deferring shall increase and ascertain the condemnation.

But if we should look under the skirt of the prosperous and prevailing tyrant, we should find, even in the days of his joys, such allays and abatements of his pleasure, as may serve to represent him miserable, even in the hour of his prosperity, and independent of his final infelicities. How often have we seen a young and healthy person warm and ruddy under a poor and thin garment, when at the same time an old rich person hath been cold and paralytic under a load of sables and the skins of foxes ! It is the body that makes the clothes warm, not the clothes the body : and the spirit of the man creates felicity and content, not any spoils of a rich fortune wrapped about a sickly and uneasy soul. Appolodorus was a traitor and a tyrant, and the world wondered to see a bad man apparently so fortunate ; but they knew not that he nourished scorpions in his breast, and that his liver and his heart were eaten up with spectres and images of death : his thoughts were full of interruptions, his dreams of illusions ; his fancy was abused with real troubles and fantastic images, imagining that he saw the Scythians flaying him alive, his daughters like pillars of fire dancing round about a caldron in which himself was boiling, and that his conscience accused him of being the cause of all these evils. And although all tyrants may not have such accusing and fantastic consciences, yet all tyrants shall die and come to judgment; and though such a man may be feared, he is not at all to be envied.— " Envy thou not the oppressor, and choose none of his ways."

THE THRESHER'S CONFESSION ;

Or, Godliness True Happiness.

WALKING in the country, says the Rev. Mr. J——, I went into a barn, where I found a thresher at his work; I addressed him in the words of Solomon : " in all labour there is profit." Leaning upon his flail, and with much energy, he answered, " No, sir; that is the truth, but there is one exception to it : I have long laboured in the service of sin, but I got no

14*

profit by my labour."—" Then you know something of the apostle's meaning, when he asked—' what fruit had ye then in those things whereof ye are now ashamed ?' " " Thank God," said he, " I do ; and I also know, that now being freed from sin, and having become a servant unto righteousness, I have my fruit unto holiness, and the end everlasting life." How charming to meet with instances of this kind! piety found in a barn, is better than the most splendid pleasures found in a palace.

TRIALS NOT TO BE COURTED, BUT THE PROMISE ALWAYS TO BE RELIED ON.

ONE of the English martyrs was so alarmed at the thoughts of his suffering on the morrow in the midst of a fire, that it seemed to him an impossibility that he should go through the conflict ; and in order to try the experiment, he put his finger into the flame of the candle, but found he could not endure it ; and no wonder says Mr. Cecil, for that was not his call ; his dispensation did not require that he should voluntarily bring himself into pain, and much less that he should do it in a spirit of unbelief. But though he could not endure, in his own strength, even his finger in the flame, yet the next day he could give up, in the strength of God, his whole body to the fire ; and, with heroic constancy and Christian fortitude, could cheerfully resign his life in the flames : for as our day is, so shall our strength be. In the world, we are taught to expect tribulation and temptation from every quarter, though it will be our Christian duty, as well as prudence, to avoid them whenever we can. Let us beware of imitating the martyr in attempting to thrust our finger into the flame ; but to whatever degree of suffering God calls us, it is enough that HE is faithful to his promise, and will perform it.

TRIALS PRODUCTIVE OF GOOD.
I REMEMBER, says Mr. Whitfield,

some years ago, when I was at Shields, I went into a glass-house ; and standing very attentive, I saw several masses of burning glass, of various forms. The workman took a piece of glass and put it into one furnace, then he put it into a second, and then into a third. I said to him, " Why do you put this through so many fires ?" He answered, " O, sir, the first was not hot enough, nor the second, and, therefore, we put it into a third, and that will make it transparent." This furnished Mr. W. with a useful hint, that we must be tried, and exercised, with many fires, until our dross be purged away, and we are made fit for the owner's use.

NECESSITY OF DIVINE TEACHING ILLUSTRATED.

MAN is totally ignorant of himself until he is taught by the Divine Spirit. Length of years, the acquisition of human knowledge, natural powers, all leave him just where he was. Many awful and striking instances might here be mentioned, as exemplifying this awful fact; but a few shall suffice. A poor woman, near fourscore years of age, once happened to forget the Sunday, and went to spinning that morning as usual : on being reminded, soon after, what day it was, she exclaimed, " I have lived all these years, and never sinned against God before ; and must I sin against him now ?" Another woman professed to be under deep conviction, and went to a minister, crying aloud, that she was a sinner ; but when he came to examine her in what point, though he went over and explained all the Ten Commandments, she would not own that she had broken one of them.

Some time since the gentleman of A—— met at an inn, to concert measures for the reformation of the sabbath. In the course of the debate upon reform, Mr. ——— took notice, that they had gone on to seventy years in their present manner, and he could, therefore, see no propriety in urging a reform *now*

TRUTH.

Power of Truth.

An instance of this has lately occurred in Ireland, in the case of the Rev. Mr. M. Crowley, who, in searching the Scriptures with a view to refute the Protestant doctrines, has been led, from full unbiassed conviction, to embrace them. The same happy effects have uniformly attended a careful impartial study of the word of God. This was remarkably verified in the reformation from popery in the sixteenth century. I shall mention a remarkable instance of this from a work lately published.* In an act of the Scottish parliament, A. D. 1525, renewed 1535, prohibiting the importation of books containing heretical opinions, and the rehearsing and disputing about them, an exception was made as to clerks in the schools, that they might confute them. In this device the patrons of the Romish church were outwitted, for a number of these clerks were, by the perusal of the books, and by the disputation concerning them, induced to embrace the Protestant tenets.

The persons employed in the first promulgation of the gospel were a few fishermen, with a publican and a tent-maker, without authority and power to force men to obedience, and without the charms of eloquence to insinuate the belief of the doctrines they delivered; and with these disadvantages they could never have conceived the thought, much less had courage, to attempt the great impossibility of converting the whole world to Christ, and subjecting the heads of princes, and the learned and the wise, to the foot of a crucified person, without the divine assistance.

They were without authority and power. Other religions were established in several nations, by persons of the greatest eminency and credit among them. That of the Persians by Zoroaster, that of the Egyptians

* M'Crie's Life of Knox.

by Hermes, that of the Grecians by Orpheus, that of the Romans by Numa, all kings, or of great reputation for their wisdom and virtue; and they were received without contradiction. For, being correspondent to the corrupt inclinations of men, it was not strange that the princes had either capacity to invent them, or power to plant them. And in later times, Mahomet opened a way for his religion by his sword, and advanced it by conquest. Now it is no wonder that a religion so pleasing to the lower appetites, that gives license to all corrupt affections in the present life, and promises a sensual paradise suitable to beasts in the future, should be embraced by those who were subject to his arms. But the apostles were meanly born and educated, without credit and reputation, destitute of all human strength, and had only a crucified person for their leader. Christianity was exposed naked in the day of its birth, without any shelter from the secular powers.

They had not the advantage of art and eloquence to commend their religion. There is a kind of charm in rhetoric that makes things appear otherwise than they are. The best cause it ruins, the worst it confirms. Truth, though in itself invincible, yet by it seems to be overcome; and error obtains a false triumph. We have a visible proof of this in the writings of Celsus, Symmachus, Cæcilius, and others for Paganism, against Christianity. What a vast difference is there between the lies and filthiness of the one, and the truth and sanctity of the other! Yet with what admirable address did they manage that infamous subject! Although it seemed incapable of any defence, yet they gave such colours to it, by the beauty of their expressions and their apparent reasons, that it seemed plausible; and Christianity, notwithstanding its brightness and purity, was made odious to the people. But the apostles were most of them wholly unlearned. St. Paul himself acknowledges (2 Cor. ii. 4.) that he was weak in presence, and his speech was not with the enticing words of man's wisdom. A crucified Christ was all their rhetoric. Now these impotent, despicable persons were employed to subdue the world to the cross of Christ; and in that season when the Roman empire was at its height, when the most rigorous severities were used against all innovations, when philosophy and eloquence were in their flower and vigour; so that truth, unless adorned with the dress and artifice of falsehood, was despised, and a message from God himself, unless eloquently conveyed, had no force to persuade. Therefore the apostles debased themselves with a sense of their own weakness.

THE VALUE OF TIME.

It was a speech of a woman labouring under horror of conscience, when several ministers and others came to comfort her—"Call back time again; if you can call back time again, then there may be hope for me; but time is gone."

THE HAPPY UNION.

If in the church of the first-born Christians in the earthly Jerusalem, the bond of charity was so strict, that it is said " the multitude of believers were of one heart, and one soul;" how much more intimate and inseparable is the union of the saints in Jerusalem above where every one loves another as himself! It is recorded of Alexander, that entering with Hephestion his favourite, into the pavilion of the mother of Darius, who was then his prisoner, she bowed to the favourite, as having a greater appearance of majesty, thinking him to be Alexander. But being apprised of her error, she humbly begged his pardon. To whom the generous king replied, " You did not err, mother: this is also Alexander." Such was their affection, that whoever was taken of them, the other was taken in him, the less ascending in the greater, without degrading the greater in the less. This is a pic-

ture of the holy love of the blessed; but with the same difference as exists between the description of a star and a coal, and its beauty in its proper aspect. And where all is love, all is delight. The act itself is its own reward. As that benign and pleasant affection is enlarged with respect to the object, and its degrees, such is the delight that results from it. In that blessed society there is a constant receiving and returnin of love and joy.

UNBELIEF.

Unbelievers are cut off from all claim to the benefits of Christ's death. The law of faith, like that of the Medes and Persians, is unalterable. " He that believeth not the Son shall not see life." Christ died not to expiate final infidelity: this is the mortal sin that actually damns;—it charges all their guilt upon sinners;—it renders the sufferings of Christ fruitless and ineffectual to them: for it is not the preparation of a sovereign remedy that cures the disease, but the applying it. As our sins were imputed to him, upon the account of his union with us in nature, and his consent to be our surety, so his righteousness is meritoriously imputed to us, upon our union with him by a lively faith. The man that looked on the rainbow, when he was ready to be drowned, what relief was it to him, that God had promised not to drown the world, when he must perish in the waters? So, though Christ hath purchased pardon for repenting believers, and a rainbow encompasses the throne of God, (Rev. iv. 3.) the sign of reconciliation, what advantage is this to the unbeliever, who dies in his sins, and drops into the lake of fire? It is not from any defect of mercy in God, or righteousness in Christ, but from the obstinate rejection of it, that many who have heard the gospel certainly and finally perish.

UNTHANKFULNESS REPROVED.

Nothing becomes us, as dependant creatures, so much as gratitude;

yet what multitudes sit down to their meals without ever imploring the divine blessing, or giving God thanks. A suitable reproof for this neglect was rendered useful in the following instance: Mr. Baker, a mulatto preacher in Jamaica, before he was converted, was sitting down to breakfast with his wife and child, in a careless manner, without giving thanks to God for what they were going to receive. An old black man, standing at the same time at the door, perceiving their conduct, turned round to one who was near him, and said, "Whence have these people come? I could wish to learn if they know that God made them." Mr. B. overheard this, got up and said, "Old man, can you read?" "No," he replied, "but I know that both of you can."—"As you cannot read, how dare you thus reprimand me?" The old man immediately humbled himself, and said, "Master, if you will not be angry, I will tell you where to search the Scriptures, and you will find there that you are not only to thank God, but to return God love, prayer, and thanksgiving, for what you are going to receive, in the name of Jesus Christ." This made such an impression on his mind, that it led to his conversion.

DARKNESS OF THE HUMAN UNDERSTANDING.

"Now we may see," says a certain author, "how impossible it is for the natural understanding to discover the mystery of redemption, when those that had the highest reputation for wisdom were ignorant of the creation. The philosophers were divided in nothing more than in their account of the world's original. Some imagined it to proceed from water, others from fire; some from order, others from confusion; some to be from eternity, others in time. If the soul's eye be so weakened as not to see that Eternal Power which is so apparent in its effects, much less could it pierce into the will and free determinations

of God, of which there is not the least intimation or shadow in the things that are made."

A late writer who makes great pretensions to superior wisdom, says, that "Jesus of Nazareth was a man constituted *in all respects like other men;* subject to the same infirmities, the *same ignorance, prejudices,* and frailties."

Porphyry, a Platonic philosopher, who excelled as in learning and eloquence, so in malignity the most furious enemies of Christianity; yet he was, by irresistible evidence, compelled to acknowledge that Jesus Christ was a most pious and excellent person, and that, after his death, he ascended into heaven.

THE ALLELUIA VICTORY.

THIS word signifies, "Praise the Lord," or, "Praise to the Lord;" and is very proper to be constantly used by us who are dependant creatures, and under such great obligations to the Father of mercies. We have often heard of prayer doing wonders; but instances also are not wanting of praise being accompanied with signal events. The ancient Britons, in the year 420, obtained a victory over an army of the Picts and Saxons, near Mold, in Flintshire. The Britons, unarmed, having Germanus and Lupus at their head, when the Picts and Saxons came to the attack, the two commanders, Gideon-like, ordered their little army to shout *Alleluia* three times over, at the sound of which, the enemy, being suddenly struck with terror, ran away in the greatest confusion, and left the Britons masters of the field. A stone monument, to perpetuate the remembrance of this *Alleluia* victory, I believe, remains to this day in a field near Mold.

THE WORD IN SEASON.

How various are the ways by which God is pleased to work, in bringing his people to himself! What appears to us at first as a casual circumstance, we see to be his appointment for the fulfilment of his own purposes. The Rev. Mr. Henry Erskine, (father of the late Messrs. E. and R. Erskine,) when living in a retired house upon the border, in the north of England, noticed, one day as he was walking, a number of people digging peats; and upon coming to them, he observed that "they were too merry." To which one of them replied, " Sir, we suppose you are a minister, and if you will condescend to preach a sermon, we will sit down and be grave hearers."—" I fear," said Mr. Erskine, "you are not in a proper frame to hear a sermon." They, however, pressed it so much upon him, that he at last consented, and after retiring for a little while to a secret place, he came forth and preached to about thirty people, which happily issued in the conversion of eleven. Let us learn from this to embrace every opportunity of using the talent God hath given us. Who can calculate the result? Bread cast upon the water may sometimes be found, not after many, but after few days.

Mr. Philip Henry used to blame those whose irregular zeal in the profession of religion made them neglect their worldly business. "There was a pious woman," he observes, " who was convinced of this her fault, by means of an intelligent godly neighbour; who coming into the house and finding the woman far in the day in her closet, and the house sadly neglected, ' What,' saith he, 'is there no fear of God in this house?' This made a lasting impression on her mind. Thus ' A word spoken in due season, how good it is!' "

A gentleman asking a young person how she did, was answered, " Very well."—" Then," said he, "you are in the right way to heaven, for none go there but such as are very well." This gave rise to serious reflections, for she went out and wept bitterly. Walking home with her brother, on parting she told him there was no satisfaction in the world, no

happiness, but in Christ, and that she wished him this happiness. This parting conversation was made the means of his conversion to God.

A good man, overwhelmed with trouble, and unable either to extricate himself, or procure a friend in the hour of necessity, came to the resolution, as his last resource, of leaving his native country. There remained only one Lord's day more previous to his departure, and from an apprehension that it would be the last he should ever spend in his own land, it impressed him with more than usual solemnity.

When at the house of God, the text which the minister selected for the subject of his discourse was Psalm xxxvii. 3.—" Trust in the Lord, and do good; so shalt thou dwell in the land, and verily thou shalt be fed." On hearing these words he found his attention particularly arrested, nor did he feel himself less interested in the sermon, every sentence of which appeared peculiarly applicable to his circumstances, and led him to conclude the whole to be the voice of Providence.

Impressed with this conviction, he changed his purpose, and resolved to struggle against the torrent of adversity, and await the good pleasure of his God concerning him. The appointed time to favour him soon arrived. The Lord quickly turned his captivity like that of Job, and caused his latter end to be more blessed than his beginning. The text and the sermon so evidently fulfilled in his experience will very naturally lead us to adopt that beautiful expression of Solomon—" A word spoken in due season, how good it is!"

HORRORS OF WAR.
Conflagration of Moscow, 14th Sept. 1812.

THE French entered Moscow on the 14th of September, but they possessed only a heap of smoking ruins. A degree of mystery hangs over the conflagration of this ancient city: whether it was occasioned by the inhabitants, or in consequence of the defence made by them, and the bombardment of the French, is yet doubtful. The fact, however, is certain, and the grand effects of this destruction are of the most consoling nature. It is impossible, however, to contemplate without horror, an event which deprived 200,000 persons of their homes and possessions, and consigned to the agonizing tortures of the flames many thousands of persons, including a large number of sick and wounded soldiers, who had bled in the defence of their country.

The retreat of the French from Moscow exhibits a picture of disaster and human misery dreadful and horrific almost beyond example. It is stated that the cold, from the 6th of November, was so intense that in a few days more than 30,000 horses perished : the cavalry was dismounted, and the baggage without the means of conveyance. From the 9th to the 18th of November, Buonaparte lost, without counting the killed and wounded, 11 generals, 243 officers, 34,000 rank and file in prisoners, 250 pieces of cannon, and four standards, besides baggage, &c. The total loss to France and her allies in this campaign has been estimated at 400,000 men killed, disabled, and prisoners, and 5,900,000*l.* of property in equipments, &c. &c.

The loss of the Russians in soldiers (killed, wounded and prisoners) may be stated at 130,000, to which must be added 70,000 persons burnt and destroyed in various ways at Moscow ; the loss of Russian property cannot be less than 108,100,000*l.* Severe as these sacrifices appear to be, the safety and independence of Russia have been established ; and we cannot sufficiently admire the patriotism and the courage of all ranks, from the prince to the peasant, in their united determination, not only to resist, but to vanquish the common enemy.

In a German publication, the loss of men, during the late war, from 1802 to 1813—in St. Domingo, Cala-

bria, Russia, Poland, France, Spain, Portugal, Germany, &c. including the maritime war, contagious diseases, famine, &c.—is stated to amount to the dreadful sum of *five millions eight hundred thousand ! ! !*

Oh ! when will the time come that the knowledge of the Lord shall cover the earth, and men shall learn war no more ! Hasten, O Lord, this golden age !

The Battle of Moskwa, 7th Sept. 1812.

This battle was fought at Moskwa, or, more properly speaking, Borodino, for it was in the neighbourhood of the village of that name. The details of it need not be given here. The Russian army was commanded by Prince Bragation, who was fully sensible that on the issue of it the greatest consequences depended. The battle was obstinately contested. It began at six in the morning, and lasted till nearly the evening. The French were victorious, according to their own account, but the Russian statement clearly proved that victory, so far as it consisted in keeping possession of the field of battle, rested with the Russians. Buonaparte, in fact, retreated after the battle to Mojaisk, where his 18th bulletin, containing the account of the action was dated. The loss on both sides was immense. The French lost above 30,000 men, the Russians nearly 50,000 ! Many generals fell on both sides.

The Battle of Smolensko, 17th Aug. 1812.

This town, which lay on the road to Moscow, was taken by storm, and the most dreadful carnage ensued. It was soon on fire, and, to use the words of Buonaparte himself, " it afforded the French a sight similar to that which an eruption of Vesuvius presents to an inhabitant of Naples." The city was nearly destroyed, and all the inhabitants who had not time to escape were massacred. Those who did escape fled towards Moscow, where the people were employed in throwing up lines of defence, expecting the approach of the conqueror, who was above three hundred miles distant.

When a soldier was brought before Lamacus, a commander, for misbehaviour, and pleaded he would do so no more, Lamacus answered, *Non licet in bello bis peccare ;—*" no men must offend twice in war."

How desirable then is peace ! It is recorded of a certain cavalier, who had acted a signal part in the war of the *great rebellion*, and who at length died fighting by the side of his king, that when alone, and pacing about his chamber, he was frequently heard to ingeminate the word *peace*. "Peace!" said he, "dear peace ! when shall we know thee again !"

An account of the wars between England and France with the terms of their duration, since the one which commenced in 1110, and which continued two years—1141, one year—1161, twenty-five years—1211, fifteen years—1224, nineteen years—1294, five years—1332, twenty-one years—1368, fifty-two years—1422, forty-nine years—1492, one month—1512, two years—1521, six years—1549, one year—1557, two years—1562, two years—1627, two years—1665, one year—1689, ten years—1702, eleven years—1744,four years—1756, seven years—1776,seven years—1793, nine years—and lastly, in 1803, near eleven years, making within a period of 704 years, 270 years of war ; of which 27 have fallen within the present reign.

THE WRESTLER OVERTHROWN.

It is awful to reflect on the influence which illicit pleasures have had, not merely on the young and unthinking, but on the wise and intelligent part of mankind. Even good men have fallen victims to their passions, and gone with sorrow to the grave. Samson the strongest man, and David the most pious, both slain by unlawful embraces. So we are told, that a mighty wrestler, who had won a crown at Olympus for contending prosperously, was observed to turn his head and go forward with his face upon his shoulder to behold a fair woman that was present ; and he lost the glory of his strength, when he became so weak that a female could turn his head about, which his adversary could not. "These," says Bishop Taylor, "are the follies and weakness of man, and they are dishonourable to religion, namely, that a man should contend nobly and do handsomely, and then be taken in a base and dishonourable action, and so, as it were, mingle venom with his delicious ointment.

NECESSITY OF WATCHFULNESS.

The eye was formed for noble and delightful purposes, to admire, to survey, to distinguish, to guard, to direct, to enjoy. But how often is this useful organ diverted to base and sinful ends. Even good men have found it the inlet of evil; so that they have had occasion to pray, "turn away mine eyes from beholding vanity." How prudent then to imitate holy Job, in making a covenant with our eyes. Scipio would not venture to behold his fair captive, but in the presence of her mournful husband, to whom he honourably restored her. Even Alexander the Great would not see the beautiful daughters of Darius, lest the conqueror of the world should be tempted by their charms. Zaleusus, the Locrian legislator, ordained that the crime of adultery should be punished with the loss of the offender's eyes. But a greater than these hath enjoined us to pluck out our own eyes if they offend, that is, to restrain and mortify its sinful lusts.

THE WORLD INSUFFICIENT TO MAKE MEN HAPPY.

"The greatest vanity of this world," says Bishop Taylor, "is remarkable in this, that all its joys summed up together are not big enough to counterpoise the evil of one sharp disease, or to allay a sorrow." For imagine a man great in his dominion, as Cyrus, rich as Solomon, victorious as David, beloved like Titus, learned as Tristmegistus, powerful as all the Roman greatness; all this, and the results of all this, give him no more pleasure in the midst of a fever or the tortures of the stone, than if he were only lord of a little dish, and a dishfull of fountain water. Indeed the excellency of a holy conscience is a comfort and a magazine of joy so great, that it sweetens the most bitter portion in the world, and makes tortures and death not only tolerable but amiable; and therefore to part with this treasure whose excellency is so great for the world, which is so inconsiderable and vain, as not to have in it recompense enough for the sorsows of a sharp disease, is a bargain fit to be made by none but fools and madmen. Antiochus Epiphanes, and Herod the Great with his grandchild Agrippa, are sad instances of this great truth; to each of which it happened that the grandeur of their fortune, the greatness of their possessions, and the increase of their estate, disappeared, and expired like camphire, at their arrest by those several sharp diseases, which covered their head with cypress, and hid their crowns in an inglorious grave.

THE WORLD RENOUNCED.

THE precepts of Christianity may appear very severe to the devotees of this world. The restraints which it imposes may seem very unnecessary to them. But he who knows, that the world lieth in wickedness, that it is every way prejudicial to the interests of the soul; that it hath ruined its thousands and tens of thousands, sees nothing but kindness and mercy in the prohibitions of the Christian religion, and that he only can be happy who keeps himself unspotted from the world. When Dionysius of Syracuse invited Plato to come and witness the splendour and festivity of his court, the Grecian sage replied, "philosophy will not allow Plato to visit Dionysius." So when the world tempts the Christian, he can say, "my

religion will not allow me to comply with the world." And in this let it be remembered the Christian feels no regret, for "this is the victory that overcometh the world, even our faith."

Such is the nature of divine grace, that it teaches us to renounce every thing which is derogatory to the divine glory and the interest of our own souls. Nor is this of a compulsory nature but a voluntary act. We are made willing in the day of divine power; willing to leave the world, to oppose sin, to walk in the divine commands, and live to his praise. And can any thing be more reasonable than to renounce an evil for a good; an enemy for a friend, a state of danger for a state of safety. Aristippus cast his gold into the sea, saying, "it is better these things perish by Aristippus, than Aristippus by these things." So a Christian can say, "it is better give up the world, than to be conquered and ruined by it."

Genuine faith influences us to deny ourselves, to renounce the world, to cherish holiness, to bear reproach, and to look beyond the present scene to the world of light and eternal glory. Such an effect will be produced more or less on all who possess this divine grace. The Marquis of Vico in Italy, when he was come to years and to the knowledge of Jesus Christ, refused to be called the son and heir to a marquis, a cupbearer to an emperor, and nephew to a Pope, and chose rather to suffer affliction, persecution, banishment, loss of lands, living, wife, children, honours, and preferments, than to enjoy the sinful pleasures of Italy for a season; esteeming the reproach of Christ greater riches than all the honours of the most brilliant connections, and all the enjoyments of the most ample fortune, for he had respect unto the recompense of the reward!

Seneca, contemplating the beauty and greatness of those orbs of light above, cast down his eyes to find out the earth hardly visible at that distance, and breaks forth into a philo-sophical disdain : Is it this to which the great designs and vast desires of men are confined. Is it for this, there is such disturbance of nations, wars, and shedding of blood? O folly, O fury, of deceived men! to imagine great kingdoms in the compass of an atom, to raise armies, to divide a point of earth with their sword! It is just as if the ants should conceive a field to be several kingdoms, and fiercely contend to enlarge their borders, and celebrate a triumph in gaining a foot of earth, or a new province to their empire." And from hence he excites men to ascend in their thoughts, and take an intellectual possession of the material heavens, as most worthy of their minds. But the soul that is raised by faith looks beyond the starry heavens. How much more justly is it filled with noble wonder at the divine and truly great things in the spiritual world, and looks down on the lower scene of things, and all that has the name of felicity here, as sordid and vile.

LOVE OF THE WORLD

ECCLESIASTICAL historians relate that in the time of the persecution by Decius, the rich men among the Christians, were most easily and miserably foiled ; the love of the world was a dangerous snare in their hearts, of their revolting back to pagan idolatry and the bondage of Satan. And, in the time of the Arian persecution how many who by their titles and office were specially obliged to be valiant for the truth, and to contend earnestly for the faith, yet did accommodate their profession to their aspiring ambition and greedy avarice! The standard of their religion was the pith of the state : they had a political faith, and appeared either Orthodox or Arian, as the public favour shone upon truth or heresy.

What are all earthly things when compared to those of a heavenly nature! When one was asked, whether he did not admire the goodly structure of a stately house, he an-swered, "no! for," saith he, " I have been at Rome, where more magnificent fabrics are to be seen." Thus when Satan would present the things of this world, as delightful and engaging, we can say they are of no value in our estimation, having seen by faith the temple of God above, a house not made with hands, eternal in the heavens.

VANITY OF THE WORLD.

IT was the saying of a rich man, though the people hated and taunted him, yet when he came home and looked upon his chests, *"Egomet mihi plaudi domi."* With how much better reasons do believers bear out external injuries ! What inward contentment, when they consider themselves truly enriched with the favour of God! And as this makes them contemn the contempts that the world puts upon them, so likewise it breeds in them a neglect and disdain of those poor trifles, that the world admires. The sum of their desires is, that the rays of the love of God may shine constantly upon them. The favourable aspect and large proffers of kings and princes would be unwelcome to them, if they should stand betwixt them and the sight of that sun ; and truly they have reason. What are the highest things the world affords? What are great honours, and great estates, but great cares and griefs, well dressed and coloured over with a show of pleasure, which promise contentment and perform nothing but vexation? That they are not satisfying, is evident ; for the obtaining of much of them only whets the appetite, and teaches men to desire more. Neither are they solid. Will not the pains of a gout, of a strangury, or some such malady (to say nothing of the pains of a guilty conscience) blast all these delights? What relish finds a man in large revenues, and stately buildings, in high preferments, honourable titles, when either his body or his mind is in anguish? And besides the emptiness of all these things, you know they want one main point, *continuance.* But the loving kindness of God possesses every requisite to make the soul happy.

THE WORLD A SEA

WE are all of us too prone to seek for happiness in earthly things. We vainly imagine that in change of situation or circumstances we shall have less care and fewer troubles; forgetting that every place, every situation, hath its peculiar difficulties. Should worldly prosperity, however, attend us, as disciples of Christ we should remember where we are; and that while in the world we must expect to meet with tribulation. A friend of the famous Mr. J. Dod being raised from a mean estate to much worldly greatness, Mr. Dod sent him word that, "this was but like going out of a boat into a ship; and he should remember, that while he was in the world, he was still on the sea." Let us then wisely prepare for difficulties, and learn to cast all our cares on Him who holds the winds in his fists, who stills the waves of the sea, and who has promised to guide his people safe into the haven of rest.

THE PRESENT WORLD A STATE OF EXILE TO A GOOD MAN.

A HOLY indifference of affection to present things, makes it easy to part with them, and death less fearful to us. David, though a king, declares, he was a stranger on earth, not only with respect to his transient condition, but his inward disposition; and that he was as a weaned child from the admired vanities of the world. Chrysostom, in a letter to Ciriacus, who was tenderly sensible of his banishment, wrote to him, "you now begin to lament my banishment, but I have done so for a long time; for since I knew that heaven was my country, I have esteemed the whole earth a place of exile. Constantinople, from whence I am expelled, is as distant from paradise, as the desert to which they send me."

MISCELLANEOUS.

IT is represented as the peculiar glory of Theodosius, that he seated majesty and love in the same throne. "But how distant is the greatest monarch in the world from the Son of the eternal God, the Prince of the kings of the earth! Love brought him down from his throne in heaven, where he was adored by the angels, and united him to our nature in our lowly state; that we might be raised to his kingdom, and united to him in glory."

One of the ancient Romans highly celebrates the astronomers who discovered the true causes of the eclipses of the sun and moon, and thereby freed the world from the double darkness of ignorance and fear; for before that discovery, men believed the obscuring of those great lights to be the fainting fits of nature, and mortal symptoms threatening an universal calamity. But what prayer and blessing is due to our Saviour, who hath given us infallible assurance that the death of the righteous is not, as the heathen world imagined, an irreparable loss of life, but a short eclipsing of this low and mean light that is common to sensitive creatures, to be restored more excellent and permanent in heaven, where those stars shine in the divine presence forever. " Thanks be to God which gives us the victory through our Lord Jesus Christ." This should render him infinitely precious to us, and inflame our hearts with desires equal to our obligations to serve him.

The Psalmist indemnified himself by an intercourse with the people of God for the injury done him by the great. " I am," said he, " a companion of all them that fear thee, and of them that keep thy precepts. Suffer me to sanctify here, the profane praise, which Lucian gave Pompey, " the gods are for Cæsar, but Cato is for Pompey." Yes, the approbation

Z

of Cato is preferable to that of the gods! I mean those imaginary gods who frequently usurp the rights of the true God.

Is it a testimony of great military skill in a general to range an army composed of divers nations that have great antipathies between them, in that order which is necessary to secure a victorious battle? And is it not a testimony of infinite providence to dispose all the hosts of heaven and earth, so as that they should join successfully for the preservation of nature? It is astonishing that any should be of such a reprobate mind, as not to be convinced by the sight of the world, a visible word, that more gloriously illustrates the perfections of the Creator, than the sublimest eloquence, that conceals what it designs to represent. When Sophocles was accused by his ungrateful sons, that his understanding having declined with his age, he was unfit to manage the affairs of his family, he made no other defence before the judges, but recited part of a tragedy newly composed by him, and left it to their decision, whether there was a failure in his intellectual powers. Upon which he was not only absolved, but crowned with praises.

A musical amateur of eminence, who had often observed Mr. Cadogan's inattention to his performances, once said to him, "come, I am determined to make you feel the force of music; pay particular attention to this piece." It was played. "Well, what do you say now?" "Why, just what I said before." "What! can you hear this, and not be charmed? Well, I am quite surprised at your insensibility: *where are your ears?*" "Bear with me, my lord!" replied Mr. Cadogan, "since I too have had my surprise. I have often from the pulpit set before you the most striking and affecting truths: I have sounded notes that have raised the dead:—I have said, 'surely he will feel' now; but you never seemed charmed with my music, though infinitely more interesting than yours.

—I too have been ready to say, with astonishment, *Where are your ears?*"

God is more angry at a sin committed by his servants, than at many by persons who are enemies; and an uncivil answer from a son to a father, from an obliged person to a benefactor, is a greater indecency, than if any enemy should storm his house, or revile him to his face. Augustus Cæsar taxed all the world, and God took no public notice of it; but when David taxed and numbered a petty province, it was not to be expiated without a plague: because such persons, besides the direct sin, add the circumstance of ingratitude to God, who hath redeemed them from their vain conversation, and from death and hell; and consigned to them the inheritance of sons, giving them his grace and Spirit, with many periods of comfort, and a certain hope, and visible earnest of immortality. Nothing is baser than that such a person, against his reason, against his interest, against his God, against so many obligations, against his general practice, against his very habits and acquired inclinations, should do a dishonourable action.

To expect to give a just idea of Christianity by any quality as detached from the whole, would be to resemble a certain Athenian, who having a palace to sell, took out a single brick from the wall, and produced it at the auction, as a specimen of the edifice.

The temperamental lust is the root from whence many others spring and are fed; and the eradicating of that, takes away the strength and life of other vicious affections. The king of Syria commanded his captains not to fight against small or great, but only against the king of Israel, and after he was slain, the victory over his army was presently obtained. Let us direct our zeal against the besetting sin, for all the servile lusts must fall and die with that. When Mithridates, the king of Pontus, a fierce implacable enemy of the Romans, was killed, their joy was exuberant in sacrifices and feasts, accounting that an army of enemies were extinguished in his single death.

"As often as I have been among vain men," said one, "I returned home, less a man than I was before." Real Christians can find no pleasure in associating with the wicked.— Though in the present state they cannot be entirely secluded from them, yet they are desirous of avoiding all intimate connexion with them. In moments of depression, the tempted Christian has found this almost the only evidence of grace he could lay hold of. Weak perhaps in faith, destitute of any high enjoyment, much harassed by the enemy, he will still appeal to his Lord, and say, " do I not love them that love thee, and have I not avoided them that hate thee ?" This made a good woman at the point of death, say, " O Lord, let me not go to hell, where the wicked are : for thou knowest I never loved their company here." And what Christian will not join the Psalmist in saying, " depart from me, ye evil doers; for I will keep the commandments of my God."

It is not for want of power that God spares the wicked, but because they are always in his hands, and he can make them as miserable as they are sinful when he pleases. It is not through the neglect of justice, but for the wisest and most holy reasons, as shall appear in the last day, when a decisive, irreversible judgment shall be pronounced and immediately inflicted upon them before the world. When an actor at Athens spoke with admiration of riches, as the most valuable acquisition, and of the felicity of rich men, the people were in an uproar at the immorality of the speech, and were ready to chase him from the stage. But the poet himself appeared and desired them to stop their fury till they saw the catastrophe, the wretched end of that sordid miser. Thus we are apt to accuse the ways of God when the wicked flourish, but we should stop our tumultuous thoughts, for their end will absolve Divine Providence from all undue reflections upon the account of their temporal happiness.

Dioclesian, the last and the worst of the Roman persecuting emperors, observed, that the more he sought to blot out the name of Christ, the more legible it became; and that whatever of Christ he thought to eradicate, it took the deeper root, and rose the higher in the hearts and lives of men. Those who have been, as it were, in the arms of God, are as men made of fire, walking in stubble : they consume and overcome all opposition ; nay, difficulties are but as whet-stones to their fortitude.

The Rev. Mr. M. was educated for the bar. His conversion arose from the following circumstance. He was desired one evening by some of his companions, who were with him at a coffee-house, to go and hear Mr. John Wesley, who they were told was to preach in the neighbourhood ; and then to return and exhibit his *manner* and *discourse* for their entertainment. He went with that intention, and just as he entered the place, Mr. Wesley named as his text, "prepare to meet thy God," with a solemnity of accent, which struck him, and which inspired a seriousness that increased as the good man proceeded in exhorting his hearers to repentance. He returned to the coffee-room, and was asked by his acquaintance, "if he had taken off the old methodist." To which he answered, " *No, gentleman, but he has taken me off*," and from that time he left their company altogether, and in future associated with serious people, and became himself a serious character.

It was Cicero's just censure of Homer, that whereas he should have raised earth to heaven by instructing men to live according to the purity of the gods, he forced down heaven to earth, and represented the gods to live like men in this region of impurity. It is the highest glory of man to be made the image of God in moral excellencies; and it is the vilest contumely to God to fashion him according to the image of man's vicious affections.

The Christian Race.

Among the West Indians, some are reported to be so swift in running that no horse can keep pace with them; and they have a constant rule in their diet, to eat no beast, or bird, or fish, that is slow in motion, fancying that it would transfuse a sluggishness into them. The Christian life is, by the apostle, compared to a race; and earthly things, by an inseparable property of nature, so load and depress the soul, that it cannot with vigour run the race set before us. The believer therefore, who contends for the high prize of his calling, and is true to his end, will be temperate in all things. Nay, he will not only be circumspect, lest these things should interfere with his great design, but wisely manage them in a subserviency to it.

The true Balance.

In the reign of king Charles I. the goldsmiths of London had a custom of weighing several sorts of their precious metal before the privy council. On this occasion, they made use of scales poised with such exquisite nicety, that the beam would turn (the master of the company affirmed) at the two-hundreth part of a grain. Noy, the famous attorney-general, standing by, and hearing this, replied, "I should be loth then to have all my actions weighed in those scales." With whom I heartily concur, says the pious Hervey, in relation to myself. And since the balances of the sanctuary, the balances in God's hand, are infinitely more exact. O what need have we of the merits and righteousness of Christ to make us acceptable in *his* sight and passable in *his* esteem!

It was prudent counsel that one of the ancients gave for composing a book, that the author frequently reflect upon the title, that it may correspond in all the parts with his original design. "Thus it becomes a man often to consider the end of his being, that the course of his life may have a direct tendency to it, and the more excellent our end is, the more constraining is the necessity to prosecute it. It is of great efficacy to reflect upon ourselves, whither do my thoughts and desires tend? For what do I spend my strength and consume my days? Will it be my last account, how much by my prudence and diligence I have exceeded others in temporal acquisitions?" If a general were at play while the armies are engaging, would it be a noble exploit for him to win the game, while his armies for want of a conductor lost the victory? Will it be profitable for a man to gain the world and lose his own soul? Let conscience answer in truth.

It has been observed of Phocion, that he never appeared elated in prosperity or dejected in adversity; he never betrayed pusillanimity by a tear, or joy by a smile.

It is said of Mr. William Fuller, the banker in London, that in the course of his life, and at his death, he gave to the support of the cause of religion, in different ways, to the amount of sixty thousand pounds!

When the great Physician of souls appeared in the fulness of time, he demonstratively proved himself to be that divine person, whom prophets predicted, and to whose praise psalmists had sung. He went about doing good, and healed all manner of diseases, and every species of iniquity that could infect the soul. When the *Grecian* painter *Zeuxis*, presented gratuitously his incomparable pictures, his vanity prompted him to give this reason for his conduct; "that his performances were above all price." But *Jesus* being *Lord of all*, performed his mighty works of healing freely, and without a reward: because it was impossible to propose any to him, which could either merit his favour or claim his acceptance; and we do not find that a single person, among all the multitudes which he healed, was so insensible of the worth of the remedy or dignity of the physician, as to make him so degrading an offer. He healed for nothing; and those whom he healed could give him nothing but what his own bounty had previously conferred upon them.

Dr. Crow, chaplain to Bishop Gibson, bequeathed him two thousand five hundred pounds; but the bishop understanding the doctor had left some poor relations, nobly resigned the whole legacy in their favour.

The worthy Mr. Thornton, of Clapham, it is said, expended annually two thousand pounds in the distribution of religious books only, and his charities reached to the remotest part of the globe. John Baptist Joseph Languet, vicar of St. Sulpice at Paris, sometimes disbursed the sum of a million of livres in charities, in a single year. When there was a general dearth in 1725, he sold, in order to relieve the poor, his household goods, his pictures, and some curious pieces of furniture that he had procured with great difficulty.

While human reason is not to be despised, we must ever remember, it is not to be idolized. Man, in his present state, is a disordered being; his understanding is clouded, and his reasoning powers are injured by the fall. To suppose we can know every thing, and especially divine things, by the mere effort of reason is absurd. Revelation, as it was necessary, so it has been vouchsafed to mankind; those therefore who take this as their rule, are certain to obtain true knowledge; but those who refuse it, must still wander on in error. As divine revelation is given, so divine influence is promised. As all systems, both in creation and Providence, are maintained, and carried on by a constant supernatural energy; so the mind lies dead, dark, and insensible, until it becomes the subject of divine operation.

Several learned men tried to persuade a great scholar to believe in Christianity, but it seems all their la-
bour was in vain. A plain honest person, however, managed the argument in a different manner; by referring not so much to logical reasoning as to the work of the divine Spirit; so that at last the scholar exclaimed, "when I heard no more than human reason, I opposed it with human reason; but when I heard the Spirit, I was obliged to surrender." Thus it is that the wisest trusting to their own wisdom are lost; while those who are taught of the Spirit, know the way of God in truth.

It is of great importance how parents act towards their children. A wanton young lady once told her vicious mother, who was standing by her bed-side, "that it was too late to speak of God to her; for," says she, "you have undone me, and I am going to hell before, and you will certainly come after." Plato, seeing a child doing mischief in the streets, went immediately and corrected its father for it. That father who does not correct his child, when he does amiss, is himself justly corrected for his faults, and it is the pattern of God's judicial proceedings; for as he visits the iniquities of the fathers upon the children who *imitate them;* so he visits the iniquities of the children upon the fathers, who *countenance and indulge them.*

It is too common with some professors, under a pretence of magnifying the grace of God, to excuse their want of zeal, and their negligence in the duties of religion, by pleading that they can do nothing without the sensible influence of grace upon their minds.

I once heard a zealous minister (now with God) talking in his sleep, which was a very customary thing with him, and lamenting this disposition in some professors, which he thus reproved, "I am a poor creature, says one, and I can do nothing," says another. No, and I am afraid you *do not want to do much.* I know you have no strength of your own, but how is it you do not cry to the Strong for strength?"

Philip, king of Macedon, being urged to assist, by the credit and authority he had with the judges, a person whose reputation would be quite lost by the sentence that was going to be pronounced against him, " I had rather," says he, " that he should lose his reputation than I mine."

The persevering Cynic.

However a Christian may suffer from painful dispensations of Divine Providence ; however God may smite and chastise him ; yet he can find happiness no where but in him. It is said that Diogenes became a disciple of Antisthenes, who was at the head of the Cynics. Antisthenes at first refused to admit him into his house, and even struck him with a stick. Diogenes calmly bore the rebuke and said, " Strike me, Antisthenes ; but never shall you find a stick sufficiently hard to remove me from your presence, whilst there is any thing to be learnt, any information to be gained from your conversation and acquaintance." Such firmness recommended him to Antisthenes, and he became his most devoted pupil. So the Christian can say, that nothing shall ever separate him from Him who is the source of all his knowledge, and safety, and joy.

The learned Cordwainer.

It is credibly reported of the Rev. Nehemiah Cox, once pastor of the Church at Cranfield, in Bedfordshire, and author of a discourse on the covenants, (printed in 1684,) that he followed the business of a cordwainer, and was persecuted for preaching the gospel as a non-conformist. When he came upon his trial at Bedford assizes, he first pleaded in Greek, and then in Hebrew ; upon which the judge calling for the indictment, wherein he was styled, " Nehemiah Cox, cordwainer," expressed his surprise, and declared that none there could answer him ; and, upon Mr. Cox arguing that it was but fair that he should plead in what language he pleased, he was dismissed.

We transcribe this anecdote from the appendix to a funeral sermon preached by Dr. Ryland, on occasion of the death of the Rev. J. Symonds, of Bedford, (1788,) who says that he has frequently heard the above anecdote repeated in conversation in the town and neighbourhood of Bedford, and with this addition, that the judge should say to the counsellors, " well, this cordwainer has wound you all up, gentlemen !"

Self-condemnation.

While the proud pharisee boasts of his fancied righteousness, and trusts in his own works for salvation, the true believer is deeply humbled under a view of his own unworthiness. He mourns over the manifold infirmities of his nature ; and knows that it is by grace alone he can be saved. His conduct indeed may be uniform, so that none can accuse him ; yet he condemns himself, and his imperfection in all he does. A patriarch of Alexandria, being introduced to an old religious person in his hermitage, asked him what he found in that desert. To which he answered, " to judge and condemn myself perpetually ; that is the employment of my solitude ;" the patriarch answered, " there is no other way." Now, though there is no necessity to seclude ourselves from society, or to retire into a wilderness ; yet the only way to heaven is through the valley of humiliation. It is thus only that we can appreciate the gospel of Christ, and see the suitableness of his righteousness, and the absolute necessity of his grace. Living and dying, therefore, this must be our language—" God be merciful to me a sinner !"

The Aged Christian.

An aged Christian in much distress of mind was once complaining to a friend, of his miserable condition ; and among other things, said, " that which troubles me most is, that God will be dishonoured by my fall." His friend hastily caught at this, and used it for the purpose of comforting him : " art thou careful of the honour of

God?—and dost thou think that God hath no care of thee and of thy salvation?" A soul forsaken of God cares not what becomes of the honour of God; therefore be of good cheer : if God's heart were not towards thee, thine would not be towards God; or towards the remembrance of his name.

The attentive Children.

Perhaps more attention should be paid to the rising generation in an address from the pulpit than what is ordinarily done. They may under the divine blessing receive more benefit than we suspect. A child after being remarkably attentive to the sermon, was observed to weep when going to bed, on the Lord's day evening. On being asked the cause, the little one replied, "because I am so wicked, and Jesus Christ has been so good to us as the minister said."— Another child, six years old, having heard a minister preach on the ministry of angels, said to her friends, "I am not afraid to go to bed now, (though before very fearful,) for Mr. —— said, 'the angels watch over us while we are asleep,'" and this actually cured her of her fears. Another, about seven years old, hearing the same minister preach on secret worship, went home and retired to her closet, and ever since has continued to pray and read the scriptures in private. It is good, therefore, for children to be under the word; the seed may be sown which shall afterwards spring up and produce abundance of fruit.

Miss Dinah Dowdney of Portsea, who died at nine years of age, one day in her illness, said to her aunt, with whom she lived, "when I am dead, I should like Mr. Griffin to preach a sermon to children to persuade them to love Jesus Christ, to obey their parents, not to tell lies, but to think about dying, and going to heaven. I have been thinking," said she, "what text I should like him to preach from—2 Kings, iv. 26. You are the Shunamite; Mr. G. is the prophet, and I am the Shunamite's

child. When I am dead, I dare say you will be grieved. Though you need not. The prophet will come to see you, and when he says, 'How is it with the child?' you may say, 'IT IS WELL.' I am sure it will then be well with me, for I shall be in heaven, singing the praises of God. You ought to think it well too." Mr. G. accordingly fulfilled the wish of this pious child.

The Crown of Thorns.

It was the custom of some heathen nations to bring their sacrifices to the altars, crowned with garlands; but thorns were the garlands with which the great sacrifice, the Redeemer, was crowned. These thorns it is probable, were very painful and fetched blood from his head, and formed a part of the sufferings he endured for his people. But if he endured such pain and misery for us, what shall we not endure for him? for is it fit that the head should be crowned with thorns, and the members with rosebuds? Godfrey of Boulogne, first king of Jerusalem, refused to be crowned with a crown of gold, saying, "It became not a Christian there, to wear a crown of gold, where Christ, for our salvation, wore a crown of thorns." So it doth not become us as his followers to look for great things here. "The servant is not greater than his lord! If they have persecuted me they will also persecute you." May we be enabled to endure the cross and despise the shame. Amen.

Compassion.

We are informed by a certain historian, of two brothers, one of whom for a capital crime was condemned to die, but upon the appearance of the other, who had lost an arm in the successful defence of his country, and the presentation of the remaining stump, the judges were so affected with a grateful recollection of his past services, as freely for his sake to pardon his guilty brother.

Thus our exalted Redeemer appearing "on the throne as a Lamb that had been slain," Rev. 5. 6. "with scars of honour in his flesh, and triumph in his eyes," silently but powerfully reminds His heavenly Father of his bitter sufferings, and the important design of them, even the salvation of his people. Nor does he thus appear in vain.

When the London apprentices came before Henry VIII. pleading pardon for their insurrection, the monarch, moved by such a sight, and their cry, "mercy, mercy," said, "take them away, I cannot bear it!" If such a king could be moved by such a plea, how forcible must the sinner's plea be in the ears of Jesus Christ?

Force of Conscience.

The conscience that is now stupified by sensuality will make furious reflections upon the folly of the sinner's choice, and be more tormenting than the infernal fiends. When Crœsus, the rich king of Lydia, was bound to the stake, and the fire kindled for his burning, he lamentably called out, "Solon, Solon, Solon;" and being asked the reason of it, declared, that in the height of his prosperity, that wise Grecian had advised him to prepare for a revolution from his glory and greatness, into a miserable state, and his neglect of that counsel was more tormenting than the loss of his kingdom. How piercing will the remembrance be to lost souls of their despising the instructions, warnings, and gracious methods of the divine wisdom, to have prevented their ruin ; that mercy that was so often and so rebelliously resisted. This will be the hell of all hells!

Curiosity Reproved.

"Vain curiosity ought not to be indulged ; and when it is, it seldom escapes punishment."

Nitocris, a celebrated queen of Babylon, ordered herself to be buried over one of the gates of the city, and placed an inscription on her tomb, which signified, that her successor would find great treasures within, if ever they were in need of money, but that their labours would be ill repaid if ever they ventured to open it without necessity. Cyrus opened it, through curiosity, and was struck to find within these words ! "If thy avarice had not been insatiable, thou never wouldst have violated the monuments of the dead."

Caution to be used in judging others.

In the primitive church as well as now, there was much difference of opinion as to some non-essential and inferior things in religious services : we either lay too much stress on some things or too little on others. To cultivate the spirit of devotion is the great object : if the means which my brother uses in order to prosecute this, are somewhat different from mine, why should I judge him if we arrive at the same end ? In defining the operation of religious principle, one observes, I am afraid of becoming an Albert Durer. Albert Durer gave rules for forming the perfect figure of a man. He marked and defined all the relations and proportions. Albert Durer's man became the model of perfection in every academy in Europe, and now every academy in Europe has abandoned it, because it is supposed no such figure was ever found in nature. I am afraid of reducing the variety, which to a certain degree, may be of God's own forming, to my notion of perfection. "You must maintain and cultivate a spirit of devotion." I say to all, "but be ye judges, as conscientious men, of the particular means suited to your circumstances."

The duty of attending to our Calling.

Whatever be our condition in the present world, our great object must be to serve God : whether we are rich or poor, masters or servants, young or old, single or married, in private or public stations, this is the grand end we must keep in view. Nor is there any state in life, however low and mean, that will exempt a man from his duty. Phidias was a famous sculptor ; he excited the admiration of men, because he could show his extraordinary skill not only in gold, and marble, and ivory, but in mean materials, in wood or ordinary stone. Thus a Christian is to glorify his God and Saviour in the lowest as well as the highest station in life ; therefore, said the apostle, let every man wherein he is called therein abide with God.

The Crucifix, or human Ceremonies.

Should any apply the Jewish science of ceremonies to the Christian religion, and pretend to set off the service and attract the eyes of fine folks in the world, they would oppose the wise designs of Jesus Christ, which was to supply the wants of the poor with the goods of the church. Into two extremes, both contrary to the spirit of Christianity, this *science* leads people ; they who can afford it, *oppose* the humility of Christ by a profusion of grandeur, all inconsistent with the simplicity of Christ ; they who cannot *oppose* the dignity of Christ, by applying in his worship a kind of mean cast-off finery : thus a Greek bishop, who pretended he could not perform public worship without a crucifix, and not being able to procure one, contrived to make one on the spot with two bits of broken lath ; as if the God he adored had been a finical being of small understanding and great ostentation. How little was the true glory of the church understood by this man ! The prophet Isaiah, indeed, speaks of its glory as superior to all others.— " Arise, shine ; for thy light is come, and the glory of *the Lord* is risen upon thee."

The Divine Attributes the Object of Faith, not of Reason.

Man's ignorance of the manner in which divine mysteries exist, is no sufficient plea for infidelity, when the scripture reveals that they do exist. For reason, which is limited and restricted, cannot frame a conception that is commensurate to the essence

and power of God. This will appear more clearly by considering the mysterious excellencies of the divine nature, the certainty of which we believe, though the manner we cannot understand ; as that his essence and attributes are the same, without the least shadow of composition ; yet his wisdom and power are to our apprehensions, distinct, and his mercy and justice in some manner opposite; that his essence is entire in all places, yet not terminated in any ; that He is above the heavens; and beneath the earth, yet hath no relation of high or low, distant or near ; that He penetrates all substances, but is mixed with none ; that He understands, yet receives no ideas within himself; that He wills, yet has no motion that carries him out of himself; that in Him time hath no succession, that which is past is not gone, and that which is future, is not to come. That He loves without passion, is angry without disturbance, repents without change. The perfections of God are above the capacity of reason fully to understand, yet essential to the Deity. Here we must exalt faith and abase reason.

Security of a Christian.

How noble is the triumph of the Christian ! Although exposed to manifold difficulties, and persecuted by powerful and dangerous enemies, yet he knows he is safe; yea, even though death is before him, and he fall a martyr to truth, he can still rejoice.

Socrates, when unrighteously persecuted to death, said of his enemies, with a courage becoming the heart of a Christian, " They may kill me, but they cannot hurt me." So a Christian may truly say ; for nothing can eventually injure him, for his life is hid with Christ in God.

Temptation.

In whatever situation we are, or whatever progress we have made in the good way, we must not expect to be exempt from temptations. The enemy knows well how to adapt them to our age, feelings, constitution, views, circumstances, and senses.— We have, however, the divine promises of support, so that the weakest need not despair. Let us remember that under the divine blessing, they will only be rendered profitable to humble us, but excite dependence, as well as fit us to sympathize with others.

Deceitfulness of the Heart.

" I find more solid truth in that one scripture," says the pious Haliburton, " which tells us that 'the heart is deceitful above all things, and desperately wicked,' than in many volumes of idle and unscriptural notions reared up on the subtle arguings of men, whose eyes have never been opened to see the plague of their own hearts, and who therefore run out in asserting such an ability, and power, and inclination to good in man, as neither scripture, nor the experience of such as have their eyes in the least measure opened, admits of. However, if others will think that there are in them such good inclinations, I will quit my part in them. Woful experience convinces me, and obliges me to acknowledge to my own shame, that I never looked towards the Lord's way, save when he drew me. " I was as a bullock unaccustomed to the yoke ;" I never went longer in it than the force lasted : I inclined to sit down, and sat indeed down at every step : no great sign I had any heart to the way ! I never got up again, but when the Lord's power was anew put forth. I all this while never went one step but with a grudge : I frequently looked back to Sodom ; I have been as a backsliding heifer ; I was grieved for what I left behind. My heart clave to what my light had the greatest opposition to. Thus I was one of them that rebel against light. I often refused where the command was plainest. When I was brought into a strait, I betook myself rather to any shift than to Christ. Sin bit me, and yet I loved : my heart deceived me often ; and yet I trusted in it, rather than in God. God dealt with me in a way of kindness ; but when he spake to me in my prosperity, I would not hear : He smote me ; and I went on frowardly : I never parted with any sin, till God beat me, and drove me from it, and hedged in my way. Surely this looks like the heart, deceitful above all things, and desperately wicked."

Happiness.

We were not sent into this world with orders to make ourselves miserable, but with abilities, and directions, and helps, to search out the best possibilities of happiness which remain to beings fallen from that state of moral and mental rectitude in which man was created ; to make the best of the ruins of that perfect world whose beauty he had marred, and whose capacity of conferring felicity he had fatally impaired. Human life, therefore, abounding as it does in blessings and mercies, is not the blissful vision which youthful fancy images, or poetry feigns, or romance exhibits. It is in a considerable measure compounded of painful and of dull realities, and not a splendid tissue of grand events or brilliant exploits ; it is to some an almost unwearied state of penury, to many a series of cares and troubles, to all a state of probation. But the primeval punishment, the sentence of labour, like the other inflictions of Him who in judgment remembers mercy, is transformed into a blessing. And whether we consider the manual industry of the poor, or the intellectual exertions of the superior classes, we shall find that diligent occupation, if not criminally perverted from its end, is at once the instrument of virtue, and the secret of happiness. Men cannot be safely trusted with a life of leisure.

Holiness needful to enter Heaven.

If an unregenerate body cannot

enter the kingdom of heaven, much less an unregenerate soul. An infamous person in the civil law may be excepted against, as not fit to be an heir; and shall the law of man be purer than the law of God? Tiberius once said to a person that requested death, rather than long imprisonment, "I am not yet reconciled to thee, that I should show thee such a favour." And can wicked men, who are constantly insulting God, imagine that he can be so reconciled to them, as either to take them to heaven, or even to annihilate them, and deliver them from all misery when they die?

Controversy.

Controversial discussions are not only harmless, but useful, provided truth be the inspiring motive, and charity the medium of conducting them. Truth is frequently beaten out by conflicting blows, when it might have contracted rust and impurity by lying quiet, uninquired into and unassailed. We are in danger of growing negligent about a truth which is never attacked, or of surrounding it with our own fancies, and appending to it our own excrescences; while the assailant teaches even the friendly examiner to clear the principle of all foreign mixtures, and by giving it more purity, to give it wider circulation.

Inordinate Affection to the World.

The pleasures of the world exceedingly unfit a man for the discharge of his duty toward God; and those who are inordinately attached to them, seldom or ever set God before their eyes. Like children, who, when their minds are ardent for play, are very unwilling to go to school; so when men's minds are set upon pleasure, their hearts are entirely alienated from every thing of a divine and holy nature. Even *Jerome* complains of himself, that though he was in a desolate wilderness, yet his fancy conveyed him to the dances of the Roman ladies. What must it be then with persons fond of pleasures! Let them, as one observes, sequester themselves ever so much, yet their fancies are filled with corporeal resemblances. Carnal pleasures make the heart fat, and so render the soul unable to engage in spiritual exercises. As it is said of the dullest of all animals, that the heart is the fattest; so it is with men fond of the world; their heart is more indisposed towards God and his services than any others.

Defective Theology.

A theology which depresses the standard, which overlooks the motives, which dilutes the doctrines, softens the precepts, lowers the sanctions, and mutilates the scheme of Christianity; which merges it in undefined generalities; which makes it consist in a system of morals that might be interwoven with almost any religion, (for there are few systems of religion which profess or teach immorality,) a theology which neither makes Jesus Christ the foundation, nor the Holy Spirit the efficient agent, nor inward renovation a leading principle, nor humility a distinguishing characteristic; which insists on a good heart, but demands not a renewed heart; which inserts virtues into the stock of the old nature, but insists not on the necessity of a changed nature;—such a theology is not that which the costly apparatus of Christianity was designed to present to us. But such a system is Socinianism.

"It is observable," says Dr. Bates, "that those who most excelled in natural wisdom were the greatest despisers of evangelical truth. The proud wits of the world chose rather to be masters of their own, than scholars to another. They made reason their supreme rule, and philosophy their highest principle, and would not believe what they could not comprehend. They represented Christians under scornful titles as captives of a blind belief, and derided their faith as the effect of folly; and rejected revelation, the only means to convey the knowledge of divine mysteries to them. They presumed by the light and strength of their own reason and virtue to acquire felicity, and slighted the doctrine that came from heaven to discover a clear way thither, and divine grace that was necessary to lead and assist them."

Linnæus.

The great Linnæus had the following inscription placed over the door of the hall in which he gave his lectures. " *Innocui vivite! Numen adest.*" Live guiltless—God observes you.

Riches.

We see the advantages of those men that are puffed up with riches and honours, but we see not their troubles and vexations. " I wish, I wish," says one, "that those who desire riches, would consult with rich men; they would then, to be sure, be of another opinion."

Mercies acknowledged.

" Say ye unto your brethren *Ammi*, and to your sisters, *Ruhamah*." Hosea ii. 1. Say it, to brethren and to sisters, upon every opportunity, and with the utmost importunity, that it may make impression upon their spirits, and not be as a seal set upon the water, nor as rain falling upon a rock, that leaves no sign behind it.

The Grecians being delivered out of servitude by Flaminius the Roman general, cried out, " Soter, Soter," that is, " Saviour, Saviour," with such a courage, that the very birds of the air, astonished thereat, fell to the ground. The people of Israel gave such a loud shout at the return of the ark, that the earth rang again. A drowning man being pulled out of the water by *Alphonsus*, King of *Arragon*, and rescued from so great a death, cried out (as soon as he came again to himself) by way of thankfulness, *Arragon, Arragon !* Let us cry aloud, *Ammi, Ruhamah*, hitherto God hath helped us, who were lately

(with those Israelites in the wilderness) *talking of our graves.* Say therefore with the Psalmist, " Because thou hast delivered my soul from death, mine eyes from tears, my feet from falling, I will walk before the Lord in the land of the living."

Scriptures, the use of.

A pious minister, conceiving that all his labours among the people of his charge were wholly in vain, was so extremely grieved and dejected, that he determined to leave his flock, and to preach his farewell sermon ; but he was suddenly struck with the words, Luke x. 6. " And if the son of peace be there, your peace shall rest upon it : if not, it shall turn to you again ?" He felt as if his Lord and Master had addressed him thus · " ungrateful servant, art thou not satisfied with my promise, that my despised peace shall return to you again ? Go on then to proclaim peace,"— which accordingly he did, with renewed vigour and zeal. Thus, how useful doth God render his own word in consoling and directing the minds of his people under their seasons of perplexity and sorrow.

Promises.

And this is God's dealing with mankind ; he promises more than we could hope for ; and when he hath done that, he gives us more than he hath promised. God hath promised to give to them that fear him, all that they need, food and raiment ; but he adds out of the treasures of his mercy, variety of food, and changes of raiment ; some to get strength, and some to refresh ; something for them that are in health, and something for the sick. And though skins of bulls, and stags, and foxes, and bears, could have drawn a veil thick enough to hide the apertures of sin and natural shame, and to defend us from heat and cold, yet when he addeth the fleeces of the sheep and beavers, and the spoils of silk-worms, he hath proclaimed that although his promises are the bounds of our certain expectation, yet they are not the limits of his loving-kindness : and if he does more than he hath promised, no man can complain that he did otherwise, and did greater things than he said. Thus God acts ; and therefore so also must we, imitating that example, and transcribing that copy of divine .ruth, always remembering that His *promises are Yea and Amen.*

Mercy of God.

God's mercies are above all his works, and ours too. All his attributes sit at the feet of mercy again. Neh. ix. 17. " Thou art a God ready to pardon ;" or rather, as in the original, "a God of pardons :" in which last expression there is a very great emphasis, as it shows that mercy is essential unto God : and that he is incomparable in forgiving iniquity, transgression, and sin. As a circle begins every where and ends no where, so do the mercies of God. When Alexander encamped before a city, he used to set up a light, to give notice to those within that if they came forth to him while that fire lasted, they should have quarter ; if otherwise, no mercy was to be expected. But such is the mercy and patience of God to sinners, that he sets up light after light, and waits year after year. When they have done their worst against him, then he comes with his heart full of love, and makes a proclamation of grace, that, if now at last they will accept of mercy they shall have it.

It is the observation of Solomon, *God made man upright, but he sought out many inventions* ; especially to palliate and hide, or to excuse faults. Sin in its native deformity is so foul, that men employ a great deal of art and study, either to conceal it under a veil of darkness, or a deceitful mask of virtue, or by various excuses to lessen its guilt and ignominy. Adam made an apron of fig leaves to cover his nakedness, a resemblance of his care to hide his sin ; David could not expect to deceive God ; but to hide his adultery with Bathsheba

from men, he sends for Uriah from the army, that he might have gone home to his wife. It is observed of Cæsar and Pompey, whose ambitious spirits aspired to sovereign power, that they made use of some ensigns of royalty to accustom the people by degrees to them, yet were crafty to hide their design. Cæsar sometimes appeared publicly with a wreath of laurel on his head ; but lest the people from his wearing that appearance of a crown should be jealous of his intention, pretended it was only to supply his want of hair, and cover his baldness. Pompey wore a white fillet curiously wrought about his leg, under a pretence that his leg was hurt, but in truth, because it was a diadem, a royal ornament, for which he was reproached by some strict observers. There are innumerable arts used to cover men's respective sins. I shall only instance one that is usually practised. How do many, like the crafty lapwing that flutters at a distance from its nest, appear zealous against the visible sins of others, that under the shadowy deceit they may hide their own ? Their words feathered with severe censure, fly abroad, wounding the reputation of others for less faults, that they may not be suspected to be guilty of worse sins secretly cherished by themselves.

Ceremonies.

WHAT is the shining of the true church ? Doth a church shine, when church service is raised from a decent and primitive simplicity, and decorated with pompous ceremonies, with rich furniture and gaudy vestments ? Is the church then beautiful ? Yes, indeed ; but all the question is, whether this be the proper genuine beauty or no, whether this be not strange fire, as the fire that Aaron's sons used, which became vain, and was taken as strange fire ? Methinks it cannot be better decided than to refer it to John in his book of the Revelation. We there find a description of two several women, the one riding in state arrayed in purple, decked with gold and precious stones and pearls, Rev. xii. 3. the other in rich attire too but of another kind, chap xii. clothed with the sun, and a crown of twelve stars on her head ; the decoration of the one was all earthly, the other all celestial. Why need she borrow light and beauty from precious stones, that is clothed with the sun and crowned with the stars ? She wears no sublunary ornaments ; but, what is more noble, she treads upon them, and the moon is under her feet. Now which of these two is the spouse of Christ? You can easily resolve the question ; the truth is, those things seem to deck religion, but they undo it. Observe where they are most used, and we shall find little or no substance of devotion under them ; as we see in that apostate church of Rome. This painting is dishonourable to Christ's spouse ; and, besides, it spoils her natural complexion. The superstitious use of torches and lights in the church by day is a kind of shining, but surely not commanded here. No, it is an affront done both to the sun in the heavens and to the sun of righteousness in the church.

The last Judgment.

Take away the hopes and fears of an hereafter, and what antidote is of force against the power of inherent lusts ? What can disarm the world of its allurements? How can man void of innocence, and full of impurity, resist the delights of sin, when the inclinations from within are as strong as temptations from without ? How greedily will he perceive the advantages of this mortal condition, and strive to gratify all his sensual appetites ? The Romans, when the fear of Carthage that aspired to a superiority in empire, was removed, presently degenerated from military valour and civil virtues, into softness and luxury. So if men were absolved from the fear of a judgment to come, no restraint would be strong enough to bridle the impetuous re-

solutions of their depraved will. If there were no dread of punishment after death, there is no species of iniquity that would not be continued until death. Human laws, however rigorous, would be found altogether insufficient to bind society together, and this world would be converted into a hell.

Necessity of Vigilance against the Attacks of Satan.

The activity and diligence of Satan are equal to his malice. The spirits of darkness never slumber or sleep ; they are not capable of weakness or weariness as our faint flesh is. The grand adversary is restless in following his pernicious designs. What is recorded of Marcellus, the Roman general, is applicable to Satan: if he obtains a victory, he fiercely insults and pursues it ; and if he be repulsed, he returns afresh. His spite is never spent. He tempted our Saviour with distrust of God's providence, with presumption and vain glory ; and being foiled in all attempts, it is said, *he departed for a season*, and afterwards made use of Peter as his instrument, to make him decline his sufferings for the salvation of men.

The fabled charioteer, who usurped his father's empire for a day, is not more illustrative of *their* presumption, who virtually snatching the reins of government from God, would involve the earth in confusion and ruin, than the denial which the ambitious supplicant received to his mad request, is applicable to the goodness of God in refusing to delegate his power to his creatures. " My son, the very tenderness I show in denying so ruinous a petition, is the surest proof that I am indeed thy father."

A friend sympathising with Dr. Kerr, of Madras, in his embarrassments and distress, and solicitous to relieve it, forwarded to him by the post of a letter, of which the following is a copy, containing a bank note of five hundred pagodas (two hundred pounds.)

"5th March, 1795.

"A friend to virtue takes this method of contributing to its relief. It will be sufficient satisfaction to him to know, by a line in the Courier, that A. B. has received the favour of *a Christian*."

The Blind American Preacher.

"The first emotions which touched my breast were those of mingled pity and veneration. But ah! how soon were all my feelings changed! the lips of Plato were never more worthy of a prognostic swarm of bees than were the lips of this holy man! It was a day of the administration of the sacrament; and his subject of course was the passion of our Saviour. I had heard the subject handled a thousand times : I had thought it exhausted long ago. Little did I suppose, that in the wild woods of America I was to meet with a man whose eloquence would give to this topic, a new and more sublime pathos than I had ever before witnessed!

"As he descended from the pulpit to distribute the mystic symbols, there was a peculiar, a more than human solemnity in his air and manner, which made my blood run cold, and my whole frame shiver!

"He then drew a picture of the sufferings of our Saviour; his trial before Pilate; his ascent up Calvary; his crucifixion, and his death. I knew the whole history, but never until then, had I heard the circumstances so selected, so arranged, and so coloured. It was all new, and I seemed to have heard it for the first time in my life ; his enunciation was so deliberate, that his voice trembled on every syllable, and every heart in the assembly trembled in unison. His peculiar phrases had that force of description, that the original scene appeared to be at that moment acting before our eyes! we saw the very faces of the Jews, the staring, frightful distortions of malice and rage! we saw the buffet : my soul kindled

with a flame of indignation ; and my hands were involuntarily and convulsively clenched !

"But when he came to touch on the patience, the forgiving meekness of our Saviour ; when he drew to the life his blessed eyes streaming in tears to heaven, his voice breathing to God a soft and gentle prayer of pardon on his enemies, 'Father, forgive them, for they know not what they do !'— the voice of the preacher, which had all along faltered, grew fainter and fainter, until his utterance being entirely obstructed by the force of his feelings, he raised his handkerchief to his eyes, and burst into a loud and irrepressible flood of grief. The effect is inconceivable, the whole house resounded with the mingled groans, and sobs, and shrieks of the congregation !

"It was some time before the tumult had subsided so far as to permit him to proceed. Indeed, judging by the usual but fallacious standard of of my own weakness, I began to be very uneasy for the situation of the preacher, for I could not conceive how he would be able to let his auditors down from the height to which he had wound them, without impairing the solemnity and dignity of his subject, or perhaps shocking them by the abruptness of the fall. But, no: the descent was as beautiful and sublime as the elevation had been rapid and enthusiastic.

"The first sentence, with which he broke the awful silence, was a quotation from Rousseau, 'Socrates died like a philosopher, but Jesus Christ like a God!'"

It is no less our interest, than our duty, to keep the mind in a habitual posture of submission to the will of of God. "Adam," says Dr. Hammond, "after his expulsion, was a greater slave in the wilderness than he had been in the inclosure." If the barbarian ambassador came expressly to the Romans to negotiate for his country permission to be their servants, declaring that a voluntary submission even to a foreign power, was preferable to a wild and disorderly freedom; well may the Christian triumph in the peace and security to be obtained by a complete subjugation to him who is emphatically called *the God of order.*

It is the observation of a certain philosopher concerning sensual persons, that they have reason in the faculty and habit, but not in the use and exercise. The conscience or understanding declares our duty, that it is absolutely necessary to obey God; and men assent to it in general; but when this principle is to be applied to practice in particulars that are ungrateful to the corrupt will, lust draws a veil over it, that it may not appear to check the sensual inclination. Whilst the mind, seduced by the senses, is intent upon the pleasing object, it does not simply and intensely consider the divine command: but conscience is brought under the control of the tempestuous passions. The light of reason, as well as divine revelation, discovers that the blessed beginning, and happy end of man, is to be like God, and to enjoy his love; but when there is a competition between his favour, and the things of the world, the carnal heart suppresses the dictates of the mind, and makes a blindfold choice of things present and sensible, as if man were all earth, and there was no spark of heaven in him.

The heathens are charged by the apostle Paul, *That they held the truth in unrighteousness.* The notion of God as the supreme lawgiver, and to be obeyed according to the law impressed upon his conscience, was a natural truth, and should have reigned in their hearts and lives: but they would not suffer it to exert its power in ordering their actions. There is a natural miracle seen in Egypt every year. When the river Nile overflows the plains, many living creatures are half formed, and part remains slimy earth without life or motion.

Altera pars vivit, rudis est pars altera tellus.

Such monsters were the unrighteous heathens; half men in their understanding, and half mud in their filthy affections. And there are innumerable such monsters in the Christian world.

Christian Zeal.

Christian zeal will prompt us to every useful exertion, and if we do not always succeed, we must not despair; " I will try and attempt every thing," says Brutus, " I will never cease to recall my country from this state of servility. If the event be favourable it will prove matter of joy to us all; if not, yet I, notwithstanding, shall rejoice." So the zealous and active mind will never cease in the use of means for the happiness of man, and the glory of God. If success be granted, he will rejoice abundantly, and if not, still he will have the satisfaction of at least making the generous attempt. Nothing can be more interesting and affecting than the discourse of our Lord with his disciples, recorded in Luke xxxiv. 13, &c. " I have been intimate," says the admirable Cowper, " with a man of fine taste, who confessed to me, that though he could not subscribe to the truth of Christianity itself, yet he never could read the above account of our Lord's appearance to the disciples, without being wonderfully affected by it. What must they find then whose eye penetrates deeper than the letter?"

Poverty is always better than profaneness.—A poor man, who is honest and good, stands on a far more elevated scale than the most opulent man who is base and impious. Yet poverty is not desirable, as it exposes to many inconveniences.

We cannot however, easily account for the singularity of men. That which many think an evil, others imagine to be a good. What some avoid as unpleasant, others seek as beneficial. Thus, for instance, riches in general are sought after with avidity yet poverty has been courted by some. Tubero, a Roman consul, son-in-law of Paulus, the conqueror of Perseus, is celebrated for his poverty, in which he seemed to glory as well as the rest of his family. Sixteen of the Tuberos with their wives and children lived in a small house, and maintained themselves with the produce of a little field which they cultivated with their own hands. But how many thousands of Christians have endured poverty, rather than comply with the world. Here indeed is a holy singularity. The riches of this world become contemptible, if they impede our progress in the way to heaven. Rather let me be poor, and obedient to the will of God, than to possess all the wealth of the universe, and forget him.

The following is part of a letter from a young minister, written two days before his death.

"Never have I felt more of the efficacy of the blood of Christ than I do now; the atonement is so full, that there remains no more conscience of sins; hence is that boldness in the Lord. This is excellent doctrine; honourable to God, and supporting to man! Preach it, my friend! Earnestly preach! While I have life I will speak it; for it is a faithful saying, and worthy of all acceptation. When you pray, be sure remember me. Come to see me, nor think it the melancholy entertainment of seeing a sick man. I am well; I am as I should be. Expect then to find me pleasant and cheerful; and yet I am almost sick—but it is only with the fear of being well. I dread to go back to life again. I cannot bear health and prosperity; no; all is now well through infinite goodness. God has spoken peace, and that is enough. Health and long life in such a world as this, how burdensome the thought! How good has this sickness been to me; evermore shall I bless God for it. That wondrous being (whose name is love) seems to be designing and doing more for me than ever before! How sweet are my hours of solitude! in prayer I meet him—in meditation I hold him fast, and cannot let him go; but with Abraham continue with him till he leave off speaking.

My joys for the future, be all from heaven. I have enough of earthly things, and count them but loss and dung, compared with the excellency of the knowledge of Christ Jesus my Lord. It is only with respect to a future life I value my friend, with whom I hope to spend a pleasant and everlasting day! Farewell!"

"Friends," said Socrates, "there is no friend." And a friend is a changeable creature, saith another: all in changeable colours as the peacock, as often changed as moved. Besides, many friends are not more fickle than false; like deep ponds clear at the top, and all muddy at the bottom. *Fide ergo: sed cui vide.* Try before you trust: and when you have tried your utmost, trust not over far, lest you cry out at length, as Queen Elizabeth did, "in trust, I have found treason:" or Julius Cæsar, when stabbed by Brutus among others, "what thou, my son Brutus?" He was slain in the senate house, with twenty-three wounds, given mostly by persons whose lives he had preserved.

It is reported of Agesilaus, that coming to help the king of Egypt in his distress he was despised by the Egyptians, because of the plainness of his person, and the homeliness of his attire; for they thought that they should see the king of Sparta such an one as the king of Persia was, bravely habited and pompously attended: so did the Jews expect a Messiah like one of the mighty monarchs of the earth; and they are strongly possessed with the fond conceit of an earthly kingdom. Hence when they saw Mahomet arising in such power, they were ready to cry him up for the Messiah. *The rich hath many friends, saith Solomon; but the poor is hated, even of his own neighbour,* Prov. xiv. 20. Christ came to his own; but his own received him not. It was once disputed among the Romans in their senate, whether Christ, having done many wonderful works, should be received into the number of the gods? But their historian adds, that

Aa

they declined to do it, because he preached poverty, and made choice of poor men to be his followers, such as the world careth not for.

Consistency of Character.

Nothing can be more indecent and absurd than to pretend the relation and respect of disciples to such an holy master as Jesus Christ, and yet by disobedience to deny him. When the bloody spectacles of the gladiators were first brought to Athens, one of their wise men advised the masters of their prizes, that they should remove the statue and altar of *mercy* out of the city, there being such an incongruity between the goddess they professed to worship, and that cruel sacrifice of men for the sport of the people. And would it not be more in character for those who are not afraid to violate his most holy laws, and to contradict the pattern of Christ, to give up their profession, and to take some other more complying with their lusts. It is not the title of a Christian that sanctifies those who pollute and defame it. It is not the wearing the livery of Christ that can honour those who stain it by their filthiness ; but it is an aggravation of their guilt. It is an inconceivable indignity to the Saviour, and revives the old calumnies of the heathens, as if the gospel were a sanctuary for criminals when those *that call him Lord,* do not what he commands them.

Self Reproach.

When a certain parent made his will, he said, " I leave such an estate to my eldest son, though he has been so disobedient, and though I am fearful he will misapply it." This so affected the son that he burst into tears, and said, " God forbid I should," and from that time became a new man.

The Report Discredited.

It was the charge brought against the prophets and priests in Jeremiah's day, that they cried " peace, peace, when there was no peace." How awful is it when the ministers of the sanctuary are unfaithful to their charge, and deceive the people to their ruin; when, instead of giving the sound of alarm, they lull them in carnal security, till destruction and misery overtake them. A report once prevailed in a certain town of Italy that the enemy was coming to storm it; upon which the inhabitants made a law that forbade such a report to be credited ; and when the enemy really arrived, no one mentioned it, or took up arms in his own defence, and the town was easily taken. Thus it is with the impenitent ; they are taught to believe there is no danger, until at last they are swept away without remedy.

St. Austin relates of Marcellinus that he hung Christ's picture, and the picture of Pythagoras together; and many there are, says Mr. Brooks, not only in Rome, but in England, yea, I am afraid in London, who join Christ and their works together, Christ and their prayers together, Christ and their teachers together, Christ and their mourning together, Christ and their alms together.

No system demands obedience like the gospel, and no other system can furnish motives equal to it. This makes a Christian victorious over his temptations : the unsummed heaps of the miser's den, cannot draw forth his soul to sin, even though opportunity should concur, for God is there; and in the language of a celebrated French author,* he says, " I fear my God, and I fear none but him ! !" Christ concludes the whole with that capital aphorism by which we are informed how impossible it is to divide the affections between God and the world, or indeed any other object. He must be the supreme object both of love and worship, or he is not our God—" No servant can serve two masters, for either he will hate the one and love the other, or else he will hold to one and despise the other : ye *cannot serve* God and Mammon.'

* Racine.

Services rewarded.

When a valiant soldier lost his arm in battle, his commander was so well pleased with him, that he presented him with an arm of gold as an honourable reward for his services.'

A pious Welsh minister many years ago being about to publish a sermon, previously consulted Mrs. Hannah More, how many thousand copies he ought to print. He felt not a little shocked at her advising him to reduce his thousands to hundreds; scores she dared not to advise. As she had foreseen, not half a dozen were sold, except a few charitably taken off his hands by his friends. At her return soon after from the metropolis, he hastened to her with all the ardour of impatience, and seriously inquired, whether she had observed any material reformation at the court end of the town, since the publication of his discourse! So true is the poet's maxim,

"None but an author knows an author's cares,
Or fancy's fondness for the child she bears."
                                        Cowper.

Amyclas was the name of the master of the ship in which Cæsar embarked in disguise. When Amyclas wished to put back to avoid a violent storm, Cæsar unveiling his head, discovered himself, and bidding the pilot pursue his voyage, exclaimed, *Cæsarem vehis, Cæsarisque fortunam;* You convey Cæsar, and the fortunes of Cæsar are at issue.

The Youth converted.

It is generally known that Mr. Whitfield frequently preached in the open air. In Philadelphia, he often stood on the outside steps of the court-house, and from that station addressed admiring thousands, who crowded the streets below. On one of these occasions, young Rodgers, afterwards Dr. Rodgers, was not only present, but pressed as near to the person of his favourite preacher as possible; and to testify his respect, held a lantern for his accommodation. Soon after the sermon began, he became so absorbed in the subject, that the lantern fell from his hand, and was dashed to pieces; and that part of the audience in the immediate vicinity of the speaker's station were not a little discomposed by the occurrence.

A subsequent circumstance, connected with this event, and not less remarkable, is worthy of being recorded. Mr. Whitfield, in the course of his fifth visit to America, about the year 1754, on a journey from the southward, called at St. George's in Delaware, where Mr. Rodgers was then settled in the gospel ministry, and spent some time with him. In the course of this visit, Mr. Rodgers, being one day riding with his visitant, in a close carriage, in which the latter usually travelled, asked him whether he recollected the occurrence of the little boy, who was so much affected with his preaching as to let his lantern fall: Mr. Whitfield answered, " O yes! I remember it well; and have often thought I would give any thing in my power to know who that little boy was, and what had become of him." Mr. Rodgers replied, with a smile, " I am that little boy!" Mr. Whitfield, with tears of joy, started from his seat, took him in his arms, and with strong emotions remarked that he was the fourteenth person then in the ministry whom he had discovered in the course of that visit to America, of whose hopeful conversion he had been the instrument.

What are all earthly things when compared to those of a heavenly nature! When one was asked whether he did not admire the goodly structure of a stately house, he answered, "No; for I have been at Rome, where more magnificent fabrics are to be seen." Thus when Satan would present the things of this world as delightful and engaging, we can say, they are of no value in our estimation, having seen by faith the temple of God above, a house not made with hands, eternal in the heavens.

Some Christians have died with

more joy than they lived, and triumphed over the last enemy with the vocal praises of God; others with silent offerings have quietly commended their spirits into his hand. Some have inward refreshings and support; others exuberant joys and ravishments, as if the light of glory shined into them, or the veil of flesh were drawn, and their spirits were present with the invisible world. Some of the martyrs in their cruelest sufferings felt such impressions of confidence and alacrity, that as in the house of Lamech there were recorded at the same time two discordant callings by the two brothers; Jubal, the inventor of the harp and organ, and Tubal-cain, the first artificer in brass and iron. The one practised on instruments of music, breathing harmonious sounds and melodies; the other used hammers and anvils, making noise and tumult. So in some persons whilst the heaviest strokes fell on their bodies, their souls were ravished with joy and exultation.

SIR THOMAS MORE.

A PERSON who had a suit in chancery, once sent Sir Thomas More two silver flagons, not doubting of the acceptableness of the present. On receiving them, Sir Thomas called one of his servants, and told him to fill those two vessels with the best wine in his cellar; and turning round to the servant who had presented them, "tell your master," replied the inflexible magistrate, "that if he approves my wine, I beg he would not spare it!"

Timeo Danaos et dona ferentes.

Such was his diligence in conducting the business of a court of chancery, that though he found it full of causes, yet before he resigned the office, after determining one cause, and calling for the next, he was told that there was not another depending, which circumstance he ordered to be entered upon record. This gave occasion to the following epigram:

When *More* some years had chancellor been,
　No *More* suits did remain;
The same shall never *More* be seen,
　Till *More* be there again.

DOCTOR BARROW.

THE celebrated Lord Rochester one day met Dr. Barrow in the Park, and being determined as he said, to put down *the rusty piece of divinity*, accosted him by taking off his hat, and, with a profound bow, exclaimed, "Doctor, I am yours to my shoe tie." The doctor, perceiving his aim, returned the salute with equal ceremony, "My lord, I am yours to the ground." His lordship then made a deeper congee, and said, "Doctor, I am yours to the centre." Barrow replied, with the same formality, "My lord, I am yours to the antipodes;"—on which Rochester made another attempt, by exclaiming, "Doctor, I am yours to the lowest pit of hell." "There, my lord," said Barrow, "I leave you," and immediately walked away.

It is related of Hobbes, "the philosopher of Malmsbury," who was atheistically inclined, that he had the most dreadful apprehensions of death, which he called "taking a leap in the dark." Dr. Wallis relates of him, that discoursing one day with a lady in high life, Hobbes told her, "that were he the master of the world, he would give it all to live one day longer." She expressed her astonishment that a philosopher who had such extensive knowledge, and so many friends to gratify or oblige, would not deny himself one day's gratification of life, if by that means he could bequeath to them such ample possessions. His answer was, "what shall I be the better for that, when I am dead? I say again, if I had the whole world to dispose of, I would give it to live one day." How different is the language of the real Christian? "Having a desire to depart and to be with Christ, which is *far better*"—far better than the highest enjoyments that can be attained in this world!

THE END.

Other Solid Ground Titles

Printed in the United States
64688LVS00004B/19-30

9 781932 474848